YO-CCH-973

THE
HISTORIA REGUM BRITANNIE
OF GEOFFREY OF MONMOUTH
II

The First Variant Version

THE
HISTORIA REGUM BRITANNIE
OF GEOFFREY OF MONMOUTH

ISSN 0267-2529

I

Bern, Burgerbibliothek, MS. 568

Edited by Neil Wright

THE
HISTORIA REGUM BRITANNIE
OF
GEOFFREY OF MONMOUTH
II

The First Variant Version:
a critical edition

Edited by Neil Wright

D. S. BREWER

Introduction and editorial matter © Neil Wright 1988

First published 1988 by D. S. Brewer
240 Hills Road, Cambridge
an imprint of Boydell & Brewer Ltd
PO Box 9, Woodbridge, Suffolk IP12 3DF
and of Boydell & Brewer Inc.
Wolfeboro, New Hampshire 03894-2069, USA

ISBN 0 85991 212 4

British Library Cataloguing in Publication Data

Geoffrey, *of Monmouth, Bishop of St. Asaph*
    The historia regum Britannie of
    Geoffrey of Monmouth. – (Historia regum
    Britannie, ISSN 0267-2529;2)
    2 : The first variant version : a critical
    edition
    1. England – Kings and rulers   2. Great
    Britain – History – to 1066
    I. Title   II. Wright, Neil   III. Series
    936.2′009′92   DA135
    ISBN 0-85991-212-4

Library of Congress Cataloging-in-Publication Data
(Revised for volume 2)

Geoffrey, of Monmouth, Bishop of St. Asaph, 1100?–1154.
    The Historia regum Britannie of Geoffrey of Monmouth.
    Text in Latin; editorial matter in English.
    Bibliography: v. 1, p.
    Includes indexes.
    Contents: 1. Bern, Burgerbibliothek, MS. 568 – 2. The
first variant version, a critical edition.
    1. Great Britain – History – To 449.   2. Legends, Celtic.
3. Arthur, King.   4. Merlin.   I. Wright, Neil.
II. Burgerbibliothek Bern. Manuscript. 568.   III. Title.
DA140.G353   1985   942.01′3   84-24170
ISBN 0-85991-211-6 (v. 1)

♾ Printed in Great Britain
on long life paper made to the full American Standard
by St Edmundsbury Press, Bury St Edmunds

CONTENTS

To the memory of Lewis Morris and Evan Evans
without whose happy intervention in the
Galfridian tradition J. Jay Parry would
not have recognised the significance of
this text

Published with the assistance of
the Eugène Vinaver Memorial Trust Fund

Editor's Preface

The First Variant version of the *Historia Regum Britannie* is a most important witness to the early reception of Geoffrey of Monmouth's pseudo-history; but it is also a sobering example of the manifold difficulties which have still to be surmounted by Galfridian scholarship. The text-history of the First Variant version, for instance, is of considerable complexity. Although the Variant survives in only eight known manuscripts, it presents in microcosm many of the problems characteristic of the mediaeval Latin text. The eight manuscripts fall into two main groups, both of which testify to the freedom with which the text might be treated; and the question of the relationship of the two branches is complicated by problems of contamination (which certainly occurred in at least one manuscript). Moreover, the possibility of the influence of the vulgate text is ever present; indeed, three of the manuscripts bear witness to major acts of conflation, in two cases with the vulgate *Historia* itself and in the other with yet a further variant version. It is not, therefore, surprising that the only previous attempt to edit the First Variant version – that of Jacob Hammer – resulted in a text which was seriously distorted by the inclusion of a mass of vulgate material, while the true readings of the Variant were consigned to the apparatus. This new edition, which presents the first full examination of the text-history of the First Variant, seeks to redress the balance by providing an accurate text securely based on all known manuscript witnesses.

The First Variant also raises severe problems of date and authorship, which Hammer's edition did little to solve. Indeed, these problems have been compounded by the question of the First Variant's relationship to the *Roman de Brut*, Wace's vernacular version of Geoffrey's *Historia*. Suggestions as to the date of the First Variant have ranged from the view that it was Geoffrey's source (hence written before 1135–8) to the assertion that it was a conflation of the vulgate text and Wace's poem (hence post-1155). It is argued here that the First Variant is a reworking of the vulgate *Historia* by an unknown author; and that it was completed at some time before 1155,

vii

since Wace's *Roman de Brut* demonstrably draws on both the First Variant and vulgate texts. With regard to Wace, it is hoped that this conclusion will encourage a reassessment of the way in which he combined the First Variant and vulgate texts with other matter found solely in the *Roman de Brut*. The implications for the First Variant text itself are considerable. If the pre-1155 dating is accepted, the Variant version must have been written within Geoffrey's lifetime and so, like Henry of Huntingdon's *Epistola ad Warinum*, represents a near-contemporary response to the *Historia Regum Britannie*. The chief aim of the First Variant is unquestionably to abbreviate, though not drastically so; but, although it sometimes (inevitably) introduces errors and contradictions, the resulting text is by no means devoid of literary interest. Frequent reminiscences of the bible and Classical texts (independent of the vulgate) indicate that the abbreviator was an educated man. He was also interested in historical matters, for he had recourse to Bede and Landolfus Sagax and tried on occasion to reconcile the Galfridian version of events with these more orthodox historical authorities. Furthermore, his fondness for biblical allusion lends the First Variant in many passages (especially speeches) a tone rather more moral than that of Geoffrey's original. In sum, the First Variant does not abbreviate its source slavishly, but often recasts the *Historia* freely in a manner quite different from that of Geoffrey himself.

The present edition conforms closely to the format of the initial, single-manuscript text which serves as the basis for this series. In particular, the text of the First Variant has been divided, as exactly as possible, into the two hundred and eight chapters (first employed by Faral) used in my previous edition, so that the contents of both First Variant and vulgate texts can be compared with ease. Discussion of the literary borrowings and reminiscences found in the vulgate text itself must of necessity be postponed until the completion of the ultimate goal of this project, a comprehensive edition of Geoffrey's *Historia* based on all the manuscripts, which will also contain a full commentary; however, since the independent use of biblical, Classical, and historical allusions is so important a characteristic of the First Variant version, a complete list (and assessment) of its non-vulgate borrowings (including a number not recorded by Hammer) has been included in the introduction of this volume. Also, whereas in my previous, single-manuscript edition the description of Bern MS. 568, on which it was based, had necessarily to be as complete as possible, in the present work the eight First-Variant manuscripts are not treated so exhaustively, as they are to be examined in detail in the descriptive catalogue of Geoffrey manuscripts which is currently being prepared by Julia Crick.

viii

The author wishes to thank all those who have aided in the production of this volume: above all the Trustees of the Vinaver Fund whose continued generous sponsorship has made this edition possible. I am also most grateful to Julia Crick, Dr David Dumville, Dr Tony Hunt, Dr Michael Lapidge, and Dr Brynley F. Roberts, all of whom have kindly read parts of this edition, discussed its contents with me, or otherwise provided assistance both physical and moral. A paper based on the introduction of this volume was read at a seminar on the transmission of Latin texts held in the University of Cambridge in April 1987; I should like to express my gratitude to Professor Michael Reeve and the other participants for a number of helpful suggestions made on that occasion. My heaviest debt is as ever owed to Dr Richard Barber, upon whose ready ear and seemingly inexhaustible patience I have confidently relied at all stages. Finally, my sincere thanks are due to Dr Janet Seeley for her unstinting encouragement and support at all times during the preparation of this volume.

INTRODUCTION

I *The First Variant version of the* Historia Regum Britannie: *contents, date, and authorship*

In 1951 Jacob Hammer published – albeit in seriously mangled form – a text of the *Historia Regum Britannie* which differed considerably from that hitherto regarded as the standard version of Geoffrey's *Historia*.[1] Hammer referred to the former as the First Variant version[2] and to the latter as the vulgate, terms which have since gained general acceptance among Galfridian scholars. Yet despite this agreement, basic questions concerning the genesis of the First Variant version have, since the appearance of Hammer's edition, elicited widely divergent responses from his critics. There has thus far been no consensus of opinion on such fundamental issues as exactly how the text of this Variant relates to that of the vulgate, when and with what motives the Variant was composed, and who was responsible for it. Indeed, so diverse have been the various hypotheses advanced in answer to these questions that it will be necessary to summarize them here before attempting to resolve the problems which they raise.

Hammer himself, in the introduction to his edition, devoted some space to an examination of the relationship of the First Variant text to the vulgate. He catalogued, giving a few examples in each case, the following details as characteristic of the Variant: additional material, sometimes drawn from older sources; a fondness for biblical phraseology; some speeches abbreviated or omitted, or, conversely, paraphrased or completely altered in form and content; and a tendency to tone down or omit unpleasant details.[3]

---

[1] *Geoffrey of Monmouth: Historia Regum Britanniae. A Variant Version* (henceforth referred to as *Variant Version*).
[2] Hammer used this term because he had discovered another variant version, which he was editing at the time of his death; see Emanuel, 'Geoffrey of Monmouth's *Historia Regum Britanniae*: a Second Variant Version'.
[3] Hammer, *Variant Version*, pp. 8–12.

Hammer nowhere explicitly discussed the question of the priority of the Variant or vulgate text or of the dating of the Variant, but it is clear that he considered the latter to be a reworking (of the vulgate) for which Geoffrey of Monmouth was not responsible; he referred to the Variant's 'author' as an 'unknown Welsh redactor' (this merely on the strength of parallels between the Variant and Welsh versions of the *Historia*) and as a 'chronicler who, though inspired by Geoffrey, refused to reproduce him slavishly'.[4] The view that the First Variant postdated the vulgate is implicit in these statements, and it may be concluded that Hammer saw the Variant as a later – probably considerably later – redaction of the *Historia*.

The first scholar to address the question of the date of the Variant version directly was Robert Caldwell, who devoted two articles to this problem. The first of these was primarily concerned with the interrelationship of the Variant with the *Roman de Brut* of Wace.[5] While it had long been recognised that Wace's poem was essentially a vernacular version of Geoffrey's *Historia*,[6] Caldwell maintained that there were clear indications that the *Roman de Brut* had closer links with the Variant version than with the vulgate. He showed first that the 'additional material' in the Variant, cited by Hammer to illustrate the differences between it and the vulgate, was also present in the *Roman de Brut*; and secondly that some of the additions which (Margaret Houck had argued)[7] were made by Wace to his source could in fact also be found in the Variant. Further comparison of the *Roman de Brut* with the Variant version led Caldwell to conclude that Wace had drawn principally on the Variant (but not exclusively, as some passages in the second half of the poem, especially that part dealing with the reign of Arthur, were clearly derived from material found solely in the vulgate).[8] This conclusion provided evidence for the date of the Variant, since the *Roman de Brut* was completed in 1155.[9] According to Caldwell, therefore, the Variant version must have been written before that date and, indeed, within the lifetime of Geoffrey himself (who died probably in 1155).[10] As to the question of authorship, Caldwell accepted Hammer's in-

[4] *Ibid.*, p. 19.
[5] Caldwell, 'Wace's *Roman de Brut*'; Wace's poem is edited by Arnold, *Roman de Brut*.
[6] Ulbrich, 'Über das Verhältnis'; Waldner, *Waces Brut*; Arnold, 'Wace et l'*Historia Regum Britanniae*'.
[7] Houck, *Sources*, pp. 215–60 (especially 228–37).
[8] 'Wace's *Roman de Brut*', pp. 680–81.
[9] *Roman de Brut*, lines 14863–6, 'Puis que Deus incarnatiun / Prist pur nostre redemptiun / Mil e cent cinquante e cinc anz / Fist mestre Wace cest romanz'.
[10] Wright, *Historia Regum Britannie*, I.x.

ference that the Variant was not produced by Geoffrey, while rejecting – rightly in my view – Hammer's ill-founded assertion that it was demonstrably the work of a Welshman.

In a second article,[11] Caldwell refined his approach to the dating of the Variant version. Turning his attention to its relationship with the vulgate, he argued that the absence from the vulgate of some material found in the Variant and the inclusion in the Variant alone of some passages drawn directly from prior sources (Bede and Landolfus Sagax) could best be explained if the vulgate were regarded as a reworking of the Variant. Elsewhere, Caldwell stated that the Variant 'looks like an early draft put together from original sources' and the vulgate 'like a deliberate revision'.[12] In his opinion, then, the Variant version antedated not only Wace's *Roman de Brut*, but also the vulgate *Historia Regum Britannie* itself, probably published in 1138.[13] However, Caldwell apparently did not modify his acceptance of Hammer's view that the Variant could not be the work of Geoffrey. His hypothesis therefore involved the difficulty of maintaining that the Variant represented a version of the *Historia* composed by an unknown author at some time before Geoffrey compiled the vulgate text – a difficulty which Caldwell made no attempt to resolve.

Caldwell's arguments were vigorously countered by Pierre Gallais.[14] The latter regarded Caldwell's claim that the Variant version preceded the *Roman de Brut* as a serious challenge to Wace's originality, since it threatened to reduce the status of the romance poet to that of a 'compilateur'.[15] Gallais accepted that, by reason of its style, the Variant could not have been written by Geoffrey himself, but he rejected the proposition that an unknown author could have produced such a version prior to the appearance of the vulgate text; accordingly, the Variant must have been composed after 1138 and, if Caldwell were right in seeing it as Wace's prime source, before the latter began work on the *Roman de Brut* (viz, Gallais suggested, around 1150). However this seemed too short a time to Gallais, who thought it unlikely that a revision of the *Historia* by an author other than Geoffrey would have been made so soon after the publication of the vulgate text or, for that matter, in Geoffrey's lifetime. Furthermore, a

---

11 'The use of sources'; it is regrettable that Caldwell's paper was published in abstract form which did not set out his arguments in full.
12 Parry and Caldwell, 'Geoffrey of Monmouth', p. 87.
13 Wright, *Historia Regum Britannie*, I.xii–xvi.
14 'La *Variant Version*'.
15 *Ibid.*, p. 4.

painstaking comparison of that part of the *Roman de Brut* concerned with Arthur and the corresponding sections of the vulgate and First Variant texts[16] led Gallais to a conclusion diametrically opposed to that of Caldwell: namely that the Variant version drew on Wace's *Roman de Brut* and was, therefore, composed after 1155. While Gallais made no attempt to date the Variant version more precisely, he tentatively suggested that stylistic comparison with the works of late twelfth- and early thirteenth-century writers (such as Gerald of Wales, Walter Map, or Gervase of Tilbury) might produce interesting results.

Gallais's arguments were themselves attacked by Hans-Erich Keller,[17] who advocated a return to the position adopted by Caldwell, though in a qualified form. Keller held that comparison of the treatment of the proper and place-names in the Variant and the *Roman de Brut* indicated that Caldwell had been right to suppose that Wace had used the Variant. He also accepted Caldwell's contention that the Variant, though not written by Geoffrey, antedated the vulgate text. Elaborating another suggestion made by Caldwell,[18] Keller identified the two versions of the *Historia* (viz vulgate and Variant) with two sources (supposedly in Latin) mentioned by Geffrei Gaimar who compiled, probably shortly before 1140, the *Estoire des Engleis*, another vernacular verse work based in part on Geoffrey of Monmouth's *Historia*.[19] Keller maintained that Gaimar referred to the vulgate as 'le livere Walter Espac', and to the Variant version as 'le bon livere de Oxenforde / Ki fust Walter l'arcediaen'.[20] On the strength of this latter identification, Keller concluded that the source of the *Historia Regum Britannie* was not, as Geoffrey alleged, an ancient Welsh- or Breton-language book in the possession of Walter archdeacon of Oxford,[21] but rather the Variant, composed before 1138 and possibly, Keller suggested, written by Archdeacon Walter himself.

Caldwell's position also finds support from R. William Leckie, Jr., who has devoted an important study to the impact of Geoffrey's *Historia* on twelfth-century littérateurs and historians.[22] Leckie highlighted Geoff-

[16] *Ibid.*, pp. 4–30.
[17] 'Wace et Geoffrey de Monmouth'.
[18] 'Wace's *Roman de Brut*', p. 682.
[19] Edited by Bell, *L'Estoire* (see pp. li–lii on the date of Gaimar's poem).
[20] *L'Estoire*, lines 6442 and 6458–9. The problems posed by Gaimar's two sources are discussed by Bell, pp. liii–liv; for a counter-argument that Gaimar refers very imprecisely to only one source (Geoffrey's *Historia*), see Tatlock, *The Legendary History*, pp. 453–5.
[21] Wright, *Historia Regum Britannie*, I.xvii–viii.
[22] *The Passage.*

rey's innovative treatment of the transfer of power from the native British to their English foes; since Geoffrey's account directly contradicted those of accepted authorities such as Bede, it inevitably drew from contemporary and near-contemporary authors various attempts to resolve this problem or to reach a compromise solution. In the course of examining these responses to Geoffrey's narrative, Leckie maintained that the Variant version at several points manifested a concern to deal with the problems raised by the vulgate text and must, therefore, have postdated the *Historia*.[23] Furthermore, he argued that the *Roman de Brut* also exhibited a similar, yet distinct, approach which, according to Leckie, could not have arisen independently but must represent an attempt to modify the Variant.[24] Leckie, then, upheld Caldwell's conclusion that the Variant was composed before 1155. Since he had rejected Caldwell's argument that the Variant was earlier than the vulgate, Leckie preferred to view the First Variant as a later recension compiled by an unknown redactor (working at some time between 1138 and the early 1150s).

The diverse and contradictory nature of these various hypotheses serves to underline the great difficulties with which questions about the date, authorship, and purpose of the First Variant version present us. Indeed, none of the views set out above is beyond criticism. Hammer's comparison of the vulgate and Variant texts was far from comprehensive, while his pronouncements – such as they were – on the date and authorship of the Variant were nowhere supported by rigorous argument. Caldwell's comparison of the Variant with the *Roman de Brut* was more thorough, but he offered no real evidence for his assertion that the undeniable parallels between the two texts demonstrated that Wace had relied on the Variant version, rather than vice versa. Similarly, his arguments in favour of the priority of the Variant over the vulgate fell far short – at least in the form in which they were published – of conclusive proof; furthermore, Caldwell made no attempt to resolve the serious difficulties which this theory engendered. Gallais, on the other hand, compared vulgate, Variant, and the *Roman de Brut* with great care, but his examination was nevertheless incomplete, being based only on the Arthurian section of the texts (which is precisely the part of Wace's poem which makes most use of the vulgate *Historia* and thus considerably clouds the exact nature of the relationship of the *Roman de Brut* and the Variant text). The suspicion must also be entertained that Gallais's investigation may have been prejudiced by the desire to safeguard

---

[23] *Ibid.*, pp. 102–9 (also 25–8).
[24] *Ibid.*, pp. 109–17.

Wace's claims to literary originality. Keller's comparison of the *Roman de Brut* and the Variant was also incomplete, since in his case it was limited to their treatment of names – an area of notorious difficulty because of the vagaries of mediaeval scribal practice. Further, his identification of Gaimar's 'bon livere de Oxenforde' with the Variant version and his assertion that the latter, compiled by Archdeacon Walter, represents Geoffrey's source is wild speculation. Even Leckie's careful and otherwise cogent arguments about the literary-historical relationship of the vulgate, the Variant, and Wace's *Roman de Brut* are based only on parts of those texts, rather than on their entirety.

The paramount objection is that none of the critics has examined all aspects of the problem comprehensively in order to achieve a solution compatible with all the available evidence. Such a comprehensive approach must be directed to answering three crucial questions. Was the Variant version composed before or after the vulgate? Was the Variant written by Geoffrey himself or by another author? And was the Variant used by Wace, or does it rather reflect the influence of the *Roman de Brut* and consequently postdate that text? Clearly, the first two questions can, since conclusive external evidence is lacking, only be addressed after the Variant and vulgate texts have been compared more carefully than has so far been the case; moreover, the results of such a comparison may also provide additional important evidence, useful in conducting a much needed reinvestigation of the relationship of the Variant to Wace's *Roman de Brut*.

With these aims in view, the vulgate and Variant texts have been compared systematically and the results set out in Table I. However, before these results and their broader implications can be examined, a number of definitions must be made. Let us begin with the terms 'vulgate' and 'Variant' themselves. 'Vulgate' is here used to denote that version of the *Historia Regum Britannie* found in all editions prior to that of Hammer (irrespective, that is, of minor variations in the dedication of the *Historia*); in the present work, the vulgate is quoted from the text of the Bern manuscript, already edited in this series, which is, except in point of some small details, essentially a representative of the standard version of the *Historia*.[25] By the term 'Variant version' is meant the uncontaminated text printed here, as opposed to that of Hammer's edition which drew heavily on a manuscript interpolated with the vulgate.[26] In the present edition, as in that

---

[25] For a discussion of the points of difference, see Wright, *Historia Regum Britannie*, I. liv–ix.

[26] See below, p. xcii.

of the Bern manuscript which preceded it, the text has been divided into the two hundred and eight chapters first used in the edition of Edmond Faral;[27] this permits a close, chapter-by-chapter comparison of the vulgate and Variant texts.

Such a comparison reveals that the similarities and differences between the vulgate and Variant can best be assessed by dividing the chapters into ten categories. While this classification is mechanical and occasionally – of necessity – generalising, it has the advantage of affording an overview of the relationship of the texts in question, both more accessible and complete than any hitherto possible; but, it must be stressed, it is hoped that readers will supplement its findings by their own close reading of the texts. The ten categories mentioned above are represented in Table I by the letters A–J. These categories can themselves be subdivided into three groups. In the first of these (A–F), the subject-matter is essentially the same in vulgate and Variant texts, and the differences between them are limited to methods of treatment. In this group, the categories, which are not necessarily mutually exclusive, are as follows.

A   chapter containing material common to vulgate and Variant, and cast in similar style.
B   chapter containing material common to vulgate and Variant, but with differences of style and diction.
C   chapter containing material common to both texts, but in less full form in the Variant.
D   chapter common to both texts, but found in extremely brief form in the Variant.
E   chapter containing a speech or speeches common to both texts, but found in fuller form in the Variant.
F   chapter (or material contained in that chapter) common to both texts, but found in a different order in the Variant.

The second group consists of two types of chapter, the chief characteristic being that some or all of the material in the chapter is found only in the vulgate.

G   entire chapter found only in the vulgate.
H   chapter containing material found only in the vulgate.

Finally, the third group also has two categories, but in this case the chapters exhibit material found only in the Variant.

[27] *La Légende*, III.63–301.

I   chapter containing material found only in the Variant, and drawn from a recognisable source.

J   chapter containing other material found only in the Variant.

The distribution of these ten categories throughout the two hundred and eight chapters of the *Historia* is set out in Table I.

Table I

Block diagram showing the number of chapters in each of the ten categories.

No. of chapters

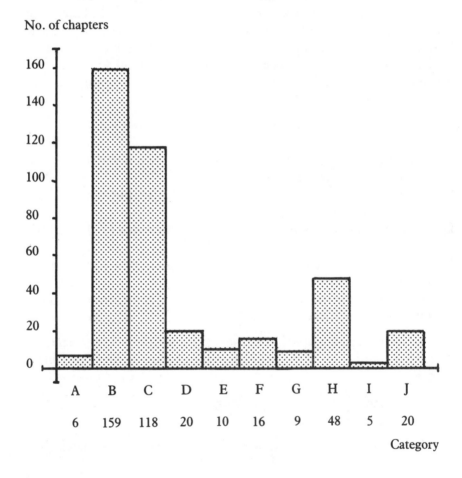

	A	B	C	D	E	F	G	H	I	J
	6	159	118	20	10	16	9	48	5	20

Category

Complete list of chapters in each category.

A   Chapters   112, 113, 114, 115, 116, 117

B   Chapters   7, 8, 9, 10, 13, 14, 16, 18, 20, 21, 22, 24, 27, 30, 31, 32, 33, 34, 36, 37, 38, 40, 41, 42, 43, 44, 45, 46, 47, 50, 51, 53, 54, 55, 56, 57, 58, 59, 60, 61, 62, 63, 64, 65, 66, 67, 68, 69, 72, 73, 74, 75, 78, 80, 83, 84, 85, 86, 87, 88, 89, 91, 93, 94, 95, 96, 97, 98, 99, 100, 101, 103, 104, 105, 106, 108, 111, 118, 119, 120, 121, 122, 123, 124, 125, 126, 127, 128, 129, 130, 131, 132, 133, 134, 136, 137, 138, 139, 140, 141, 142, 143, 144, 145, 146, 147, 148, 149, 150, 151, 152, 153, 154, 155, 156, 157, 158, 159, 161, 162, 163, 164, 165, 166, 167, 168, 169, 170, 171, 172, 173, 174, 175, 176, 177, 178, 179, 180, 182, 183, 184, 186, 188, 189, 190, 191, 192, 193, 196, 197, 198, 199, 200, 201, 203, 204, 205, 206, 207

C   Chapters   6, 7, 9, 10, 11, 12, 13, 14, 15, 17, 18, 19, 21, 22, 23, 24, 25, 26, 27, 28, 29, 31, 32, 33, 34, 35, 36, 37, 38, 39, 40, 41, 43, 44, 45, 46, 47, 48, 50, 51, 52, 54, 56, 57, 58, 59, 60, 62, 64, 65, 66, 67, 68, 69, 70, 74, 75, 76, 78, 79, 80, 85, 86, 87, 88, 91, 97, 98, 102, 103, 104, 105, 106, 107, 108, 119, 123, 124, 125, 126, 127, 128, 129, 134, 135, 137, 139, 142, 143, 144, 145, 146, 147, 148, 152, 154, 155, 156, 157, 158, 159, 165, 166, 167, 168, 169, 170, 172, 173, 175, 176, 177, 196, 201, 202, 205, 206, 207

D   Chapters   49, 71, 77, 81, 82, 83, 90, 92, 120, 131, 132, 140, 141, 171, 174, 178, 181, 194, 195, 208

E   Chapters   35, 41, 62, 63, 121, 136, 161, 174, 200, 203

F   Chapters   5, 21, 27, 29, 93, 102, 161, 162, 163, 164, 177, 179, 184, 186, 187, 204

G   Chapters   1, 2, 3, 4, 109, 110, 160, 185, 187

H   Chapters   10, 15, 22, 30, 34, 37, 49, 52, 62, 69, 70, 71, 77, 79, 81, 82, 83, 85, 90, 91, 92, 100, 104, 119, 120, 132, 140, 141, 146, 147, 156, 157, 166, 170, 171, 173, 174, 175, 177, 178, 190, 191, 193, 194, 195, 196, 202, 208

I   Chapters   5, 6, 54, 59, 86

J   Chapters   39, 43, 46, 72, 94, 101, 130, 137, 145, 146, 161, 164, 172, 186, 188, 189, 203, 204, 207, 208

Category A – that is, chapters in all respects the same in the vulgate and Variant texts – is entirely limited to §§ 112–17, or the body of the *Prophetie Merlini*. It should be noted that § 118, which is in effect a continuation of the *Prophetie*, is also very similar in both texts, although there are minor variations of style and vocabulary. The *Prophetie* were probably composed around 1135, released before the *Historia* itself, and circulated not only as *Historia Regum Britannie*, §§ 109–117 (or –118) but also separately in the form of a *libellus*;[28] it was probably because of this status as a discrete work, as well as their obscurity, that the *Prophetie* proper (that is, excluding the introductory §§ 109–111) are found without modification in both the vulgate and Variant texts.

Category B is unquestionably the largest, since it contains no fewer than one hundred and fifty-nine chapters; clearly, one of the major distinctions between vulgate and Variant lies in the differing stylistic treatment of similar material. These differences can range from comparatively minor instances of word-order and vocabulary to passages in which one text (be it vulgate or Variant) is manifestly a reworking of the other. Some examples will serve to illustrate these differences. In the first passage (quoted below from the vulgate and Variant texts), the differences amount to little more than minor variation.

Historia Regum Britannie, § 183, vulgate

[183] Cui successit Malgo omnium fere ducum Britannie pulcherrimus, multorum tirannorum depulsor, robustus armis, largior ceteris, et ultra modum probitate preclarus nisi sodomitana peste uolutatus sese Deo inuisum exhibuit. Hic etiam totam insulam obtinuit et sex comprouintiales occeani insulas, Hiberniam uidelicet atque Hislandiam, Godlandiam, Orchades, Norguegiam, Daciam, adiecit dirissimis preliis potestati sue.

Variant

[183] Huic successit Malgo omnium fere ducum Britannie pulcherrimus et probitate preclarus, nisi sodomitica peste fedatus Deo sese inuisum exhibuisset: multorum tamen tyrannorum depulsor, robustus armis, largior ceteris. Hic totam Britanniam sibi subiugauit; adiacentes quoque insulas, Hyberniam uidelicet atque Hyslandiam, Gothlandiam, Orcades, necnon Norwegiam, et Daciam, durissimis preliis sue potestati adiecit.

In each text, this chapter comprises two sentences. The first of these provides an excellent example of variety of word- or (in this case) clause-order, since the element 'multorum tyrannorum ... largior ceteris' is found early in the sentence in the vulgate, and at its end in the Variant. There is also some variation of vocabulary: *huic* in the Variant, *cui* in the vulgate; *fedatus*

---

28 Wright, *Historia Regum Britannie*, I.x–xi.

in the Variant, and the more emotive *uolutatus* in the vulgate.[29] This latter tendency is more pronounced in the second sentence: *Britanniam* (Variant), *insulam* (vulgate); *sibi subiugauit* (Variant), *obtinuit* (vulgate); *adiacentes insulas* (Variant), *sex comprouintiales occeani insulas* (vulgate). But here too there are differences of word-order: *durissimis preliis sue potestati adiecit* (Variant); *adiecit dirissimis preliis potestati sue* (vulgate).

In the chapter quoted above, these differences do not appear to have been motivated primarily by a desire for abbreviation or expansion (although the fifty-one words of the vulgate slightly outnumber the fifty of the Variant), but rather simply by reasons of style. Indeed, in another similar example (*Historia Regum Britannie*, § 198, quoted below) the Variant version is in fact fuller (seventy-one words) than the vulgate (sixty-five). Yet the familiar process of reordering of words and clauses and the substitution of another word (or words) for its (or their) synonym is again present and is, if anything, more pronounced in this chapter.

Historia Regum Britannie, § 198, vulgate

[198] Habita igitur uictoria Caduallo uniuersas Anglorum prouincias peruagando ita debachatus est in Saxones ut ne sexui quidem muliebri uel paruulorum aetati parceret; quin omne genus Anglorum ex finibus Britannie abradere uolens quoscumque reperiebat inauditis tormentis afficiebat. Deinde commisit prelium cum Offrico qui Aeduuino successerat atque interemit illum et duos nepotes eius qui post ipsum regnare debuerant sed et Caduanum regem Scottorum qui eis auxiliari uenerat.

Variant

[198] Confecto itaque prelio et uictoria patrata uniuersas Cadwallo prouincias Saxonum perlustrans ita in totum Saxonum Anglorum genus debachatus est et omnis exercitus eius ut ne quidem sexui muliebri uel paruulorum etati parceret, multos inauditis tormentis afficiens, ceteros diuersis mortibus puniens. Post hec commisit prelium cum Osrico qui Edwino successerat et interfecit eum et duos nepotes eius quos post illum regnare sperabat sed et Eadanum regem Scotorum qui eis in auxilium uenerat.

The extent which these stylistic variations can on occasion reach is well illustrated by *Historia Regum Britannie*, § 55, which contains the text of a letter supposedly sent by Cassibellanus in reply to Julius Caesar. As com-

---

[29] The vulgate text derives this word (and much of the chapter) directly from Gildas; see Wright, 'Geoffrey of Monmouth and Gildas', pp. 10–11 and 38–39.

parison of the two texts (set out below) reveals, the differences of form – and in this case also, to some degree, of content, although the gist of the chapter remains the same – make it clear that one version, even if it is not immediately clear which, must be a reworking of the other.

Historia Regum Britannie, § 55, vulgate

[55] Cassibellanus rex Britonum Gaio Iulio Cesari. Miranda est, Cesar, Romani populi cupiditas quicquid est auri uel argenti sitiens; nequit nos infra pericula occeani extra orbem positos pati quin etiam census nostros appetere presumat quos hactenus quiete possedimus. Nec hoc quidem sufficit nisi postposita libertate subiectionem ei faciamus perpetuam seruitutem subituri. Obprobrium itaque tibi petiuisiti, Cesar, cum communis nobilitatis uena Britonibus et Romanis ab Enea defluat et eiusdem cognationis una et eadem catena prefulgeat qua in firmam amiciciam coniungi deberent. Illa a nobis petenda esset non seruitus, quia eam potius largiri didicimus quam seruitutis iugum deferre. Libertatem namque in tantum consueuimus habere quod prorsus ignoramus quid sit seruituti obedire. Quam si ipsi dii conarentur nobis eripere, elaboraremus utique omni nisu resistere ut eam retineremus; liqueat igitur dispositioni tue, Cesar, nos pro illa et pro regno nostro pugnaturos si, ut comminatus es, infra insulam Britannie superuenire inceperis.

Variant

[55] Cassibellaunus rex Britonum Gaio Cesari. Miranda est, Cesar, Romanorum cupiditas que quicquid est usquam auri uel argenti in toto orbe terrarum siciens nos extra orbem positos preterire intactos non patitur. Censum exigis, tributarios nos facere queris qui perpetua libertate hactenus floruimus, qui a Troiana nobilitate sicut Romani descendimus. Obprobrium generi tuo, Cesar, si intelligis, postulasti qui hisdem ortos natalibus iugo seruitutis premere non erubuisti. Libertatem autem nos in tantum consueuimus et tam nobis ab antecessoribus familiaris est ut quid sit in genere nostro seruitus penitus ignoremus. Quam libertatem si dii ipsi quoque conarentur auferre, nos omni nisu elaboraremus ne quod nobis tamquam insitum a natura par cum diis tanto tempore tenuimus, per hominem mortalem amitteremus. Liqueat igitur tibi, Cesar, pro regno nos et libertate, dum uita comes fuerit, indefessos communiter stare etiam mortem subire paratos si tempus dissolucionis forte nostre institerit.

The recasting, though more extensive here, follows the pattern already apparent in previous passages. There are, however, on this occasion some new elements. First, one can observe in the Variant version a slight tendency to rhymed, parallel clauses (*floruimus . . . descendimus; postulasti . . . erubuisti*). Secondly, in the phrase 'dum uita comes fuerit' (which also occurs in Variant, §174), the Variant exhibits a biblical echo not present in the vulgate text: compare 2 Kings (4 Reg.) 4.16, 'si *uita comes fuerit*'. As Hammer observed, this fondness for the bible is characteristic of the Variant, which frequently includes biblical phraseology or allusions absent from the vulgate.[30] The same is also true of some Classical borrowings,

---

[30] *Variant Version*, pp. 9–10. Hammer's edition reported a considerable number of biblical (and Classical) borrowings, but drew no distinction between those common to both texts and those found in the Variant alone. For this reason, a list of the biblical allusions and echoes unique to the Variant (including some not noted by Hammer) is included here. Compare First Variant, §15, '*do . . .* naues et *frumentum, uinum et oleum*' and Hosea 2.8, '*dedi* ei *frumentum et uinum et oleum*'; §18, '*a* summo *usque deorsum*' and Mark 15.38, '*a* sursum *usque deorsum*'; §19, '*uolens eam penitus delere*' and Deuteronomy 7.23, '*donec penitus deleantur*'; §25, '*secessit in partes* Cornubie' and Matthew 2.22, '*secessit in partes* Galilaeae'; §31, '*in senectute bona*', also Genesis 25.8; §34, '*terraque* omnis *siluit in conspectu eius*' and 1 Maccabees 1.3, '*siluit terra in conspectu eius*'; §39, '*ab australi plaga*', also Joshua 18.5; §43, 'Nec *cessauit gladius* eius *a mane usque ad uesperam*' and 1 Maccabees 9.73, '*cessauit gladius* ex Israhel' and 9.13, '*a mane usque ad uesperam*' (also Exodus 18.13); §48, '*cum ualida manu*', and 2 Kings (4 Reg.) 18.17, '*cum manu ualida*'; §61, '*ad iracundiam . . . prouocauerunt*', also 1 Ezra 5.12; §61, '*in merorem conuersus est*' and James 4.9, '*conuertatur* et gaudium *in maerorem*'; §62, '*non reddens malum pro malo*' and 1 Peter 3.9, '*non reddentes malum pro malo*'; §69, '*in superbiam elatus*' (also §75) and 1 Timothy 3.6, '*in superbia elatus*'; §69, '*usque in senectutem*' and Ecclesiasticus 46.11, '*usque ad* [var. in] *senectutem*'; §70, '*Collecto . . . exercitu*', also 2 Maccabees 12.38; §70, '*in* magnam *multitudinem creuerunt*' and Genesis 48.16, '*crescant in multitudinem*'; §73, '*hereditario iure*', also Leviticus 25.46; §78, '*pulcram ualde ac formosam*' and Ester 1.11, '*pulchra ualde*' and 2.15, '*formonsa ualde*'; §87, '*terram hereditate possiderent*' and Ezekiel 33.25 (also 33.26), '*terram hereditate possidebitis*'; §94, '*uir gnarus*', also Genesis 25.27; §95, '*usque ad crapulam et ebrietatem*' and Luke 21.34, '*in crapula et ebrietate*'; §95, '*furore repleti*' and Ecclesiasticus 39.16, '*furore . . . repletus*'; §97, '*quorum fama . . . diuulgabatur*' and Luke 4.37, '*diuulgabatur fama* de illo'; §99, '*fideles . . . in* mea *dilectione*' and Wisdom 3.9, '*fideles in dilectione*'; §103, '*sub optentu* pacis' and Mark 12.40, '*sub obtentu . . .* orationis'; §107, '*spiritus inmundi*', also Mark 3.11; §120, '*ut arene maris* comparari posset' and Genesis 41.49, '*ut harenae maris* coaequaretur'; §134, '*ut ueritas coniectoris probaretur*' (also §142, '*ut ueritas . . . coniectoris . . .* completeretur') and Genesis 40.22, '*ut coniectoris ueritas probaretur*'; §136, '*liberemus animas nostras*', also 1 Maccabees 9.9; §136, '*Dei uiui*', also 2 Corinthians 3.3; §136, '*Confitentes peccata* nostra' and Matthew 3.6, '*confitentes peccata sua*'; §136, '*si Deus pro nobis, quis contra nos?*', also Romans 8.31 (cited verbatim); §151, '*sonitu buccine*', also 1 Chronicles 15.28; §161, '*conspectui tuo* pareat' and Psalms 16.15, '*apparebo conspectui tuo*'; §169, 'tamquam *futurorum presagus*' and Genesis 41.11, '*praesagum futurorum*'; §§184/6, '*et desolata est terra ab omni specie* sua' and Ezekiel 19.7, '*et desolata est terra*' and 1 Thessalonians 5.22, '*ab omni specie* mala'; §188, '*uerbum uite*' and Acts 5.20 (and 7.38), '*uerba uite*'; §197, '*uerbis consolatoriis*' and Zechariah 1.13, '*uerba consolato-*

primarily from Vergil. In *Historia Regum Britannie*, § 14, in the vulgate text Mempricius warns the Trojans that they should not 'inter Danaos manere' but at the same point in the Variant we find instead 'inter Danaum inuisum genus cohabitare'; this latter version is clearly an allusion to *Aeneid* I.28, 'Et *genus inuisum* et rapti Ganymedis honores' (where, by contrast, the phrase is applied to the Trojans themselves).[31] Other Classical borrowings found only in the Variant are drawn, to give one example in each case, from Lucan (First Variant, § 60, 'eorum ... *uesanam rabiem*'; and *De Bello Ciuili* V.190–91, '*rabies uaesana* per ora / Effluit'),[32] Ovid

---

ria'; § 204, '*terram desiderabilem*', also Jeremiah 3.19 (in addition to Psalms 105.24 and Zechariah 7.14); see also nn. 41, 59, 62, and 63 below. Classical allusions unique to the First Variant (again including several not recorded in Hammer's edition) are listed in nn. 31–6 below.

31 Compare also First Variant, § 9, '*nil tale uerentes*' (also §§ 12 and 175) and *Aeneid* IX.207, '*nil tale uerebar*'; § 13, '*stricto ferro*' and *Aeneid* IV.580 (also X.715); § 13, '*arma capescentes*' and *Aeneid* III.234, '*arma capessant*'; § 18, 'utrum *pacem ferrent an arma*' and *Aeneid* VIII.114, '*pacemne* huc *fertis an arma*'; § 21, '*pectore pectus* ... alisit' and *Aeneid* XI.615, '*Pectora pectoribus* rumpunt'; § 31, '*magna stipati* militum *caterua*' (also § 41, 'armatorum *stipatus caterua*') and *Aeneid* I.497, '*magna* iuuenum *stipante caterua*'; § 36, '*armato milite* inuaserat' and *Aeneid* II.20, '*armato milite* complent' (this phrase is also found in vulgate §§ 88 and 90; see Wright, 'Geoffrey of Monmouth and Gildas', p. 15, n. 40); § 43, '*accensi ira*' and *Aeneid* XII.946, 'furiis *accensus* et *ira*'; § 60, '*haut segnis*' (and § 173, 'non segnis'), also *Aeneid* III.513; § 80, 'quibus *permissa* fuerat ... *potestas*' and *Aeneid* IX.97, 'cui tanta deo *permissa potestas?*'; § 81, '*post fata* Octauii' and *Aeneid* IV.20, '*post fata* Sychaei'; § 98, '*uiros ignote* lingue magneque stature ... *aduenisse*' and *Aeneid* VII.167–8, 'ingentis *ignota* in ueste ... / *Aduenisse uiros*'; § 108, '*conticuerunt omnes*' and *Aeneid* II.1, '*Conticuere omnes*'; § 123, '*Clamor* ad *sydera tollitur*' and *Aeneid* XI.745 (also XII.462), '*Tollitur* in caelum *clamor*' and II.488, 'ferit aurea *sidera clamor*' (but compare too *Ilias Latina*, 142–3 [also 593–4], '*ad sidera clamor* / *Tollitur*'); § 147, 'lancea ... rigida *latoque ferro*' and *Aeneid* I.313 (also XII.165), '*lato* ... hastilia *ferro*'; § 155, '*letali uulnere*', also *Aeneid* IX.580; § 159, 'si quid de uobis *merui*' and *Aeneid* IV.317, '*Si* bene *quid de* te *merui*'; § 165, '*sanguinis riui*' and *Aeneid* XI.668, '*Sanguinis* ... *riuos*'; § 167, '*uinctis manibus post terga*' and *Aeneid* II.57, '*manus* ... *post terga reuinctum*' (also XI.81, '*Uinxerat et post terga manus*'); § 173, '*scuta galeasque*' and *Aeneid* I.101, '*Scuta* uirum *galeasque*'; § 174, '*paratus* ... pro uobis *occumbere*' and *Aeneid* II.61–2, '*paratus* / ... *occumbere* morti'; § 174, '*ad tartara misit*' and *Aeneid* VI.543, '*ad* ... *Tartara mittit*' (cf. VIII.563; XI.397; XII.14); § 178, '*finem rebus dubiis inponere*' and *Aeneid* IV.639, '*finemque imponere*' and VI.196, '*dubiis* ne defice *rebus*' (also XI.445); § 203, '*flectere lumina*' and *Aeneid* IV.369, '*lumina flexit*'.

32 Compare also First Variant, § 9, 'uidens *stragem suorum*', § 43, 'indoluerunt de *strage suorum*', § 60, 'uidens *stragem suorum*', and § 167, '*strages suorum* facta est' (the phrase also being found in the vulgate text, § 173) and *De Bello Ciuili* IV.797, 'ceciditque in *strage suorum* (but cf. also Statius, *Thebaid* III.169, 'digesta *strage suorum*'); § 21, '*in iram accensus*' and *De Bello Ciuili* III.133–4, '*in iram* / ... *accensus*'; § 40, '*supprema die* adueniente' and *De Bello Ciuili* X.41, 'Occurrit *suprema dies*'; § 43, '*flectit iter*', also *De Bello Ciuili* VIII.471.

(First Variant, § 84, 'nemora et *saltus uenatibus apta*' and *Heroides* V.17, '*saltus uenatibus aptos*'),[33] Statius (First Variant, § 136, 'circumueniemus eos inopinate *nichil tale . . . timentes*'; and *Achilleid* I.567, '*nil tale timenti*'),[34] and probably Sallust (First Variant, § 93, '*semotis omnibus arbitris*'; and *Bellum Catilinae* 20.1, '*omnibus arbitris* procul *amotis*').[35] It is also possible that the Variant contains independent echoes of Cicero, Horace, Terence, Seneca, and Sidonius Apollinaris.[36] Too much should not, at this stage, be made of these biblical and Classical allusions unique to the Variant, since other such echoes and quotations of the bible and of Classical authors are either shared by both texts or found solely in the vulgate; and, indeed, such borrowings are characteristic of Geoffrey's literary technique.[37] It must be noted, however, that these independent echoes con-

[33] Compare also First Variant, § 17, '*flante secunda aura*' and *Ex Ponto* II.3.26, '*flauit* uelis *aura secunda*'; § 36, '*rabie uentorum* pulsus' and *Metamorphoses* V.7, '*uentorum rabies*' (but cf. also Statius, *Thebaid* VII.810, '*uentorum rabiem*'); § 43, '*fulgere ad lune radios*' and *Metamorphoses* IV.99–100, '*ad lune radios . . . /* Uidit'; § 88, '*uulgus inerme* cedentes' (also, in the same chapter, 'super *uulgus inerme*') and *Ars Amatoria* III.46, 'Traditur armatis *uulgus inerme* uiris'; § 130, '*functique epulis*' and *Metamorphoses* IV.765, '*epulis functi*'; § 137, '*quis enim ignem celare* potest' and *Heroides* XVI.7, '*quis enim celauerit ignem*' (describing the flame of love in both cases); § 158, '*silencium rupit*' and *Metamorphoses* I.208, '*silentia rupit*'; § 173, '*ruunt sine lege*' and *Metamorphoses* II.204, 'Hac *sine lege ruunt*'.

[34] The same phrase is found in both the Variant and vulgate texts in § 66. Compare also First Variant, § 21, '*exertis brachiis*' and *Achilleid* I.346, '*exsertaque bracchia* uelat'; § 41, '*brachia* materna *collo* filii *innectit*' and *Thebaid* IV.26–7, 'certant *innectere collo /* Bracchia'; § 41, '*carpens oscula*' and *Thebaid* III.711, '*carpens . . . oscula*'.

[35] Compare also First Variant, § 18, 'Mox *oritur ingens clamor*' and *Bellum Iugurthinum* 57.3, '*clamor ingens oritur*'; § 42, '*conuenerunt* omnes *reguli* Francorum *in unum* exercitum' and *Bellum Iugurthinum* 11.2, '*reguli in unum conuenerunt*'; § 76, '*fide interposita*' and *Bellum Iugurthinum* 32.1, '*interposita fide*'; § 103, '*sceleris* sui *conscios*' and *Bellum Catilinae* 34.2, 'tanti *sceleris conscius*'; § 132, 'si *dictis facta* compensaret' and *Bellum Catilinae* 3.2, '*facta dictis* exaequanda sunt' (but compare too Plautus, *Pseudolus* 108, '*Dictis facta* suppetant'); § 172, '*ira commotus*', also *Bellum Catilinae* 31.6.

[36] Compare, respectively, First Variant, § 55, '*insitum a natura*' and Cicero, *Pro Sulla* 83, 'tamen hoc *natura est insitum*'; § 107, '*stuprum intulit*', also Cicero, *De Officiis* III.9.38; § 94, '*uerba . . . auribus . . . instillauit*' and Horace, *Epistulae* I.8.16, '*auriculis* hoc *instillare* memento'; § 81, '*filiam locare*' and Terence, *Phormio* 645–6, '*filiam / . . . locaret*'; § 196, '*pannis obsitum*' and Terence, *Eunuchus* 236, '*pannis* annisque *obsitum*'; § 63, 'Nulla uirtus clemencia dignior est imperatori' and Seneca, *De Clementia* I.3.3, 'Nullum tamen clementia . . . magis quam regem aut principem decet' (also I.5.2, 'Est . . . clementia . . . maxime . . . decora principibus'); § 62, 'in pace ferus est ut leo et in bello timidus ut lepus' and Sidonius Apollinaris, *Epistolae* V.7.5, 'in praetoriis leones, in castris lepores'.

[37] On Geoffrey's biblical borrowings, see Feuerherd, *Geoffrey of Monmouth und das alte Testament*; Hammer, 'Geoffrey of Monmouth's use'; and Fowler, 'Some biblical influences'. On his knowledge of Vergil, see Tausendfreund, *Vergil*; and, for particular verbal

stitute an important element of the different handling in the Variant of material common to both texts.

Category C – chapters the contents of which are found in less full form in the Variant version – is (like category B) large, with one hundred and eighteen examples. In these chapters the subject-matter of both vulgate and Variant texts is again basically similar; the differences lie not so much in style as in the Variant offering a more compressed, less detailed account than that of the vulgate. This tendency is immediately apparent in the following examples, one drawn from the beginning of a chapter dealing with the siege of Sparatinum (*Historia Regum Britannie*, § 11), the other a complete chapter concerning the origin of the name 'Pendragon' (*Historia Regum Britannie*, § 135).

(i) *Historia Regum Britannie*, § 11, vulgate

[11] Et obsessi in edito murorum astantes totis uiribus nituntur ut ipsorum machinationes contrariis machinationibus repellant. Et nunc tela nunc sulphureas tedas eicientes sese unanimiter defendere intendunt. Cum autem parata testudine murus suffoderetur, Greco igne atque calidarum aquarum aspersione hostes retrocedere cogebant. Cybi tandem penuria et cotidiano labore afflicti legatum ad Brutum miserunt postulantes ut eis in auxilium festinaret. Timebant enim ne in debilitatem redacti oppidum deserere cogerentur. Brutus ergo opem subuectare affectans internis anxietatibus cruciatur quia tot milites non habebat quot sibi ad campestre prelium committendum sufficerent. Callido deinde usus consilio proponit castra hostium noctu adire ipsosque soporatos deceptis eorum uigilibus interficere.

Variant

[11] Obsessi uero a muris uiriliter resistentes telis omnium generum ac sulphureis tedis eorum machinaciones repellebant. Tandem cibi penuria et cotidiano labore afflicti legatum ad Brutum mittunt postulantes ut eis in auxilium festinaret ne debilitate coacti opidum deserere cogerentur. Brutus ergo audiens suos in unum collegit et ad succurrendum oppidanis uiriliter

---

reminiscences, Faral, *La Légende*, II (*passim*) and Wright, 'Geoffrey of Monmouth and Gildas', p. 6 (also 'Geoffrey of Monmouth and Gildas revisited', p. 162, n. 27). Examples of Geoffrey's imitation of Statius and Lucan (in addition to the explicit quotation of the latter in vulgate, § 62) are discussed by Faral, *La Légende*, II.134 and Tatlock, *The Legendary History*, pp. 405–6, respectively. Other vulgate borrowings from Classical authors are reported in Hammer's edition, but they are not there distinguished from echoes found only in the First Variant version.

hortatur. Sed quia tantum non habuit exercitum ut campestre prelium inire aduersus hostes auderet, callido usus consilio proponit castra eorum noctu adire ipsosque soporatos deceptis eorundem uigilibus interficere.

(ii) *Historia Regum Britannie*, § 135, vulgate

[135] At Uther frater eius conuocato regni clero et populo cepit diadema insule annitentibusque cunctis sublimatus est in regem. Reminiscens autem expositionis quam Merlinus de supradicto sydere fecerat iussit fabricari duos drachones ex auro ad similitudinem drachonis quem ad radium stelle inspexerat. Qui ut mira arte fabricati fuerunt, obtulit unum in ecclesia prime sedis ecclesie Wintonie; alterum uero sibi ad ferendum in prelia retinuit. Ab illo itaque tempore uocatus fuit Uther Pendragon quod Britannica lingua capud drachonis sonamus. Iccirco hanc appellationem receperat quia Merlinus eum per drachonem in regem prophetauerat.

Variant

[135] Ueniens ergo Uther Wintoniam conuocato clero et populo omnibus expetentibus et acclamantibus illum regem fieri suscepit dyadema regni Britannie et in regem sublimatus est. Reminiscens autem interpretacionis Merlini quam de sydere fecerat iussit fabricari duos drachones ex auro purissimo et unum in ecclesia episcopali Wintonie obtulit; alterum sibi ad ferendum in prelia retinuit. Ab illo ergo tempore appellatus est Utherpendragon, hoc est Britannice 'capud draconis', sicut Merlinus eum per drachonem in regem prophetauerat.

Indeed, some chapters in the Variant – those which I have designated as category D – are very considerably shorter than their vulgate counterparts. These chapters number no fewer than twenty-one. The relationship between the Variant and vulgate in such cases can best be appreciated by comparing *Historia Regum Britannie*, §§ 131 and 181 in both texts, as set out below.

(i) *Historia Regum Britannie*, § 131, vulgate

[131] Eodem tempore Pacentius filius Uortegrini qui in Germaniam diffugerat commonebat omnem armatum militem illius regni in Aurelium Ambrosium patremque suum uindicare uolebat. Promittebat enim infinitam copiam auri et argenti si auxilio eorum sibi Britanniam subdidisset. Denique cum promissis suis uniuersam iuuentutem corrupisset, parauit maximum nauigium applicuitque in aquilonaribus partibus insule ac eas uastare incepit. Cum id regi nuntiatum fuisset, collegit exercitum suum obuiamque perrexit

atque seuientes hostes ad prelium prouocauit. Qui ultro ad prelium uenientes commiserunt pugnam cum ciuibus sed uolente Deo deuicti fuerunt et
in fugam compulsi.

Variant

[131] Eodem tempore Pascencius Uortigerni filius qui in Germaniam diffugerat congregato undecumque exercitu nauigioque comparato applicuit in
aquilonaribus Britannie partibus atque eas uastare cepit. Sed rex Aurelius ut
audiuit, collecto exercitu ei obuiam uenit et commissa pugna deuictus Pascencius fugit.

(ii) *Historia Regum Britannie*, § 181, vulgate

[181] Cui successit Aurelius Conanus, mire probitatis iuuenis et ipsius
nepos, qui monarchiam totius insule tenens eiusdem diademate dignus esset
nisi foret ciuilis belli amator. Auunculum etenim suum qui post Constantinum regnare debuit inquietauit atque in carcerem posuit eiusque duobus
filiis peremptis obtinuit regnum tertioque regni sui anno defunctus est.

Variant

[181] Conanus uero regni dyademate insignitus, dignus laude si non foret
ciuilis belli amator, post multa facinora ab illo perpetrata secundo regni sui
anno obiit.

In the passages above, the Variant version is the shorter simply because it is
less detailed; however, in the majority of similar cases the reason is rather
that the chapters in question also belong to category H – chapters, that is,
containing material (whole passages or episodes) found only in the vulgate
text. While this latter category will be discussed in full below,[38] it is con-
venient to set out here a list of those chapters which are very much shorter
in the Variant, together with a brief indication of their contents, in order to
establish precisely which chapters are so handled. The chapters and their
contents are as follows.

Historia Regum Britannie,

§ 49	reign of Gorbonianus
§ 71	reign of Coillus
§ 77	passions of British martyrs

---

[38] Below, p. xxxix.

The question of why these particular chapters are found in a form so much shorter in the Variant text is one to which we must return later.

Before this examination of categories B, C, and D can be concluded, it must be stressed that the dividing line between the effects, in one text or the other, of stylistic reworking and a fuller (or less full) treatment of common material is apt to become blurred, as is demonstrated by some of the passages already quoted. In fact a significant number of chapters – one hundred and four – exhibits both processes at work and hence belongs to both categories B and C (or D). As an illustration, compare, for example, chapter 105 in both vulgate and Variant texts.

Historia Regum Britannie, § 105, vulgate

[105] Non impune tamen hoc egerunt pagani quia multi eorum perempti fuerunt dum neci ceterorum imminerent. Eripiebant enim Britones ex tellure lapides et fustes atque sese defendere uolentes proditores illidebant. Aderat ibi consul Claudiocestrie uocabulo Eldol qui uisa proditione sustulit palum quem forte inuenerat et defensioni uacauit. Quemcumque attingebat cum illo confringens ei membrum quod percutiebat dirigebat confestim ad tartara. Alii caput, alii brachia, alii scapulas, compluribus etenim crura elidens terrorem non minimum inferebat. Nec prius ab illo loco abscessit donec septuaginta uiros consumpto palo interfecit. Nam cum tante multitudini resistere nequiuisset, diuertit sese ab illis atque ciuitatem suam petiuit. Multi hinc et inde ceciderunt sed uictoriam habuerunt Saxones. Britones namque nichil tale premeditati inermes aduenerant, unde minime resistere potuerunt. Ut igitur inceptum nefandum peregerunt Saxones, uoluerunt interficere Uortegirnum sed mortem comminantes ligauerunt eum petieruntque ciuitates suas atque munitiones pro uita. Quibus ilico quicquid affec-

tauerunt concessit ut uiuus abscedere sineretur. Cumque id iureiurando confirmatum fuisset, soluerunt eum a uinculis atque urbem Londonie primitus adeuntes ceperunt. Ceperunt deinde Eboracum et Lindocolinum necnon et Guintoniam, quasque prouincias deuastantes. Inuadebant undique ciues quemadmodum lupi oues quas pastores deseruerunt. Cumque ergo tantam cladem inspexisset Uortegirnus, secessit in partibus Kambrie inscius quid contra nefandam gentem ageret.

Variant

[105] Dum autem fieret quasi de ouibus hec cedes, Britones qui euadere periculum potuerunt aut fugiendo aut lapides in hostes mittendo et palis et fustibus defendendo plures interemerunt. Eldol uero consul Claudiocestrie sustulit palum quem forte offenderat et defensioni uacauit et multos per palum confractis ceruicibus ad tartara legauit; nec prius destitit donec .lxx. ex illis palo suo interfectis diuertit se ab eis equumque uelocem ascendens ciuitatem suam quam cicius potuit adiit. Peracto itaque scelere uoluerunt regem ipsum interficere mortemque comminantes uinxerunt eum fortiter loris postulaueruntque sibi ciuitates et castra municionesque regni omnes contradi si mortis periculum euadere uellet. Cumque id iureiurando confirmasset, soluentes eum a uinculis Urbem Trinouantum primitus adeuntes susceperunt, deinde Eboracum et Lyndocolinum necnon et Wentanam ciuitatem. Ut ergo ab eis euadere potuit Uortigernus, secessit in partibus Kambrie, ignorans quid sibi agendum foret contra nefandam gentem.

Category E consists of chapters in which the Variant, although containing material essentially similar to that in the vulgate, offers a fuller, rather than a less full, version. As Hammer noted, the passages in which this occurs all consist of speeches.[39] There are ten such speeches in the Variant text, which are found in the chapters listed below.

Historia Regum Britannie,

§35	speech of *fabricatores mendacii* to Brennius
§41	speech of Conwenna (or Tonwenna)
§62	speech of Androgeus
§63	further speech of Androgeus
§121	speech of Hengist
§136	speech of Gorlois
§161	speech of Auguselus
§174	speech of Arthur
§200	speech of Margadud
§203	speech of Cadwaladr

[39] *Variant Version*, pp. 10–11.

In some of these speeches the version found in the Variant is only slightly fuller than that of the vulgate. In that in *Historia Regum Britannie*, § 35, for example, apart from the sort of stylistic variation already familiar from category B, the only material unique to the Variant worthy of note comprises the clause 'fedus quod tibi dedecori est *et contra generositatem tuam fecisti et fac consilio procerum tuorum ut ducas* filiam', compared with 'fedus quod tibi dedecori est et duc filiam' in the vulgate. Of the other speeches listed, those of Conwenna (*Historia Regum Britannie*, § 41), Androgeus (§§ 62 and 63), Arthur (§ 174) and Margadud (§ 200) similarly exhibit clauses or slightly more substantial portions of text unique to the Variant. The remaining four speeches, however, are different both in treatment and tone in the Variant text and deserve more detailed consideration. As an example, both versions of the speech of Cadwaladr (in *Historia Regum Britannie*, § 203) are set out below.

Vulgate

Ipse etiam rex Cadualadrus cum nauigio miserabili Armoricam petens predictum planctum hoc modo augebat: 'Ue nobis peccatoribus ob nimia scelera nostra quibus Deum offendere nullatenus diffugimus dum penitentiae spatium habebamus. Incumbit ergo illius potestatis ultio quae nos ex natali solo exstirpat quos nec olim Romani nec deinde Scoti uel Picti nec uersute proditionis Saxones exterminare quiuerunt. Sed in uanum patriam super illos tociens recuperauimus cum non fuit uoluntas Dei ut in ea perpetue regnaremus. Ipse uerus iudex cum uidisset nos nullatenus a sceleribus nostris cessare uelle ac neminem genus nostrum a regno expellere posse, uolens corripere stultos indignationem suam direxit qua propriam nationem cateruatim deserimus. Redite ergo Romani, redite Scoti et Picti, redite ambrones Saxones: ecce patet uobis Britannia ira Dei deserta quam uos desertam facere nequiuistis. Non nos fortitudo uestra expellit sed summi regis potentia quam numquam offendere distulimus.'

Variant

Ipse quoque rex Cadwalladrus ad Armoricam cum paucis nauigio effugit et inter nauigandum fertur has lugubres uoces ad Deum protulisse: 'Ue nobis miseris et peccatoribus, qui ob immania scelera nostra quibus Deum offendimus hanc tribulationem et dispersionem patimur; gentem et patriam amittimus. Timendum est ualde nobis ne post hanc celestem patriam perdamus et eterna hereditate priuemur. Domine, miserere nobis; tempus et locum penitencie misericorditer permitte. Ne irascaris nimis ut, si uel terrena caremus et presenti hereditate, illa omnino ne frustremur ad quam boni omnes quos in hac uita eligisti laborant peruenire. Exterminat nos de terra nostra potestas ulcionis tue, quos nec olim Romani uel quelibet gens robustior eradicare potuit. Uere peccauimus ultra modum coram te et angelis tuis qui digni non sumus ut conuersi ad penitenciam terras quas incoluimus inhabitemus. Expellimur flagello iracundie tue quia serui nequissimi spreuimus, dum licuit, ueniam misericordie tue. Experimur nunc seueritatem iudicantis qui, dum tempus habuimus, noluimus flectere lumina ad paternitatem uocantis. Frustra patriam nostram aduersus hostes te adiuuante tociens expugnauimus, tociens expulsi te donante recuperauimus, si sic olim decreueras uniuersum genus nostrum extirpare de terra uiuencium. Sed placabilis esto, quesumus, super maliciam nostram et conuerte luctum nostrum in gaudium ut de periculo mortis erepti uiuentes tibi Domino Deo nostro, cuius serui esse debemus, in perpetuum famulemur. Redeant ergo Romani, redeant Scoti et Picti, redeant Saxones perfidi et ceteri, quibus patet Britannia ira Dei deserta, quam illi desertam facere nequiuerunt. Non nos fortitudo illorum expellit sed summi regis indignacio et potencia.'

In the vulgate text, Cadwaladr's soliloquy takes the form of a lament. Its main thrust is that the loss of Britain was caused by God's retribution, meted out for the sins of the British, rather than by wars with the Romans, Picts and Irish, and English; it ends with a bitter invitation to these latter to enjoy their unmerited gains. In the Variant text, the speech retains this basic framework, but the addition of further elements of piety lend it more the character of a prayer (it being addressed, indeed, 'ad Deum'): Cadwaladr fears that the loss of Britain is only the prelude to the loss of a place in heaven and prays directly to God to avert this; the theme of divine retribution also receives more elaborate treatment in the Variant;[40] the final address to Britain's foes is made indirectly in the Variant (*redeant* as opposed to the vulgate's *redite*), while at the same time being prefaced by another direct prayer for God's mercy. Moreover, precisely these elements unique to the Variant contain, as Hammer noted in his apparatus, a plethora of biblical borrowings and allusions, entirely appropriate to their setting.[41] In this case, the fondness for biblical borrowings, which (as we

---

[40] Note, for example, the rhetorical balance and rhyme 'seueritatem iudicantis ... paternitatem uocantis'; cf. p. xxiii above.

[41] Compare 'hanc *tribulationem* et dispersionem *patimur*' and 2 Corinthians 4.8, 'in omnibus *tribulationem patimur*'; 'et *eterna hereditate* priuemur' and Hebrews 9.15, 'repromissionem accipiant ... *aeternae hereditatis*'; '*Domine, miserere nobis*', also Tobias 8.10; '*locum penitencie* ... permitte' and Job 24.23, 'dedit ei Deus *locum penitentiae*'; '*Ne irascaris*', also Genesis 18.32; '*coram* te et *angelis* tuis' and 1 Timothy 5.21, '*coram* Deo et ... electis *angelis*'; 'extirpare *de terra uiuencium*' and Psalms 51.7, 'euellet te ... *de terra uiuentium*'; '*placabilis esto* ... *super* maliciam nostram' and Exodus 32.12, '*esto placabilis super* nequitia populi'; 'et *conuerte luctum nostrum in gaudium*' and Esther 13.17 (cited verbatim); '*de periculo* mortis *erepti*' and 2 Corinthians 1.10, '*de* tantis *periculis eripuit* nos'.

have seen) is typical of the Variant text, serves a clear dramatic purpose; the presence of such allusions in Cadwaladr's speech is entirely suited to the character of the speaker – the last king of the British, soon to die at Rome in an odour of sanctity.

Of the remaining three speeches found in a fuller form in the Variant, that of Gorlois of Cornwall (§ 136) also manifests a religious tone quite absent from the vulgate text;[42] this religious element is again appropriate to the dramatic context in which the speech occurs – that of conflict between the christian British and the pagan English. The speech of Auguselus (§ 161), although it is more vigorous in the Variant version, lacks any such pious touches. However, perhaps the most striking example of the different handling of speeches in the Variant occurs in § 121. Both versions of the passage in question are set out below.

Vulgate

[121] At Hengistus cum aduentum ipsius comperisset, reuocata audatia commilitones suos elegit atque unumquemque animans hortabatur eos uiriliter resistere nec congressum Aurelii abhorrere. Dicebat autem ipsum paucos ex Armoricanis Britonibus habere cum numerus eorum ultra .x. milia non procederet. Insulanos uero Britones pro nichilo reputabat cum tociens eos in preliis deuicisset. Proinde promittebat suis uictoriam et ob ampliorem numerum securitatem. Aderant enim circiter ducenta milia armatorum. Et cum omnes hoc modo inanima⸗set, iuit obuiam Aurelio in campo qui dicebatur Maubeti quo ipse Aurelius transiturus erat.

Variant

[121] At Hengistus conuocans in unum Saxones suos sic hortabatur eos, dicens: 'Nolite terreri, fratres et commilitones mei, a superuenientibus pueris quorum audacia nullis adhuc populis nota temerario se ausu in nos bellatores notissimos et exercitatissimos ingerere festinat. Nolite, inquam, timere eorum de diuersis nacionibus congregatam multitudinem quorum in preliis multociens experti estis inbellem inualitudinem. Mementote uictores semper extitisse et de eis stragem non modicam cum paucis peregisse. Dux quoque eorum qui indoctum ducit exercitum necdum ad uirilem peruenit etatem, magis puerilibus exercitatus lusibus quam bellis. Fauentibus ergo diis nostris inuictissimis et fugari et prosterni necesse est illos qui necdum arma ferre nouerunt et quorum inbecillis est bellandi astucia.' Et cum omnes hoc modo animasset Hengistus, dato signo in hostes iter tendit ut subitum et furtiuum impetum in illos faceret Britonesque incautos et inparatos occuparet.

---

[42] See also n. 30 above.

As is immediately apparent, Hengist's speech is in *oratio obliqua* in the vulgate, but is reported in *oratio recta* in the Variant; this change of form combines with the obvious changes of content – such as the greater emphasis placed by the Variant on Hengist's over-confident contempt for all the British as inexperienced, and the omission of his respect for the prowess of the Breton contingent – to render the Variant version the more vivid.

It is clear, then, that some of the speeches found in fuller form in the Variant version constitute another important aspect of the stylistic differences between the two texts and will need to be considered when the relationship between them is discussed.

Category F, the last of those concerning matter common to both texts, comprises chapters in which all or part of their content is found in a different order in the vulgate and Variant. There are sixteen such chapters. Let us begin with those chapters in which only a part of their content is involved: these all exhibit the apparent transposition (in one text or the other) of sentences or larger blocks of text either within the same chapter (a feature which on a smaller scale is characteristic, as we have seen, of the stylistic differences between vulgate and Variant) or, more often, to another adjacent chapter. In most such cases, the more coherent narrative structure is found in the Variant version, although we should be wary of drawing any firm conclusions from this fact at the present stage. Two examples – the first from the beginning of § 27, the second §§ 179–80 entire – serve to illustrate these transpositions.

(i) *Historia Regum Britannie*, § 27, vulgate

Deinde trans Hunbrum condidit urbem quam de nomine suo uocauit Kaer Ebrauc, id est ciuitas Ebrauci. Et tunc Dauid rex regnabat in Iudea et Siluius Latinus in Italia et Gad, Nathan, et Asaph prophetabant in Israel. Condidit etiam Ebraucus urbem Alclud uersus Albaniam et oppidum Montis Agned, quod nunc Castellum Puellarum dicitur, et Montem Dolorosum.

Variant

Deinde trans Humbrum condidit ciuitatem quam de nomine suo uocauit Kaerebrauc, id est ciuitas Ebrauci. Edificauit et aliam ciuitatem Alclud nomine uersus Albaniam et oppidum Montis Agned – quod nunc Castellum Puellarum dicitur – et Montem Dolorosum. Et tunc Dauid rex regnabat in Iudea et Siluius Latinus in Ytalia et Gad, Nathan, et Asaph in Israel prophetabant.

[179] Illo igitur insignito insurrexerunt Saxones et duo filii Modredi nec in eum preualere quiuerunt. Sed post plurima prelia diffugiendo unus Londonias, alter uero Guintoniam ingressus, eas obtinere ceperunt. Tunc defunctus est sanctus Daniel Bangoriensis ecclesie religiosissimus antistes et .N. Gloecestrensis episcopus in archiepiscopatum Londoniarum erigitur. Tunc obiit sanctissimus Urbis Legionum archiepiscopus Dauid in Meneuia ciuitate infra abbatiam suam; quam pre ceteris sue dioceseos monasteriis dilexerat quia beatus Patricius, qui natiuitatem eius prophetauerat, ipsam fundauit. Dum ibi apud confratres suos moram faceret, subito languore mortuus in eadem ecclesia sepultus est. Pro eo ponitur in metropolitana sede Kinocus Lampaternensis ecclesie antistes et ad altiorem dignitatem promouetur. [180] At Constantinus insecutus est duos filios Modredi et Saxones potestati sue subiugauit et predictas ciuitates cepit. Et alterum iuuenem Guintonie in ecclesia sancti Amphibali diffugientem ante altare trucidauit; alium uero Londoniis in quorumdam fratrum cenobio absconditum atque tandem iuxta altare inuentum crudeli morte affecit. Exin quarto anno sententia Dei percussus iuxta Utherpendragon infra lapidum structuram sepultus fuit; que haut longe Salesberia mira arte composita Anglorum lingua Stanhenge nunccupatur.

Variant

[179/180] Postea duo filii Modredi cum Saxonibus qui remanserant, alter Londoniam, alter uero Wintoniam ingressi contra Constantinum munire ceperunt. At Constantinus cum armata manu Britonum ciuitatibus adueniens Saxones potestati sue subiugauit et alterum iuuenem Wintonie in ecclesia sancti Amphibali delitescentem trucidauit, alterum uero Londoniis in quodam cenobio absconditum crudeli morte multauit. Tunc temporis sanctus Daniel Bangornensis ecclesie religiosus antistes migrauit ad Dominum. Tunc quoque sanctus Dauid obiit Urbis Legionum archiepiscopus sepultusque est in Meneuia ciuitate infra monasterium suum, quod pre ceteris sue dioceseos dilexerat pro eo quod beatus Patricius, qui natiuitatem eius prophetauerat, ipsum fundauit. Subrogatur sedi illius Kinnocus Lampaternensis ecclesie antistes et ad altiorem dignitatem in metropolitanum promouetur. Cum autem duobus annis regnasset Constantinus, tertio anno interfectus est a Conano et infra structuram lapidum, que Saxonica lingua Stanheng nuncupatur, iuxta cenobium Ambrii sepelitur.

In the first of the chapters quoted here (§ 27), the historical synchronism of events in Britain with those in Italy and Israel obtrudes in the vulgate text into the account of the building activities of Ebraucus; this awkwardness is avoided in the Variant, where the synchronism follows the details of the

building programme. Similarly, in §§ 179–80, the passage devoted to episcopal obits and successions interrupts in the vulgate the narrative of Constantine's campaign against Mordred's sons; but in the Variant text the
passage is more neatly appended to that narrative. The remaining Variant
chapters which contain material in a different order from that in the vulgate, or material found in a different chapter in the vulgate, are, with the
exception of those already quoted, listed below (with details of the matter
distinctive to them).

Historia Regum Britannie (Variant version)

§ 5	part of the final (Variant) sentence is found in vulgate § 2 (which chapter is absent from the Variant text)
§ 21	the episodes of the first distribution of land in Britain and the wrestling-match of Corineus and Gogmagog are transposed
§ 29	contains chronological matter found in vulgate § 28
§ 93	contains a part of Gozelinus's speech found in vulgate § 92 (otherwise absent from the Variant text)
§ 102	contains a short version of the account of the mission of St Germanus (vulgate § 100)
§ 177	contains an account of the siege of Winchester (vulgate § 178, in addition to having sentences transposed
§ 204	contains a passage about Æthelstan, first English ruler of Britain (vulgate § 207)

However, on two occasions, at *Historia Regum Britannie*, §§ 159–64
and 184–7 respectively, whole chapters, or the greater portions thereof, are
found in different positions in the two texts; this – together with other
minor transpositions of the type already discussed – results in important
differences of narrative structure in the passages in question. The first of
these passages is concerned with the reaction of Arthur and his nobles to
the demands of Roman ambassadors and with the assembly of British and
Roman forces for the ensuing hostilities. The second deals with the
devastation of Britain by Gormund and its effects on the religion and
ascendency of the British population. The differences between the vulgate
and Variant texts of these two extensive passages can best be appreciated if
the sequence of chapters (and parts of chapters) in both texts is set out for
comparison.

(i) *Historia Regum Britannie*, §§ 159–64, vulgate

§ 159	Arthur's speech
§ 160	Hoel's reply

§ 161	Auguselus's speech
§ 162 (i)	catalogue of British forces
(ii)	dismissal of Roman ambassadors
§ 163	catalogue of Roman forces
§ 164 (i)	Roman advance on Britain
(ii)	Arthur's dream

Variant

§ 159	Arthur's speech (in different form)
[§ 160	absent from Variant text]
§ 162 (ii)	dismissal of the Roman ambassadors
§ 163	catalogue of Roman forces
§ 164 (i)	Roman advance on Britain (combined with § 163 above)
§ 161	Auguselus's speech (with different introductory matter and form)
§ 162 (i)	catalogue of British forces (including one sentence from vulgate § 160)
§ 164 (ii)	Arthur's dream

(ii) *Historia Regum Britannie*, §§ 184–7, vulgate

§ 184	devastation of Britain
§ 185	condemnation of British civil faction
§ 186 (i)	flight of British population to far West
(ii)	British clerics abandon Loegria
§ 187 (i)	British loss of supremacy
(ii)	establishment of three British and three English rulers

Variant

§ 184	devastation of Britain
[§ 185	absent from Variant text]
§ 186 (ii)	British clerics abandon Loegria (in different form and combined with § 184)
§ 186 (i)	British population flee to far West
[§ 187 (i)	absent from Variant text (except for one clause found in § 186 [i])]
[§ 187 (ii)	entirely absent from Variant text, which has a different passage at this point]

In the first of these passages (§§ 159–64), the Variant text offers a narrative which is simpler (in that Hoel's speech is absent) and differently balanced (in that the dismissal of the Roman envoys and the mustering of Roman forces precedes Arthur's military preparations rather than vice versa as in the vulgate text). These differences are, though on a larger scale, very much in line with the minor, but similar, structural divergences already discussed. The second passage (§§ 184–7) is more complex, since the Variant text there reflects a historical perspective different from that of the vulgate. A similar difference of perspective is apparent in the presence in Variant § 204 of material found in the vulgate text in § 207; the significance of these latter divergences is an important question to which we must return later.[43]

Having completed our examination of the first group of categories, we may proceed to the second. This latter group consists of two categories (G and H), comprising respectively chapters either wholly or partially absent from the Variant version. Category G, vulgate chapters entirely (or almost entirely) lacking in the Variant, contains only nine examples. The vulgate chapters concerned are as follows.

Historia Regum Britannie,

§§ 1–4	prologue and dedication(s) of the *Histora* (save for one clause from vulgate § 2 found in Variant § 5)
§§ 109–10	prologue and dedication to the *Prophetie Merlini*
§ 160	Hoel's speech (except for one clause found in Variant § 162)
§ 185	condemnation of British civil faction
§ 187	British loss of ascendency (except for one clause found in Variant § 186)

Seven of the above chapters are of the same type, which may explain their absence from the Variant text: vulgate §§ 1–4 and 109–10, being prefatory or dedicatory, comprise statements of authorial intention on Geoffrey's part; § 185, a denunciation, is also composed in the authorial voice (although Geoffrey does not name himself on this occasion). As we shall see,[44] the almost total absence of such personal material, on a large or a small scale, must be regarded as characteristic of the Variant version.

Of the remaining two chapters, the first (§ 160) – one clause of which is, in fact, found in Variant § 162 – is entirely composed of a speech; its absence should therefore be considered in the light of the large number of speeches wanting in the Variant, discussed in category H below. Similarly, the second chapter (§ 187) is not completely missing from the Variant, since, as we

43 Below, pp. lxvi–lxx.
44 Below, p. xli.

have seen,[45] a part of it is found in the previous chapter in that version. Moreover, this chapter occurs in a passage which will need to be discussed in detail when we consider the historical aims of the Variant version.[46]

Category H, the second within this group, is by far the larger, since it includes forty-eight chapters. These chapters, which in the vulgate contain subject-matter absent from the Variant text, can themselves be divided into two groups.

The first of these groups comprises chapters in which speeches, or sometimes entire episodes whose core consists of one or more elaborate speeches, are found only in the vulgate text. The chapters in question, and the speeches and/or episodes involved, are as follows.

Historia Regum Britannie,

§ 79	speech of Roman exiles to Constantine
§ 81	description of Mauricius and his speech to Maximianus
§ 82	Maximianus's arrival in Britain
§ 83	reception of Maximianus
§ 90	speech of Archbishop Guizelinus in London
§ 92	speeches of Guizelinus and Aldroenus of Brittany
§ 119	speech of Ambrosius (save for one sentence present in the Variant)
§ 132	two short speeches before Ambrosius's death
§ 141	speech of Uther
§ 146	speech of Arthur at Badon
§ 147	speech of Dubritius at Badon
§ 178	details of the battle of Camblan including: dispositions; speeches of Arthur and Modred (reported in *oratio obliqua* in the vulgate); some elements of the fighting
§ 191	speech of Brian
§ 194	speech of Solomon of Brittany
§ 195	reply of Cadwallo

These speeches (and related material) present in the vulgate text, but entirely absent from the Variant, considerably outnumber those speeches in which the Variant exhibits a more elaborate treatment of *oratio recta* common to both texts;[47] the absence of speeches, then, is the trait more typical of the Variant.

45 Above, p. xxxvii.
46 Below, pp. lxvi–lxx.
47 Above, p. xxx.

The Variant text lacks not only the speeches set out above but also a considerable amount of other material found in the vulgate. This material, together with the chapter in which it is found (in the vulgate), is listed below.

Historia Regum Britannie,

§ 10	details of the siege of Sparatinum
§ 15	Immogen's lament and Brutus's consolations
§ 22	Lud's altercation with Nennius about the naming of London (including a reference to Gildas)
§ 30	synchronising reference to Elijah
§ 34	reference to Gildas's account of the Molmutine Laws
§ 37	details of battle of *nemus Calaterium* between Brennius and Belinus
§ 49	description of the reign of Gorbonianus
§ 52	description of the reign of Gorbonianus's son
§ 62	details (and praise) of the final resistance of Cassibellanus to Caesar (including a quotation of Lucan)
§ 69	description of Aruiragus (including a quotation of Juvenal)
§ 70	statement of Geoffrey's disinterest (in the *Historia*) in the history of the Scots and Irish
§ 71	description of the reign of Coillus
§ 77	details of the passions of St Alban and other martyrs
§ 85	details of the British occupation of Armorica
§ 91	details of the massacre of British by Picts and Irish (including rhetorical moralising in the authorial voice)
§ 100	mission of Germanus of Auxerre (found, in part, in Variant, § 102)
§ 104	burial of the British leaders assassinated by Hengist
§ 120	eulogy of Ambrosius and a description of Scotland
§ 140	construction of a litter for Uther
§ 156	mention of the three archbishops and the British heroes present at Arthur's crown-wearing at Caerleon
§ 157	descriptive details of Arthur's court
§ 166	details of Gawain's battle with the Romans
§ 170	Roman dispositions at Siesia and a catalogue of their leaders
§ 171	details of initial clashes at Siesia
§ 173	list of British casualties
§ 174	further details of fighting at Siesia
§ 175	authorial comment on the justice of the British victory at Siesia
§ 177	reference to Geoffrey by name

§186	statement of the author's intention of translating an account of the exile of British clerics in Brittany
§190	Ethelfrid's repudiation of his wife
§193	Cadwallo's illness on Guernsey and the eating of a slice from Brian's thigh
§196	attempted rescue of Brian's sister
§202	reference to Bede and the length of Cadwaladr's reign
§208	references to Caradoc of Llancarvan, William of Malmesbury and Henry of Huntingdon, and to Geoffrey's alleged source, the *liber uetustissimus*

It is not easy to discern precisely why these details were omitted in the Variant or, conversely, added in the vulgate. Some patterns do, however, emerge. As we have seen when discussing vulgate chapters entirely missing from the Variant, passages composed in the authorial voice or containing self-reference on Geoffrey's part are generally absent from the Variant version. Thus the Variant not only lacks the chapters introductory to the *Historia* proper and to the *Prophetie Merlini*, and the condemnation of civil strife in §185, but also similar personal material found in §§70, 91, 175, 177, 186, and 208 (listed above).

Another type of material sometimes absent from the Variant consists of battle-descriptions and related passages (as in §§10, 37, 91, 166, 170, 171, and 174); this point should not, however, be overemphasised, as the Variant does contain other such passages, often indeed stylistically different and as vigorous as their counterparts in the vulgate.[48] Rather, the absence of these battle-episodes should be seen as part of a general tendency for some of the more rhetorical and emotionally charged passages in the vulgate text to be absent from the Variant. The omission from the Variant (or the addition in the vulgate) of some battle-descriptions is, then, in line with that of the speeches listed above, as well as that of other emotive passages (such as those at §§15, 62, 77, and 91, and perhaps 193 and 196). Possibly too, the absence from the Variant of a number of references and points of detail, including (in addition to those found in passages already discussed) those in §§22, 30, 34, 156, 157, and 202, should also be viewed as a result of the same tendency, although it must be stressed that the Variant version, as we shall see, does include other details not found in the vulgate text. Finally, before we leave this category, it should be noted that in some cases the lack of the above passages, whether speeches or other episodes,

---

[48] Compare, for instance, the treatment of the battle between Aurelius and Hengist in Variant and vulgate, §123.

means that the Variant chapters are very much shorter than their vulgate counterparts; I have already listed such chapters in category D.[49]

The final group of categories comprises Variant chapters which, unlike the majority of those already discussed, contain material not present in the vulgate text. Since in no case is an entire chapter found only in the Variant, this group consists of two categories: I, chapters containing material unique to the Variant and drawn from a recognisable source; and J, chapters containing other material unique to the Variant.

Category I is relatively small, as only five chapters (§§ 5, 6, 54, 59, and 86) belong to it. In all these chapters, the Variant exhibits borrowings from earlier historical sources. In one case, that of the description of Britain in § 5, the vulgate and Variant texts are almost completely different, since the former draws freely on the *De Excidio Britanniae* of Gildas,[50] the latter practically verbatim on Bede's *Historia Ecclesiastica Gentis Anglorum*.[51] I set out the vulgate and Variant texts for comparison below, together with the relevant portions of *Historia Ecclesiastica* I.1 (I omit the Gildasian passage since I have discussed Geoffrey's use of it at length elsewhere).[52]

Historia Regum Britannie, § 5, vulgate

[5] Britannia insularum optima in occidentali occeano inter Galliam et Hiberniam sita octoginta milia in longum, ducenta uero in latum continens quicquid mortalium usui congruit indeficienti fertilitate ministrat. Omni etenim genere metalli fecunda campos late pansos habet, colles quoque prepollenti culture aptos in quibus frugum diuersitates ubertate glebe temporibus suis proueniunt. Habet nemora uniuersis ferarum generibus repleta quorum in saltibus et alternandis animalium pastibus gramina conueniunt et aduolantibus apibus flores diuersorum colorum mella distribuunt. Habet etiam prata sub aeriis montibus ameno situ uirentia in quibus fontes lucidi per nitidos riuos leni murmure manantes pignus suauis soporis in ripis accubantibus irritant. Porro lacubus atque piscosis fluuiis irrigua est et absque meridiane plage freto quo ad Gallias nauigatur tria nobilia flumina, Tamensis uidelicet et Sabrine necnon et Humbri, uelut tria brachia extendit quibus transmarina commertia ex uniuersis nationibus eidem nauigio feruntur. Bis denis etiam bisque quaternis ciuitatibus olim decorata erat quarum quedam dirutis menibus in desertis locis squalescunt, quedam uero adhuc integre templa sanctorum cum turribus perpulcra proceritate erectis continent in

49 Above, p. xxviii–ix.
50 Edited by Winterbottom, *Gildas*.
51 Edited by Colgrave & Mynors, *Bede's Ecclesiastical History*.
52 Wright, 'Geoffrey of Monmouth and Gildas', pp. 5–7 (and 34–5).

quibus religiosi cetus uirorum ac mulierum obsequium Deo iuxta christian-
am tradicionem prestant. Postremo quinque inhabitatur populis: Norman-
nis uidelicet atque Britannis, Saxonibus, Pictis et Scotis. Ex quibus Britones
olim ante ceteros a mari usque ad mare insederunt donec ultione diuina
propter ipsorum superueniente superbiam Pictis et Saxonibus cesserunt.
Qualiter uero et unde applicuerunt restat nunc parare ut in subsequentibus
explicabitur.

Variant

[5] Britannia insularum optima quondam Albion nuncupata est: in occidentali occeano inter Galliam et Hyberniam sita octingenta milia passuum in
longum, ducenta uero in latum continens. Terra opima frugibus et arboribus
et alendis apta pecoribus ac iumentis; uineas etiam quibusdam in locis germinans sed et auium ferax terra, fluuiis quoque multum piscosis ac fontibus
preclara copiosis. Habet et fontes salinarum, habet et fontes calidos, uenis
quoque metallorum eris ferri plumbi et argenti fecunda. Eratque quondam
ciuitatibus nobilissimis .xx. et .viii. insignita. Insula hec Britones et Pictos et
Scotos incolas recepit. Britones autem a quibus nomen accepit in primis a
mari usque ad mare totam insulam insederunt; qui de tractu Armenicano ut
fertur Britanniam aduecti sunt. Qualiter uero et unde uel ubi applicuerunt
restat calamo perarare sequendo ueterum hystorias qui a Bruto usque ad
Cadwaladrum filium Cadwalonis actus omnium continue et ex ordine
texuerunt.

Bede, *Historia Ecclesiastica* I.1

Brittania occeani insula, cui quondam Albion nomen fuit, ... per milia passuum .dccc. in boream longa, latitudinis habet milia .cc.... Opima frugibus
atque arboribus insula, et alendis apta pecoribus ac iumentis, uineas etiam
quibusdam in locis germinans, sed et auium ferax terra marique generis
diuersi, fluuiis quoque multum piscosis et fontibus praeclara copiosis ...
Habet fontes salinarum, habet et fontes calidos, ... etiam uenis metallorum,
aeris ferri plumbi et argenti, fecunda ... Erat et ciuitatibus quondam .xx. et
.viii. nobilissimis insignita ... In primis autem insula Brettones solum, a quibus nomen accepit, incolas habuit; qui de tractu Armoricano, ut fertur, Britanniam aduecti australes sibi partes illius uindicarunt.

Clearly, one of the above versions of *Historia Regum Britannie*, § 5 (either
the Gildasian or the Bedan) must have been substituted for the other, although once again it is not immediately plain whether the substitution occurred in the Variant or the vulgate text.

In the remaining four chapters, the Variant contains historical details additional to, rather than in place of, those found in the vulgate. In § 6, both versions of which are set out below, these details concern legendary Roman history.

Historia Regum Britannie, § 6, vulgate

[6] Eneas post Troianum bellum excidium urbis cum Ascanio filio suo diffugiens nauigio Italiam adiuit. Ibi cum a Latino rege honorifice receptus esset, inuidit Turnus rex Rutilorum et cum illo congressus est. Dimicantibus ergo illis preualuit Eneas peremptoque Turno regnum Italie et Lauiniam filiam Latini adeptus est. Denique suprema die illius superueniente Ascanius regia potestate sublimatus condidit Albam super Tyberim genuitque filium cuius nomen erat Siluius. Hic furtiue ueneri indulgens nupsit cuidam nepti Lauinie eamque fecit pregnantem.

Variant

[6] Eneas post Troianum excidium cum Ascanio filio fugiens Ytaliam nauigio deuenit ibique a Latino susceptus cum Turno Dauni Tuscorum regis filio dimicans eum interemit. Regnumque Ytalie et Lauiniam filiam Latini adeptus est. De cuius etiam nomine Lauinium oppidum quod struxerat appellauit et regnauit Eneas Latinis annis .iiii.. Quo uita discedente regnum suscepit Ascanius qui et Iulus eiusdem filius erat; quem apud Troiam ex Creusa filia Priami regis genuerat et secum in Ytaliam ueniens adduxerat. Qui Ascanius derelicto nouerce sue Lauinie regno Albam Longam condidit deosque et penates patris sui Enee ex Lauinio in Albam transtulit. Symulacra Lauinium sponte redierunt. Rursus traducta in Albam, iterum repecierunt antiqua delubra. Educauit autem Ascanius summa pietate Postumum Siluium fratrem suum ex Lauinia procreatum et cum .xxx. annis et .iiii. regnasset, Siluium reliquid heredem. Hic furtiue indulgens ueneri nupserat cuidam nepti Lauinie eamque fecerat pregnantem.

In this case, the additional information in the Variant text is borrowed, again often verbatim, from the *Historia Romana* of an eleventh-century writer, Landolfus Sagax.[53]

---

[53] Edited by Crivellucci, *Landolfi Sagacis Historia Romana* (see I.xxxvii–viii for the date of the work). The borrowing from Landolfus in the First Variant was first noted by Caldwell, 'The use', p. 123. Hammer, *Variant Version*, p. 24, compared instead Paul the Deacon's *Historia Romana* I.1 (edited by Droysen, *Eutropi Breviarium*, pp. 6–7); but, although Landolfus's work is primarily a continuation of Paul the Deacon's *Historia*, it adds material, such as the story in this passage of Ascanius's household gods, which is derived from Nepotianus's *Epitoma librorum Valerii Maximi* (edited by Kempf, *Valerii Maximi Facto-*

Capta igitur Troia Eneas Ueneris et Anchise filius ad Italiam uenit tertio anno post Troie excidium. Cum Turno Dauni Tuscorum regis filio dimicans, eum interemit eiusque sponsam Lauiniam, Latini regis filiam, in coniugio accepit, de cuius etiam nomine Lauinium oppidum, quod construxerat, appellauit. Regnauit igitur Eneas Latinis annis tribus.

Quo uita decidente [var. decedente] regnum suscepit Ascanius, qui et Iulus, eiusdem Enee filius, quem apud Troiam ex Creusa coniuge filia Priami regis genuerat et secum in Italiam ueniens adduxerat. Qui Ascanius derelicto nouerce sue Lauinie regno Albam Longam condidit et Siluium Posthumum fratrem suum Enee ex Lauinia filium summa pietate edocauit [var. educauit] deosque penates patris sui Enee ex Lauio [sic] in Albam Longam transtulit; simulacra uero Lauium sponte redierunt. Rursus traducta in Albam Longam iterum repetiuere antiquiora delubra. Deinde Ascanius Iulum filium procreauit, a quo familia Iuliorum exorta est. Paruulus quia necdum regendis ciuibus idoneus erat, cum triginta et octo annis regnasset Ascanius, Siluium Posthumum fratrem suum regni reliquid heredem.

In the three other chapters in question, the Variant draws once more on Bede's *Historia Ecclesiastica*. When recounting Caesar's two invasions of Britain (§§ 54 and 59), the Variant text offers additional details – the circumstances and date of the first invasion, and the number and type of Caesar's ships on both occasions – which are manifestly derived from Bede (not only from the relevant chapter of the *Historia Ecclesiastica* but also from the recapitulation at the end of that work), as the clear verbal parallels show.[54]

(i) *Historia Regum Britannie*, § 54, vulgate

[54] Interea contigit, ut in Romanis repperitur historiis, Iulium Cesarem subiugata Gallia ad litus Rutenorum uenisse.

---

rum, pp. 592–624, at 606). The First Variant follows Landolfus's account of this incident very closely (and cannot, therefore, independently be combining Paul the Deacon and Nepotianus, both of whom are reworked by Landolfus).

[54] In addition to the major borrowings set out here, the description in the First Variant of Maximianus as '*uim sui furoris* exacuens' (§ 86, the phrase being absent from the vulgate) is evidently modelled on *Historia Ecclesiastica* II.7, '*uim sui furoris* ... abstraxit' (though Bede there refers to a fire).

Variant

[54] Interea contigit, ut in Romanis reperitur hystoriis, Iulium Cesarem subiugata Gallia in Britanniam transisse. Sic enim scriptum est: anno ab urbe condita sexcentesimo nonagesimo tercio, ante uero incarnacionem Domini anno sexagesimo, Iulius Cesar primus Romanorum Britannias bello pulsauit, in nauibus onerariis et actuariis circiter octoginta aduectus. Cum enim ad litus Rutenorum uenisset . . . .

Bede, *Historia Ecclesiastica* I.2

Uerum eadem Brittania Romanis usque ad Gaium Iulium Caesarem inaccessa atque incognita fuit. Qui anno ab Urbe condita sescentesimo nonagesimo tertio, ante uero incarnationis Dominicae tempus anno sexagesimo, . . . uenit ad Morianos, unde in Brittaniam proximus et breuissimus transitus est, et nauibus circiter onerariis atque actuariis .lxxx. praeparatis in Brittaniam transuehitur.

and *Historia Ecclesiastica* V.24

Anno igitur ante incarnationem dominicam sexagesimo Gaius Iulius Caesar primus Romanorum Brittanias bello pulsauit et uicit; nec tamen ibi regnum potuit obtinere.

(ii) *Historia Regum Britannie*, § 59, vulgate

[59] Emenso itaque biennio parat occeanum iterum transfretare et sese in Cassibellaunum uindicare.

Variant

[59] Paratis itaque omnibus que ad tantum negocium pertinebant biennio emenso nauibusque sexcentis utriusque commodi comparatis iterum Britanniam adiit.

Bede, *Historia Eccelsiastica* I.2

Regressus in Galliam legiones in hiberna dimisit ac sescentas naues utriusque commodi fieri inperauit. Quibus iterum in Brittaniam primo uere transuectus . . . .

Lastly, in § 86, which is concerned with Maximianus (as Geoffrey calls the historical Magnus Maximus), the Variant version, again following Bede,[55]

---

[55] Given the evident use of Bede in Variant, §§ 54 and 59, there is (*pace* Caldwell, 'The use', p. 124) no reason to suppose that the Variant here relies on Landolfus rather than Bede.

but on this occasion more freely and with some awkwardness,[56] contains a passage on Gratian, Valentinian, and Maximianus's death, which is not present in the vulgate.

Historia Regum Britannie, § 86, vulgate

Ipse uero cum ceteris commilitonibus suis ulteriorem Galliam adiuit grauissimisque preliis illatis subiugauit eam necnon et totam Germaniam in omni prelio uictoria potitus. Thronum autem imperii sui apud Treueros statuens ita debachatus est in duos imperatores, Gracianum et Ualentinianum, quod uno interempto alterum ex Roma fugauit.

Variant

Ipse deinde cum suis ulteriorem Galliam penetrans grauissimis preliis illatis subiugauit eam necnon et totam Germaniam, ciuitate Treueri solium imperii sui constituens. Postea in Gratianum et Ualentinianum imperatores uim sui furoris exacuens uno interempto alterum a Roma fugauit. Ipse uero Rome imperator creatus .xl. ab Augusto imperium rexit anno ab incarnacione Domini trecentesimo septuagesimo .vii.. Ualentinianus autem, frater Gratiani, ad Theodosium in orientem fugiens imperio per Theodosium restitutus est et Maximianum subinde apud Aquileiam fratrem uindicans interfecit.

Bede, *Historia Ecclesiastica* I.9

Anno ab incarnatione Domini .ccclxxvii. Gratianus quadragesimus ab Augusto post mortem Ualentis sex annis imperium tenuit. ... [Maximus] imperator creatus in Galliam transit. Ibi Gratianum Augustum subita incursione perterritum, atque in Italiam transire meditantem, dolis circumuentum interfecit fratremque eius Ualentinianum Augustum Italia expulit. Ualentinianus in Orientem refugiens a Theodosio paterna pietate susceptus mox etiam imperio restitutus est, clauso uidelicet intra muros Aquileiae, capto atque occiso ab eis Maximo tyranno.

Before passing on to the last category, it should be noticed that the above borrowings unique to the Variant version twice involve internal inconsistences not found in the vulgate text. In § 5, the statement, borrowed from Bede, that the British population first migrated to Britain from Armorica

---

[56] It is far from clear in the Variant whether the sentence, 'Ipse uero Rome imperator creatus .xl. ab Augusto imperium rexit anno ab incarnacione Domini trecentesimo septuagesimo .vii.' describes (correctly, with Bede) Gratianus or (erroneously) Maximianus himself (who is also referred to as 'Ipse' at the beginning of the passage).

flatly contradicts the Trojan origin-story so prominent at the beginning of the *Historia*;[57] and in § 86, the note, again from Bede, that Maximianus was killed at Aquileia (as was historically true of Maximus) runs counter to the claim made in *Historia Regum Britannie*, §§ 88–89 (in both texts) that he died at Rome.

Category J is larger than I; it consists of twenty chapters, all of which contain significant material unique to the Variant version. The chapters and passages concerned are listed below.

Historia Regum Britannie,

§ 39	description of the marshy nature of Britain
§ 43	details of the battles of Brennius and Belinus against the Romans (the presence of the British revealed by moonlight reflected off their armour; the mission of Gabius and Porsenna to Apulia and Italy)
§ 46	description of Ireland and details of its colonization
§ 72	details of the conversion of Lucius and the British
§ 94	details of Vortigern's part in the coronation of Constans
§ 101	details of Vortimer's third victory over the English (explaining its occurrence in Kent)
§ 130	details of Merlin's transportation of the *Chorea Gigantum* (which is moved by a spell rather than physical means)
§ 137	details of Uther's infatuation for Igerna (which is inspired by the devil and compared to that of David for Bathsheba); reflections on the effects of love
§ 145	Arthur requires the English to leave behind their arms before retiring from Britain to the Continent
§ 146	the English, as a consequence unarmed, seize weapons from the British population
§ 161	Arthur's request for aid from his nobles
§ 164	Arthur entrusts the interpretation of his dream to God
§ 172	greater emphasis on the paganism of some of the peoples subject to Rome
§§ 186–7	Loegria renamed Anglia after the English; creation of an unspecified number of English kings
§ 188	details of Augustine's conversion of the English

[57] Unless, that is, we assume (as does Wace, *Roman de Brut*, lines 793–6) that Armorica was merely the location of the Trojans' last Continental adventure before sailing to Britain. But there is no such suggestion in the relevant chapters of the Variant (§§ 17–20); rather the Trojans there set sail from Aquitaine (as in the vulgate text).

§ 189	details of the martyrdom of the monks of Bangor
§ 203	details of the plague which drove the British from the island
§ 204	details of English rule under Æthelstan
§ 207	details of the ultimate fate of the British
§ 208	reference in the colophon to the author of the *Historia* as Geoffrey Arthur

It must be stressed that the list set out above reveals the blurring inevitably involved in the proposed division of a complex literary work into a number of fixed categories; as we have seen, minor verbal additions are to some extent characteristic of the stylistic differences between the two texts (discussed in category B), and also of those speeches found in fuller form in the Variant version (examined in category E).[58] But, although it is sometimes difficult to draw the distinction precisely, the passages listed above are as far as possible limited to those which represent important matter unique to the Variant.

It is not easy to advance a single explanation of why these details should either have been added in the Variant text or suppressed in the vulgate. In some cases, it seems that the usual tendency for matters of detail present in the vulgate text to be missing from the Variant is simply reversed, as (for example) in the following description of Ireland found only in Variant § 46.[59]

Ubi cum uenissent, inuenerunt terram opimam et apricam nemoribus et fluminibus riuisque et omni Dei munere opulentam; ceperuntque continuo ibi tabernacula sua edificare et terram colere. . . .

Other passages of this type occur in §§ 43, 94, 146, 186, 187, and 188 (although these latter three chapters also reflect the differing historical perspective of the Variant, discussed below),[60] 203, 204, and 207. In other cases, the Variant offers such details by way of an explanation: that the construction of roads in Britain had been neglected because of the marshy nature of the island (§ 39); that Vortimer's third battle took place in Kent because the English had retreated thither from Scotland (§ 101); that, since

---

[58] Above, pp. xx and xxx respectively.

[59] I have not been able to trace these geographical details to any source (such as Orosius or Solinus). However, the somewhat odd expression *tabernacula edificare* in this passage constitutes a further biblical echo unique to the Variant: compare Exodus 1.11, '*aedificaueruntque* urbes *tabernaculorum* Pharaoni'.

[60] Below, pp. lxvi–lxx.

the English had been disarmed by Arthur, they acquired new weapons by taking them from the British (§§ 146–7). These explanatory notes are somewhat akin to the differences of structure between the two texts (category F above), where the Variant often has the more logical sequence of events; indeed, the additional passage in § 161 is clearly related to, and forms an integral part of, the differing ordering of §§ 159–64 in the Variant text.[61] The remaining elements unique to the Variant, however, have the effect of putting the episodes in which they occur into a different light. For example, in vulgate § 130 Merlin dismantles the *Chorea Gigantum* by means of *sue machinationes* which, we infer, are no more than mechanical means more effective than those already fruitlessly employed by the British, although the passage remains slightly obscure. There is no such uncertainty in the Variant version where Merlin's methods are those of a true magician; he achieves his end merely by 'paulisper insusurrans motu labiorum tamquam ad oracionem'.[62] This passage is not, however, typical of these details unique to the Variant. Most often they lend the Variant a tone more markedly pious or christianising than the vulgate, as in §§ 137 (where, however, the comparison of Uther to David precedes an independent echo of Ovid; see n. 33 above), 164, 172, and 189, and especially in § 72, the conversion of the British, both versions of which are set out for comparison below.

Historia Regum Britannie, § 72, vulgate

[72] Natus est ei unicus filius nomine Lucius. Qui cum defuncto patre regni diademate insignitus fuisset, omnes actus bonitatis illius imitabatur ita ut ipse Coilus ab omnibus censeretur. Exitum quoque suum preferre uolens principio epistulas suas Eleutero pape direxit petens ut ab eo christianitatem reciperet. Serenauerunt enim mentem eius miracula quae tyrones Christi per diuersas nationes faciebant. Unde in amorem uere fidei anhelans pie peticionis effectum consecutus est. Siquidem beatus pontifex comperta eius deuotione duos religiosos doctores Faganum et Duuianum misit ad illum; qui uerbum Dei incarnatum predicantes abluerunt ipsum babtismate sacro et ad Christum conuerterunt. Nec mora concurrentes undique nationum populi exemplum regis insequuntur eodemque lauacro mundati celesti regno restituuntur. Beati igitur doctores cum per totam fere insulam paganismum deleuissent, templa que in honore plurimorum deorum fundata fuerant uni

---

[61] Above, p. xxxvii.
[62] This passage contains another biblical echo found only in the Variant: cf. Judith 13.6, 'et *labiorum motu* in silentio dicens'.

Deo eiusque sanctis dedicauerunt diuersisque cetibus ordinatorum repleuerunt. Fuerunt tunc in Britannia .xxviii. flamines sed et tres archiflamines
quorum potestati ceteri iudices morum atque phanatici submittebantur. His
etiam ex precepto apostolici ydolatriam eripuerunt et ubi erant flamines
episcopos, ubi archiflamines archiepiscopos posuerunt. Sedes autem
archiflaminum in nobilibus tribus ciuitatibus fuerunt, Lundoniis uidelicet
atque Eboraci et in Urbe Legionum, quam super Oscam fluuium in Glamorgancia ueteres muri et edificia sitam fuisse testantur. His igitur tribus euacuata supersticione .xxviii. episcopi subduntur. Diuisis quoque parrochiis
subiacuit metropolitano Eboracensi Deira et Albania quas magnum flumen
Humbri a Loegria secernit. Londoniensi metropolitano submissa est
Loegria et Cornubia. Has duas prouincias seiungit Sabrina et Kambria, id est
Gualia, que Urbi Legionum subiacuit. Denique restauratis omnibus redierunt antistites Romam et cuncta que fecerant a beatissimo papa confirmari
impetrauerunt. Confirmatione igitur facta reuersi sunt in Britanniam cum
pluribus aliis comitati quorum doctrina Britonum fideles in Christo in breui
corroborati sunt. Eorum nomina et actus in libro reperiuntur quem Gildas
de uictoria Aurelii Ambrosii inscripsit. Quod autem ipse tam lucido tractatu
parauerat nullatenus opus fuit ut inferiori stilo renouaretur.

Variant

[72] Interim natus est ei unicus filius cui nomen Lucius impositum est. Hic
post mortem patris regni dyademate insignitus omnem uiam prudencie
atque actus patris bonosque mores insecutus ab omnibus ad quos fama bonitatis illius peruenerat amabatur et colebatur. Audiens quoque christianitatem Rome et in aliis terris exaltari primus omnium regum Britonum Christi
nomen affectans epistulas dirigit Eleutherio pape, petens ut ad se mitteret
personas tales a quibus christianitatem suscipere deberet. Serenauerant enim
mentem eius miracula que Christi discipuli et predicatores per diuersas
nacionum gentes ediderant. Et quidem in omnem terram exiuit sonus eorum
et in fines orbis terre uerba eorum. Et quia ad amorem uere fidei hanelabat,
pie peticionis effectum consecutus est. Siquidem predictus pontifex gloriam
in excelsis Deo canens duos religiosos doctores, Faganum et Duuianum, de
latere suo misit Britanniam qui uerbum Dei caro factum et pro hominibus
passum regi populoque predicarent et sacro baptismate insignirent. Nec
mora concurrentes undique populi diuerse nacionis exemplum regis sequentes lauacro sacro intinguntur atque omnipotenti Deo subduntur, ydola
despicientes et minutatim confringentes. Beati igitur doctores cum paganismum de gente Britonum in maiori parte deleuissent, templa que in honore
plurimorum deorum fundata fuerant mundatis ruderibus uni Deo consecrauerunt et uiris religiosis custodienda tradiderunt. Fuerunt tunc in Britannia per regiones constituti .xxviii. flamines et tres archiflamines qui thura
diis ex ritu gentilium cremabant atque libamina de pecudibus litabant. Hec

li

itaque ex apostolica doctrina ydolatrie eripientes episcopos ubi erant flamines, archiepiscopos ubi archiflamines consecrauerunt. Sedes principales
archiflaminum sicut in nobilioribus ciuitatibus fuerant, Londoniis scilicet et
Eboraci et in Urbe Legionum – que super Oscham fluuium in Glamorgancia
sita est, ita in hiis tribus euacuata supersticione tribus archiepiscopis dedicauerunt; in reliquis episcopos ordinauerunt diuisisque parrochiis unicuique ius suum assignauerunt. Metropolitano Eboracensi Deira et Albania,
sicut magnum flumen Humbri eas a Loegria secernit, in parrochiam cessit.
Londoniensi uero submissa est Loegria et Cornubia, quas prouincias
seiungit Sabrina a Kambria, id est Gualia, que Urbi Legionum subiacuit.
Hiis ita Dei nutu constitutis redierunt Romam antistites prefati et cuncta que
fecerant a beato papa confirmari impetrauerunt. Palliis itaque ac ceteris
honoribus decenter ab ecclesia Romana insigniti reuersi sunt in Britanniam
cum pluribus uiris religiosis comitati quorum doctrina et predicacione gens
Britonum in fide Christi roborata et aucta est; quorum actus in libro quem
Gildas hystoriographus composuit lucide scripti reperiuntur.

In this passage, the Variant exhibits not only its by now familiar penchant
for biblical vocabulary and allusion,[63] but also an interest in pagan rites
combined with a hostility towards them, and, in the detail of the *pallia*
despatched from Rome, a further statement of the orthodoxy of the alleged
foundation of Britain's three archiepiscopal sees. Clearly, this aspect of the
material unique to the Variant text is closely allied to its independant
biblical borrowings and also to such of its speeches as have additional
religious emphasis or content.

Finally, one of the passages in category J merits special attention. This is
§ 208, the colophon of the *Historia*. Despite the absence elsewhere in the
Variant text of personal material found in the vulgate, which is in fact mir-
rored by the lack in this passage (in the Variant) of the vulgate's explicit
reference to historians contemporary with Geoffrey and to his single, al-
legedly British-language, source in the possession of Archdeacon Walter,
Geoffrey is here mentioned by name only in the Variant text, in which the
chapter takes the following form.

---

[63] Compare 'omnem *uiam prudencie* ... insecutus' and Proverbs 9.6, 'ambulate per *uias*
[var. *uiam*] *prudentie*'; 'in omnem terram exiuit sonus eorum et in fines orbis terre uerba
eorum', also Psalms 18.5 (quoted verbatim); 'gloriam in excelsis Deo' and Luke 2.14, 'gloria
in altissimis Deo' and 19.38, 'gloria in excelsis'; 'de latere suo' and 1 Kings 3.20, 'de latere
meo'; 'uerbum Dei caro factum' and John 1.14, 'uerbum caro factum'.

Regum autem eorum acta qui ab illo tempore in Guualliis successerunt et fortunas successoribus meis scribendas dimitto ego, Galfridus Arthurus Monemutensis, qui hanc hystoriam Britonum de eorum lingua in nostram transferre curaui.

In this passage, Geoffrey is named *Galfridus Arthurus Monemutensis* rather than *Gaufridus* (or *Galfridus*) *Monemutensis* as in the vulgate text (at §§ 3, 110, and 177, none of these references being found in the Variant). It is, however, impossible to draw any firm conclusions about the date or authorship of the Variant from its use of Geoffrey's by-name Arthurus. Certainly Geoffrey referred to himself as *Galfridus Arturus*, or *Galfridus Artur*, (although never, so far as we know, in conjunction with the adjective *Monemutensis*) when witnessing charters,[64] but in his writings he preferred the forms *Gaufridus Monemutensis* (in the vulgate *Historia*) and *Gaufridus de Monemuta* (in the later *Vita Merlini*).[65] Moreover, the use of the form *Galfridus Arthurus* is not restricted to Geoffrey himself; it is also employed by his contemporaries Henry of Huntingdon and Robert of Torigni, as well as by later writers such as William of Newburgh, Gerald of Wales, and Matthew Paris.[66] Nothing positive, then, can be inferred from the appearance of the name in this form in the Variant version. Indeed, although the colophon asserts that the Variant text was, like the vulgate, the work of Geoffrey of Monmouth, this claim could just as well be due to a later redactor as to Geoffrey himself.

After this detailed and of necessity complex examination of the data contained in Table I, a brief recapitulation is in order. The differences between the two texts fall under two main headings.

First, the Variant text is shorter, with one hundred and ninety-nine (Faral) chapters as against the two hundred and eight of the vulgate. Furthermore, one hundred and thirty-eight of the chapters in the Variant are briefer than their vulgate counterparts, twenty being very markedly so. This comparative shortness on the part of the Variant text is primarily caused by the absence of the following material: the prefaces, both to the *Historia* and to the *Prophetie Merlini*; most personal details, self-references, and statements of intention by the author; a considerable

---

64 Wright, *Historia Regum Britannie*, I.x.
65 Edited by Clarke, *Life*, line 1526.
66 Tatlock, *The Legendary History*, pp. 438–9.

number of other, often rhetorical passages – chiefly speeches, descriptions, or emotive episodes. The Latin of the Variant text is also generally more compressed than that of the vulgate.

Secondly, the Variant is almost everywhere characterised by differences of style and an independent treatment of much of the subject-matter common to both texts, coupled on some occasions with the inclusion of material not found in the vulgate text. In fact, the only chapters found in almost identical form in both texts are those comprising the body of the *Prophetie Merlini*; but this is hardly surprising, as the latter had independent status as a work of notorious difficulty separate from the *Historia*. Of the remaining chapters of the Variant version, no fewer than one hundred and fifty-nine show stylistic variations, consisting for the most part of minor differences of sentence-structure, vocabulary, and sometimes biblical and Classical borrowings not found in the vulgate text. In sixteen chapters, passages appear in different positions in the Variant text; and in two cases this results in major episodes having a structure entirely different from that of the vulgate. As to those elements found only in the Variant text, these fall into three types. Twelve Variant speeches appear in a fuller form – sometimes much fuller, but more often only slightly fuller – than in the vulgate text; they are, however, outnumbered by those vulgate speeches which are not present in any form in the Variant version. In four chapters, the Variant borrows independently from Bede, and, in another, from Landolfus Sagax. These borrowings consist entirely of historical matter (absent from the vulgate), save in one case (§ 5) where material from Bede is found in the place of a more elaborate passage derived in the vulgate from Gildas. A further twenty chapters contain other unique material, much of which has a religious tone in harmony both with the Variant's biblical allusions and with the contents of some of the speeches which it includes in a fuller form.

With the findings of this close examination of the Variant and vulgate texts in mind, we must now return to the problems of authorship and date of the Variant version. The first of these problems turns entirely on comparison of the two texts themselves, but the question of dating rests on the Variant's relationship not only to the vulgate text but also to Wace's *Roman de Brut*. It is undeniably the case that there are close contacts between the Variant version and Wace's poem. As we have seen, Robert Caldwell demonstrated that some divergencies, between the *Roman de Brut* and its supposed source, the vulgate *Historia*, in fact tally closely with precisely the elements characteristic of the Variant version; and he noted further points of similarity between the Variant text and the *Roman de*

Brut.[67] Caldwell concluded that the Variant was Wace's source and could therefore be dated prior to 1155, when the *Roman de Brut* was completed.[68] Caldwell's view was supported by Keller and Leckie,[69] but countered by Gallais, who defended Wace's claim to originality by maintaining that the Variant was instead dependent upon the *Roman de Brut*.[70] The problem, therefore, is to determine whether the relationship between the Variant version and the *Roman de Brut* affords any firm evidence (especially in the light of our close investigation of the contents of the Variant) for the priority of one text over the other.

Let us begin by examining the full implications of Caldwell's and Gallais's theories. In the opinion of the former, the Variant text, already in existence by the 1150s, formed the basis of Wace's vernacular poem. This position is slightly complicated by the presence in the *Roman de Brut* of some elements found only in the vulgate text (primarily from §118 onwards and particularly in the Arthurian section).[71] Wace must, therefore, also have had access to a vulgate text (in some form) and have combined both sources in his poem. This supposition need not create untoward difficulty, since two extant manuscripts of the Variant version bear witness to very similar acts of conflation.[72] Nor does this model seriously threaten – as Gallais feared – our estimation of Wace as a creative artist, since it is precisely in the free recasting of its sources that the achievement of the *Roman de Brut* lies.[73] There are, therefore, no fundamental objections to Caldwell's position.

Conversely, Gallais's view that the Variant version depends on Wace's poem raises several grave problems. If the *Roman de Brut* were indeed, as Gallais maintained, the source of the Variant text, it might be expected that the latter would be simply a Latin translation of Wace's vernacular poem. But this is not the case. The Variant text is clearly not independent of the vulgate: the close verbal similarities between the two, which outweigh

---

[67] Above, p. xii and n. 5.

[68] Above, n. 9

[69] Above, p. xiv.

[70] Above, p. xiii.

[71] Caldwell, 'Wace's *Roman de Brut*', pp. 680–2.

[72] Below, pp. lxxviii and lxxix. Neither of these manuscripts can itself account for Wace's conflation; both postdate his poem and, moreover, one (Cardiff MS. 2.611) includes vulgate elements absent from the *Roman de Brut*, while the *Roman de Brut* contains vulgate details not found in the other (Aberystwyth, NLW, MS. 13210).

[73] On Wace's methods, see Jirmounsky, 'Essai d'analyse'; and Houck, *Sources*, pp. 167–214.

their various dissimilarities, cannot have arisen by coincidence. It follows that the Variant must, according to Gallais's interpretation, represent a conflation of the vulgate text and the *Roman de Brut*, in which elements found uniquely in Wace's poem were translated into Latin and interpolated into the vulgate text, while vulgate elements not present in the *Roman de Brut* were deleted. Gallais offered no explanation of why the vernacular poem should be conflated with its Latin source in this way; indeed, this hypothesis includes a number of inconsistencies. Examination of the vulgate material supposedly omitted by Gallais's conflator reveals that references to Geoffrey of Monmouth by name (in *Historia Regum Britannie*, §§ 1–3, 109–10, and 177) have been rejected from the Variant text, just as they were by Wace. Why, then, does the Variant retain, albeit in abbreviated form, the attribution to Geoffrey in the final chapter (§ 208), even though this attribution is not found at the end of the *Roman de Brut* (lines 14859–65)?[74] Much vulgate matter omitted by Wace is indeed missing from the Variant;[75] but the body of the *Prophetie Merlini*, omitted from the *Roman de Brut*, is found in full in the Variant text.[76] Why did the hypothetical conflator omit the former material but not the latter? One of the best known additions made by Wace to his vulgate source is King Arthur's Round Table, which is first mentioned in the *Roman de Brut*.[77] Yet there is no reference to the Round Table in the Variant text; why was so singular a detail (in addition to several others)[78] passed over by the conflator? Why too does the Variant fail to include two striking episodes from the *Roman de Brut*, namely the firing of Cirencester by sparrows (lines 13710–44) and

---

[74] There is *prima facie* every reason to suppose (against Gallais, 'La *Variant Version*', p. 18, n. 2) that the Variant text did in its original form contain this attribution and that this version of § 208 was not added by a later scribe.

[75] For example, the details of Mauricius's mission to Maximianus and the latter's arrival in Britain; compare *Historia Regum Britannie*, §§ 81–3 (vulgate and Variant texts), and *Roman de Brut*, lines 5849–72.

[76] *Roman de Brut*, lines 7535–42; *Historia Regum Britannie*, §§ 111–17 (vulgate and Variant texts).

[77] Lines 9747–60; for a discussion of the passage and its context, see Schmolke-Hasselmann, 'The round table', especially pp. 46–53.

[78] For instance, the foundation of Exeter by Julius Caesar (*Roman de Brut*, lines 4825–8), Taliesin's prophecy of the birth of Christ (4855–76), and the discovery of the True Cross by Constantine's mother, Helen (5720–4), none of which has any counterpart in the Variant (even though the final episode is fully in keeping with the religious tone of the latter). Other elements found only in the *Roman de Brut* are listed by Gallais himself; see 'La *Variant Version*', pp. 11–12.

the 'fish-tail' miracle performed by St Augustine (13583–624)?[79] Finally, it will be remembered that the *Roman de Brut* includes some vulgate elements which are not found in the Variant version.[80] Gallais's hypothesis offers no explanation for their absence from the Variant, since there is no clear reason why the alleged conflator should have chosen arbitrarily to omit this material, even though it was found in both Wace's poem and the vulgate text. In short, the form and content of the Variant version cannot coherently be accounted for by Gallais's supposition that the Variant postdates the *Roman de Brut*.

A further example of the difficulties engendered by Gallais's position is afforded by the treatment in all three texts of the events following the Roman embassy to Arthur (§§ 159–64 in the vulgate text). As we have seen,[81] in these chapters the order of events in vulgate and First Variant texts differs as follows.

Historia Regum Britannie, §§ 159–64, vulgate

§ 159	Arthur's speech
§ 160	Hoel's reply
§ 161	Auguselus's speech
§ 162 (i)	catalogue of British forces
(ii)	dismissal of Roman ambassadors
§ 163	catalogue of Roman forces
§ 164 (i)	Roman advance on Britain

Variant

§ 159	Arthur's speech
[§ 160	absent from Variant text]
§ 162 (ii)	dismissal of Roman ambassadors
§ 163	catalogue of Roman forces
§ 164 (i)	Roman advance on Britain
§ 161	Auguselus's speech (in different form)
§ 162 (i)	catalogue of British forces

In the *Roman de Brut* (lines 10775–11162) the narrative structure is as follows:

10775–10904 Arthur's speech
10905–10954 Hoel's reply

79 These episodes are discussed by Houck, *Sources*, pp. 265–87, 290–1, and 301–7.
80 Above, n. 71.
81 Above, p. xxxvi.

Wace, then, is partially in agreement with the First Variant (against the vulgate text) in so far as he recounts both the dismissal of the Roman envoys and the gathering of Roman troops before then describing the British contingents. However, in the *Roman de Brut* the mustering of the British forces is not prefaced (as it is in the Variant version) by a speech by Auguselus of Scotland; instead, this speech and also Hoel's reply to Arthur (which is absent from the Variant) in Wace's poem precede the dismissal of the Roman ambassadors (as they do in the vulgate text). If, as Gallais maintained, the First Variant were closely following the *Roman de Brut*, we should be faced with two insoluble problems. Why is Hoel's speech (present in both the vulgate text and the *Roman de Brut*) inexplicably absent from the Variant version? And further, why, once it had been decided to omit Hoel's speech, was Auguselus's speech not also simply dropped rather than being for no obvious reason transferred to a new position before the description of the various British contingents? If, on the other hand, we accept Caldwell's solution, these difficulties disappear. Wace, who was at this point using both the Variant and vulgate versions of the *Historia*, followed the overall structure of the Variant (which is regularly his base-text) – hence the dismissal of the Roman envoys and the preparation of the imperial army precede the catalogue of British forces in both the *Roman de Brut* and the Variant version. However, Wace wished to supplement the (as we have seen, generally more compressed) Variant version by reference to the vulgate text. Noticing that Hoel's speech was absent from the Variant version, he restored it to its (vulgate) position following Arthur's address; he also transferred Auguselus's speech (which in the *Roman de Brut* combines elements from both the vulgate and Variant versions of Auguselus's oration) to the position which it occupied in the vulgate text, very probably in order to balance Hoel's speech.[82] The narrative sequence of the *Roman de Brut* can, therefore, cogently and economically be accounted for by assuming with Caldwell that it represents a conflation (effected not without skill) of the Variant and vulgate

[82] Compare Wace's treatment of *Historia Regum Britannie*, § 158, where the speech of Cador of Cornwall (*Roman de Brut*, lines 10737–64) is similarly balanced by a reply by Gawain (10765–72) which is not found in either the vulgate or the Variant text.

texts. Conversely, the structure of the First Variant in these chapters defies logical explanation if we accept Gallais's claim that the latter was a Latin version closely based on Wace's poem.

Further arguments against Gallais rest on the use in the Variant (independently of the vulgate) of the works of Landolfus Sagax and Bede.[83] Details about Ascanius and the foundation of Alba Longa, derived from Landolfus, are found in both the Variant text (§6) and the *Roman de Brut* (lines 9–114). The presence of these details in Wace's poem (where the information in question is more diffused) is readily explicable if, as Caldwell supposed, the Variant text was Wace's source. Gallais's theory demands a highly contorted explanation: first, that Wace supplemented the vulgate text with details drawn from Landolfus; and second, that whoever was responsible for the Variant version recognised Wace's source as Landolfus's *Historia Romana*, identified and consulted the passage in question, and, completely rejecting Wace's reworking, incorporated it into his text almost verbatim. While this latter interpretation is not, perhaps, impossible, it is far less convincing than Caldwell's simpler explanation.

Passages which in the Variant exhibit Bedan material not found in the vulgate (§§5, 54, 59, and 86) also militate against Gallais's position. The first of these passages, consisting of a description of Britain (§5), is not found in the poem by Wace who dispensed with Geoffrey's opening geographical excursus. If the Variant were indeed dependent on the *Roman de Brut*, ought it not (like Wace) to omit §5, or otherwise to retain that chapter in its vulgate form? Why instead did the author of the Variant independently substitute a version based on Bede? The next two passages both concern Caesar's invasions. Both the Variant text (§59) and the *Roman de Brut* (lines 4225–8) state, exactly as Bede does, the number and type of ships in Caesar's second invasion fleet. Similarly, the Variant (§54) reports verbatim from Bede the date of Caesar's first attack and the number of his ships; Wace records the same date and number, but in two different and widely separated passages (*Roman de Brut*, lines 3827–30 and 3965–6 respectively). Again it is simpler to suppose that Wace in the poem repositioned these elements from the Variant text, than that a hypothetical conflator recognised both details as originating from Bede, checked them in the *Historia Ecclesiastica*, and reunited them in the Variant text. In §86 the Variant contains a note, derived from Bede, on the career of Maximianus (the historical Magnus Maximus) and (correctly) his death at Aquileia; this

---

[83] Discussed above, pp. xliv–xlvii.

account contradicts the version found later in both Variant and vulgate texts (§§ 88–9) that Maximianus died at Rome. In the *Roman de Brut*, lines 5986–9, which correspond to the end of *Historia Regum Britannie*, § 86, there is (as in the vulgate) no mention of Maximianus's death; yet lines 6117–26, which correspond to the end of § 88 and the beginning of § 89, do contain, like the Variant text (in § 86), non-vulgate details drawn from Bede (for example, Theodosius's aid to Valentinianus) and report Maximianus's death as occurring not, as in both the vulgate and Variant texts (at this point), in Rome but at Aquileia, as in Bede's *Historia Ecclesiastica* and the Variant text (in § 86). Therefore the material derived from Bede is in Wace's poem found at a point corresponding to *Historia Regum Britannie*, §§ 88–9; and the contradiction between Bede and the vulgate *Historia* over the place of Maximianus's death is eliminated (correctly according to the facts of the historical Magnus Maximus's life). If, as Gallais has maintained, the Variant version was derived from Wace, why was the Bedan material from *Roman de Brut*, lines 6117–26 (corresponding to *Historia Regum Britannie*, §§ 88–9), repositioned in § 86, where it is not in its proper chronological place? Why, moreover, was the vulgate's claim that Maximianus died at Rome preferred to Wace's assertion – which was accurate (with reference to Magnus Maximus) and found support from Bede's account – that this event occurred in Aquileia? The only possible answer is that the supposed conflator, after illogically repositioning the Bedan passage in § 86 (which is in itself an unlikely act), made the gross error of failing to eliminate the contradiction between Wace's (Bedan) account and that of the vulgate in § 88; but such a hypothesis does not fit well with the extraordinary care with which the supposed conflator is alleged to have checked Wace's sources. It is far simpler to suppose that Wace noticed the discrepancy between §§ 86 and 89 of the Variant text and (correctly identifying Maximianus with Magnus Maximus) solved the problem by omitting the erroneous statement in § 89 and substituting for it the more historically correct material from (Variant) § 86. If so, the Variant must have been Wace's source.

A further serious objection to Gallais's position has been raised by Leckie, who noted that an important distinction between the vulgate and Variant texts is the manner in which they handle the passage of dominion from the British to the English.[84] In the Variant version (§§ 186–7), this transition is first marked by the donation of power to the English by the African king Gormund and the subsequent renaming of *Britannia* as

---

[84] See n. 23 above and, especially, pp. lxvi–lxx below.

Anglia; but in the vulgate text (§§ 186–7) this change of name is not mentioned and Gormund's donation denotes rather a division of the previously united kingdom between a number of British and English rulers.[85] According to the vulgate (§ 207), the first English king to control the whole of Loegria was Æthelstan (who reigned from 924 to 939); in the Variant this reference to Æthelstan is found in the reign of the seventh-century King Cadwaladr (§ 204), with whom Æthelstan is thus erroneously represented as contemporaneous.[86] In both of these important passages, the *Roman de Brut* is largely in agreement with the Variant version. Wace records the change of name from Britain to England in lines 13375–84 and 13631–52 (the latter lines corresponding to *Historia*, § 187). Similarly, Æthelstan is treated in lines 14719–74 (especially 14757–74), at a point, that is, corresponding to Variant § 204, not vulgate § 207; but Wace (unlike Geoffrey) makes the identity of the king (and hence his tenth-century date) clear by giving additional biographical details, absent from both vulgate and Variant.[87] Wace also mentions Æthelstan in another passage (lines 13929–46) which has no counterpart in the Variant version. If the Variant version depended on the *Roman de Brut*, it is very difficult to account for the presence in the Variant of only one of these passages dealing with Æthelstan; it is even more difficult to explain how, in that case, the error of misdating Æthelstan could possibly have arisen in the Variant, since his identity is clearly stated in the *Roman de Brut*. But if, as Leckie argued, the Variant version is the source of the *Roman de Brut*, there is no obstacle to the supposition that Wace, having recognised Æthelstan as the historical, tenth-century English ruler, retained his source's reference to Æthelstan – at a point corresponding to § 204 (not 207, as in the vulgate) – but at the same time introduced another passage on this king and further information about his life in order to correct the Variant's chronological error in assigning him to the seventh century.[88]

[85] Both passages are set out below, pp. lxvii and lxviii respectively.

[86] Below, pp. lxviii and lxix respectively.

[87] Discussed by Houck, *Sources*, pp. 251–3.

[88] Indeed, Wace's dependence on the Variant would explain an apparent contradiction in his poem: the phrase which introduces Æthelstan's reign, 'A cel tens' (*Roman de Brut*, line 14757), which Arnold, *Le Roman*, II.816, described as 'pas heureuse' (because it implies 'in the reign of Cadwaladr'), in fact corresponds closely to 'Ab illo ergo tempore' (Variant, § 204) and hence sits awkwardly with Wace's later explicit identification of Æthelstan as the tenth-century English king. Otherwise we must assume (as does Leckie, *The Passage*, p. 114) that Wace intended 'A cel tens' to refer very loosely to the period after the spread of English culture (described in *Roman de Brut*, lines 14739–56).

The combined weight of the preceding arguments must tip the scales conclusively against Gallais and in favour of Caldwell's assertion that the Variant version of the *Historia* was Wace's source. Hence the Variant was in existence in Geoffrey of Monmouth's lifetime, since he died probably in 1155, the year of the completion of the *Roman de Brut*. Is it then possible that the Variant text represents either an early draft of the vulgate or a later revision, made in either case by Geoffrey himself? The former suggestion was advanced by Caldwell on the strength of differences between the use of sources in the two texts.[89] In fact, Caldwell's hypothesis is ruled out by close examination of those passages in which the vulgate and Variant texts share the same sources. In such passages, the vulgate usually agrees closely with the wording of its source, whereas the Variant version recasts freely and often abbreviates. I have discussed elsewhere the treatment in vulgate and Variant texts of borrowings from Gildas;[90] but the same tendency is also manifest in a passage, in § 188 of both texts, derived from Bede.[91] The passages in question are set out below along with their Bedan source.

Historia Regum Britannie, § 188, vulgate

Inter ceteras erat quedam nobilissima in ciuitate Bangor in qua tantus fuisse fertur numerus monachorum ut, cum in .vii. portiones esset cum prepositis sibi prioribus monasterium diuisum, nulla harum portio minus quam trecentos monachos haberet qui omnes labore manuum suarum uiuebant.

Variant

... inter quos erat abbas Dinoot nomine liberalibus artibus inbutus in Bangor ciuitate presidens bis mille fere monachis. Qui per diuersas mansiones diuisi labore manuum uictum sibi acquirebant et in .vii. porciones dividebant prout singulis quibusque opus erat; sed et nulla porcionum minus continebat quam .ccc. monachos.

Bede, *Historia Ecclesiastica* II.2

Erant autem plurimi eorum de monasterio Bangor in quo tantus fertur fuisse numerus monachorum ut cum in .vii. portiones esset cum prepositis sibi rectoribus monasterium diuisum, nulla harum portio minus quam .ccc. homines haberet qui omnes de labore manuum suarum uiuere solebant.

---

[89] Above, p. xiii.
[90] 'Geoffrey of Monmouth and Gildas', pp. 26–8 and 36–8.
[91] For a discussion of Geoffrey's use of Bede in the vulgate *Historia*, see Wright, 'Geoffrey of Monmouth and Bede'.

If the Variant text represents an early draft of the *Historia* made by Geoffrey himself, how did it come about that the Bedan borrowing set out above is more fully integrated (in terms of style) in the Variant text than in the vulgate? Moreover, if the vulgate is the later text, why should Geoffrey reject his initial, more complete recasting in favour of less free, almost verbatim borrowing? In the passage above, then, and, moreover, in the case of other borrowings shared by both texts,[92] it seems that the author of the Variant version has recast not the sources themselves but the vulgate text, including any borrowings which it contains. The Variant version is therefore a reworking of the vulgate text; and it follows that, if Geoffrey were responsible for the Variant version, it cannot represent his early draft of the *Historia*, but must instead be a later revision of the vulgate text.

Let us consider the possiblity that Geoffrey may have produced such a reworking of the vulgate text. This hypothesis is not wholly implausible. The dedication of the *Historia Regum Britannie* (§§ 3–4) is found in three different forms, all arguably due to Geoffrey himself;[93] he was possibly also responsible for a revised version of the dedication to the *Prophetie Merlini* (§§ 109–10),[94] as well perhaps as a further (more radical) revision of the initial dedication.[95] It might therefore be held that Geoffrey could also have been the author of the Variant version, which exhibits such recasting on a larger scale. There are, however, several objections to this argument. Faral noted that among the features characteristic of Geoffrey's Latin prose is the frequent linking of a clause to that preceding it by the repetition of the main verb of that previous clause in the form of a participle (or a gerund),[96] as in the following example (from § 166):

> ipsos a tergo cedunt, cesos prosternunt, prostratos despoliant, despoliatos pretereunt.

Gallais, who also noticed this stylistic mannerism in the vulgate text, pointed out that it is very seldom employed in the Variant;[97] in § 166 of that

---

[92] Compare, for example, the passage in vulgate and Variant, § 198 (set out above, p. xxi), which is based on *Historia Ecclesiastica* II.20 (Wright, 'Geoffrey of Monmouth and Bede', pp. 41–2 and 58).

[93] These are set out for comparison in my *Historia Regum Britannie*, I.xiii–xiv.

[94] Printed by Faral, *La Légende*, III.189.

[95] See Hammer, 'Remarks', pp. 529–30, and Wright, *Historia Regum Britannie*, I.xii, n. 17.

[96] *La Légende*, II.397, n. 2.

[97] 'La *Variant Version*', p. 8, n. 1.

text, for example, the passage quoted above is represented only by the words *multos strauerunt* and other such vulgate passages are regularly so treated in the Variant version. It seems unlikely that, if the Variant version were a revision made by Geoffrey, he should have suppressed in this way a stylistic device of which he was demonstrably so fond in the vulgate text. The vulgate text also manifests a certain liking for hexameter rhythm; in § 147, for example, Arthur's spear Ron is described in words which form an internally rhymed hexameter line ('Hec erat ardua lataque lancea, cladibus apta') and in § 21 part of the wrestling bout of Corineus and Gogmagog has a metrical form ('adnectens crebris afflatibus aera uexant'). In the Variant version both clauses are recast so that the hexameter metre is largely disrupted (respectively, 'hec erat rigida latoque ferro, hostium cladibus apta' and 'annectunt crebris flatibus auras uexantes'). It is difficult to see why, if Geoffrey himself were responsible for the Variant, he should deliberately have eliminated these embellishments when revising the vulgate text.[98]

There are other important stylistic differences between the two texts. One characteristic of the Variant version is a certain artless repetitiousness, the same word or words appearing (without obvious rhetorical point or emphasis) more than once in the same, or adjacent, (Faral) chapters. Elsewhere I have drawn attention to Variant, §§ 89–92 which contain the following repetitions (among others):[99] *laboriosis expeditionibus, frequentibus expeditionibus, laboriosis occursibus* (all in § 90), and *laboriosam in Britanniam expeditionem* (§ 91); *erraticos latrunculos* (§ 90) and *ab incursione erraticorum hostium* (§ 91). Although the general level of such repetition in the Variant text is not usually as high as in these chapters, casual examination of Variant, §§ 8–14 (chosen at random), reveals further repetition not found in the vulgate text: *iugo seruitutis premi* and *iugo seruitutis teneri* (§ 8); *uiriliter resistentes* and *uiriliter hortatur* (§ 11); *ea que itineri necessaria forent* and *que itineri neccesaria fuerint* (§ 14). While some stylistic formulae can be found in the vulgate text,[100] this careless repetitiousness in the Variant version is largely alien to Geoffrey's normal prac-

[98] Indeed, the change (in § 147) from *lataque* to *latoque ferro* introduces into the Variant an echo of the *Aeneid* (see n. 31 above), a fresh literary resonance which suggests a purpose different from that of Geoffrey.

[99] 'Geoffrey of Monmouth and Gildas', pp. lxiii.

[100] Such as that noted above, p. lxiii, and a tendency to connect three substantives by *atque* and *necnon et* (for example, § 52, 'Loth uidelicet atque Urianus necnon et Anguselus': see also Faral, *La Légende*, II.397, nn. 1 and 2); repetition of phrases does sometimes occur in the vulgate text, but never on the same scale as in the Variant version and rarely within one chapter.

tice. The Variant version also contains a considerable number of examples of the *nominatiuus pendens*, in which a noun and/or participle in the nominative is very loosely attached to the main clause of the sentence (where in Classical Latin an ablative absolute might be used), as for example in §154, 'Quo adueniens Riculfus rex cum suis, prelium commissum est grande'.[101] In contrast, such loose – and, strictly speaking, incorrect – syntactical construction is generally avoided in the vulgate text. Another distinction between the two texts lies in their choice of vocabulary. In §18, for example, the vulgate text employs the word *guerra*, derived from the vernacular, while the Variant has the purer (and more elevated) word *arma*;[102] in this case, the choice of vocabulary in the Variant is more conservative than that in the vulgate. However, the Variant version also exhibits a number of specialised or striking words and phrases which are not found in the vulgate. Comparison of the two texts reveals the following examples unique to the Variant: *barones* (§38), *centuria* (§§19 and 43), *curialiter* (§40), *decurio* (§66), *erarium* (§§63 and 158), *ex senatus consultu* (§81), *exsufflabunt odio* (§14), *minutatim* (§72), *palorum caribdis* (§60), *patriota* (§7), *receptui lituum sonans* (§20; also *receptui canens*, §60), *rudus* (*-eris*, 'rubble') (§72), *rumigerulus* (§138), *sabanus* (§132), *tepide rexit* (§28), *triclinium* (§196) – the list could probably be expanded. In addition to such vocabulary unique to itself, the Variant, as we have seen, almost everywhere exhibits simple synonyms for words found at the same point in the vulgate.[103] In short, the Latin vocabulary of the Variant version bears the stamp of a mind other than Geoffrey's. These differences of style and expression, the greater repetitiousness of the Variant text, and its preference for non-Galfridian vocabulary, coupled with its independent Classical and biblical allusions (already discussed),[104] in effect preclude Geoffrey's authorship of the Variant version.

---

101 Other examples are found in: §15, 'Nec mora adductus, optio ei datur'; §31, 'Apud quam moratus, ... orta est discordia'; §61, 'iuuentus noster ludos mutuos componens, inter ceteros inierunt duo nepotes'; §69, 'congressusque cum Romanis, totum diem consumpserunt'; §76, 'prelium committentes, dissipatus est Allectus'; §77, 'Perueniens ... hec examinatio ... passus est sanctus Albanus'; §81, 'Consilium ... sumens, fuerunt qui'; §108, 'Uolens ... turrim edificare, non possunt fundamenta', §129, 'Lauati ... lapides ... infirmitates curabat'; §136, 'Superueniens ... rex Uther ... congrediuntur Saxones Britonibus'; §143, 'iuxta flumen ... congressi, utrorum exercitus ... cecidit'; §143, 'Arthurus ... premunitus ... partem ... interfecerunt'.

102 In fact the latter word there forms part of a Vergilian reminiscence found only in the Variant text: see n. 31 above.

103 Examples are listed by Gallais, 'La *Variant Version*', p. 7, n. 1.

104 Above, pp. xxiii–xxvi.

For reasons of style, then, we must conclude that the Variant version was produced by someone other than Geoffrey of Monmouth. In that case there remains the question of whether the Variant text was the source of the vulgate *Historia* or a later reworking of the vulgate text. Although the treatment of sources common to both texts, which has already been examined,[105] argues very strongly in favour of the latter view, we cannot entirely discount the possibility, however remote, that Geoffrey was dissatisfied with the free use made of these sources by a writer who had preceded him and therefore substituted passages more closely based on the originals. However, if we suppose that the Variant version represents Geoffrey's source, considerable difficulties arise. Geoffrey first published the *Prophetie Merlini* separately in (or perhaps before) 1135 and in this form they were used by Orderic Vitalis in 1135/6,[106] some two or three years before the date at which the *Historia* itself probably appeared. Since the *Prophetie* are found in almost identical form in both the vulgate and Variant texts, the latter must itself have been written by 1135 at the latest, if it was Geoffrey's source.[107] But if the Variant version had been in existence so long, why in January 1139 was Henry of Huntingdon so surprised on discovering the *Historia Regum Britannie* at Le Bec? We can only conclude that, if the Variant version was indeed Geoffrey's source, it was not circulated before the appearance of the vulgate *Historia*; in that case the Variant would represent a private draft, on which Geoffrey later based his *Historia*, but which was prepared by someone other than Geoffrey – the most obvious candidate arguably being Archdeacon Walter, Geoffrey's Oxford colleague, who was himself much interested in history. But how, then, did the Variant version come into circulation at all? And why – apart from supposed doubts about the reaction of readers to a work of dubious historicity (which the rapidly achieved popularity of the *Historia* shows to have been largely groundless) – should anyone allow Geoffrey to claim (or steal) the credit for a composition which was not for the most part his own?

Speculations such as these are, in fact, rendered unnecessary by the cogent arguments against the priority of the Variant over the vulgate text

105 Above, p. lxii.
106 See Wright, *Historia Regum Britannie*, I.xi.
107 Unless, of course, we assume that the *Prophetie* were indeed written by Geoffrey and then incorporated by another author into the Variant text. But since Geoffrey claims in the preface of the *Prophetie* (§ 109) already to have been at work on the *Historia* at the time of the publication of the *Prophetie*, this hypothesis would mean that the vulgate and Variant texts were produced simultaneously, which is extremely implausible.

advanced by Leckie.[108] He drew attention to the late date at which, according to Geoffrey, power was transferred from the British to the English. Before the appearance of the *Historia Regum Britannie*, the conventional view – largely derived from Bede – was that this transfer of power occurred at some point in the earlier sixth century at the latest (not long, that is, after the arrival of the English and the battle of Mount Badon).[109] In the vulgate text of the *Historia*, however, the British are not seriously weakened until the ravages of the African king Gormund (which Geoffrey assigns to the later sixth century)[110] who hands over Loegria to the English (§ 186):

> Postquam autem, ut predictum est, infaustus tyrannus cum innumerabilibus Affricanorum militibus totam fere insulam uastauit, maiorem partem eius, que Loegria uocabatur, prebuit Saxonibus quorum consilio applicuerat. Secesserunt itaque Britonum reliquie in occidentalibus regni partibus, Cornubia uidelicet atque Gualiis, unde crebras et ferales irruptiones incessanter hostibus fecerunt.

Even after the donation of Gormund, the British, although they have suffered a serious set-back, do not entirely lose control to the English. Instead, each racial group is governed by its own rulers (§ 187):

> Amiserunt deinde Britones regni diadema multis temporibus et insule monarchiam nec pristinam dignitatem recuperare nitebantur; immo partem illam patrie que adhuc eis remanserat non uni regi sed tribus tyrannis subditam ciuilibus preliis sepissime uastabant. Sed nec Saxones diadema regni adhuc adepti sunt qui tribus etiam regibus subditi quandoque sibi ipsi quandoque Britonibus inquietationem inferebant.

Indeed, the British in some measure regain control under their last great king, Cadwallon (§§ 197–201), and are not entirely ousted until the later seventh century, when Cadwallon's son, Cadwaladr, and the majority of the British population flee from a Britain ravaged by plague. The English are reinforced from the Continent and occupy all the island (except Wales, Scotland, and possibly Cornwall) as its masters (§ 204):

---

108 See above, p. xv, n. 23.
109 Leckie, *The Passage*, especially pp. 5–19.
110 Gormund's depredations are not precisely dated by Geoffrey; but, after Arthur dies in A.D. 542, Constantinus and Aurelius Conanus reign for four and three years respectively, and are succeeded by Wortiporius, Malgo, and Kareticus (the object of Gormund's attacks), the lengths of whose reigns are not specified.

Quorum [sc. Saxones] residui, cum tam feralis lues cessauisset, continuum morem seruantes nuntiauerunt conciuibus suis in Germania insulam indigena gente carentem facile eis subdendam si in illam habitaturi uenirent. Quod cum ipsis indicatum fuisset, nefandus populus ille collecta innumerabili multitudine uirorum et mulierum applicuit in partibus Nordhamhimumbrie et desolatas prouintias ab Albania usque Cornubiam inhabitauit. Non enim aderat habitator qui prohiberet preter pauperculas Britonum reliquias quae superfuerant, quae infra abdita nemorum in Gualiis commanebant. Ab illo tempore potestas Britonum in insula cessauit et Angli regnare ceperunt.

Even despite the fact that the English gain control at this time, it is not until the reign of Æthelstan (in the tenth century) that a single English ruler governs all Loegria (§ 207):

At Saxones sapientius agentes, pacem et concordiam inter se habentes, agros colentes, ciuitates et opida aedificantes et sic abiecto dominio Britonum, iam toti Loegrie imperauerunt duce Adelstano qui primus inter eos diadema portauit. Degenerati autem a Britannica nobilitate Gualenses numquam postea monarchiam insulae recuperauerunt.

In the Variant version, the stages of this transfer of power have been given a different emphasis. The donation of Gormund marks not merely the end of British rule in Loegria but also the replacement of the name Britannia by Anglia, derived from that of the victorious English. Thus English control of Loegria (even though this control is essentially contradicted by the events of Cadwallon's reign) constitutes in the Variant version a more important step towards the passage of dominion, if indeed it does not signal the transition itself (§§ 186/7):

Postquam infaustus ille tyrannus totam regionem illam deuastauit, Saxonibus tenendam dimisit atque ad Gallias cum Ysembarto transiuit. Hinc Angli Saxones uocati sunt qui Loegriam possederunt et ab eis Anglia terra postmodum dicta est. Britonibus enim fugatis ac dispersis amisit terra nomen Britannie sicque Angli in ea super reliquias Britonum regnare ceperunt et Britones regni dyadema in perpetuum amiserunt nec postea pristinam dignitatem recuperare potuerunt. Seccesserant itaque eorum reliquie partim in Cornubiam, partim in Guallias, ubi nemoribus obtecti in montibus et speluncis cum feris degentes longo tempore delituerunt donec reuocata audacia irrupciones in Anglos Saxones crebras facere conati sunt et sic diu perseuerauere ut nec Saxones in illos, nec illi in Saxones preualerent. Creati sunt interea plurimi reges Anglorum Saxonum qui in diuersis partibus Loegrie regnauerunt; inter quos fuit Edelbertus rex Cancie, uir illustris et magne pietatis.

Despite the greater weight attached to the donation of Gormund in the Variant version, the latter, like the vulgate text, also reports the passage of dominion in Cadwaladr's reign. However, the Variant account has a significant difference. After the departure of Cadwaladr for Brittany, control of the island passes to the English under Æthelstan, whom they make king and who is thus represented as a contemporary of Cadwaladr (§ 204):

> Quorum [sc. Saxones] residui, cum feralis illa lues cessasset, miserunt in Germaniam propter conciues suos ut desolacionem suam aliis ciuibus supplerent. Illi uero nichil hesitantes, ut audierunt terram ab incolis orbatam, festinato itinere cum innumerabili multitudine uirorum ac mulierum nauigantes applicuerunt in partibus Nordamhumbrie et ab Albania usque in Cornubiam uniuersam terram occupauerunt. Nec enim supererat quisquam qui prohiberet uel commaneret in locis desertis preter paucas reliquias Britonum qui superfuerunt et de prefata mortalitate euaserunt uel postea nati sunt. Illi abdita nemorum inhabitant in Gualiis tantum et in Cornubia commanentes. Ab illo ergo tempore potestas Britonum cessauit et Angli in totum regnum regnare ceperunt, Adestano rege facto qui primus inter eos dyadema portauit. Pacem et concordiam tamquam fratres inter se habentes agros coluerunt, ciuitates et oppida reedificauerunt et magistratus et potestates in urbibus constituentes leges quas de terra sua aduexerant subiectis populis tradiderunt seruandas; ducatus et honores prout Britones ante habuerant inter se diuidentes summa pace et securitate terram desiderabilem incoluerunt.

The vulgate material relating to Æthelstan (§ 207) is thus found (in somewhat modified form) in § 204 of the Variant text.

The differences of narrative structure set out above cannot easily be accounted for if we suppose that the Variant version was the antecedent of the vulgate text. Clearly, the author of the Variant text believed that the transfer of power from the British to the English was largely effected by Gormund's donation. Why, then, does his subsequent account of the British recovery under Cadwallon contradict this belief? And why does he record a second passage of dominion in the seventh century? Moreover, the misdating of Æthelstan to Cadwaladr's reign is explicable only if the author of the Variant version was entirely ignorant of the identity of the former as an English king of the tenth century. But if our author was unaware of this king's historical importance in being the first to rule over a single, unified kingdom of England, why did he mention Æthelstan at all? Conversely, no such difficulties are encountered if we suppose that the Variant version is a reworking of the vulgate text. By giving Gormund's

donation more emphasis than it receives in the vulgate text and by effectively shifting the transfer of power to an earlier date (in §§ 186/7), the
author of the Variant version has attempted to reconcile the vulgate
account of the passage of dominion, unparalleled before Geoffrey's time,
with the accepted, Bedan version (and this sits well with the other evidence
for his interest in Bede); the resultant discrepancy with the Variant version's account of Cadwallon's reign shows that this attempted reconcilia-
tion was superficial, rather than comprehensively carried out. In the same
way, the misdating of Æthelstan came about because of a failure to recognise this king – named in the vulgate, but not specifically dated[111] – as
belonging to the tenth century and because of a desire to mark the transition from a British to an English supreme ruler as early as possible, in this
case immediately after Cadwaladr's flight. The treatment of the passage of
dominion in the Variant version can therefore be explained only if the latter
is a reworking, in this respect a somewhat crude and poorly executed
reworking, of the vulgate text.

The results of the preceding discussion permit us finally to answer the
three crucial questions, about the genesis of the Variant version, raised by
its relationships with the vulgate text and Wace's *Roman de Brut*.[112] The
Variant version was not Geoffrey's source nor was it written by Geoffrey
himself; it is a redaction of the vulgate text made by an unknown contemporary of Geoffrey at some time between 1138, the probable publication-
date of the *Historia*, and the early 1150s – certainly no later than 1155, since
the Variant version was used extensively in Wace's *Roman de Brut*, which
was completed in that year.[113]

Now that we have established that the First Variant is a reworking of the
vulgate *Historia*, we may more clearly perceive its literary aims. Indeed, it
is instructive to compare the First Variant with another contemporary

---

[111] Despite this vagueness, it is extremely unlikely that Geoffrey was himself unaware of
Æthelstan's tenth-century date. Certainly it is impossible that in the vulgate text his reign is
envisaged as occurring as early as the seventh century. After the death of Cadwaladr at
Rome in A.D. 689 (§ 206), Yvor and Yni return to Britain and battle against the English for
sixty-nine years (viz, until A.D. 758). There follows an unspecified period of further decline
for the British (§ 207, 'Barbarie ... irrepente') and of consolidation for the English, resulting
finally in unity under Æthelstan.
[112] See above, p. xvi.
[113] Indeed, if the First Variant was, as has been claimed, also used by Geffrei Gaimar, then it
must have been in existence by 1139; but, as we have seen (p. xvi above), there is no real
evidence to support the speculative identification of the Variant as one of the two sources on
which, according to Gaimar, the lost portion of his poem was based.

work which recasts the *Historia*, Henry of Huntingdon's *Epistola ad Warinum*.[114] This letter, later incorporated in Henry's *Historia Anglorum*, was based on notes made by Henry at Le Bec in January 1139 when Robert of Torigni gave him his first sight of Geoffrey's *Historia*. The *Epistola* offers primarily a very abbreviated version of the vulgate text. However, it also exhibits major stylistic changes (including independent literary echoes) and structural deviations from its source (deviations which led some scholars to suggest – mistakenly, in my view – that the text of the *Historia* used by Henry at Le Bec was itself non-standard). Moreover, some of the modifications made by Henry were, as I have argued elsewhere, evidently determined by a desire to reconcile elements of Geoffrey's History with Bede or with Henry's own *Historia Anglorum*. Henry, then, not only abbreviated the *Historia Regum Britannie*, but also to some degree reshaped it according to his own literary and historiographical ends. The First Variant is directly comparable. It is evident from the passages discussed in detail above that it too aims to abbreviate and stylistically to recast the vulgate *Historia*, although in its case the abbreviation is by no means as drastic as in the *Epistola ad Warinum*. Most chapters in the First Variant are more compressed than their vulgate counterparts and, as we have seen, speeches, battle-descriptions, and other emotive details are frequently omitted. At the same time, in the Variant version Geoffrey's Latinity is almost everywhere recast. On occasion entire episodes are restructured to give a smoother or more coherent narrative (as, for example, in §§ 27 and 179/80). Sometimes material (frequently including independent citation or echoing of the bible) is added in the Variant, often in speeches; this lends a more moral tone than in the vulgate, as, for example, in the speeches of Gorlois (§ 136) and Cadwaladr (§ 203), the account of Britain's conversion to christianity (§ 72), or the story of Uther's illicit passion for Igerna (§ 137).[115] This free restructuring in the First Variant runs parallel to Henry of Huntingdon's recasting of the vulgate in the *Epistola ad Warinum*. The First Variant also adds historical material and, like the *Epistola*, tries to some extent to reconcile the vulgate

---

114 A version of this letter is included in Robert of Torigni's *Chronicon*, ed. Delisle, *Chronique*, I.97–111; for an interim edition of the text of the *Epistola* found in Henry's own *Historia Anglorum*, see Wright, 'The place' (where the arguments advanced here are set out in full).

115 The handling in the Variant version of the last of these episodes is discussed by Morris, 'Uther and Igerne', p. 76.

account with other historical works. Supplementary details of the legendary history of Rome were derived from Landolfus Sagax, while matter dealing with the invasions of Julius Caesar and the career of Maximianus/ Maximus was borrowed from Bede. The First Variant also offers a different account of the parentage of the British eponymous hero Brutus which conforms more readily to the information given by Landolfus;[116] and, as we have seen, the handling of the transfer of power from British to English in the Variant is clearly intended to harmonize better with the accepted Bedan version of events. However, these attempts to reconcile the *Historia* with other sources are, like those in the *Epistola ad Warinum*, only sporadic. They do not represent a comprehensive effort to solve all the historical problems raised by Geoffrey's construct. In many places where Geoffrey's account largely or wholly contradicts that of Bede (as, for example, in the reigns of Constantinus and Constans),[117] the First Variant follows the vulgate closely. Furthermore, the historical material added in the Variant on at least two occasions contradicts other passages in that text, while its treatment of the passage of dominion is not entirely self-consistent and involves a serious error of dating.[118] Evidently, historical information was incorporated into the First Variant in a rather haphazard manner according to the whim of its author rather than by a coherent plan to create an ideologically more orthodox version of the *Historia*. Other attempts in the Variant to modify Geoffrey's narrative also have unhappy results. According to Geoffrey's account of British dispositions at the battle of Siesia (in vulgate § 168), the main army was divided into a number of formations, the fourth of which was commanded by Hoelus of Armorica and Gawain, while the reserve was led by Arthur himself and a further, mounted reserve was entrusted to Morvid of Gloucester; indeed, it was the intervention of Morvid's force (in §175) which later decided the battle. However, in Variant §168, this cavalry reserve is commanded not by Morvid but by Hoel, and the fourth British formation is under Gawain 'and two counts' ('cum duobus comitibus'). Yet when this latter force is attacked (in §173), it is led by Gawain and Hoel; and (in §175) the commander of the reserve cavalry is named as Morvid. In other words, the initial modification in

---

[116] Below, pp. xcix–ci.
[117] Cf. Wright, 'Geoffrey of Monmouth and Bede', pp. 45–7.
[118] A more radical attempt to solve the difficulties raised by the Galfridian and Bedan accounts of the transfer of power was made by another contemporary, Alfred of Beverley; see Leckie, *The Passage*, pp. 86–92.

Variant §168 was forgotted by §§173 and 175 with the result of a contradiction in the narrative. The First Variant is, then, primarily an abbreviated and recast version of the vulgate, which on occasion and by no means consistently reflects the moral outlook and historical interests of its redactor.

Can the redactor of the First Variant version be identified more precisely? A number of candidates may be considered. Wace was the first writer indisputably to have employed the First Variant: is it possible that the Variant represents a much altered Latin version of the vulgate *Historia* made by Wace and on which he later based the *Roman de Brut*? This hypothesis is open to a number of objections. First, why should Wace have gone to the trouble of preparing his own elaborate Latin version (including, it will be remembered, independent biblical and Classical allusions and verbatim borrowings from Bede and Landolfus Sagax) rather than simply translating the *Historia* directly into the vernacular? Secondly, the First Variant and the *Roman de Brut* by no means agree exactly; as we have seen, the *Roman de Brut* contains material absent from the First Variant, material which Wace added both independently and under the influence of the vulgate text. It seems very odd that, if the First Variant were a draft made by Wace, it should have needed such extensive reworking in the *Roman de Brut* itself. In fact, text-historical evidence precludes Wace's authorship. As we shall see, Wace used a First-Variant manuscript of a type which demonstrably contains an interpolation (which is reproduced by Wace);[119] his manuscript of the First Variant must therefore have stood at at least one remove from the archetype; and Wace cannot himself have been responsible for the First Variant version. Perhaps we should instead consider the possiblity that one of Geoffrey's contemporaries with known historical interests may have been responsible for the Variant version. Among the major historians, William of Malmesbury seems a most unlikely candidate. We may doubt whether William ever took Geoffrey's pseudo-history seriously; even if he did, a competent historian such as William would hardly have produced a reworking which included the glaring error of representing Æthelstan as a seventh-century ruler. The case for Henry of Huntingdon might at first sight appear stronger. Not only was Henry interested, indeed 'amazed', by his discovery of the *Historia Regum Britannie* at Le Bec, but he also produced a précis of Geoffrey's work, the *Epistola ad Warinum*, which he incorporated into the

<hr>

119 Below, pp. xcix–ci and ciii–iv.

later editions of his own *Historia Anglorum*. Could it be that the First Variant is another text by Henry, a longer reworking of the *Historia*? This is hardly likely. Both the *Epistola* and the First Variant sometimes differ from the vulgate in point of narrative structure; but these differences do not agree in each text. It seems impossible that both texts should have made entirely differing, independent alterations to the vulgate if they were produced by the same author. Similarly, the *Epistola* contains a number of historical modifications which are not found in the First Variant (for example, a closer identification of the British king Brennius with Brennus, the Gaulish chieftain on whom Geoffrey undoubtedly modelled that character);[120] conversely, other modifications in the First Variant are not present in the *Epistola*. The quite different attempts in both texts to recast historical elements therefore argue conclusively against Henry's authorship of the First Variant. Another possibility is that the Variant version was produced by Walter, archdeacon of Oxford. As Geoffrey's colleague at Oxford,[121] Walter would certainly have had the opportunity to consult (and rework) the *Historia*; and Walter's proficiency in rhetoric and history (Geoffrey describes him in the vulgate *Historia Regum Britannie*, §2 as, 'uir in oratoria arte atque in exoticis historiis eruditus') could have provided the stimulus for such a reworking. Although such a hypothesis is attractive, it is hard to see why Walter should have wished to modify the historical narrative of the *Historia* in the manner found in the First Variant. Walter, who, according to Geoffrey, owned the alleged Breton- (or Welsh-) language source of the *Historia* (as well as providing information orally), was evidently Geoffrey's collaborator and quite possibly connived with him to float his audacious pseudo-history. He thus had every opportunity to suggest that Geoffrey should add material (for example from Landolfus or Bede) or change the narrative structure of the *Historia* during its composition. There seems to be little reason why Walter should later have himself modified his friend's work or have tried (in, as we have seen, a somewhat half-hearted way) to reconcile its contents with other historical authorities. At best, the case for Walter's authorship of the First Variant must remain unproven. It is safest, therefore, to conclude provisionally that the redactor of the First Variant version was a writer well read in the

120 Tatlock, *The Legendary History*, p. 305.
121 Legge, 'Master Geoffrey', pp. 23–4 and 26.

bible and the Classics, of conventional christian piety,[122] and with an interest in history which manifests itself in his use of Bede and Landolfus; his identity, however, remains unknown.

Finally we must address the question of the circulation and success of the Variant version. For its circulation in the twelfth century we must rely entirely on the evidence of the writers to whom it was known. It seems that the Variant was available early in Normandy. At some date before 1155 it was used by Wace, who was resident in Caen; however, it is uncertain whether Wace, a Jerseyman by birth, acquired a copy of the Variant in Caen[123] or in southern England, where (Houck argued) he may have travelled.[124] The First Variant was also known to John of Hauville (Hauville-en-Roumais near Rouen) whose hexameter poem *Architrenius*[125] was written in winter 1184/5, when John was probably already at the cathedral school in Rouen. In *Architrenius* V.409–10, John describes Corineus's first landfall (with Brutus) in Britain as follows, 'superis auraque fauentibus utens / Litora felices intrat Totonesia portus'. This reference to favourable gods and breezes is not found in the vulgate *Historia*, § 20, which mentions only winds ('Prosperis ergo uentis promissam insulam exigens in Totonesio litore applicuit'), but is present in Variant, § 20, 'Prosperis denique uentis diis fauentibus terram diuinitus promissam petunt et in portu Derte fluminis qui Totonesium dicitur applicant'.[126] However, in an earlier passage (*Architrenius* I.268–7) John refers to Gogmagog's gigantic size, 'Bis senis [sc. cubitis] Frigios potuit mouisse ruentis / Gemagog arduitas'. The giant's height is not mentioned in the Variant text, but a reference to his twelve cubits is found in the vulgate, § 21, 'Geomagog stature .xii. cubito-

---

[122] Note that the First Variant does not always reflect Geoffrey's occasionally anti-monastic tone (Tatlock, *The Legendary History*, pp. 267–8); the Variant, for example, lays greater emphasis on the martyrdom of the British monks at Leicester (§ 189). This does not, however, prove that the redactor of the Variant was a regular monk – unlike Geoffrey who was very probably a secular canon (of the collegiate church of St George, Oxford).

[123] The presence of the vulgate *Historia* (also employed by Wace) at Caen might easily be explained by the town's connexion with one of the dedicatees of the work, Robert of Gloucester, who became governor of Caen in 1135 (Houck, *Sources*, p. 163), or by early links between Caen and Oxford (Foreville, 'L'école'), where Geoffrey probably wrote the *Historia*; but these associations cannot readily account for the possible availability at Caen of the First Variant.

[124] *Sources*, pp. 219–28 and 284–7.

[125] Edited by Schmidt, *Johannes de Hauvilla*; on the date of the poem, see *ibid.*, p. 22.

[126] Cf. *ibid.*, p. 329.

rum'.[127] It seems then that John of Hauville had access to a First-Variant manuscript (at Rouen?), although, like Wace, he also knew the vulgate text.[128]

If we turn to the evidence of the surviving manuscripts, which mostly date from the thirteenth and fourteenth centuries, a different picture emerges. Of the eight manuscripts, only one (or perhaps two) was not written in the British Isles. Three (or perhaps four) of the manuscripts were produced at or owned by Cistercian houses; but this need not in itself necessarily mean that the Cistercians played a particularly active part in the dissemination of the First Variant version.[129]. On the other hand, the Variant version was certainly well known in Wales. In one manuscript (E), the Variant text was added after that book had reached Wales. Another manuscript (c) preserves parts of a conflated text compounded from the First Variant and the vulgate by Brother Madog of Edeirnion. Two other manuscripts (D and R) contain Welsh glosses. This manuscript-evidence is supported by that of the Welsh *Brutiau*; for although these translations are based primarily on the vulgate *Historia*, the Variant text clearly also exercised an influence on at least some recensions of the *Brutiau*.[130] Only one manuscript of the Variant (R) is certainly Continental, originating from Italy or southern France. This branch of the tradition may also lie behind a very much abbreviated and interpolated version of the First Variant made for Filippo Maria, duke of Milan, by Galeazzo di Correggio in the late fourteenth century.[131] Although, then, the bulk of surviving manuscripts is British, the First Variant was not entirely unknown on the Continent after its early availability in Normandy.

---

[127] *Ibid.*, p. 295. There is no record of Gogmagog's size in the *Roman de Brut*; so John cannot have expanded the Variant text by reference to Wace (cf. Schmidt, *Johannes de Hauvilla*, p. 77, n. 147).

[128] Indeed, *Architrenius* V.410 ('Litora felices intrat Totonesia portus') seems to echo both texts simultaneously; cf. 'in Totonesio litore' (vulgate, §20) and 'in portu Derte fluminis' (Variant, §20).

[129] For the role of a Cistercian abbey (Sawley) in the transmission of texts dealing with British history, see Dumville, 'Celtic-Latin texts'.

[130] Parry, 'A variant version', pp. 368–9; Huws and Roberts, 'Another manuscript', pp. 150–1; Wright, 'The parentage'. It is also possible that near the end of the twelfth century the First Variant was known to Lazamon, resident on the English–Welsh border; see Le Saux, 'Lazamon's *Brut*', pp. 121–32.

[131] Barber, 'The manuscripts', p. 163. Galeazzo's text is too much reworked itself to serve as a witness to the First Variant version, but it seems that its exemplar belonged to the group represented by the manuscripts aHR. An edition of Galeazzo's work will appear later in this series.

There remains the question of the popularity of the First Variant. It is clear that the Variant, which is found in only eight of the more than 220 extant manuscripts of the *Historia*, was never as successful as the vulgate text and never, so far as we can tell, threatened to overshadow it. However, the Variant was known and copied and did exert influence, on Wace, John of Hauville, the Welsh *Brutiau*, and even in fourteenth-century Italy. It is significant that the Variant was the main text on which Wace based the *Roman de Brut*, since he draws only supplementary material (almost exclusively in the second half of the poem) from the vulgate *Historia* (which therefore he perhaps acquired later than the Variant, when his poem was well under way). This suggests that the Variant, which was produced relatively soon after the appearance (in 1138) of the vulgate text, may have benefited from the immediate enthusiasm with which the *Historia* was greeted and have come into circulation because of popular demand for Geoffrey's work. Such rapid dissemination would also sit well with manuscript-evidence that a text of the Variant with minor interpolation and recasting was already in existence before 1155, since Wace's manuscript appears to have been of this type.[132] But if the Variant did enjoy early popularity, it does not seem to have lasted. In essence, the Variant is an abbreviation of the vulgate text. Its sporadic attempts to modify the historical content of the vulgate became largely irrelevant when Geoffrey's *Historia* was, as Leckie has argued, increasingly accepted as a historical authority.[133] The chief distinction between vulgate and Variant texts thus became the latter's omissions. The natural reaction was to supplement these omissions by reintroducing the missing vulgate material, an approach which Wace had adumbrated by his simultaneous use of both the Variant and vulgate texts in the latter half of the *Roman de Brut*. No fewer than six of the eight extant Variant manuscripts contain some vulgate additions, although in two cases on a minor scale and in a third case possibly to repair physical damage. But two manuscripts bear witness to major acts of conflation, with the vulgate in one manuscript and with the Second Variant in the other. The manuscript-evidence, then, suggests that by the thirteenth and fourteenth centuries the First Variant had, although it was still copied, become something of a poor relation of the vulgate *Historia*. However, the Variant could still exercise some influence, as the following instance demonstrates. London, British Library, MS. Royal 4.C.xi

---

[132] Below, p. ciii–iv.
[133] *The Passage*, especially p. 119.

contains the Second Variant version of the *Historia Regum Britannie* in a copy of the second half of the twelfth century (fos 222r–249r).[134] In this manuscript §§ 1–5 were, for reasons which remain unclear, placed at the end of the text. At the end of § 5 (fo 249r), after the concluding words 'ut in sequentibus explicabitur', a fourteenth-century scribe has added the words (from the First Variant, § 5) 'historias qui a Bruto usque ad Cadwalladrum filium Cadwallonis actus omnium continue et ex ordine texuerunt. Explicit prohemium'. This brief addition indicates the availability to the annotator of a copy of the First Variant version of the *Historia*.

II *The Manuscripts*

The eight manuscript-witnesses to the First Variant (and the sigla used in this edition) are as follows.[135]

a: Aberystwyth, National Library of Wales, MS. 13210 (*olim* Phillipps 26233) was written in the second half of the thirteenth century by a known scribe, William of Woodchurch, at the Cistercian abbey of Robertsbridge (Sussex),[136] as we learn from a colophon on fo 64v: 'Hanc hystoriam Brittonum scripsit frater Willelmus de Wodecherche laicus quondam conuersus Pontis Roberti cuius anima requiescat in pace. Amen'. This volume comprises some sixty-four folios whose contents are: Dares Phrygius, *De Excidio Troiae* (fos 1r–10v); *Historia Regum Britannie*, 'correcta et abbreuiata' according to the closing rubric (fos 10v–64r); an etymological table of British place-names drawn from the *Historia* (fo 64r/v).[137] Four leaves have been lost between fos 62 and 63, the resulting lacuna running from *Historia*, §§ 186/7 ('cum feris'), to § 203 ('edentes et bibentes'). The volume was once (and perhaps originally) bound with two other manuscripts presumed to be of common origin with it: Phillipps 26641, containing a version of William of Malmesbury's *Gesta Regum Anglorum*;[138] and

---

134 Ward & Herbert, *Catalogue*, I.227.

135 The manuscripts are described in greater detail by Crick, *A Summary Catalogue*.

136 Davies, *Handlist*, IV.503–4; Huws & Roberts, 'Another manuscript'; Ker, *Medieval Libraries*, pp. 160 and 296.

137 Dumville, 'Anecdota'; Huws & Roberts, 'Another manuscript', p. 148.

138 Sotheby & Co., *Catalogue of Manuscripts on Vellum, Paper and Linen*, 21/11/72, lot 539; now deposited in Edinburgh, as National Library of Scotland, MS. Acc. 9193/13, cf. Ker & Watson, *Medieval Libraries*, p. 58 and n. 2.

Phillipps 26642, containing the *Topographia Hibernie* of Giraldus Cambrensis.[139] These, bound together, were in the mid-sixteenth century in the possession of Archbishop Matthew Parker.[140] It was probably Parker who added two notes in MS. a: fo 11r, 'hic liber multum uariat a communi Galfrido quamuis in multum concordant'; and fo 64r, 'et cum uulgari Galfrido non concordat'.[141]

The Robertsbridge text of the *Historia Regum Britannie* represents a conflation of the First and Second Variants, the latter being used extensively from §61. In the sixteenth century, the prologue and dedication of the *Historia* (vulgate, §§ 1–3, the dedication being that to Robert of Gloucester alone) were copied in the margin of fo 10v by the same scribe who added the dedication of William of Malmesbury's *Gesta Regum Anglorum* on fo 64v. The text is divided into eleven books as follows: Preface, §5; I, §§ 6–22; II, §§ 23–34; III, §§ 35–53; IV, §§ 54–72; V, §§ 73–89; VI, §§ 90–108; VII, §§ 111–117; VIII, §§ 118–142; IX, §§ 143–164a; X, §§ 161–176; XI, §§ 177–208.[142] This manuscript is only a partial witness to the text of the First Variant, the fact of conflation limiting its evidential value. It is cited in my apparatus only in so far as its readings demonstrate its place within the text-history of the First Variant.

c: Cardiff, South Glamorgan Central Library, MS. 2.611 is a book now containing 132 folios quired in twelves but wanting at least one quire at each end and a leaf after fo 87. It was written in a rather current Gothic textura hand in the late thirteenth or early fourteenth century.[143] Opinions have varied as to its origin, whether the Franco-German border or Wales.[144] A Welsh gloss of sixteenth-century date establishes its probable presence in Wales, and some fifteenth-century annotations in a characteristically 'English' hand might indeed equally well have been written in Wales.

The book's contents are an acephalous copy of Dares Phrygius, *De Excidio Troiae* (fos 1r–9r), followed by a *Genealogia Troianorum* (found also in MSS. D, fos 10v–11r, and E, pp. 56–7) and a complex hybrid version

---

139 Sotheby & Co., *Catalogue of Manuscripts*, 25/11/69, lot 455.
140 Huws & Roberts, 'Another manuscript', pp. 147–8.
141 *Ibid.*, p. 148.
142 For the restructuring of §§ 160–164 in the First Variant, see p. xxxvi above.
143 Ker, *Medieval Manuscripts*, II.357–8; Hammer, *Variant Version*, pp. 8 and 12–19; Dumville, 'The origin'.
144 The former provenance was suggested by E. G. H. Millar, *apud* Hammer, *Variant Version*, p. 8, n. 10; the latter ('or perhaps England') is upheld by Ker, *Medieval Manuscripts*, II.358.

of the *Historia Regum Britannie* (fos 10r–130v), compounded from, on the one hand, a text of the First Variant conflated with the vulgate and, on the other, the vulgate itself, and preceded (fos 9v–10r) by a 26-line poem ascribing the work (viz, the initial conflation of the First Variant and vulgate texts) to Brother Madog of Edeirnion.[145] This version of the *Historia* is not divided into books. The manuscript ends with sundry Merlin-prophecies and a four-line *Epithaphium Arturi* (fos 130v–132v).[146]

The prehistory of this version of the *Historia* seems extraordinarily complex, with clear hints of north-English and Scandinavian elements in its make-up.[147] On the other hand, there appears to be sufficient evidence of a Welsh dimension in its history to allow the possibility that the extant text was created in Wales and the manuscript copied there.[148]

This version of the *Historia* is no more than a partial witness to the text of the First Variant, for that text is used only in §§ 5–108 and (very sparingly) in §§ 178–208. The nature of the conflation and rewriting limit the value of its testimony for the edition of the First Variant. It is here cited only in so far as its readings demonstrate its place within the text-history of the Variant version.

D: Dublin, Trinity College, MS. 515 (E.5.12) was written in the late thirteenth or early fourteenth century in an unidentified British scriptorium – so much, at least, is indicated by its script. The total appearance of the book has suggested an origin in a Cistercian house, but this has not been established with certainty. The volume comprises sixty-nine folios, the original text appearing on fos 12r–65v.[149]

The original contents (initially foliated 'i–x' followed by 'i–xliii') were Dares Phrygius, *De Excidio Troiae* (fos 12r–21r), the First Variant version of the *Historia Regum Britannie* (fos 21r–65v), and an English king-list (fo 65v) extending from Alfred of Wessex to Edward I (1272–1307). A regnal length is given for Henry III (1216–72), albeit over an erasure, but none has

---

[145] Walther, *Initia*, no. 18633. This poem is also found (in a sixteenth-century hand) in Cambridge, Corpus Christi College, MS. 281, fo iiv (James, *A Descriptive Catalogue*, II.45), although the text of the *Historia Regum Britannie* in that manuscript is not of the First Variant. On the probable identity of Madog, see Williams, 'Cyfeiriad'; Jenkins, *The Dictionary*, pp. 607–8; and Parry, *History*, pp. 56–7.

[146] Walther, *Initia*, no. 7952 (the order of the verses there being different from those in c).

[147] Dumville, 'The origin', pp. 317–21.

[148] Huws & Roberts, 'Another manuscript', p. 151.

[149] Abbott, *Catalogue*, p. 78; Hammer, *Variant Version*, pp. 6–7.

(in the original hand) been entered for his son. In as much as it does not conflict with the palaeographical conclusion, it is a reasonable deduction that the writing of this manuscript was achieved in Edward I's reign.

Matter was added at the beginning and end of the manuscript, partly in an informal bookhand and partly in a fourteenth-century Anglicana script. At the beginning are found: a diagram of the arts and sciences (fo 1r); the letter of Alexander to Aristotle (fos 1v–3r); *Prophetia Aquile Sephtonie* (fos 3r–3v); an acephalous copy of Walter Map's *Dissuasio Ualerii ad Ruffinum philosophum ne uxorem ducat*, beginning, 'est pastor Admeti' (fos 5r–7v);[150] *Genealogia ab Adam ad Cadwaladrum* (fos 10r–10v), also found in MS. E, pp.54–6; *Genealogia Troianorum* (fos 10v–11r), also found in MSS. c, fos 9r–10v, and E, pp 56–7; an unidentified text, 'Uir quidam magnus . . . pro posse defecit' (fo 11v) (fos 4r/v, 8r–9v being blank). At the end of the volume are added: the epitaph of Ceadwalla of Wessex (from Bede's *Historia Ecclesiastica Gentis Anglorum* V.7)[151] (fo 66r); a chronicle from Romulus to Julius Caesar (fo 66r); *Modus confitendi peccata* (fos 66v–69v).

The text of the *Historia Regum Britannie* is divided into eleven books indicated by large capitals, as follows:[152] Preface, §5; I, §§6–22; II, §§23–34; III, §§35–53; IV, §§54–89; V, §§90–97; VI, §§98–108; VII, §§111–117; VIII, §§118–142; IX, §§143–164a; X, §§161–176; XI, §§177–208. It was subjected to at least one level of subsequent mediaeval 'correction'. Hammer saw in this the work of the original scribe and two later annotators,[153] but it is far from clear that his division of the hands is correct. The marginal and interlinear additions may perhaps all be explained as the work of a single annotator, writing now more, now less formally. They appear to display: (1) the results of sporadic collation against another copy of the First Variant, which must have belonged to the group represented by MSS. aHR, and also in a few cases (for example, in §§29, 40, and 50) against a manuscript of the vulgate text, although it is possible that the collated manuscript was itself a conflated text (such as we find in MS. c or, in a

---

[150] Edited by James, *Walter Map*, pp.288–312; on the separate transmission of the *Dissuasio*, see *ibid.*, pp.xlvii–ix. I owe the identification of this text to Julia Crick.

[151] This is not the same version of the epitaph as that found in another Galfridian manuscript (Paris, BN lat. 6040, fo 59v), which is printed by Hammer, 'An unrecorded *epitaphium*'.

[152] *Pace* Hammer, *Variant Version*, p.6. The capital at §116 [31] does not seem to mark a book-division (cf. n.173 below).

[153] *Variant Version*, p.6.

different way, in MS. a); (2) marginal updatings or revisions of Welsh name-forms in the text of the *Historia*; (3) at least two quotations (fos 52v and 53v) from the *Historia Brittonum*; (4) miscellaneous other name-forms; (5) a substantial marginal annotation on fo 39ra in Middle Welsh, 'Seuerus a wnayth gweyd keyn e ar draus enis Predeyn rac kenedel kidraul guaul ueyth'. Both this annotation (on Severus) and a marginal note on fo 53v (naming Gawain's mother as Goear) are seemingly influenced by the Welsh *Brutiau*.[154] The sum of these annotations makes clear that the annotator was a Welshman with a keen interest in names. Occasionally his observations miss their mark, providing false updatings of the main text's often mangled Welsh name-forms; but these demonstrate a knowledge of Welsh nomenclature even if they reflect adversely on his grasp of Welsh historical philology.

E: Exeter, Cathedral Library, MS. 3514 is a thirteenth-century codex comprising some 268 folios, quired largely in twelves, the complexities of whose history have only recently begun to be appreciated. It is now recognised that the volume was created in two stages.[155] Its core was pp. 223–450, containing a group of episcopal and abbatial lists (pp. 223–6)[156] followed by a text of Henry of Huntingdon's *Historia Anglorum* (pp. 226–450).[157] This part was written by two scribes in the mid-thirteenth century in an unidentified British scriptorium; its exemplar was very probably the book which is now London, Lambeth Palace, MS. 327,[158] written *ca* 1200,[159] of unknown origin (perhaps, on the evidence of the episcopal lists, in the province of Canterbury)[160] but by the fifteenth century in the possession of the Augustinian canons of Bourne (Lincolnshire).[161]

Later in the thirteenth century, Exeter 3514 received an extensive series of additions (written in a number of hands) which were so placed as to surround the original book: these new leaves now constitute pp. 1–222,

---

[154] Cf. Griscom & Jones, *The Historia*, pp. 354 and 444 (respectively); also Parry, *Brut*, p. xi.
[155] Ker, *Medieval Manuscripts*, II.822–5 (at 822).
[156] Dumville, 'An early text', pp. 10–13; Sarah Foot (Newnham College, Cambridge) is currently working on these lists.
[157] Greenway, 'Henry of Huntingdon', p. 106.
[158] *Ibid.*, p. 114; Todd, *A Catalogue*, p. 43.
[159] Ker, *Medieval Libraries*, p. 11.
[160] Dumville, 'An early text', p. 12.
[161] Ker, *Medieval Libraries*, p. 11.

451–534. The joins had been effected by the early fourteenth century, as we can see from a table of contents added on fo iir.[162] In front of the original manuscript were placed pseudo-Methodius, *De fine saeculi* (pp. 1–6); a composite Anglo-French history probably of Bury St Edmunds origin (pp. 9–30);[163] pseudo-Bede, *Imago Mundi* (pp. 36–53); genealogies, including *Genealogia ab Adam ad Cadwalladrum* and *Genealogia Troianorum*, (pp. 54–8) with fourteenth-century marginalia of Welsh interest; list-texts about English history (pp. 58–60, continuing into a lacuna of one folio); *Genealogia regum Francie* (pp. 61–66); Dares Phrygius, *De Excidio Troiae* (pp. 67–93); Geoffrey of Monmouth's *Historia Regum Britannie* in the First Variant version (pp. 94–218). Behind the manuscript of Henry's *Historia Anglorum* was placed another series of historical texts, *Historia Normannorum et Regum Anglorum* (pp. 450–504), and Welsh chronicles and genealogies (pp. 507–528).[164]

Wherever the original manuscript was written, it is clear that when the additions were made the book had reached Wales. The genealogies include two of Welsh origin, one 'ad probandum quod Lewlinus princeps Wallie fuit cognatus Dei'![165] Llywelyn ap Gruffydd ruled from 1246 to 1282. At the other end of the book two Welsh chronicles and other matter of Welsh interest (pp. 507–528) confirm the Welsh origin of the additions. Investigation of *Cronica de Wallia* (pp. 507–519) has shown that it was probably composed, and therefore all these texts added, at the Cistercian abbey of Whitland.[166] The codex bears a number of marks of its later history, but the only one of these which has proved susceptible of interpretation indicates that in the second half of the fifteenth century it belonged to John Russell, bishop of Rochester (1476–80) and subsequently of Lincoln (1480–94).[167]

The date of the original manuscript (pp. 223–450) has been determined palaeographically since the names in the lists on pp. 223–226 were not up to date at the time of copying.[168] On the other hand, there is reason to think that the dates offered by some of the additions do provide reasonable clues to the period of execution of the work. The Anglo-French history which

[162] Ker, *Medieval Manuscripts*, II.822.
[163] Dumville & Lapidge, *The Annals*, pp. xx–xxi and l–lii.
[164] Jones, '"Cronica"'; Hughes, *Celtic Britain*, pp. 76–9 (and references cited there); Bromwich, *Trioedd*, p. 542; Roberts, 'Pen Penwaedd'.
[165] Not recorded by Jones, '"Cronica"', or Bartrum, *Early Welsh Genealogical Tracts*.
[166] Hughes, *Celtic Britain*, p. 79.
[167] Ker, *Medieval Manuscripts*, II.824–5; Emden, *Biographical Register*, pp. 1609–11; Fryde *et al.*, *Handbook*, pp. 268 and 256.
[168] Ker, *Medieval Manuscripts*, II.823.

occupies pp. 9–30 contains a genealogical table ending with three of King Edward I's sons, born 1266–73, who died young (1271–84),[169] and an account of French kings to Phillipe IV (1285–1314).[170] The pedigree of Llywelyn ap Gruffydd (p. 56) has already been mentioned. On p. 58 a genealogy of English kings ends with Henry III (1216–72).[171] And the concluding Welsh chronicle ends abruptly in the annal for 1285.[172] A date of writing in the 1280s would not conflict with this evidence.

The text of the First Variant in this manuscript is divided into ten books, to be indicated by large capitals (which were in fact never added), as follows: Preface, §5; I, §§6–22; II, §§23–34; III, §§35–53; IV, §§54–89; V, §§90–108; VI, §§111–117(or 118); VII, §§118(or 119)–142; VIII, §§143–164a; IX, §§161–176; X, §§177–208.[173] The textual character of this copy of the *Historia* will be discussed further below.[174] Here, however, attention must be focused on some additions made to this text by another scribe. The character of the First Variant is such that it lacks §§1–3/4 and 109–110 of the vulgate *Historia*, viz the preface (with either single or double dedication) to the whole work and that to the *Prophetie Merlini*. These were added to the Exeter copy,[175] on pp. 94 and (in the margin) 158, the same fourteenth-century scribe[176] providing also a marginal quotation of St Augustine, *De Ciuitate Dei* XV.23 (on *incubi*) (p. 158), and a brief marginal commentary on the *Prophetie* (pp. 159–160).[177] Secondary scribal activity has also resulted in a partial redivision by (marginal) rubrics of the text into books[178] and chapters, and in marginal notation of British kings in a numbered sequence.[179] I give here, for the sake of completeness, the Exeter 3514 texts of the prefaces to the *Historia* and the *Prophetie Merlini*.

---

[169] John, Henry, and Alphonso: see Fryde *et al.*, *Handbook*, p. 38.

[170] Ker, *Medieval Manuscripts*, II.822.

[171] *Ibid.*, II.823.

[172] *Ibid.*, II.824.

[173] Other spaces for capitals at §§8, 16 (including the initial lines of the verses in that chapter), and 116 [31] (cf. n. 152 above) do not appear to indicate book-divisions.

[174] Below, p. xcv.

[175] Hammer's erroneous statement (*Variant Version*, p. 6) that the preface of the *Historia* is incomplete in E (beginning 'paginam illinissem') was obviously occasioned by the omission of the first text-column (on p. 94) from his photostat!

[176] Ker, *Medieval Manuscripts*, II.823.

[177] Printed by Hammer, 'Bref commentaire'.

[178] Hammer, *Variant Version*, pp. 5–6 (at 6); the redivision is: I, §§6–22; II, §§23–34; III, §§35–53; IV, §§54–72; V, §§73–?; µVIλ (no rubric), §§?–142; VII, §§143–?.

[179] Hammer, *Variant Version*, p. 6.

§§ 1–3 (p. 94)

[1] <C>um mecum multa de multis sepius animo reuoluens in hystoriam regum Britannie inciderim, in mirum contuli quod infra mencionem quam de eis Gildas et Beda luculento tractatu fecerant nichil de eis regibus qui ante incarnacionem Christi inhabitauerant, nichil de Arthuro ceterisque compluribus qui post incarnacionem successerunt reperissem, cum et gesta eorum digna eternitate laudis constarent et a multis populis quasi inscripta iocunde et memoriter predicentur. [2] Talia uero et de talibus multociens cogitanti obtulit Walterus Oxenefordus archideaconus, uir in ceatoria[180] arte et in exoticis hystoriis eruditus, quendam Britannici sermonis librum uetustissimum qui a Bruto[181] primo rege Britonum usque ad Cadwaldum filium Cadwallonis actus omnium continue et ex ordine perpulcris oracionibus proponebant [sic]. Rogatu itaque illius ductus, tametsi infra alienos ortulos falerata uerba non collegerim, agresti tamen stilo propriisque calamis contentus codicem illum in Latinum sermonem transferre curaui. Nam si ampulosis dictionibus paginam illinissem, tedium legentibus ingererem dum magis in exponendis uerbis quam in hystoria intelligenda ipsos commorari oporteret. [3] Opusculo igitur meo, Roberte dux Glauuernie, faueas ut sic te doctore, te monitore corrigatur: quod non ex Galfridi Momninutensis fonticulo cenceatur exortum, sed sale Minerue tue conditum illius dicatur edicio quem Henricus illustris rex Anglorum generauit, quem philosophia liberalibus artibus erudiuit, quem innata probitas in milicia militibus prefecit. Unde Britannia tibi nunc temporibus nostris acsi alterum Henricum adepta interno congratulatur affectu.

§§ 109–110 (p. 158)

[109] Nondum autem ad hunc locum hystorie perueneram, cum de Merlino diuulgato rumore compellebant me contemporanei mei undique prophetias eius edere, maxime autem Alexander Lincolniensis episcopus, uir summe religionis et prudencie. Non erat alter in clero siue in populo cui tot nobiles famularentur quos mansueta pietas ipsius et benigna largitas in obsequium suum aliciebat. Cui cum satis esse preelegissem, prophetias transtuli et eidem cum huiusmodi literis direxi. [110] Coegit me, Alexander Lincolniensis episcopus, nobilitatis tue dilectio prophetias Merlini de Britannico in Latinum transferre antequam historiam perarrassem quam de gestis regum Britannorum inceperam; proposueram enim illam prius perficere istud quia[182] opus subsequenter explicare ne, dum uterque labor incumberet, sen-

---

[180] Glossed (in text) 'id est seatoria, a secis dicta [...] fuit primo' and (in margin) 'scema <->atis id est scriptura'.
[181] *Buto* with suprascript *r* MS.
[182] sic (for -*que*) MS.

lxxxv

sus meus ad singula minus fieret. Attamen quoniam securus eram uenie quam discrecio subtilis ingenii tui donaret, agrestem calamum meum labellis apposui et plebeia modulacione ignotum tibi interpretatus sum sermonem. Admodum autem admiror quod id pauperi stilo dignatus es[183] committere cum tot doctiores, tot discreciores uirga potestatis tue coherceat, qui sublimioris carminis delectamento aures misericordie tue mulcerent. Et ut omnes philosophos tocius Britannie insule preteream, tu solus es – quod non erubesco fateri – qui pre cunctis audaci lira caneres, nisi te culmen honoris ad cetera negocia uocaret. Quoniam ergo placuit ut Galfridus Monumutensis fistulam suam in hoc uaticinio sonaret, modulacionibus suis fauere non diffugias. Et siquid inordinate siue uiciose protulerit, ferula camenarum tuarum in rectum auertas concentum.

H: London, British Library, MS. Harley 6358 is a composite codex, created in modern times, of which the relevant portion (fos 2–59) was written in the early thirteenth century. It comprises some eighty-six folios.[184] Its text of the *Historia Regum Britannie* (fos 2r–58v) displays the peculiarity that it falls into two quite distinct sections: fos 2r–41v contain a text of the First Variant (albeit with minor vulgate additions in §§ 60 and 91), as far as the middle of § 149, divided into chapters and books; fos 42r–58v, by a new scribe, contain the vulgate text divided into books but not chapters. The book-division (indicated by rubrics) in the First Variant section, §§ 5–149, is as follows: Preface, § 5; I, §§ 6–21; II, §§ 22–34; III, §§ 35–53; IV, §§ 54–73; V, §§ 73–97; VI, §§ 98–108; VII, §§ 111–117; VIII, §§ 118–142; IX, §§ 143–?.

It seems clear that the exemplar used for fos 2–41 was damaged: in the last (fifth) quire of this section (fos 34–41) every one of the sixteen pages lacks one line of text, not as a result of physical loss in H itself, which is undamaged, but evidently as a result of scribal inattention to loss in his exemplar. The scribe must have been very faithful to the layout of his exemplar, copying page for page, line for line; if he had not, the lacunae would occur at different points on each page of H. This fact seems sufficient to render extremely unlikely Jacob Hammer's statement that the scribe of H, fos 34–41, 'evidently copied from an exemplar which was already a copy of a mutilated manuscript':[185] it is in the highest degree

---

183 The variant reading *eras* is noted in the margin.
184 Ward & Herbert, *Catalogue*, I.235–6; Hammer, *Variant Version*, p. 7.
185 *Ibid.*, p. 7.

improbable that two successive copies, presumably by different scribes, would each be so faithful to its exemplar.

That eight folios of H's exemplar were thus damaged may suggest at once a reason why the First Variant text was abandoned after fo 41v. We may suppose that at this point the exemplar was so damaged that it could no longer be used or, indeed, that the remainder of the text was lost from it. In either eventuality a fresh exemplar would have to be sought, and this turned out to be a vulgate text.

Another theory of the genesis of the extant codex remains possible, however. The present form could result from physical loss of text from the beginning of H's vulgate text; but this alternative hypothesis, that the First Variant section was added after the loss of material from the second (vulgate) portion of the text, is rendered highly improbable by the textual condition of fos 41v–42r. The question turns on a clause in § 149 which in the First Variant has the form '.lx. rupes feruntur esse', while in the vulgate text it runs 'sexaginta rupes manifestum est esse'. The text in H is '.lx. rupes ma[fo 42r]nifestum est esse', with the word *manifestum* divided between fos 41v and 42r; moreover, the element *ma-* (on 41v) is written over an erasure (presumably of the First Variant's *fer-*). The text of fo 41v has therefore been modified to effect a junction with that of fo 42r. Since fos 34–41 of H were, as we have seen, so faithful a copy of their exemplar, it seems a coincidence beyond belief that these folios containing First Variant §§ 5–149 could have been used to supplement an incomplete vulgate text, in which (by chance) the pre-existing text (of § 149) abutted so neatly with them. It is far more likely that the vulgate text (fos 42r–58v) was copied with the aim of completing the First Variant folios, the difference of diction beween the vulgate and First Variant texts of § 149 necessitating a minor modification at the end of fo 41v so that the transition could be made smoothly.

Official correction is much in evidence in this codex, as are alterations by a later scribe. It belonged in the fifteenth century to one Richard Blysset (fo 59v).[186]

The readings of this manuscript are fully reported as far as the end of fo 41v. The text of fos 42–58, which contains no First Variant matter, has been left for consideration with other manuscripts of the vulgate.

P: Aberystwyth, National Library of Wales, MS. 2005 (Panton 37) is an eighteenth-century manuscript of ninety-six folios containing various

[186] Wright, *Fontes*, pp. 74 and 466.

notes and extracts.[187] Fos 63r–72v comprise a description (with excerpts) by Evan Evans[188] of a First-Variant manuscript, now lost. Evans gives the following information about the manuscript and its contents (fos 63r–64v).

An account of a curious manuscript which now belongs to Doctor Treadway Nash near Bevere Worcester 1773 bought out of the library of the late Mr Lewis Morris[189] of Penbryn in Cardiganshire. This seems to be the first edition of Galfrid's history, and differs very much from the printed copies.[190]
This manuscript was bought by me Lewis Morris of Gallvadog in Cardiganshire of Thomas Osborn bookseller of Grays Inn July 1753 It contains these several heads.
1 Of the nature and property of animals from Aristotle.
2 Dares Phrygius of the Siege of Troy.
3 Galfridus Arthurius Monemutensis's translation of the history of Britain out of Welsh into Latin, with Merlin's prophecies without the common preface found in other copies, and letter to the Bishop of Lincoln, or the conclusion, where Malmsbury and Huntingdon and Caradog of Llan Garvan are mentioned. It is divided like the Heydelberg edition into twelve books, but not always distinguished, nor in chapters. It is more like the British Tyssilio than any of the printed copies.
4 A commentary or explication of Merlin's prophecies. [N.B. These are set down paragraph by paragraph in red letters with Galfrid's explanations different from the printed copies.]
5 Latin verses on Ireland, Scotland, etc beginning Regnum Scotorum.
6 The Articles of Munster A.D. 1310.
7 Verses of the Sibylls concerning the coming of Christ.
8 Giraldus Cambrensis's topography of Ireland.
9 Giraldus Cambrensis of the Conquest of Ireland.
This book once belonged to the Monastery of the Virgin Mary near Dublin[191] and differs much from the printed copies especially in Galfridus's history.

---

[187] Evans, *Report*, II.843–5; Parry, 'A variant version'; Hammer, *Variant Version*, pp. 4–5 and 8.
[188] Jenkins, *Dictionary of Welsh Biography*, pp. 229–31.
[189] *Ibid.*, pp. 661–2.
[190] From this point Evans apparently transcribed Morris's notes directly from the manuscript.
[191] The Cistercian abbey of St Mary, Dublin: see Gwynn & Hadcock, *Medieval Religious Houses*, pp. 122 and 130–1.

In the leaf before the beginning of the book is the following account in text-hand.[192]

Liber communitatis domus alme Uirginis Marie juxta Dubliniam. In isto uolumine continentur Aristotilis Tractatus de natura et proprietatu animalium. Daretis Excidium Trojanum. Historia Britonum a Galfrido Arturio translata. Prophetice [sic] Merlini de duobus draconibus. Topographia Hybernica. Duo libri expugnationis Hyberniae Gyraldi Barii Cambrensis. Sum Patricii Dowdal x Julii accomodat. Wilielmo Ryano.

Evans, 'in order to show what difference there is betwixt this and the printed copies' (fo 69r), transcribed the following chapters, 5–8(part), 54–55, and 206–208 (fos 65r–72v). The textual character of P's extracts of the *Historia* will be discussed later.[193] Here, however, it must be noted that we cannot be entirely certain how faithfully the original text was reported by Evans (who may have been influenced by the vulgate edition with which he clearly also worked). We may, for example, doubt whether the First Variant text was, as is claimed, divided into the twelve books of Commelin's edition[194] ('but not always distinguished'), since none of the other First Variant manuscripts contains that book-division. The extracts themselves show no more than that the fourth book began at § 54. Evans occasionally had difficulty interpreting the abbreviations in his source manuscript: some of them he attempted to reproduce, for example *īstū* (for *insitum*) and *īstnctē* (erroneously, for *institerit*), both on fo 70v; and sometimes he added, in square brackets, a conjecture as to their meaning, for example *c'ie [q<aero> an ciuitatis]* (for *curie*) on fo 72r.

R: Paris, Bibliothèque de l'Arsenal, MS. 982 (7.H.L.) is a large-format manuscript comprising 188 folios, written (on the evidence of its script) in Italy or southern France in the second half of the fourteenth century.[195] The inscription (now barely legible) 'A Bele Viegne' (fo 188r) indicates that the book once belonged to Jean Le Bègue, clerk of the court of the Chambre des Comptes, who compiled inventories of the French royal library in 1411

---

[192] This sentence is most probably Evans's; if it was written by Morris, then Evans must have been working with a description (and excerpts) prepared by Morris himself and may never have seen Morris's manuscript.

[193] Below, pp. cx–cxi.

[194] For Commelin's book-division, see Wright, *Historia Regum Britannie*, I.liii and 172–4.

[195] Martin, *Catalogue*, II.205–7; Laistner & King, *A Hand-list*, pp. 81 and 100; Haenel, *Catalogi*, p. 306, no. 489; Potthast, *Bibliotheca*, I.138.

and 1413.[196] It later belonged to the Collège de Navarre, Paris.[197] The principal contents of this largely historical book are: Orosius, *Historiarum contra paganos libri septem* (fos 1r–42v); Isidore, *Chronica* and *Historiae* (fos 42v–53r); Rodrigue Ximenes, *Chronicon*, with continuation (fos 54r–97r); miscellaneous *Historiae nationum* (fos 97r–112r); an added glossary A–G (fos 112v–114r); Bede, *Historia Ecclesiastica Gentis Anglorum* (fos 115r–160v); a letter of St Jerome, no. 73 (fos 160v–161v); Bede, *Expositio super Tobiam* (fos 161v–164r); Dares Phrygius, *De Excidio Troiae* (fos 165r–168v); *Historia Regum Britannie* in the First Variant version (fos 168v–188r). Fos 53v, 114v, 164v, and 188v are blank.

The copy of Bede's *Historia Ecclesiastica*, followed by Jerome's Letter 73, has been thought to derive from the former MS. Phillipps 2701, a manuscript written at Nonantola in Italy in the ninth century and remaining there until the sixteenth or seventeenth century.[198] If it is the immediate exemplar of R, then our manuscript almost certainly shares a Nonantolan origin.

It is possible that the exemplar of R's copy of the First Variant may have had Welsh connexions since there is present within its text of the *Historia* (§94) a Welsh gloss (*guar*) on the *Vor-* element of the name Vortigern (fo 176v; compare fo 185v, where *ensis Arthuri* is an intrusive gloss on the name *Caliburno* two lines earlier in §174). R's text of the First Variant has also been modified in other ways: the *Vera Historia de Morte Arthuri*[199] has been inserted into the text between §§178 and 179 (fos 186r–186v); and §207 is found in a recast, abbreviated form (fo 188r). The text of the *Historia* in this manuscript is divided by rubrics into eleven books: Preface, §5; I, §§6–22; II, §§23–34; III, §§35–53; IV, §§54–72; V, §§73–89; VI, §§90–108; VII, §§111–117; VIII, §§118–142; IX, §§143–164a; X, §§161–176; XI, §§177–208.

S: Edinburgh, National Library of Scotland, MS. Adv. 18.4.5 is written in a late thirteenth- or early fourteenth-century hand of uncertain (but British) origin.[200] It comprises some ninety folios. The book's contents are: pseudo-Aristotle, *Secretum Secretorum* (fos 1r–29v); Dares Phrygius, *De*

---

196 Hallaire, 'Quelques manuscrits'.
197 For a survey of volumes from the Collège de Navarre now in the Bibliothèque de l'Arsenal, see Martin, *Catalogue*, VIII.510–18.
198 Colgrave & Mynors, *Bede's Ecclesiastical History*, pp. lxix–lxx.
199 Ed. Lapidge, 'An edition'. See also Barber, 'The *Vera Historia*'; Lapidge, 'Additional manuscript evidence'; and Barber, 'The manuscripts'.
200 Cunningham, 'Latin Classical manuscripts', pp. 74–5.

Excidio Troiae (fos 29v–40r); and the First Variant version of the *Historia Regum Britannie* (fos 40r–90v). The body of the *Prophetie Merlini* (§§ 113 [9], *seruitutis*, to 117 [73], *cornua*) is missing from this manuscript's text of the First Variant owing to the excision of three folios after fo 67; in the upper margin of fo 67v is found the following explantory note in a sixteenth-century hand, 'hic absciduntur obscene predictiones Merlini. Utpote per concilium Tridentinum ultimum condemnate'. The text is divided into ten books (indicated by large capitals) as follows: Preface, § 5; I, §§ 6–34; II, §§ 35–43 (to 'occupare temptant.'); III, §§ 43–53; IV, §§ 54–89; V, §§ 90–108, VI, §§ 111–117; VII, §§ 118–142; VIII, §§ 143–164a; IX, §§ 161–176; X, §§ 177–208. Another scribe added marginal headings and, at the head of fo 56v and the foot of fo 66r, material drawn from the vulgate text (§§ 68 and 104, respectively). At the bottom of fo 58v, the same scribe noted 'hic deficit [?] de martyrio sancti Albani martyris', evidently comparing vulgate, § 77.

III *Editions and text-history*

The peculiarities of individual First-Variant manuscripts attracted a degree of attention relatively early: in the sixteenth century, Archbishop Matthew Parker noted (if the hand is his) that the text of MS. a differed from the vulgate *Historia*;[201] in the late eighteenth century, Evan Evans made excerpts (in MS. P) from Lewis Morris's (now lost) manuscript precisely with the aim of illustrating the differences between its text and the printed editions;[202] a century later, H. L. D. Ward described some of the divergences of MS. H from the vulgate text.[203] It was not, however, until 1932 that parts of the First Variant version appeared in print, when John J. Parry published a generally accurate transcription of the extracts in MS. P.[204] Parry's hope that the manuscript from which these excerpts were made 'may some day come to light, so that its peculiarities may be fully studied'[205]

---

201 Above, p. lxxix.
202 Above, p. lxxxix.
203 Ward & Herbert, *Catalogue*, I.235.
204 'A variant version'. Errors are few, *praecla* (p. 365) probably being a misprint (of *praeclara*); Parry does, however, fail to recognise an abbreviated form of *aliter* (p. 365, n. 1).
205 *Ibid.*, p. 369.

was realised, in a different way, by Jacob Hammer. In 1943, Hammer, in a survey of the text-history of Geoffrey's *Historia*, announced the discovery of four other First-Variant manuscripts, c, E, H, and D (which he erroneously characterised as 'an abbreviation of the above three');[206] from MS. E he there printed First Variant, §§ 5–8, 94, and 206–8.

Hammer's researches resulted in the publication in 1951 of an edition of the First Variant version using all five manuscripts known to him (cDEHP), but based primarily on c 'to offer as full a text as possible'.[207] Hammer's reporting of these manuscripts was generally very reliable and errors of transcription rare.[208] However, his decision to rely primarily on the conflate MS. c, even though he was aware that it was heavily interpolated with the vulgate, was fatal to the usefulness of his edition.[209] The choice of c meant that Hammer printed not the pure First Variant but a vulgate text of §§ 109–177 and a text of §§ 1–108 and 178–208 in which the First Variant was very heavily interpolated with the vulgate. Much of the genuine First Variant text of MSS. DEHP was thus, in §§ 6–118, consigned to the apparatus of Hammer's edition. Indeed, in the latter part of the *Historia*, Hammer was forced to abandon this arrangement; he printed §§ 119–208 twice, separating the almost exclusively vulgate text of c (and, from § 149, the vulgate section of H) from the First Variant text of MSS. DEP (and H to § 149), which differed too extensively to be reported in an apparatus. Hammer had also to print c's mainly vulgate version of § 5 separately from the First Variant text of DEHP. In effect, Hammer's edition of the First Variant can conveniently be consulted only in §§ 119–208; in the case of §§ 5–118, readers are forced to reconstruct the text from the apparatus as they read.

Hammer's edition has other serious deficiencies. In one passage, the vulgate exercised a particularly unfortunate influence. As we have seen, a peculiarity of the First Variant is the reorganisation of the narrative structure of §§ 159–164.[210] Hammer noted this reorganisation but, since it did not correspond to the text of cH, both of which are entirely vulgate at this point, he transposed the relevant portions of text when printing the pure Variant MSS. D and E.[211] A characteristic feature of the First Variant was

---

[206] 'Remarks', pp. 530–5.
[207] *Variant Version*, p. 20.
[208] For example, *permanent* for H's *permanerent* (p. 87, n. 54); see also Parry's review, p. 239.
[209] See the reviews by Parry (p. 238) and Frappier (p. 127).
[210] Above, p. xxxvi.
[211] *Variant Version*, pp. 238–40.

thus entirely eliminated from Hammer's edition (save for a brief note in his apparatus). Another feature of the Variant text was disguised because Hammer did not distinguish those literary borrowings common to the vulgate and First Variant texts from the considerable number of literary echoes found only in the Variant. Hence his collection of *fontes* – otherwise a most valuable contribution to the study of the *Historia* – entirely fails to demonstrate the freedom with which the redactor independently introduced literary reminscences into the Variant.[212]

A further serious limitation of Hammer's edition is his apparent indifference to the problem of the textual relationship of the manuscript-witnesses known to him. He remarked only that D and E 'are doubtless descended from the same parent'[213]; he also considered that the extracts in P were made from a 'very close relative of DEH'.[214] He did not, however, note that the text of First-Variant §§ 5–149 preserved in MS. H often differs substantially from that of D and E; nor did he discuss the affiliation of DEHP with the text of the Variant to which c is a partial witness. Since the appearance of Hammer's edition, three more First-Variant manuscripts (aRS) have come to light. It has also become clear that Wace's *Roman de Brut* is largely based on the First Variant and is therefore the earliest known witness. As a vernacular translation (also depending in part on the vulgate text), Wace's poem must be treated with extreme caution; nevertheless it can shed valuable light on the type of text used by Wace shortly before 1155. Clearly, then, reconsideration of the text-history of the First Variant version is long overdue.

Collation of the eight extant manuscript-witnesses reveals that they fall into two principal groups, namely aHR and DES, while MSS. c and P occupy intermediate positions which must be discussed in detail later.[215] The distinction between the two main groups is for the most part limited to differences of word-order and the use of synonyms, although such divergences occur throughout the text. But before seeking the origin of these divergences, the relationship of the manuscripts within each of the two main groups must be established more clearly.

In the case of the group aHR, a, or more precisely the Variant exemplar on which the conflated text of that manuscript was based, and H (§§ 5–149)

---

[212] With the exception, that is, of some biblical echoes discussed by Hammer, *ibid.*, pp. 9–10.

[213] *Ibid.*, p. 7.

[214] *Ibid.*, p. 8.

[215] Below, pp. cv–cxi.

are evidently very closely related. They share lacunae in §5, 'ac fontibus preclara copiosis'; §37, 'ceteri quoque … fuga delituerunt'; §41, 'Nec mora … transfretauerunt'; and §43, 'eos oppugnare … a tergo'. They also agree in error, for example reading *facit* for *faciet* in §112[4] and *Moricanis* for *Armoricanis* in §121 (in both cases against not only R but also DES and the vulgate text). However, both a and H also contain independent omissions: a lacuna in H, §12, 'si quis … me et' is not paralleled in a; and an omission from a, §43, 'cum Britonibus … Romam rediret' is not present in H, which contains the clause in question. Clearly, then, the conflate MS. a (second half of the thirteenth century) was not based on H itself (early thirteenth-century). It is also unlikely that a's text derived directly from H's exemplar since it shows no sign of the damage which characterised that book,[216] unless of course copying occurred before that damage took place. It seems, then, that a and H are derived from a common parent which was characterised by a number of lacunae found in both its descendents. What of the relationship of MS. R to the parent of aH? While R generally agrees very closely with aH, it does not contain any of their lacunae. It appears therefore that R derives from an exemplar more complete than that of aH and is the best witness in this group. However, R does occasionally agree with aH in error: in §107, aHR have 'de deo sacratis' for the correct reading 'de deo Socratis' (cDES and the vulgate text); and in §149, aHR give the erroneous form *laci* (for *lacus*) where DES read *loci*. All three manuscripts (aHR) must therefore ultimately derive from a common ancestor. A further pointer in this direction is that a, unlike H, has the same book-division as R and indeed shares some rubrics with the latter.[217] It seems then that a and R preserve the original book-division of their common ancestor, while that division was modified in H (or, more likely, in its exemplar).[218] Corroborative evidence to this effect is supplied by the text of Dares Phrygius, *De Excidio Troiae*, which precedes the First Variant in MSS. a (fos 1r–10v) and R (fos 165r–168v). In both manuscripts, this text begins 'Incipit [*om. a*] epistola Cornelii ad Crispum Salustium in Troianorum hystoria que in Greco a Darete hystoriographo tracta [facta *R*] est'; and ends 'Explicit excidium Troie [Troie excidium *a*]'. Trial collation of the opening and closing chapters reveals that the version of Dares's history in aR differs from that printed by Meister (the preface, for example, beginning 'Cum multa Athenis studiosissime agerem' as against Meister's 'Cum

216 Above, p. lxxxvi.
217 Above, pp. lxxix and xc respectively.
218 Above, p. lxxxvi.

multa ago Athenis curiose').[219] The version in aR appears to be related to that found in London, British Library, MS. Burney 216, fos 89r–93v, of the twelfth century.[220] It seems, then, that in their Dares-text aR preserve another characteristic of their ancestor which must also have contained the same non-standard version; by the same token this Dares-text must have been omitted from H or its exemplar, a further indication that H is in some respects a less reliable witness than aR to the common ancestor of this group. Finally it must be noted that the exemplar from which a and H descend may arguably have been influenced on one occasion by the vulgate text. In § 116 [51], the First Variant (witnesses R and DES) reads 'asinus … horrido rugitu populum patrie terrebit', *rugitu* in the Variant text replacing the very rare word *rechanatu* found in the vulgate; a and H read in this passage *rachanatu* and *rechanatu* respectively. However, it is equally possible – and perhaps more likely – that this word was interpolated independently in both manuscripts, that is in the course of conflation with the Second Variant version in a, and as one of the vulgate additions which were made to the text of H.[221]

If we turn to the other main group (DES), it is clear that all three of those manuscripts are very closely related. They share a corruption in § 72 where, instead of 'secernit in … quas prouincias', they have only 'et Cornubia' (which is incomprehensible). Two of the manuscripts, D and E (the text of S being lost because of physical damage at this point), share a lacuna in § 115 [23], omitting 'Mulieres incessu … superbia replebitur'. Furthermore a substantial passage (chiefly comprising a description of the persecutions under Diocletian) in § 77 ('latronum seuitiam … Urbis Legionum ciues') is missing from the text of DES (although it is present in the margin of D); however, judgement as to whether this is as a result of a lacuna in DES or the addition of material in aHR must be suspended until the relationship of the two main families has been discussed in detail. DES also frequently agree in error: they give the date of Caesar's first British invasion as 'ante … incarnationem Domini .l. anno' rather than 'anno .lx.' as in aHR and Bede (the source of the First Variant version in this passage);[222] in § 157, DES read *gladiorum*, where aR's *gaudiorum* must be correct; and in § 174, DES read

219 The fact that Meister does not report the version of *De Excidio Troiae* found in aR (nor that in cDES: below, pp. xcvi and cv) shows how badly a modern re-edition of Dares's text is needed.

220 Ward & Herbert, *Catalogue*, I.16–17.

221 Above, pp. lxxix and lxxxvi respectively.

222 Above, pp. xlv–xlvi.

the nonsensical *galeati* for *calcati* in aR. Moreover, in DES (fos 12r–21r, pp. 67–93, and fos 29v–40r, respectively) the First-Variant text is preceded by a version of Dares Phrygius, *De Excidio Troiae*, which differs substantially from that found in aR and, indeed, in Meister's edition. This text begins 'Daretis Frigii Entelli historia de uastacione Troie incipit a Cornelio nepote Salustii de Greco in Latinum sermonem translata'; and ends 'Hactenus [Actenus *E*; Athenis *S*] id Dares Frigius [Frigius Dares *D*] mandauit litteris'. The preface of this version too differs from the text printed by Meister (and that found in aR); for example, it begins 'Cum multa uolumina [uolumina multa *S*] legerem Athenis curiose'; this very idiosyncratic version of Dares's History appears to be closely related to that found in London, British Library, MS. Burney 280, fos 20v–38v, of *ca* 1300.[223] DES must therefore descend from a common parent, which shared their lacunae and also contained the same variant text of Dares Phrygius (entirely different from that in aR). While DES are closely related, no one of these manuscripts can be a direct copy of either of the others since each of the three contains unique omissions. D omits the clauses 'et ad propria rediret' (§34) and 'ut auxilium Cesari ferret' (§62). E has a lacuna in §34 ('Deinde duxit ... ex ipsis esset'). S contains corruptions in §55 ('positum preterire intactum' for 'terrarum sitiens ... preterire intactos') and §63 ('dominum mecum et auunculum' for 'ut dominum ... captum uinculis') and has a lacuna in §76 ('tradidit se ... ut uiui de'). All three manuscripts must therefore derive independently from a common ancestor. There are, however, some indications that S is more closely related to E than to D. In §69, for example, E and S share the name-form *Kaerpenhuelgdit* (for *Kaerpenhuelgoit*); and in §98, where D (and aHR) reads 'longis nauibus' and E has 'magnis nauibus et longis', S reads 'magnis nauibus'.

We must now consider the relationship of the two groups, aHR and DES. Since the chief distinction between these families lies in variations of word-order and the use of synonyms, one might be tempted to regard the two families as quite separate recensions of the original text, both possibly due to the redactor of the First Variant version himself. This hypothesis is unlikely, however. First, there are indications that both groups descend from a single ancestor which already contained a degree of corruption. For example, in §168, all extant First-Variant witnesses (aDERS only) give the following text: 'At Lucius Hiberus dux Romanorum tales casus moleste ferens animum diuersis cruciatum cogitationibus nunc hoc, nunc illud reuoluens'. The text is evidently corrupt since, if *reuoluens* governs *ani-*

223 Ward & Herbert, *Catalogue*, I.21–2.

mum, then *hoc* and *illud* are otiose, and vice versa. The vulgate text reads in §168: 'animum suum diuersis cogitationibus uexatum *hunc huc, nunc illuc* reuoluit'; indeed, the passage echoes Vergil, *Aeneid* VIII.20, 'Atque *animum nunc huc* celerem, *nunc* diuidit *illuc*.[224] Clearly, then, the vulgate readings *huc* and *illuc* must be restored to the First-Variant text for the meaningless *hoc* and *illud*.[225] A second example is less clear-cut. In §206, the vulgate text reads 'filium autem suum Iuor ac Yni nepotem … dirigeret'. When reporting the names 'Iuor ac Yni' in this passage, the extant First-Variant witnesses (aDERS)[226] are divided between 'Iuor [Inor *R*] Ayni' (aR) and 'Iuorum [Yuorum *E*] uel' (DES). The readings of both families appear to represent scribal efforts to make sense of a corrupt exemplar. However, it is just possible that aR here preserve the text of the archetype of the First Variant, which may have substituted 'filium … Iuor Ayni nepotem' ('his son Ivor, nephew of Ayni [or Aynus]') for 'filium … Iuor ac Yni nepotem ('his son Ivor and nephew Yni'), possibly because of corruption in the vulgate manuscript from which the redactor of the First Variant worked. If such were the case, then only DES share a corruption in §206. Indeed, it is also possible, although perhaps unlikely, that the error in §168 was already present in the archetype of the First Variant and arose through carelessness on the part of the readactor himself rather than in the course of transmission. We cannot therefore be entirely sure of the status of the corruptions shared by the two families, aHR and DES. Do they indicate that both are descended from a common ancestor which stood at at least one remove from the archetype, or do they rather reflect the text of the archetype itself? If the second hypothesis were correct, then the two families might still represent separate recensions (based on the archetype). This second hypothesis, however, is precluded by MS. c which, as we shall see,[227] shows textual affinities with both groups. Since it is highly unlikely that the First-Variant element of c is a conflation of aHR- and DES-type manuscripts, c must represent an intermediate stage in the transmission of the First-Variant text: hence one family (be it aHR or DES) must be a more faithful witness to the archetype, while the other is a reworking of the First Variant version.

---

[224] This reminiscence was not noted by Hammer, *Variant Version*, pp. 177 and 245.

[225] Hammer, *ibid.*, p. 245, prints the text of DE without comment.

[226] This passage is also present in P which reads 'Ifor Ann' (the name-forms possibly owing more to Evan Evans than to his exemplar).

[227] Below, pp. cv–cix.

There is strong *prima facie* evidence that aHR stand closer to the original First-Variant text than DES. If the text of both groups is compared with the vulgate, aHR on a great number of occasions agree with the vulgate text against DES. A chapter chosen at random (§37) contains the following examples: aHR 'ut *sponsa* [sponsa sponsi *R*] et regnum', DES 'ut uxor et regnum', vulgate 'ut regnum et *sponsa*'; aHR '*sin autem* testatus est', DES 'si non testatus est', vulgate '*Sin autem* testatur'; aHR 'quod uocatur *Calaterium*, DES 'quod uocatur Calaterinum', vulgate 'quod uocatur *Calaterium*'. Similar agreement between aHR and the vulgate is found throughout the text. Indeed, one passage exhibiting such agreement merits close attention. In §137, Gorlois of Cornwall, when threatened by Uther Pendragon, attempts to find protection for himself and his wife Igerna. In aHR the narrative has the following form.

> At Gorlois ... castrum quoddam muniuit ubi se cum ualida manu suorum inclusit et uxorem suam, pro qua magis timebat, in oppido Tintagol super litus maris sito et undique uallibus preruptis ac mari circumsepto cum custodibus reclusit.

According to aHR, Gorlois occupies an unspecified *castrum*, while Igerna is guarded at Tintagel. In the corresponding passage in DES, the narrative structure is different in that Gorlois's *castrum* is identified as Tintagel, which is therefore represented as the refuge of both Igerna and her husband.

> At Gorlois ... castrum quoddam muniuit ubi se cum ualida manu suorum et uxorem, pro qua magis timebat, inclusit, scilicet in opido Tintageol super litus maris sito et undique uallibus preruptis ac mari circumsepto.

Of these two versions, that of aHR is closer to the vulgate text, in which Igerna is entrusted to the safety of Tintagel, while Gorlois enters the castle of Dimilioc.

> Et cum magis pro uxore sua quam pro semetipso anxiaretur, posuit eam in oppido Tintagol in litore maris quod pro tuciore refugio habebat. Ipse uero ingressus est castellum Dimilioc.

Not only do aHR, although they omit the name Dimilioc, agree with the vulgate text (against DES), but DES's version is internally inconsistent. By placing both Gorlois and Igerna in Tintagel, DES considerably cloud the subsequent dénouement which turns on the seduction of Igerna (at Tintagel) by the disguised Uther, while Gorlois is killed (at Dimilioc) during the king's absence. According to DES, all these events took place at Tintagel: and we are left to speculate about Gorlois's activities during the night on which Uther enjoyed his wife. The close agreement of aHR with the vulgate in this and other passages suggests therefore that they preserve a better text of the original First Variant version (itself a reworking of the vulgate text) than that of DES, which appears to have been subjected to a degree of recasting with, on at least one occasion, unfortunate results.

However, the possibility that the text found in MSS. aHR was instead at some stage contaminated with the vulgate must also be considered. Might not the family DES be the more faithful witness to the First Variant version, while aHR contain a text which has been subjected to 'correction' against the vulgate? Another divergence between the two families is crucial to the resolution of this problem. The divergence occurs in §6, in a passage dealing with the birth of Brutus, eponymous founder of the British people.[228] In the vulgate text, Geoffrey, following the pseudo-Nennian *Historia Brittonum*, represents Brutus as the son of Silvius. This Silvius was, according to Geoffrey, son of Ascanius, son of the Trojan hero Aeneas, who was therefore Brutus's great-grandfather. However, no son of Ascanius named Silvius was known to mediaeval historiography outside the pages of Geoffrey's *Historia* or his source, the *Historia Brittonum*. Conventional histories of Rome's legendary period, such as, for example, that of Landolfus Sagax, do make reference to a Silvius; but he is Silvius Postumus, Aeneas's son by Lavinia, so called because of his birth after his father's death. We have already seen that the First Variant version, in the passage in question (§6), borrows extensively from Landolfus;[229] drawing on his History, the Variant there records both the birth of Silvius Postumus after Aeneas's death and, later, Postumus's designation as heir to his half-brother Ascanius in Alba Longa. It is the question of the relationship of Silvius Postumus to Brutus which divides the two families of First-Variant manuscripts. The text of the first group (aHR) runs as follows.

> Educauit autem Ascanius summa pietate Postumum Siluium fratrem suum de Lauinia procreatum et, cum .xxx. annis et .iiii. [.xxxiii. annis *aH*][230] regnasset, Siluium reliquid heredem. Hic furtiue indulgens ueneri nupserat quidam nepti Lauinie eamque fecerat pregnantem. Cumque id Ascanio compertum esset [compertum esset Ascanio *aH*] ...

[228] See further Wright, 'The parentage', where this problem is discussed in detail.
[229] Above, p. xliv.
[230] On the disagreement of R and aH here, see p. cvii below.

There is in aHR no mention of a son of Ascanius named Silvius and it is clear from Landolfus's History (which the First Variant here follows closely) that Ascanius's heir is his half-brother Silvius Postumus. According to aHR, then, this same Silvius Postumus was Brutus's father (by Lavinia's niece) and Brutus was Aeneas's grandson (rather than great-grandson as in the vulgate text). The other group of manuscripts (DES) offers a different version of events, as follows.

> Educauit autem Ascanius summa pietate Postumum Siluium fratrem suum ex Lauinia procreatum et, cum .xliii. annis regnasset, Siluium reliquit heredem. Et Ascanius cum .xv. esset annorum, genuerat filium quem uocauit Siluium a Siluio fratre suo Postumo. Hic furtiue indulgens ueneri nupserat cuidam nepti Lauinie eamque fecerat pregnantem. Cumque id Ascanio patri suo compertum fuisset...

According to DES, there were two Silvii, Silvius Postumus (as in Landolfus) and Silvius, son of Ascanius (as in the vulgate text), who in this case was named after his uncle; DES also agree with the vulgate text that Brutus, as the son of the second Silvius, was Aeneas's great-grandson.

Which of these contradictory accounts is the original? If, as other evidence has suggested, aHR have priority, then Silvius, son of Ascanius, must have been suppressed when material from Landolfus was added to the First-Variant text; possibly the redactor, regarding the vulgate's Silvius as a doublet of (or an error for) Landolfus's Silvius Postumus, decided to bring Geoffrey's account more closely into line with that of a standard authority (this would sit well with his attempts to reconcile Geoffrey and Bede, for example).[231] In that case, the second Silvius, son of Ascanius, must have been restored to the text of DES under the influence of the vulgate (and perhaps also because of the difficulty that Postumus, who was supposedly the progenitor of the Roman royal dynasty, is later killed by his son Brutus in aHR's text). On the other hand, if the original version was that of DES, then the First Variant recognised two Silvii (Landolfus's Silvius Postumus and Geoffrey's Silvius, son of Ascanius); and the second of these must subsequently have been suppressed in aHR (for the reasons already stated).

Either explanation is plausible. But can we decide between them? There is a further reference to the parentage of Brutus in *Historia Regum Britannie*, §54, where Julius Caesar comments on the common ancestry of the

---

231 Above, pp. xlv–xlvi and lxvi–lxix.

Romans and Britons. The vulgate text is 'illis autem Brutus, quem Silvius, Ascanii filii Enee filius, progenuit'. In this passage Brutus appears as the son of Silvius, son of Ascanius and thus Aeneas's great-grandson, exactly as in vulgate § 6. In the First Variant version (§ 54), this passage reads in all the extant manuscripts[232] 'illis autem Brutus, Siluii Enee filius'. The meaning here is not immediately clear. Brutus may be referred to as 'son of Silvius [son of] Aeneas' (*filii* being deliberately omitted or having dropped out). Or, more likely, he is represented as the son of Silvius Aeneas. This latter, fourth king of the Latins, was conventionally identified as the son of Silvius Postumus (who was supposedly the third king of the Latins). However, in another passage in the vulgate *Historia* (§ 22), Geoffrey refers to 'Siluius Eneas, Enee filius, ... Latinorum tertius'. An identical reference is found in the same chapter in the Variant (§ 22, where all the manuscript-witnesses are in agreement).[233] It seems, then, that in the Variant, §§ 54 and 22, Silvius Aeneas may be treated as identical with his namesake Silvius Postumus (particularly as both are identified as Aeneas's son). But whichever of these interpretations is correct in Variant, § 54, it is clear that the reference to Brutus's parentage in that chapter can be consistent only with the version of § 6 found in aHR (where Brutus is the son of Silvius Postumus).[234] It is highly improbable that DES can contain the true First-Variant text if they agree with the vulgate in § 6, yet contradict that text in § 54 where they agree with the other First-Variant witnesses (aHR) against the vulgate. Given that the vulgate account of Brutus's genealogy in § 54 has clearly been modified in the First Variant (on the evidence of all the manuscripts), it is impossible that the modified passage should contradict DES's version of events in § 6, if they there preserve the original text. It seems then that aHR's internally more consistent version is the original, while DES contain a (vulgate) interpolation in § 6.

There is, moreover, one more passage in which the text of DES was arguably influenced by the vulgate. In §§ 186/7 aR (H no longer being a witness) record the defeat of the British by the English as follows: 'et Britones regni dyadema *in perpetuum* amiserunt nec postea pristinam

---

232 With the exception of c (which reads 'Brutus et Siluius Enee filius') and D ('Brutus Siluii Enee filii'); in D *Siluii* is dotted and the vulgate text 'filius Siluii, filius [sic] Ascanii' has been added in the margin.

233 With the exception of H which reads 'Eneas, Anchise filius, ... Latinorum tertius' (evidently as the result of scribal 'correction').

234 Especially as there is no reason at all to identify Silvius Aeneas with Ascanius' son Silvius.

dignitatem recuperare potuerunt'. We have already seen how one aim of the redactor of the First Variant version was to try to harmonize the Galfridian and Bedan accounts of the passage of dominion by representing that event as occurring as early as possible in the narrative.[235] In aR, British power is marked as effectively ceasing after the donation of Gormund (in §§ 186/7), despite the later British recovery under Cadwallon. The text of aR is thus fully in accord with the historiographical aims of the First-Variant redactor. In DES, on the other hand, the passage in question has a different form: 'et Britones regni diadema amiserunt nec postea pristinam dignitatem *nisi post longum tempus* recuperare potuerunt'. The version of DES is more equivocal and more easily reconciled with the subsequent recovery under Cadwallon. This version is also closer to that of the vulgate, § 187: 'Amiserunt deinde Britones regni diadema *multis temporibus* et insule monarchiam nec pristinam dignitatem recuperare nitebantur'. The most likely explanation for this discrepancy is that the version of aR, which is more consistent with the aims of the First Variant, is the original, while the text of DES has been slightly modified under the influence of the vulgate *Historia*.

If, then, the text of the group aHR stands closer to that of the archetype, while that of DES is a revision, can we ascertain at what stage in transmission this revision may have been effected? The earliest witness to the First Variant version, Wace's *Roman de Brut* (completed in 1155) offers some assistance in answering this question. Since Wace's poem is a free translation of the First Variant into the vernacular (and, indeed, also makes use of the vulgate *Historia*), the evidence of its text must always be treated with circumspection. Nevertheless, two passages in particular enable us to form some impression of the type of First-Variant manuscript with which Wace must have worked. We have already seen that an account of the persecution under Diocletian is found (in § 77) in only one group of First-Variant manuscripts, aHR (although it is present in the margin in D).[236] A passage devoted to this persecution is also found in Wace's poem. It might, however, be maintained that Wace derived his account from the vulgate *Historia*; but, although Wace used the vulgate text extensively in the second half of his poem, in the first half (where this passage occurs) he employed the vulgate very seldom, relying almost exclusively on the First Variant. And, while there is no clear indication that Wace's account of the

235 Above, pp. lxvi–lxix.
236 Above, p. xcv.

persecution draws on the vulgate text, there are in the passage in question strong parallels between Wace's poem and the Variant text of aHR. In aHR, the account in §77 begins:

Hiis diebus orta est persecucio Dyocletiani in christianos et edicto eius grassante per uniuersum orbem missus est Maximianus Herculius trans Alpes in Gallias edicta principis facturus …

With this compare *Roman de Brut*, lines 5579–84.

> Ço fu par Diocletian,
> Qui enveia Maximian,
> Par cruelté e par enjurie,
> Pur tuz les crestïens destruire
> Ki aveient abitement
> Ultre Mont Geu, vers occident

There are evident verbal parallels between the two passages: (*missus est* and *enveia*; *trans Alpes* and *Ultre Mont Geu*). Indeed, I have not been able to trace the reference to the Alps to any other source. Certainly it is not found at this point (§77) in the vulgate text, which reads:

Superuenerat Maximianus Herculius, princeps milicie predicti tyranni, cuius imperio omnes subuerse sunt ecclesie …

In recounting Diocletian's persecution, then, Wace drew on a First-Variant text which, like aHR, included an account of that event. Must this imply that his manuscript was related to aHR?

The second relevant passage of the *Roman de Brut* is that dealing with legendary Roman history (lines 9–148); these lines relate the birth of Silvius Postumus (74–80) and the story of Ascanius's household-gods (89–104), both derived directly from the First Variant.[237] It will be remembered that the two families of First-Variant manuscripts diverge when recounting the birth of Brutus, one group (aHR) representing Brutus as the son of Silvius Postumus, the other (DES) making him son of Ascanius's son Silvius. The account of Brutus's conception in the *Roman de Brut* (lines 107–117) is as follows:

---

[237] Above, p. xliv.

Aschanius, quant il fina,
Silvium [viz, Postumus], sun frere, herita,
Ki esteit de Lavine nez,
Puis ke Eneas fu finez.
Un fiz aveit Aschanius
Ki refu numez Silvius;
Le nun de sun uncle porta;
Mais poi vesqui e poi dura.
Il out amee une meschine
Celeement, niece Lavine;
Od li parla, cele conçut.

Wace's account here agrees entirely with that of manuscripts DES. In this passage he must therefore have been using a text of the DES-type.

How can this conclusion be reconciled with the evidence of the previous passage that Wace apparently followed a manuscript akin to the aHR-group? We may consider three possible explanations: (1) that Wace worked from an aHR-type text which he independently modified by the reintroduction from the vulgate *Historia* (§6) of Silvius, son of Ascanius; and that this modification may then (after 1155) have influenced the DES-group; (2) that Wace possessed two First-Variant manuscripts (or perhaps a conflate manuscript combining the two groups) and that both families were already in existence by 1155; (3) that Wace used a manuscript of the DES-group which contained the account of Diocletian's persecution (as in aHR) and so preserved a better text than DES (from which that account has dropped out). The first of these explanations is highly unlikely. There is absolutely no reason to suppose that Wace's *Roman de Brut* influenced the DES-group rather than vice versa; DES do not, for example, contain a single one of the numerous passages and details unique to Wace's poem. Moreover, Wace shares with DES the non-vulgate statement that Ascanius's son Silvius was so named after his uncle Silvius Postumus; Wace must therefore have worked directly from a DES-type text rather than using the vulgate text independently. It is also extremely implausible that Wace used two First-Variant manuscripts (as well as the vulgate text) while composing his poem; and that the period between the composition of the First Variant (after 1138) and its use by Wace (shortly before 1155) could have seen not only the genesis of the two distinct families of First-Variant manuscripts but also the creation of a conflate text combining both. Rather, Wace's poem points to the revised First Variant text represented by group-DES already being in existence by 1155, but in a more complete form than is found in the extant witnesses.

The existence of a DES-type text superior to that preserved in MSS. DES themselves is corroborated by the evidence of MS. c. This manuscript must be used with great caution, for its text is First-Variant only in §§ 5–108 and 178–208, and is moreover heavily interpolated with the vulgate in those chapters. Nevertheless, in passages where the text of c is undeniably First-Variant, it is unmistakably related to DES. Two examples of this relationship, chosen at random, will serve to show that, where the two families aHR and DES diverge in respect of word-order or the use of synonyms, c very often agrees with DES. In §7, where aHR read 'tria castella que sibi pater suus moriens donauerat', both c and DES have 'tria castella que pater suus sibi moriens donauerat'; and in §6, where aHR read 'in Albam transtulit', cDES have 'in Albam Longam detulit'. A further point of contact between c and DES lies in the text of Dares Phrygius's *De Excidio Troiae* found in MS. c (fos 1r–9r). Although this text is acephalous in c, it has the *explicit* 'Hactenus id Dares Frigius mandauit litteris', which agrees very closely with that of the Dares-text found in DES. Trial collation of the final chapter of Dares's work in c reveals that it is in fact identical to the text found in DES, which is, as we have seen, a highly idiosyncratic version of *De Excidio Troiae*;[238] c therefore contains the same non-standard Dares-text which must also have been present in the common ancestor of DES. However, despite c's evident close relationship with DES, in other passages c aligns itself with MSS. aHR, as in the following examples. In §14, where the text of DES is 'Brutus autem, ut predictum est, tentorium regis agressus', c and aHR read 'Brutus autem tentorium regis, ut predictum est, agressus' (which is closer to the vulgate text 'At Brutus tentorium regis, ut predictum est, nactus'); and in §50, where DES have 'fratri dissimilis extitit', acHR read 'germano dissimilis extitit' ('germano' again being the reading of vulgate, §50). MS. c, therefore, agrees now with DES, now with aHR.

The intermediate position of c could be explained in one of two ways. The exemplar on which the conflate text in MS. c was based may have contained a text of the First Variant more reliable than that of either group, DES or aHR. If that were so, both aHR and DES would represent revisions of the original First-Variant text, since the agreement of c with aHR would signal recasting (or corruption) in DES, while c's agreement with DES would denote similar reworking (or corruption) in aHR. However, this hypothesis does not sit well with the strong indications, which have

---

[238] Above, p. xcvi.

already been discussed, that the text of group aHR is superior to that of DES, nor with the very close relationship of c to DES in that both contain the same non-standard Dares-text (as opposed to the similarly distinctive version associated with aR). Indeed, there is undeniable evidence that, in some cases where c is in agreement with DES, the text of aHR has better authority. In the passage from §6 (cited above), for example, where cDES have 'in Albam Longam detulit' and aHR 'in Albam transtulit', the First Variant's source, the *Historia Romana* of Landolfus Sagax (who is quoted verbatim in this passage) has 'in Albam Longam *transtulit*.[239] In the light of the borrowing from Landolfus, it is not easy to see how the original First-Variant text could have read *detulit* (as in cDES), while the reading *transtulit* in aHR (*and* Landolfus) is due to revision.[240] But this difficulty disappears if we suppose that aHR here preserve the original (Landolfian) text, which has been revised in cDES. Similarly, in the three passages in §37 (already discussed)[241] where aHR agree with the vulgate text against DES, c twice concurs with aHR (viz, in having *sin autem* for DES's *si non*, and *Calaterium* for DES's *Calaterinum*); but, in the first example, c agrees with DES in reading 'ut uxor et regnum' rather than aHR's 'ut *sponsa* et regnum' (*sponsa* being the vulgate reading). This is only one of several cases in which c agrees with DES against aHR and the vulgate.

The First-Variant text of MS. c, then (in as far as it is recoverable), is not superior to both the families, aHR and DES. It belongs to the DES-group, but preserves (as indicated by its intermittent agreement with aHR) a somewhat better text than the other surviving witnesses of its group (DES). It is therefore important to note that in §77 MS. c includes an account of Diocletian's persecution. Although the text of c at this point certainly contains vulgate interpolation (at the end of the chapter), the beginning of its account is unmistakably First-Variant in that it agrees almost verbatim with that in MSS. aHR. The textual condition of c thus lends support to the evidence of Wace's *Roman de Brut* that the description of Diocletian's persecution (found in aHR) not only formed part of the archetype of the First Variant version but was also originally present in the DES-type text (although it has fallen out of DES themselves).

There is one further indication of the superiority of the First Variant text of c over that of DES. This occurs in §6, in a passage dealing with the

---

[239] Crivellucci's apparatus (p. 6) does not record any manuscript variants for *transtulit*.
[240] Conversely, there is no difficulty in supposing that *Longam* was added in DES (or perhaps fell out from aHR).
[241] Above, p. xcviii.

length of Ascanius's reign in Alba Longa before he handed over power to Silvius Postumus. The passage is again derived from Landolfus, who states (as do other authorities, such as Paul the Deacon and Jerome in his *Chronicon*) that Ascanius ruled for 38 years. However, no First-Variant manuscript agrees with Landolfus. The extant witnesses fall into three groups: DES (and P) give the length of Ascanius's reign as 44 years; aH give 33 years; and cR read 34 years. It is striking that R, the best witness from the aHR-group, and c are here in agreement. Moreover, Wace's *Roman de Brut* similarly gives Ascanius's reign as 34 years (line 105, '[Ascanius] *Trente e quatre* anz maintin la terre'). The earliest and most reliable witnesses all therefore agree. Moreover, it is relatively easy to see how 34 (*.xxxiiii.*) could in the course of transmission have been corrupted to 33 (*.xxxiii.*) in the common exemplar of aH and to 44 (*.xxxxiiii.*) in that of DES. However, although c's reading is undoubtedly superior to that of DES, it is less clear whether the 34 years of cR and Wace arose because of an easy corruption of the figure 38 (*.xxxviii.*) borrowed from Landolfus, which must have occurred in a common ancestor of all the extant witnesses (and so provides further evidence that they all stand at at least one remove from the archetype); or whether the figure 34 was already present in the archetype, either through a slip on the redactor's part or as a result of authorial policy (although in that case there is no obvious motive for Landolfus's conventional figure of 38 years having been changed to 34).[242] In any event it is clear that c's reading is again superior to that of DES and identical to that of the DES-type text used by Wace.

There is, however, one remaining problem raised by the question of the relationship of c to DES. We have seen that one characteristic of the revised First Variant text of MSS. DES is the representation (in §6) of Brutus as the son of Ascanius's son Silvius (as in the vulgate *Historia*), a modification which was already present in the DES-type manuscript used by Wace shortly before 1155. One would therefore expect c to agree with DES in containing this modification. In fact, c agrees closely with aHR, the passage in question running as follows:

[242] A similar problem is raised by the length of Aeneas's reign as recorded in Variant, §6. The orthodox Classical and mediaeval view was that Aeneas reigned for three years, this figure being given by the First Variant's source, Landolfus (see p. xlv above). Yet in all the First-Variant manuscripts and in Wace (*Roman de Brut*, line 69) the figure is four years (with the exception of P which has three, but this may well be a correction made by Evan Evans). It is again unclear whether the redactor of the First Variant deliberately changed Landolfus's figure or whether Aeneas's four-year reign arose because of corruption in the common ancestor of the extant witnesses.

Educauit autem Ascanius summa pietate Siluium Postumum fratrem suum ex Lauinia procreatum. Et cum 34 annis regnasset, Siluium reliquit heredem unicum. Hic furtiue indulgens ueneri nupserat cuidam nepti Lauinie eamque fecerat pregnantem. Cumque id Ascanio conpertum esset...

The agreement of c with aHR in representing Brutus as the son of Silvius Postumus has considerable implications for the genesis of the DES-family of manuscripts. Since c frequently agrees with DES against aHR and the vulgate (and Landolfus on one occasion), it must like DES be a reworking of the original First-Variant text. However, it is also clear that the equally frequent agreement of c with aHR against DES cannot be explained simply in terms of the text-type DES being a more corrupt descendant of a c-type ancestor; for c does not contain the important modification to Brutus's genealogy which characterises DES. It follows that the text of DES must constitute a further reworking of that witnessed by c. This in turn implies considerable scribal activity with regard to the First Variant version in the relatively short period between its completion (sometime after 1138) and Wace's use of a DES-type manuscript (shortly before 1155). Not only must the original First-Variant text have been reworked to produce the revised text on which MS. c was based (this step arguably also embracing the association of the First Variant with the non-standard Dares-text found in cDES), but this reworked text must later have undergone further revision, including the change to Brutus's parentage, resulting in the DES-type text evidently used by Wace.

The only alternative to this hypothesis is to suppose that the First-Variant text on which c was based did in fact include the modification to Brutus's parentage (as in DES), but that it was eliminated from c in the course of interpolation with the vulgate (by Brother Madog of Edeirnion). This supposition receives some support from a further modification found, only in c, earlier in §6. Landolfus, the source of the First Variant version in this passage, records Ascanius's alternative name Iulus (or less correctly Iulius), referring to him as 'Ascanius, qui et Iulus, eiusdem Enee filius' (*Historia Romana*, I.2). This information is reproduced in the First Variant, §6, in the form, 'regnum suscepit Ascanius qui et Iulus eiusdem filius erat' (there are some minor variations in the manuscripts).[243] The by-name Iulus helps to explain Ascanius's position as ancestor of the Julian

---

[243] Only R has *Iulus*, the other manuscripts reading *Iulius*; in H, the passage has been doctored to read 'regnum Ascanius qui et Iulius eiusdem filius accepit' (*accepit* being suprascript over underpointed *erat*).

family (and so of Julius Caesar). This connexion is made clearer by Lan-dolfus's subsequent statement (which concurs with Paul the Deacon's History and Jerome's *Chronicon*) that Ascanius had a son who was also named Iulus (or Iulius): 'Deinde Ascanius Iulum filium procreauit a quo familia Iuliorum exorta est' (*Historia Romana*, I.2). This historical detail is not present in the First Variant version, where MSS. aHR suppress all reference to Ascanius's offspring, and DES mention only Silvius, the son assigned to Ascanius by the vulgate *Historia*. In c, however, the passage alluding to Ascanius's second name, Iulus, has a form quite different from that found in the other manuscripts, namely 'regnum suscepit Ascanius – et Siluius Iulius eiusdem filius dictus erat'. The meaning of this passage is not immediately clear. Are we to understand that Ascanius was also known as Silvius Julius (with *eiusdem* referring to Aeneas, as in Landolfus and the other First-Variant witnesses)? This is unlikely since there is no suggestion elsewhere that Ascanius was also known as Silvius, which might have inspired this change. More likely c's meaning is that Ascanius's son (namely Landolfus's Iulus) was called Silvius Julius (*eiusdem* in this case referring to Ascanius himself). If so, c may be attempting to identify Ascanius's son Iulus with the son Silvius, attributed to him by the vulgate *Historia* and First-Variant manuscripts DES. Furthermore, it is then possible that c, when it records that Ascanius made Silvius his heir, means to refer not to his half-brother Silvius Postumus, but rather to his own son Silvius Julius; in that case, c would agree with DES in representing Ascanius's son Silvius (more precisely Silvius Julius) as Brutus's father. If this is the intention, then the modified passage in c could arguably be based on a DES-type text including the vulgate interpolation in §6, although the vulgate interpolation itself was omitted from c as part of its attempt to reidentify DES's Silvius as Ascanius's 'historical' son Iulus. There are, however, two objections to this hypothesis. It is not made explicit in c that Ascanius's heir was Silvius Julius rather than Silvius Postumus. Moreover the text of c, when describing Ascanius's discovery of Brutus's conception, 'Cumque id Ascanio compertum esset', agrees exactly with that of R (cf. also aH's 'Cumque id compertum esset Ascanio'); c does not agree with the reading of DES, 'Cumque id Ascanio patri suo compertum fuisset', where their text is that of the vulgate (save for the addition of *suo*). Thus c is here in agreement with aHR, which probably better preserve the original First-Variant text in this passage, and disagrees with DES, whose text has been influenced by the vulgate. In the light of these objections, it is safest to accept the prior conclusion that, while c is related to the DES-group, the text of MSS. DES resulted from a further revision of that witnessed by c.

Finally, we must consider the eighteenth-century extracts preserved in MS. P and their place in the text-history of the First Variant version. In the first of these extracts (§§ 5–8), the affiliation of P is clear: P is regularly in agreement with DES (also frequently with cDES) and only very rarely with aHR. Like DES, P represents Brutus as the son of Silvius, son of Ascanius, against aHR (and, very probably, c). MS. P also erroneously gives the length of Ascanius's reign in Alba Longa as 44 years, again in agreement with DES and against c and the other manuscripts.[244] It seems then, on this evidence, that P is a close relative of DES.

However, in the second of P's extracts (§§ 54–55) the position is entirely reversed. MS. P now agrees more closely with aH (or acHR) and especially with H. At the beginning of § 54, for example, only H and P read 'Interea contigit Cesarem' as against 'Interea contigit, ut in Romanis historiis repperitur, Iulium Cesarem' in all the other manuscripts.[245] Similarly at the end of § 55, aHP agree in having 'tempus nostre resolucionis' (where they may be influenced by II Timothy 4.6, 'tempus meae resolutionis instat') against all the other witnesses, respectively: 'nostre dissolucionis tempus forte' in DES, 'tempus nostre dissolucionis forte' in c, and, most significantly, 'tempus dissolucionis forte nostre' in R (the best witness of the aHR-family). This change of allegiance cannot be explained simply by making P, like c, a relative of DES but preserving a less corrupt version of their text (and so agreeing with acHR). In § 54, P records the *ab urbe condita* date of Caesar's first invasion of Britain as 623, exactly as in aH. This is an error for the correct date AUC 693 which is found in all the other manuscripts (except c which has 694) and is secured by the passage of Bede's *Historia Ecclesiastica* on which the First Variant here depends.[246]. The second extract in P is therefore very closely textually related to aH.

The final extract in P (§§ 206–208) is more difficult to classify because it agrees now with DES and now with aR (and with c where that manuscript is a witness). However, P's agreement in these chapters with acR may simply mean that its text is less corrupt than that of DES. This is evidently the case at the end of § 206, where 'anno incarnationis', the reading of DES, is certainly corrupt, since 'anno ab incarnatione', found in P and acR, agrees verbatim with both the vulgate text and Bede's *Historia Ecclesi-*

---

[244] Above, p. cvii.
[245] However, it is possible that a's exemplar may also have read 'Interea contigit Cesarem', the fuller (vulgate) clause being added in the course of interpolation with the Second Variant which occurred in a.
[246] Above, p. xlvi.

astica, which is the source of this passage.[247] Moreover, there is one clear indication that P's text is closely related to that of DES. In §207, P agrees with DES in reading, 'Sed illi Britones qui in parte boreali Anglie remanserunt a Britannica lingua degenerati numquam Loegriam ...', while the text of aR and c is quite different, being once again closer to the vulgate.[248] It seems then that P's final extract is, like its first, more closely allied to DES.

There is only one possible explanation for the textual affiliations of P's extracts. The close agreement of P's second excerpt with H can have come about only through the conflation of P's otherwise DES-type text with an H-type manuscript. P's second extract cannot simply preserve a better text of §§54–55 than that found in the other witnesses of the DES-group; in that case P would agree not only with H (and a), but also with R (and probably with c). The fact that P there regularly agrees with H against all the other manuscripts can mean only that in §§54–55 P's text derives directly from an H-type manuscript. Conversely, P's other extracts are clearly closely related to DES. We must conclude therefore that P was based on a hybrid manuscript. Since we possess only extracts from that manuscript, we cannot be sure of the extent of conflation in its text nor indeed whether the manuscript contained a basically DES-type text (as the opening and closing extracts suggest) or an H-type text in which damage at the beginning and end was perhaps made good by use of an exemplar akin to DES. We must therefore provisionally conclude that P is a hybrid witness, although this conclusion might have to be modified should Lewis Morris's untraced manuscript, on which P's excerpts were based, ever come to light.

The results of the preceding survey of surviving First-Variant manuscripts may now be set out in the following tentative stemma.

To recapitulate, the text-history of the First Variant version may be summarized as follows. The original text (α) must have been written after the appearance in 1138 of the vulgate *Historia*, of which it is a revision. Shared corruptions in the surviving witnesses demonstrate that all extant manuscripts are ultimately derived from a common exemplar. It is not, however, entirely clear whether these corruptions were already present in the arche-

---

[247] See Wright, 'Geoffrey of Monmouth and Bede', pp. 44–5 and 59.

[248] Of these witnesses, aR read 'Degenerati autem a Britannica nobilitate Gualenses qui in parte boriali Anglie remanserunt numquam postea Loegriam ...', while c has 'Degenerati autem Britanni qui in parte boriali insule remanserunt numquam postea Loegriam ...'; the vulgate text in this passage reads 'Degenerati autem a Britannica nobilitate Gualenses numquam postea monarchiam insule recuperauerunt'.

First Variant Version. Stemma

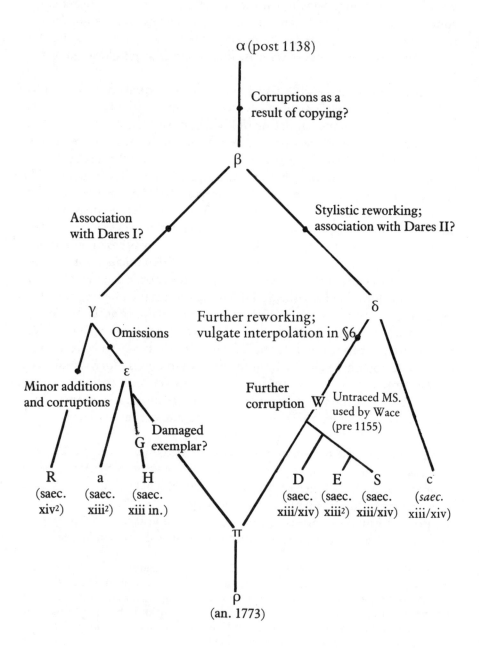

α (post 1138)

Corruptions as a
result of copying?

β

Association
with Dares I?

Stylistic reworking;
association with Dares II?

γ

Omissions

Further reworking;
vulgate interpolation in §6

δ

ε

Minor additions
and corruptions

Further
corruption

W Untraced MS.
used by Wace
(pre 1155)

Damaged
G exemplar?

R
(saec.
xiv²)

a
(saec.
xiii²)

H
(saec.
xiii in.)

D
(saec.
xiii/xiv)

E
(saec.
xiii²)

S
(saec.
xiii/xiv)

c
(*saec.*
xiii/xiv)

π

ρ
(an. 1773)

type (α) or, as is perhaps more likely, arose as a result of copying; in which case, all the manuscripts must descend from a common exemplar (β) which stood at at least one remove from the archetype. From this shared ancestor – whether the archetype (α) or merely a hyparchetype (β) – stem two families of manuscripts: from one exemplar (γ) is derived the group aHR, and from another (δ) the group cDES. The chief distinction between these two families lies in differences of word-order and vocabulary. But it is also clear that the First Variant text was associated in γ with a non-standard version of Dares Phyrgius's *De Excidio Troiae* (Dares I), while in δ the Variant was associated with a different non-standard recension of the same text (Dares II). However, it is impossible to determine whether both these associations were made during transmission or whether one or other of the Dares-texts was originally found with the First Variant in the archetype.

Of the two families, aHR seem to preserve the better text of the First Variant, being closer to the vulgate text and the Variant's other sources. Within this family R is, apart from minor corruptions and additions, the best witness. The two other manuscripts, a and H, both of which have been independently conflated with other texts of the *Historia*, derive from a common ancestor (ε), which was characterised by a number of minor corruptions and lacunae also found in aH (where R's text is neither corrupt nor lacunose). The precise relationship of H to ε is somewhat problematical. H is a very close copy of a damaged exemplar. The text preserved by MS. a shows that its exemplar (ε) was not damaged in this way, but it remains possible that H was copied after subsequent damage to ε. However, since a shares the same book-division and some rubrics with R, it seems very likely that this book-division was also found in ε. MS. H has a slightly different book-division; but it is uncertain whether this division was already found in H's damaged exemplar or was a modification introduced by the scribe of H (who certainly made a number of 'corrections' to the text). H, then, may either have been copied very faithfully from a damaged exemplar (ζ) derived from ε, or, perhaps less likely, may be a slightly modified copy of ε itself, made after that exemplar suffered damage.

The history of the second family of manuscripts is more complicated. Four of these manuscripts (cDES) certainly derive from a common ancestor (δ) in which the First Variant had been subjected to a degree of stylistic recasting and was associated with a non-standard Dares-text (Dares II). This recasting must have occurred early, since the (untraced) First-Variant manuscript (w) used by Wace when composing the vernacular *Roman de Brut* (completed in 1155) was closely related to DES.

However, the reworking must have been carried out in at least two stages. The First-Variant elements preserved in c bear witness to a text closely allied to that of DES but which was less heavily reworked and did not contain an important vulgate interpolation in § 6 (as we have seen, counter-arguments that this interpolation was originally present in c's exemplar but was suppressed in c itself are far from convincing); the First-Variant text on which c was based was also more complete than that surviving in DES, preserving, for instance, a passage on Diocletian's persecution which is missing from DES. Wace's First-Variant source-text (w) also bears witness to a more complete DES-type text than that surviving in those manuscripts, as it too must have contained the passage dealing with Diocletian's persecution. However, Wace's exemplar also included the vulgate interpolation in § 6 which is characteristic of DES. The combined evidence of c and Wace's source-text (w) thus shows that by 1155 the First Variant version had already been revised at least twice. The considerable scribal activity which this implies accords well with the suggestion, which has already been advanced, that the First Variant may have owed its initial popularity to the immediate success of the *Historia Regum Britannie* and at the outset have been copied frequently in order to answer the demand for that text. This activity may also imply that the First Variant was produced quite shortly after the appearance of the *Historia* in 1138, particularly if, as may be the case, the minor corruptions shared by all extant witnesses go back not to the archetype, but to a hyparchetype (β) which stood at at least one remove from the original text. The family cDES, then, bears witness to a considerable reduplication of copies of the First Variant version between 1138 and 1155. DES themselves are clearly closely related to the text (w) used by Wace, although their shared corruptions prove that they are descended from a common parent textually inferior to w. Finally, the text preserved in the eighteenth-century MS. P suggests that its excerpts were drawn from a hybrid text (π). Its first and last extracts are clearly related to DES (although P's text in §§ 206–208 seems to be slightly superior to theirs); however, P's central extract belongs to the aHR-group, being most closely related to H. In so far as the text-history of the First Variant version can be understood from the evidence of the extant witnesses, the only possible explanation is that P's exemplar was a conflate text combining the two main manuscript-families, although we must enter the proviso that this conclusion might need revision if Lewis Morris's manuscript were ever discovered.

It is clear from the preceding summary that the manuscript-family aHR constitutes a more reliable witness to the text of the First Variant than does cDES (and the fragments in P). Of the group aHR, the best manuscript is unquestionably R; not only is the First Variant text of H incomplete (breaking off in §149), while that of a is (from §60) heavily interpolated with the Second Variant version, but R's text often preserves better readings than that of aH. The present critical edition, which is based on a full collation of all known First-Variant manuscripts, for this reason relies primarily on MS. R. However, on those occasions when R contains minor corruptions or omissions, the readings of a and H (where their text is First Variant) have been accepted into the text, particularly when they are supported by DES. The group DES has also been used to correct obvious errors in R in §§149–208, where H, whose text is vulgate from §149, is no longer a witness, and the partial witness a, which indeed contains a lacuna running from §§186/7 to 203, cannot entirely be relied upon. The apparatus included in this edition is intended to be comprehensive, giving the reader as complete a picture as possible of the variant readings and spellings of the complete manuscript-witnesses to the First Variant. However, the partial witnesses a and c, which contain heavy interpolation from the vulgate *Historia* and from the Second Variant version respectively, are cited in the apparatus only in as far as their readings demonstrate their place in the text-history of the First Variant. (Complete editions of the versions of the *Historia* found in MSS. a and c will appear later in this series.) It must be stressed that the text printed here represents the pure First Variant, and that it does not contain vulgate or other interpolations of the sort that disfigure Jacob Hammer's edition; readers of this volume will therefore at last be able to appreciate clearly the true contents and structure of the First Variant version.

The text transmitted by the surviving manuscript-witnesses is largely free from serious corruption so that editorial emendation (indicated in this edition by the use of angle-brackets) has been necessary in only a very few passages. It should be noted here that all other use of the term correction in the apparatus refers to scribal activity. Unlike Hammer, I have not introduced Classical Latin orthography into the text, since this system was foreign to mediaeval scribal practice. I have therefore reproduced closely the orthography of the best MS. (R), except in a few cases where its orthography is very idiosyncratic and also of some proper names which are not spelt consistently in R; although this policy sometimes involves the use of slightly unfamiliar forms, it is dictated by the need for editorial consistency. All abbreviations have been expanded silently, with the exception of some abbreviated name-forms which, since they help to establish the textual affiliation of the manuscripts concerned, have been recorded in the apparatus. Modern punctuation has been introduced in order that the text may be followed with the minimum of difficulty, but the sentence-structure of the manuscripts has as far as possible been retained. Finally, since the surviving manuscripts subdivide the First Variant into varying numbers of books of different length, it is uncertain which, if any, of these book-divisions was originally employed by its redactor. Accordingly, the text printed here has been divided into the two hundred and eight chapters, first employed by Edmond Faral, which were used in my previous single-manuscript edition. Cases where parts of a chapter have been transposed in the First Variant, or appear in a different chapter, have already been set out and discussed in detail above; on the rare occasions where transposition or omission leads to a blurring of consecutive chapters in the First Variant, the chapters in question have been run together (as in §§ 179/180 or 191/2, for example). It is intended that this arrangement will allow the reader conveniently and swiftly to compare the First Variant text with that of the vulgate already printed in this series.

BIBLIOGRAPHY

ABBOTT, T. K.   *Catalogue of the Manuscripts in the Library of Trinity College, Dublin* (Dublin 1900)

ARNOLD, Ivor (ed.)   *Le Roman de Brut de Wace* (2 vols, Paris 1938/40)

ARNOLD, I.   'Wace et l'*Historia Regum Britanniae*', *Romania* 57 (1931) 1–12

BARBER, R.   'The manuscripts of the *Vera Historia de Morte Arthuri*', *Arthurian Literature* 6 (1986) 163–4

BARBER, R.   'The *Vera Historia de Morte Arthuri* and its place in Arthurian tradition', *Arthurian Literature* 1 (1981) 62–77

BARTRUM, P. C. (ed.)   *Early Welsh Genealogical Tracts* (Cardiff 1966)

BELL, Alexander (ed.)   *L'Estoire des Engleis by Geffrei Gaimar* (Oxford 1960)

BROMWICH, Rachel (ed. & transl.)   *Trioedd Ynys Prydein. The Welsh Triads* (2nd edn., Cardiff 1978)

CALDWELL, R. A.   'The use of sources in the *Variant* and vulgate versions of the *Historia Regum Britanniae* and the question of the order of the versions', *Bibliographical Bulletin of the International Arthurian Society* 9 (1957) 123–4

CALDWELL, R. A.   'Wace's *Roman de Brut* and the *Variant Version* of Geoffrey of Monmouth's *Historia Regum Britanniae*', *Speculum* 31 (1956) 675–82

CLARKE, Basil (ed. & transl.)   *Life of Merlin. Geoffrey of Monmouth, Vita Merlini* (Cardiff 1973)

COLGRAVE, Bertram & MYNORS, R. A. B. (edd. & transl.)   *Bede's Ecclesiastical History of the English People* (Oxford 1969)

CRICK, Julia   *A Summary Catalogue of the Manuscripts of Geoffrey of Monmouth's Historia Regum Britannie* (Cambridge 1988)

CRIVELLUCCI, Amadeo (ed.)   *Landolfi Sagacis Historia Romana* (2 vols, Rome 1912/13)

CUNNINGHAM, I. C.   'Latin Classical manuscripts in the National Library of Scotland', *Scriptorium* 27 (1973) 64–90

DAVIES, W. Ll. (ed.)   *Handlist of manuscripts in the National Library of Wales* (Aberystwyth 1943–   )

DELISLE, Léopold (ed.)   *Chronique de Robert de Torigni, Abbé du Mont-Saint-Michel, suivie de divers opuscules historiques* (2 vols, Rouen 1872/3)

DROYSEN, H. (ed.)   *Eutropi Breviarium ad urbe condita cum versionibus Graecis et Pauli Landolfique additamentis* (Berlin 1879)

DUMVILLE, D.N. 'An early text of Geoffrey of Monmouth's *Historia Regum Britanniae* and the circulation of some Latin histories in twelfth-century Normandy', *Arthurian Literature* 4 (1984) 1–36

DUMVILLE, D.N. 'Anecdota from manuscripts of Geoffrey of Monmouth', *Arthurian Literature*, forthcoming

DUMVILLE, D.N. 'Celtic-Latin texts in northern England, c.1150–c.1250', *Celtica* 12 (1977) 19–49

DUMVILLE, David & LAPIDGE, Michael (edd.) *The Annals of St Neots with Vita Prima Sancti Neoti* (Cambridge 1985)

DUMVILLE, D.N. 'The origin of the C-text of the Variant Version of the *Historia Regum Britannie*', *Bulletin of the Board of Celtic Studies* 26 (1974–6) 315–22

EMANUEL, H.D. 'Geoffrey of Monmouth's *Historia Regum Britanniae*: a Second Variant Version', *Medium Ævum* 35 (1966) 103–11

EMDEN, A.B. *A Biographical Register of the University of Oxford to A.D. 1500* (3 vols, Oxford 1957–9)

EVANS, J. Gwenogvryn *Report on Manuscripts in the Welsh Language* (2 vols, London 1898–1910)

FARAL, Edmond *La Légende Arthurienne. Etudes et Documents* (3 vols, Paris 1929)

FEUERHERD, Paul *Geoffrey of Monmouth und das alte Testament mit Berucksichtigung der Historia Britonum des Nennius* (Halle a.S. 1915)

FOREVILLE, R. 'L'école de Caen au XIe siècle et les origines normandes de l'université d'Oxford', in *Etudes médiévales offertes à M. le Doyen Augustin Fliche de l'Institut par ses amis, ses anciens élèves, ses collègues* (Montpellier 1952), pp. 81–100

FOWLER, D.C. 'Some biblical influences on Geoffrey of Monmouth's historiography', *Traditio* 14 (1958) 378–85

FRAPPIER, J. [review of J. Hammer (ed.), *Geoffrey of Monmouth: Historia Regum Britanniae. A Variant Version*], *Romania* 74 (1953) 125–8

FRYDE, E.B., *et al. Handbook of British Chronology* (3rd edn., London 1986)

GALLAIS, P. 'La *Variant Version* de l'*Historia Regum Britanniae* et le *Brut* de Wace', *Romania* 87 (1966) 1–32

GREENWAY, D.E. 'Henry of Huntingdon and the manuscripts of his *Historia Anglorum*', *Anglo-Norman Studies* 9 (1986) 103–26

GRISCOM, Acton & JONES, R.E. (edd.) *The Historia Regum Britanniae of Geoffrey of Monmouth with Contributions to the Study of its Place in Early British History together with a Literal Translation of the Welsh Manuscript No. LXI of Jesus College, Oxford* (New York 1929)

GWYNN, Aubrey & HADCOCK, R.N. *Medieval Religious Houses: Ireland* (London 1970)

HAENEL, Gustav   *Catalogi librorum manuscriptorum qui in bibiliothecis Galliae, Helvetiae, Belgii, Britanniae M., Hispaniae, Lusitaniae asservantur* (Leipzig 1830)

HALLAIRE, E.   'Quelques manuscrits de Jean Le Bègue', *Scriptorium* 8 (1954) 291–2

HAMMER, J.   'An unrecorded *Epitaphium Ceadwallae*', *Speculum* 6 (1931) 607–8

HAMMER, J.   'Bref commentaire de la *Prophetia Merlini* du ms 3514 de la Bibliothèque de la Cathédrale d'Exeter (Geoffrey de Monmouth, *Historia Regum Britanniae* l.VII)', in *Hommages à Joseph Bidez et à Franz Cumont* (Bruxelles 1948), pp. 111–19

HAMMER, Jacob (ed.)   *Geoffrey of Monmouth: Historia Regum Britanniae. A Variant Version* (Cambridge, Mass. 1951)

HAMMER, J.   'Geoffrey of Monmouth's use of the Bible in the *Historia Regum Britanniae*', *Bulletin of the John Rylands Library* 30 (1946/7) 293–311

HAMMER, J.   'Remarks on the sources and textual history of Geoffrey of Monmouth's *Historia Regum Britanniae* with an excursus on the *Chronica Polonorum* of Wincenty Kadlubek (Magister Vincentius)', *Bulletin of the Polish Institute of Arts and Sciences in America* 2 (1943/4) 501–64

HOUCK, Margaret   *Sources of the Roman de Brut of Wace* (Berkeley, Cal. 1941)

HUGHES, Kathleen   *Celtic Britain in the Early Middle Ages. Studies in Scottish and Welsh Sources* (Woodbridge 1980)

HUWS, D. & ROBERTS, B.F.   'Another manuscript of the Variant Version of the "Historia Regum Britanniae"', *Bibliographical Bulletin of the International Arthurian Society* 25 (1973) 147–52

JAMES, Montague Rhodes   *A Descriptive Catalogue of the Manuscripts in the Library of Corpus Christi College Cambridge* (2 vols, Cambridge 1912)

JAMES, M.R. (ed. and transl.)   *Walter Map, De Nugis Curialium. Courtiers' Trifles* (Oxford 1983)

JENKINS, R.T. (ed.)   *The Dictionary of Welsh Biography down to 1940* (London 1959)

JIRMOUNSKY, M.   'Essai d'analyse des procédés littéraires de Wace', *Revue des Langues Romanes* 63 (1925) 261–96

JONDORF, G. & DUMVILLE, D.N. (edd.)   *France and the British Isles in the Middle Ages and Renaissance* (Woodbridge forthcoming)

JONES, T. (ed.)   '"Cronica de Wallia" and other documents from Exeter Cathedral Library MS. 3514', *Bulletin of the Board of Celtic Studies* 12 (1946–8) 27–44

KELLER, H.   'Wace et Geoffrey de Monmouth: problème de la chronologie des sources', *Romania* 98 (1977) 379–89

KEMPF, Karl (ed.)   *Valerii Maximi Factorum et Dictorum Memorabilium libri novem cum Iulii Paridis et Ianuarii Nepotiani epitomis* (2nd edn., Stuttgart 1966)

KER, N.R. *Medieval Libraries of Great Britain. A List of Surviving Books* (2nd edn., London 1964)

KER, N.R. *Medieval Manuscripts in British Libraries* (4 vols, Oxford 1969–)

KER, N.R. & WATSON, A.G. *Medieval Libraries of Great Britain. A List of Surviving Books. Supplement to the Second Edition* (London 1987)

LAISTNER, M.L.W. & KING, H.H. *A Hand-list of Bede Manuscripts* (Ithaca, N.Y. 1943)

LAPIDGE, M. 'Additional manuscript evidence for the *Vera Historia de Morte Arthuri*', *Arthurian Literature* 2 (1982) 163–68

LAPIDGE, M. (ed.) 'An edition of the *Vera Historia de Morte Arthuri*', *Arthurian Literature* 1 (1981) 79–93

LECKIE, R.W. *The Passage of Dominion: Geoffrey of Monmouth and the Periodization of Insular History in the Twelfth Century* (Toronto 1981)

LEGGE, M.D. 'Master Geoffrey Arthur', in *An Arthurian Tapestry*, ed. K. Varty (Glasgow 1981), pp. 22–27

LE SAUX, Françoise 'Lazamon's *Brut*: the poem and its sources' (unpubl. Ph.D. dissertation, Lausanne 1988)

LOOMIS, R.S. (ed.) *Arthurian Literature in the Middle Ages. A Collaborative History* (Oxford 1959)

MARTIN, Henry *Catalogue des Manuscrits de la Bibliothèque de l'Arsenal* (8 vols, Paris 1885–99)

MEISTER, Ferdinand (ed.) *Daretis Phrygii De Excidio Troiae Historia* (Leipzig 1873)

MORRIS, R. 'Uther and Igerne: a study in uncourtly love', *Arthurian Literature* 4 (1984) 70–92

PARRY, J.J. 'A variant version of Geoffrey of Monmouth's *Historia*', in *A Miscellany of Studies in Romance Languages and Literatures presented to Leon E. Kestner*, edd. M. Williams & J.A. de Rothschild (Cambridge 1932), pp. 364–9

PARRY, J.J. (ed. and transl.) *Brut Y Brenhinedd: Cotton Cleopatra Version* (Cambridge, Mass. 1937)

PARRY, J.J. & CALDWELL, R.A. 'Geoffrey of Monmouth', in *Arthurian Literature in the Middle Ages*, ed. R.S. Loomis (Oxford 1959), pp. 72–93

PARRY, J.J. [review of J. Hammer (ed.), *Geoffrey of Monmouth: Historia Regum Britanniae. A Variant Version*], *Journal of English and Germanic Philology* 51 (1952) 237–42

PARRY, Thomas *History of Welsh Literature* (Oxford 1955)

POTTHAST, August *Bibliotheca Historica Medii Aevi. Wegweiser durch die Geschichtswerke des europäischen Mittelalters bis 1500* (2 vols, Berlin 1896)

ROBERTS, B.F. 'Pen Penwaedd a Phentir Gafran', *Llên Cymru* 13 (1974–81) 278–81

SCHMIDT, P.G. (ed.) *Johannes de Hauvilla, Architrenius* (München 1974)

SCHMOLKE-HASSELMANN, B.   'The round table: ideal, fiction, reality', *Arthurian Literature* 2 (1982) 41–75

TATLOCK, J.S.P.   *The Legendary History of Britain. Geoffrey of Monmouth's Historia Regum Britanniae and its Early Vernacular Versions* (Berkeley, Cal. 1950)

TAUSENDFREUND, E.G.H.   *Vergil und Gottfried von Monmouth* (Halle a.S. 1913)

TODD, Henry J.   *A Catalogue of the Archiepiscopal Manuscripts in the Library at Lambeth Palace* (London 1812)

ULBRICH, A.   'Über das Verhältnis von Wace's *Roman de Brut* zu seiner Quelle des Gottfried von Monmouth *Historia Regum Britanniae*', *Romanische Forschungen* 26 (1909) 181–259

VARTY, Kenneth (ed.)   *An Arthurian Tapestry. Essays in Memory of Lewis Thorpe* (Glasgow 1981)

WALTHER, Hans   *Initia Carminum ac Versuum Medii Aevi Posterioris Latinorum. Alphabetisches Verzeichnis der Versanfänge mittellateinischer Dichtungen* (Göttingen 1959)

WARD, H.L.D. & HERBERT, J.A.   *Catalogue of Romances in the Department of Manuscripts in the British Museum* (3 vols, London 1883–1910)

WILLIAMS, I.   'Cyfeiriad at y Brawd Fadawg ap Gwallter?', *Bulletin of the Board of Celtic Studies* 4 (1927–9) 133–4

WILLIAMS, M. & de ROTHSCHILD, J.A. (edd.)   *A Miscellany of Studies in Romance Languages and Literatures presented to Leon E. Kestner* (Cambridge 1932)

WINTERBOTTOM, Michael (ed. & transl.)   *Gildas: The Ruin of Britain and Other Works* (Chichester 1978)

WRIGHT, Cyril Ernest   *Fontes Harleiani. A Study of the Sources of the Harleian Collection of Manuscripts preserved in the Department of Manuscripts in the British Museum* (London 1972)

WRIGHT, N.   'Geoffrey of Monmouth and Bede', *Arthurian Literature* 6 (1986) 27–59

WRIGHT, N.   'Geoffrey of Monmouth and Gildas', *Arthurian Literature* 2 (1982) 1–40

WRIGHT, N.   'Geoffrey of Monmouth and Gildas revisited', *Arthurian Literature* 4 (1984) 155–63

WRIGHT, Neil (ed.)   *The Historia Regum Britannie of Geoffrey of Monmouth, I: A Single-manuscript Edition from Bern, Burgerbibliothek, MS. 568* (Cambridge 1984)

WRIGHT, N.   'The parentage of Brutus in Geoffrey of Monmouth's *Historia Regum Britannie* and related texts', forthcoming

WRIGHT, N.   'The place of Henry of Huntingdon's *Epistola ad Warinum* in the text-history of Geoffrey of Monmouth's *Historia Regum Britannie*: a preliminary investigation', in *France and the British Isles in the Middle Ages and Renaissance*, edd. G. Jondorf & D.N. Dumville (Woodbridge forthcoming)

HISTORIA REGUM BRITANNIE: FIRST VARIANT VERSION

SIGLA

Complete witnesses

D   Dublin, Trinity College, MS. 515 (E.5.12), fos 21r–65v
E   Exeter, Cathedral Library, MS. 3514, pp. 94–218
H   London, British Library, MS. Harley 6358, fos 2r–58v [§§ 5–149(part) only]
P   Aberystwyth, National Library of Wales, MS. 2005 (Panton 37), fos 63r–72v [§§ 5–8(part), 54–55, 206–208 only]
R   Paris, Bibliothèque de l' Arsenal, MS. 982 (7.H.L.), fos 168v–188r
S   Edinburgh, National Library of Scotland, MS. Adv. 18.4.5, fos 40r–90v [§§ 5–113(part), 117(part)–208]

Partial witnesses

a   Aberystwyth, National Library of Wales, MS. 13210 (*olim* Phillipps 26233), fos 10v–64r
c   Cardiff, South Glamorgan Central Library, MS. 2.611, fos 9v–130v

[5] [1] Britannia[2] insularum optima quondam Albion nuncupata est: in occidentali occeano[3] inter Galliam[4] et Hyberniam[5] sita octingenta[6] milia passuum in longum, ducenta[7] uero in latum continens. Terra [8]opima frugibus[8] et arboribus et[9] alendis apta pecoribus ac iumentis;[10] uineas[11] etiam[12] [13]quibusdam in locis[13] germinans [14]sed et[14] auium ferax terra, fluuiis quoque multum piscosis[15] [16]ac fontibus[17] preclara[18] copiosis.[16] Habet et fontes salinarum,[19] habet et [20]fontes calidos,[20] uenis quoque metallorum eris[21] ferri plumbi[22] et argenti fecunda. Eratque[23] quondam[24] ciuitatibus nobilissimis [25].xx. et .viii.[25] insignita. Insula hec Britones[26] et Pictos et Scottos[27] incolas recepit. Britones[28] autem[29] a quibus nomen accepit[30] in primis a mari usque ad mare totam insulam insederunt; qui de tractu Armenicano[31] ut fertur [32]Britanniam aduecti sunt.[32] Qualiter uero et unde uel ubi applicuerunt restat calamo[33] perarare[34] sequendo ueterum hystorias[35] qui[36] a Bruto usque ad Cadwaladrum[37] filium Cadwalonis[38] actus [39]omnium continue[39] et ex ordine texuerunt.

§§1–3/4 of the vulgate text are not present in the First Variant version.

✳   ✳   ✳

§5 [1] *Incipit hystoria Brittonum tracta ab antiquis libris Brittonum* a; *Hystoria Britonum* c; *Incipit historia [hystoria D] Britonum [Brytonum D] a Galfrido Arturo [Arturo* deleted (or highlighted?) E; *Arthurio* P] *Monemutensi* [altered to *Monemuthensi* by suprascript *h* in D] *de Britannica lingua in Latinum translata* DEPS; *Incipit prologus in hystoriam Britonum* H; *Incipit hystoria Britonum ab antiquis Britonibus tracta* R. [2] acDPRS; <*B*>*ritannia* E; *Brittannia* H. [3] acDEHRS; *oceano* P. [4] acDEHRS; *Gallyam* P. [5] cERS; *Hiberniam* aDH; *Yberniam* P. [6] acR; *.dccc.* DEHPS. [7] acR; *.cc.* DEHPS. [8...8] D (& Bede; see Introduction, p.xliii); *frugibus* with *optima* suprascript a; *optima frugibus* EPRS (with the marginal note *aliter opima* in P); *frugibus opima* H. [9] aDEPRS; om. H. [10] aDEHRS; *jumentis* P. [11] aDHPRS; *ueneas* E. [12] aDEHPS; *quoque* R. [13...13] R (& Bede); *in locis quibusdam* aH; *in quibusdam locis* DEPS. [14...14] aDEHRS; *set* (or *sed t*) P. [15] aDEHRS; *piscosis habundans* P. [16...16] DEPRS; om. aH. [17] R (& Bede); om. aH; *fontibus aqua* DEPS. [18] DERS; om aH; *praeclara* P. [19] aDEHPS; *alinarum* R. [20...20] DEPS (& Bede); *calidos fontes* aHR. [21] aDEPRS; *eris* H. [22] aDEPRS; *et plumbi* H. [23] aDHS; *Erat* P; *Erat quoque* ER. [24] aDEHPS; *quendam* R. [25...25] R (& Bede); *.xxviii.* aDEHPS. [26] aDEPRS; *Brittones* H. [27] aEHR; *Scothos* D; *Scotos* PS. [28] aDEPRS; *Brittones* H. [29] aDHPRS; om. E. [30] aDHPRS; *recepit* E. [31] aDEHRS; *Armoricano* P. [32...32] aHR (*Brittaniam* in H); *aduecti sunt Britanniam* DEPS. [33] aDEHPS; *stilo uel calamo* R. [34] acDEHP (after deleted, modified *parare* in P); *parare* RS. [35] aDRS; *historias* EHP. [36] aDEHPS; *que* R. [37] aDPR; *Cadwalladrum* ES; *Kadwaladrum* H. [38] aPR; *Caduualonis* D; *Cadwallonis* ES; *Kaduallonis* H. [39...39] aDEHRS; *omni conamine* P.

[6] [1] Eneas[2] post Troianum[3] excidium cum Ascanio filio[4] fugiens
Ytaliam[5] nauigio deuenit[6] ibique a Latino susceptus cum Turno Dauni[7]
Tuscorum regis filio dimicans eum interemit. Regnumque Ytalie[8] et
Lauiniam filiam Latini adeptus est. De cuius etiam nomine Lauinium[9]
oppidum[10] quod struxerat[11] appellauit et regnauit Eneas Latinis[12] annis
.iiii..[13] Quo uita discedente[14] regnum suscepit[15] Ascanius qui et Iulus[16]
eiusdem[17] filius[18] erat;[19] quem apud Troiam ex Creusa filia Priami regis
genuerat et secum in Ytaliam[20] ueniens adduxerat.[21] Qui Ascanius
derelicto [22]nouerce sue Lauinie[22] regno [23]Albam Longam condidit
deosque et penates patris sui Enee[24] ex Lauinio in[23] [25]Albam transtulit.[25]
Symulacra[26] Lauinium sponte redierunt.[27] Rursus[28] traducta[29] in Albam,
iterum repecierunt[30] antiqua delubra. Educauit autem Ascanius summa
pietate Postumum[31] Siluium[32] fratrem suum ex[33] Lauinia procreatum et
cum [34].xxx. annis et .iiii.[34] regnasset, Siluium reliquid[35] heredem.[36] Hic[37]
furtiue indulgens ueneri nupserat cuidam nepti Lauinie[38] eamque
fecerat pregnantem.[39] Cumque id [40]Ascanio compertum esset,[40] precepit[41] magis suis explorare quem sexum puella concepisset. Dixerunt[42]
magi ipsam[43] grauidam esse puero qui et [44]patrem et matrem[44]

§6 [1] *Incipit narratio* aR; *Incipit hystorie Britonum liber primus* H; *Enea post Trojanum
excidium* P; no rubric in cDES. [2] acDHPRS; <E>*neas* E. [3] acDEHRS; *Trojanum* P.
[4] aDEHRS; *filio suo* cP. [5] DEPRS; *Italiam* acH. [6] acDEHR; *deuenere* P; *aduenit* S.
[7] aDEH; *Clauii* P; *Dami* R; *Latini* S. [8] cDRS; *Italie* aEH; *Ytaliae* P. [9] acHP; *Lauinii*
D; *Launni* (?) E; *Launum* R; *Lauini* S. [10] aHPR; *opidum* cDES. [11] acDEHRS;
extruxerat P. [12] HR (& Landolfus; see Introduction, p. xlv); *super Latinos* a; *in
Lauinio* c; *Lacio* D; *in Latio* EP; *in Latino* S. [13] DEHR; *quatuor* aS; 4 c; .iii. P.
[14] aDEPS; *descedente* c; *decedente* H; *descendente* R. [15] aDEPRS; om. H. [16] R; *Iulius*
acDEHS; *Julius* P. [17] acDEHRS; *ejusdem* P. [18] aHR; *filius dictus* cDEPS. [19] ac-
DEPRS; *erat* underpointed with *accepit* suprascript H. [20] cDPRS; *Italiam* aEH.
[21] acHPRS; *adduxerat* (in text) with *ab* in margin D; *abduxerat* E. [22...22] acDEHRS
(*Lauinie* altered from *Lauine* in E); *nouercae suae Lauiniae* P. [23...23] acDEHPR; om. S.
[24] acDEHR; *Eneae* P; om. S. [25...25] aHR; *Albam Longam detulit* cDEPS. [26] R;
Simulacra acDEHS; *Simulac* P. [27] acDEHPR; *redeunt* S. [28] acDEHRS; *Rursum* P.
[29] acDEPRS; *traducto* H. [30] R; *repetiuerunt* aH; *repetierunt* cDEPS. [31] EHPRS;
Postumium a; *Posthumum* D. [32] acDEHRS; *filium* P. [33] cDEPS (& Landolfus); *de*
aHR. [34...34] R; .xxxiii. *annis* aH; *34 annis* c; .xliii. *annis* DEPS. [35] aHRS; *reliquit* cDES.
[36] acHR; *heredem* [*haeredem* P]. *Et Ascanius cum* .xv. [.xi. S] *esset* [*eratP*] *annorum,
genuerat filium quem* [*qui* P] *uocauit Siluium a Siluio fratre suo Postumo* [*Posthumo* P]
DEPS. [37] acDEPRS; *Hic* with *Siluius* suprascript H. [38] acDEHRS; *Lauiniae* P.
[39] acDEHRS; *praegnantem* P. [40...40] cR; *compertum esset Ascanio* aH; *Ascanio patri
suo compertum fuisset* DEPS. [41] acDEHRS; *praecepit* P. [42] aDERS; *Dixeruntque* cP;
Dixerunt autem H. [43] cDEPRS; *illam* aH. [44...44] cDEPRS; *matrem et patrem* aH.

interficeret: [45]pluribus quoque[45] terris [46]in exilium[47] peragratis[46] ad summum tandem culmen honoris perueniret.[48] Nec fefellit eos uaticinium suum. Nam ut dies partus uenit,[49] edidit[50] mulier puerum[51] et mortua est pariendo. Traditur[52] autem puer [53]ad nutriendum[53] et uocatur Brutus. Et cum esset .xv.[54] annorum, comitabatur[55] patri in uenatu sagittamque[56] in ceruos dirigens inopino ictu sagitte[57] patrem interfecit.

[7] Indignantibus ergo parentibus in exilium pulsus est Brutus. Exulatus itaque nauigio tendit[1] in Greciam[2] ubi progeniem Heleni filii Priami inuenit que[3] sub potestate Pandrasi [4]regis Grecorum[4] in seruitute tenebatur. Pyrrus[5] etenim[6] Achillis filius post euersionem Troie[7] ipsum Helenum cum pluribus aliis inde secum in uinculis adduxerat[8] ut[9] necem patris sui in ipsos uindicaret.[10] Agnita igitur Brutus suorum conciuium prosapia moratus est apud eos. Ibique in tantum milicia[11] et probitate uigere cepit ut inter omnes patriotas ualde amaretur. Diuulgata itaque per uniuersam terram fama probitatis ipsius[12] ceperunt [13]ad eum confluere omnes[13] qui de genere[14] Troianorum[15] ibidem morabantur, orantes ut si fieri posset a seruitute Grecorum[16] liberarentur. Quod fieri posse asserebant si ducem haberent qui eorum multitudinem in bello [17]contra Grecos[17] gnauiter[18] regere[19] nosset.[20] In tantum enim infra patriam multiplicati erant ut .vii. milia[21] cum[22] armis exceptis paruulis et mulieribus computarentur.[23] Preterea erat quidam [24]nobilissimus iuuenis[25] [24] in Grecia[26] nomine

45...45 aHPR; *pluribusque* cDS; *pluribus qui* E. 46...46 acDHPRS; *peragratis in exilium* E. 47 acDPRS; *exilio* H. 48 acDHPRS; *peruenit* E. 49 cHR; *aduenit* aDES; *aduenere* P. 50 cDEPRS; *enixa est* aH. 51 acDEHPS; *p puerum* R. 52 acDEPRS; *Traditus est* H. 53...53 cDEHR; *nutriendum* a; *nutriendus* PS. 54 aHPR; *24* c; *.xi.* DES. 55 acDEHPS; *committabatur* R. 56 DERS; *Sagittam* aH; *sagitamque* c; *sagittarum* P. 57 acDEHRS; *sagittae* P.

§7 1 acDEHRS; *tetendit* P. 2 acDEHRS; *Graeciam* P. 3 acDEHRS; *qui* suprascript P. 4...4 acDERS; *Grecorum regis* H; *regis Graecorum* P. 5 aHR; *Pirrus* cDEPS. 6 aEHPRS; *enim* cD. 7 acDEHRS; *Trojae* P. 8 cR; *abduxerat* aDEHP; *adduxer* S. 9 acDEHPS; *in* R. 10 acDEHPR; *iudicaret* S. 11 cEHR; *militia* aDPS. 12 aHR; *eius* c; *illius* DEPS. 13...13 acDEPRS; *omnes ad eum confluere* H. 14 acDEHRS; *gente* P. 15 acDEHRS; *Trojanorum* P. 16 acDEHRS; *Graecorum* P. 17...17 acDEHRS; om. P. 18 aDE; *grauiter* cHPS; *grauatim* (?) R. 19 acEHPRS; *gerere* D. 20 acHR; *posset* DES; *possit* P. 21 acDEHRS; *millia* P. 22 acDEHRS; *in* (preceded by deleted *paruulis*) P. 23 aDEPRS; *computabantur* c; *conputarentur* H. 24...24 acHR; *iuuenis nobilissimus* DEPS. 25 acHR (& DES); *juuenis* P. 26 acDEHRS; *Graecia* P.

Assaracus qui partibus eorum fauebat, ex Troiana[27] matre natus. Hic tria castella que [28]sibi pater suus moriens[28] donauerat contra fratrem suum uiriliter tenebat; que[29] ei conabatur auferre frater quia ex concubina natus fuerat. Erat[30] autem ille [31]patre et matre[31] Grecus et asciuerat[32] regem ceterosque Grecos parti sue fauere. Inspiciens[33] ergo Brutus et[34] uirorum multitudinem et munitionum[35] opportunitatem[36] securius peticioni[37] illorum acquieuit.[38]

[8] Erectus[1] itaque Brutus in ducem conuocat Troianos[2] undique et oppida[3] Assaraci[4] muniuit. Ipse uero et[5] Assaracus cum maxima multitudine uirorum ac[6] mulierum que[7] eis adherebant[8] nemora et colles occupant.[9] Deinde [10]per litteras[11] regem in hec uerba[10] affatur:[12] 'Pandraso regi Grecorum [13]Brutus dux reliquiarum Troie[13] salutem. Quia indignum fuerat gentem preclaro genere Dardani ortam iugo seruitutis premi et tractari aliter quam nobilitatis eius serenitas expeteret, sese infra abdita nemorum recepit malens ferino ritu, carnibus[14] uidelicet et herbis, uitam cum libertate tueri quam diuiciis[15] et deliciis affluens iugo seruitutis teneri. Quod si celsitudinem tuam offendit, non est imputandum[16] eis cum communis sit intencio[17] captiuorum [18]uelle ad pristinam dignitatem[18] redire. Misericordia itaque motus amissam libertatem largiri digneris et loca que occupauit[19] inhabitare permittas. Sin autem concede ut ad aliarum terras nationum[20] [21]cum pace liberi[21] abscedant.'[22]

---

27 acDEHRS; *Trojana* P. 28...28 aHR; *pater suus moriens sibi* cDEPS. 29 acDEHRS; *qui* P. 30 aHR; *Fuit* DES; *Fuerat* P. 31...31 acDEPRS; *et patre* H. 32 acHPRS; *acciuerat* DE. 33 aDEHRS; *Incipiens* cP. 34 acDEHRS; om. P. 35 acDHPS; *municionum* E; *municionem* R. 36 PR; *oportunitatem* acEHS; *opertunitatem* D. 37 aDEHR; *petitioni* cPS. 38 R; *adquieuit* acDEHS; *adquiesceuit* P.

§8 1 acDHPRS; <*E*>*rectus* E. 2 acDEHRS; *Trojanos* P. 3 aHPR; *opida* cDES. 4 cDPR; *Asaraci* aEHS. 5 acDEHRS; om. P. 6 acDEHPR; *et* S. 7 acDEPRS; *qui* H. 8 aceEHPRS; *adherebat* D. 9 cEPRS; *occupabant* a; *occupat* D; *ocupant* H. 10...10 cDEPRS; *regem in hec uerba per litteras* aH. 11 cDERS; *literas* P. 12 acHR; *profatur* DEPS. P's first extract ends here with the note 'Thus far the first chapter in this MSS. The Latin verses of Diana's oracle etc are the same as in the printed copies'. 13...13 aHR; *Brutus reliquiarum Troie dux* c; *dux reliquiarum Troie Brutus* DES. 14 acDEHR; *carnalibus* with *al* underpointed S. 15 cER; *diuitiis* aDHS. 16 aDR; *inputandum* cEHS. 17 ERS; *intentio* acDH. 18...18 acDEHS; *ad pristinam dignitatem uelle* R. 19 acDHR; *occupant* E; *cupauit* (?) S. 20 acDHR; *nacionum* ES. 21...21 acHR; *liberi cum pace* DES. 22 cHRS; *abcedant* aDE.

[9] Lectis igitur[1] litteris Pandrasus[2] eorum quos in seruitutem[3] tenuerat admiratus[4] audaciam continuo procerum suorum consilio[5] exercitum colligere decreuit ut armis eos arctaret[6] qui terras eius insolenter occupauerant. Oppidumque[7] mox Sparatinum adiit; cui Brutus cum tribus milibus fortium[8] Troianorum obuius ex inprouiso[9] inuasit et irruptionem[10] in Grecos et stragem magnam fecit. Porro Greci stupefacti nil tale uerentes omnes in partes dilabuntur et fluuium Akalon[11] qui prope fluebat transire festinant; in quo multi periclitati interierunt.[12] Quos diffugientes [13]Brutus insequitur[13] et partim in undis, partim super[14] ripam ferro prosternit. Antigonus autem frater Pandrasi uidens stragem suorum indoluit reuocauitque[15] uagantes socios[16] in turmam et feroci impetu in seuientes[17] Troas[18] se interserit. Densaque acie incedens hortatur suos uiriliter resistere telaque letifera totis uiribus contorquet.[19] Troes[20] uero audacter[21] insistentes cedem miserandam peregerunt et Antigonum [22]captum retinuerunt.[22]

[10] Brutus igitur uictoria potitus oppidum[1] sexcentis[2] militibus muniuit, nemorum abdita petens ubi Troiana plebs cum mulieribus et pueris[3] delitescebant.[4] At Pandrasus ob fugam suam fratrisque capcionem[5] grauiter merens nocte illa populum dilapsum coadunare non cessauit. Et cum postera[6] lux illucesceret,[7] oppidum[8] obsidere[9] progressus est in quo Brutum et [10]fratrem suum Antigonum[10] [11]estimabat clausos[11] assultumque[12] menibus intulit distributo exercitu per turmas in circuitu.

§9 [1] acDEHS; *ergo* R. [2] acDEHS; *Prandasus* R. [3] aHR; *seruitute* cDES. [4] acDERS; *ammiratus* H. [5] acDEHS; *concilio* R. [6] acDEHR; *artaret* S. [7] R; *Oppidum* aH; *Opidumque* cDES. [8] aDHRS; *forcium* cE. [9] cEHRS; *improuiso* aD. [10] aDHRS; *irrupcionem* cE. [11] aDERS; *Alzalou* c; *Achaloy* H. [12] acDEHS; *perierunt* R. [13]...[13] acEHRS; *insequitur Brutus* D. [14] acEHRS; *supra* D. [15] acDEHS; *reuocantesque* underpointed before *reuocauitque* in R. [16] acDHRS; *secios* E. [17] acDEHS; *seuientem* R. [18] cDERS; *Troias* aH. [19] cDERS; *retorquet* aH. [20] acDERS; *Troiani* H. [21] acDERS; *audaciter* H. [22]...[22] acEHRS; *retinuerunt captum* D.

§10 [1] aH; *opidum* cDES; *oppidis* R. [2] R; *de* aH; *600* c; *.dc.* DE; *.dcc.* S. [3] acEHRS; *mulieribus* deleted from text (with *paruulis* in margin) D. [4] acDEHS; *diletescedebant* R. [5] ER; *captionem* acDHS. [6] cDERS; *postera die* aH. [7] DES; *illucesseret* a; *illuscesceret* cH; *illusceret* R. [8] HR; *opidum* acDES. [9] cDERS; *insidere* aH. [10]...[10] R; *Antigonum* aH; *Antigonum fratrem suum* cDES. [11]...[11] acHR; *clausos estimabat* DES. [12] aDEHS; *insultumque* c; *asultumque* R.

[11] Obsessi uero a muris uiriliter resistentes[1] telis omnium generum ac sulphureis[2] tedis[3] eorum machinaciones[4] repellebant. Tandem cibi[5] penuria et cotidiano labore afflicti legatum ad Brutum mittunt postulantes ut eis in auxilium festinaret ne debilitate coacti oppidum[6] deserere cogerentur. Brutus ergo[7] audiens suos in unum collegit et ad succurrendum oppidanis[8] uiriliter hortatur. Sed quia tantum non habuit exercitum ut campestre prelium [9]inire aduersus hostes[9] auderet, callido usus consilio[10] proponit castra eorum noctu adire ipsosque soporatos deceptis eorundem uigilibus[11] interficere.[12] Aduocato itaque secreto[13] Anacleto Antigoni[14] socio, quem cum[15] Antigono[16] captum tenebat, euaginato gladio[17] in hunc modum affatus est: 'Egregie iuuenis, finis uite tue[18] Antigonique adest nisi que tibi dixero [19]fideliter executus[19] fueris. Uolo ergo[20] per te in sequenti nocte uigiles Grecorum caute decipere ut tuciorem[21] aditum aggrediendi ceteros habeam. Tu uero callide [22]negotium huiusmodi[22] agens in secunda noctis hora uade ad obsidionem[23] manifestaturus fallacibus uerbis te Antigonum a carceribus et uinculis meis abstraxisse[24] et usque ad conuallem nemorum eduxisse illumque nunc[25] inter frutices delitere nec longius abire posse propter insequentes Troianos qui aditus uiarum circumdederunt ne ad fratrem liberatus redeat. Sicque deludens adduces[26] eos usque ad conuallem hanc ubi [27]te et eos[27] operiemur.'

[12] Anacletus ergo uiso gladio qui inter hec uerba morti sue imminebat[1] perterritus ualde promisit [2]iureiurando sese rem quam intimauerat[2] executurum si sibi et Antigono uita daretur. Confirmata

---

§11 [1] acDEHRS (corrected from *insistentes* in D). [2] acEHRS; *sulfureis* D. [3] aDEHS; *thedis* c; *cedis* R. [4] ER; *machinationes* aDHS; *machinas* c. [5] aH; *sibi* cR; *ibi* DE; *ubi* S. [6] aHR; *opidum* cDES. [7] acDEHS; *uero* R. [8] a; *opidanis* cDES; *oppidonis* H; *oppidanos* R. [9]...[9] aHR; *aduersus hostes inire* cDES. [10] acDEHS; *concilio* R. [11] aHR; *uigiliis* c; *custodibus* DES. [12] acDEHS; *interficeres* R. [13] cDES; *secreto in parte* aR; *secreto in partem* H. [14] acDERS; *Antigonis* H. [15] DERS; *eum* (?) a; *cum* underpointed with *ut* suprascript H. [16] acDERS; *attigit* H. [17] acHR; *gladio eum* DES. [18] acDEHS; *sue* R. [19]...[19] cDERS (*exequtus* in c); *executus fideliter* aH. [20] acDEH; *igitur* RS. [21] cERS; *tutiorem* aDH. [22]...[22] aHR; *hoc modo negocium* c; *huiusmodi negocium* DES. [23] aDEHS; *obsedionem* cR. [24] acDEHR; *obtraxisse* S. [25] acDEHR; *uinctum* S. [26] aHR (corrected from *adducens* in a); *deduces* cDES. [27]...[27] acHR; *eos et te* DES.

§12 [1] aDHRS; *iminebat* cE. [2]...[2] cR; *se iureiurando rem quam intimauerat* a; *iureiurando sese quam intimauerat rem* DES; *se iureiurando rem quam interminauerat* H.

itaque huiusmodi[3] prodicione[4] [5]uersus obsidionem se agere cepit[5] Anacletus[6] et, cum iam prope castra incederet, ab exploratoribus Grecorum tenetur et agnoscitur.[7] At ille ingentem leticiam simulans, 'Subuenite,' ait, 'uiri et [8]si quis est non falsus amicus, et[8] Antigonum uestrum de manibus Troianorum eripite. Quem usque ad conuallem hanc proximam nocte [9]hac de[9] carcere Bruti extractum eduxi et ecce inter uepres et[10] nemorum densa delitescit[11] timens ne a Troianis iterum comprehendatur.' Audientes autem Greci Anacleti uerba nichil hesitantes accelerant, arma arripiunt, et illum usque ad conuallem[12] festinantes secuntur;[13] illis denique inter[14] frutecta progredientibus emergit[15] se Brutus cum armatis cateruis[16] et prosilit in medium repente factoque impetu occupat perterritos[17] nil[18] tale uerentes ac cede durissima[19] affecit; ulteriusque progressus per tres turmas [20]socios suos diuisit[20] obsidionem Grecorum disturbare[21] parans precepitque ut singule turme singulas castrorum partes adirent sine tumultu: nec cedem cuiquam inferrent donec ipse cum sua cohorte[22] tentorio regis potitus lituo signum daret.

[13] Edocti itaque omnes Bruti oratione[1] infra castra se recipiunt. Nec mora insonante lituo enses euaginant et stricto ferro hostes semisopitos [2]inuadunt; trucidant[2] quosdam arma capescentes,[3] quosdam inermes et[4] sompno oppressos haut[5] segniter interficiunt.[6] Ad gemitus moriencium[7] euigilant ceteri et cum aliis stupefacti ab hostibus ceduntur. Neque enim tempus arma capiendi uel spacium[8] fugiendi dabatur, cum Troes armati eos undique circumuenientes tamquam[9] oues [10]in caulis[10] iugulabant. Quibus autem fuge beneficium contigit, scopulis elisi sub noctis tenebris precipitabantur. Cadentibus crura uel brachia frangebantur.

[3] aEHRS; *huius* cD. [4] ER; *proditione* acDHS. [5...5] R; *obsidionem uersus se agere cepit* a; *obsidionem uersus se cepit agere* c; *se uersus obsidionem agere cepit* DES; *uersus se agere coepit* H. [6] cHR; *Antigonus* a; *A* DES. [7] acHR; *cognoscitur* DES. [8...8] aR; *si quis est non falsus amicus me et* cDES; om. H. [9...9] acDEHS; *de hac* R. [10] acDERS; *et frutecta et* H. [11] acDEHS; *deletescit* R. [12] acDERS; *uallem* H. [13] acHRS; *sequntur* DE. [14] aHR; *per* cDES. [15] acH; *euergit* DERS. [16] aHR; *suis* c; *uiris* DES. [17] acDER; *perteritos* HS. [18] acDEHS; *nile* R. [19] acDER; *dirissima* H; *dirissima* (altered from *durissima*) S. [20...20] aHR; *diuisit socios* cDES. [21] acEHR; *desturbare* DS. [22] acDEHS; *chorte* R.

§13 [1] acDHRS; *oracione* E. [2...2] acDEHR; *inuadunt et trucidant et* S. [3] cDERS; *capessentes* aH. [4] acDERS; om. H. [5] acDEHS; *aut* R. [6] acDEHS; *interficiunt, inuadunt* R. [7] cER; *morientium* aDHS. [8] acDER; *spatium* HS. [9] R; *tanquam* acDEHS. [10...10] HR; *in caulas* ac; *infra caulas* DES.

Cui neutrum horum contingebat inscius quo fugam faceret in[11] prope [12]fluentibus fluuiis[12] submergebatur.[13] Uixque infortunium quisquam euadere potuit. Namque[14] oppidani[15] [16]quoque commilitonum[16] aduentu applaudentes[17] insiliebant armati atque cladem duplicabant.[18]

[14] Brutus autem [1]tentorium regis, ut predictum est,[1] aggressus sociis interfectis ipsum [2]uiuum retinere[2] curauit. Ut ergo sub [3]luce aurore[3] ruina tanta patuit, Brutus magno fluctuans gaudio spolia peremptorum sociis iuxta modum cuiusque distribuere precepit. Deinde cum Pandraso oppidum[4] ingreditur mortuorum cadauera sepelienda tradens. Postera autem die dux inclitus Brutus maiores natu[5] conuocans[6] quesiuit ab eis quid de rege Pandraso agendum adiudicarent[7] quidque ab eo petendum laudarent. Qui mox diuersis affectibus capti, pars partem regni ad inhabitandum petere hortabatur,[8] pars uero licentiam[9] abeundi et ea que itineri necessaria forent. Cumque[10] [11]diu in ambiguo[11] res extitisset, surrexit unus Menbricius[12] nomine ceterisque[13] asculantibus ait: 'Utquid hesitatis, patres et fratres, in hiis[14] que saluti nostre sunt utilia? Ultima hec sententia[15] nobis tenenda est, licencia[16] uidelicet abeundi, si uobis posterisque[17] uestris uitam et pacem adipisci desideratis. Nam si eo pacto uitam concesseritis Pandraso[18] ut per eum partem Grecie adepti inter Danaum inuisum genus cohabitare deliberatis,[19] numquam[20] diuturna pace fruemini dum fratres et filii et nepotes eorum quibus tantam intulistis stragem uobis inmixti[21] uel uicini fuerint. Memores cedis[22] parentum eterno uos exsufflabunt odio; nec uobis[23] minores uires habentibus facile erit resistere dum generatio[24] eorum multiplicata generationi[25] succedet.[26] Eorum enim numerus

---

[11] acDEHS; *ut* R. [12...12] HR; *fluuiis fluentibus* acDES. [13] acDRS; *submergebantur* E; *mergebantur* H. [14] aDERS; *Nam uel* c; *Nanque* H. [15] aHR; *opidani* cDES. [16...16] cR (*comilitonum* in c); *commilitonum* aH; *commilitonum quoque* DES. [17] acDHRS; *plaudentes* E. [18] acDER; *dupplicabant* HS.

§14 [1...1] acHR; *ut predictum est tentorium regis* DES. [2...2] acHR; *retinere uiuum* DES. [3...3] acDEHR; *lucis aurora* S. [4] aHR; *opidum* cDES. [5] acDEHS; *natus* R. [6] aHR; *aduocans* cDES. [7] acDERS; *iudicarent* H. [8] aDEHS; *hortabantur* cR. [9] aDHRS; *licenciam* cE. [10] acDERS; *Cum* H. [11...11] aHR; *duo in ambiguo* c; *in ambiguo diu* DS; *in ambiguo die* E. [12] cHRS; *Membritius* a; *Membricius* DE. [13] cDERS; *ceteris* a; *et ceteris* H. [14] cDERS; *his* aH. [15] acDHRS; *sentencia* E. [16] acERS; *licentia* DH. [17] aHR; *et posteris* cDES. [18] acDEHRS (corrected from *Pndraso* in D). [19] acDRS; *desideratis* underpointed before *deliberatis* in E; *deliberatis* altered to *deliberetis* in H. [20] acDERS; *nunquam* H. [21] acHRS; *immixti* DE. [22] acHS; *cede* DER. [23] acDEHS; *nobis* R. [24] acDHRS; *generacio* E. [25] acDHRS; *generacioni* E. [26] acDEHR; *succedit* S.

cottidie[27] augebitur, uester uero minuetur. Laudo itaque et consulo in parte mea, si ceteris uidebitur, ut petatis[28] ab illo[29] filiam suam primogenitam, quam Innogen uocant, ut duci nostro[30] copuletur et aurum et argentum, naues et frumentum et que itineri neccesaria[31] fuerint. Et si impetrare[32] poterimus, licencia[33] sua[34] alias naciones[35] petamus.'

[15] Ut ergo finem dicendi fecit, acquieuit[1] tota multitudo atque suasit ut Pandrasus in medium adduceretur.[2] Nec mora adductus,[3] optio[4] ei datur eligendi aut filiam suam, sicut predictum est, Bruto coniugem dare[5] aut suum interitum et fratris. Qui[6] respondens ait: 'Nichil michi uita prestancius,[7] nichil[8] iocundius censeo et, licet inuitus et coactus sub mortis periculo externo[9] uiro et hosti filiam meam karissimam[10] daturus sim,[11] solacium[12] tamen[13] habeo quia[14] probo eam[15] copulo et nobili quem ex genere Priami et Anchise creatum fama declarat. Do ergo ei[16] filiam meam primogenitam Innogen, do etiam aurum et argentum, naues et frumentum, uinum et oleum, et quicquid[17] itineri[18] dixeritis esse neccesarium. Et si a proposito uestro[19] diuertentes cum Grecis commanere uolueritis, terciam regni mei partem [20]ad inhabitandum uobis[20] concedo. Sin autem cetera prosequar[21] in uestra deliberacione.'[22] Conuentione[23] itaque[24] facta diriguntur legati per uniuersa Grecie litora[25] colligere naues; que collecte [26]trecente .xxiiii.[26] erant numero et omni mox genere farris honerantur.[27] Filia[28] Bruto maritatur; quisque[29] prout dignitas expetebat auro et argento donatur[30] et peractis cunctis erectis uelis secundis uentis abscedunt.[31]

---

[27] R; *cotidie* acDEHS. [28] acDEHS; *pietatis* R. [29] aHR; *eo* cDES. [30] acDEHS; *meo* R. [31] cDERS; *necessaria* aH. [32] acDERS; *inpetrare* H. [33] cERS; *licentia* aDH. [34] acDERS; *uestra* H. [35] ER; *nationes* acDHS.

§15 [1] acR; *adquieuit* DEHS. [2] acH; *duceretur* DES; *duceretur* (with *ad* in margin) R. [3] cHR; *adductus est et* a; *adducto* DES. [4] aDHRS; *opcio* E. [5] acDERS; *daret* H. [6] acDEHS; *et* R. [7] cEHRS; *prestancius* aD. [8] acDHR; *nil* E; *uel* S. [9] acDEHR; *extraneo* S. [10] aDERS; *licet inuitam* c; *carissimam* H. [11] aDHR; *sum* cES. [12] acDERS; *solatium* H. [13] acDERS; *inde* H. [14] acEHRS; *quod* D. [15] DEHR; *uiro eam* a; om. S. [16] acDERS; om. H. [17] acDEHS; *quidquid* R. [18] aHR; *itineri uestro* cDES. [19] acHR; om. DES. [20]...[20] R; *uobis ad habitandum* c; *uobis ad inhabitandum* aDEHS. [21] DEHR; *persequar* a; *prosequantur* cS. [22] ER; *deliberatione* acDHS. [23] acDHRS; *Conuencione* E. [24] aHR; *autem* cDES. [25] DERS; *littora* acH. [26]...[26] R; *370* c; *.cccxxiiii.* aDEHS. [27] cR; *onerantur* aDEHS. [28] HR; *Filia Innogen* a; *Filia regis* cDES. [29] acDEHS; *quisquis* R. [30] acDHRS; *dotatur* E. [31] ERS; *abcedunt* acD; *abscedunt* altered to *abcedunt* H.

[16] Prospero[1] itaque [2]uentorum flatu[2] duobus diebus et una nocte[3] sulcantes maria applicuerunt [4]in quandam insulam Leogetiam uocatam[4] que ab incursione piratarum[5] uastata ac[6] omni habitatore deserta antiqua tamen retinebat delubra. In qua feras diuersorum generum reperientes[7] copiose[8] naues suas uenacione[9] refecerunt.[10] Uenientes autem ad quandam[11] desertam ciuitatem, templum Dyane[12] in ea reperiunt[13] ubi ymago[14] eiusdem dee responsa querentibus dabat. Qui mox litatis uictimis a numine futuri itineris presagia requirunt: que uel qualis[15] patria eis sedes certe mansionis debeatur. Communicatoque omnium[16] assensu assumpto [17]Brutus secum[17] Gerione augure et .xii. maioribus natu, circumdatus[18] tempora[19] uittis,[20] abdita templi penetrans ante uetustissimum delubrum, ubi ara dee statuta[21] fuerat, uas sacrificii uino plenum et [22]sanguine candide cerue[22] dextra[23] tenens erecto uultu ad effigiem numinis silencium[24] in hec uerba dissoluit:

'Diua[25] potens nemorum, terror siluestribus apris,
  Cui licet anfractus[26] ire per ethereos
Infernasque domos, terrestria iura resolue;[27]
  Et dic quas terras nos habitare uelis.
Dic certam sedem qua te uenerabor in euum,
  [28]Qua tibi[28] uirgineis templa dicabo choris.'[29]

Hec[30] ubi nouies dixit, circuiuit[31] aram quater fuditque uinum quod tenebat in foco iuxta morem litantium[32] ibi accenso. Postea recubuit super pellem cerue quam ante aram extenderat inuitatoque sompno obdormiuit. Eratque[33] tunc quasi [34]tertia noctis hora.[34] Tunc uisum est illi deam astare [35]ante ipsum[35] et sese sic affari:

§16 [1] acDHRS; <P>rospero E. [2...2] aHR; cursu cDES. [3] acDERS; noctu H. [4...4] aR; in quandam insulam nomine Leogeciam [Loegeciam c; Leogetiam D] cDES; ad insulam Loegiam uocatam H. [5] acDEHS; pirratarum R. [6] cDEHS; et a; ab R. [7] acEHRS; inuenientes D. [8] acR; copiosa DEHS. [9] ER; uenatione acDHS. [10] acDERS; referserunt H. [11] acDEHS; qndam R. [12] cR; Diane aDEHS. [13] acHR; repererunt D; reperierunt E; repperierunt S. [14] cDERS; imago aH. [15] c; om. aDEHRS. [16] acDHRS; omni E. [17...17] acHR; secum Brutus DES. [18] acDEHS; circumdatis R. [19] acE; timpora DH; timpera RS. [20] aDEHS; uictis c; uitis R. [21] acDEHS; statua R. [22...22] acDHRS; candide cerue sanguine E. [23] cDERS; dextera aH. [24] cDERS; silentium aH. [25] acHR; Quia DS (with Diua in margin of D); <Q>uia E. [26] acH; amfractus D; affractus ES; amphractus R. [27] cDES; resolue (with uel reuolue suprascript) a; reuolue HR. [28...28] acDEHS; Quae (with tibi in margin) R. [29] acDEHR; coris S. [30] acDEHS; Quod R. [31] acEHRS; circumiuit D. [32] aDHRS; littancium c; litancium E. [33] cDERS; Erat aH. [34...34] aHR; noctis tercia hora cES; noctis hora tercia D. [35...35] R; ante eum aH; om. cDES.

'Brute,[36] sub occasu solis trans Gallica regna
  Insula in occeano[37] est [38]undique clausa mari:
[39]Insula in occeano est[39] [38] habitata gygantibus[40] olim,
  Nunc deserta quidem, gentibus apta tuis.
Hanc pete: namque tibi sedes erit illa perhennis;
  Hic[41] fiet natis altera Troia tuis.
Hic de prole tua reges nascentur, et ipsis
  Tocius[42] terre subditus orbis erit.'

Tali uisione [43]dux expergefactus[43] uocatis sociis rem per ordinem narrauit ut sibi[44] dormienti contigerat.

[17] Dehinc[1] ad naues repedauit et flante secunda aura prospero cursu [2].xxx. dierum[2] spacio[3] uenerunt ad Affricam, deinde ad Lacum Salinarum et ad Aras Philistinorum. Hinc nauigauerunt inter Ruscicadam[4] et Montes Azare. Ibi ab incursione piratarum[5] maximum[6] passi sunt periculum. Uictoriam tamen adepti spoliis eorum ditati sunt. Porro flumen Malue[7] transcurrentes applicuerunt in[8] Mauritaniam. Quam penuria cibi et potus e[9] nauibus egressi uastauerunt a mari usque ad mare. Inde refertis[10] nauibus petierunt Columpnas Herculis ubi Syrenes,[11] monstra maris, apparuerunt eis; que[12] ambiendo naues fere obruebant. Elapsi tamen inde Hyspanie[13] horas pretermeant ubi iuxta litora[14] [15]inuenerunt quatuor[16] generationes[17] [15] de exulibus Troianis[18] que Antenoris fugam comitate[19] fuerant. Quorum[20] dux [21]Corineus dictus erat,[21] uir magne uirtutis et audacie. Agnita itaque inuicem[22] ueteris originis prosapia associatus est eis cum maxima populi parte cui

---

[36] acDHRS; <B>rute E. [37] acDHRS; occiano E. [38]...[38] aDERS; om. cH. [39]...[39] DR; Insula in occeano est deleted (with Fertilitate uirens suprascript) a; om. cH; Insula in occiano E; Insula est in occeano S. [40] R; gigantibus acDEHS. [41] aDEHR; Hec cS (altered from Hic in S?). [42] acEHRS; Totius D. [43]...[43] acEHRS; expergefactus dux D. [44] acDEHR; sicut S.

§17 [1] acDEHR; Deinde S. [2]...[2] acDEHS; dierum .xxx. R. [3] acDERS; spatio H. [4] acDERS; Rusciscadam H. [5] acDEHS; pirratarum R. [6] acDEHRS (corrected from maxiemum in R). [7] acDERS; Malne H. [8] aHR; om. cDES. [9] acH; om. DES; de R. [10] aHR; refectis cDES. [11] acDHR; Serenes E; Sirenes S. [12] acDHRS; qui E. [13] acERS; Hispanie DH. [14] DER; littora acHS. [15]...[15] acDEHS; .iiii. generaciones inuenerunt R. [16] acHS; .iiii. DE (& R). [17] acDHS; generaciones E (& R). [18] acDERS; Troianorum H. [19] acDEHS; concomitate R. [20] acDEHS; Quarum R. [21]...[21] aHR; dictus erat Corineus cDES. [22] aHR; om. cDES.

presidebat. Deinde Aquitaniam[23] a dextra pretereuntes ostium[24] Ligeris[25] ingressi anchoras fixerunt. Moratique sunt[26] [27].vii. diebus[27] situm regni explorantes.

[18] Regnabat tunc in Aquitannia[1] Gofarius[2] rex Pictus. Hic cum audisset fama indicante externam gentem in fines regni sui applicuisse, misit nuncios[3] ad explorandum utrum pacem ferrent an arma. Nuncii[4] autem classem petentes obuiauerunt Corineo egresso iam cum ducentis[5] uiris ad uenandum. Mox allocuti eum cur sine licentia[6] saltus regis [7]ad uenandum inuasissent[7] – statutum enim [8]ab antiquo[9] fuerat[8] neminem sine principis iussu ibidem debere feras capere – Corineus respondit se prohibicionem[10] [11]nescire sui regis[11] neque etiam huiuscemodi[12] rei alias[13] prohibicionem[14] audisse, sed nequaquam fieri debere. Quo dicto unus ex illis Ymbertus[15] nomine curuato arcu sagittam in ipsum direxit. Uitauit eam Corineus[16] impetumque [17]faciens in Ymbertum[17] ipso arcu quem tenebat capud[18] ei[19] in frusta[20] conscidit.[21] Diffugientesque[22] socii Gofario[23] necem Ymberti[24] nunciauerunt et hostes fortissimos aduentasse. Rex ergo[25] contristatus [26]statim collegit[26] exercitum grandem ut in ipsos animaduerteret mortemque nuncii[27] uindicaret. At Brutus diuulgato eius aduentu naues munit, mulieres et paruulos infra transtra[28] iubet commanere. Ipse autem cum multitudine uirorum bellatorum obuius regi Gofario[29] progreditur. Initoque certamine dira pugna utrobique committitur. Et cum [30]diei multum[30] in

[23] EHR; *Aquitanniam* aD; *Acquitanniam* c; *Acquitaniam* S. [24] aERS; *hostia* c; *hostium* DH. [25] acDEHR; *Legeris* S. [26] cDERS; *sunt ibi* aH. [27]...[27] acEHRS; *diebus .vii.* D.

§18 [1] DER; *Aquitania* aHS; *Acquitannia* c. [2] DERS; *Gofferauus* c; *Goffarius* H. [3] R; *nuntios* aH; om. c; *nuncium suum* D; *nuncium* ES. [4] acDERS; *Nuntii* H. [5] aR; *200* c; *.cc.* DEHS. [6] aDHRS; *liccencia* c; *licencia* E. [7]...[7] aR; *inuasissent ad uenandum* cDEHS. [8]...[8] acEHRS; *fuerat ab antiquo* D. [9] cERS (& D); *antiquis* aH. [10] ER; *prohibitionem* aDH; *prohibitioni* c; *prohibitationem* S. [11]...[11] cDHRS; *sui regis nescire* aE. [12] aDR; *huius* c; *huiuscemode* E; *huiusce* H; *huius* with *se* suprascript S. [13] cDERS; *alias se* aH. [14] ER; *prohibitionem* acDH; *prohibitationem* S. [15] R; *Nubertus* aDEH; *Imbertus* cS. [16] acDHRS; *C* E. [17]...[17] c; *faciens in Nubertum* aH; *in Nubertum faciens* DE; *faciens in Imbertum* R; *in Imbertum faciens* S. [18] ERS; *caput* acDH. [19] acDERS; *eius* H. [20] aDHS; *frustra* cER. [21] aDR; *concidit* cEHS. [22] R; *Diffugientes* acH; *Diffugientes autem* DES. [23] aDR; *Gofferano* c; *Gofforio* ES; *Goffario* H. [24] R; *Nuberti* aDEH; *Imberti* cS. [25] acDEHR; *uero* S. [26]...[26] aHR; *collegit statim* cDS; *collegit* E. [27] DERS; *Nuberti* a; *Imberti* c; *nuntii sui* H. [28] aDER; *castra* cHS (*ca–* over an erasure in S). [29] DR; *Gofferano* c; *G* E; *Goffario* HS. [30]...[30] R; *multum diei* acDEHS.

agendo consumpsissent, puduit Corineum Aquitanos[31] tam audacter in eos resistere, Troianos non triumphare. Unde sumpta audacia seuocauit in dextram[32] partem prelii suos[33] et facto agmine celerem impetum[34] in hostes facit ipsosque dextra leuaque cedit et penetrata cohorte cunctos in fugam coegit. Fortuna[35] ei amisso[36] gladio bipennem administrauit[37] qua cunctos quos attingebat[38] a summo usque deorsum findebat. Miratur Brutus, mirantur socii, mirantur etiam[39] hostes audaciam uiri et uirtutem. Qui bipennem post fugientes librans timorem illorum hiis[40] uerbis cohercebat:[41] 'Quo fugitis, timidi, quo segnes[42] abitis? Reuertimini, o[43] reuertimini et congressum cum Corineo facite. Proth[44] pudor! Tot milia hominum[45] solum[46] fugitis?[47] Sed habete solacium[48] quod dextra[49] hec solebat Tyrenos[50] gygantes[51] et fugare et prosternere ac ternos[52] atque[53] quaternos ad tartara trudere.' Ad hec uerba Corinei quidam consul nomine Suardus[54] cum trecentis[55] militibus impetum[56] faciens Corineum undique circumdedit. At Corineus non oblitus bypennis[57] in ipsum consulem erectam uibrat percussumque a summo usque [58]ad ymum[58] in duas partes[59] dissecuit. Sed et confestim irruens in ceteros bipennem rotat stragem maximam[60] faciens et nunc hac nunc illac[61] discurrens huic [62]brachium cum manu[62] amputat, illi scapulas a corpore separat, alii[63] capud[64] truncat. Omnes in ipsum solum et ipse solus in omnes ruit.[65] Quod Brutus cernens a longe [66]motus probitate uiri[66] cucurrit cum turma et [67]auxilium ei[67] subrogat. Mox oritur ingens clamor et crebri ictus multiplicantur et fit cedes durissima.[68] Nec mora uictoriam adepti sunt Troes et regem Gofarium[69] cum suis in fugam uertunt.

---

[31] aHR; *Aquitannos* c; *Aquitaneos* DES. [32] cDERS; *dexteram* aH. [33] aR; *et suos* c; *socios* DES; *sui* H. [34] aDERS; *cursum* c; *inpetum* H. [35] aR; *Fortunaque* cDES; *Fortuna enim* H. [36] acDHR; *ammisso* ES. [37] DR; *amministrauit* acES; *aministrauit* H. [38] acDHRS; *attigebat* E. [39] acDEHR; *et* S. [40] cDERS; *his* aH. [41] acDEHR; *chohercebat* S. [42] acDEHRS (corrected from *signes* in S). [43] DERS; *Aquitani* a; *obsecro* c; *a* H. [44] cDRS; *proh* aEH. [45] HR; om. acDES. [46] acDERS; om. H. [47] acDEHS; *figitis* R. [48] acDERS; *solatium* H. [49] cHRS; *dextera* aDE. [50] R; *Tyrrenos* aD; *terrenos* cH; *Tirrenos* ES. [51] aDHR; *gigantes* cES. [52] acDEHS; *trinos* R. [53] acDERS; *et* H. [54] ERS; *Suhardus* acDH. [55] aR; *300* c; *.ccc.* DEHS. [56] acDERS; *inpetum* H. [57] R; *bipennis* acDEHS. [58...58] R; *ad imum* aDES; *imum* c; *deorsum* (with *ad imum* suprascript) H. [59] acDHRS; om. E. [60] aHR; *magnam* cDES. [61] acDEHS; *illas* R. [62...62] aHR (*bracchium* in R); *manum cum brachio* cDES. [63] acDERS; *illi* H. [64] cRS; *caput* aDEH. [65] DERS; *irruit* acH. [66...66] DERS; *probitate uiri motus* aH; *motus amore et probitate uiri* c. [67...67] acEHRS; *ei auxilium* D. [68] acHR; *dirissima* DES. [69] aR; *Gofferanum* c; *Gof* D; *G* ES; *Goffarium* H.

[**19**] Fugiens itaque Gofarius[1] partes Galliarum[2] adiuit[3] ut ab amicis et cognatis auxilium peteret.[4] Erant tunc temporis .xii. reges in Gallia quorum regimine tota patria pari dignitate regebatur. Qui benigne suscipientes eum promittunt sese unanimiter[5] expulsuros a finibus Aquitannie[6] externam gentem. Brutus autem[7] uictoria letus peremptorum spoliis socios ditat et in turmas et centurias resociatos per patriam ducit et dilatat uolens eam penitus delere. Agros igitur[8] depopulatur,[9] ciuitates incendit[10] et gazas absconditas inde extrahit,[11] stragem miserandam ciuibus ac[12] plebanis infert. Dumque tali clade Aquitanie[13] partes infestaret, uenit ad locum ubi nunc est ciuitas Turonorum quam, ut Homerus testatur, ipse prior construxit atque ibidem castra metatus est ut, si necessitas urgeret,[14] se suosque infra ipsa castra reciperet. Peractis itaque castris post biduum[15] ecce Gofarius[16] cum immenso[17] exercitu collecto ex omni Galliarum parte aduentauit.

[**20**] Torua[1] igitur lumina[2] in castra Troianorum retorquens tristis in hec uerba erupit: 'Proth[3] fatum triste! Castra etiam in regno meo statuerunt ignobiles[4] exules. Armate uos, uiri,[5] armate celeriter et per ordinatas turmas ad[6] pugnam incedite. Nulla mora erit quin[7] semimares istos uelud[8] oues intra caulas capiemus atque[9] captos[10] captiuos per regna nostra[11] mancipabimus.' Armauerunt[12] se omnes[13] ad preceptum regis Gofarii[14] et per duodena agmina statuti[15] hostes inuadunt. Hostes econtra dispositis cateruis[16] eos audacter suscipiunt. [17]In congressu[17] ergo preualuerunt Troes et cedem magnam ex[18] hostibus fecerunt fere ad[19] duo milia hominum. Galli autem, quia eorum [20]maior numerus

---

§19 [1] aR; *Gofferanus* c; *Gof* D; *G* ES; *Goffarius* H. [2] acDEHR; *Gallearum* S. [3] aHR; *adiit* cDES. [4] acDEHRS (corrected from *peterent* in H). [5] acHR; om. DES. [6] cDER; *Aquitanie* aHS. [7] cDERS; om. aH. [8] acDERS; *itaque* H. [9] acDRS; *deppellatur* with first *l* underpointed E; *depopulat* H. [10] aDHRS; *a* underpointed before *incendit* c; *ascendit* E. [11] aH; *subtrahit* c; *extraxit* DRS; *abstraxit* E. [12] cDERS; *et* aH. [13] aDHRS; *Aquitannie* cE. [14] acDEHS; *urget* corrected from *urseget* R. [15] acDEHS; *biennium* R. [16] aR; *Gofferanus* c; *Gofar* D; *G* ES; *Goffarius* H. [17] DHR; *inmenso* ac; *uniuerso* ES.

§20 [1] acH; *Toruo* DERS. [2] acH; *lumine* DERS. [3] cDR; *Proh* aEHS. [4] acDERS; *ignobiles uiri et* H. [5] aDHR; *o uiri* cES. [6] acDEHR; *in* S. [7] acDEHR; om. S. [8] aR; *uelut* cDEHS. [9] aHR; *et* cDES. [10] cDERS; om. aH. [11] acDEHS; *uestra* R. [12] acDHR; *Armauerant* ES. [13] aHR; *socii omnes* cDES. [14] aR; *Gofferani* c; *Gof* D; *G* ES; om. H. [15] acHR; *statim* DES. [16] aHR; *turmis* cDES. [17...17] acHR; *Ingressu* DES. [18] acDHRS; *in* E. [19] acEHRS; *usque ad* D. [20...20] aHR; *numerus maior erat* c; *maior erat numerus* DES.

14

erat[20] et magis ac magis augmentabatur,[21] undique conuenientes impetum in Troas acriter fecerunt[22] et eos in castra regredi coegerunt. Obsessi itaque a Gallis sub noctis silentio[23] consilium inierunt[24] ut Corineus cum suis per quedam diuortia[25] intempesta nocte egrederetur et in nemore[26] quod prope erat usque ad diem deliteret[27] ut, cum Brutus diluculo egressus cum eis dimicaret, ipse cum[28] cohorte gentis sue inprouisus[29] a dorso superueniret et sic utrimque[30] attonitos Gallos inuaderent. Quod ita factum est. Et dum mane die illucescente[31] Brutus cum [32]gente sua[32] de castris exiens cum Gallis decertaret, mutuis uulneribus prosternuntur et, antequam Corineus cum suis se exercitui manifestaret, cecidit nepos Bruti Turnus nomine, uir [33]magne audacie,[33] quo fortior siue audacior[34] nullus excepto Corineo inter[35] Troas aderat. Hic solus solo gladio sexcentos[36] uiros strauerat; sed ab irruenti multitudine dum eos persequitur[37] a suis auulsus multis uulneribus confossus est. De nomine itaque ipsius ciuitas Turonis uocabulum sumpsit quia ibidem sepultus est Turnus. Interea superueniente Corineo[38] a tergo hostes inuadit.[39] Troes audaciores et multo acriores propter mortem Turni uindicandam[40] insurgentes sternunt Gallos et trucidant undique sine intermissione. Tandem fugam arripiunt Galli et campum deserere[41] festinant; quos Troes animosi [42]usque ferientes insecuntur.[42] Patrata igitur uictoria Brutus receptui lituum sonans reuerti et coadunari[43] ad castra facit suos [44]decernitque cum eis[44] naues[45] repetere ne – iterum hostes conglobati et pluriores prioribus effecti[46] – sustinere eos nequirent[47] sed magis periclitarentur. Contione[48] itaque peracta[49] classem repetunt et de[50] preda [51]diuiciarum diuersarum[51] eam replent. Prosperis denique uentis diis[52] fauentibus terram diuinitus

[21] aHR; *augmentabantur* cDES. [22] acDHRS; *fecerunt uel coegerunt* E. [23] aDHS; *silencio* cE; *sylencio* R. [24] acDEHS; *inerunt* R. [25] aDHRS; *diuorcia* cE. [26] DES; *nemus* acHR. [27] aDEHS; *delitesceret* c; *diliteret* R. [28] acDERS; *in* H. [29] aHRS; *diluculo* c; *improuisus* DE. [30] acDR; *utrinque* EH; *utrique* S. [31] aDS; *illuscescente* cH; *illucessente* E; *illucente* R. [32]...[32] aHR; *suis* cDES. [33]...[33] acEHRS; *audacie magne* D. [34] cDERS; *audatior* aH. [35] aDEHS; om. c; *in* R. [36] R; *scescentos* a; *secentos* c; *.dc.* DEH; *.dcc.* S. [37] aHR; *persequeretur* cDES. [38] acDHR; *C* ES. [39] acHR; *inuadunt* DES. [40] acDEHS; *iudicandam* R. [41] acDEHS; *dissereres* R. [42]...[42] aR; *ferientes usque insecuntur* cDES (*insecuntur in* c); *usquequaque insequuntur* H. [43] acDEHRS (corrected from *coadnari* in E). [44]...[44] aHR; *discernitque cum eis* c; *decernitque* DS; *decreuitque* E. [45] acDEHR; om. S. [46] acHR; *effecti essent* DES. [47] acDEHR; *nequierunt* S. [48] aDEH; *Concione* c; *Conticione* R; *Contentione* S. [49] aHR; *facta* cDES. [50] acDHRS; *dum* E. [51]...[51] R; *diuersarum diuitiarum* aDHS; *diuersarum diuiciarum* cE. [52] acEHRS; om. D.

promissam petunt et in⁵³ portu Derte⁵⁴ fluminis qui Totonesium⁵⁵ dicitur⁵⁶ applicant.

[21] Insule huic tunc ¹nomen Albion¹ erat² que a nemine exceptis paucis gygantibus³ inhabitabatur. Diffusi itaque ⁴Troes per patriam⁴ gygantes⁵ reperiunt quos statim ad cauernas moncium⁶ fugant. Quadam autem die dum in eodem portu nauium⁷ diis libamina⁸ ex more soluunt et uictimis cesis⁹ festiuum diem celebrant,¹⁰ superuenit Goemagog¹¹ gygas¹² cum aliis .xx. gygantibus¹³ illos a sacrificio incepto disturbans et quosdam¹⁴ de Bruti sociis lapidibus et conchis¹⁵ obruerunt. At Troes undique confluentes omnes interfecerunt preter solum Goemagog.¹⁶ Hunc ergo¹⁷ Brutus uiuum conseruari¹⁸ precepit uolens uidere luctam inter ipsum et Corineum. Corineus uero¹⁹ audiens de montibus accurrit et uidens gygantem²⁰ ad luctandum prouocat. Inito deinde²¹ certamine hinc stat Corineus tunica succinctus, hinc²² stat gygas²³ ad luctam paratus; et²⁴ exertis²⁵ brachiis alter in alterum tendens dorsa uinculis²⁶ brachiorum annectunt²⁷ crebris flatibus auras uexantes. Nec mora Goemagog²⁸ Corineum²⁹ totis uiribus astringens pectore pectus illius alisit³⁰ fortiter tribus Corineo fractis³¹ costis. Mox ille in iram accensus ³²reuocat uires³² et toto conamine amplexatus de litore³³ proximo super rupes excussit.³⁴ At ille per abrupta silicum ruens in frusta³⁵ dilaceratus expirauit³⁶ fluctusque sanguine maculauit.³⁷ Locus ergo ille ³⁸nomen ex

---

⁵³ acDEHS; om. R. ⁵⁴ aDEHS; *Derce* c; *Dercerte* R. ⁵⁵ DHS; *Totoniensium* a, *Totonensium* c; *Totenesium* E; *Tonesium* R. ⁵⁶ acHR; *appellatur* DES.

§21 ¹...¹ aR; *Albion nomen* cDES; *nomen Albyon* H. ² acDERS; om. (erased?) H. ³ DHR; *gigantibus* acES. ⁴...⁴ cDERS; *per patriam Troes* aH. ⁵ DHR; *gigantes* acES. ⁶ cERS; *montium* aDH. ⁷ aHR; om. cDES. ⁸ acDEHS; *labamina* R. ⁹ acDEHS; *celsis* R. ¹⁰ cDES; *celebrarent* aHR. ¹¹ aDEH; *Geomagog* c; *Gemagog* R; *Gogmagog* S. ¹² aDHR; *gigas* cES. ¹³ aDHR; *gigantibus* cES. ¹⁴ acDEHRS (corrected from *quodam* in R). ¹⁵ HR; *contis* aDES; *concis* c. ¹⁶ aDEH; *Geomagog* c; *Gemagog* R; *Gogmagog* S. ¹⁷ acHR; *enim* DES. ¹⁸ R; *reseruari* aH; *seruari* c; *seruare* DES. ¹⁹ aHR; *hec* c; *ergo* DES. ²⁰ aDEHR; *gigantem* cS. ²¹ aEHRS; *denique* c; *inde* (with *deinde* in margin) D. ²² acDHR; *hic* ES. ²³ aDHR; *gigans* c; *gigas* ES. ²⁴ acDERS; om. H. ²⁵ aDEHS; *exercis* c; *erectis* R. ²⁶ aHRS; *uinclis* cDE. ²⁷ aDERS; *adnectunt* c; *annectens* over an erasure H. ²⁸ aDEH; *Geomagog* c; *Geomemagog* R; *Gogmagog* S. ²⁹ acDERS (corrected from *Corieneum* in a); om. H. ³⁰ aR; *illisit* c; *lesit* DES; *allisit* H. ³¹ acDEHR; *fractus* (perhaps corrected to *fractis*) S. ³²...³² aHR; *uires renouat* c; *uires reuocat* DES. ³³ aDERS; *littore* H. ³⁴ aDERS; *proiecit* H. ³⁵ aDHS; *frustra* cER. ³⁶ aDEHR; *exspirauit* cS. ³⁷ acDERS; *commaculauit* H. ³⁸...³⁸ aH; *ex casu ipsius nomen* c; *ex casu illius nomen* DES; *nomen de casu illius* R.

casu illius[38] sortitus est usque in[39] presentem diem. Hinc Troes agros incipiunt colere, domos edificare ut in breui tempore terram diu inhabitatam[40] censeres. Postea Brutus de nomine suo insulam Britanniam[41] appellat, sociosque suos Britones.[42] Unde postmodum loquela gentis que prius Troiana nuncupabatur dicta [43]Britannica est.[43] Corineus quoque ad occidentem portionem[44] regni sortitus ab appellatione[45] nominis sui Corineiam[46] uocat; que nunc uel a cornu Britannie[47] quia ceu cornu ea pars terre [48]in mari producta est[48] uel per corruptionem[49] predicti nominis Cornubia appellatur.[50]

[22] Potitus tandem regno Brutus affectauit ciuitatem edificare. Ad quam edificandam[1] congruum querens locum peruenit ad Thamensem[2] fluuium locumque nactus est proposito suo perspicuum. Condidit itaque[3] ibidem ciuitatem eamque Nouam Troiam uocat;[4] que postmodum per corruptionem[5] uocabuli [6]Trinouantum dicta est.[6] Condita ergo ciuitate muniuit[7] eam ciuibus [8]iure uicturis[8] deditque legem qua pacifice tractarentur. Regnabant tunc in Troia filii Hectoris expulsis Antenoris reliquiis. Preerat in Iudea Heli[9] sacerdos et archa testamenti capta erat a Philisteis. Regnabat in Ytalia Siluius[10] Eneas, Enee[11] filius, auunculus Bruti, Latinorum tercius.[12]

[23] Cognouerat[1] autem Brutus Innogen uxorem suam et ex ea genuit tres[2] filios quorum nomina erant Locrinus, Albanactus,[3] Kamber. Mortuo autem Bruto .xxiiii. [4]anno aduentus sui[4] in Britanniam[5]

[39] acHR; *ad* DES. [40] acER (corrected from *inhabitam* in a); *habitatam* DS; *inhabitatam habitabilem* H. [41] acDERS; *Brittanniam* H. [42] cR; *Britannos* aDES; *Brittannos* H. [43...43] aHR (*Brittannica* in H); *est Britannica* cDES. [44] acDHRS; *porcionem* E. [45] acDHRS; *appellacione* E. [46] aDE; *Coreneam* c; *Corneam* H; *Coreneiam* R; *Corineam* S. [47] acDERS; *Brittannie* H. [48...48] acHR; *producta est in mari* DES. [49] acDHRS; *corrupcionem* E. [50] acDEHRS; after *appellatur*, *Explicit liber primus. Incipit secundus* (with *De edifi<atione> Lundoni<arum>* in margin) H.

§22 [1] acDHRS; *edificandum* E. [2] aDR; *Tamensem* c; *Thamense* EHS. [3] acDHRS; *corrupcionem* E. [6...6] acHR; *dicta est Trinouantum* DES. [7] acDEHRS (corrected from *muniit* in D). [8...8] aDHRS; *conuicturis* c; *iure curie uicturis* E. [9] RS; *Hely* acDEH. [10] acDERS; om. H. [11] acDERS; *Anchise* H. [12] cDR; *tertius* aEHS. After *tercius, Explicit liber .i.. Incipit liber .ii.* in a; *De diuisione Anglie et Wallie <et> Scotie* in H; and *Explicit liber primus. Incipit secundus* in R.

§23 [1] aDHRS; *Cognouit* c; *<C>ognouerat* E. [2] acDERS; *.iii.* H. [3] acDEHS; *Albancus* R. [4...4] acHR; *aduentus sui anno* DES. [5] acDERS; *Brittanniam* H.

17

sepelierunt eum filii sui infra urbem quam[6] condiderat et diuiserunt regnum Britannie[7] inter se et [8]habuit quisque[8] partem suam: Locrinus, qui et primogenitus, sortitus est eam partem que postea de nomine suo appellata[9] est Loegria;[10] Kamber autem partem illam que est[11] ultra Sabrinum flumen,[12] que nunc Gualia[13] dicitur, sed de nomine suo prius[14] Kambria[15] nomen retinuit[16] – unde adhuc gens illa[17] lingua[18] Britannica[19] sese Kambro[20] appellat; Albanactus iunior possedit partem[21] que de nomine suo Albania dicta est, sed nunc Scocia[22] appellatur.

[24] Illis deinde concordi pace inter se regnantibus[1] applicuit [2]Humber rex[2] Hunorum in Albaniam et commisso prelio cum Albanacto interfecit eum et magnam[3] gentis sue partem. Ceteri uero[4] ad Locrinum diffugerunt. Locrinus igitur[5] audito rumore indoluit ascitoque[6] fratre[7] Kambro cum magno exercitu perrexit uindicare fratrem suum. Rex autem Hunorum eis obuius fuit circa Humbrum fluuium et congressu facto compulsus est rex Hunorum cum suis fugam arripere quousque in flumen precipitatus est et nomen [8]suum flumini[8] reliquit.[9] Locrinus itaque et Kamber potiti uictoria naues hostium petunt, spolia diripiunt, et sociis largiuntur. Tres puellas ibidem[10] mire pulcritudinis inuenerunt, quarum una fuerat[11] filia regis Germanie quam predictus Humber cum ceteris rapuerat dum patriam uastaret. Erat nomen illius Estrildis et tante pulcritudinis fuit[12] quod [13]nulla ei[13] in pulcritudine comparari posset.[14] Amore itaque illius[15] captus Locrinus precepit eam sibi seruari ut in uxorem duceret. Quod[16] cum Corineo compertum esset, indignatus est quoniam Locrinus pactus ei antea fuerat sese filiam ipsius ducturum. Adiit ergo regem et bipennem in dextra[17] manu librans

6 acDEHS; *qua* R. 7 acDERS; *Brittannie* H. 8...8 cDERS; *quisque habuit* a; *accepit unusquisque* H. 9 acHR (corrected from *appella* in a); *dicta* DES. 10 acDHR; *Leogria* ES. .11 acDEHS; om. R. 12 acDHS; *fluuium* ER. 13 DHRS; *Guallia* a; *Wallia* c; *Guuallia* E. 14 acDERS; om. H. 15 aceEHRS; *Cambria* D. 16 cDEHS; *tempore longo retinuit* a; *tempore retinuit* R. 17 acDERS; om. H. 18 acDEHS; *ligua* R. 19 acDERS; *Brittannica* H. 20 aHR; *Kembre* c; *Cambra* D; *Kambra* ES. 21 aHR; *partem suam* cDES. 22 cER; *Scotia* aHS; *Scothia* D.

§24 1 acDERS; *uiuentibus* H. 2...2 acDERS; *rex Humber* H. 3 acHR; *maximam* DES. 4 acDERS; *autem* H. 5 acDEHR; *uero* S. 6 DHS; *accersitoque* a; *accitoque* c; *accito* E; *ac scitoque* R. 7 acDERS; *fratre suo* H. 8...8 aDEHS; *suum flumen* c; *sui fluuii* R. 9 acDEHR; *reliquid* S. 10 aceEHRS; *ibi* D. 11 aHR; *fuit* cDES. 12 acHR; *erat* DES. 13...13 aEHRS; *nulla* c; *ei nulla* D. 14 acDEHS; *posat* (for *poscat?*) R. 15 acHR; *ipsius* D; *eiusdem* ES. 16 acDHRS; *Et* E. 17 DERS; *dextera* aH; om. c.

taliter illum[18] allocutus est iratus:[19] 'Heccine[20] rependis michi, Locrine, ob tot uulnera[21] que in obsequio patris tui perpessus sum dum prelia cum ignotis [22]committeret gentibus:[22] ut filia mea postposita barbaram sibi[23] preponeres? Non inpune[24] feres dum uigor huic inerit dextre que tot gygantibus[25] causa mortis extitit.' Hoc[26] autem iterum iterumque replicans[27] librabat bipennem quasi percussurus, cum [28]utrorumque sese[28] interposuerunt amici. Sedato uero Corineo Locrinum[29] regem quod pepigerat exequi laudauerunt acsi coegissent. Duxit itaque Corinei filiam Locrinus nomine Guendoloenam; nec tamen[30] Estrildis[31] amoris[32] oblitus est sed facto intra[33] Urbem Trinouantum subterraneo[34] inclusit eam ac [35]seruandam familiaribus suis[35] tradidit ibique furtiuam uenerem agens .vii. annis eam frequentauit. Quocienscumque[36] igitur adibat illam, fingebat se uelle occulta libamina diis suis reddere.[37] Interea grauida facta est Estrildis ediditque filiam mire pulcritudinis quam uocauit Habren. Grauida etiam facta[38] est Guendoloena[39] genuitque[40] filium cui impositum est nomen Maddan.[41] Hic Corineo auo suo[42] traditus est nutriendus,[43] cuius doctrinam et mores executus est.

[25] Subsequente deinde tempore defuncto Corineo deseruit Locrinus[1] Guendoloenam[2] et Estrildem[3] in reginam sublimauit.[4] Indignata ergo[5] Guendoloena[6] secessit in partes Cornubie collectaque totius[7] patrie iuuentute cepit Locrinum[8] inquietare consertoque tandem[9] utrorumque[10] exercitu commiserunt[11] prelium iuxta flumen Sturam ibique Locrinus ictu sagitte occubuit. Mortuo itaque Locrino Guendoloena[12] suscepit regni gubernacula paterna furens[13] insania. Iubet deinde

18 acEHRS; *eum* D. 19 acDEHR; *aratur* (deleted) S. 20 acDEHR; *Eccine* S. 21 acDEHS; *wlnera* R. 22...22 acDEHS; *gentibus committeret* R. 23 aHR; om. cDES. 24 acEHRS; *impune* D. 25 DHR; *gigantibus* acES. 26 acDHS; *Hec* E; *Hunc* R. 27 acDERS; *repplicans* H. 28...28 aR; *inter utrumque* c; *utroque se* DES; *utrorum sese* H. 29 acDHRS; *Locr* E. 30 aHR; *tum* c; *tunc* DES. 31 acR; *Estrildidis* DES; *Estrilde* H. 32 acHR; *amorem* DES. 33 acHR; *infra* DES. 34 acDEHS; *subterrandre* (?) R. 35...35 aHR; *familiaribus suis seruandam* cDES. 36 aDERS; *Quociensque* c; *Quotienscumque* H. 37 aHR; *offerre* cDES. 38 acDEHR; om. S. 39 aDEHS; *Gwendolena* c; *Guendolena* R. 40 acDEHR; *genuit* S. 41 aDERS; *Madan* cH. 42 acDEHR; om. S. 43 DERS; *nutriendum* aH; *ad nutriendum* c.

§25 1 cDS; om. aHR; *Locr* E. 2 acHRS; *Guendol* DE. 3 cH; *Estrildam* aR; *Estrildidem* DES. 4 cDERS; *sullimauit* aH. 5 aDEHR; *igitur* c; *est* S. 6 aHR; *Gwendolena* c; *Guendol* DE; *Guendolis* S. 7 aDHRS; *tocius* cE. 8 acDHRS; *Locr* E. 9 acHR; om. DES. 10 acDERS; *utrinque* H. 11 acDERS; *comiserunt* H. 12 aH; *Gwendolena* c; *Guendol* DE; *Guendolena* R; *Guendolis* S. 13 acDEHR; *fruens* S.

Estrildem[14] et filiam eius precipitari in fluuium[15] Sabrine fecitque edictum ut flumen[16] nomine puelle uocaretur in posterum, tantum honoris tribuens pro eo quod eam genuerat Locrinus uir suus. Unde usque in hodiernum diem appellatum est flumen Sabrina a nomine [17]Habren puelle[17] per corruptionem.[18] Regnauit deinde Guendoloena .xv. annis, cum Locrinus[19] antea [20]secum .x.[20] regnasset annis;[21] et, cum uidisset Maddan[22] filium suum etate adultum, sceptro[23] regni insigniuit eum contenta regione Cornubie[24] dum uiueret. Tunc Samuel propheta regnabat in Iudea et [25]Siluius Eneas adhuc uiuebat et Homerus clarus habebatur.[25]

[26] Insignitus igitur[1] Maddan[2] uxore[3] [4]ex ea genuit[4] duos filios, Menbricium[5] et Malim,[6] regnumque[7] cum pace .xl. annis tenuit. Quo defuncto [8]discordia orta est[8] inter [9]predictos fratres[9] propter regnum quia uterque totum possidere uolebat. Menbricius[10] ergo Malim[11] fratrem suum in dolo simulata pace colloquio postulans inter proloquendum ipsum[12] interfecit solusque regni monarchiam adeptus in tantam tyrannidem[13] exarsit ut quemque fere nobilissimum interficeret. Sed et totam progeniem suam exosus [14]quemcumque suspectum in regni successione[14] habebat aut ui aut dolo perimebat. Relicta etiam propria coniuge ex qua inclitum iuuenem Eubraucum[15] genuerat sese sodomitico[16] operi – proth[17] nefas![18] – subdidit.[19] Tandem[20] .xx. regni

[14] cH; *Estrildam* aR; *Estrildidem* DES. [15] acHR; *flumen* DES. [16] acHR; om. DES. [17...17] acHR; *puelle Habren* DES. [18] aDHRS; *corrupcionem* cE. [19] aHRS; *Locrino autem* D; *Locr* E. [20...20] HR; *secum* (followed by an erasure?) a; *secum 20* c; *.x.* DES. [21] acDEHR; om. S. [22] aDERS; *Madan* cH. [23] acDEH; *sceptus* (sic) R; *susceptu* S. [24] cDERS; om. aH. [25...25] acDHRS; *Homerus clarus habebatur et Siluius Eneas adhuc uiuebat* E.

§26 [1] acHR; *ergo* DES. [2] aDERS; *Madan* cH. [3] aDERS; *regno duxit uxorem et* c; *duxit uxorem et* H. [4...4] acDHRS; *genuit ex ea* E. [5] aHR; *Menpricium* c; *Menpritium* DES. [6] DHR; *Maucium* c; *Malin* aES. [7] aHR; *et regnum* DES. [8...8] acHR; *orta est* DES. [9...9] acHR; *fratres predictos discordia* DS; *ipsos fratres discordia* (with *predictos* in margin) E. [10] aHR; *Mempricius* c; *Menpritius* D; *Menpricius* ES. [11] HR; *Mausium* c; *Malin* aDES. [12] acEHRS; *eum* D. [13] acDRS; *tirannidem* EH. [14...14] aHR (*sucessione* in a); *quemcumque in regni successione suspectum* c; *et quemquam quem in regni successione suspectum* DS; *cum quemquam quem in regni successione suspectum* E. [15] aDER; *Ebraucum* cH; *Eubrancum* S. [16] acDHRS; *sodomatico* E. [17] cR; *proh* aDEHS. [18] acDERS; *nephas* H. [19] acDEHS; *subdit* R. [20] acDEHS; *et tandem* R.

sui anno dum uenatum iret, a sociis auulsus in quandam conuallem a multitudine rabidosorum[21] luporum dilaceratus interiit. Tunc [22]Saul regnabat in Iudea[22] et Eristeus[23] in Lacedemonia.[24]

[27] Defuncto itaque Membricio[1] Eubraucus[2] filius suus,[3] uir magne stature et mire fortitudinis regimen[4] Britannie[5] suscepit et .lx.[6] annis rexit.[7] Hic primus post Brutum classem in partes Gallie direxit prouinciasque mari proximas cede uirorum et predacionibus[8] affecit ditatusque auri argentique[9] copia spoliisque diuersis in Britanniam[10] reuersus est. Deinde trans Humbrum condidit ciuitatem quam de nomine suo uocauit[11] Kaerebrauc[12] id est ciuitas[13] Ebrauci.[14] Edificauit et aliam ciuitatem Alclud[15] nomine uersus Albaniam et oppidum[16] Montis Agned[17] – quod nunc Castellum Puellarum dicitur – et [18]Montem Dolorosum.[18] Et tunc Dauid rex regnabat in Iudea et Siluius Latinus[19] in Ytalia[20] et[21] Gad, Nathan, et Asaph in Israel prophetabant. Genuit quoque .xx. filios ex .xx.[22] coniugibus necnon[23] et .xxx. filias. Erant autem nomina[24] filiorum eius:[25] Brutus Uiride Scutum, Margadud,[26] Sisillius,[27] Regin,[28] Moruid,[29] Bladud,[30] Iagon,[31] Bodloan, Kincar,[32] Spaden, Gaul, Dardan,[33] Eldad,[34] Iuor,[35] Cangu, Hector, Kerin, Rud, Assarach,[36] Buel. Nomina autem filiarum: Gloigin,[37] Innogin,[38] Otidas, Guenlian, Guardid,[39] Angarad,[40] Guenlodee, Tangustel,[41] Gor-

21 acDEH; *rabiosorum* R; *rabidorum* S. 22...22 cDERS; *regnabat in Iudea Saul* aH. 23 aH; *Eristenus* c; *Ericteus* DES; *exens* R. 24 acH; *Lacedemona* DES (*with sub quo militavit Hercules* added in margin of D); *Lacedoemonia* R.

§27 1 HR; *Menbritio* a; *Mepricio* c; *Mempritio* DE; *Menpricio* S. 2 aDE; *Ebraucus* c; *Ebrauchus* H; *Eubranius* R; *Eubrancus* S. 3 acEHRS; *eius* D. 4 acDHRS; *regnum* E. 5 acDERS; *Brittannie* H. 6 DEHR; *.xl.* aS; *30* c. 7 acDHR; *erexit* E; *e* [altered to *eam*] *rexit* S. 8 ER; *predationibus* acDHS. 9 cERS; *et argenti* aDH. 10 acDERS; *Brittanniam* H. 11 acDERS; om. H. 12 acDER; *Kaerebrauch* (with *appellauit* suprascript) H; *Kaerebranc* S. 13 aHR; *ciuitatem* cDES. 14 acEHR; *Eubrauci* D; *Ebranci* S. 15 acDR; *Alelud* EH; *Aldud* S. 16 aR; *opidum* cDEHS. 17 acDEHS; *Agneo* R. 18...18 acDERS; *Mons Dolorosus* H. 19 acDES; *Latinis* HR. 20 cDEHR; *Italia* aS. 21 acHR; om. DES. 22 aHR; *20* c; *.ix.* DES. 23 acHR; om. DES. 24 acDERS; om. H. 25 acDEH (with *nomina* suprascript in H); om. R; *suorum* S. 26 acDS; *Marcadud* E; *Margad* H; *Mardadiid* R. 27 acDEHR; *Sisilius* S. 28 acH; *Reghin* DES; *Regra* R. 29 aEHS; *Moriud* cD; *Monud* R. 30 aHR; *Balduc* c; *Blandiud* DES. 31 aS; *Lagon* cDEH; *Magon* R. 32 aHR; *Kyngar* c; *Kinear* DES. 33 acDEHS; *Bardan* R. 34 acDEHS; *Edad* R. 35 cHRS; *Inor* a; *Luor* DE. 36 acDEHR; *Assarac* S. 37 acDEHS; *Glorgin* R. 38 aHR; *Inogin* c; *Innogen* DES. 39 a; *Guaurdid* c; *Guanardid* DES; *Guardit* H; *Gamdid* R. 40 aH; *Agharad* c; *Angarat* DE; *Angaard* R; *Angarath* S. 41 aDEHS; *Tanguistil* c; *Tangustes* R.

21

gon, Medlan,[42] Methael,[43] Ourar,[44] Mailure,[45] Kambreda, Ragan,[46] Gad, Ecub,[47] Nest, Chein,[48] Stadud, Gladus,[49] Ebrein,[50] Blangan,[51] Abalac,[52] Angues,[53] Galaes[54] – omnium pulcerrima[55] –, Edra, Anor, Stadialis,[56] Egron.[57] Has omnes direxit pater[58] in Ytaliam[59] ad Siluium [60]Albam qui post Siluium[60] Latinum [61]regnabat. Fueruntque ibi maritate nobilibus Troianis quorum cubilia [62]et Latine et Sabine[62] diffugiebant.[61] At filii duce Assaraco fratre duxerunt[63] classem in Germaniam et[64] auxilio Siluii[65] Albe usi[66] subiugato populo adepti sunt regnum.

[28] Brutus autem [1]cognomento Uiride Scutum[1] cum patre remansit regnique[2] gubernacula post illum adeptus .xii.[3] annis regnauit. Huic[4] successit Leil filius suus, pacis amator et equitatis. Qui urbem constituit de nomine suo Kaerleil[5] in aquilonali[6] parte Britannie.[7] Uixit[8] Leil post [9]sumptum regnum[9] .xxv. annis sed [10]regnum in fine[10] tepide rexit. Quocirca ciuilis discordia [11]in regno orta est.[11]

[29] Post hunc regnauit filius suus Rudhudibras[1] .xxxix. annis. Iste[2] populum a[3] ciuili discidio in concordiam reuocauit condiditque Kaer-kein,[4] id est Cantuariam urbem,[5] et Kaergueint,[6] id est Guentoniam,[7] atque[8] oppidum[9] Montis Paladur,[10] quod nunc Sephtonia[11] dicitur. Ibi[12]

---

[42] acDERS; *Methlan* H. [43] acH; *Methabel* DES; *Meth Athel* R. [44] acHS; *Durar* DER. [45] aHR; *Ora Ylur* c; *Melure* DES. [46] acHR; *Ragau* DES. [47] aHR; *Eruli* c; *Echub* DES. [48] HR; *Chem* aE; *Cheim* c; *Kein* D; *Ehem* S. [49] acHR; *Gladius* DS; *Gladuis* E. [50] HR; *Ebrem* acDES. [51] aDEHR; *Rugan* c; *Blangam* S. [52] R; *Aballac* aDEHS; *Abalalc* c. [53] aHR; *Agnes* cDES. [54] acDES; *Galahes* H; *Banlaes* R. [55] R; *pulcherrima* acDEHS. [56] R; *Stadiald* a; *Stadralis* cDES; *Stahalt* H. [57] acR; *Edron* DES; *Egrom* H. [58] acHR; om. DES. [59] R; *Italiam* acDEHS. [60...60] acDERS (*Siluium* corrected from *Siluinum* in D); om. H. [61...61] cDERS; *regnabat* a; om. H. [62...62] R; om. aH; *Latine et Sabine* c; *Sabine et Latine* DES. [63] acDEHS; *dixerunt* R. [64] acDEHR; *in* S. [65] acDES; om. H; *Siluii* R. [66] acDEHR; *usi* altered to *ubi* in S.

§28 [1...1] acHR; *Uiride Scutum cognomento* DES. [2] acEHRS; *regni* D. [3] aDERS; *12* c; *.xxii.* H. [4] acDEHS; *Hic* R. [5] acDHRS; *Kairleil* E. [6] aDEHR; *aquilonari* c; *aquilonati* S. [7] acDERS; *Brittannia* H. [8] aH; *Uixit autem* c; *Uixit quoque* DES; *Uix* R. [9...9] acDEHS; *regnum sumptum* R. [10...10] acHR; *in fine regnum* DES. [11...11] aHR; *orta est* c; *orta est in regno* DES.

§29 [1] acEHRS; *Rudhudibras* (in text) with *Runhirwas* in margin D. [2] acEHRS; *Ipse* D. [3] acDEHS; om. R. [4] DHR; *Kaerkem* aES; *Kaerkeint* c. [5] aHR; *ciuitatem* cDES. [6] aHR; *Kaerweint* c; *Kaerguent* DE (with *Kaerwynt* suprscript in D); *Kaerguetus* (?) S. [7] aDEHRS (with *Wyntoniam* suprascript in D); *Wintoniam* c. [8] acHR; *et* DES. [9] aHR; *opidum* cDES. [10] acDEHR; *Paladure* S. [11] ER; *Scepthonia* a; *Sceptonia* c; *Scephtonia* D (in text: *Sceptesburch* in margin) & S; *Scehptonia* H. [12] acDHRS; *Ibique* E.

tunc, ut dicitur, aquila locuta est dum murus edificaretur.[13] Tunc Salomon cepit edificare templum Domini in Ierusalem[14] et Aggeus, [15]Amos, Ieu, et Ioel et Azarias[15] prophetabant.[16] Et[17] tunc Siluius Epit<us>[18] patri[19] Albe in Ytalia[20] successit.

[30] Successit deinde Bladud filius Rudhudibre rexitque[1] regnum pacifice .xx. annis. Hic edificauit urbem Kaerbadum[2] que nunc Bada[3] nuncupatur; fecitque ibidem[4] calida balnea ad usus mortalium, quibus[5] prefecit numen Minerue. In cuius ede[6] inextinguibiles posuit ignes qui numquam deficiunt in fauillas. Sed ex quo tabescere incipiunt in saxeos globos feruentes uertuntur. Quod per nigromantiam[7] artem addidicit[8] facere: adeo[9] ingeniosus fuit. Multa[10] et[11] alia prestigia fecit et ad ultimum ceu Dedalus alis sibi factis per aera uolare presumpsit. Unde summo[12] infortunio lapsus cecidit super templum Appollinis[13] infra Urbem Trinouantum menbrisque[14] confractis[15] miserabiliter[16] expirauit.[17]

[31] Quo defuncto Leir filius eiusdem in regem erigitur qui .lx.[1] annis [2]uiriliter regnum[2] rexit. Edificauit[3] autem[4] super flumen[5] Soram[6]

---

[13] aHR; *fabricaretur* cDES. After *fabricaretur*, *Tunc Capis filius Epiti Ytalia regnabat* added (from the vulgate text) in margin of D. [14] acDERS; *Hierusalem* H. After *Ierusalem*, *et regina Saba uenit audire sapientiam eius* added (from vulgate text, §28) in margin of D. [15...15] DES; *et Amos et Ieu et Iohel et Azarias* a; *et Amos et Ieu et Ioel et Zacarias* c; *et Amos et Abbacuc et Iohel et Zacharias* H; *et Amos, Ieu, [...] Ioel, Azarias* R. [16] acDEHS; *prophetauit* (with *-abant* suprascript) R. [17] acDEHS; *tunc* deleted before *Et* in R. [18] my correction; *Epiti* aR; *Egipti* c; *Egypti* DES (with *Epytus* suprascript in D); *Epyti filius* H. [19] acDEHS; *patris* R. [20] DR; *Italia* aEHS; *Ytaliam* c.

§30 [1] acDEH; *rexque* R; *rexit* S. [2] acHR; *Kaerbaelum* DES (with *Kayrbadum* in margin of D). [3] aDERS; *Bado* c; *Bathonia* H. [4] acHR; *ibi* DES. [5] acDEHS; om. R. [6] acDERS; *sede* H. [7] DHR; *nigromanticam* a; *nigromantiam* altered to *nigromanticam* cS; *nigromanciam* E. [8] cDERS; *didicit* a; *addidit* H. [9] acEHRS; *adeo enim* D. [10] acDERS; *Multa quidem* H. [11] aEHRS; om. c; *etiam* D. [12] acDERS; *supremo* H. [13] cERS; *Apollinis* aDH. [14] HR; *membrisque* acDES. [15] aHR; *fractis* cDES. [16] acHR; *mirabiliter* DES. [17] acDEHR; *exspirauit* S. After *expirauit*, *Tunc propheta orauit ne plueret super terram annos .iii. et menses sex* added from vulgate text (in modified form) in margin of D.

§31 [1] aDEH; *60* c; *.xl.* RS. [2...2] aR; *regnum uiriliter* cDEHS. [3] acDERS; *et edificauit* H. [4] acDERS; om. H. [5] acHR; *fluuium* DES. [6] aDERS; *coram* c; *Suram* H.

ciuitatem de nomine eius dictam Kaerleir; Saxonice uero Leirchestra[7] nuncupatur. Huic nate sunt tres[8] filie denegata masculini sexus prole: nomina earum Goronilla,[9] Regau,[10] Cordeilla.[11] Pater eas paterno amore[12] sed magis iuniorem[13] Cordeillam[14] diligebat. Cumque in senectutem[15] uergere cepisset, cogitauit regnum suum ipsis diuidere et cum parte regni maritis copulare. Sed ut sciret que illarum parte regni pociore[16] dignior esset, interrogationibus[17] suis singulas temptauit, scilicet que magis illum diligeret.[18] Interroganti igitur Goronilla[19] maior natu numina celi testata est ipsum se magis diligere quam uitam suam. Cui pater: 'Quoniam senectutem meam uite tue preposuisti, te karissimam[20] filiam[21] maritabo iuueni quemcumque elegeris in regno meo cum tertia parte regni.' Deinde Regau[22] secunda exemplo sororis sue beniuolenciam[23] patris captans iureiurando respondit[24] [25]se super[25] [26]omnes creaturas[26] eum[27] diligere. Credulus ergo pater eadem[28] dignitate qua[29] primogenitam cum tertia[30] parte regni maritare spopondit.[31] At Cordeilla [32]iunior cum intellexisset[32] sororum[33] adulacionibus[34] acquieuisse,[35] temptare cupiens patrem respondit: 'Est uspiam, pater mi, filia que patrem suum plusquam patrem presumat diligere? Nempe ego [36]semper dilexi te sicut[36] patrem et adhuc a proposito non desisto; et si ex[37] me amplius[38] extorquere uis, audi [39]amoris certitudinem[39] quem tecum habeo et interrogationibus[40] tuis finem inpone.[41] Etenim quantum[42] habes tantum[43] uales tantumque te diligo.' Porro pater [44]iratus eam[44] ex iracundia aut derisione [45]taliter responsum dedisse[45] indignans stomachando ait: 'Quoniam sic patris senectutem spreuisti

---

[7] aR; *Leicestre* c; *Leircestra* DH; *Leircestria* E; *Leicestra* S. [8] aDERS; *3* c; *.iii.* H. [9] ES; *Gonorilla* aDH; *Gorenilla* c; *Gorozilla* R. [10] aHR; *Ragau* cDES. [11] acDEHR; *Cordeuilla* S. [12] acHR; *amore amauit* DES. [13] aDES; om. c; *minorem* HR. [14] acDEHR; *Cordeuillam* S. [15] acHRS; *senectute* DE. [16] cEHRS; *potiore* aD. [17] acDHRS; *interrogacionibus* E. [18] acHR; *diligebat* DES. [19] ERS; *Gonorilla* aDH; *Gorenilla* c. [20] acDERS; *carissimam* H. [21] acHR; *filiam meam* DES. [22] aHR; *Ragau* DES. [23] cERS; *beniuolentiam* aDH. [24] acDERS; *re iurando* deleted before *respondit* in H. [25...25] acDEHS; *super se* R. [26...26] acHR; *creaturas omnes* DES. [27] acDHRS; om. E. [28] acDEHRS (corrected from *eandem* in S). [29] acEHRS; *qua et* D. [30] aDERS; *3* c; *.iii.* H. [31] acHS; *spospondit* DER. [32...32] acDHS; *cum intellexisset iunior* E; *minor cum intellexisset* R. [33] acDERS; *sorores* H. [34] ER; *adulationibus* acDHS. [35] acERS; *adquieuisse* DH. [36...36] R; *semper te dilexi ut* acH; *te semper dilexi ut* DES. [37] aHR; *a* cDES. [38] acDHRS; om. E. [39...39] acDERS; *amorem certitudinis* H. [40] acDHRS; *interrogacionibus* E. [41] HR; *impone* acDS; *pone* E. [42] cDERS; *tantum* aH. [43] cDERS; *quantum* aH. [44...44] aR; *iratus* c; *iratus putans* DES; *ratus eam* H. [45...45] acHR; *tale dedisse responsum* DES.

ut uel eo amore quo me sorores tue diligunt dedignata es respondere, ego [46]dedignabor te in tantum ut[46] in regno meo cum sororibus tuis[47] partem non habebis.[48] Quippe cum te plusquam ceteras hucusque dilexerim, tu me minus quam cetere diligere fateris.' Nec mora consilio[49] procerum suorum predictas puellas dedit unam duci Cornubie et alteram regi Albanie. Quibus post decessum[50] suum totam regni monarchiam concessit. Contigit interea quod Aganippus rex Francorum uxore carens audita fama pulcritudinis Cordeille nuncios[51] dirigit regi[52] Britonum[53] ut illam sibi coniugio copularet. Pater autem [54]nondum filie responsionibus[54] oblitus ait se eam sibi[55] daturum,[56] sed sine dote: duabus etenim prioribus regnum suum diuiserat. Quod cum Aganippo regi[57] intimatum[58] fuisset,[59] amore uirginis inflammatus[60] remisit iterum ad regem dicens[61] se satis auri et argenti et terre possidere neque[62] dote alia indigere nisi tantummodo[63] puelle nobilis[64] coniugio de qua sibi postmodum heredes procrearet. Confirmato igitur nuptiali[65] federe mittitur Cordeilla ad regem Aganippum et ei in uxorem coniungitur. Post multum uero temporis ut Leir rex senio[66] affectus[67] torpere cepit, insurrexerunt in eum[68] duces quibus filias priores[69] locauerat et abstulerunt ei regnum et regiam potestatem. Concordia tamen[70] inter eos habita rex Albanie Maglaunus[71] alter generorum illum secum retinuit cum .xl.[72] militibus ne inglorius[73] esset propter [74]filiam eius coniugem suam.[74] Moram itaque [75]apud eum illo[75] faciente indignata aliquanto[76] filia sua Goronilla ob multitudinem[77] militum secum commorancium,[78] quia ministris eiusdem[79] conuiciabantur,[80] maritum suum affata iussit[81] patrem suum contentum esse debere

[46...46] aR; *in tantum te dedignabor ut* c; *dedignabor in tantum te ut* DES; *dedignabor te in tantum quod* H. [47] acDHRS; *tui* E. [48] acDEHRS; after *habebis, arum* [?] *largitione* added in margin of D. [49] acDHS; *concilio* E; *consilium* R. [50] acDEHS; *discessum* R. [51] cDERS; *nuntios* aH. [52] aHR; *ad regem* cDES. [53] acDERS; *Brittonum* H. [54...54] aHR; *filie responsionum nondum* c; *filie responsionibus nondum* DES. [55] aHR; om. cDES. [56] aDHRS; *daturum sibi* c; *daturam* E. [57] aHR; om. cDES. [58] cDEHR; *nunciatum* aS. [59] aHR; *esset* cDES. [60] acDEHR; bis in S. [61] acDEHRS (corrected from *ducens* in S). [62] aDEHR; *nec* cS. [63] acHR; om. DES. [64] acDES; om. HR. [65] aDHRS; *nupciali* cE. [66] cDERS; *senio corpore* a; *senio corporis* H. [67] acDEHS; *confectus* R. [68] DERS; *illum* acH. [69] aHR; *predictas* cDES. [70] acHR; *autem* DES. [71] acDES; *Maglaunius* H; *Maglauuus* R. [72] aHR; *40* c; *.lx.* DS; *sexaginta* E. [73] acDERS; *ingloriosus* H. [74...74] R; *filiam suam coniugem eius* cDS; *filiam eius uxorem suam* aH; *suam coniugem* E. [75...75] aHR (*aput* in H); *apud illum eo* cDES. [76] cDHRS; *aliquando* aE. [77] acDEHR; *multitudineque* S. [78] ERS; *commorantium* aDH; *commanencium* c. [79] acDERS; *eius* H. [80] acDERS; *conuitiabantur* H. [81] acDEHS; *misit* (?) R.

obsequio .xxx.[82] militum. Indignatus ille relicto Maglauno[83] secessit ad Henninum[84] ducem Cornubie, sponsum alterius filie. Apud[85] quem moratus, infra annum orta est discordia inter utrorumque famulos; unde iussus est a filia pater senex [86]familiam totam[86] deserere preter .v.[87] qui ei obsequio[88] satis essent. Porro pater ultra quam dici potest tunc [89]anxius et tristis[89] reuersus est iterum ad primogenitam[90] sperans mutato animo se cum tota familia honorifice uelle retinere. At illa per numina celi iurauit quod nullatenus secum commaneret nisi [91]relictis omnibus solo[91] milite contentus esset. Paruit ille tristis et cum solo milite illi adhesit. Recordatus subinde honoris pristini et dignitatis amisse detestando miseriam ad quam redactus erat cogitare cepit quod iuniorem filiam[92] expeteret. Estimans[93] eam pietate posse moueri[94] paterna transfretauit ad Gallias et in transfretando hec apud se [95]cogitando memorabat:[95] 'O irreuocabilia[96] seria fatorum, quo solito cursu fixum iter tenditis? Cur, inquam, me ad instabilem felicitatem promouere[97] uoluistis,[98] cum maior pena sit [99]ipsam amissam[99] recolere quam sequentis infelicitatis presentia urgeri? O irata[100] fortuna! O[101] Cordeilla[102] filia, quam uera sunt dicta illa que questionibus meis sapienter respondisti: ut quantum haberem tantum ualerem tantumque me diligeres! Dum igitur habui quod dare[103] possem, uisus fui ualere hiis[104] qui non michi sed[105] donis meis applaudebant. Interim dilexerunt me, sed[106] abeuntibus[107] [108]muneribus et ipsi abierunt. Sed[109] qua fronte tamen, filia mea karissima, tuam audebo faciem uidere uel me ipsum tibi presentare qui quasi uilem et abiectam te deterius[110] et sine dote quam sorores tuas inter extraneos locare curaui?' Dum ergo hec et hiis[111] similia in mente uolueret, applicuerunt in Gallias et uenit Karitiam[112] ubi [113]filia sua erat.[113] Cum autem ueniret ad urbem ubi ipsa

---

[82] DHRS; *triginta* aE; *30* c. [83] acDERS; *Maglaunio* H. [84] DERS (with *Henuinum* in margin of D); *Henuinum* aH; *Hennium* c. [85] acDERS; *Aput* H. [86...86] aHR; *totam familiam* cDES. [87] aDHRS; *quinque* c; *quinque milites* E. [88] cDERS; *in obsequio* aH. [89...89] acDEHS; *tristis et anxius* R. [90] acDEHS; *primogenitum* R. [91...91] acDEHS; *solo relictis omnibus* R. [92] acDERS; *filiam suam* H. [93] acHR; *estimansque* DES. [94] ac-DEHR; *pietate* underpointed before *moueri* in S. [95...95] aR; *memorabat dicens* DES; *cogitans memorabat* H. [96] acDERS; *inreuocabilia* H. [97] acDEHS; *promouere me* R. [98] cDERS (corrected from *uoluisti* in S); *uoluisti* aH. [99...99] acHRS; *ipsa amissa* DE. [100] acHR; *irrita* DES. [101] acDEHR; om. S. [102] acDERS; *Chordeilla* H. [103] acDEHR; *non* underpointed after *dare* in S. [104] cDERS; *his* aH. [105] acDHRS; *set* E. [106] acDHRS; *set* E. [107] cDERS; *abientibus* aH. [108...108] acDHRS; bis with *uacat* in margin E. [109] acDHRS; *Set* E. [110] acDEHS; *decernis* R. [111] DERS; *his* aH. [112] a; om. c; *Karmam* (with *Kariciam* in margin) D; *Karinam* E; *Kariciam* H; *Karina* R; *Karniam* S. [113...113] aDERS (with *filia* omitted from E); *filia sua carissima erat* c; *erat filia sua* H.

tunc manebat, erubuit ingredi ad eam[114] solus in paupere ueste retinensque pedem per nuncium[115] qui solus armiger sibi adherebat indicauit eius aduentum, hystoriam[116] miserie sue pandens. Manifestato itaque patris infortunio contrita[117] est corde et[118] fleuit amare celerique [119]consilio usa[119] tradidit clam nuncio[120] qui hec sibi indicauerat[121] auri argentique copiam, precipiens ut ad aliam ciuitatem patrem[122] deduceret ibique[123] se[124] infirmum fingeret ac balneis[108] et [125]optimis cibis[125] indulgeret et foueret uestibusque melioribus ornaret. [126]Iussit quoque[126] ut .xl.[127] milites pariter[128] secum retineret et tunc demum regi[129] Aganippo uiro suo aduentum suum et causam aduentus per internuncios[130] manifestaret. Quo facto atque completo secundum regine preceptum[131] post paucos dies notificato regi eius aduentu ueniunt ad eum rex et regina magna stipati militum caterua atque honorifice illum susceperunt. Dederuntque ei potestatem in toto regno suo donec in [132]pristinam dignitatem[132] illum[133] restituissent. Interea collecto grandi [134]per totam Galliam exercitu[134] Cordeilla cum patre in Britanniam[135] transiit commissoque prelio cum generis[136] triumpho potitus est [137]atque dominium tocius regni adeptus.[137] Tribus[138] annis post imperauit genti Britonum[139] restituens quemque[140] potestati[141] sue. Defuncto autem eo in senectute bona suscepit Cordeilla regni gubernacula sepeliuitque patrem[142] in quodam subterraneo[143] supra fluuium Sora[144] infra[145] Leirchestriam.[146] Erat autem subterraneum illud in honore bifrontis Iani dedicatum ubi gens[147] ydolatrie[148] data totius[149] anni opera in sollempnitate eiusdem dei auspicabantur.[150]

---

114 acEHRS; *ipsam* D. 115 acDERS; *nuntium* H. 116 acERS; *historiam* DH. 117 acDERS; *contristata* H. 118 cER; *ac* aDHS. 119...119 acDERS; *usa consilio* H. 120 acDERS; *nuntio* H. 121 acDEHR; *nuntiauerat* S. 122 acDEHS; *de parte* (?) R. 123 acDEHS; om. R. 124 acDEHS; *sese* R. 125...125 acDEHS; *aliis cibis optimis* R. 126...126 acDERS; *Iussitque* H. 127 aHR; *40* c; *.lx.* DES. 128 aHR; om. cDES. 129 acHR; om. DES. 130 DER; *internuntios* acHS. 131 aHR; *uoluntatem* cDES. 132...132 acEHRS; *pristinum statum* D. 133 DERS; *ipsum* acH. 134...134 acDERS; *exercitu per totam Galliam* H. 135 cDERS; *Brittanniam* aH. 136 cDERS; *generibus* aH. 137...137 R; *atque totius* [*tocius* c; corrected from *toti* in H] *regni dominium adeptus* [*adeptus est* c] acH; *ac dominium totius* [*tocius* E] *regni adeptus est* DES. 138 DERS; *tribusque* acH. 139 acDERS; *Brittonum* H 140 aH; *quecunque* c; *unumquemque* DES; *queque* R. 141 acDHRS; *dignitati* E. 142 acDERS; *patrem suum* H. 143 acDEHS; *subterreineo* R. 144 aHR; *Soram* cDES (with *sub fluuio Sora* in margin of D). 145 acDEHS; *inter* R. 146 R; *Leirchestram* a; *Leicestriam* c; *Leicestram* D; *Leircestriam* EH; *Laucestram* S. 147 acEHRS; *gentes* D. 148 aDR; *ydolatre* c; *idolatrie* EHS. 149 acDHRS; *tocius* E 150 acDHR (corrected from *auspiscabantur* in c); *auspitabantur* ES.

[32] Mortuo quoque[1] Aganippo rege Cordeilla regnum Britannie[2] per quinquennium in [3]pace bona[3] rexit donec a filiis sororum suarum inquietata, Margano[4] uidelicet et Cunedagio[5] – hiis[6] enim nominibus insigniti erant – post [7]multa prelia commissa[7] ad ultimum deuicta ab eis et capta miserias[8] carceris sortita est; ubi ob amissionem regni dolore obducta sese interemit. Exinde[9] partiti sunt [10]iuuenes regnum[10] et pars illa[11] que est trans Humbrum[12] cessit Margano;[13] alia uero pars regni que uergit ad occasum submittitur Cunedagio.[14] Emenso deinde biennio accesserunt quibus regni turbatio[15] placebat ad Marganum[16] animumque illius[17] pulsabant, dicentes dedecus et iniustum fore, cum primogenitus esset, totius[18] regni dominium non habere. Cumque sic a[19] peruersis hominibus incitatus[20] esset, duxit exercitum per prouincias [21]Cunedagii ferroque[21] et incendio uastare cepit. Orta igitur[22] [23]inter fratres discordia[23] obuius uenit [24]Morgano Cunedagius[24] cum maxima[25] exercitus multitudine factoque congressu cedes [26]inmensa utrimque[26] facta est et Marganus[27] in fugam uertitur. Quem secutus Cunedagius[28] fugientem a[29] prouincia in prouinciam tandem intercepit eum in pago Kambrie et eo interfecto de nomine suo illi pago usque in[30] hodiernum diem nomen dedit.[31] Potitus itaque uictoria Cunedagius[32] monarchiam tocius[33] regni adeptus .xxxiii. annis gloriose rexit. Tunc Ysaias[34] et Osee[35] prophetabant et[36] Roma condita est a geminis fratribus Remo et Romulo .xi. kalendis Maii.[37]

§32 [1] acDEHR; *quippe* S. [2] acDERS; *Brittannie* H. [3...3] aHR; *bona pace* cDES. [4] aHR; *Morgano* c; *Morgauno* (with *Maglauni et Goronille filio* suprascript) D; *Margauno* ES. [5] DERS (with *filio Henuini et Ragau* suprascript in D); *Conedagio* acH. [6] cDERS; *his* aH. [7...7] R; *multis preliis commissis* acDEHS. [8] acDEHS; *miseriis* R. [9] cDERS; *Exin* aH. [10...10] cDERS; *regnum iuuenes* aH. [11] aHR; *ea* cDES. [12] acDEHRS; after *Humbrum, uersus Katenesiam* (from the vulgate text) in margin of D. [13] aHR; *Morgano* c; *Margauno* DS; *Marganno* E. [14] DERS; *Conedagio* acH. [15] acDHRS; *turbacio* E. [16] aDHR; *Morganum* c; *Margaunum* ES. [17] acHR; *ipsius* DES. [18] aDHRS; *tocius* cE. [19] acDEHR; om. S. [20] acHR; *excitatus* DES. [21...21] acDERS; *partemque Conedagii ferro* H. [22] aDHRS; *autem* c; *ergo* E. [23...23] acDEHS; *discordia inter fratres* R. [24...24] cR; *Margano Conedagius* aH; *Margauno Cunedagius* DES. [25] acDEH; *magna* RS. [26...26] cS; *utrimque inmensa* a; *immensa utrimque* D; *inmensa utrinque* E; *utrinque inmensa* H; *immensa utrumque* R. [27] aHR; *Morganus* c; *Margaunus* DES. [28] acDERS; *Conedagius* H. [29] acDEHS; *de* R. [30] acDEHR; om. S. [31] acDEHRS; after *dedit, et est Glamorgantia* (?) added in margin of D. [32] acDERS; *Conedagius* H. [33] cER; *totius* aDHS. [34] aERS; *Ysayas* cH; *Isaias* D. [35] acHR; *Iosue* DES (with *Osee* in margin of D). [36] acDHRS; *Item* E. [37] acDERS; *May* H.

[33] Postremo defuncto Cunedagio[1] successit ei Riuallo[2] filius eius, iuuenis fortissimus et prudens, qui regnum cum diligencia[3] gubernauit. In tempore eius cecidit pluuia sanguinea per tres[4] dies et muscarum affluencia[5] homines moriebantur. Riuallo[6] successit Gurgustius[7] filius eius: cui Sisillius; [8]cui Iago[8] Gurgustii nepos; cui Kinmarcus[9] Sisillii[10] filius;[11] cui Gorbodiago.[12] Huic nati sunt duo[13] filii, Ferreus[14] et Porrex, inter quos orta est contencio[15] regni, uiuente adhuc patre sed uergente in senium. At Porrex regni cupiditate accensus fratrem suum dolo interficere parat. Quod cum illi compertum fuisset,[16] uitatis insidiis transfretauit in Gallias ususque auxilio Suardi[17] regis Francorum reuersus est et cum fratre dimicauit. Pugnantibus autem illis [18]interfectus est Ferreus[18] et omnes sui. Porro mater eorum nomine [19]Indon de[19] morte filii commota quia arcius[20] eum diligebat in odium et iram aduersus uictorem fratrem[21] incitata est. Nacta ergo tempus uindicandi filium aggreditur sompno oppressum cum ancillis suis et in plurimas sectiones[22] dilacerauit.[23] Exinde ciuilis discordia multo tempore populum afflixit[24] et regnum quinque[25] regibus submissum[26] est qui sese mutuis cladibus infestabant.

[34] Succedente[1] tempore surrexit[2] quidam iuuenis [3]Dumwallo Molmucius[3] nomine, filius Clotenis ducis Cornubie, specie et audacia omnes reges Britannie[4] excellens. Qui ut patris hereditatem suscepisset, [5]surrexit in Pinnerem[6] regem Loegrie[5] et facto congressu interfecit eum. Deinde conuenerunt Rudaucus rex Kambrie atque Staterius rex

§33 [1] acDERS; *Conedagio* H. [2] HR; *Riwallo* aDES; *Kadwallo* c. [3] cER; *diligentia* aDHS. [4] acDERS; *.iii.* H. [5] cER; *afflucentia* aDHS. [6] HR; *Riwallo* aS; *Kadwallo* c; *Riuuall* DE. [7] aDERS; *Gurgucius* c; *Gurgustus* H. [8]...[8] acES; *cui Yago* D; *cui Iago* (?) H; *Cunago* R. [9] aHR; *Kunarocus* c; *Kimarcus* DS; *Kimmartus* E. [10] acDHRS; *Sisilli* E. [11] acDEHRS (with *nepos* in margin of D). [12] acEHRS; *Gorbodugo* D. [13] acDERS; *.ii.* H. [14] acDEHR; *Ferrex* S. [15] ER; *contentio* acDHS. [16] acDEHS; *esset* R. [17] acR; *Suhardi* DEHS (altered from *Suardi* in E). [18]...[18] aHR; *Ferreus interfectus est* cDES. [19]...[19] aE; *Iudon de* c; *Ydon de* D; *Inden de* H; *Uidon de* R; *Iudondri* S. [20] R; *artius* aES; *arctius* cDH. [21] acDERS; *fratrem suum* H. [22] acDERS; *seditiones* H. [23] cDERS; *dilacerant* aH. [24] acDEHS; *affluxit* R. [25] R; *.v.* aDEHS; *4* c. [26] acEHR; *summissum* DS.

§34 [1] acEHRS; *Succedente ergo* D. [2] acDEHR; *surexit* S. [3]...[3] R; *Dunwallo Molinucius* a; *Dumwallo Molinticius* c; *Dunwallo Molmutius* DES; *Dunuuallo Molmitius* H. [4] acDERS; *Brittannie* H. [5]...[5] cDERS; *in Pinnerem regem Loegrie insurrexit* aH. [6] ERS; *Pumerem* c; *Pynnerem* D.

Albanie confirmatoque [7]inter se federe[7] duxerunt[8] exercitus suos in terram Dumwallonis[9] omnia depopulantes. Quibus uenit obuius Dumwallo[10] cum .xxx. milibus uirorum [11]et prelium[11] commisit. Ut autem multum diei[12] pugnatum est et adhuc uictoria staret utrisque in ambiguo, [13]seuocauit Dumwallo ad se[13] sexcentos[14] audacissimos iuuenes et armis interemptorum[15] armauit eos. Ipse quoque proiectis illis quibus armatus erat similiter fecit. [16]Deinde duxit eos in cateruas hostium quasi[17] ex ipsis essent.[16] Nactus ergo locum quo[18] Rudaucus et Staterius erant, commilitonibus indixit[19] ut in ipsos irruerent et fortiter ferirent. Facto itaque impetu perimuntur [20]predicti duo[20] reges et plures alii cum illis. At Dumwallo[21] timens ne a suis opprimeretur proiectis hostium armis et suis resumptis ad suos reuertitur et ruens acriter in hostium cateruas uictoria potitus est fugatis partim cesisque partim hostibus terraque omnis siluit in conspectu eius. Cumque[22] totam Britanniam[23] dominio suo subiugasset, fecit sibi dyadema[24] ex auro et regnum in pristinum statum reduxit. Hic leges que Molmuntine[25] dicuntur inter Britones[26] statuit que[27] usque ad hoc tempus inter Anglos celebrantur. Statuit quoque inter cetera[28] ut templa deorum et ciuitates tali dignitate[29] pollerent ut quicumque fugitiuus siue reus ad ea confugeret, liber ab omni impedimento[30] et securus abiret [31]et ad propria rediret.[31] Decretum est etiam ut in itinere templi et ciuitatis et fori necnon[32] et culture aratri eadem lex haberetur. Cessabant ergo in diebus eius[33] latronum mucrones et raptorum rapine nec erat usquam qui uiolentiam alicui inferret.[34] Hac pace et quiete cum .xl. annis regnum administrasset, diem clausit ultimum in Urbe Trinouantum et prope templum Concordie sepultus est,[35] quod ipse ad confirmacionem[36] legum construxerat.[37]

[7...7] acERS (bis, with first occurrence deleted in R); om. aH. [8] acDEHS; *dux dixerunt* R. [9] cR; *Dunwallonis* aDE; *Dunuuallonis* H; *Dunuallonis* S. [10] cR; *Dunwallo* aDE; *Dunuuallo* HS. [11...11] aDHRS; *preliumque* cE. [12] acDHRS; *die* E. [13...13] R; *seuocauit Dunwallo* a; *uocauit Dumwallo ad se* c; *seuocauit ad se Dunwallo* DES; *seuocauit Dunuuallo ad se* H. [14] R; *scecentos* a; *600* c; *.dc. uiros* DES. [15] acDEHS; *interemptos* R. [16...16] acDHRS; om. E. [17] acDHS; om. E; *quas* R. [18] aDERS; *in quo* c; *ubi* H. [19] aR; *ait* c; *dixit* DEHS. [20...20] aR; *duo predicti* cDS; *duo* E; *.ii. predicti* H. [21] cDR; *Dunwallo* aES; *Dunuuallo* H. [22] acDERS; *Cunque* H. [23] acDERS; *Brittanniam* H. [24] cDR; *diadema* aEHS (corrected from *deadema* in a). [25] cDES; *Molmirtine* (?) a; *Molmitine* H; *Molumitine* R. [26] cDERS; *Brittones* aH. [27] acDEHS; *qui* R. [28] acDEHRS; after *cetera, ut beatus Gildas commemmorat* added in margin of D. [29] acDEHS; *honore* R. [30] acDERS; *inpedimento* H. [31...31] acEHRS; om. D. [32] acDEHS; om. R. [33] acHR; *illius* DES. [34] acDEHRS (corrected from *inferrent* in S). [35] DEHS; om. acR. [36] ER; *confirmationem* acDHS. [37] acDEHRS: after *construxerat, Explicit liber .ii.. Incipit .iii.* aH; and *Explicit liber secundus. Incipit liber .iii.* R.

[35] Dumwalloni[1] successerunt filii [2]eius duo[2] Belinus et Brennius.[3] Qui cum de regno inter se contenderent, censuerunt proceres terre regnum hac ratione diuidendum ut Belinus in parte sua Loegriam et Kambriam necnon et Cornubiam possideret. Erat enim primogenitus poscebatque[4] Troiana consuetudo ut hereditatis dignior pars ei proueniret. Brennius uero minor[5] Nordhamhumbriam[6] ab Humbro usque Cathenesiam[7] obtineret[8] et fratri subderetur. Confirmato igitur[9] super hiis[10] federe rexerunt terram cum pace et iusticia per quinquennium. Interea surrexerunt adulatores quidam, mendacii fabricatores, Brennium adeuntes et sic affantes: 'Utquid te [11]occupat ignauia[11] qua fratri Belino subiciaris, cum idem pater et mater [12]eademque generis nobilitas[12] te ei parificet? Adde quod in[13] milicia[14] preuales tociens[15] expertus uires tuas in duce Morianorum Cheulfo[16] terra marique Albanorum prouinciam uastante; cui resistere et de[17] regno[18] fugare potuisti. Rumpe ergo fedus[19] quod tibi dedecori[20] est et contra generositatem tuam fecisti et fac consilio procerum tuorum ut ducas filiam Elfingii regis Norgueguensium[21] et ipsius[22] auxilio dignitatem amissam recuperes.' Ut igitur[23] hiis[24] et aliis animum iuuenis corruperunt,[25] acquieuit[26] consiliis[27] eorum et transiens in Noruegiam[28] duxit regis filiam.

[36] Quod cum fratri nunciatum esset, indignatus quod sine sui licentia se[1] inconsulto id egisset adiit cum exercitu Nordamhumbriam[2] occupauitque conprouincialium ciuitates et municiones[3] et custodibus suis tradidit custodiendas. Porro Brennius peracto negotio[4] cum uxore et

§35 [1] c; *Dunwalloni* aDS; *<D>unwalloni* E; *Dunuuallo* H; *Dumwallo* R. [2...2] aR; *eius* cDES; *eius .ii.* H. [3] acDEHS; *Briennius* R. [4] cDEHS; *possebatque* a; *possedebatque* R. [5] aHR; *iunior* cDES. [6] DH; *Nordanhunbriam* a; *Nordanhumbriam* c; *Nordamhimbriam* ES; *Nordarihumbriam* R. [7] R; *Catanesiam* aH; *Catenesiam* c; *ad Catinesiam* DES. [8] aR; *possideret* cDES; *optineret* H. [9] acDEHR; *itaque* S. [10] cDRS; *his* aH; *hoc* E. [11...11] aHR; *ignauia occupat* cDES. [12...12] R; *eadem generis nobilitas ac;* *eademque gentis nobilitas* DES; *eadem generis nobilitate* H. [13] acDERS; om. H. [14] cEHRS (corrected from *malicia* in R); *militia* aD. [15] ER; *totiens* acDHS. [16] acDE; *Cheulpho* H; *Theulfo* RS. [17] cR; *e* aDEHS. [18] acEHRS; *regione* D. [19] acEHRS; *moras* deleted before *fedus* in D. [20] acDERS; *dedecus* H. [21] R; *Norguensium* aH; *Norweigensium* c; *Norguegensium* DS; *Norguegencium* E. [22] acDERH; *iupius (?)* S. [23] acDERS; om. H. [24] cDERS; *his* aH. [25] aDEHS; *corrumperunt* c; *corripuerunt* R. [26] cDERS; *adquieuit* aH. [27] aHR; *consilio* cDES. [28] ER; *Norguegiam* aDH; *Norwegiam* cS.

§36 [1] aDERS; *seque* c; *et se* H. [2] cDERS; *Nordanhunbriam* a; *Nordanhumbriam* H. [3] ERS; *munitiones* acDH. [4] acDHRS; *negocio* E.

magnis copiis Norguegensium[5] parato nauigio redit Britanniam.[6] Rumor enim innotuerat[7] de fratre quia urbes et municiones[8] suas armato milite inuaserat; cumque iam in altum equora sulcaret, Gudlacus[9] rex Dacorum[10] ex insidiis prosiliens inuasit classem et dimicans cum Brennio cepit forte nauem in qua puella fuerat illatisque uncis[11] illam[12] intra[13] consocias[14] naues attraxit. [15]Ardebat enim eius amore[15] et duxisset eam uxorem nisi Brennius prepedisset. Interea ruunt ex aduerso uenti factoque turbine nauigium dissipant et in diuersa litora compellunt. Rex autem Dacorum [16]ui tempestatis[16] actus quinque[17] dierum cursu rabie uentorum pulsus [18]applicuit cum puella[18] in Britanniam[19] nesciens quam esset nactus patriam. Captus itaque[20] a pagensibus ductus est ad Belinum regem, qui et ipse super maritima fratris aduentum prestolabatur. Erant autem cum naue Gudlaci[21] tres[22] alie naues quarum una fuerat[23] ex Brennii nauigio lapsa; quorum hominum relatu rei causa et infortunium patuit[24] Belino.[25] Captus igitur [26]rex Gudlacus[26] cum puella et ceteris qui[27] in nauibus erant custodie mancipatur.[28]

[37] Emensis deinde aliquot[1] diebus ecce Brennius resociatis nauibus in Albaniam applicuit. Qui cum audisset et uxoris retencionem[2] et regni [3]sui occupationem,[3] misit nuncios[4] fratri ut sponsa[5] et regnum [6]restituerentur sibi;[6] [7]sin autem[7] testatus est celi numina se totam Britanniam[8] a

[5] DERS; *Norguengensium* a; *Norwegiensium* c; *Norguensium* H. [6] cDERS; *Brittanniam* aH. [7] acDEHS; *innouerat* R. [8] ERS; *munitiones* acDH. [9] acDER; *Guthlacus* H; *Gudlachus* S. [10] acDERS; *Dachorum* H. [11] acDEHS; om. (but with space left) R. [12] acDEHS; *illamque* R. [13] acEHRS (*intra* before *illam* in c); *inter* D. [14] aDEHR; *ad socias* c; *consorcias* S. [15...15] acDERS; *Amore enim eius ardebat* H. [16...16] acDES (*tempestatis* corrected from *tempestatiis* in S); *in tempestate* H; *in tempestatis* R. [17] R; *.v.* aDEHS; *4* c. [18...18] acHR; *cum puella applicuit* DES. [19] cDERS; *Brittanniam* aH. [20] cDERS; *enim* aH. [21] acDERS; *Guthlaci* H. [22] acDERS; *.iii.* H. [23] cDERS; *fuit* aH. [24] acEHRS; *patuit* [with *tuit* extended into margin] *tum* (?: over an erasure) D. [25] acDERS; *Bellino* H. [26...26] aR; *Gudlacus rex* cDES; *rex Guthlacus* H. [27] acDEHS; *que* R. [28] aR; *mancipantur* cDEHS.

§37 [1] acDEHS; *aliquos* R. [2] ERS; *retentionem* aH; *retentioni* c; *re/retentionem* D. [3...3] aHR; *occupationem* cD; *occupacionem* ES. [4] cDERS; *nuntios* aH. [5] aH; *uxor* cDES; *sponsa sponsi* R. [6...6] cDERS; *restituerentur* a; *sibi restitueretur* H. [7...7] acHR; *si non* DES. [8] cDERS; *Brittanniam* aH.

mari usque ad mare ferro et igne uastaturum. Audiens ergo Belinus negauit[9] plane quod petebat collectoque omni exercitu[10] uenit [11]obuiam fratri[11] pugnaturus. Brennius quoque fidens in Norguegensibus[12] suis et exercitu undecumque[13] collecto occurrit illi obuiam[14] in nemore quod uocatur Calaterium,[15] ubi congredientes magnam cedem[16] utrimque[17] fecerunt. Postremo preualentibus Britonibus[18] diffugiunt[19] Norguegenses[20] [21]uulnerati ad naues,[21] Belino[22] insequente et [23]stragem magnam[23] patrante. Ceciderunt[24] in illo conflictu .xv. milia hominum nec ex residuis mille superfuerunt[25] qui illesi abscederent. At Brennius uix unam nauim nactus, ut fortuna dedit,[26] Gallicana litora[27] petiuit; [28]ceteri quoque quo casus eos[29] ducebat fuga delituerunt.[28]

[38] Cum igitur [1]Belino uictoria[1] cessisset, conuocauit regni proceres infra Eboracum consilio illorum[2] tractaturus quid de rege Dacorum[3] faceret. Mandauerat namque[4] illi ex carcere quod sese regnumque Dacie[5] sibi submitteret [6]tributumque singulis annis daret,[6] si liber cum amica sua[7] sineretur abire, pactumque [8]hoc federe iuramenti[8] et obsidibus datis firmaret. Audita igitur huiuscemodi pactione consilio et assensu baronum[9] rex Dacorum e[10] carcere solutus liber cum suis abire permittitur atque in Daciam sospes rediit.

[39] Rex itaque Belinus[1] tocius[2] Britannie[3] dominio potitus leges quas

[9] aHR; *negabat* cDES. [10] acHR; *exercitu suo* DES. [11...11] cDERS (with *patri* underpointed before *fratri* in R); *fratri obuiam* aH. [12] DERS; *Norguensibus* aH; *Norwegiensibus* c. [13] acDERS; *undecunque* H. [14] acDERS; om. H. [15] acHR; *Calaterinum* DES (with *Kalaterium* in margin of D). [16] acDEHS; *cena* underpointed before *cedem* in R. [17] acDRS; *utrinque* EH. [18] cDERS; *Brittonibus* aH. [19] aHR; *diffugerunt* cDES. [20] DERS; *Norguenses* aH; *Norweigenses* c. [21...21] acHR; *ad naues uulnerati* DES. [22] acDERS; *Bellino* H. [23...23] acR; *magnam stragem* DES; *stragem maximam* H. [24] acDERS; *et ceciderunt* H. [25] acDHS; *fuerunt* underpointed before *superfuerunt* in E; *fuerunt super* R. [26] acDERS; *dederat* H. [27] DERS; *littora* acH. [28...28] cDERS; om. aH. [29] R; om. cDES (& aH).

§38 [1...1] aHR; *uictoria Belino* cDES. [2] DERS; *eorum* acH. [3] cD; *Daco* aEHR; *Dac* S. [4] acDERS; *nanque* H. [5] cHRS; *Datie* aDE. [6...6] acDEHS; om. R. [7] aHR; om. cDES. [8...8] aR (*hic* in R); *fidei iuramenti* c; *hoc fidei iuramento* DES; *iuramento* H. [9] acDERS; *baronum suorum* H. [10] acDEHS; *de* R.

§39 [1] acDERS; *Bellinus* H. [2] cEHR; *totius* aDS. [3] cDERS; *Brittannie* aH.

pater adinuenerat[4] confirmauit, addens quoque[5] ut strata uiarum[6] que ducebant ad ciuitates ex cemento et lapidibus fabricarentur[7] – que scilicet a Cornubiensi mari usque ad Catinensium[8] litus in[9] introitu Albanie, id est ab australi plaga in septemtrionem,[10] protenderentur.[11] Iussit etiam[12] aliam[13] fieri [14]in latitudinem[14] regni[15] a Meneuia[16] urbe que super Demeticum mare sita est usque ad Portum Hamonis, id est ab oriente in occidentem, ut ducatum preberet[17] ad urbes[18] infra positas. Alias quoque duas[19] [20]ex obliquo terre uias[20] construere precepit[21] ut utroque latere accessus ad urbes et municipia paterent. Erat enim terra lutosa et aquosa, utpote insula intra mare sita; nec ante Dunwallonem[22] patrem Belini[23] extiterat quisquam qui uiarum aut pontium curam haberet in toto regno. Deinde sanciuit[24] eas Belinus omni honore omnique[25] dignitate iurisque sui esse precepit ita ut de illata super eas uiolencia[26] supplicium sumeretur. Siquis autem [27]scire desiderat[27] omnia que de ipsis[28] statuerit,[29] legat[30] Molmuntinas[31] leges, quas Gyldas[32] hystoriografus[33] de Britannico[34] in Latinum,[35] rex uero Aluredus de Latino in Anglicum transtulit,[36] et reperiet[37] luculenter scripta que optat.

[40] Belino autem regnum cum pace et tranquillitate regente frater eius Brennius [1]in Gallias, ut predictum est,[1] appulsus principes regni[2] .xii. tantum militibus commitatus[3] adiit casum suum singulis ostendens

---

[4] aDEHS; *aduenerat* with *in* added suprascript c; *inuenerat* R. [5] aDEHRS; after *quoque, quia de uiis que ad ciuitates ducebant orta est dissensio* added from the vulgate text (in modified form) in margin of D. [6] DERS; om. aH. [7] aHR; *fierent* DES. [8] aR; *Cathenesium* c; *Catinesium* DES; *Katinensium* H. [9] acDEHS; om. R. [10] aDERS; *septemptrionem* c; *septentrionem* H. [11] a; *procederetur* c; *protenderetur* DEH; *procederentur* R; *protenderet* S. [12] acDEHR; *et* S. [13] acHR; *alia* DES. [14]...[14] acHR; *a latitudine* DES. [15] acHR; *regni id est* DES. [16] acDEHR; *menia* S. [17] acHR; *preberent* DES. [18] acDEHS; *urbes et municipia* R. [19] acDERS; *.ii.* H. [20]...[20] aHR; *uias ex obliquo terre* cDES. [21] acDHRS; *cepit* (with *pre−* suprascript) E. [22] aS; *Dunwallum* c; *Dunwall* DE; *Dunuuallum* H; *Dumwallum* R. [23] acDERS; *Bellini* H. [24] aEHRS; *sanxciuit* c; *sanxiuit* D. [25] acDEHR; *omni* S. [26] ERS; *uiolentia* aDH; *iniuria* c. [27]...[27] aHR; *desiderat scire* cDES. [28] aHR; *eis* cDES. [29] aHR; *preceperat* c; *preceperit* DES. [30] acDEHR; om. S. [31] DES; *Molinutinas* a; *Molmontinas* c; *Molmitinas* H; *Molitunas* R. [32] HR; *Gildas* acDES. [33] R; *hystoriographus* aS; *historigraphus* c; *historiographus* DH; *hystorigraphus* E. [34] acDERS; *Brittanno* H. [35] acHRS; *Latinum* (with *transtulit* in margin) D; *Latinum transtulit* E. [36] acDEHR; *transtulit* (with *legat* added suprascript) S. [37] cDERS; *repperiet* aH.

§40 [1]...[1] acHR (*dictum* in c); *ut dictum est in Gallias* DES. [2] cDERS; om. aH. [3] cERS; *comitatus* aDH.

atque [4]auxilium ab eis petens[4] quo honorem amissum recuperare queat. Uenit tandem ad Seginum[5] [6]Allobrogum ducem[6] a quo gratanter susceptus, tum[7] quia nobili prosapia ortus, tum[8] quia curialiter erat edoctus, per temporis spacium[9] retentus est. Erat enim pulcher aspectu, uenatu et aucupatu omnibus precellens. Cum igitur[10] in amiciciam[11] et familiaritatem ducis incidisset, statuit dux consilio suorum fidelium unicam filiam quam habebat [12]sibi copulare,[12] cum ducatu Allobrogum si masculino careret[13] herede. Nec mora desponsatur ei puella principesque terre ei subduntur. Et uix annus[14] emensus erat; supprema[15] die adueniente mortuus est dux.[16] Brennius itaque principatu potitus[17] quos prius [18]amicicia[19] et obsequiis[18] illexerat largicionibus[20] donorum accumulat.[21]

[41] Procedente ergo[1] tempore [2]collecto per omnem Galliam[2] exercitu in Britanniam[3] profectus est; congregato in Neustriam ab omni litore[4] nauigio inde[5] secundis uelis in Britanniam[6] applicuit. Diuulgato autem eius[7] aduentu Belinus[8] armatorum stipatus caterua prelium cum illo[9] commissurus obuius uenit. Sed[10] cum hinc inde cohortes se ad bellum pararent,[11] mater amborum ducum[12] Tonwenna[13] nomine adhuc uiuens se mediam aciebus interserit[14] per dispositas incedens turmas. Estuabat enim filium uidere quem multo tempore non uiderat. Ut igitur[15] tremulis gressibus ad locum quo ipse erat peruenit, brachia materna collo filii innectit, optata carpens oscula, nudatisque[16] uberibus illum in hunc modum affata est, sermonem [17]impediente singultu:[17] 'Memento,

4...4 acH; *auxilium petens ab eis* DES; *ab eis auxilium petens* R. 5 aH; *Segetium* c; *Siginum* DES; *Segnium* R. 6...6 aDEHS; *ducem Allobrogum* c; *Allobrogum aut* (?) R. 7 aDERS; *est tum* c; *tam* H. 8 cDERS; *tu* a; *tam* H. 9 acDER; *spatium* HS. 10 aHR; *ergo* cDES. 11 cER; *amicitiam* aDHS. 12...12 aR; *ei copulare* cDES; om. (with *ei dare* in margin) H. 13 acDEHS; *carent* R. 14 acDEHS; *annis* R. 15 acEHS; *suprema* D; *subprema* R. 16 aEHS; *dux Sigumus* c; *Siginus* D; *dux Segnius* R. 17 cDERS; *potito* aH. 18...18 acEHRS; *obsequiis et amicicia* D. 19 cERS; *amicitia* aH. 20 ERS; *largitionibus* acDH. 21 acDEHRS; after *accumulat*, *et quod Allobroges pro maximo habebant profusus erat in dandis cibis, nulli ianuam suam prohibens* added from vulgate text in margin of D.

§41 1 aDEHRS; *itaque* c. 2...2 aHR; *per totam Galliam collecto* cDES. 3 cDERS; *Brittanniam* aH. 4 DERS; *littore* acH. 5 acDEHR; *in* S. 6 cDERS; *Brittanniam* aH. 7 acDHR; om. ES. 8 acDHR; *Bel* ES. 9 acEHRS; *eo* D. 10 acDHRS; *Set* E. 11 aDEHS; *parent* modified to *pararent* by suprascript *ar* c; *parent* R. 12 aDEHS; om. c; *ducorum* R. 13 aDES; *Conwenna* c; *Tonuuenna* H; *Conwennia* R. 14 acDERS; *interserat* H. 15 acDEHS; *ergo* R. 16 acDEHR; *nudatis* S. 17...17 acDES; *inpediente singultu* H; *singultu impediente* R.

fili, memento uberum istorum[18] que suxisti maternique uteri unde[19] te rerum opifex in hominem cum non esses creauit. Anxietatum[20] igitur[21] quas pro te pertuli reminiscens peticioni[22] mee acquiesce[23] atque inceptam iram compesce. [24]Nam quod[24] dicis te a nacione[25] tua per fratrem tuum expulsum, si[26] rei ueritatem consideres, tu ipse te expulisti non ille, sicut nosti, quando regem Norguegensium[27] eo inconsulto ut fratrem grauares adisti. Denique fugiens ad summum honoris culmen prouectus es. Plus profecisti in fuga quam si stares in patria. Subditus namque illi partem regni que tibi contigerat possidebas et adhuc, si uoluisses, habere potuisses. Quam ut dimisisti, par sibi[28] aut maior factus es regnum Allobrogum adeptus. Quid igitur fecit nisi quod [29]ex paupere te[29] in sublimem[30] [31]erexit ducem?[31] Adde quod gentem barbaram super eum[32] adduxisti qui[33] te et illum[34] forsitan regno priuassent si partes uestras[35] debiliores aspexissent.'[36] Brennius igitur super [37]matris lamentationibus[37] motus sedato animo acquieuit[38] et deposita galea secum ad fratrem perrexit. Belinus[39] quoque pacifico uultu abiectis armis [40]obuiam ei[40] uenit et in amplexus cum osculo pacis se inuicem brachiis fraternis innexuerunt. [41]Nec mora amici [42]facti sunt[42] et Urbem Trinouantum pariter[43] ingressi sunt. Ibique consilio capto communem exercitum parant et cum magno nauigio [44]ad Gallias simul[44] transfretauerunt.[41]

[42] Quod cum per naciones[1] diuulgatum fuisset,[2] conuenerunt omnes reguli Francorum in unum exercitum contra eos ut bellando [3]eos ui[3] de terra sua eicerent. At Belino[4] et Brennio uictoria fauente fractis cateruis atque diffusis[5] Franci fugam arripiunt. Fugientes ergo Francos Bri-

[18] acDERS; om. H. [19] acDEHR; *in quo* S. [20] acEHRS; *Anxietates* D. [21] DERS; om. aH; *ergo* c. [22] DEHR; *petitioni* acS. [23] ER; *adquiesce* acDHS. [24]...[24] aDEHR; *Namque* c; *Nam que* S. [25] ER; *natione* acDHS. [26] acDERS; om. H. [27] DERS; *Norguensium* aH; *Norwegiensium* c. [28] aHR; *ei* cDS; om. E. [29]...[29] aHR; *te ex paupere* cDES. [30] acDHR; *sullimem* ES. [31]...[31] acDEHRS (with the vulgate reading *promouit regem* in the margin of D). [32] acDERS; *illum* H. [33] acDERS; *que* H. [34] HR; *ipsum* acDES. [35] acDERS; *nostras* H. [36] cDERS; *inuenissent* aH. [37]...[37] aHR; *lamentationibus matris* cS; *lamentacionibus matris* DE. [38] cR; *adquieuit* aDEHS. [39] acDERS; *Bellinus* H. [40]...[40] aDERS; *obuius* c; *ei obuiam* H. [41]...[41] cDERS; om. aH. [42]...[42] DES; om. cR (& aH). [43] DES; om. cR (& aH). [44]...[44] cR; om. aH; *simul ad Gallias* DES.

§42 [1] cER; *nationes* aDHS. [2] acHR; *esset* DES. [3]...[3] cDES; *eos* aH; *in eos* R. [4] acDHR; *Bel* ES. [5] acDHRS; *difusis* E.

tones[6] et Allobroges insecuntur,[7] cedunt, interimunt et quosdam capiunt; captos[8] compedibus et manicis ferreis tradunt, [9]ipsos quoque[9] regulos dedicioni[10] coegerunt urbibusque euersis et municionibus[11] captis totum Gallie regnum[12] infra annum submiserunt.

[43] Postremo petentes Romam Ytaliam[1] ferro et igne depopulantur.[2] Erant tunc temporis Rome duo[3] consules creati Gabius et Porsenna; qui cum nullam fiduciam resistendi super gentem suam haberent, assensu et consilio senatorum concordiam et amiciciam[4] petentes auri et argenti [5]copia plurimisque diuersis donariis[5] largiendo quod petebant impetrauerunt,[6] singulis annis tributum de Ytalia[7] et censu[8] Romanorum paciscentes.[9] Acceptis itaque obsidibus et [10]federe firmato[10] in Germaniam[11] duxerunt[12] exercitum ad bellandos[13] eiusdem terre populos. Exeuntibus autem illis de Romanorum finibus terrore sullato[14] piguit Romanos[15] prefati federis et resumpta audacia a tergo [16]eos oppugnare ceperunt. Germanis itaque a fronte resistentibus et Ytalis[17] a tergo[16] infestantibus terror inuasit Britones et Allobroges. In tanta tamen[18] anxietate positi festino utuntur consilio fratres ut Belinus scilicet [19]cum Britonibus suis oppugnare Germanos insisteret, Brennius uero cum suis Romam rediret et[19] rupti federis iniuriam in Romanos uindicaret. Reuerso ergo[20] Brennio in Ytaliam[21] Romani, qui ad [22]Germanos auxiliandos[22] exercitum Allobrogum et Britonum per notas uias preterierant, Romam redire ceperunt et Brennium precedere festinabant. Belinus autem precognito per exploratores eorum transitu Alpium itinera occupat uallemque nactus qua[23] hostes futura nocte transituri erant infra illam cum suis delituit omnem strepitum suorum[24]

---

6 acDERS; *Brittones* H. 7 cERS; *insequuntur* aH; *insequntur* D. 8 acERS; *captosque* DH. 9...9 acDERS; *ipsosque* H. 10 ER; *deditioni* acDHS. 11 ERS; *munitionibus* acDH. 12 acDEHS; *regnum sibi* R.

§43 1 DRS; *Italiam* acEH. 2 R; *depopulant* acDEHS. 3 acDERS; *.ii.* H. 4 cDERS; *amicitiam* aH. 5...5 cHR (*plurimisque et* in R); *copiam plurimaque diuersa donaria* aDE; *copiam plurima diuersa donaria* S. 6 acDERS; *inpetrauerunt* H. 7 cDERS; *Italia* aH. 8 cR; *censum* aH; *de censu* DES. 9 cDERS; *pasciscentes* aH. 10...10 DERS; *firmato federe* aH; *federe confirmato* c. 11 acDHRS (corrected from *Germanniam* in S); *Germanniam* E. 12 cRS; *direxerunt* aDEH. 13 aR; *debellandos* cH; *debellandum* D; *bellandum* ES. 14 R; *sublato* acDEHS. 15 acDEHS; *Romanis* R. 16...16 cDERS; om. aH. 17 DR; om. aH; *Italis* cES. 18 aDERS; *autem* c; *tum* H. 19...19 cDERS; om. a; *Germaniam subiuugaret et Brennius* H. 20 acDEHR; *igitur* S. 21 cDHRS; *Italiam* aE. 22...22 acDEHS; *auxiliandos Germanos* R. 23 acDEHS; *quam* R. 24 acDEHS; *eorum* R.

compescens. Uenientes itaque Ytali[25] ad eundem locum nil tale uerentes[26] insidias Belini compererunt.[27] Et cum uallem[28] [29]armis hostium fulgere ad lune radios[29] cernerent, stupefacti in fugam uersi[30] sunt. Quos gradu propero[31] insequens Belinus [32]stragem non modicam[32] illucescente[33] aurora incepit Ytalis[34] inferre. Nec cessauit gladius eius a mane usque ad uesperam Romanos cedere donec nox superueniens eorum impetum compescuit[35] atque diremit. Prostratis itaque Romanis atque dispersis flectit iter post Brennium atque Romam petit. Ut igitur communem exercitum simul fecerunt, Romam undique obsidione cinxerunt;[36] inuadentes muros machinis ad terram prosternunt et [37]Romanis immensum terrorem[37] inferunt. Romani ergo [38]econtra uiriliter[38] resistentes a muris propulsabant fundibulis[39] et balistis eorum ferocem audaciam et lapidibus immensis[40] muros infestantes obruebant. Quod cum duces ambo [41]Brennius et Belinus[41] aspexissent,[42] indolue-runt de strage suorum[43] et accensi ira obsides, quos a Romanis susceperant .xxiiii.[44] ex nobilioribus, patibulis ante portas affixerunt. At Romani proteruiores propter contumeliam filiorum et nepotum effecti freti legatione[45] consulum, [46]Gabii scilicet[46] et Porsenne, qui ut congre-garent exercitum de Apulia[47] et Ytalia[48] precesserant, eadem die qua illos[49] adesse nouerunt eis in auxilium statutis agminibus urbem egrediuntur et cominus[50] cum ducibus congrediuntur. Hinc Gabius et Porsenna, hinc Romani hostes inparatos[51] occupare temptant. Porro[52] fratres ambo[53] cum cladem commilitonum[54] tam subito illatam inspexis-sent, conuocato exercitu in turmas et centurias[55] suos[56] resociauerunt et

[25] DS; *Itali* acEHR. [26] cDERS; *timentes* aH. [27] aDERS; *comperierunt* c; *conpererunt* H. [28] acDERS; *conuallem* H. [29...29] aHR; *hostium armis fulgere ad lune radios* c; *hostium armis ad lune radios fulgere* DES. [30] acDEHS; *reuersi* R. [31] DERS; *prospero* acH. [32...32] acDEHS; *non modicam stragem* R. [33] DS; *illuscescente* acH; *illucessente* E; *illuscente* R. [34] DR; *Italis* acEHS. [35] acDERS; *conpescuit* H. [36] acHR; *cinxerunt et* DES. [37...37] acHR (*inmensum* in cH); *inmensum terrorem Romanis* DES. [38...38] cH; *contra uiriliter* a; *uiriliter econtra* DES; *econtra* R. [39] cDES; *fundibalis* a; *fradibulis* H; *fundabilis* R. [40] acDERS; *inmensis* H. [41...41] aHR; om. c; *Belinus et Brennius* DES. [42] aceEHS (over an erasure in a); *inspexissent* D; *asspexissent* R. [43] aDEHS; om. c; *eorum* R. [44] aHR; *et .xxiiii.* c; *scilicet .xxiiii.* DES. [45] acDES; *legacione* H; *legacionem* R. [46...46] ERS; *Gabii* aDH; *scilicet* (with *Gabii* in margin) c. [47] acDRS; *Apulea* E; *Appulia* H. [48] cDRS; *Italia* aEH. [49] DERS; *illum* aH; *eos* c. [50] aHRS; *comminus* cDE. [51] ER; *imparatos* acDS; *inperatores* H. [52] acDHRS; <*P*>orro E. [53] acHR; om. DES. [54] acDEHS; *suorum commilitonum* R. [55] cDERS; *centuriones* aH. [56] acDEHR; *suas* S.

irrupcionem[57] in hostes audacter facientes retrocedere coegerunt. Postremo innumerabilibus utrimque[58] cesis uictoria [59]cessit fratribus.[59] Interempto namque in certamine Gabio et Porsenna capto[60] urbem uictores subintrant, diuersi generis opibus ditati.[61]

[44] Capta itaque, sicut[1] dictum est, Roma Belinus in Britanniam[2] reuersus est. Brennius uero in Ytalia[3] remansit populum [4]inaudita tyrannide premens.[4] Cuius uitam et actus textus Romane hystorie[5] declarat. Belino autem in Britanniam[6] reuerso renouare cepit urbes ueteres ubicumque[7] collapse fuerant et quasdam nouas edificare ubi prius non fuerant. Inter quas condidit unam super Uscham[8] flumen prope Sabrinum mare que Kaerusch[9] appellata metropolis Demecie[10] facta est; que[11] postea a Romanis Urbs Legionum dicta est pro eo quod [12]in eadem legiones Romanorum[12] hyemare[13] solebant. Fecit etiam in Urbe Trinouantum portam mire fabrice super ripam Thamensis fluuii quam[14] postea Saxones Angli Belnesgata[15] appellauerunt. Desuper uero portam [16]edificauit turrim[16] mire magnitudinis portumque subtus nauibus ydoneum.[17] Leges quoque paternas in regno renouauit[18] et firmas teneri precepit constanti iusticie[19] indulgens. In diebus eius tanta copia terram refecit quantam[20] nec retro ulla etas habuisse meminit, nec subsequens subsecuta[21] fuit. Cum ergo summa tranquillitate rexisset populum, ultimum clausit diem in Urbe Trinouantum. Cuius corpus combustum in aureo cado repositum in summitate turris quam fecerat decenter [22]collocatum est.[22]

---

[57] ER; *irruptionem* acDHS. [58] acDRS; *utrinque* EH. [59...59] acDERS; *fratribus prouenit* H. [60] acDHRS; bis in E. [61] cDERS; *impletam* a; *refertam* H.

§44 [1] acDEHR; *sicud* S. [2] cDERS; *Brittanniam* aH. [3] cDRS; *Italia* aEH. [4...4] aHR (*tirannide* in aH); *premens inaudita tirannide* c; *inaudita premens tyrannide* [*tirannide* E] DES. [5] cDR; *historie* aEHS. [6] cDERS; *Brittanniam* aH. [7] acDEHR; *ubi* S. [8] DERS; *Huscham* aH; *Oscham* c. [9] aDERS; *Kaeroysk* c; *Kaeruch* with supscript *s* H. [10] cR; *Demetie* aDEHS. [11] acDEHS; *quo* R. [12...12] aHR; *legiones Romanorum in ea* cDES. [13] cDR; *hiemare* aHS; *yemare* E. [14] acDEHS; *qua* R. [15] HS; *Belinesgata* a; *Belinesgade* c; *Belnesgate* DE; *Belnesgato* R. [16...16] aHR; *turrim edificauit* cDES. [17] cDR; *idoneum* aEHS. [18] acDERS; *reuocauit* H. [19] DER (preceded by underpointed *ind* in R); *iustitie* acHS. [20] acDEHS; *quantum* R. [21] acEHRS; *consecuta* D. [22...22] acDES; *collatum est* H; *est collocatum* R.

[45] Successit ei filius eius[1] Gurguint[2] Barthruc[3] nomine, uir modestus et prudens, qui[4] per omnia patris actus imitans pacem et iusticiam amauit. Interea contigit[5] Dacos non reddere tributum quod diebus patris et pacti sunt reddere et sibi[6] persoluebant. Quod grauiter ferens transiuit[7] cum magna classe[8] in Daciam.[9] Afflictoque durissimis[10] preliis populo regem Dacorum interfecit et regnum pristino iugo subdidit.[11]

[46] Ea tempestate cum dispositis omnibus pro uoluntate sua domum per insulas Orcadum[1] rediret, inuenit ibi .xxx. naues uiris et mulieribus plenas. Causam ergo[2] aduentus eorum querens, accessit ad illum[3] dux classis eiusdem Partholoum[4] nomine et [5]adorato eo[5] ueniam rogauit et pacem. Qua impetrata[6] dixit[7] se ex partibus[8] Hyspaniarum[9] expulsum et maria circuire ut locum mansionis inueniret. Petiit ergo ut porciunculam[10] Britannie[11] ad inhabitandum[12] prestaret ne odiosum iter maris diucius[13] pererraret; quod[14] iam per annum unum et dimidium fecerat. Quo audito[15] rex [16]haut peticioni eius[16] defuit[17] et ad inhabitandam non Britanniam[18] sed Hyberniam[19] eis[20] [21]indulsit insulam,[21] que intacta adhuc hominum accessu fuerat, ductoresque eis de suis tradidit qui eos illuc usque dirigerent. Ubi cum uenissent,[22] inuenerunt terram opimam[23] et apricam[24] nemoribus ac fluminibus riuisque[25] et omni Dei munere opulentam; [26]ceperuntque continuo[26] ibi tabernacula sua edifi-

§45 [1] acDHR (eius suprascript in R); om. E; suus (over an erasure?) S. [2] cDEHR; Gurguient (with the i suprascript) a; Gurgiunt S. [3] DS; Barhtruc a; Barbedruc c; Bartruch E; Bartrue H; Barchruch R. [4] acDEHS; que R. [5] acDEHS; contingit R. [6] DERS; sibi etiam aH; om. c. [7] acHR; transiit DES. [8] acDEHS; classa R. [9] acDHRS; Datiam E. [10] cR; dirissimis aDEHS (altered from durissimis in D). [11] acHR; restituit DES.

§46 [1] cDERS; Orchadum aH. [2] acHR; modo DE (with uero in margin in D); uero S. [3] aHR; eum cDES. [4] ERS; Partholoim a; Partholomi c; Partholoita D; Parcholoun H. [5...5] acDEHR; adoratis [?] eum S. [6] acDERS; inpetrata H. [7] acHR; dicit DES. [8] acDERS; parte H. [9] cDRS; Hispaniarum aEH. [10] ER; portiunculam acDHS. [11] cDERS; Brittannie aH. [12] acDEHS; hinhabitandum R. [13] cERS; diutius aDH. [14] acDHRS; quia E. [15] acDEHRS; after audito, eos ex Hyspania uenisse et Basclenses uocatos esse didicisset added from vulgate text (in modified form) in margin of D. [16...16] aDEHS; petitioni eius haut c; hanc peticionem eius R. [17] acDEHR; non suprascript before defuit in S. [18] cDERS; Brittanniam aH. [19] cERS; Hiberniam aDH. [20] acDEHS; om. R. [21...21] aHR (insulam corrected from insultam in R); insulam indulsit cDES (idulsit in c). [22] acHR; uenirent DES. [23] cDEHS; optimam aR. [24] acDERS; apris eam H. [25] aHR; om. cDES. [26...26] acDHRS; ceperunt continuoque E.

care et terram colere creueruntque et multiplicati sunt ibidem usque in hodiernum diem. Gurguint[27] uero rex peracto uite sue cursu mortuus est et sepultus[28] in Urbe Legionum.

[47] Post hunc[1] Guizelinus dyadema[2] regni suscepit; quod satis modeste[3] omni tempore uite sue rexit. Erat ei[4] nobilis uxor[5] Marcia nomine omnibus artibus erudita; que inter plurima proprio ingenio reperta[6] legem quam Britones[7] Marcianam[8] appellant adinuenit. Hanc rex Aluredus inter cetera transtulit et Saxonica lingua[9] Merchenelaga[10] uocauit. Mortuo autem Guizelino gubernaculum regni predicte regine remansit. Erat enim [11]ei filius[11] .vii. annorum Sisillius[12] nomine cuius etas nondum apta erat regimini.[13] Sed[14] postquam adoleuit in uirum dyademate[15] regni[16] potitus est. Mortuo Sisillio[17] Kinewarus[18] filius suus regnum obtinuit.[19] Cui successit Danius[20] eiusdem frater.

[48] Huic successit Morpidus[1] ex concubina[2] genitus.[3] Is probitate famosissimus esset nisi plus nimio crudelitati indulsisset. Iratus namque modum non habebat nec cuiquam parcebat sed proprio telo interficiebat. Pulcher tamen erat aspectu et in dandis muneribus profusus nec erat alter tante fortitudinis in regno. Temporibus eius applicuit[4] quidam [5]dux Morianorum[5] cum magna classe armatorum in

---

[27] cDEHR; *Gurguent* a; *Gurgiunt* S. [28] acDEHS; *sepultus est* R.

§47 [1] acDHRS; *hec* E. [2] DES; *diadema* acH; *dyodema* R. [3] cDERS; *honeste* aH. [4] acDEHS; *enim* R. [5] acEHRS; *uxor* (in text) with *mater* in margin D. [6] acDEHS; om. R. [7] cDES; *Brittones* aH; *Britones reperta* R. [8] acEHRS; *Martianam* D. [9] acDEHS; *ligua* R. [10] DERS; *Marchenelaga* ac; *Merthenelaga* H. [11...11] cDRS; *filius ei* aH; *filius* E. [12] acDEHS; *Sisillus* R. [13] acDEHS; *regnum* R. [14] acDHRS; *Set* E. [15] cDERS; *diademate* aH. [16] acDEHRS (corrected from *regnum* in R). [17] acDEHS; *Sisillo* R. [18] R; *Kimarus rex* a; *Kynowarus* c; *Kineuarus* DE (with *Kymarus* in margin of D); *Kinuuarus rex* H; *Kinerarus* S. [19] DR; *optinuit* acEHS. [20] acDHRS; *Danius* (with *Morpidus* suprascript) E.

§48 [1] HRS; *Morwidus* a; *Morwynus* c; *Morpidus* (with *Merwidus* suprascript) D; *Morpidus* (with *Danius* suprascript) E. [2] aEHRS; *concubina Tagusla nomine* c; *concubina* with *id est Tangusteia* (from the vulgate text) suprascript in D. [3] acDEHS; *natus* R. [4] acDEHS; *applicauit* R. [5...5] cDERS; *Morianorum dux* aH.

Nordanhymbriam[6] et deuastare [7]cepit patriam.[7] Cui Morpidus[8] occurrens cum ualida manu Britonum[9] congressus est et uictoria potitus; ipse solus plus in prelio illo profecit quam maxima[10] pars sui exercitus. Et post uictoriam uix superfuit ullus[11] quem propriis manibus non interficeret[12] ut[13] uel sic[14] truculentiam suam saciaret.[15] At postquam perimendo fatigatus est, uiuos excoriari precipiebat[16] et excoriatos comburi.[17] Inter hec seuicie[18] sue acta contigit a parte Hybernici[19] maris beluam inaudite magnitudinis et feritatis aduenisse que incolas secus maritima repertos misere[20] lacerabat et deuorabat. Cuius fama cum aures eius pulsasset, accessit ad illam solus[21] uiribus fidens et congressus est cum illa. At cum omnia tela[22] in ea[23] consumpsisset,[24] arreptum[25] faucibus apertis ipsum[26] uelud[27] pisciculum belua[28] deuorauit.

[49] Genuerat ipse[1] [2]quinque filios[2] quorum primogenitus Gorbonianus[3] nomine solium[4] regni suscepit. Nullus ea tempestate iustior erat[5] aut amancior[6] equi nec qui populum maiori diligencia[7] tractaret. Inter hec et plurima innate probitatis ipsius bona debita nature soluens ab hac luce migrauit et in Urbe Trinouantum sepultus est.

[50] Successit illi[1] Archgallo[2] frater eius qui in actibus suis germano[3] dissimilis extitit. Nobiles namque deponere, ignobiles exaltare affec-

[6] HR; *Nordanhimbriam* a; *Northumbriam* c; *Nordamhumbriam* DS; *Nordanhumbriam* E. [7...7] acHR; *patriam cepit* DES. [8] HRS (with *cui* repeated after *Morpidus* in R); *Morwidus* a; *Morwinus* c; *Morpidus* (with *Morwidus* suprascript) D; *Morpidus* (with *Danius* suprascript) E. [9] cDERS; *Brittonum* aH. [10] acDERS; *magna* H. [11] aHR; *unus* cDES. [12] acDEHR; *interfecit* S. [13] acDEHS; *ubi* R. [14] aDERS; *sibi* c; *sic* (suprascript) H. [15] acDERS; *satiaret* H. [16] acDEHR; *precepit* S. [17] acDERS; *conburi* H. [18] cER; *seuitie* aDS; *sententie* H. [19] cEHRS; *Hibernici* aD. [20] aHR; *miserabiliter* cDES. [21] acDHRS; *solis* E. [22] acHR; *tela sua* DES. [23] acDERS; *eam* H. [24] acDEHRS (with *inutiliter* suprascript and *accelerauit monstrum illud* added from the vulgate text in the margin of D). [25] acEHS; *arreptum* (altered to *arreptumque*) D; *areptis* R. [26] cDERS; *illum* aH. [27] ERS; *uelut* acDH. [28] aHR; om. cDES.

§49 [1] acDEHS; *enim ipse* R. [2...2] RS; *filios .v.* aH; *5 filios* c; *.v. filios* DE. [3] aHR; *Gorbodianus* c; *Gordianus* DES (with *Gorbonianus* in margin of D). [4] acDEHS; *solum* R. [5] acDEHRS (suprascript, with *illo* added, in H). [6] cERS; *amantior* aDH. [7] cER; *diligencia* aDHS.

§50 [1] acHR; *ei* DES. [2] cR (with the *h* underpointed in c); *Ardigallo* aDEHS. [3] acHR; *fratri* DES.

tauit et quibusque sua auferre, thesauros accumulare non destitit[4] donec [5]regni forciores[5] diucius[6] ferre non ualentes eum a solio deposuerunt et Elidurum fratrem suum[7] in regem erexerunt. Qui postea propter misericordiam quam in fratrem fecit Pius uocatus est. Nam ubi Archgallo[8] per quinquennium notos et ignotos prouinciales circuisset[9] ut amissum honorem per [10]eorum auxilium[10] recuperaret nec a quoquam exauditus fuisset,[11] paupertate cogente reuersus est ad [12]fratrem Elidurum regem.[12] Cui [13]mox rex[13] occurrens in nemore Calaterio[14] amplexatus est eum, oscula dans innumera.[15] Et ut aliquamdiu fraternis amplexibus et fletibus inuicem [16]consolati sunt,[16] duxit illum[17] [18]secum Elidurus[18] in ciuitatem Aldclud[19] et in thalamo suo occuluit et [20]egrotare finxit se,[20] nuncios[21] mittens per tocius[22] regni barones ut ad se uisitandum uenirent. Qui cum uenissent, precepit ut unusquisque singulatim[23] et sine strepitu [24]thalamum ingrederetur.[24] Dicebat enim sermonis tumultum plurimum capiti[25] nociturum. Singulis ergo quiete ingredientibus precipiebat [26]Elidurus satellitibus[26] ad hoc preparatis ut capita[27] truncarentur [28]extractis gladiis[28] nisi se iterum fratri suo[29] Archgalloni[30] sicut prius fuerant[31] submitterent.[32] Sic igitur[33] separatim de cunctis agens omnes Archgalloni[34] [35]mediante timore[35] pacificauit. Confirmato itaque omnium[36] federe duxit fratrem ad Eboracum cepitque [37]dyadema de capite suo[37] et fratris[38] capiti imposuit.[39] Unde postea, quia pius in fratrem extitit, [40]nomen Pius suscepit.[40]

---

4 acDHRS; *desistit* E. 5...5 cERS; *regni fortiores* aD; *fortiores regni* H. 6 cERS; *diutius* aDH. 7 acHR; *eius* DES. 8 cR; *Ardigallo* aDEHS. 9 acDEHR; *circuiuisset* S. 10...10 acHR; *auxilium eorum* DES. 11 acDEHS; *esset* R. 12...12 cDERS (*Elid'* in E); *fratrem suum Elidurum regem* a; *fratrem suum regem Elidurum* H. 13...13 cDERS; *rex mox* aH. 14 acDEHS; *Colaterio* R. 15 DEH; *in munera* aR; *communia* c; *et munera* S. 16...16 acH; *sunt consolati* DES; *solati sunt* R. 17 aHR; *eum* cDES. 18...18 R; *Elidurus secum* aH; *Elidurus* cDES (*Elid'* in E). 19 aDER; *Alclud* c; *Alelud* H; *Aladud* S. 20...20 a; *se egrotare finxit* c; *egrotare se finxit* DES; *egrotare finxit eum* HR. 21 cDERS; *nuncios* aH. 22 cEHR; *totius* aS; *uniuersi* D. 23 aEHS; *singillatim* cD; *sigillatim* R. 24...24 aHR; *ingrederetur* c; *ingrederetur thalamum* DE; *ingrederetur talamum* S. 25 EHRS; *capiti suo* acD. 26...26 aHR; *satellitibus Elidurus* DES (*Elid'* in E). 27 cDERS; *capite* aH. 28...28 cDERS; om. aH. 29 aHR; om. cDES. 30 cR; *Ardigalloni* aDEHS. 31 acDEHS; *fuerunt* (tampered?) R. 32 acDEHRS (corrected from *submitterentur* in D). 33 acEHRS; *ergo* D. 34 cR; *Ardigalloni* aDEHS. 35...35 acDEHS; *timore mediante* R. 36 aDHR; *omni* cES. 37...37 aHR (*diadema* in aH); *de capite suo dyadema* cDES (*diadema* in cE). 38 acDEHS; *fratri* R. 39 cDRS; *inposuit* aEH. 40...40 aHR; *pium nomen accepit* c; *Pius nomen accepit* DES (after *accepit*, *Solebat ipse uersa uice ignobiles deponere, nobiles autem exaltare* added from the vulgate text in margin of D).

43

Regnauit deinde Archgallo[41] .x. annis et ab antecepta nequicia[42] correptus iustior et micior[43] omnibus[44] apparuit. Superueniente denique languore obiit[45] et in urbe Kaerleir[46] sepultus est.

[51] Erigitur[1] Elidurus[2] iterum in regem et pristine dignitati restituitur. Sed dum Gorbonianum [3]primogenitum fratrem[3] in omni bonitate sequeretur, duo [4]residui fratres eius[4] Ingenius[5] et Peredurus[6] illum lacessere[7] et infestare bello[8] temptant.[9] Congressi[10] itaque potiti sunt uictoria et ipsum captum turri Urbis Trinouantum custodie[11] mancipauerunt. Deinde partiti regnum in duo diuiserunt; Ingenio[12] ab Humbro flumine usque in occidentem tota[13] terra cessit, [14]Pereduro[15] Albania usque Humbrum. Emensis autem .vii. annis obiit Ingenius[16] et totum regnum cessit[14] Pereduro;[17] ipsumque post temporis spatium[18] [19]mors repentina[19] surripuit. [20]Elidurus igitur[20] carcere ereptus tertio[21] in regni solium sublimatur.[22] Et cum totum tempus uite sue bonis[23] moribus et pietate iusticiaque explesset, ab hac luce migrans exemplum pietatis successoribus reliquid.[24]

[52] Eliduro successit nepos eius,[1] Gorboniani filius, auunculum[2] moribus et prudencia[3] imitatus. Post hunc regnauit Marganus Archgallonis[4] filius. Qui etiam [5]exemplo parentum[5] serenatus gentem suam [6]cum tranquillitate rexit.[6] Cui successit Eumanius[7] frater suus. Hic

---

[41] cR; *Ardigallo* aDEHS. [42] cDERS; *nequitia* aH. [43] RS; *mitior* acDEH. [44] aHR; om. cDES. [45] acDEHS; *obit* R. [46] acDEHS; *Kerleir* R.

§51 [1] aHR; om. c; *Eligitur* DES. [2] acDHRS; *Elid'* E. [3...3] aHR; *fratrem suum primogenitum* cDES. [4...4] cDERS; *fratres eius residui* aH. [5] cERS; *Iugenius* aDH. [6] acHRS; *Paredurus* DE. [7] cE; *lacescere* aDS; *lassescere* H; *lascescere* R. [8] cDERS; om. aH. [9] acDEHS; *temptauit* R. [10] acDEHR; *Generosi* S. [11] acDHRS; om. E. [12] cERS; *Iugenio* aDH. [13] acDERS; om. H. [14...14] acDEHS; om. R. [15] acH; *Pareduro* DE; om. R; *ipsumque post temporis spatium* deleted after *Pereduro* in S. [16] ES; *Iugenius* aDH; om. R. [17] aHRS; *Pareduro* DE. [18] acHRS; *spacium* DE. [19...19] acEHRS; *repentina mors* D. [20...20] DERS (*Elid'* in E); *Elidurus* aH; *Elidurusque* c. [21] aEHRS; *tercio* cD. [22] aDRS; *solimatur* (or *sblimatur?*) c; *sullimatur* EH. [23] acHR; *in bonis* DES. [24] aR; *dereliquit* c; *reliquit* DEHS.

§52 [1] acDEHRS; *Reyn nomine* added in margin of D. [2] acR; *patrem et patruum* DS; *patrem et patrum* E; *awunculum* H. [3] cER; *prudentia* aDHS. [4] cR; *Ardigallonis* aDEHS. [5...5] aHR; *parentum exemplo* cDES. [6...6] acDEHS; *rexit cum tranquillitate* R. [7] R; *Enimaunus* a; *Ennianus* c; *Emmannus* DES (with *Eynianus* in margin of D); *Enmaunus* H.

tractando iniuste populum et cum tyrannide[8] exercens[9] .vi. regni sui anno a regia sede depositus est.[10] In loco cuius positus est cognatus eius Idwallo,[11] Ingenii[12] filius;[13] cui[14] successit Runo[15] Pereduri[17] filius; huic Gerontius[17] Eliduri filius; post hunc Catullus[18] filius suus;[19] post Catullum[20] Coillus;[21] post Coillum Porrex; Porreci[22] successit Cherin.[23] Huic nati fuerunt[24] tres[25] filii, Fulgenius[26] uidelicet et Eldadus[27] necnon et Andragius.[28] Qui omnes alter post alterum regnauerunt. Post hos successit Urianus Andragii[29] filius; cui Eliud;[30] cui Cledaucus;[31] cui Clotenus;[32] cui Gurgucius;[33] cui Merianus; cui Bledudo;[34] cui Capenronius;[35] cui Sisillius;[36] cui Bledgabred.[37] Hic omnes cantores quos retro etas habuerat et in modulis et in musicis instrumentis excessit[38] ita ut deus ioculatorum[39] diceretur. Post hunc regnauit Archmail[40] frater[41] suus; post hunc Eldol; huic successit Redion;[42] cui Rederchius; cui Samuil[43] Penissel; cui Pir;[44] cui Capoir;[45] cui Eligueillus,[46] Capoiri[47] filius, uir in omnibus actibus modestus et prudens.[48]

8 acDRS; *tirannide* EH. 9 acDEHS; *existens exercens* R. 10 acDEHRS; after *depositus est*, *Postposita enim iusticia tirannidem exercere preelegit* added from the vulgate text in margin of D. 11 acDERS; *Ituuallo* H. 12 cERS; *Iugenii* aD; *Iugeni* H. 13 acDEHRS; after *filius, Hic Eyniauni euentu correctus ius atque rectitudinem colebat* added from the vulgate text in margin of D. 14 cDERS; om. aH. 15 acDEH; *Rono* R; om. S. 16 acHRS; *Pareduri* DE. 17 aDEHS; *Genentius* c; *successit Geroncius* R. 18 aR; *Catellus* cDES; *Katullus* H. 19 aDEHR; *eius* c; om. S. 20 aHR; *Catellum* cDES. 21 acDERS; *Koillus* H. 22 RS; *Porrecti* acDEH. 23 aEHRS; *Kerin* c; *Cherin* altered to *Cherein* D. 24 acDERS; *sunt* H. 25 acDERS; *.iii.* H. 26 acEHRS; *Fulgentius* (with *Sulgenius* in margin) D. 27 R; *Eldanus* aH; *Eldaldus* cDES. 28 acEH (following deleted *En* in c); *Andragius* (with *Androgeus* suprascript) D; *Endgagius* (with *E* underpointed and *A* suprascript) R; *Endragius* S. 29 acDEHRS (with *Androgei* suprascript in D). 30 aDERS; *Cliud* c; *Heliud* H. 31 aDEHS; om. c; *Dedaucus* R. 32 DHR; *Dotenus* aS; *Dotennus* c; *Cloteus* E. 33 cR; *Gurgutius* aDEHS. 34 acDERS; *Bledud* H. 35 ES; *Capeuione* altered to *Capeuioenus* a; *Caipenroneus* c; *Capp oenus* altered (by suprascript *cui*) to *Capp cui Oenus* D; *Capeiuoenus* H; *Capemeonus* (or *Capeineonus?*) R. 36 aDEHS; *Sissilius* c; *Sisillus* R. 37 acDERS (with *Blethgeurit* in margin of D); *Bledgaberd* S. 38 acDHRS; *excusserat* E. 39 acDHRS; *iaculatorum* E. 40 R; *Arthinail* a; *Archinaus* c; *Aromail* DES (with *Arthnail* in margin of D); *Arkinail* H. 41 acHR; *filius* DES. 42 aDEHR; *Reidion* c; *Ridion* S. 43 cDEHRS (with the *m* underpointed in D); *Samiul* a. 44 cDERS; *Peir* aH. 45 acDERS; *Kapoir* H. 46 acEHRS; *Digueillus* D. 47 c; *Capoirri* a; *Capoir* DES; *Caipoiri* H; *Capouri* R. 48 acDEHRS; after *prudens, qui super omnia rectam iusticiam inter populos exercebat* added from the vulgate text in margin of D.

[53] Post hunc Heli[1] filius eius, regnumque .xl. annis rexit. Hic tres[2] generauit filios, Lud[3] scilicet, Cassibellaunum,[4] Nennium. Quorum primogenitus, [5]id est[5] Lud,[6] regnum post obitum patris suscepit. Hic gloriosus urbium edificator existens renouauit[7] et[8] sublimauit[9] pre ceteris muros Urbis Trinouantum et plurimis turribus[10] eam circumcinxit. Precepitque ciuibus ut palacia[11] in eadem[12] construerent ita ut non esset in longe positis regnis ciuitas que huic posset[13] parificari. Iste Lud[14] bellicosus et satis probus extitit et in dandis epulis profusus; et cum plures ciuitates possideret, hanc pre ceteris ornauit. Unde postmodum de nomine suo Kaerlud dicta est ac deinde per corrupcionem[15] nominis[16] Kaerlondem.[17] Succedente[18] tempore[19] per commutacionem[20] linguarum dicta est Lundene[21] et postea Lundres, applicantibus alienigenis qui patriam linguam in suam commutauerunt. Defuncto tandem Lud corpus eius reconditum[22] est in predicta ciuitate iuxta portam illam[23] que[24] adhuc de nomine suo Portlud[25] Britannice,[26] Saxonice uero Ludesgata[27] nuncupatur.[28] Nati[29] fuerant ei [30]filii duo, Androgeus et Tenuantius[30]. Qui cum [31]etate adhuc[31] iuniores regni administracioni[32] minime sufficerent, Cassibellaunus[33] [34]eorum auunculus[34] loco illorum[35] in regnum sublimatur.[36] Mox dyademate[37] insignitus tanta cepit largitate ac[38] probitate pollere ut fama eius[39] undique diuulgaretur, etiam in externa[40] regna. Nepotibus deinde adultis et ad

§53 [1] cHR; *Hely* a; *Beli* DS; *Bely* E. [2] acDERS; *.iii.* H. [3] aEHRS; *Llud* cD. [4] aDH; *Cassibelaunum* corrected from *Cassibelaunus* c; *Cassibelaunum* E; *Cassibellannum* R; *Cassibellanum* S. [5...5] aDERS; om. cH. [6] aERS; *Llud* cD; *Lhud* H. [7] acDEHS; *reuocauit* R. [8] acDHR; om. ES. [9] acDR; *sullimauit* EH; *sullimauitque* S. [10] acDEHRS (corrected from *turris* in R). [11] cDERS; *palatia* aH. [12] aHR; *ea* cDES. [13] acDHRS; *possit* E. [14] aDERS; *Llud* c; *Hlud* H. [15] ER; *corruptionem* aDHS. [16] aDEHS; om. cR. [17] aES; *Kaerlondein* c; *Kaerlunden* DH; *Kaerlandem* R. [18] acEHRS; *et succedente* D. [19] acDEHRS; after *tempore*, *decoratum est et nomine Lundeyn dicta est deinde* added in margin of D. [20] DERS; *commutationem* ac; *communicationem* H. [21] acDEHRS; *ab Anglis* suprascript in D. [22] acDERS; *conditum* H. [23] acEHRS; om. D. [24] acDEHS; *qui* R. [25] DES; *Porhlud* aH; *Porthllud* c; *Porlud* R. [26] cDERS; *Brittannice* aH. [27] aHR; *Leudegade* c; *Ludegate* DES. [28] acHR *appellatur* DES. [29] H; *Nam* aDERS; *Deinde nati* c. [30...30] aHR (*Tenuatius* in R); *duo filii Androgeus et Tenuancius* c; *duo filii Tenuantius et Androgeus* D; *duo filii Tenuancius et Androcheus* E; *duo filii Tenuancius et Androgeus* S. [31...31] aHR; *adhuc etate* cDES. [32] DERS (corrected from *administracione* in R); *administrationi* aH; *aministracioni* c. [33] DH; *Cassibelaunus* acE; *Cassibellannus* R; *Cassibellanus* (altered from *Cassibellannus*) S. [34...34] acHR; *patruus eorum* DES. [35] acEHS; *eorum* DR. [36] cDR; *sullimatur* aEHS. [37] cDRS; *diademate* aEH. [38] cDES; *atque* aH; *et* R. [39] aHR; *illius* cDES. [40] aHR; *extrema* cDES.

uirilem etatem excretis pietati indulgens noluit illos omnino expertes regni esse sed in partes tamquam[41] asciuit,[42] Urbem Trinouantum cum ducatu Cancie[43] tribuens Androgeo,[44] ducatum Cornubie Tenuancio.[45] Ipse dyademate[46] prelatus ipsis et tocius[47] regni principibus imperabat.[48]

[54][1] Interea[2] contigit, [3]ut in Romanis reperitur hystoriis,[4] Iulium[3] Cesarem[5] subiugata[6] Gallia in Britanniam[7] transisse.[8] Sic[9] enim scriptum est: anno ab urbe condita [10]sexcentesimo nonagesimo tercio,[10] ante[11] uero incarnacionem[12] Domini [13]anno sexagesimo,[13] [14]Iulius Cesar[14] primus Romanorum Britannias[15] bello pulsauit, in nauibus onerariis et actuariis circiter octoginta[16] aduectus.[17] Cum enim ad litus[18] Rutenorum uenisset[19] et illinc [20]Britanniam insulam[20] aspexisset, quesiuit a circumstantibus que patria, que gens inhabitasset. Cumque nomen regni didicisset et populi, ait:[21] 'Hercle! Ex eadem prosapia nos Romani descendimus quia[22] ex Troiana[23] gente processimus. Nobis Eneas[24] post destructionem Troie[25] primus pater fuit, illis[26] autem Brutus, Siluii[27] Enee[28] filius.[29] Sed,[30] nisi[31] fallor,[32] ualde a nobis degenerati sunt nec

---

41 cR; *tantum* a; *tanquam* DEHS. 42 acDEHS; *assciuit* R. 43 cER; *Cantie* aDHS. 44 cDERS; *Andrageo* a; *Androgeno* H. 45 cERS; *Tenuatio* a; *Tenuantio* DH. 46 DRS; *diademate* acEH. 47 cER; *totius* aDHS. 48 acDEHRS; after *imperabat, Explicit liber tertius [.iii.* H]. *Incipit liber* [om. aR] *quartus [.iv.* H] aHR (followed by the rubric *Iulius Cesar* in R).

§54 P's second extract begins here with the note: 'I shall here transcribe another chapter as a specimen from the body of the MSS, which is that of the arrival of Julius Caesar and the Romans, in order to show what difference there is betwixt this and the printed copies'. 1 No rubric in acDHRS; *Incipit liber .iiii.* added in margin of E; *De primu aduentu Caesaris in Britanniam. Liber .iiii.* P. 2 acDHPRS; *<I>nterea* E. 3...3 acDERS; om. HP. 4 acDRS; *historiis* E; om. HP. 5 acDEHRS; *Caesarem* P. 6 acDEHRS; *subjugata* P. 7 cDEPRS; *Brittanniam* aH. 8 acDHPRS; *transsisse* E. 9 aDEPRS; *Sicut* cH. 10...10 R (& Bede; see Introduction, p. xlvi); *secentesimo .xxiii.* a; 694 c; *.dcxciii.* DES; *.dcxxiii.* HP. 11 acDEHPRS (corrected from *anno* [?] in P). 12 ER; *incarnationem* acDHPS. 13...13 R (& Bede); *anno .lx.* aHP; 60 *anno* c; *.l. anno* DES. 14...14 acDEHRS; *Julius Caesar* P. 15 DEPRS; *Brittannias* aH; *Britones* c. 16 R; *.lxxx.* aDEHPS; 80 c. 17 acDERS; *aduentatus* H; *aduectatus* P. 18 acDEHRS; *littus* P. 19 acEHPS; *aduenisset* D; *peruenisset* R. 20...20 PR; *Brittanniam insulam* aH; *Britanniam* cDES. 21 acDEHRS; *ate* (underlined) P. 22 acDEHRS; *qui* P. 23 acDEHRS; *Trojana* P. 24 acDEHRS; *Aeneas* P. 25 acDEHRS; *Trojae* P. 26 acDEHRS; *filius* P. 27 aEHPRS; *et Siluius* c; *Siluii* underpointed, with *filius Siluii, filius Ascanii* added in margin D. 28 acDEHRS; *Aeneae* P. 29 acEHPRS; *filii* D. 30 acDHPRS; *Set* E. 31 acDEHRS; *ni* P. 32 acDEHPS; *fallo* R.

quid sit milicia[33] nouerunt cum infra occeanum[34] extra orbem[35] commaneant. Leuiter cogendi erunt tributum nobis dare et obsequium Romane[36] dignitati prestare.[37] Prius[38] tamen per nuncios[39] requirendi sunt ut Romanis subiciantur[40] et uectigal reddant ut cetere[41] gentes.' Quod cum litteris regi[42] Cassibellauno[43] intimasset,[44] indignatus rex epistulam[45] suam ei remisit hec uerba continentem:

[55] 'Cassibellaunus[1] rex Britonum[2] [3]Gaio Cesari.[3] Miranda est, Cesar, [4]Romanorum cupiditas[4] que[5] quicquid[6] est usquam[7] auri uel[8] argenti in toto orbe [9]terrarum siciens[10] nos extra orbem[11] positos preterire intactos[9] non patitur.[12] Censum exigis, tributarios [13]nos facere queris[13] qui[14] perpetua [15]libertate hactenus[15] floruimus, qui a Troiana[16] nobilitate sicut Romani descendimus. Obprobrium[17] generi tuo, Cesar,[18] si intelligis, postulasti qui hisdem[19] ortos natalibus iugo[20] seruitutis premere[21] non erubuisti.[22] Libertatem [23]autem nos[23] in tantum consueuimus [24]et tam[24] nobis ab antecessoribus[25] familiaris est[26] ut quid sit in genere[27] nostro seruitus penitus ignoremus. Quam libertatem si dii [28]ipsi quoque[28] conarentur auferre, nos omni nisu[29] elaboraremus[30] ne quod[31] nobis tamquam[32] insitum[33] [34]a natura[34] [35]par cum[35] diis [36]tanto

[33] acDERS; *militia* HP. [34] aDHRS; om. c; *occianum* E; *oceanum* P. [35] acDEHP; *urbem* RS. [36] acDEHRS; *Romanae* P. [37] acDEHRS; *praestare* P. [38] acDEPRS; *Primitus* H. [39] cDERS; *nuntios* aHP. [40] acDEHRS; *subjiciuntur* P. [41] acDEHRS; *caeterae* P. [42] acDEHRS; *suis* P. [43] aDH; *Cassibelauno* cE; *Cassibellano* PS; *Cassibellanno* R. [44] acDEHRS; *nunciasset* P. [45] acDEHRS; *epistolam* P.

§55 [1] acDH; *Cassibelaunus* E; *Cassibellanus* PS; *Cassibellannus* R. [2] cDEPRS; *Brittonum* aH. [3...3] aDEHS; *Gaio Iulio Cesari* c; *Caio Caesari* P; *Gayo Cesari* R. [4...4] acEHPRS; *cupiditas Romanorum* D. [5] acDEHRS; *qui* P. [6] acDEHPS; *quidquid* R. [7] acDEHRS; *usque* P. [8] acDEHRS; *et* P. [9...9] acDEHPR; *positum preterire intactum* (both *positum* and *intactum* tampered) S. [10] acER; *sitiens* DHP; om. S. [11] acDEHP; *urbem* R; om. S. [12] acDEHRS; *patietur* P. [13...13] acHPR; *queris nos facere* DES. [14] acDEHRS; *quum* P [15...15] acHPR; *hactenus libertate* DES. [16] acDEHRS; *Trojana* P. [17] acDEHRS; *Opprobrium* P. [18] acDEHRS; *Caesar* P. [19] aDR; *isdem* cHP; *hiisdem* E; *eisdem* S. [20] acDEHRS; *jugo* P. [21] aDEHPS; *subdere* c; *primere* R. [22] acDHPRS; *eribuisti* E. [23...23] aHPR; *animos* c; *autem* DES. [24...24] acDEHRS; *traditam* P. [25] acDHPS; *ancessoribus* E; *antecessoribus nostris* R. [26] acDEHPR; om. (with *existit* suprascript) S. [27] acDEHRS; *ipso genere* P. [28...28] acHPR; *quoque ipsi* DES. [29] acDEHS; *nisi* P; *uisu* R. [30] acDEHRS; *elaboremus* P. [31] acDEHPRS (corrected from *quid* in P). [32] R; *tanquam* acDEHPS. [33] acDEHRS; *instinctum* (underlined) followed by [*istū*] (= *insitum*) P. [34...34] R; *a natura est* acDES; *est a natura* H; *a ♄* [= *natura*] *est* P. [35...35] aHR; *et cum* c; *et par cum* DE; *partum* P; *quod partum* S. [36...36] acHPR (with *tanto* over an erasure in P); *tantopere* DE; *tanto opere* S.

tempore[36] tenuimus, per hominem[37] mortalem amitteremus.[38] Liqueat[39] igitur tibi, Cesar,[40] pro regno nos et libertate, [41]dum uita comes fuerit,[41] indefessos communiter[42] stare, etiam[43] mortem subire paratos si [44]tempus dissolucionis forte nostre[44] institerit.'[45]

[56] Hiis[1] itaque lectis Cesar nauigium parat. Uentis et mari se committens uela erigit ac aura flante prospera in hostio[2] Thamensis[3] fluuii cum toto nauigio applicuit. Uix terram attigerant,[4] et ecce Cassibellaunus[5] rex cum omni [6]Britonum exercitu[6] Dorobernum[7] aduenit, paratus pugnancium[8] copiis[9] non impiger[10] occurrere Cesari. Aderat secum[11] Belinus princeps milicie[12] sue cuius consilio et prouidencia[13] tocius[14] regni monarchia tractabatur.[15] Duo quoque nepotes sui, uiri strenuissimi, Androgeus uidelicet[16] dux Trinouantum et Tenuancius[17] dux Cornubie, latus eius stipabant necnon tres sibi subditi reges, Eridionis[18] Albanie et Guertaet[19] Uenodocie Britaelque[20] Demecie.[21] Qui omnes ad libertatem tuendam animati dederunt consilium ut in hostes antequam [22]se castris[22] munissent[23] haut[24] [25]segnis insiliret[25] et[26] a regno suo eos uiuaciter perturbaret. Dispositis[27] itaque agminibus ad bellum intrepidi procedunt,[28] hostibus [29]se cominus[29]

---

[37] acDEHRS; *hostem* P. [38] acHPR; *amittamus* DE; *ammittamus* S. [39] acDEHRS; *Liceat* P. [40] acDEHRS; *Caesar* P. [41...41] acDEHRS; *cum uita comite fn'ie [sic MS. q.]* P. [42] acEHRS; *comiter (?)* D; *contra* P. [43] aDEHR; *et* cPS. [44...44] R; *tempus nostre [−ae P] resolucionis [resolucionis a]* aHP; *tempus nostre dissolucionis forte* c; *nostre dissolucionis tempus forte* DES. [45] acDEHRS; *ĩstnctē [sic MS. q]* P; P's second extract ends at this point.

§56 [1] cDERS; *His* aH. [2] cDHR; *ostio* aES. [3] cDHRS; *Tamensis* aE. [4] aDERS (corrected from *attingerant* in S); *attigerat* c; *attigerunt* H. [5] aD; *Cassibelaunus* cE; *Kassibellaunus* H; *Cassibellannus* R; *Cassibellanus* S. [6...6] R; *Brittonum exercitu* aH; *exercitu Britonum* cDES. [7] aDERS; *Doroberniam* c; *Dorobernium* H. [8] ER; *pugnantium* aDHS; *pungnancium* c. [9] cDERS; *more* a; *cohorte* H. [10] acDERS; *inpiger* H. [11] acDERS; *tunc* H. [12] cER; *militie* aDHS. [13] cER; *prouidentia* aDHS. [14] cER; *totius* aDHS. [15] acDERS; *tradebatur* H. [16] aHR; *scilicet* cDES. [17] cR; *Tenuantius* aDEH; *Tenonancius* S. [18] a; *Cridionus* c; *Cridious (with Cridoo in margin)* D; *Eridious* E; *Eridion* H; *Eridioris* R; *Eridionus* S. [19] DR (with *Gweyctah<...>* in margin of D); *Guernaet* aH; *Gurthaet* c; *Guerthaec* E; *Guertaet* S. [20] acDERS (with *Buthathel* in margin of D); *Britoelque* H. [21] cEHRS; *Demetie* aD. [22...22] acH; *castris se* DES; *se in castris* R. [23] acDEHS; *muniuissent* R. [24] acDEHS; *aut* R. [25...25] DEHS; *segnes insilirent* a; *segniter insiliret* c; *segnius insiliiet (or insiluet?)* R. [26] acDERS; *om.* H. [27] acDEHR; *Depositis* S. [28] acHR; *incedunt* DES (altered from *accedunt* in E). [29...29] aHS; *se comminus* cDE; *cominus se* R.

offerunt; pila pilis obuiant ac tela omnium generum utrimque[30] uibrantur. Hinc inde mox corruunt uulnerati[31] telis infra uitalia receptis. Manat[32] tellus cruore moriencium[33] ac super ipsa cadauera ferociter[34] pugnatur. Concurrentibus[35] itaque cateruis optulit[36] casus Nennium et Androgeum[37] duces cum Cantuariis[38] quibus preerant aciei in qua Cesar erat inserere. Et cum ictus mixtim[39] ex utraque parte multiplicarent, sors dedit Nennio[40] congressum in ipsum Cesarem faciendi. Irruens ergo[41] in illum toto conamine letatur se posse uel solum ictum tanto uiro inferre. Quem Cesar ut[42] uidet[43] impetum in se uelle facere, pretenso clipeo excepit et nudato gladio quantum uires dederunt ipsum super cassidem et scutum quo erat ille protectus tanto[44] conamine percussit ut gladius [45]inde extrahi[45] [46]a Cesare nequaquam[46] posset. Irruentibus ergo turmis coactus est Cesar [47]gladium Nennio[47] relinquere. Nennius itaque gladio imperatoris[48] insignitus [49]in eo[49] pugnauit toto[50] certamine et quemcumque eo percuciebat[51] letaliter uulnerabat.[52] Illi ergo in hunc modum [53]hostes prosternenti[53] obuiauit Labienus Romanorum tribunus et a Nennio peremptus est. Sicque dimicantibus Romanis et Britonibus[54] magna cedes ex utraque parte facta est plurima parte diei.[55] Nocte superueniente castra petunt Romani telorum ictibus grauiter uulunerati[56] et [57]labore diurno[57] mirabiliter[58] fatigati sumuntque[59] mox consilium nocte eadem naues ingredi et ad Gallias redire.

---

[30] acD; *utrinque* EH; *utrumque* R; om. S. [31] acDEH; *wlnerati* RS. [32] acDERS; *Manabat* H. [33] cER; *morientium* aDH; *morientum* S. [34] acEHRS; *atrociter* D. [35] acDEHR; *Conuenientibus* (corrected from *Conuenirentibus*) S. [36] acEHRS; *obtulit* D. [37] acDEHR; *Andgrogeum* S. [38] DERS (with *et ciuibus Urbis Trinouantum* added from vulgate text in margin in D); *cateruis* aH; *Cantuariis et ciuibus Trinouantum* c. [39] acDEHR; *mixturi* S. [40] acDEHS; *Nennino* R. [41] acDERS; om. H. [42] acDEHR; om. S. [43] HRS; *uidit* acDE. [44] acDERS; om. H. [45...45] acHR; *extrahi inde* DES. [46...46] ac-DES (*nequacquam* in c); *nequaquam a Cesare* H; *a Cesare non* R. [47...47] acEHRS; *Nennio gladium* D. [48] acDERS; *inperatoris* H. [49...49] aDERS; *eo* c; *est in quo* H. [50] acDEHS; *tanto* R. [51] acER; *percutiebat* DHS. [52] acDEHS; *wlnerabat* R. [53...53] aR; *in hostes properanti* c; *hostes prostranti* DEHS. [54] cDERS; *Brittonibus* aH. [55] ac-DEHRS (with *cedente tandem uictoria Britonibus* in margin of D). [56] acDEH; *wlnerati* RS. [57...57] acHR; *diurno labore* DES. [58] acEHRS; *mirabilit* D. [59] acEHR; *sumptumque est* DS.

[57] Abeuntibus itaque Romanis Britones[1] quidem gratulantur[2] de uictoria sed contigit statim dolere et tristari,[3] Nennio uiro egregio ac bellicoso de uulnere Cesaris infra .xv. dies moriente. Quem in Urbe[4] Trinouantum delatum sepelierunt iuxta aquilonalem[5] portam,[6] exequias ei regias facientes[7] pro eo quod frater[8] regis erat,[9] gladium quoque Cesaris quem in congressu scuto suo retinuerat in sepulcro[10] [11]iuxta illum[11] ob memoriam probitatis collocantes. Nomen gladii scriptum erat in eo Crocea Mors quoniam uix[12] eo [13]quis percussus[13] [14]mortis periculum poterat euadere.[14]

[58] Cesare itaque in Gallias appulso rebellionem[1] moliuntur[2] Galli, dominium Romanorum formidantes.[3] Fuge enim eorum fama diuulgata minus terrori[4] erant[5] quorum dominium inuiti et[6] coacti susceperant. Crebrescebat[7] quoque [8]fama cotidie[8] totum mare [9]Britonum nauibus[9] plenum[10] ad fugam Romanorum insequendam. Audaciores[11] igitur effecti cogitabant qualiter Cesarem a finibus suis arcerent. Quod Iulius callens[12] timuit[13] anceps bellum cum feroci[14] populo committere[15] apertisque[16] thesauris maiores atque nobiliores terre muneribus donauit[17] promissisque maioribus sibi eos allexit, pollicens si fortuna iuuante [18]a Britannia subiugata uictor[18] rediret[19] populo libertatem, exheredatis[20] restitutionem,[21] principibus munificencie[22] largitatem uelle facere. Sicque delinitos[23] et pacificatos in tantum amorem sibi omnes

---

§57 [1] cDERS; *Brittones* aH. [2] acDERS; *congratulantur* H. [3] acDHRS; *contristari* E. [4] aHR; *Urbem* cDES. [5] DHR; *aquilonem* altered to *aquilonanem* a; *acquilonarem* c; *aquilonem* E; *aquilonatem* S. [6] acHR; *partem* DES. [7] acHR; *ferentes* DES. [8] aDERS; *nepos* c; *filius* H. [9] DERS; *esset* aH; *esset et filius* c. [10] acDHRS; *sepulchro* E. [11]...[11] acDERS; *illius* H. [12] acHR; om. DES. [13]...[13] acDEHS; *percussus qui* R. [14]...[14] aHR; *mortem poterat euadere* c; *mortis periculum uix euadere poterat* DES.

§58 [1] acDERS; *rebellare* H. [2] acDEHS; *molliuntur* R. [3] acEHRS; *formidantes* (with *abicientes* suprascript) D. [4] acDHRS; *terroris* E. [5] HR; *quam ante erant* a; *iam erant* c; *illis erant* DS; *illis erat* E. [6] acHR; *atque* DES. [7] aDES; *et crescebat* c; *Crescebat* HR. [8]...[8] cDES; *cotidie fama* aH; *fama cottidie* R. [9]...[9] cR; *Brittonum nauibus* aH; *nauibus Britonum* DES. [10] cDERS; om. aH (with *coopertum* before *Brittonum* in a). [11] cDER; *Audatiores* aHS. [12] acDEHRS (with *callidus* suprascript in D). [13] aHR; *noluit* cDES. [14] acDERS; *feroce* H. [15] acDEHR; *conmittere* S. [16] aEHRS; *sed apertis* c; *apertis* preceded by *sed* suprascript D. [17] acDRS; *dotauit* E; *ditauit* H. [18]...[18] R; *a Brittannia subiugata* aH; *a Britannia uictor subiugata* c; *uictor a Britannia subiugata* DES. [19] acDEHS; *rediretur* R. [20] acDEHS; *exheredatis* R. [21] acHRS; *restitucionem* DE. [22] cR; *munificentie* aDHS; *munifice* E. [23] acDEHS; *delimitos* R.

deuinxit[24] ut non solum [25]non rebellare[25] sed etiam Britonum[26] iniuriam et ferocem audaciam[27] se cohercere et uindicare secum promitterent.

[59] Paratis itaque omnibus que ad tantum negocium[1] pertinebant biennio emenso nauibusque sexcentis[2] utriusque [3]commodi comparatis[3] iterum Britanniam[4] adiit et per Thamensem[5] fluuium prosperis uelis euectus[6] Urbem Trinouantum primo aggredi temptat.[7] Uerum Britones[8] premuniti ita alueum fluminis palis ferreis per totum amnem[9] fixis constipauerunt ut nulla nauis[10] illesa et sine periculo transmeare flumen[11] posset.

[60] Uenientes ergo Romani[1] ad illam palorum caribdim infiguntur palis, perforantur naues, aquis absorbentur; et in hunc modum plures periclitantur. Cesar uidens stragem suorum indoluit[2] et dimisso itinere aluei quod ceperat ad terram diuertere classem imperat. Qui uix elapsi de periculo paucis submersis terram subeunt, nauibus egrediuntur, castra figunt.[3] Et ecce Cassibellaunus[4] haut segnis comparatis[5] copiis descendit in prelium datoque signo irruit in Romanos et eos [6]cedere audacter cepit.[6] Romani autem, quamquam[7] periculum passi, uiriliter Britonum[8] primam inuasionem sustinuerunt et eos a castris procul pepulerunt;[9] audaciam pro muro habentes non minimam ex hostibus stragem fecerunt. At Britones[10] suorum agminibus constipati, multo maiorem numerum armatorum[11] quam prius conflauerant[12] ita ut[13] estimarentur tricies maiorem numerum habere; augmentabantur preterea omni hora superuenientibus turmis undique. Cesar autem uidens eorum multitudinem atque uesanam rabiem non posse sustinere

[24] acDEH; *conuinxit* R; *coniunxit* S. [25...25] RS; *rebellare* aDEH; *ipsum* [added in margin] *debellare* c. [26] cDERS; *Brittonum* aH. [27] cR; *audatiam* aDEHS.

§59 [1] ER; *negotium* acDHS. [2] R; *cescentis* a; *600* c; *.dc.* DEHS. [3...3] acDEHS; *commodius paratis* R. [4] cDERS; *Brittanniam* aH. [5] cDRS; *Tamensem* aE; *Thamense* H. [6] acDEHR; *euectis* S. [7] cDER; *temptauit* a; *temptant* HS. [8] cDERS; *Brittones* aH. [9] aEHR; *ampnem* cDS. [10] acDERS; om. H. [11] acDHRS; om. E.

§60 [1] cDERS; *naues* aH. [2] cDERS; *condoluit* aH. [3] acDEHR; *fugiunt* S. [4] aD; *Cassibelaunus* cE; *Kassibelaunus* H; *Cassibellannus* R; *Cassibellanus* S. [5] cDERS; *paratis* aH. [6...6] acDEHS; *audacter cepit cedere* R. [7] acDEHR; *postquam* S. [8] cDERS; *Brittonum* aH. [9] a; *propulerunt* c (omitting *procul*); *pulerunt* DEHS (altered from *puluerunt* in S); *pulserunt* R. [10] cDERS; *Brittones* aH. [11] acHR; om. DES. [12] acHR; *habentes* DES. [13] acDEHR; *ut iam* S.

receptui canens certamen diremit;[14] suos ad castra redire coegit ne
maius periculum sustinerent. Nauesque[15] protinus ingreditur et ad
Gallias aura flante prospera quantocius[16] deuenit.[17] Ibi prope litus
turrim[18] ingressus, quam [19]antea sibi[19] preparauerat propter dubios belli
euentus, tuto se collocauit loco. Turri illi Odnea[20] nomen erat, ubi
exercitum misere dilaceratum longa admodum quiete refecit et proceres terre ad se collocutum uenire fecit.

[61] Cassibellaunus[1] autem secundo de Romanis triumphans magno
exultans gaudio statuit uota diis omnipotentibus soluere atque pro
tanto euentu sacrificiorum ritus adimplere. Monuit itaque omnes qui
erant in exercitu ut constituto termino conuenirent ad Urbem Trinouantum cum uxoribus et filiis et caris suis quatinus[2] ibidem pro
adepta uictoria dies exultacionis[3] secum agerent. Cumque omnes
absque[4] mora aduenissent, diuersa libamina facientes prout cuique
suppetebat litauerunt. Numerus[5] holocausti[6] illius comprehensus[7] est in
.xl. milia[8] uaccarum et centum[9] milia ouium et .xxx. milia siluestrium
ferarum cuiusque[10] generis collectarum, preterea diuersorum generum
uolatilia que numero comprehendi difficile fuit. Libaminibus itaque
diis[11] pro more peractis refecerunt se residuis epulis ut fieri assolet[12] in
huiusmodi sacrificiis atque perfuncti[13] diuersorum generum ferculis[14]
quod reliquum[15] fuit diei ludis exultantes[16] indulserunt. Interea contigit
inclitos[17] iuuenes palestra exercitari;[18] inter quos erat nepos regis
Hireglas[19] nomine, alter uero Androgei ducis nepos Euelinus dictus.
Qui[20] cestibus[21] contendentes inuicem se ad iracundiam indignando

---

[14] acDHRS; *dirimit* E. [15] acDEHR; *Naues* S. [16] acEHR; *quantotius* D; *prospera*
deleted after *quantocius* in S. [17] acDE; *deuenit. Ut canit poeta: 'Territa quesitis
ostendit terga Brittannis'* (Lucan, *De Bello Ciuili*, II.572; quotation derived from the
vulgate text, §62) H; *aduenit* RS. [18] acDEHS; *turim* R; [19]...[19] R; *sibi antea* aH; *ipse
antea sibi* c; *ipse antea* DES. [20] aHR; *Odena* c; *Ydonea* DES (with *Odnea* in margin
of D).

§61 [1] aD; *Cassibelaunus* cE; *Kassibellaunus* H; *Cassibellannus* R; *Cassibellanus* S.
[2] acDEHS; *quatenus* R. [3] DER; *exultationis* acHS. [4] cDERS; *sine* aH. [5] acDEHS;
Numerus autem R. [6] cDHRS; *holocasti* a; *holochausti* E. [7] acDERS; *conprehensus* H.
[8] acDEHS; om. R. [9] aR; *100* c; *.c.* DEHS. [10] acDEHS; *cuiuscumque* R. [11] aHR; om.
cDES. [12] acDERS; *solet* H. [13] acDEHS; *per finem* R. [14] acDHS; *epulis* underpointed
before *ferculis* in E; *ferculum* R. [15] acEHRS; *residuum* D. [16] acDERS; *exultantantes*
H. [17] acDEHS; *multos* R. [18] aDEHS; *exerceri* c; *excitari* R. [19] cR; *Herelglas* a;
Hirelglas DES (altered to *Hirglas* D); *Hyrelglas* H. [20] acDHRS; *Que* E. [21] acDEHRS
(corrected from *celestibus* in S).

prouocauerunt. Quorum alter Euelinus Androgei nepos Hireglas[22] [23]regis nepotem gladio arrepto[23] interfecit. Perturbata igitur curia rumor ad Cassibellaunum[24] regem peruenit et de leticia qua prius fluctuabat in merorem conuersus est. Aduocatoque Androgeo precepit[25] ut nepos suus [26]Euelinus sibi[26] ad iusticiam protinus[27] presentaretur et sententiam[28] quam proceres [29]dictarent subiret.[29] Cumque animum regis ira commotum dubitasset[30] Androgeus, respondit sese[31] suam curiam habere et in illa definiri[32] debere [33]calumpniam suorum.[33] Si igitur[34] morem antiquitus statutum intemeratum custodire[35] uellet, die[36] statuto presto erat ut in curia sua iuuenem legibus coherceret[37] et de presenti calumpnia satisfaceret. Rex indignans recessit iratus, Androgeo gladium et mortem comminatus. Nec distulit quin mox terras et possessiones eius ferro et flammis[38] uastaret. Androgeus ergo iram regis sustinere non ualens per internuncios[39] cepit regem[40] compellare[41] et eius iracundiam mitigare. Sed cum furorem eius [42]nullatenus posset[42] refrenare, diuersis cogitacionibus[43] angebatur[44] qualiter regi ualeret resistere. Itaque omni alia spe decidens auxilium Cesaris expetere decreuit litterasque illi [45]in hanc direxit sententiam:[45] 'Gaio[46] Cesari Androgeus dux Trinouantum post optatam[47] mortem optandam salutem. Penitet me[48] aduersum[49] te egisse dum regem meum ad [50]Romanos expellendos[50] [51]de terra nostra[51] uiribus meis [52]adiutus sum.[52] Si enim [53]me bello[53] subtraxissem, Cassibellaunus[54] Romanorum uictor non extitisset. Cui post triumphum tanta irrepsit superbia ut me per quem triumphauit a finibus meis exterminare[55] presumat. Numina celorum testor me non promeruisse iram illius, nisi dicar promereri quia

[22] R; *Hirelglas* aDES (altered to *Hirglas* in D); *Hirglas* c; *Hirelglam* H. [23...23] aHR (*arepto* in R); *nepotem regis arrepto gladio* cDES (*arepto* in ES). [24] aDR; *Cassibelaunum* cE; *Kassibellaunum* H; *Cassibellanum* S. [25] acHR; om. DES. [26...26] acHR; *ei* DES. [27] aHR; om. cDES. [28] aDHRS; *sentenciam* cE. [29...29] acHR; *protinus dictarent subiret precepit* DES. [30] acHR; *dubitaret* DES. [31] acDERS; om. H. [32] aDEHS; *deffiniri* cR. [33...33] acDHRS; *suorum calumpniam* E. [34] acDEHS; *ergo* R. [35] acEHRS; *custodiri* D. [36] acDHRS; *de* E. [37] acDEHR; *choherceret* S. [38] acDERS; *igne* H. [39] cDERS; *internuntios* aH. [40] acEHRS; om. D. [41] acDERS; *compellere* H. [42...42] acHR; *posset nullatenus* DES. [43] ER; *cogitationibus* acDHS. [44] acDEHS; *augebatur* R. [45...45] aHR; *in hanc sententiam direxit* c; *direxit in hanc sententiam* DES (*sentenciam* in E). [46] aDEHS; *Gaio Iulio* c; *Gayo* R. [47] acDHS (corrected from *optantam* in H); *preoptatam* E; *aptatam* R. [48] acH; *me Cesar* DES; *te* underpointed (with *me* suprascript) R. [49] aHR; *aduersus* cDES. [50...50] cDERS; *expellendos Romanos* aH. [51...51] acDERS; *dextera mea et* H. [52] acDERS; *adiuui* H. [53...53] cDERS; *me a bello* a; *bello me* H. [54] D; *Cassibellaunus rex* a; *Cassibelaunus* cE; *Kassibelaunus* H; *Cassibellannus* R; *Cassibellanus* S. [55] acDHR; *eterminare* ES.

diffugio nepotem meum [56]curie sue tradere[56] iudicandum morte;[57] quem iniuste iratus exoptat dampnare. Quod ut manifestius discrecioni[58] tue liqueat, causam rei aduerte. Contigerat nos ob leticiam[59] triumphi libamina diis patriis offerre. In quibus dum celebraremus [60]que agenda sunt[60] sollempnia,[61] iuuentus nostra [62]ludos mutuos[62] componens, inter ceteros inierunt duo[63] nepotes nostri palestram exemplo aliorum ducti. Cumque meus triumphasset, succensus est alter [64]iniusta ira[64] festinauit- que eum percutere. At ille uitato ictu cepit socium per manum qua extractum ensem tenebat, uolens eripere ne sibi noceret. Interea cecidit nepos regis super mucronem confossusque morti subiacuit.[65] Quod cum regi notum esset, precepit ut puerum [66]meum traderem curie sue[66] ad ulciscendum nepotem suum ut pro homicidio supplicio plecteretur. Cui dum[67] contradixissem, uenit cum exercitu terras meas et possessiones ferro et igni[68] uastare. Unde a serenitate maiestatis tue auxilium peto quatinus per te dignitati mee restitutus, tu per me Britannia[69] pociaris.[70] De[71] hoc autem nichil hesitaueris quia omnis abest prodicio.[72] Ea enim condicione[73] mouentur[74] mortales ut post inimicicias[75] amici fiant, et post fugam ad triumphum accedant.'

[62] Hiis[1] Cesar inspectis consilium mox[2] capit a familiaribus suis ne uerbis solummodo[3] Androgei inuitatus Britanniam[4] adiret nisi tales dirigerentur[5] obsides quibus securius incederet. Nec mora misit ei Androgeus [6]Sceuam filium[6] suum et .xxx. nobiles iuuenes ex propin- quis suis. Transiens itaque Cesar applicuit in Rutupi[7] Portu et terram ingrediens uenit inprouisus[8] usque Dorobernum. Interea [9]obsidere Cassibellaunus[10] Urbem Trinouantum[9] parat. Sed ut Cesaris aduentum

56...56 R; *curie sue* aH; *tradere curie sue* DES. 57 aDHRS; *morti* cE. 58 cERS; *celsitudini* aH; *discretioni* D. 59 aDEHR; *letitiam* cS. 60...60 acDES; *agenda* H; *que agendo sunt* R. 61 acDHRS; *solempnia* E. 62...62 acDEHS; *mutuos ludos* R. 63 acDERS; *.ii.* H. 64...64 acDEHR; *et iusta iraque* S. 65 aDEHR; *succubuit* c; *iacuit* preceded by suprascript *sub*— S. 66...66 aH; *meum curie sue traderem* cDES; *curie meum traderem sue* R. 67 acDERS; *cum* H. 68 acDRS; *igne* EH. 69 cDRS; *Brittannia* aH; *Britanniam* E. 70 acERS; *potiaris* DH. 71 acDEHS; om. R. 72 DER; *proditio* acHS. 73 cDER; *conditione* aHS. 74 acDERS; *uouentur* H. 75 cDERS; *inimicitias* aH.

§62 1 cDERS; *His* aH. 2 acHR; om. DES. 3 acDEHR; *solum* S. 4 cDERS; *Brittan- niam* aH. 5 acDEHS; *dirigentur* R. 6...6 a; *Scenam filium* cERS; *filium suum Sceuam* D; *Cenam filium* H. 7 aDERS; *Rutubi* cH. 8 acHRS; *improuisus* DE. 9...9 DERS; *Cassibellaunus [Kassibellaunus* H] *Urbem Trinouantum obsidere* aH; *obsidere Cassibe- launus Trinouantum* c. 10 D; *Cassibelaunus* E; *Cassibellannus* R; *Cassibellanus* S.

cognouit, exercitum congregat;[11] ei ire obuiam festinat. Ut igitur uallem prope Doroberniam[12] intrauit, aspexit in eadem Romanorum castra et tentoria fixa: ductu etenim[13] Androgei illuc conuenerant. Nec mora aduenientes Britones[14] statuerunt se per cateruas, cum Romanis pugnaturi. Androgeus autem cum .v. milibus armatorum in prope sito[15] nemore delituit [16]ut auxilium Cesari ferret.[16] Ut ergo hinc inde[17] conuenerunt, tela iaciunt et inuicem uulnerantur;[18] et dimissis telis iam cominus[19] certamen ensibus[20] agere meditantur, cum Androgeus nemore[21] egrediens cum suis Cassibellauni[22] aciem a tergo inuadit. Unde Britones[23] attoniti stacionem[24] suam dimittere et aciem dirimere coacti sunt. Fugam itaque[25] ualidam simul arripientes[26] montem petunt in loco prope situm, rupibus et coriletis obsitum, cuius summitatem nacti ab hostibus se tuentur et iaculis ac lapidibus tanquam de munitione[27] celsa in terram proiectis[28] a se longius propellunt.[29] Cesar itaque montem obsedit et Britones[30] undique circumuallauit,[31] obstruens uias et aditus ne quis eorum euadat,[32] memor dedecoris fugarum preteritarum. O admirabile genus[33] Britonum,[34] qui[35] ipsum cui totus mundus nequiuit resistere bis fugere coegerunt; deuicti[36] quoque et fugati resistunt, parati mortem pro patria et libertate subire. Emenso igitur[37] die primo ac secundo, cum non haberent quid comederent obsessi, cum fame captionem[38] Cesaris formidantes et iram eius abhorrentes, misit nuncios[39] Cassibellaunus[40] Androgeo orans ut sese[41] cum Iulio pacificaret ne dignitas gentis sue, quarum stirpe ortus erat,[42] ipso deleto deleretur. Mandauit etiam supplicans se nondum[43] promeruisse ut mortem suam optaret, licet inquietudinem sibi intulisset. [44]At Androgeus[44] nunciis[45] respondens ait: 'Dii celi et terre, orat[46] me nunc herus meus cui prius

---

[11] acHR; *congregat et* DES. [12] acHR; *Dorobernum* DES. [13] acERS; *enim* DH. [14] cDERS; *Brittones* aH. [15] acDHS; *situ* E; *cito* R. [16...16] acEHRS; om. D. [17] acHR; *et inde* DES. [18] acDEH; *wlnerantur* RS. [19] aHRS; *comminus* cDE. [20] aHR; om. cDES (with *ensibus* suprascript before *agere* in D). [21] aHR; *de nemore* cDES. [22] aDH; *Cassibelauni* cE; *Cassibellanni* R; *Cassibellani* (corrected from *Cassibellanum*) S. [23] cDERS; *Brittones* aH. [24] DER; *stationem* acHS. [25] acDEHR; *illam* S. [26] DERS; *accipientes* aH; *aripientes* c. [27] acHS; *municione* DE; *mutacione* R. [28] cDES; *proicientibus* aHR. [29] cDERS; *expellunt* aH. [30] cDERS; *Brittones* aH. [31] acDEHS; *circumualuerit* R. [32] acDEHRS (corrected from *euadadat* in S). [33] acDHRS (over an erasure in S); *ergo* E. [34] cDERS; *Brittonum* aH. [35] acEHRS; *quod* D. [36] acDHRS; *diuicti* E. [37] aDEHS; *itaque* c; *ergo* R. [38] acDHRS; *capcionem* E. [39] cDERS; *nuntios* aH. [40] aD; *Cassibelaunus* cE; *Kassibellaunus* H; *Cassibellannus* R; *Cassibellanus* S. [41] acHR; *se* DES. [42] acDEHS; *eat* R. [43] acHR; *non* DES. [44...44] aH; *Androgeus autem* cDES; *Sed an Andgrogeus* R. [45] cDERS; *nuntiis* aH. [46] acDEHR; *orant* S.

56

despectui eram et⁴⁷ quem iniuriis lacessierat! Pacificarine⁴⁸ ⁴⁹Cesari se per me⁴⁹ desiderat rex Cassibellaunus⁵⁰ qui exustis⁵¹ ferro et flammis possessionibus meis ceu⁵² pro nichilo ducens exheredare cogitarat?⁵³ Non est ualde timendus ⁵⁴terre princeps⁵⁴ uel diligendus qui in pace ferus est ut leo et in bello timidus ut lepus. Uereri tamen debuerat ne illum iniuriose tractaret per quem tantus uir, uidelicet Romanus imperator⁵⁵ ac tocius⁵⁶ orbis uictor, bis deuictus ⁵⁷est et fugatus.⁵⁷ Insipiencia⁵⁸ obducitur⁵⁹ qui commilitones quibus triumphat iniuriis et⁶⁰ contumeliis infestat. Non enim unius ducis est uictoria, immo omnium commilitonum qui pro duce suo se et sanguinem suum fundunt. Quiescat ergo ⁶¹rex uester amodo⁶¹ presumere se uictorem absque aliis extitisse per quos tota uictoria patrata est. Et ego, licet ⁶²indigne me⁶² exacerbasset, pacificabo eum Cesari, non reddens malum pro malo. Satis uindicata est iniuria quam michi intulit cum ⁶³misericordiam meam⁶³ et auxilium supplex imploret.'⁶⁴

[63] Hec¹ dicens festinus² uenit ad Cesarem amplexisque ³eius genibus³ sic allocutus est eum: 'Ecce, satis uindicasti te, Cesar, in Cassibellaunum,⁴ cum ad dedicionem⁵ et tributum reddendum compulisti. Quid amplius ⁶ab eo exigere censes⁶ quam subiectionem sui et uectigal Romane dignitati? Nulla uirtus clemencia⁷ dignior est imperatori.⁸ Esto igitur ei propicius⁹ et clemens et non reddas ei secundum opera sua.' Cumque ad hec uerba Androgei Cesar nichil respondisset sed quasi surda aure illum¹⁰ preterisset, indignatus Androgeus ¹¹Cesari iterum¹¹ ait: 'Hoc solum me pepegisse tibi, Cesar, memini ut submisso

---

⁴⁷ acDERS; om. H. ⁴⁸ aDEHS; *Pacificari* c; *Pacificari nunc* R. ⁴⁹...⁴⁹ acHR (*Cessari* in R); *per me Cesari* DES. ⁵⁰ aD; *Cassibelianus* c; *Cassibelaunus* E; *Kassibellaunus* H; *Cassibellannus* R; *Cassibellanus* S. ⁵¹ acDEHRS (corrected from *exustus* in S). ⁵² acDEHR; *seu* S. ⁵³ aDHR; *me cogitaret* c; *cogitauerat* ES. ⁵⁴...⁵⁴ aHR; *princeps terre* cDES. ⁵⁵ acDERS; *inperator* H. ⁵⁶ cERS; *totius* aDH. ⁵⁷...⁵⁷ acHR; *ac fugatus est* DES. ⁵⁸ cER; *Insipientia* aDHS. ⁵⁹ aHR; *enim obducitur* cDES. ⁶⁰ acHR; *uel* DES. ⁶¹...⁶¹ acHR (*ammodo* in R); *amodo rex noster* DES. ⁶²...⁶² aHR; *me indigne* cDES. ⁶³...⁶³ acHR; *meam misericordiam* DES. ⁶⁴ acDERS; *inploret* H.

§63 ¹ acDEHS; *Hic* R. ² acDEHS; *festinans* R. ³...³ aHR; *genibus* c; *genibus eius* DES. ⁴ aDR; *Cassibelaunum* cE; *Kassibellaunum* H; *Cassibellanum* S. ⁵ ER; *deditionem* acDHS. ⁶...⁶ acHR; *exigere censes ab eo* DES. ⁷ cER; *clementia* aDHS. ⁸ acDERS; *inperatori* H. ⁹ acDERS; *propitius* H. ¹⁰ cDERS; om. aH. ¹¹...¹¹ aHR; *iterum Cesari* cDES.

Cassibellauno[12] Britanniam[13] Romano imperio[14] subdere laborarem; ecce, quod pepigi habere potes. Quid ultra tibi debeo? Nolit celi terreque rector [15]ut dominum meum et auunculum [16]se tali iusticie[16] offerentem paciar[17] aut captum uinculis[15] teneri aut dira morte interimi. Non est facile Cassibellaunum[18] [19]interfici me uiuente,[19] cui auxilium in tanta necessitate denegare non possum, nisi peticionem meam [20]pro eo benigne[20] susceperis.' Hac ergo[21] oratione[22] mitigatus Cesar concessit Androgeo[23] quod petebat. Datis itaque obsidibus et tributo de Britannis[24] quoque[25] anno tria[26] milia librarum argenti erario[27] [28]Romano assignato[28] concordes facti[29] Cesar et Cassibellaunus[30] dextras[31] sibi inuicem dederunt et oscula pacifica; sicque contione[32] separata quisque [33]in sua cum gaudio[33] remearunt.[34] Cesar autem[35] tota hyeme[36] in Britannia[37] remansit; uere redeunte in Galliam[38] transfretauit. Inde Romam cum omni exercitu suo se contulit sicut in hystoria[39] legitur Romanorum. Postea cum Cassibellaunus[40] .vii. annis superuixisset,[41] mortuus est et in[42] Eboraco[43] sepultus.

[64] Cui successit[1] Tenuancius[2] dux Cornubie: nam Androgeus frater eius Romam cum Cesare profectus fuerat. Qui dyademate[3] insignitus[4] regnum cum diligencia[5] quoad uixit tractauit. Post illum Kimbelinus[6] filius suus, miles strenuus,[7] suscepit imperium; quem Cesar Augustus

---

[12] aDR; *Cassibelauno* cE; *Kassibellauno* H; *Cassibellanno* S. [13] cDERS; *Brittanniam* aH. [14] acDERS; *inperio* H. [15...15] acDEHR; *dominum meum et auunculum* S. [16...16] aHR; *tali iusticie se* cDE; om. S. [17] aER; *patiar* cDH; om. S. [18] aD; *Cassibelaunum* cE; *Kassibellaunum* H; *Cassibellanum* RS. [19...19] acDES; *me uiuente interfici* H; *interficere me uiuente* R. [20...20] acHRS; *pro eo digne* D; *benigne pro eo* E. [21] cDERS; *igitur* aH. [22] acDHRS; *oracione* E. [23] acDEHR; *Andgrogeo* S. [24] cDERS; *Brittannis* aH. [25] aEHS; *quocumque* c; *quoquo* D; *queque* R. [26] aRS; *3* c; *.iii.* D (with *.xxx.* in margin) and E; *.iiii.* H. [27] aDEHS; *errario* cR (corrected from *erragrio* in R). [28...28] acDERS; *assignato Romano* H. [29] acDERS; *facti sunt* H. [30] a; *Cassibelaunus* c; *Cassibell'* DES; *Kassibellaunus* H; *Cassibellannus* R. [31] acEHRS; *dextras* (with *−que* suprascript) D. [32] acDH; *concione* E; *contitione* R; *contentione* S. [33...33] cDERS; *cum gaudio in sua* aH. [34] aDER; *remeat* corrected from *remaneat* c; *remeauit* HS. [35] acDEHR; *itaque* S. [36] DR; *yeme* c; *hieme* aEHS. [37] cDERS; *Brittannia* aH. [38] aHR; *Gallias* cDES. [39] acDRS; *historia* EH. [40] a; *Cassibelaunus* c; *Cassibell'* DES; *Kassibellaunus* H; *Cassibellannus* R. [41] cDERS; *uixisset* aH. [42] acDHRS; om. E. [43] acDERS; *Eburaco* H.

§64 [1] acDEHS; *concessit* R. [2] cERS; *Tenuantius* aDH. [3] DRS; *diademate* aEH; *dyamete* c. [4] acDEHS; *insingnitus* R. [5] cER; *diligentia* aDHS. [6] acDRS; *Kimbellinus* E; *Kembelinus* H. [7] aDERS; *strenuissimus* c; *strennuus* H.

58

Rome nutrierat, armis[8] decorauerat. Hic in tantam [9]amiciciam Romanorum[9] uenerat ut, cum posset tributum eorum detinere, gratis dabat.[10] Hiis[11] diebus natus est saluator noster Iesus Christus in Bethleem[12] sicud ewangelica[13] narrat hystoria.[14]

[65] Huic Kimbelino[1] nati sunt duo[2] filii, Gwiderius[3] et Aruiragus;[4] et[5] cum rexisset feliciter .x. annis regnum Britannie,[6] moriens dimisit sceptrum regni Gwiderio[7] primogenito. Hic cum tributum Romanis denegaret, missus est Claudius imperator a senatu cum exercitu[8] ad Britanniam[9] ut iterum subiugaret eam et tributum redderet. Princeps milicie[10] Claudii Lelius[11] Hamo uocabatur cuius consilio et ope[12] Claudius nitebatur.[13] Uenientes ergo[14] in Britanniam[15] applicuerunt Porcestriam ciuitatem supra mare sitam.

[66] Quam cum [1]obsedisset Claudius[1] et portas eius muro preclusisset[2] ut uel sic fame[3] afflictos ciues eius dedicioni[4] cogeret, superuenit Gwiderius[5] cum exercitu Britonum[6] commissoque prelio cum Romanis maiorem partem exercitus [7]et ipsum[7] Claudium ad naues fugere coegit. Sed inter[8] bellandum[9] Hamo prefatus [10]princeps milicie[10] uersuto usus consilio proiectis[11] armis propriis capit Britannica[12] arma defunctorum[13] in bello et quasi ex ipsis contra suos pugnabat, exhortans Britones[14] ad insequendum Romanos, citum promittens de illis triumphum. Nouerat

[8] acEHRS; *et* suprascript before *armis* in D. [9...9] cDERS; *Romanorum amicitiam* aH. [10] acDERS; *daret* H. [11] cDERS; *His* aH. [12] acDEHR; *Bethlehem* S. [13] cRS; *euangelica* aH; *euuangelica* DE. [14] acDERS; *historia* H.

§65 [1] acEHRS; *Kymbelino* D. [2] acDERS; *.ii.* H. [3] R; *Guiderinus* a; *Gwider* c; *Guider* DEHS. [4] aDEHS; *Auigarus* c; *Aruiragrus* R. [5] acDERS; *hic* H. [6] cDERS; *Brittannie* aH. [7] acR; *Guiderio* DEH; *Guiderino* S. [8] acDEHR; *Britonum* underpointed after *exercitu* in S. [9] cDERS; *Brittanniam* a; *Brittannias* H. [10] cER; *militie* aDHS. [11] acDEHS; *Leluus* R. [12] acDEHR; *opere* S. [13] aDER; *utebatur* cHS (in margin in c; tampered with in S?). [14] cDERS; *igitur* aH. [15] cDERS; *Brittanniam* aH.

§66 [1...1] acHR; *Claudius obsedisset* DES. [2] aHR; *obstruxisset* c; *exclusisset* DES. [3] aHR; om. cDES. [4] ER; *deditioni* acDHS. [5] acR; *Guiderius* DEHS. [6] cDERS; *Brittonum* aH. [7...7] aHR; *ipsumque* DES. [8] acEHRS; *in inter* D. [9] acEHRS; *bellando* D. [10...10] cR; *princeps militie* aH; *militie princeps* D; *milicie princeps* ES. [11] aHR; *abiectis* cDES. [12] cDERS; *Brittannica* aH. [13] cDES; *interfectorum* aH; *defunctorum uel interfectorum* R. [14] cDERS; *Brittones* aH.

enim linguam[15] Britannicam[16] quam didicerat Rome inter obsides Britonum.[17] Deinde[18] accessit paulatim iuxta regem adituque inuento quod cogitarat[19] expleuit et regem nichil[20] [21]tale timentem[21] mucrone percussum suffocauit. Elapsus[22] deinde ab[23] hostium cuneis[24] sese inter suos recepit. Frater[25] autem regis[26] Aruiragus[27] ut illum peremptum inuenit, deponens arma sua regiis se induit armis hinc inde Britones[28] [29]ad perstandum[29] exhortans tamquam[30] esset Guiderius. Qui nescientes casum regis stragem non minimam[31] de hostibus usque ad naues persequendo egerunt. Cedentibus itaque Britonibus[32] diuiduntur[33] Romani in duas partes: Claudius cum quadam parte suorum naues ingreditur; Hamo autem,[34] quia naues ingredi non licuit, nemorum[35] tutamina petit. Aruiragus igitur[36] existimans in comitatu[37] Hamonis Claudium esse persequitur[38] fugientes de loco ad[39] locum nec cessauit eos insequi usque ad litus maris. Ibi dum in portu nauium Hamo se de equo misisset ut in [40]una naue[40] mercatorum ascenderet et de instante[41] mortis periculo se eriperet, mox superuenit Aruiragus et stricto ense[42] eum interfecit nomenque dedit loco qui usque hodie Portus Hamonis appellatur.

[67] Interea Claudius resociatis sociis[1] oppugnat predictam ciuitatem — que tunc Kaerperis, nunc autem Porcestria dicitur. Nec mora menia diruit[2] ciuibusque[3] subactis insecutus[4] est Aruiragum iam Wintoniam[5] ingressum. Obsedit ciuitatem diuersisque[6] machinis oppugnat.[7] Aruiragus uero se obsessum indignans copias suorum per cateruas[8] disponit apertisque[9] portis ad preliandum educit; sed interuenientibus ex utraque parte maioribus natu concordiam facere statuerunt ne strages[10]

[15] acDEHS; *lingua* R. [16] cDERS; *Brittannicam* aH. [17] cDERS; *Brittonum* aH. [18] acDHRS; *Denique* E. [19] aHRS; *cogitauerat* cDE. [20] aEHRS; *nil* cD. [21...21] acDEHS; *timentem tale* R. [22] acDHRS; *Elapsis* E. [23] acDEHS; *ad* R. [24] aHR; *cateruis* cDES. [25] acDHRS; *Aruigarus* added before *Frater* in E. [26] acDEHRS (corrected from *regit* in R). [27] aHR; om. cDES. [28] cDERS; *Brittones* aH. [29...29] acDERS; om. H. [30] R; *tanquam* acDEHS. [31] acEHRS; *modicam* D. [32] cDERS; *Brittonibus* aH. [33] aHR; *diuisi sunt* cDES. [34] acDEHS; om. R. [35] acDEHS; *in* deleted before *nemorum* in R. [36] acDEHS; *ergo* R. [37] aDEHR; *commitatu* cS. [38] acHR; *prosequitur* DES. [39] acHR; *in* DES. [40...40] aR; *naui una* c; *unam nauem* DEHS. [41] acHR; *instanti* DES. [42] acDERS; *gladio* H.

§67 [1] aDERS; *suis* c; *turmis* H. [2] acDERS; *dirimit* H. [3] acDHRS; *ciuibus* E. [4] acDERS; *insequtus* H. [5] acDHRS; *Wyntoniam* E. [6] cDERS; *diuersis* aH. [7] aDEHS; *oppungnat* cR. [8] acDERS; *turmas* H. [9] acDERS; *apertis* H. [10] aDEHS; *strage* R.

¹¹populi amplior¹¹ fieret. Requisitus Claudius pacemne¹² an bellum mallet, respondit se saluo Romano¹³ honore malle pacificari; neque enim ¹⁴adeo humanum cruorem¹⁴ siciebat¹⁵ ut extra rationem¹⁶ eos debellare uellet. Ductis igitur¹⁷ usque¹⁸ ad id loci sermonibus pactus est Claudius sese filiam suam Aruirago daturum, tantum ut ¹⁹se cum regno¹⁹ Britannie potestati Romane subiectum cognosceret. Postpositis ergo²⁰ debellacionibus²¹ utrimque²² suaserunt maiores natu Aruirago huiuscemodi²³ pactionibus adquiescere.²⁴ Paruit itaque et subiectionem Cesari fecit.

[68] Confestim Claudius Romam mittens natam suam ut Aruirago sponsaretur¹ adduci precepit. Interea ²auxilio Aruiragi usus² Orcades et proximas Britannie insulas potestati Romane acquisiuit.³ Porro emensa hieme⁴ redierunt legati cum filia Genuissa nomine et Aruirago nuptiali⁵ copulata thoro celebrarunt nuptias⁶ iuxta Sabrinum fluuium in confinio Demecie⁷ et Loegrie. Unde rex locum eundem ⁸celebrem post se⁸ esse cupiens suggessit Claudio ut ibidem ciuitas edificaretur et de nomine eius Kaerglou⁹ – ¹⁰id est Claudiocestria¹⁰ – appellaretur. Quidam tamen ipsam traxisse nomen a Gloio duce aiunt quem Claudius in illa generauerat;¹¹ cui post Aruiragum¹² gubernaculum Demetici¹³ ducatus cessit. Hiis¹⁴ itaque patratis reuersus est Claudius Romam, ubi tunc temporis Petrus¹⁵ apostolus de Anthiochia¹⁶ ueniens predicationem¹⁷ ewangelii¹⁸ Romanis intimabat.¹⁹

---

^{11...11} DES; *amplior populi* aH; *populi maior* R. ¹² aEHRS; *pacem* D. ¹³ aDEHS; *humano* deleted before *Romano* in R. ^{14...14} aHR; *humanum cruorem adeo* DES. ¹⁵ EHRS; *scicebat* a; *sitiebat* D. ¹⁶ aDHRS; *racionem* E. ¹⁷ aDEHS; *itaque* R. ¹⁸ aDHRS; om. E. ^{19...19} cDEHS; *cum se regno* a; *cum regno se* R. ²⁰ acDEHR; om. S. ²¹ aER; *debellationibus* cDHS. ²² acDHS; *utrinque* E; *utrumque* R. ²³ acDHRS; *huiusmodi* E. ²⁴ aHR; *acquiescere* cDES.

§68 ¹ acHR; *desponsaretur* DES. ^{2...2} aR; *usus Cesaris auxilio* c; *Aruiragi usus auxilio* DES; *auxilium Aruiragi usus* H. ³ R; *adquisiuit* acDEHS. ⁴ aHRS; *hyeme* cDE. ⁵ acDHRS; *nupciali* E. ⁶ acDHRS; *nupcias* E. ⁷ cR; *Demetie* aH; *Demetice* DES. ^{8...8} acH; *post se celebrem* DES; *celebrem posse* R. ⁹ acDHR (with *Kayrgloyn* in margin of D); *Kayrglou* E; *Kaerclou* S. ^{10...10} acDERS; *a Claudio* H. ¹¹ aHR; *genuerat* c; *generauit* DES. ¹² aDEHR; *Auiragum* c; *Aruiragum* corrected from *Aruirago* in S. ¹³ aDERS; *Demecie* c; *Demetie* (over an erasure) H. ¹⁴ cDERS; *His* aH. ¹⁵ cDEHS; *sanctus Petrus* R. ¹⁶ cRS; *Antiochia* DEH. ¹⁷ cDHRS; *predicacionem* E. ¹⁸ cRS; *euangelii* aDH; *euuangelii* E. ¹⁹ cDEHRS; after *intimabat*, *misitque Marcum euange-listam in Egiptum predicare euangelium quod scripserat* added (from vulgate text) in margin of S.

[69] Post discessum Claudii a Britannia[1] Aruiragus in superbiam elatus despexit Romane potestati subiacere. Missus est igitur[2] Uespasianus[3] a senatu in[4] Britanniam[5] ut Aruiragum [6]et gentem[6] rebellem compesceret et tributum restitueret. Cum autem nauigaret et in Rutupi[7] Portu applicare uellet, Aruiragus de aduentu illius[8] premunitus[9] a portu eum[10] prohibuit; retraxit igitur se Uespasianus[11] a[12] portu illo[13] retortisque uelis in Totonesio litore[14] se contulit et exiens in terram ciuitatem[15] Kaerpenhuelgoit,[16] que nunc Exonia uocatur, adiit. Cumque[17] eam .vii. diebus obsedisset, superuenit Aruiragus cum exercitu forti; congressusque cum Romanis, totum diem consumpserunt ambo exercitus lacessentes[18] inuicem uulneribusque[19] utrimque[20] lacerati. Superueniente noctis crepusculo quieuerunt; mane autem facto mediante Genuissa regina [21]concordes effecti sunt[21] Uespasianus[22] et Aruiragus. Hyeme[23] uero emensa nauigauit Uespasianus[24] in Galliam[25] et inde Romam rediit. Rexit[26] deinde Aruiragus regnum Britannie[27] cum pace et tranquillitate[28] usque in senectutem uergens dilexitque[29] senatum et gentem Romanam propter uxorem suam quam diligebat; que de Romanis, sicut[30] predictum est, originem duxerat.[31] Ut igitur dies uite sue expleuit, mortuus est et sepultus Claudiocestrie in templo quod in honorem Claudii dicauerat.

[70] Successit Aruirago filius suus Marius, uir mire prudencie[1] et sapientie.[2] Regnante itaque[3] illo quidam[4] rex Pictorum [5]nomine Rodric[5] de Scithia[6] adueniens cum magna classe applicuit in Albaniam[7] cepitque prouinciam[8] uastare. Collecto igitur Marius exercitu obuiam ei uenit et

§69 [1] cDERS; *Brittannia* aH. [2] acDEHR; *ergo* S. [3] cDHS; *Uaspasianus* aE; *Uespesianus* R. [4] acHR; *ad* DES. [5] cDERS; *Brittanniam* aH. [6...6] acHR; om. DES. [7] DERS; *Rutubi* acH. [8] acH; *illorum* DES; *eius* R. [9] cDERS; *premonitus* aH. [10] acHR; *eos* DES. [11] acDHRS; *Uaspasianus* E. [12] acHRS; *de* DE. [13] aHR; *suo* cDES. [14] DER; *littore* acHS. [15] acEHRS; om. D. [16] acDR; *Kaerpenhuelgdit* ES; *Kaerpenhelgoit* H. [17] acDEHR; *Cum* S. [18] c; *lacescentes* aHR (altered to *lasescentes* in H); *laciscentes* DES. [19] aDEH; *vulneribus* c; *wlneribusque* R; *wlneribus* S. [20] acDR; *utrinque* ES; om. H. [21...21] aHR; *concordes facti sunt* cES; *facti sunt concordes* D. [22] acDHRS; *Uaspasianus* E. [23] cDER; *Hieme* aHS. [24] acDHRS; *Uaspasianus* E. [25] acHR; *Gallias* DES. [26] aHR; *Rex* cDES. [27] cDERS; *Brittannie* aH. [28] aHR; *tranquillitate regens* DES. [29] acHR; *dilexit* DES. [30] acR; *sicud* DEHS. [31] acHR; *duxit* DES.

§70 [1] cEHRS; *prudentie* aD. [2] acDHRS; *sapiencie* E. [3] acDEHS; *namque* R. [4] acDHRS; om. E. [5...5] aHR; *Rodric nomine* cDES. [6] aDHS; *Scitia* c; *Cichia* E; *Scicia* R. [7] cR; *Albania* aDEHS. [8] aHR; *in prouinciam* c; *patriam* DES (over an erasure in E).

congressus cum illo[9] interfecit eum[10] et uictoria potitus erexit lapidem in signum triumphi[11] in loco qui postea de nomine suo dicta est Westmaria;[12] in quo titulus scriptus memoriam eius usque in hodiernum diem testatur. Perempto uero Rodric[13] dedit deuicto populo qui cum eo uenerat partem Albanie ad[14] inhabitandum; que pars Cathenesia[15] nuncupatur. Erat autem [16]terra deserta,[16] nullo habitatore antea culta. Cumque uxores non haberent, a Britonibus[17] [18]natas et[18] cognatas uxores sibi petentes repulsam[19] passi sunt. Transeuntes igitur in Hyberniam[20] duxerunt de populo illo uxores ex[21] quibus orta soboles in magnam[22] multitudinem creuerunt; et exinde Picti Britanniam[23] incoluerunt. At Marius cum totum regnum [24]summa pace[24] composuisset,[25] cepit cum Romanis dilectionem habere, tributa soluens et exemplo patris incitatus iusticiam[26] et leges paternas atque omnia honesta sectabatur.

[71] Cumque cursum uite sue explesset, moriens filio suo Coillo[1] regni gubernaculum dimisit. Hic ab infancia[2] Rome nutritus mores Romanorum edoctus in amiciciam[3] eorum incidit et tributa libenter eis[4] reddens [5]aduersari eis in nullo[5] uolebat.[6]

[72] Interim[1] natus est[2] ei[3] unicus filius cui nomen Lucius impositum[4] est. Hic post mortem patris regni dyademate[5] insignitus omnem uiam[6] prudencie[7] atque actus patris bonosque[8] mores insecutus[9] ab omnibus ad quos fama [10]bonitatis illius[10] peruenerat amabatur et colebatur.

[9] acEHRS; *eo* D. [10] acEHRS; *illum* D. [11] cDERS; *uictorie sue* a; *tituli triumphi* H. [12] acDER (corrected from *Westmamaria* in a); *Westimaria* H; *Westrimaria* S. [13] acDEHR; *Rodrico* S. [14] acDEHS; om. R. [15] R; *Katanesia* aH; *Katenesia* cDES. [16...16] acDEHS; *deserta terra* R. [17] cDERS; *Brittonibus* aH. [18...18] acDEHS; *et natas* R. [19] acDEHS; *repulsas* R. [20] aDERS; *Hiberniam* cH. [21] acHR; *de* DES. [22] acHR (after *multitudinem* in c); *maximam* DES. [23] cDERS; *Brittanniam* aH. [24...24] DERS; *cum pace summa* aH; *in suma pace* c. [25] acDERS; *conposuisset* H. [26] aDERS; *iusticias* cH.

§71 [1] acDERS; *Koillo* H. [2] ER; *infantia* acDHS. [3] DERS; *amicitiam* aH; *amicitia* c. [4] acHR; om. DES. [5...5] acH; *in nullo eis aduersari* DES; *in nullo aduersari eis* R. [6] acDEHS; *nolebat* R.

§72 [1] acDERS; *Interea* H. [2] acDHRS; om. E. [3] aDERS; *illi* c; om. H. [4] aDERS; om. c; *inpositum* H. [5] DER; *diademate* acHS. [6] acDERS; om. H. [7] cERS; *prudentie* aD; *prudentiam* H. [8] acDERS; *et bonos* H. [9] acDERS (corrected from *insecutos* in R); *insequtus* H. [10...10] acDEHS; *illius bonitatis* R.

¹¹Audiens quoque¹¹ christianitatem Rome et in aliis regnis¹² exaltari¹³ primus omnium regum Britonum¹⁴ Christi nomen affectans epistulas dirigit¹⁵ Eleutherio pape, petens ut ad se ¹⁶mitteret personas tales¹⁶ a quibus christianitatem suscipere deberet. Serenauerant¹⁷ enim mentem eius miracula que¹⁸ Christi discipuli et predicatores per diuersas nacionum¹⁹ gentes ediderant. Et quidem²⁰ in omnem terram exiuit sonus eorum et in fines orbis terre uerba eorum. Et quia ad amorem ²¹uere fidei²¹ hanelabat,²² pie peticionis²³ effectum²⁴ consecutus²⁵ est. Siquidem predictus pontifex gloriam²⁶ in excelsis Deo canens duos religiosos doctores, Faganum et Duuianum,²⁷ de latere suo misit Britanniam²⁸ qui uerbum Dei caro²⁹ factum et pro hominibus passum regi populoque predicarent et sacro baptismate insignirent. Nec mora concurrentes ³⁰undique populi diuerse nacionis³⁰ exemplum regis sequentes³¹ lauacro sacro³² intinguntur atque omnipotenti Deo subduntur, ydola³³ despicientes et minutatim confringentes. Beati igitur doctores cum paganismum³⁴ de gente Britonum³⁵ in maiori parte deleuissent,³⁶ templa que in honore plurimorum deorum fundata fuerant³⁷ mundatis³⁸ ruderibus³⁹ uni Deo consecrauerunt et uiris religiosis custodienda tradiderunt. Fuerunt⁴⁰ tunc in Britannia⁴¹ per regiones constituti .xxviii.⁴² flamines et⁴³ tres archiflamines qui thura diis ex ritu gentilium cremabant atque libamina de pecudibus litabant. Hec⁴⁴ itaque⁴⁵ ex⁴⁶ apostolica doctrina ydolatrie⁴⁷ eripientes episcopos ubi erant flamines, ⁴⁸archiepiscopos ubi⁴⁹ archiflamines⁴⁸ consecraue-

¹¹...¹¹ acHR; *Audiensque* DES. ¹² acHR; *terris* DES. ¹³ acDEHRS (corrected from *exalutari* in D). ¹⁴ cDERS; *Brittonum* aH. ¹⁵ cDERS; *direxit* aH. ¹⁶...¹⁶ aHR; *personas mitteret tales* c; *personas tales mitteret* DES. ¹⁷ acDEHS; *Serenauerunt* R. ¹⁸ acDHRS; *qui* E. ¹⁹ ER; *nationum* acDHS (corrected from *nationes* in S). ²⁰ acDERS; *quod* H. ²¹...²¹ cDERS; *fidei uere* a; *Dei* H. ²² cDR; *anelabat* aES; *anhelabat* H. ²³ aDER; *petitionis* cHS. ²⁴ acDEHR; *affectum* S. ²⁵ acDERS; *consequutus* H. ²⁶ cDERS; *gloria* aH. ²⁷ cDERS (or perhaps *Dumanum* in D); *Dumianum* a; *Dimianum* H. ²⁸ cERS; *Brittanniam* aH; *in* suprascript before *Britanniam* in D. ²⁹ acDES; *carnem* HR. ³⁰...³⁰ aHR (*nationis* in aH); *populi undique diuerse nationis* c; *populi diuerse nacionis undique* DES (*nationis* in D). ³¹ acDERS (before *regis* in c); *insequentes* H. ³² acDHRS; *sancto* E. ³³ cDERS; *idola* aH. ³⁴ acDERS; *paganissnum* H. ³⁵ cDERS; *Brittonum* aH. ³⁶ acDEHRS (corrected from *deleuisserunt* in S). ³⁷ aHR; *erant* cDES. ³⁸ acHRS (corrected from *mundati* in S); *mundata* D; *mundati* E. ³⁹ acDERS; *rudibus* H. ⁴⁰ aHR; *Fuerant* cDES. ⁴¹ cDERS; *Brittannia* aH. ⁴² DRS; *.xxxviii.* aH; *28* c; *uiginti octo* E. ⁴³ acDEHS; *archiepiscopos* deleted before *et* in R. ⁴⁴ aDEHR; *Hos* c; *Hii* S. ⁴⁵ acDEHS; *uero* R. ⁴⁶ acDEHR; om. S. ⁴⁷ acDE (*ydolatrie* before *ex apostolica* in c); *idolatrie* H; *e* deleted before *ydolatrie* in R; *ydolatriam* S. ⁴⁸...⁴⁸ acDERS; om. H. ⁴⁹ acR; *ubi erant* DES; om. H.

runt. Sedes principales[50] archiflaminum sicut in nobilioribus [51]ciuita-
tibus fuerant,[51] Londoniis[52] scilicet et Eboraci et in Urbe Legionum,[53]
que super Oscam[54] fluuium in Glamorgancia[55] sita est, ita in hiis[56]
tribus euacuata supersticione tribus archiepiscopis dedicauerunt;[57] in
reliquis episcopos ordinauerunt diuisisque[58] parrochiis[59] [60]unicuique ius
suum[60] assignauerunt. Metropolitano Eboracensi Deira[61] et Albania,
sicut magnum flumen [62]Humbri eas[62] a Loegria[63] [64]secernit, in parrochiam cessit.[65] Londoniensi[66] uero submissa est Loegria et Cornubia,
quas prouincias[64] [67]seiungit Sabrina[67] a Kambria, [68]id est Gualia,[68] que
Urbi Legionum subiacuit. Hiis[69] ita[70] Dei nutu constitutis redierunt
Romam antistites prefati[71] et cuncta que fecerant a beato papa
confirmari impetrauerunt.[72] Palliis itaque ac[73] ceteris[74] honoribus decenter ab ecclesia Romana insigniti reuersi sunt in Britanniam[75] cum
pluribus uiris religiosis[76] comitati quorum doctrina et predicacione[77]
gens Britonum in fide Christi roborata et aucta est; quorum actus in
libro quem Gyldas[78] hystoriographus[79] composuit lucide[80] scripti[81]
reperiuntur.[82]

[73] Interea gloriosus ille rex Lucius cum cultum uere fidei crescere et
exaltari in regno suo uidisset, magno fluctuans gaudio possessiones et
territoria, que prius templa ydolorum[1] possederant,[2] in meliorem usum
uertens ecclesiis fidelium habenda concessit augmentauitque[3] illas

[50] acDERS; *principalis* H. [51]...[51] cDERS; *fuerant ciuitatibus* aH. [52] acDERS; *Lundoniis*
H. [53] acDEHS; *Legionum Carlium* R. [54] aEHR; *Oscham* cDS. [55] cDES; *Damorgantia*
a; *Clamorgantia* H; *Clammorgancia* R. [56] cDERS; *his* aH. [57] RS; *dicauerunt* acDEH.
[58] aHR; *distinctis* c; *diuersisque* DES (with *diuisis* in margin in D). [59] acDEHR;
parochiis S. [60]...[60] aERS; *unicuique suam ita* c; *ius suum unicuique* DH. [61] aDR; *Deiria*
cEHS. [62]...[62] acDERS; *Humbreas* H. [63] acDEHR; *Leogria* S. [64]...[64] acHR; *et Cornubia*
DES. [65] acR; om. DES; *secessit* H. [66] cR; *Lundoniensi* aH; om. DES. [67]...[67] cR;
Sabrina seiungit aH; *seiungit Sabrina* (altered by erasure from *Sabrinam?*) D; *seiungit
Sabrinaque* E; *seiungit Sabrinam* S. [68]...[68] HR; *id est Guallia* a; *id est Wallia* c; om.
DES (with *id est Wallia* in margin of D). [69] cDER; *His* aHS. [70] acDEHS; *itaque* R.
[71] acDEHS; *prefata* R. [72] acDERS; *inpetrauerunt* H. [73] acEHRS; *a* corrected to *ac* D.
[74] acDERS; *ceterisque* H. [75] cDERS; *Brittanniam* aH. [76] acDEHS; *religiosi* R.
[77] aERS; *predicatione* cDH. [78] R; *Gildas* acDEHS. [79] aDRS; *historiographus* cEH.
[80] aDHR; *luci* E; *luculenter* S. [81] aDR; *descripti* ES; *scripta* H. [82] acDEHRS; after
reperiuntur, *Explicit liber quartus* [.iiii. H]. *Incipit liber* [om. HR] *quintus* [.v. H]
aHR.

§73 [1] acDER; *idolorum* H; *deorum* S. [2] cDES; *possiderent* a; *possederent* H;
possiderant R. [3] acR; *ampliauitque* DE; *et augmentauit* H; *ampliauit* S.

⁴amplioribus agris⁴ et mansis⁵ omnique libertate donauit.⁶ Peracto igitur⁷ feliciter uite sue cursu ab hac luce migrauit in urbe Claudiocestrie et in ecclesia prime sedis honorifice sepultus est anno ab incarnatione⁸ Domini ⁹centesimo quinquagesimo .vi..⁹ Defuncto eo contencio¹⁰ inter Britones¹¹ orta est quis heres eius esse deberet. Carebat enim sobole que ei¹² ¹³hereditario iure¹³ succederet.

[74] Sed¹ ut² Rome nunciatum est, misit senatus Seuerum senatorem duasque legiones cum illo ut patria³ Romane potestati restitueretur. Mox ut terram ingressus est, rebellabant Britones⁴ aduersus eum. Quorum pars sibi continuo submissa est; pars autem⁵ que subici ⁶Romane potestati⁶ renuit trans Humbrum usque in Scociam⁷ ab ipso⁸ imperatore⁹ fugata est. At illa duce Fulgenio¹⁰ omni nisu Seuero resistens irrupciones¹¹ molestas consociatis¹² sibi Pictis in regnum Deire,¹³ dum¹⁴ procul abesset,¹⁵ faciebat.¹⁶ Quam irrupcionem¹⁷ grauiter ferens imperator iussit uallum construi¹⁸ inter Deiram¹⁹ et Albaniam ut uel sic eorum²⁰ impetus arceretur ne longius nocere posset. Facto igitur uallo a mari usque ad mare Fulgenius,²¹ quia ²²terram sibi obstrui²² uidet, marinum²³ petit auxilium. Nauigauitque²⁴ in Scithiam²⁵ ut Pictorum auxilio dignitati²⁶ restitueretur. Reuersus itaque cum magno nauigio ²⁷Eboracum obsedit,²⁷ ubi magna pars Britonum²⁸ Seuerum deserens Fulgenio²⁹ adhesit. Sed Seuerus conuocatis ³⁰ceteris Britonibus³⁰ atque Romanis uiriliter adiit obsidionem; congressique³¹ pariter,

⁴...⁴ acDEHS; *agris amplioribus* R. ⁵ acHR; *mansis siue mansionibus* D; *mansionibus* ES. ⁶ acDHRS; *dotauit* E. ⁷ acDHRS; *ergo* E. ⁸ acDHRS; *incarnacione* E. ⁹...⁹ R; *157* c; *.clvi.* aDEHS. ¹⁰ aEHRS; *contentio* cD. ¹¹ cDERS; *Brittones* aH. ¹² cDERS; *sibi* aH. ¹³...¹³ acDEHS; *iure hereditario* R.

§74 ¹ acDHRS; *Set* E. ² acDHRS; *ur* E. ³ acDEHRS (corrected from *patriam* in S). ⁴ cDERS; *Brittones* aH. ⁵ cDERS; om. aH. ⁶...⁶ acHR; *potestati Romane* DES. ⁷ cERS; *Scotiam* aDH. ⁸ acDEHS; om. (from text), *ipso* in margin R. ⁹ acEHRS; *inperatore* H. ¹⁰ acEHRS; *Sulgenio* D. ¹¹ ER; *irruptiones* acDHS. ¹² cHR; *consotiatis* a; *resociatis* DES. ¹³ acDEHS; *Dene* R. ¹⁴ acDERS; om. H. ¹⁵ acDER; *abesse* HS. ¹⁶ acHR; *faciebant* DES. ¹⁷ ER; *irruptionem* acDHS. ¹⁸ acDERS; *constitui* H. ¹⁹ acDEHS; *Deniam* R. ²⁰ acDEH; *illorum* RS. ²¹ acEHRS; *Sulgenius* D. ²²...²² acEHS; *obstrui sibi terram* D; *terram obstrui* R. ²³ acDEHR; *marimum* S. ²⁴ acDEHR; *Nauigauit* S. ²⁵ DR; *Sithiam* aEHS; *Sciciam* c. ²⁶ cDERS (after *restitueretur* in c); om. aH. ²⁷...²⁷ acHR; *obsedit Eboracum* DES. ²⁸ cDERS; *Brittonum* aH. ²⁹ acEHRS; *Sulgenio* D. ³⁰...³⁰ acDERS (*Brittonibus* in a); *Brittonibus ceteris* H. ³¹ aDEHS; *congressisque* c; *congressusque* R.

inter pugnandum occubuit Seuerus cum pluribus suorum[32] et Fulgenius[33] letaliter uulneratus[34] est. Sepultusque est Seuerus Eboraci, sicut legiones[35] suorum Romanorum postulauerunt, cum [36]regali honore[36] et reuerencia.[37]

[75] Reliquit[1] ipse [2]duos filios post se,[2] Basianum[3] et Getam; quorum Geta[4] matre Romana generatus[5] erat, Basianus[6] Britannica.[7] Romani ergo arripientes Getam sublimauerunt[8] in[9] regem, Britanni[10] uero Basianum[11] elegerunt. Orta itaque inter eos altercacione[12] pugnare inuicem ceperunt fratres. Confestim Geta perempto Basianus[13] regno potitur. Ea tempestate erat in Britannia[14] iuuenis quidam nomine Carausius[15] ex infima gente creatus.[16] Qui cum uirtutem suam et probitatem in multis negociis[17] examinasset, profectus est Romam; petiuitque[18] a senatu et optinuit[19] ut maritima Britannie[20] ab incursione barbarica nauigio tueri liceret. Promisitque[21] rei publice augmentum in tributis. Reuersus itaque [22]cum signatis[22] cartis in Britanniam[23] mox collectis undicumque[24] nauibus cum magna iuuenum turba nouitates affectancium[25] tamquam[26] pirata[27] crudelis mare ingressus est. Proxima igitur aggressus litora[28] urbes et uillas finitimorum depopulari ferro et igne[29] non cessabat. Insulis quoque comprouincialibus[30] appulsus [31]omnia sua incolis[31] atrociter eripiebat. Sic itaque illo agente confluxit ad eum non minima multitudo perditorum hominum aliena rapere hanelancium[32] ita ut in breui tantum congregaret exercitum quantus[33] [34]uni regno[34] sufficeret possidendum.[35] Elatus ergo in superbiam petiuit

32 acDEHS; *eorum* R. 33 acEHRS; *Sulgenius* D. 34 acDEHS; *wlneratus* R. 35 acDERS; *legitimi* H. 36...36 acDERS; *honore regali* H. 37 cER; *reuerentia* aDHS.

§75 1 acDEHR; *Reliquid* S. 2...2 cDERS; *post se duos filios* aH. 3 DERS; *Bassianum* acH. 4 acDEHS; *Greca* (?) R. 5 acHR; *natus* DES. 6 DERS; *Bassianus* acH. 7 cDERS; *Brittannica* aH. 8 cDR; *sullimauerunt* aEHS. 9 acDERS; *eum in* H. 10 cDERS; *Brittanni* aH. 11 DERS; *Bassianum* acH. 12 ER; *altercatione* acDHS. 13 DERS (altered from *Bassianus* in S); *Bassianus* acH. 14 cDERS; *Brittannia* aH. 15 aDES; *Caurausius* cR; *Karausius* H. 16 aHR; *natus* cDES. 17 acDERS; *negotiis* H. 18 acDEHR; *Petiuit* S. 19 acHRS; *obtinuit* DE. 20 cDERS; *Brittannie* aH. 21 cDEHR; *Promisit* S. 22...22 aHRS (*cum* tampered in S?); *consignatis* c; *consignatis* (altered from *insignatis* ?) D; *insignatis* E. 23 cDERS; *Brittanniam* aH. 24 R; *undecumque* acDEHS. 25 cER; *affectantium* aDHS. 26 R; *tanquam* acDEHS. 27 acDEHS; *pirrata* R. 28 DERS; *littora* acH. 29 cDERS; *igni* aH. 30 cD; *comprouintionibus* a; *comprouincionalibus* ES; *conprouincialibus* H; *cum prouincialibus* R. 31...31 acHR; *incolis omnia sua* DES. 32 cR; *anhelantium* aHS; *anelantium* D; *anelancium* E. 33 acDERS; *quantum* H. 34...34 acDEHS; *in regno uni* R. 35 aHR; *ad possidendum* cDES.

a Britonibus[36] ut sese regem facerent et ipse[37] Romanos omnes de regno exterminaret. Quod cum impetrasset,[38] confestim dimicans cum Basiano[39] interfecit eum. Quippe proditus est a Pictis quos[40] [41]dux Fulgenius,[41] matris sue frater, in Britanniam[42] locauerat. [43]Nam dum[43] [44]hiis confidens[44] dimicaret, promissis et donis Carausii[45] corrupti [46]a Basiano[46] mox in ipso[47] congressu se subtraxerunt et inter Carausii[48] copias se inserentes de commilitonibus hostes facti[49] sunt. Unde Carausio[50] uictoria ocius[51] cessit. Ut autem [52]regni gubernacula Carausius[52] adeptus est, dedit [53]Pictis locum mansionis[53] in Albania,[54] ubi[55] Britonibus[56] admixti in euum subsequens permanserunt.[57]

[76] Cum ergo[1] Carausii[2] inuasio Rome [3]nunciata foret,[3] legauit senatus Allectum[4] [5]fortem uirum[5] et prudentem cum tribus[6] legionibus in Britanniam[7] ut tyrannum[8] illum[9] de regno deleret et tributum Romane potestati restitueret. Nec mora ueniens Allectus in Britanniam[10] prelium commisit cum Carausio[11] illoque interfecto regni solium suscepit. Deinde persecutus est Britones[12] qui relicta re publica Carausio[13] adheserant. Britones[14] igitur[15] id[16] grauiter ferentes erexerunt [17]in regem sibi[17] Asclepiodotum ducem Cornubie communique assensu[18] persecuti[19] sunt Allectum inueneruntque[20] eum Londonie[21] festum patriis diis celebrantem. Qui cum Asclepiodoti aduentum compe-

[36] cDERS; *Brittonibus* aH. [37] acDEHR; *prope* (?) S. [38] acDERS; *inpetrasset* H. [39] DERS; *Bassiano* acH. [40] acDEHS; *quod* R. [41...41] acERS; *dux Sulgenius* D; om. H. [42] cR; *Brittanniam* a; *Britannia* DES; *Brittannia* H. [43...43] aH; *Nam* c; *Nam cum* DES; *Nam dii* R. [44...44] R; *his confidens* aH; *hiis confidens cum* c; *hiis fidens* DE; *is fidenter* S. [45] aDERS; *Caurausii* c; *Karausii* H. [46...46] DES; *a Bassiano* acH; *ab assanio* (with the *i* underpointed) R. [47] acDEHS; *ipsa* R. [48] acDERS; *ipsas Karausii* H. [49] acDERS; *effecti* H. [50] acDERS; *Karausio* H. [51] acERS; *otius* DH. [52...52] cDERS; *Carausius regni gubernacula* aH (*Karausius* in H). [53...53] aHR; *locum mansionis Pictis* cDES. [54] acDEHS; *Albaniam* R. [55] acDERS; *ut* H. [56] cDERS; *Brittonibus* aH. [57] acDES; *permanerent* H; *submanserunt* R.

§76 [1] acDERS; *igitur* H. [2] acDERS (corrected from *Carausio* in R); *Karausii* H. [3...3] acDERS; *nuntiata fuisset* H. [4] acDHRS; *Allectu* E. [5...5] aDERS; *uirum fortem* cH. [6] acDERS; *.iii.* H. [7] cDERS; *Brittanniam* aH. [8] aDRS; *tirannum* cE; *tirannidem* H. [9] acDERS; *Karausii* H. [10] cDERS; *Brittanniam* aH. [11] acDERS; *Karausio* H. [12] cDERS; *Brittones* aH. [13] acDERS; *Karausio* H. [14] cDERS; *Brittones* aH. [15] aDEHS; *uero* c; *ergo* R. [16] acDHRS; om. E. [17...17] aHR; *sibi regem* cDES. [18] acHR; *consilio* DES. [19] acDERS; *persequti* H. [20] acDERS; *et inuenerunt* H. [21] DERS; *Lundonie* aH; *Londoniis* c.

risset,²² intermisso sacrificio egressus est ²³contra eum in campum;²³ et prelium committentes, dissipatus est Allectus cum ²⁴gente sua²⁴ fugiensque interfectus est. Liuius ergo Gallus²⁵ Allecti collega reliquos conuocans Romanos in urbe²⁶ clausis portis resistere Asclepiodoto parat, turribus ac muris armato milite munitis. Asclepiodotus obsidens ciuitatem misit ocius²⁷ nuncios²⁸ ducibus regni ut sibi festinarent in auxilium quatinus²⁹ gens Romanorum de regno exterminaretur ne amplius dominium eorum super se paterentur. Ad edictum ergo illius uenerunt Demeti, Uenedoti, Deiri³⁰ et Albani, et quicumque ex genere Britonum³¹ erant. Cumque ³²omnes simul³² conuenissent, machinis muro admotis cum balistis et sagittariis ciuitatem undique inuadentes dirutis muris ac portis urbem ingrediuntur, stragem ³³de Romanis non modicam³³ facientes. Interfectis itaque³⁴ Romanis preter unam legionem suaserunt Gallo ut deditioni se et eos traderet quatinus uiui abscedere sinerentur. Assensum ergo prebens³⁵ Gallus ³⁶tradidit se cum ceteris fide interposita ut uiui de³⁶ regno Britannie³⁷ exirent. Cumque Asclepiodotus misericorditer illis assentiret, superuenerunt Uenedoti et facto impetu omnes decollauerunt super riuum qui per³⁸ mediam fluit³⁹ ciuitatem, qui postea de nomine ducis Britannice⁴⁰ Nentgallin,⁴¹ Saxonice uero Galabroc⁴² nuncupatus est.

[77] Triumpho itaque peracto cepit Asclepiodotus regni dyadema¹ et ²capiti suo populo concedente² imposuit.³ Rexitque terram cum iusticia et pace .x. annis ⁴latronum seuiciam⁵ atque raptorum⁶ compescens.⁷ Hiis⁸ diebus orta est persecucio⁹ Dyocletiani¹⁰ in christianos et edicto

²² acDERS; *conperisset* H. ²³...²³ acDEHS; *in campum contra eum* R. ²⁴...²⁴ aHR; *suis* c; *sua gente* DES. ²⁵ acDEHS; *g Gallus* R. ²⁶ acDERS; *urbem* H. ²⁷ cER; *otius* aDH; *ocibus* deleted before *otius* in S. ²⁸ cDERS; *nuntios* aH. ²⁹ acDEHRS (corrected from *quantinus* in S). ³⁰ aDHS; *Deirici* c; *Deeri* E; *Deni* R. ³¹ cDERS; *Brittonum* aH. ³²...³² acHR; *simul omnes* DES. ³³...³³ aceEHR; *non modicam de Romanis* D. ³⁴ acHR; *igitur* DES. ³⁵ acDEHR; *prebuit* S. ³⁶...³⁶ acDEHR (*de* omitted from c); om. S (with *ut de* in margin). ³⁷ cDERS; *Brittannie* aH. ³⁸ acDEHS; om. R. ³⁹ acDHRS; *currit* E. ⁴⁰ cDER; *Brittannice* aH; *Britannie* S. ⁴¹ ES; *Uenirgallim* a; *Nantgallim* c; *Nantgallin* D; *Uenegalli* H; *Neucgallini* R. ⁴² aHR; *Gallebroc* c; *Galesbroc* D; *Galasbroc* ES.

§77 ¹ cDERS; *diadema* aH. ²...² aHR; *populo concedente capiti suo* DES; *populo concedente capiti* c. ³ acDER; *inposuit* HS. ⁴...⁴ acHR; om. DES (but passage present in margin in D). ⁵ cDR (after *raptorum* in c); *seuitiam* aH. ⁶ acHR; *impiorum* D. ⁷ acDR; *conpescens* H. ⁸ cDR; *His* aH. ⁹ R; *persecutio* acD; *persequutio* H. ¹⁰ R; *Diocletiani* ac; *Dyocliciani* D; *Dioclitiani* H.

eius grassante per uniuersum orbem missus est Maximianus Herculius trans Alpes in Gallias edicta principis facturus. Perueniens ergo[11] dira[12] hec examinatio usque in Britanniam,[13] trucidatis episcopis ac[14] sacerdotibus necnon et[15] de populo innumeris inter ceteros passus est sanctus[16] Albanus Uerolamius, Iulius quoque et Aaron Urbis Legionum ciues.[4]

[78] Surrexit[1] interea Cohel[2] dux [3]Kaercolim, id est Colecestrie,[3] in regem Asclepiodotum et conserto prelio interfecit eum regnique dyademate[4] se insigniuit. Quod ubi Rome nuntiatum[5] est, gauisus est senatus de morte illius quia[6] per omnia Romanam potestatem turbauerat atque deleuerat. Recolentes quoque dampnum quod de[7] amisso tributo sustinebant,[8] legauerunt in Britanniam[9] Constancium[10] senatorem,[11] qui antea Hyspaniam[12] Romanis subdiderat, uirum sapientem,[13] audacem, et[14] bellicis rebus studentem, rei publice fidelem. Porro Cohel[15] cum aduentum illius[16] in Britanniam[17] nosset, timuit ei [18]bello occurrere[18] quia fama ipsum[19] uirum fortem atque bellicosum ubique predicabat.[20] Direxit ergo Cohel[21] nuncios[22] Constancio[23] pacem petens et subiectionem cum tributo promittens. Acquieuit[24] Constancius[25] pacemque receptis obsidibus confirmauerunt. Emenso deinde mense uno graui egritudine correptus Cohel[26] infra .viii.[27] dies mortuus est. Constancius[28] ergo regni dyademate[29] potitus[30] duxit filiam Cohel[31] Helenam nomine, pulcram ualde ac[32] formosam artibusque[33] liberalibus edoctam. Nec erat regi Cohel[34] filius qui regni solio potiretur. Unde

---

[11] acHR; *itaque* D. [12] acHR; om. D. [13] cDR; *Brittanniam* aH. [14] aH; *atque* cD; *et* R. [15] acHR; om. D. [16] aDR; om. H.

§78 [1] acDEHR; *Surexit* S. [2] DE; *Cole* a; *Coel* c; *Choel* HRS. [3...3] a; *Caercolun* c; *Kaercolim* DE; *Kaercolin id est Kolocestrie* H; *Cholocestrie Kaercolim* R; *Kaercolin* S. [4] cDERS; *diademate* aH. [5] acHRS; *nunciatum* DE. [6] cDERS; *qui* aH. [7] aHR; *pro* cDES. [8] acEHRS; *sustinuerunt* D. [9] cDERS; *Brittanniam* aH. [10] ERS (corrected from *Constancinum* in S); *Constantium* acDH (corrected from *Constantinum* in c). [11] acDEHS; *senatorem sibi* R. [12] aDRS; *Hispaniam* cEH. [13] cDERS (corrected from *sapientes* in R); *prudentem* aH. [14] acDERS; *bellicosum et* H. [15] DES; *Cole* a; *Coel* (after *cum*) c; *Choel* HR. [16] acHR; *eius* DES. [17] cDERS; *Brittanniam* aH. [18...18] acDEHS; *occurrere bello* R. [19] acHR; *illum* DES. [20] acEHRS; *predicauerat* D. [21] DES; *Cole* a; *Coel* c; *Choel* H; *Cohes* R. [22] cDER; *nuntios* aHS. [23] ERS (corrected from *Constancino* S); *Constantio* acDH. [24] cR; *Adquieuit* aDEHS. [25] ERS; *Constantius* acDH. [26] DERS; *Cole* a; *Coel* c; *Koel* H. [27] acEHRS; *octo* D. [28] ERS; *Constantius* acDH. [29] cDERS; *diademate* aH. [30] aHR; *insignitus* cDES. [31] DRS; *Cole* a; *Coel* c; om. E; *Koel* H. [32] acDEHS; *et* R. [33] cDR; *artibus* aEHS. [34] DERS; *Cole* (added suprascript) a; *Coel* c; *Koel* H.

70

³⁵ita patri³⁵ cara³⁶ extiterat³⁷ ut artibus omnibus ³⁸inbui eam³⁸ faceret quo facilius et sapiencius³⁹ ⁴⁰post illum regnum⁴⁰ regere nosset. Cum⁴¹ igitur illam in ⁴²societatem thori⁴² recepisset, Constancius⁴³ generauit ex ea filium uocauitque⁴⁴ eum Constantinum.⁴⁵ Subsequente deinde tempore cum .xi. anni preterissent, Constancius⁴⁶ Eboraci obiit, ⁴⁷regnum filio suo Constantino⁴⁷ relinquens. Qui ut solio sublimatus⁴⁸ est, probitatem patris excedens infra paucos annos magnanimus et prudens omnibus apparuit. Latronum ac⁴⁹ tyrannorum⁵⁰ rapacitatem cohercuit et iusticiam pacemque populo donauit.

[79] Tempore itaque illo Maxencius¹ Romani imperii² curam agens tyrannidem³ grauissimam exercuit; rem publicam opprimere ac nobiles quosque⁴ senatores exterminare non destitit donec seuicia⁵ illius exterminati ad Constantinum in Britanniam⁶ diffugerunt. Qui ab eo honorifice accepti⁷ querimonias graues ⁸de Maxencio ei⁸ attulerunt. Audiens ergo Constantinus lamentacionibus⁹ eorum incitatus Romam adiit cum infinito exercitu, ducens secum tres¹⁰ Helene¹¹ auunculos,¹² Loelinum¹³ uidelicet et Trahern¹⁴ Mariumque, ipsosque¹⁵ in senatorium¹⁶ ordinem promouit.

[80] Interea surrexit¹ Octauius dux Geuisseorum² in proconsules Romane³ dignitatis quibus permissa⁴ fuerat a Constantino potestas

³⁵...³⁵ cDERS; *patri ita* aH. ³⁶ acEHRS; om. D. ³⁷ acH; *extitit* DES; *erat* R. ³⁸...³⁸ EHS; *imbui eam* ac; *eam inbui* D; *nubui eam* R. ³⁹ cER; *sapientius* aDHS. ⁴⁰...⁴⁰ aHR; *regnum post illum* cDES. ⁴¹ acEHRS; *Cumque* D. ⁴²...⁴² aHR; *thori societatem* cDES. ⁴³ cERS; *Constantius* aDH. ⁴⁴ acdEHR; *uocauit* S. ⁴⁵ acDEHS; *Constancium* R. ⁴⁶ cERS; *Constantius* aDH. ⁴⁷...⁴⁷ DERS; *Constantino filio suo regnum* aH; *regnum Constantino filio suo* c. ⁴⁸ cDR; *sullimatus* aEHS. ⁴⁹ acEHRS; *atque* D. ⁵⁰ acDRS; *tirannorum* EH.

§79 ¹ cER; *Maxentius* aDHS. ² acDERS; *inperii* H. ³ aDER; *tirannidem* cH. ⁴ aDEHRS (corrected from *quousque* in S); *quoque* c. ⁵ DER; *seuitia* aH; *seuiciam* cS. ⁶ cDERS; *Brittanniam* aH. ⁷ DES; *excepti* aHR; *recepti* c. ⁸...⁸ cER; *de Maxentio ei* aHS; *ei de Maxencio* D. ⁹ DER; *lamentationibus* acHS. ¹⁰ acDERS; *.iii.* H. ¹¹ acDHRS; *Elene* E. ¹² acDEHS; *aduunculos* R. ¹³ cDES (*Ioelinum* in D?); *Iohelinum* aHR. ¹⁴ aDERS; *Trahaern* c; *Trihern* H. ¹⁵ aH; *et ipsos* cDES; *ipsos* R. ¹⁶ aDRS; *senatorum* cEH.

§80 ¹ aDEHR; *insurrexit* c; *surexit* S. ² aDERS; *Gewisseorum* c; *Geuuisseorum* H. ³ acDHRS; *romone* E. ⁴ acDHR; *promissa* E; *commissa* S.

Britannie[5] et illis peremptis[6] solio regni potitus est. Cumque[7] id Constantino [8]nunciatum esset,[8] direxit Trahern [9]auunculum Helene[9] in Britanniam[10] cum tribus[11] legionibus ut ausum Octauii uindicaret. Appulsus[12] itaque in litore[13] iuxta urbem Kaerperis infra duos[14] dies recepit [15]ciuitatem illam[15] a ciuibus sibi redditam.[16] Deinde tendens Wintoniam[17] obuiauit illi Octauius cum [18]grandi exercitu[18] non longe a Wintonia[19] in campo qui Britannice[20] Maisuram[21] appellatur. Cepitque preliari et uictoria potitus est. Trahern[22] autem fugiens cum suis naues petit ingressusque altum mare Albaniam equoreo itinere adiit et prouinciam totam depredatus spoliis Albanorum ditatus est. Quod cum Octauio nunciatum[23] esset, resociatis suis tendit Albaniam. Sed Trahern citra Albaniam in prouincia que Westmarialanda[24] dicitur euagatus audacter [25]bello Octauium[25] suscipiens deuicit atque fugauit. Insecutusque[26] eum toto regno priuauit. At ille fugiens nauigio[27] [28]Norwegiam petit,[28] regem Gumperium[29] adiens ut auxilio eius regno Britannie[30] restitueretur.[31] Interea Trahern a quodam familiari Octauii interfectus periit. Edixerat[32] enim Octauius recedens quibusdam familiaribus suis ut [33]insidias ei[33] pararent et se de illo[34] uindicarent. Comes igitur oppidi[35] municipii[36] qui eum pre ceteris diligebat complens Octauii uotum, dum Trahern[37] ex urbe Londoniarum[38] quadam die recederet, delituit cum centum[39] militibus in quadam nemorosa[40] ualle [41]qua ille[41] transiturus erat atque pretereuntem [42]inopinate inter commi-

5 cDERS; *Brittannie* aH. 6 acDERS; *interemptis* H. 7 acDEHR; *Cum* R. 8...8 cR; *nuntiatum esset* aH; *nunciatum fuit* D; *nunciatum foret* ES. 9...9 aHR; *Helene auunculum* cDS; *Elene auunculum* E. 10 cDERS; *Brittanniam* aH. 11 acDERS; *.iii.* H. 12 acDEHS; *Apulsus* R. 13 DER; *littore* acHS. 14 acDERS; *.ii.* H. 15...15 aHR; *illam ciuitatem* c; *ciuitatem* DES. 16 acEHRS; *traditam* deleted before *redditam* in D. 17 acDHRS; *Wyntoniam* E. 18...18 acHR; *exercitu grandi* DES. 19 aDEHR; *Wyntonia* cS. 20 cDERS; *Brittannice* aH. 21 aDEHS; *Maysuriam* c; *Marsuriam* R. 22 aDEHR; *Trahaern* c; *Traern* S. 23 cDERS; *nuntiatum* aH. 24 R; *Westmariland* a; *Westinerilandia* c; *Westmarielanda* D; *Westimarielanda* ES; *Westimarialanda* H. 25...25 aHR; *Octauium bello* DES. 26 acDERS; *Insequutusque* H. 27 cDERS; om. aH. 28...28 aHR (*Noruuegiam* in H); *petit Norguegiam* cDES (*Norweiam* in c). 29 DR; *Gumbertum* a; *Gubtum* c; *Guperium* ES; *Gumpertum* H. 30 cDERS; *Brittannie* aH. 31 acDERS; *potiretur* H. 32 acDEHS; *eduxerat* R. 33...33 aHR; *insidias* [corrected from *insidians*] *illi* c; *ei insidias* DES. 34 acDEHR; *uim* deleted after *illo* in S. 35 aHR; *opidi* cDES. 36 acDERS; *municipli* H. 37 acEHRS; *Traharn* D. 38 DERS; *Lundoniarum* aH. 39 R; *.c.* aDEHS; *100* c. 40 acDEHS; *nemorassa* R. 41...41 acHR; *in qua* DES. 42...42 acHR; *inter commilitones inopinate* DES.

litones suos[42] interfecit mittensque[43] post Octauium [44]nunciauit ei[44] rei euentum. Octauius igitur gaudens reuersus est in Britanniam et dissipatis Romanis solium regni recuperauit. [45]Exin regnum cum[45] pace obtinuit;[46] copiam[47] auri et argenti [48]ac diuicias[48] innumeras[49] congregans in thesauro reposuit. Regnum itaque Britonum[50] ab illo tempore usque in diebus Gratiani[51] et Ualentiniani[52] feliciter rexit.

[81] Denique senio confectus Octauius cogitauit de regno disponere qualiter post mortem suam pace hereditaria frueretur. Neque enim[1] [2]erat ei[2] filius, sed unam tantum [3]filiam habens[3] optabat[4] eam [5]post se[5] in regni solio sublimari.[6] Consilium igitur[7] a familiaribus fidelibus[8] sumens, fuerunt qui laudarent[9] filiam locare alicui [10]nobilium Romanorum[10] ut firmiori[11] pace regnum tueretur. Fuerunt quoque qui censerent[12] Conanum Meriadocum[13] nepotem suum heredem facere, filiam uero alicui principi extra regnum cum magna auri et argenti copia copulandam. Dum ergo hec [14]inter se cum ambiguitate[14] gererent, surrexit Caradocus[15] dux Cornubie sententiamque[16] dedit pociorem[17] quatinus puella donaretur Maximiano senatori Romano, nobili ac prudenti uiro, ut heres esset regni post fata Octauii. Erat autem patre Britannus,[18] [19]filius Loelini[19] auunculi Constantini, matre uero et nacione[20] Romanus, et[21] ex[22] utraque parte regalem protrahebat dignitatem. Unde spes omnibus dabatur[23] tum propter affinitatem tum propter puelle [24]regalem et hereditariam dignitatem[24] tranquilla pace

[43] acDERS; *mittens* with *que* suprascript H. [44...44] acDERS; *nunciauit* with *ei* suprascript H. [45...45] aEH; *Exinde regnum cum* cDS; *Et in regnum tamen* R. [46] DR; *optinuit* acEHS. [47] acHR; *copiamque* DES. [48...48] R; *ac diuitias* aH; *diuiciasque* cE; *diuitiasque* DS. [49] acDRS; *innumas* E; *innumerabiles* H. [50] cDERS; *Brittonum* aH. [51] aEHRS; *Graciani* cD. [52] cHR; *Ualentiani* aD; *Ualenciani* ES.

§81 [1] cDEHR; om. aS. [2...2] aDEHS; *ei erat* c; *erat* R. [3...3] aHR; *habens filiam* cDES (*habens* bis in S). [4] acEHRS; *obtabat* D. [5...5] acDEHS; *posse* R. [6] cDR; *sullimari* aEHS. [7] DER; *inde* aH; *igitur inde* c; *ergo* S. [8] acDERS; *suis* H. [9] aHR; om. cDES. [10...10] aHR; *nobilium Romanorum laudarent* cDS; *Romanorum nobilium laudarent* E. [11] acEHRS; *firmiore* D. [12] acDEHR; *censerunt* altered to *censuerunt* S. [13] aDER; *Meriaducum* c; *Meridocum* H; *Meridiadocum* S. [14...14] DERS (*ambiguitate* corrected from *ambiguietate* in S); *cum ambiguitate inter se* aH; *inter se ambigue* c. [15] aDERS; *Karadocus* cH. [16] DERS; *sententiam* aH; *sentenciamque* c. [17] acERS; *potiorem* DH. [18] cDERS; *Brittannus* aH. [19...19] aHR; *Loelini filius* D; *Leolini filius* ES. [20] ER; *natione* acDHS. [21] acDERS; om. H. [22] acDEHS; om. R. [23] acDERS; om. H. [24...24] cDERS; *dignitatem ac [ad a] regalem et hereditariam* aH.

diebus eorum [25]post se[25] regnum Britannie[26] florere. Hiis[27] auditis Conanus qui priorem de se[28] sententiam[29] audisse gaudebat omnique nisu[30] ad regnum hanelabat,[31] totam[32] fere curiam perturbauit indignans quod contra se dux Cornubie sententiam dedisset. At Caradocus[33] uilipendens temerarii iuuenis exactionem ex consilio et uoluntate regis misit Mauricium[34] filium suum Romam ut ex senatus consultu Maximianum adduceret. Ueniens itaque Mauricius[35] Romam, inuenit Romam turbatam[36] et magnam inquietudinem inter ipsum Maximianum et duos imperatores, Gratianum uidelicet et [37]fratrem suum[37] Ualentinianum,[38] qui ambo ui[39] [40]imperii potestatem[40] usurpauerant, repulso Maximiano ab[41] imperii societate[42] quam[43] petebat. Mauricius[44] ergo euocans seorsum Maximianum intimauit ei super legacione[45] et negocio[46] pro quo uenerat.

[82] Quibus auditis Maximianus letus suscepit hanc legacionem[1] et iter arripiens cum Mauricio[2] [3]in Britanniam uenit.[3]

[83] Rex igitur Octauius cum honore summo suscipiens Maximianum dedit ei filiam suam et heredem regni constituit. Quod uidens Conanus nepos ipsius indignatus[1] secessit in Albaniam et exercitum collegit quantum potuit. Uenitque[2] cum multitudine [3]Pictorum ac Britonum[3] trans Humbrum flumen quasque prouincias depopulans. At Maximianus collecto fortiori[4] exercitu contra illum uenit et cum illo dimicans in fugam coegit et cum uictoria domum rediit.[5] Conanus iterum resociatis

[25]...[25] cDEHS; *posse* aR. [26] cDERS; *Brittannie* aH. [27] cDERS; *His* aH. [28] acEHRS; *se* suprascript in D. [29] acDHRS; *sentenciam* E. [30] acDEHS; *uisu* R. [31] cDRS; *anhelabat* aEH. [32] acDEHS; *totamque* R. [33] aDERS; *Karadocus* cH. [34] acDE; *Mauricum* HR (altered to *Mauricium* in H); *Mauritium* S. [35] acDEH; *Mauricus* R; *Mauritius* S. [36] acDERS; *perturbatam* H. [37]...[37] acDERS; om. H. [38] R; *Ualentinum* ac; *Ualentianum* DH; *Ualencianum* ES. [39] aDHR; om. cS; *in* E. [40]...[40] acEHRS; *potestatem imperii* D. [41] aHR; *ex* cDES. [42] aHR; *tercia parte et societate* c; *parte* DES. [43] acDHR; *quod* ES. [44] cDEHS; *Mauricus* R. [45] ERS; *legatione* cDH. [46] cDERS; *negotio* H.

§82 (variant §82 entirely absent from a and c) [1] ERS; *legationem* DH. [2] DEHS; *Maurico* R. [3]...[3] DERS; *uenit in Brittanniam* H.

§83 (variant §83 entirely absent from c) [1] aEHRS; *indignatus est et* D. [2] aDEHR; *Uenit* S. [3]...[3] DERS; *Brittonum ac Pictorum* aH. [4] aDHRS; *forciori* E. [5] aDEHRS (corrected from *reddiit* in S).

turmis[6] inquietabat regnum Britannie.[7] Sed Maximianus commissis preliis quandoque cum triumpho, quandoque superatus[8] abibat,[9] ut assolet in dubio [10]euentu belli.[10] Tandem annitentibus[11] [12]uiris sapientibus et[12] amicis eorum concordes facti sunt [13]et amici[13] adinuicem.

[84] Post quinquennium congregatis copiis auri et argenti ac innumerabilium diuiciarum[1] Maximianus nauigium parat atque in Galliam transiens Armoricum regnum,[2] quod nunc Britannia[3] dicitur, primitus adiit et populum[4] qui terram incolebat[5] debellare cepit. At Franci audientes duce Humbalto[6] [7]uenerunt cum exercitu;[7] et congredientes [8]pugnam inierunt[8] Franci et Britones.[9] Sed[10] Franci in[11] maiori parte debilitati[12] fugam arripiunt,[13] Britones[14] uero insequentes [15].xv. milia eorum fere[15] trucidauerunt. Maximianus itaque uictoria potitus[16] ad castra cum suis rediit[17] gratulans quia[18] [19]terram sibi[19] subdendam leuiter estimabat. Uocatoque ad se Conano separatim extra turbam subridens ait: 'Ecce,[20] subiugauimus partem Gallie, Francos deuicimus. Ecce, spem ad cetera [21]subicienda nobis[21] habemus. Festinemus ergo[22] urbes et oppida[23] nostro dominio subiugare antequam rumor[24] in ultiorem Galliam euolans aduersum[25] nos uniuersos populos excitet. Nam si regnum istud retinere poterimus, non dubito quin totam Galliam per hunc[26] aditum potestati nostre subdamus. [27]Ne igitur pigeat te[27] regnum Britannie[28] michi cessisse[29] quia quicquid[30] in illa amisisti tibi in hac patria restaurabo. Regem enim te faciam esse[31] regni huius et erit hec[32]

6 aDEHS; *turbis* R. 7 DERS; *Brittannie* aH. 8 aHR; *uictus* DES. 9 aDHRS; *adibat* E. 10...10 aDERS; *belli euentu* H. 11 aEH; *adnitentibus* D; *amittentibus* R; *annuentibus* S. 12...12 DERS; *uiris sapientibus* a; om. H. 13...13 DERS; om. aH.

§84 1 cERS; *diuitiarum* aDH. 2 acDHRS; om. E. 3 cDERS; *Brittannia* aH. 4 acDEHR; *populum* (with *Francorum* suprascript) S. 5 acDEH; *incolebant* R; *incolunt* S. 6 cDERS; *Humbaldo* a; *Imbaltho* H. 7...7 aR; *cum exercitu uenerunt* DES; *uenerunt* H. 8...8 aHR (*inierunt* corrected from *inerunt* in a); *pugnam fecerunt* c; *pugnauerunt* DES. 9 cDERS; *Brittones* aH. 10 acDHRS; *Set* E. 11 acDEHS; *cum* R. 12 acDEHR; *delitati* S. 13 acDEHR; *arripuerunt* S. 14 cDERS; *Brittones* aH. 15...15 aHR; *quindecim milia eorum* c; *fere .xv. milia eorum* DES. 16 acDEHS (*potitus* before *uictoria* in a); *petitus* R. 17 acDEHR; *reddiit* S. 18 aceEHRS; *quod* D. 19...19 acDEHS; *sibi terram* R. 20 acDERS; *Ece* H. 21...21 acHR; *nobis subdenda* DES (with a second *a nobis* deleted after *subdenda* in S). 22 acDEHS; *ergo nobis* R. 23 aHR; *opida* cDES. 24 aHR; *fama* cDES. 25 aHR; *aduersus* cDES. 26 aHR; *istum* DES. 27...27 aHR; *Ne tibi pigeat te* c; *Nec tibi pigeat* DES. 28 cDERS; *Brittannie* aH. 29 acDEHS; *concessisse* R. 30 acDEHS; *quidque* R. 31 acHR; om. DES. 32 acDHRS; om. E.

altera Britannia[33] eamque ex [34]nostro genere[34] pulsis indigenis reple-
bimus. Terra enim hec fertilis est omni[35] fructu repleta, flumina piscosa
et piscibus copiosa, nemora et saltus uenatibus apta; nec est uspiam
meo iudicio[36] gratior[37] tellus.' Ad hec submisso[38] capite grates[39] egit
Conanus[40] promisitque[41] se [42]fidelem sibi omni tempore uite sue[42] fore.

[85] Post hec conuocatis militum turmis Redonum[1] ciuitatem petunt
quam mox eadem die ciues eis[2] reddiderunt. Quidam enim eorum
audita Britonum[3] audacia et peremptorum casu[4] diffugerant ad nemora,
relictis mulierculis et infantibus.[5] Quippe ubicumque ui uel sponte
intrabant, quod erat masculini sexus interficiebant, solis mulieribus
parcentes.[6] Cumque uniuersam terram ab incolis deleuissent, munierunt ciuitates et oppida[7] suis armatis et castra in diuersis promontoriis[8]
statuerunt.

[86] Sed[1] deerant habitatores qui totam occuparent terram. Misit ergo
in Britanniam[2] et edicto precepit ut .c. milia plebanorum[3] colligerentur
sparsim per regiones regni [4]et .xxx. milia militum[4] quibus totam terram
incolendam contraderet.[5] Qui cum ad eius [6]iussionem conuenissent,[6]
distribuit eos per partes[7] regni et habitatores fecit et Conanum[8] eis in
regem promouit. Ipse deinde cum suis ulteriorem Galliam penetrans
grauissimis preliis illatis[9] subiugauit eam necnon et totam Germaniam,
[10]ciuitate Treueri[10] solium imperii[11] sui constituens. Postea in Gratianum[12] et Ualentinianum[13] imperatores uim sui furoris[14] exacuens uno
interempto[15] alterum a Roma fugauit. Ipse uero Rome imperator

33 cDERS; *Brittannia* aH. 34...34 acHR; *genere nostro* DES. 35 acHR; *et cum* DES.
36 acDERS; *iuditio* H. 37 acDHRS; *gracior* E. 38 acDHRS; *summisso* E. 39 aHR;
gratias cDES. 40 acDERS; *Konanus* H. 41 acDERS; *et promisit* H. 42...42 aHR; *omni
tempore uite sue sibi fidelem* DES.

§85 1 acDEHR; *Reddonum* S. 2 aHR; *ei* c; *eius* DES. 3 cDERS; *Brittonum* aH.
4 cDES; *casum* aHR. 5 acDEHS; *infantulis* R. 6 acDEHS; *parcebant* R. 7 aHR; *opida*
cDES. 8 acDERS; *promuntoriis* H.

§86 1 aDHRS; *Set* E. 2 cDERS; *Brittannia* a; *Brittanniam* H. 3 acHR; *plebanorum et
.xxx. milia militum* DES. 4...4 acHR (*30* in c); om. DES. 5 DERS; *traderet* ac; *crederet*
H. 6...6 acHR; *conuenissent iussionem* DES. 7 cDERS; *diuersas partes* aH. 8 acDERS;
Konanum H. 9 aHR; om. cDES (with *illatis* in margin of D). 10...10 cDERS; *ciuitatem
Treueri* a; *ciuitatem Treuerim* H. 11 acDRS; *regni* E; *inperii* H. 12 DHRS; *Gracianum*
acE. 13 acDR (altered from *Ualentianum* in D); *Ualencianum* ES; *Ualentianum* H.
14 acDEHS; *imperii* deleted before *furoris* in R. 15 aHR; *perempto* cDES.

creatus[16] .xl. ab Augusto [17]imperium rexit[17] anno ab incarnacione[18] Domini [19]trecentesimo septuagesimo .vii..[19] Ualentinianus[20] autem, frater Gratiani, ad Theodosium [21]in orientem fugiens imperio per Theodosium[21] restitutus est et Maximianum subinde apud Aquileiam[22] fratrem uindicans[23] interfecit.

[87] Interea infestabant Conanum[1] in Armorica Galli et Aquitani crebrisque irrupcionibus[2] inquietabant. Quibus ipse uiriliter resistens commissam sibi patriam ab eorum incursionibus protexit. Cumque sibi de omnibus cessisset uictoria, uolens commilitonibus suis uxores dare ut ex[3] eis nascerentur heredes qui terram hereditate possiderent, decreuit[4] ut ex Britannia[5] sortirentur uxores quibus maritarentur. Direxit ergo[6] legatos ad Dionotum[7] ducem Cornubie, qui Caradoco[8] fratri successerat, et curam huius negocii[9] amicabiliter[10] inpendit.[11] Erat iste Dionotus[12] tocius[13] regni custos [14]dum Maximianus aberat et principatum Britannie sub eo regebat dum Maximianus[14] maioribus negociis intenderet. Habebat et filiam mire pulcritudinis cui nomen erat Ursula, quam Conanus[15] sibi in uxorem delegerat.[16]

[88] Dionotus[1] igitur auditis Conani[2] legacionibus[3] paruit libens collectisque per [4]diuersas prouincias[4] filiabus nobilium numero .xi. milia, de plebanis uero .lx.[5] milia,[6] omnes conuenire in urbe Londonia[7] precepit. Inde per Thamensem[8] fluuium nauibus collocatis[9] in altum se

16 aHR; *factus* cDES. 17...17 acHR (*inperium* in H); *rexit imperium* DES. 18 ER; *incarnatione* acDHS. 19 R; *.ccclxxvii.* aEHS; *377* c; *.cclxxvii.* D. 20 aDR (altered from *Ualentianus* in D); *Ualentianus* cHS; *Ualencianus* E. 21...21 acDERS; om. H. 22 acDEHS (altered from *Aquileam* in H); *Aquileam* R. 23 acDEHS; *medicans* R.

§87 1 acDERS; *Konanum* H. 2 ER; *irruptionibus* acDHS. 3 cDERS; om. aH. 4 acDEHS; *decernit* R. 5 cDERS; *Brittannia* aH. 6 acDEHR; *igitur* S. 7 acEHRS; *Dyonotum* D. 8 aDERS; *Karadoco* cH. 9 acDERS; *negotii* H. 10 acDHR; *commitabiliter* ES. 11 HR; *impendit* a; *ostendit* cES; *confidit* (or *ofidit*?) D. 12 acDEHS; *Dyonotus* R. 13 cER; *totius* aDHS. 14...14 acR; *dum Maximianus* DEHS. 15 acDERS; *Konanus* H. 16 acDER; *delegauerat* H; *elegerat* S.

§88 1 acDEHS; *Dyonotus* R. 2 acDERS; *Konani* H. 3 ERS; *legationibus* acDH. 4...4 acHR; *prouincias diuersas* DS; *prouincias diuersis* (tampered: altered from *diuersas*?) E. 5 aDES; *60* c; *.xl.* H; *sexagintis* R. 6 acDEHS; *milibus* R. 7 cDERS; *Lundonia* aH. 8 cDERS; *Tamensem* a; *Thamense* H. 9 acEHRS; *collectis* D.

dederunt et maria[10] sulcantes uersus terram Armoricanorum[11] nauiga-
bant. Nec mora insurgunt uenti contrarii in classem illam et in[12] breui
per totum pelagus dissipauerunt. Periclitate sunt ergo quedam, in[13]
maiori parte submerse. Sed que periculum euaserunt appulse[14] sunt in
barbaras insulas[15] et ab ignota et nefanda[16] gente siue trucidate siue
mancipate sunt. Inciderant siquidem[17] in dirum exercitum Gwanii[18] et
Melge, quorum Gwanius[19] rex [20]Hunorum, Melga Pictorum rex[20]
fuerat; qui mittente Gratiano maritima[21] Germanie dira clade uexabant.
Hii itaque [22]obuiantes nauigio[22] predictarum puellarum rapuerunt eas
ad se uolentes lasciuire[23] cum eis. Sed cum abhorrerent puelle [24]eorum
immundam[24] dementiam,[25] quedam [26]absque ulla pietate ab eis[26] trucidate sunt, quedam ad exteras[27] naciones[28] uenundate.[29] Deinde cum
didicissent prefati[30] pirate Britannie[31] insulam armato milite fere
euacuatam, direxerunt iter ad illam et applicuerunt in Albaniam.
Agmine igitur facto inuaserunt regnum quod rege et defensore carebat,
uulgus[32] inerme[33] cedentes. Nam, ut predictum est, Maximianus
omnem iuuentutem ualidam secum abduxerat et colonos simul, qui si[34]
forte affuissent hostibus istis[35] resistere potuissent. Predicti[36] itaque
tyranni[37] Gwanius[38] et Melga postquam grassati[39] sunt pro uoluntate
sua super uulgus inerme,[40] urbes et municiones[41] sibi subdentes totam
[42]Britanniam suo dominio[42] subiugauerunt. Cum igitur[43] hec calamitas
Maximiano Rome nunciata[44] fuisset,[45] misit Gratianum[46] municipem
cum duabus[47] legionibus in Britanniam[48] ut auxilium ferret[49] oppressis.

---

[10] acEHRS; *terram* deleted before *maria* in D. [11] cD; *Morianorum* altered to
Moricanorum a; *Moricanorum* EHRS (with *Armoricanorum* suprascript in S). [12] cDH;
om. aERS. [13] acEHRS; *et in* D. [14] acDEHS; *apulse* R. [15] aHR; *nationes* cDS (with *et
insulas* suprascript in D); *naciones* E. [16] aHRS; *nephanda* cDE. [17] acDEHS; *enim* R.
[18] acR; *Guanii* DES; *Guanni* H. [19] acR; *Guanius* DES; *Guannius* H. [20...20] acDEHR
(with *Scotorum* over an erased *Pictorum* [?] in a); added suprascript in S. [21] acDHS;
marittima ES. [22...22] cDERS; *nauigio obuiantes* aH. [23] acDEHS; *lascisciuire* R.
[24...24] acHR; *immundam eorum* DES. [25] aDHRS; *demenciam* cE. [26...26] aHR; *ab eis
absque ulla pietate* cDES. [27] aDEHS; *externas* c; *extiras* R. [28] ER; *nationes* acDHS.
[29] aDHRS; *uenumdate* cE. [30] aHR; *predicti* cDES. [31] cDERS; *Brittannie* aH. [32] ac-
DEHS; *wlgus* R. [33] aDERS; *inherme* cH. [34] acDEHS; *se* R. [35] aHR; *illis* cDES.
[36] aHR; *Prefati* cDES. [37] cDRS; *tiranni* aEH. [38] acR; *Guanius* DES; *Guannius* H.
[39] acDHRS; *crassati* E. [40] aDERS; *inherme* cH. [41] ERS; *munitiones* acDH.
[42...42] cDERS; *Brittanniam dominio* a; *Brittanniam dominio suo* H. [43] acDEHS; *ergo*
R. [44] acDRS; *nunciatum* E; *nuntiata* H. [45] acHR; *esset* DES. [46] cEHRS; *Gracianum*
aD. [47] acDERS; *.ii.* H. [48] cDERS; *Brittanniam* aH. [49] acEHRS; *afferret* D.

Qui uenientes disturbatis hostibus qui se per totam terram tamquam[50] municipes locauerant[51] acerrima cede affectos[52] in Hyberniam[53] – quotquot [54]euasere periculum[54] – fugauerunt.

[89] Interea interfecto Maximiano Rome ab amicis Gratiani[1] et Britonibus[2] qui cum eo uenerant dissipatis et in parte necatis, Gratianus[3] regnum Britannie[4] adeptus est et tyrannidem[5] [6]non modicam[6] in populum exercuit donec cateruatim se stipantes plebani et irruentes in eum interfecerunt. Quod audientes predicti hostes ex Hybernia[7] nauigium educentes, secum Scotos,[8] Noruegienses,[9] Dacos cum magna manu conducentes Britanniam[10] a mari usque ad mare ferro ac flammis uastauerunt. Mittuntur ergo legati [11]cum epistolis Romam[11] ad senatum lacrimosis suspiriis postulantes auxilium, uouentes se in perpetuum seruituros si ab hac dira oppressione[12] hostium liberarentur. Quibus mox committitur legio[13] preteriti[14] [15]mali non immemor;[15] que ut aduenit in Britanniam,[16] cum hostibus congressa magnam multitudinem strauit atque[17] reliquos usque in Albaniam fugere coegit. Sicque Dei nutu a tam atroci oppressione[18] exempti uallum cum muro inmensum[19] inter Albaniam et Deiram[20] a mari usque ad mare construxerunt arcendis hostibus oportunum, indigenis uero magnum tutamen et defensionem facturum.[21] Erat autem tunc Albania[22] penitus barbarorum incursione uastata ita ut indigenis [23]expulsis receptaculum[23] esset omnium perditorum.[24]

[50] HR; *tanquam* acDES. [51] acDER; *locauerunt* HS. [52] acDEHS; *peraffectos* R. [53] ERS; *Hiberniam* acDH. [54...54] cDERS; *periculum euasere* aH.

§89 [1] aEHRS; *Graciani* cD. [2] cDERS; *Brittonibus* aH. [3] aERS; *Gracianus* cDH. [4] cDERS; *Brittannie* aH. [5] aDR; *tirannidem* cEHS. [6...6] acDEHS; om. R. [7] aRS; *Hibernia* cDEH. [8] cERS; *Scottos* aDH. [9] R; *Norguegienses* aH; *Norweienses* c; *Norguegenses* DE; *Norgugenses* S. [10] cDERS; *Brittanniam* aH. [11...11] aHR; *Romam cum epistolis* DES. [12] aHS (tampered in S?); *impressione* cDE (after *hostium* in c); *compressione* R. [13] acEHRS; *legio* (with *cui preerat Seuerus* suprascript and a Welsh note in margin; see Introduction, p.lxxxii) D. [14] acdEHS; *preterea* R. [15...15] aEHRS (with *non* deleted from S); *mali immemor* c; *non immemor mali* D. [16] cDERS; *Brittanniam* aH. [17] acHR; *et* DES. [18] acDEHS; *ex* deleted before *oppressione* in R. [19] HRS; *immensum* acDE. [20] aDEHS; *Deiriam* c; *Deira* R. [21] acDEHR; *futurum* S. [22] acDEHRS (corrected from *Albanie* in H). [23...23] acDEHS; *receptaculum expulsis* R. [24] acDEHRS; after *perditorum, Explicit liber quintus. Incipit liber* [om. R] *sextus* in aR.

[90] Romani[1] ergo depulsis hostibus Romam reuerti decreuerunt, denunciantes[2] Britonibus[3] nequaquam se tam[4] laboriosis expedicionibus[5] posse ulterius fatigari et ob erraticos[6] latrunculos Romanam iuuentutem ac potestatem[7] terra marique tam frequentibus expedicionibus[8] uexari; malle pocius[9] toto[10] tributo fraudari quam tot laboriosis occursionibus subiacere. Conuocatis itaque in urbe Londonia[11] optimatibus terre repedare[12] se Romam[13] profitentur.

[91] Atque ut se ab incursione erraticorum[1] hostium tueantur, turres in litore,[2] quo nauigium piratarum applicare formidabant, struendas[3] decernunt[4] ut, sicut [5]murus prefatus[5] in terra ad municionem[6] erat, ita et turres [7]a mari sibi[7] pro munimento[8] fierent. Armorum[9] quoque instruendorum[10] exemplaria[11] a Romanis habuerunt,[12] peltis[13] [14]et pilis[14] suadentes[15] seipsos, coniuges, liberos, opes, et, quod maius hiis[16] erat, libertatem ui[17] propria atque[18] armorum defensione uiriliter dimicando tuerentur. Sicque uale dicto Romani tanquam [19]ultra non[19] reuersuri profecti sunt. Quo audito Guanius[20] et Melga nauibus quibus fuerant in Hyberniam[21] uecti[22] emergentes cum Scotis[23] et Norguengensibus,[24] Dacis et Pictis, omnem Albaniam murotenus capescunt.[25] Contra hos constituuntur in edito[26] murorum rudes ad pugnam, qui leuiter prostrati atque telorum grandine territi [27]muris deiciuntur[27] et fugam arripiunt.[28] Hostes itaque deiecto ad solum muro fugientes persecun-

§90 [1] acDHRS; <R>omani E. [2] cDERS; denuntiantes aH. [3] cDERS; Brittonibus aH. [4] aHR; om. cDES. [5] ERS; expeditionibus acDH. [6] acDEHS; eraticos R. [7] acDEHR; potentem S. [8] ERS; expeditionibus acDH. [9] ERS; potius aDH; pocius se c. [10] acDEHS; om. R. [11] cDERS; Lundonia aH. [12] acDEHR; redire S. [13] aDEHRS (corrected from Roma in R); Romani c.

§91 [1] acDEHS; eraticorum R. [2] DERS; littore acH. [3] acDERS; struenda H. [4] acDEHR; decenter (with precipiunt suprascript) S. [5...5] aHR; prefatus murus cDES. [6] ERS; munitionem acDH. [7...7] aH; sibi a mari cDE; a mari usque ad mare sibi R; a mari S. [8] acDEHRS (corrected from monumento in H). [9] acDEHS; Animorum (?) R. [10] acDEHS; instrumentorum R. [11] acDEHR; exempla (altered from exemplariorum) S. [12] DES; om. acHR. [13] a; peltibus cDERS; pellibus underpointed in H. [14...14] acDERS; underpointed in H. [15] acDEHRS (with ut in margin in H). [16] cDERS; his aH. [17] acEHRS; in D. [18] acDERS; deleted from H. [19...19] acDERS; non ultra H. [20] DERS; Gwanius ac; Guaunius H. [21] ER; Hiberniam acDHS. [22] cDERS; euecti aH. [23] cERS; Scottis aDH. [24] aR; Norweiensibus c; Norguegensibus DES; Norguensibus H. [25] cRS; capessunt aDEH. [26] acDERS; edicto H. [27...27] acDERS; muri prosternuntur R. [28] acDERS; arripiunt. Facilius est enim ex miluo accipitrem fieri quam ex rustico subitum eruditum. H (sentence interpolated [in text] from earlier in vulgate §91).

tur,[29] persequendo interimunt, quosdam mancipatos carceribus tradunt et fit tanta strages quanta nullis temporibus [30]antea fuerat facta.[30] Igitur rursum nichilominus[31] misere Britonum[32] reliquie mittunt [33]Romam epistolas[33] ad Agicium[34] summum Romane[35] potestatis uirum in hunc modum: 'Agicio[36] ter consuli gemitus Britonum.'[37] Et post pauca querentes adiciunt:[38] 'Nos mare ad barbaros, barbari ad mare repellunt.[39] Interea oriuntur duo[40] [41]generum funera:[41] aut enim submergimur aut iugulamur.'[42] Uerum Romani nulla commoti pietate auxilium ferre recusant, pretendentes eorum sepissime laboriosam [43]in Britanniam expedicionem[43] et preterea de tributis fraudacionem.[44] Legati tristes redeunt atque huiuscemodi repulsam denunciant.[45]

[92] Inito ergo consilio transfretauit Guizelinus Londoniensis[1] metropolitanus[2] in minorem Britanniam,[3] que tunc Armorica siue Letauia[4] dicebatur, ut auxilium a[5] confratribus[6] postularet. Regnabat tunc in illa[7] Aldroenus[8] quartus a Conano[9] primo duce. Qui uiso[10] tante reuerencie[11] uiro excepit illum cum honore cognitaque sui aduentus causa, tristis ac[12] mestus de persecutione[13] agnatorum et patrie, subsidium[14] [15]se ferre[15] quale posset promisit. Tradiditque[16] sibi Constantinum[17] fratrem suum bellicosum[18] et duo[19] milia militum[20] ex electis Britonibus.[21]

[29] cDERS; *persequuntur* aH. [30...30] R; *facta fuerat* [corrected from *fuerant* in H] *antea* aH; *antea numquam facta fuerat* c; *antea facta fuerat* DES. [31] acDERS; om. H. [32] cDERS; *Brittonum* aH. [33...33] acHR; *epistolas Romam* DES. [34] aEHR; *Agencium* c; *Agitium* DS. [35] acDEHS; om. R. [36] H; *Agitio* acDES; *Agecio* R. [37] cDERS; *Brittonum* aH. [38] acDES; *aditiunt* H; *addiciunt* R. [39] acDEHS; *prorepellunt* (with −*re*− underpointed) R. [40] acDERS; *.ii.* H. [41...41] acHR; *funerum genera* DES. [42] acDERS; *uicti debellamur* H. [43...43] cDERS (*expeditionem* in cD); *expeditionem in Brittanniam* aH. [44] aES; *fraudationem* cDH; *fraudacione* R. [45] acDERS; *denuntiant* H.

§92 [1] cDER; *Lundoniensis* aH; *Lodoniensis* S. [2] acDEHS; *episcopus metropolitanus* R. [3] cDERS; *Brittanniam* aH. [4] a; *Licania* c; *Litauia* DES; *Letania* HR. [5] acHR; *a* suprascript in D; om. ES. [6] aDEHR; *fratribus* c; *cum fratribus* S. [7] acDEHS; *Britannia* R. [8] acDERS; *Aldrogeus* H. [9] acDERS; *Konano* H. [10] acDEHS; *uise* R. [11] cEHRS; *reuerentie* aD. [12] aHR; *et* DES. [13] aDHRS; *persecucione* E. [14] aDHRS; *sub* E. [15...15] DERS; *ferre se* aH. [16] aDEH; *Tradidit* RS. [17] aDHRS; *Constantium* E. [18] aEHRS; *bellicosum* (with *uirum* in margin) D. [19] aDERS; *.ii.* H. [20] aHR; om. DES. [21] DERS; *Brittonibus* aH.

[93] Qui mare ingressi in portu Totonesio[1] applicuerunt. Nec mora collecta multitudine senum ac iuuenum atque utriusque etatis uirorum regni cum hostibus congressi uictoriam adepti sunt. Exin[2] confluxerunt[3] undique [4]prius dispersi Britones[4] et in abditis locorum latitantes factaque[5] intra[6] Silcestriam[7] concione[8] erexerunt Constantinum in regem regnique dyadema[9] capiti suo imposuerunt.[10] Tunc erumpens Guizelinus pontifex, qui illum adduxerat, in uocem leticie cantando gratulanter[11] ait: 'Christus uincit, Christus regnat, Christus imperat![12] Ecce quod desiderauimus, ecce rex Britannie[13] deserte, ecce defensio nostra – assit modo Christus!' Dimissa itaque concione[14] illa cum exultacione[15] dederunt regi suo coniugem ex nobili [16]genere Romanorum[16] ortam, quam ipse Guizelinus archiepiscopus[17] secum educauerat. De qua progenuit[18] tres[19] filios, quorum nomina sunt Constans, Aurelius Ambrosius, Utherpendragon. Constantem primogenitum tradidit ecclesie Amphibali[20] nutriendum infra Wintoniam,[21] ubi etiam monasticum [22]suscepit ordinem.[22] Ceteros, uidelicet Aurelium et[23] Utherpendragon,[24] Guizelino presuli nutriendos commisit. Cumque .x. annis[25] regnasset Constantinus, quidam Pictus qui in obsequio suo fuerat accessit ad eum quasi [26]colloquium secretum[26] habiturus in uirgulto quodam semotis omnibus arbitris[27] et cum cultro dolose interfecit eum.

[94] Defuncto itaque Constantino dissensio[1] facta est inter proceres regni de duobus fratribus, quis eorum in regem sublimaretur.[2] Erant siquidem ambo adhuc pueri infra etatem tanti culminis regendi. Cumque diu contendissent et [3]alii hunc, alii illum[3] acclamarent, accessit

§93 [1] aDERS (corrected from *Totonensi* in S); *Tottonesio* H. [2] DER; *Exinde* aHS. [3] acR; *collecti* DES (with *struxerunt* deleted after *collecti* in D); *confluxerant* H. [4...4] aHR (*Brittones* in aH); *Britones dispersi prius* DES. [5] acDEHS; *factam* R. [6] aDRS; *inter se* cE; *in* H. [7] aEHRS; *Cilcestrie* c; *Cilestriam* D. [8] cERS; *contione* aDH. [9] cDR; *diadema* aEHS. [10] acDERS; *inposuerunt* H. [11] acDHRS; om. E. [12] acDERS; *inperat* H. [13] cDERS; *Brittannie* aH. [14] ER; *contione* acDHS. [15] DER; *exultatione* acHS. [16...16] acDERS; *Romanorum genere* H. [17] acHR; om. DES. [18] aDERS; *genuit* cH. [19] acDERS; *.iii.* H. [20] acDEHRS (with *sancti* in margin in D). [21] aDERS; *Gwintoniam* c; *Guintoniam* H. [22...22] cDES; *ordinem suscepit* aH; *cepit ordinem* R. [23] cDERS; om. aH. [24] aDR; *Uthyrpendragun* c; *Utherp̄* ES. [25] cDERS; *annos* aH. [26...26] aHR; *secretum colloquium* cDES. [27] acDEHS; *arbitriis* R.

§94 [1] aDEHS; *dissencio* cR. [2] cDER; *sullimaretur* aHS. [3...3] cDER; *alii hunc et alii illum* a; *alii hunc alii alium* H; *alii illum* (with *alii illum* repeated suprascript) S.

uir gnarus[4] quidem[5] sed dolosus, Uortigernus,[6] consul[7] Gewisseorum,[8] qui et ipse ad regnum toto nisu anhelabat,[9] et persuasit optimatibus[10] regni[11] quatinus[12] Constantem primogenitum, qui in monasterio Wintoniensi[13] degebat, in[14] regem eligerent. Quod cum quidam propter monasticum ordinem abhorrerent,[15] ipse se[16] ultro [17]ad hoc opus presto esse[17] atque iuuenem de monasterio exempturum[18] spopondit.[19] Relictis ergo illis Wintoniam[20] tendit, monasterium ingreditur atque colloquium regalis iuuenis deposcit. Cumque[21] extra claustrum eductus esset, uerba huiuscemodi auribus illius secreto instillauit: 'Ecce pater tuus defunctus est et fratres tui [22]propter etatem sublimari in regem[22] nequeunt nec alium habemus preter te de genere tuo quem nobis regem eligamus. [23]Acquiesce ergo[23] [24]consilio meo[24] et, si possessionem meam augmentare[25] uolueris, suadebo populum[26] et in affectum[27] conuertam sublimandi[28] te in regem et ex hoc habitu mutatis uestibus te abstraham.' Quod cum audisset Constans, magno exultans gaudio quod petebat se libenter exequi confessus est et quicquid[29] callebat ipsum uelle iureiurando confirmauit.[30] Assumpsit itaque[31] eum Uortigernus,[32] uellent[33] nollent monachi, atque mutato habitu regiis ornamentis mox indutum Londonias[34] secum duxit. Sed tunc temporis defuncto Guizelino pontifice ecclesia illa carebat nec affuit alter qui eum inungere et[35] coronam imponere[36] presumeret. Arripiens igitur[37] ipse[38] Uortigernus[39] propter instantem necessitatem coronam capiti illius[40] manibus suis imposuit.[41]

4 acDEHS; om. R. 5 acHR; *quidam* DES. 6 acH; *Uortigernus nomine* DES; *Uortigrinus guar* R. 7 aHR; *dux* cDES. 8 cR; *Geuuisseorum* aH; *Geuisseorum* DES. 9 aDEHS; *hanelabat* c; *hanelebat* R. 10 acDHR; *obtimatibus* ES. 11 cDERS; *terre* aH. 12 acHR; *ut* DES. 13 aDR; *Gwintoniensi* c; *Uintoniensi* E; *Guintoniensi* H; *Wyntoniensi* S. 14 cDERS; om. aH. 15 acDEHRS (corrected from *abhorrent* in D). 16 acDERS; om. H. 17...17 cDERS; *presto ad hoc opus esse* a; *presto ad hoc esse opus* H. 18 cDERS; *excepturum* aH. 19 cDHS; *spondit* a; *spospondit* ER. 20 aDERS; *Gwintoniam* a; *Guintoniam* H. 21 acDEHRS (corrected from *Cum* in D). 22...22 aR (*sullimari* in a); *propter etatem in regem sublimari* c; *sullimari in regem propter etatem* DES (*sublimari* in D). 23...23 cDERS; *Adquiesce igitur* aH. 24...24 acHR; *meo consilio* DES. 25 acDEHS; *aucmentare* R. 26 aDEHR; *populo* cS. 27 acDEHR; *affectum* (with *eum* suprascript) S. 28 cDR; *sullimandi* aEHS. 29 acDEHS; *quidquid* R. 30 aDEHS; *firmauit* c; *confirmabat* R. 31 acDHRS; *ergo* E. 32 acHS (before *eum* in c); *Uortig'* DE; *Uortigrinus* R. 33 acDHRS; erasure in text (with *uellent* in margin) E. 34 acDERS; *Lundonias* H. 35 acHR; *atque* DES. 36 acDERS; *inponere* H. 37 acDHRS; *ergo* E. 38 acDEHS; om. R. 39 acHS; *Uortig'* DE; *Uortigrinus* R. 40 aHR; *ipsius* cDES. 41 acDERS; *inposuit* H.

[95] Sublimatus[1] itaque Constans totam regni curam[2] Uortigerno[3] commisit necnon et semetipsum consilio et moderationi[4] eiusdem tradidit. Elapso autem[5] tempore, cum totas regni habenas ipse Uortigernus[6] pro uoto moderaretur, [7]cepit apud se[7] deliberare et intenta mente excogitare qualiter quod desiderabat de regno compleret. Uidebat namque congruum tempus adesse quo id ad effectum duceret, cum ei tocius[8] regni dominium cederet[9] et regis Constantis[10] fatuitas pateret uniuersis. Quippe in claustro enutritus[11] nullam dispensacionis[12] curam uel prouidenciam[13] regni gerebat, omnia Uortigerno[14] tantum committens. Duo autem fratres illius tamquam[15] [16]in cunis adhuc nutriebantur.[16] Preterea regni proceres maiores natu mortibus diuersis omnes fere obierant[17] et erat terra omni consilio destituta nisi quantum[18] in se erat. Hec itaque[19] in animo uoluens excogitauit fraudem praui consilii et accessit quadam die ad Constantem,[20] dolenti similis dicens: 'Moueor propter te, karissime domine, quia regnum tuum inquietare affectant collaterales insulani, et maxime Norguegenses et Daci. Rumor enim[21] et fama [22]late uagans[22] innotuit terram hanc carere uiris et senioribus morte deletis et te ipsum nichilominus iuuenem cum fratribus tuis puerili inniti[23] consilio. Quamobrem prouida te [24]oportet uti[24] deliberacione[25] quatinus ab imminentibus[26] hostibus antequam quod moliuntur[27] incipiant premunitus eripiaris et regnum[28] in[29] pace et tranquillitate perseueret.' Cui Constans, 'Nonne,'[30] ait, 'omnia dispositioni[31] tue commisi? Fac ergo quecumque[32] ad salutem meam et regni pacem noueris utilia[33] fore.' Ad hec Uortigernus:[34] 'Si in manum meam commiseris municiones[35] terre, urbes et

---

§95 [1] cDR; *Sullimatus* aEHS. [2] acDERS (*curam* before *regni* in c); *curiam* H. [3] acHS; *Uortig'* DE; *Uortigrino* R. [4] acDHRS; *moderacioni* E. [5] acDERS; *itaque* H. [6] acHS; *Uortig'* DE; *Uortigrinus* R. [7...7] acDEHS (*modera* deleted after *se* in S); *apud se cepit* R. [8] cER; *totius* aDHS. [9] aHR; *cessisset* cDES. [10] cDERS; om. aH. [11] acDEHR; *est nutritus* S. [12] ERS; *dispensationis* acDH. [13] cERS; *prouidentiam* aDH. [14] acHS; *Uortig'* DE; *Uortigrino* R. [15] R; *tanquam* acDEHS. [16...16] aDE; *cunis adhuc nutriebantur* c; *in cunis adhuc iacebant* H; *adhuc nutriebantur in cunis* R; *iuuenes adhuc nutiebantur* S. [17] acDEHRS (corrected from *obierat* in H). [18] acDEHS; *in* deleted before *quantum* in R. [19] acEHRS; *omnia* D. [20] acDERS; *Constancium* H. [21] aHR; *etenim* c; om. DES. [22...22] acEHRS; *longe uagans et late* D. [23] DHRS; *initi* a; *inuiti* c; *meriti* E. [24...24] DERS; *uti oportet* acH. [25] ER; *deliberatione* acDHS. [26] aDHRS; *iminentibus* cE. [27] aDEHS; *molliuntur* R. [28] acDEHS; *in regnum* R. [29] acDERS; *cum* H. [30] acDEHR; *Nomine* deleted before *Nonne* in S. [31] acDHRS; *disposicioni* E. [32] acEHRS; *quodcumque* D. [33] acHR; *utiliora* DES. [34] acHS; *Uortig'* DE; *Uortigrinus* R. [35] ER; *munitiones* acDHS.

castra et cetera quibus regnum [36]ab incursione hostium[36] tuear,[37] thesauros quoque quibus milites et uiri bellicosi per uniuersas terre regiones disponantur, non uereor eo[38] te roborari[39] consilio ut [40]facile caueas hostium circumueniencium[40] temeritatem.' Respondit rex: 'Sicut tibi omnem regni curam commisi, ita fac ad libitum tuum uniuersa[41] que dixisti.' 'Oportet ergo,' ait ille, 'te aliquos ex Pictis tecum in familia habere et curiam tuam talibus munire custodibus qui mediatores inter te et hostes existant et eorum machinaciones[42] explorent quo tucius[43] in domo et[44] in curia esse possis.' Hec dicens misit [45]ocius nuncios[45] in Scociam[46] inuitans Pictos ad regis [47]presidium. Quibus adductis honorabat eos Uortigernus[48] supra omnes regis[49] [47] familie tirones[50] et donariis ditabat; cibis et potibus, quibus [51]gens illa[51] nimis indulgebat,[52] cottidie[53] usque ad crapulam et ebrietatem replebat. Unde Uortigernum[54] [55]magis pro rege habebant[55] quam ipsum Constantem. Inebriati ergo[56] per plateas et uicos tanquam fanatici acclamabant: 'Dignus est Uortigernus[57] imperio,[58] dignus[59] Britannie[60] sceptro!'[61] Sub hiis[62] autem fauoribus diu latere non potuit uersuti [63]ac dolosi uiri[63] animus, utpote qui [64]ad argumenta[64] sue nequitie[65] hec omnia preparabat. Quadam ergo die[66] dum inebriati ex more fuissent [67]Picti, accessit[67] Uortigernus[68] subtristis, simulans [69]se uelle de regno Britannie[69] recedere ut ampliores acquireret[70] possessiones et[71] sibi suisque possent stipendia sufficere. Neque enim[72] id tantillum quod possidebat quinquaginta[73] militibus ut unusquisque modicum quid acciperet satis esse

---

[36...36] acDEHS; *hostium ab incursione* R. [37] DES; *tueatur* acHR. [38] aDERS; om. cH. [39] aHR; *coroborari* c; *corroborari* DES. [40...40] acHR (*circumuenientium* in aH); *caueas hostium circumuenientium facile* DES. [41] DERS; *omnia* acH. [42] ERS; *machinationes* acDH. [43] cERS; *tutius* aD; *securus* H. [44] acDEHS; om. R. [45...45] cER; *nuntios otius* aH; *otius nuntios* DS. [46] cER; *Scotiam* aDHS. [47...47] acDERS; om. H. [48] acS; *Uortig'* DE; om. H; *Uortigrinus* R. [49] acDER; om. H; *regie* (tampered?) S. [50] acEHR; *tyrones* DS. [51...51] acDEHS; *illa gens* R. [52] acHR; *indulget* DES. [53] R; *cotidie* aDEHS; om. c. [54] acS; *Uortig'* DE; *plus Uortigernum* H; *Uortigrinum* R. [55...55] DERS; *pro rege habebant magis* a; *pro rege magis habebant* c; *pro rege habebant* H. [56] acDERS; *uero* H. [57] achS; *Uortig'* DE; *Uortigrinus* R. [58] acDERS; *inperio* H. [59] aHR; *dignus est* DES. [60] cDERS; *Brittannie* aH. [61] acDEHS; *ceptro* R. [62] cDERS; *his* aH. [63...63] aHR; *uiri ac dolosi* cDES. [64...64] cDERS; *argumentum* a; *argumento* H. [65] aHRS; *nequicie* cDE. [66] acDEHS; *dum* deleted before *die* in R. [67...67] acDERS; *accessit Pictis* H. [68] achS; *Uortig'* DE; *Uortigrinus* R. [69...69] R; *se uelle e regno Brittannie* a; *se e regno Brittannie uelle* DES; *uelle se e regno Brittannie* H. [70] aDR; *quereret* c; *adquireret* EHS. [71] aDERS; *ut et* cH. [72] aHR; om. DES (with *enim* suprascript in D). [73] R; *.l.* aDEHS; *50* c.

ducebat.[74] Sic loquens Pictos ebriosos[75] ad scelus animauit et se ad hospicium[76] suum contulit, illos [77]in aula regia[77] potantes[78] dimittens.[79] Illi uero adinuicem murmurantes quod talem tamque honoratum uirum tamque munificum amitterent, arbitrantes [80]uerum esse[80] quod ille falso ac simulato ore protulerat, dixerunt furore repleti: 'Utquid monachum[81] istum uiuere permittimus? Utquid non interficimus eum ut Uortigernus[82] regno pociatur?[83] Dignus namque est imperio[84] regni et honore, dignus etiam omni dignitate qui nos ditare non cessat.'

[96] Irruentes itaque[1] thalamum[2] impetum[3] fecerunt[4] in Constantem et amputato eius capite coram[5] Uortigerno[6] detulerunt. Quod cum uidisset, in fletum quasi contristatus erupit conuocatisque[7] ciuibus [8]Londonie ciuitatis[8] – nam id in ea contigerat – iussit omnes proditores alligari atque teneri et ad ultimum decollari, qui tantum scelus perpetrauerant. Uindicta itaque de Pictis peracta fuerunt in populo qui estimarent, etsi proloqui[9] non auderent, prodicionem[10] illam et regis interfectionem per Uortigernum[11] machinatam fuisse, Pictos siquidem nullatenus nisi assensu illius tale facinus ausos fuisse. Fueruntque[12] qui eum[13] a tali crimine uerbis contradicentibus purgarent.[14] Re tandem in ambiguo relicta nutritores duorum fratrum assumentes eos fugerunt in minorem Britanniam,[15] timentes ne idem contingeret eis quod primogenito factum fuerat. Ibique eos rex Buditius[16] cum honore quo decebat[17] excepit et summa diligencia[18] educauit.

[74] aEHR; *dicebat* cD; *ducebat* altered to *dicebat* in S. [75] acHR; *ebrios* DES. [76] acDERS; *hospitium* H. [77...77] acHR; om. DES. [78] acDEHS; *portantes* R. [79] acDEHS; *dimittentes* R. [80...80] acHR; *quod uerum esset* DES. [81] acDHR; *monacum* ES. [82] acHS; *Uortig'* DE; *Uortigrinus* R. [83] cERS; *potiatur* aDH. [84] acDERS; *inperio* H.

§96 [1] aHR; *ergo* cDES. [2] aHR; *in thalamum* cDE; *in talamum* S. [3] acDERS; *inpetum* H. [4] acEHRS; *fecerunt* tampered in D. [5] acDEHR; *coronam* S. [6] acHS; *Uortig'* DE; *Uortigrino* R. [7] aHR; *Uocatis igitur* c; *uocatisque* DES. [8...8] acDES; *Lundonie ciuitatis* H; *ciuitatis Londonie* R. [9] acHR; *loqui* DES. [10] ERS; *proditionem* acDH. [11] acHS; *Uortig'* DE; *Uortigrinum* R. [12] acDEHR; *Fuerunt* S. [13] R; om. acDEHS. [14] acEHRS; *pugnarent* D. [15] cDERS; *Brittanniam* aH. [16] acD; *Hudicius* ERS; *Gudicius* H. [17] acDEHR; *debuit* S. [18] cERS; *diligentia* aDH.

[97] At Uortigernus[1] dyadema[2] regni capiti suo inponens[3] duabus cottidie[4] [5]angustiis uehementer angebatur,[5] uidelicet reatus sui conscientia[6] atque Pictorum[7] mortem suorum uindicare uolencium[8] infesta contumacia detrimentum sue gentis non modicum et totius[9] regni inquietacionem[10] sustinens. Accedebat[11] quoque ad cumulum doloris sui interminacio[12] duorum fratrum Constantis; quorum fama[13] aduentare eos in proximo super [14]se, fauentibus[14] illis [15]terre optimatibus,[15] diuulgabatur.[16]

[98] Interea applicuerunt tres[1] ciule,[2] quas longas naues dicimus, in partibus Cancie[3] plene de armatis militibus; quorum duces Horsus et Hengistus dicebantur. Eratque[4] tunc temporis Uortigernus[5] Dorobernie, que nunc Cantuaria[6] dicitur. Cui cum nunciatum[7] fuisset[8] uiros ignote lingue magneque stature in [9]longis nauibus[9] aduenisse, missis nunciis[10] [11]cum pace ad se uenire[11] fecit. Mox ut adducti sunt, uertit oculos in[12] duos[13] prefatos germanos. Nam et ipsi pre ceteris statura et decore eminebant.[14] Intuitusque[15] eos ait: 'Que patria, [16]o iuuenes, uobis[16] materna est aut que causa huc in regnum nostrum appulit?[17] Edicite!' Cui Hengistus,[18] ut erat pre ceteris amplioris et maturioris etatis persona, pro[19] omnibus respondit:[20] 'Rex tuorum nobilissime, Saxonica tellus, que una est ex regionibus Germanie, nos editos huc appulit. Causam[21] itineris [22]nostri et profectionis[22] de terra nostra, si placet audire, in pacis securitate disseremus.'[23] Concessa igitur[24] a rege

---

§97 [1] acHS; *Uortig'* DE; *Uortigrinus* R. [2] R; *diadema* acDEHS. [3] HR; *imponens* acDES. [4] R; *cotidie* acDEHS. [5]...[5] acHR; *angebatur angustiis uehementer* D; *angustiis angebatur uehementer* ES. [6] acDHRS; *consciencia* E. [7] acDEHS; *Picto* (with space left) R. [8] cER; *uolentium* aDHS. [9] aDHRS; *tocius* cE. [10] DERS; *inquietationem* acH. [11] aDEHR; *Accedat* S. [12] ERS; *interminatio* acDH. [13] acDEHS; om. R. [14]...[14] acDEHS; *fauentibus se* R. [15]...[15] acHR; *optimatibus terre* DES. [16] acDEHRS; after *diuulgabatur, Explicit liber .v.. Incipit .vi.* in H.

§98 [1] acDERS; *.iii.* H. [2] aH; *quale* c; *cymbe* D; *cimbe* E; *cuule* R; *cinbe* S. [3] cER; *Cantie* aDHS. [4] cHR; *Erat* aDES. [5] acH (*Uortigernus* before *tunc temporis* in c); *Uortig'* DES; *Uortigrinus* R. [6] acDERS; *Kantuaria* H. [7] acDERS; *nuntiatum* H. [8] aHR; *esset* cDES. [9]...[9] acDHR; *magnis nauibus et longis* E; *magnis nauibus* S. [10] cDERS; *nuntiis* aH. [11]...[11] aHR; *ad se uenire cum pace* c; *ad se cum pace uenire* DES. [12] acHR; *ad* DES. [13] acDERS; *.ii.* H. [14] HRS; *eminebat* ac; *imminebant* DE. [15] acDEH; *Intuitosque* R; *Intuitus* (followed by deleted *est*) S. [16]...[16] aHR; *iuuenes uobis* c; *uobis o iuuenes* DES. [17] cDERS; *appulerit* aH. [18] acDEHS; *Engistus* R. [19] acDERS; *pre* H. [20] acDERS; *ait* H. [21] cDER; *Causa* aH; *causamque* S. [22]...[22] acHR; *et profectionis nostri* DES. [23] aDEHS; *diceremus* cR. [24] acDEHS; *ergo* R.

[25]loquendi cum pace[25] facultate sic orsus est: 'Mos et consuetudo patrie nostre est, bone rex, ut, cum habundancia[26] uirorum [27]in ea[27] excreuerit, conueniant principes[28] terre et tocius[29] regni iuuentutem in annos .xv. aut eo amplius excretam[30] coram se uenire compellunt[31] positaque sorte pociores[32] atque fortiores[33] in exteras regiones tamquam[34] in[35] exilio relegatos dirigunt ut patria ipsa a multitudine superflua uacuetur. Est enim terra nostra fecundior hominum procreandorum[36] ubertate quam ceterorum animalium, licet ipsa quoque ferarum[37] habundancia[38] atque diuiciarum[39] copia in suo genere nequaquam fraudetur. Sic itaque a patria [40]sorte prefata[40] deiecti istis in horis Mercurio[41] duce aduecti sumus.' Audito igitur nomine Mercurii interrogauit rex qua religione deum colerent. Cui Hengistus: 'Deos patrios, [42]Saturnum, Iouem, Mercurium[42] atque ceteros quos coluerunt patres nostri ueneramur atque colimus, maxime Mercurium quem Woden[43] lingua nostra appellamus. Huic[44] maiores nostri quartam[45] feriam dicauerunt, que usque in hodiernum diem[46] lingua nostra nomen[47] Wodnesdai[48] de nomine ipsius sortita est. Post hunc colimus deam [49]inter ceteras potentissimam,[49] nomine Fream. Cui etiam dicauerunt sextam[50] feriam quam[51] de nomine ipsius Friedai[52] uocamus.'[53] 'De religione uestra, que pocius[54] irreligio dici potest,' ait Uortigernus,[55] 'uehementer doleo. De aduentu[56] autem uestro non modicum letor si moram nobiscum placuerit uobis per[57] spacium[58] temporis agere. Siue enim Deus siue[59] fortuna uos huc appulerit, congruo tempore neccessitati[60] nostre[61] auxilium ferre potestis.[62] Infestant enim nos quidam latrunculi, inimici[63] nostri, undique, quos[64] [65]uestra ope longius[65] abigere a terra nostra et in

---

[25...25] aHR; *cum pace loquendi* cDES. [26] cER; *habundantia* aDHS. [27...27] aHR; om. cDES. [28] acDEHS; *omnes principes* R. [29] cER; *totius* aDHS. [30] acDHRS; *excreta* E. [31] acDERS; *compellant* H. [32] cERS; *potiores* aDH. [33] aDHRS; *forciores* cE. [34] R; *tanquam* acDEHS. [35] aHR; om. cDES. [36] acDEHS; *procreatorum* R. [37] acDEHS; *feralis* R. [38] cERS; *habundantia* aDH. [39] cERS; *diuitiarum* aDH. [40...40] acHR; *prefata sorte* DES. [41] acDEHS; *Mercurie* R. [42...42] R (with *Mercurium* corrected from *Merculrium*); *Mercurium Iouem Saturnum* aH; *Iouem Saturnum Mercurium* cDES. [43] cDEHRS (altered from *Innoden* in H); *Wonden* a. [44] acDHRS; *Hunc* E. [45] acDERS; *.iiii.* H. [46] acDERS; om. H. [47] aDEHR; om. cS. [48] RS; *Wodnesdei* acH; *Wodenesdai* D; *Wodnesday* E. [49...49] acDERS; *ceteris potissimam* H. [50] acDRS; *.vi.* EH. [51] acDEHS; *qua* R. [52] R; *Fridai* aDHS; *Fridei* c; *Friday* E. [53] aHR; *appellamus* cDES. [54] cERS; *potius* aDH. [55] acH; *Uortig'* DES; *Uortigrinus* R. [56] acDEHRS (in margin in S). [57] acDEHS; om. R. [58] acDERS; *spatium* H. [59] cHRS; *seu* aDE. [60] cDERS; *necessitati* aH. [61] acDEHS; om. R. [62] acDEHRS (corrected from *potestatis* in S). [63] acDEHS; om. R. [64] acDEHS; *nos* deleted before *quos* in R. [65...65] acHR; *longius ope uestra* DES.

88

speluncas terre sue nequissime latitare[66] optarem aut omnino, si fieri posset, exterminare. Unde uos quotquot uenistis infra[67] regnum meum honorifice retinebo[68] et diuersis muneribus et agris ditabo.' Paruerunt barbari et federe firmato curiam repleuerunt proceribus et ualidis uiris et ad bellum strenue[69] edoctis, stipendia accepturi pro consuetudine legis sue. Nec mora emergentes ex Albania Picti exercitum grandem ualde in fines Britannorum[70] et ultra eduxerunt magnamque partem terre uastauerunt; contra quos Uortigernus[71] Saxones barbaros cum exercitu suorum dirigens[72] trans Humbrum obuius uenit illis et congressus magnam stragem ex eis faciens in fugam eos[73] coegit. Sed[74] quia consueuerant antea[75] prioribus bellis esse superiores, duriter resistendo multos Britonum,[76] plures[77] suorum[78] uulneratos ac telis confossos[79] amiserunt.

[99] Rex ergo per Saxones uictoria potitus donaria[1] sua ampliauit eis atque[2] Hengisto dedit agros et mansiones plurimas in Lindiseia[3] regione quibus se suosque sustentaret. Cumque se necessarium [4]Hengistus regi[4] sentiret et eius amicitiam atque[5] beniuolenciam[6] pro uirtute ac probitate sua erga[7] se pronam aspiceret, fidenter quadam die accessit ad eum in iocunditate[8] regia, dicens: 'Domine mi rex, patere,[9] si placet, me [10]ad te[10] pauca proloqui de statu regni atque tuorum fidelitate: comperi[11] enim[12] ex quo tibi adhesi quia pauci sunt ex tuis qui te perfecte diligant et honorem tuum defendant. Omnes fere [13]tibi malum[13] interminant, dicentes nescio quos fratres, heredes regni iustiores te,[14] in proximo ascituros[15] ex Armorico tractu ut te[16] deponant et illos promoueant. Nunc igitur, si tibi uidebitur[17] consilium

---

[66] acDERS; *actitare* H. [67] aHR; *in* cDES. [68] acDEHR; *detinebo* S. [69] acDERS; *strennue* H. [70] cDERS; *Brittannorum* aH. [71] acH; *Uortig'* DES; *Uortigrinus* R. [72] aHR; *colligens* c; *educens* DES. [73] acDERS; om. H. [74] acDHRS; *Set* E. [75] aHR; om. cDES. [76] cDERS; *Brittonum* aH. [77] acEHRS; *pluresque* D. [78] acDHRS; *suosum* (with *suorum* in margin) E. [79] acDERS; *confectos* H.

§99 [1] acDEHS; *am* deleted before *donaria* in R. [2] cDERS; *et* aH. [3] DR; *Lindeseia* acE; *Lindissea* H; *Lyndeseia* S. [4...4] aHR; *regi Hengistus* DES. [5] DERS; *et* aH. [6] cR; *beneuolentiam* aDHS; *beneuolenciam* E. [7] acDEHS; *quam* deleted before *erga* in R. [8] acDEHS; *in locum* deleted before *iocunditate* in R. [9] aDES; *patrie* c; *pater* H; *pacem* R. [10...10] acHR; om. DES. [11] acDEHRS (corrected from *cooperimur* in H). [12] acDERS; om. H. [13...13] acHR; *malum tibi* DES. [14] acDEHS; *d* deleted before *te* in R. [15] acEHRS; *ascituros* (with *expulsuros* in margin) D. [16] acDEHR; om. S. [17] acDERS; *uidetur* H.

ut de gente nostra[18] inuitemus[19] aliquos ad tuendam[20] patriam ab hostium incursione et tuorum proditione,[21] palam manifestare ne[22] dubites ut numerus[23] nostrorum augeatur in tuam fidelitatem et terreantur externi et priuati hostes cum te ac regnum tuum cinxerit[24] ac protexerit fortissimorum uirorum robur.' Ad hec Uortigernus:[25] 'Mitte ut dixisti ad terram tuam et inuita quos uolueris, tantum ut fideles uos [26]in mea dilectione semper[26] inueniam, et pete a me quod uolueris; nullam pacieris[27] repulsam.' Qui audiens regem erga se beniuolum inclinato capite gratias multimodas de beniuolentia[28] egit et adiecit: 'Ditasti,'[29] [30]inquid, 'me[30] largis mansionibus et agris sed, cum desit ciuitas aut munimentum in quo me[31] meosque in necessitate recipiam, securus non sum de uita[32] aut[33] possessione. Concedat ergo[34] dominus rex seruo suo fideli Hengisto quantum [35]corrigia una possit[35] ambire terre[36] in aliqua mansionum[37] mearum ut ibi edificem domum cum propugnaculis ad defensionem nostram si contigerit ab hostibus circumueniri. Et ego interim mittam pro uxore ac liberis et parentibus et[38] amicis ut securior de nobis, quicquid[39] commiserim,[40] existas.' Motus itaque rex peticioni eius acquieuit.[41] Nec mora missa [42]in Germaniam Hengistus legacione[42] cepit corium[43] tauri in unam redigere corrigiam.[44] Nactus[45] saxosum[46] locum ad munimentum quod magna [47]elegerat cautela,[47] circuiuit cum[48] corrigia et infra spacium[49] metatum castrum edificauit. Quod edificatum traxit[50] nomen ex corrigia:[51] Saxonice Thancastre,[52] Britannice[53] uero Kaercarrei,[54] quod Latino uerbo 'Castrum Corrigie'[55] sonat.

[18] acDEHS; *sua* deleted before *nostra* in R. [19] acDEHS; *mittemus* R. [20] acDHRS; *tuendum* E. [21] acDHRS; *prodicionem* E. [22] acDERS; *non* H. [23] acDEHS; *innumerus* (?) R. [24] acDERS; *auxerit* H. [25] acH; *Uortig'* DES; *Uortigrinus* R. [26...26] aHR; *in mea dilectione* cE; *semper in mea dilectione* DS. [27] cRS; *paciens* aE; *patiens* DH. [28] aDHRS; *beniuolencia* c; *beneuolencia* E. [29] acEHRS; *Ditastis* D. [30...30] RS; *me inquit* aH; *inquit me* cDE. [31] acDERS; *me* suprascript in H. [32] cDERS; *uita mea* aH. [33] acHR; *aut de* DES. [34] acDEHS; om. R. [35...35] acDEHS (*corigia* in cE); *possit corrigia una* R. [36] acHR; om. DES. [37] acHR; *mansione* DES. [38] acDEHS; *a* deleted before *et* in R. [39] acDEHS; *quidquid* R. [40] acDERS; *commiserimus* H. [41] acDRS; *adquieuit* EH. [42...42] acHR (*legatione* in aH); *Hengistus legatione in Germaniam* D; *Hengestus legacione in Germaniam* E; *Hengistus legacione in Germaniam* S. [43] ac-DEHS; *coreum* R. [44] aDHR; *corigiam* cES. [45] acDEHR; *Nactus est* S. [46] acDERS; *Saxones* H. [47...47] cDERS; *cautela elegerat* aH. [48] cDERS; om. aH. [49] acER; *spatium* DHS. [50] acDEHR; *taxit* S. [51] aDHRS; *corigia* cE. [52] R; *Kwangastre* a; *Thangcastre uel Dwanceastre* c; *Twangcastre* (preceded by deleted *Thancastre uel*) D; *Thancastre uel Twangcastre* E; *Wangcastre* H; *Thancastre uel Twangastre* S. [53] cDERS; *Brittannice* aH. [54] DES (with *dynas dyn carrey* in margin in D); *Kercarri* a; *Kaerygarrei* c; *Kaercorrei* H; *Caercacei* R. [55] aDHRS; *Corigie* cE.

[100] Interea reuersi[1] e[2] Germania nuncii adduxerunt .xviii.[3] naues electis militibus plenas, inter quos adducta[4] fuerat[5] filia Hengisti uocabulo[6] Ronwen[7] pulcra[8] facie ac uenusto[9] corpore.[10] Patrato igitur Hengistus edificio suo inuitauit ad prandium regem ut et[11] domum nouam et nouos [12]milites uideret.[12] Qui non distulit [13]uenire priuatim[13] et absque multitudine ut delectaretur[14] cum fideli suo Hengisto. Ut autem descendit, rex laudauit opus gnauiter[15] edificatum[16] ac milites e Germania inuitatos secum retinuit. Postquam regiis[17] epulis [18]refecti sunt,[18] egressa est puella de thalamo filia Hengisti,[19] aureum uas uino plenum manu ferens, accedensque propius[20] regi flexis genibus[21] lingua sua ait: 'Washeil,[22] [23]lauerd king.'[23] At ille mox uisa puella miratus faciem decoram cum uenusto corpore incaluit. Interrogauitque[24] interpretem suum quid puella [25]sermone suo[25] dixerat[26] et quid eodem sermone[27] respondere deberet. Cui interpres, 'Uocauit te,' ait, 'dominum regem et uocabulo salutacionis[28] honorauit. Quod autem ei[29] respondere debes ita est, "Drincheil".'[30] Respondens Uortigernus[31] ait, 'Drincheil,'[32] et iussit puellam[33] potare recepitque cyphum[34] de manu eius et ex[35] more Saxonico osculatus est eam et potauit.[36] Ab illo ergo die usque in hodiernum diem[37] remansit consuetudo illa in Britannia[38] inter[39] conuiuantes et potantes[40] ut per 'Wasseil'[41] et 'Drincheil'[42] se inuicem salutarent.[43] Rex autem multo diuersi generis potu inebriatus[44] instigante Sathana puellam adamauit et ut sibi daretur a patre postulauit, licet gentilis et non christiana esset. Hengistus[45] ergo

§100 [1] acDEHS; *reuersa* R. [2] acDH; *a* ES; *est* R. [3] aDHRS; *28* c; *octodecim* E. [4] acDEHS; *d ducta* R. [5] acHR (preceded by deleted *erat* in R); *erat* DES. [6] acHR; *nomine* DES. [7] cDES; *Ronuuen* aH; *Ronwein* R. [8] acEHRS; *pulchra* D. [9] acDEHS; *uenusta* R. [10] acDEHRS; *cuius pulchritudo nulli secunda uidebatur* added (from vulgate text) in margin in D. [11] acDEHR; om. S. [12...12] cDERS; *uideret milites* aH. [13...13] acDEHS; *priuatim uenire* R. [14] acDHR; *delectaret* ES. [15] aDEHS; *grauiter* cR. [16] acEHRS; *factum et edificatum* D. [17] acDHRS; om. E. [18...18] acHR; *sunt refecti* DES. [19] acHR; *Heng'* DES. [20] acDHRS; *propitius* E. [21] acDEHS; *poplitibus* R. [22] DERS; *Wesheil* a; *Washail* c; *Weshail* H. [23...23] D; *lauerd kin* aR; *lauert king* c; *lauerdeing* E; *llauerd king* H; *lauerd cing* S. [24] acDEHR; *Interrogauit* S. [25...25] acDHRS; *suo* (with *sermone* added in margin) E. [26] acDEHS; *dixerit* R. [27] acDEHS; *sermone suo* R. [28] acDERS (corrected from *salutauerunt* in c); *salutationis* H. [29] cDERS; om. aH. [30] aDERS; *Drinchail* cH. [31] acH; *Uortig'* DES; *Uortigrinus* R. [32] aDERS; *Drinchail* cH. [33] acDERS; *eam* H. [34] R; *ciphum* acDEH; *cifum* S. [35] acHR; om. DES. [36] acDEHS; *portauit* R. [37] cDERS; om. aH. [38] DERS; *Brittannia* aH. [39] acDEHS; om. R. [40] acDEHS; *portantes* R. [41] R; *Washeil* acDE; *Weshail* H; *Woseil* S. [42] aDERS; *Drincheal* c; *Drinchail* H. [43] acEHRS; *salutarent* altered to *salutent* in D. [44] cDERS; *inebriatus est* a; *inebriatus est et* H. [45] acHR; *Heng'* DES.

cognita regis leuitate consuluit ⁴⁶Horsum fratrem suum⁴⁶ ceterosque maiores natu de gente sua qui omnes pariter in unum consenserunt, uidelicet ut fieret regis peticio et peteret ille Cancie⁴⁷ prouinciam in dotem dari puelle. Nec mora data est puella Uortigerno⁴⁸ et Cancia⁴⁹ Hengisto,⁵⁰ nesciente Gorangono⁵¹ comite qui in eadem regnabat. Nupsit itaque rex eadem nocte ⁵²pagane puelle,⁵² nil uerescens⁵³ de sua christianitate. Que⁵⁴ cum placuisset ei, cepit eam tamquam⁵⁵ reginam habere ac diligere; unde iram et inimiciciam⁵⁶ procerum suorum et filiorum breui⁵⁷ temporis spacio⁵⁸ incurrit. Generauerat⁵⁹ namque⁶⁰ antea ⁶¹filios tres⁶¹ de uxore priore,⁶² quorum nomina erant Uortimer,⁶³ Katigern,⁶⁴ Paschent.⁶⁵

[101] Hengistus¹ autem accedens ad regem ait: 'Ego sum quasi pater tibi et consiliator² tuus esse debeo. Noli³ preterire consilium meum et omnes inimicos tuos uirtute gentis mee superabis. Inuitemus igitur⁴ ⁵adhuc, si placet,⁵ Octam⁶ filium meum e Germania cum fratruele suo Ebissa;⁷ bellatores enim uiri sunt ⁸et expugnabunt nobiscum⁸ omnes inimicos tuos maris et terre. Da eis regiones a Pictis uastatas⁹ que sunt iuxta murum inter Deiram et Scociam.¹⁰ Ibi enim locati impetum ¹¹Pictorum et¹¹ aduentancium¹² barbarorum uiriliter sustinebunt et sic in pace citra Humbrum remanebis.'¹³ Paruit¹⁴ Uortigernus¹⁵ concessitque¹⁶ inuitare quoscumque sciret ad munimentum¹⁷ milicie¹⁸ et augmen-

⁴⁶...⁴⁶ cDERS; *fratrem suum Horsum* aH. ⁴⁷ cERS; *Cantie* aD; *Kantie* H. ⁴⁸ acH; *Uortig'* DES; *Uortigrino* R. ⁴⁹ cERS; *Cantia* aD; *Kantia* H. ⁵⁰ acHR; *Heng'* DES. ⁵¹ acHR; *Gorangano* DES. ⁵²...⁵² acHR; *puelle pagane* DES. ⁵³ acDERS; *uerens* H. ⁵⁴ cDERS; *Quod* aH. ⁵⁵ DR; *quasi* c; *tanquam* aEHS. ⁵⁶ cDERS; *inimicitiam* aH. ⁵⁷ cDERS; *in breui* aH. ⁵⁸ acDER; *spatio* HS. ⁵⁹ aHR; *Genuerat* cDES. ⁶⁰ acDERS; *nanque* H. ⁶¹...⁶¹ acEHRS (.*iii.* in H); *tres filios* D. ⁶² acDERS; *priori* H. ⁶³ EHS; *Wortimerus* a; *Uortinerius* c; *Uortimerus* D; *Uotimer* R. ⁶⁴ ES; *Kartigernus* a; *Karigern* c; *Katigernus* D; *Kartigern* H; *Katigein* R. ⁶⁵ acDERS (with *Pascentius* in margin in D); *Paskent* H.

§101 ¹ acHR; *Heng'* DES. ² aHR; *consiliarius* cDES. ³ acDERS; *Noli ergo* H. ⁴ aDEHS; om. c; *ergo* R. ⁵...⁵ cDERS; *si placet adhuc* aH. ⁶ acEHS; *Ottam* D; *Hoctam* R. ⁷ acDEHS; *Eosa* R. ⁸...⁸ cDES (*expungnabunt* in c); *et expugnabunt* aH; *nobiscum et pugnabunt* R. ⁹ acDEHRS (corrected from *uastates* in S). ¹⁰ cER; *Scotiam* aDHS. ¹¹...¹¹ aHR; om. cDES. ¹² cER; *aduentantium* aDHS. ¹³ acDERS; *remanebunt* H. ¹⁴ aHR; *Paruit itaque* cDES. ¹⁵ acH; *Uortig'* DES; *Uortigrinus* R. ¹⁶ aHR; *iussitque* cDES. ¹⁷ acHRS; *monumentum* D; *monimentum* E. ¹⁸ cER; *militie* aDHS.

tum[19] sibi ualere. Missis illico[20] legatis uenerunt Octa[21] et Ebissa[22] et Cherdich[23] cum trecentis[24] nauibus armatorum uirorum. Quos omnes suscepit rex benigne magnisque ditauit muneribus. Post hos etiam[25] alii [26]atque alii per inuitacionem[27] Hengisti[28] uenerunt[26] et paulatim totam terram repleuerunt. Quod cum uidissent Britones,[29] timentes prodicionem[30] dixerunt regi nimium se indulgere atque[31] credere Saxonibus paganis, in tantum ut [32]fere iam totam[32] terram cooperirent mixti cum christianis; nec erat iam[33] facile dinoscere qui forent pagani, qui christiani. Insuper tanta multitudo emerserat ut omnibus essent terrori. Dissuadebant ergo et adiudicabant neminem illorum amplius[34] suscipere sed de hiis[35] qui superuenerant aliquos emittere. At Uortigernus,[36] quia diligebat coniugem[37] suam filiam Hengisti et per eam gentem suam, consiliis eorum[38] acquiescere[39] renuit. Uidentes igitur[40] Britones[41] [42]se apud regem[42] esse despectui et consilia eorum fore derisui, omnes unanimiter aduersus illum insurrexerunt et statim conuenientes Londonie[43] Uortimer[44] filium suum in regem erexerunt. Qui mox congregato exercitu non modico in Saxones barbaros atque paganos aciem tendit et quatuor[45] cum eis patre adherente bella gessit atque deuicit: [46]primum prelium[46] super flumen[47] Derwend;[48] secundum[49] super uadum Episfrod,[50] ubi simul congressi Horsus et Katigernus,[51] alter filius Uortigerni,[52] alterutrum se letaliter uulnerauerunt;[53] tercium[54] bellum super litus maris Cancie[55] iuxta naues ipsorum Saxonum. Diffugientes enim ab[56] Albania per longum Britannie[57] usque[58] illuc

---

[19] acDEHS; *aucmentum* R. [20] R; *ilico* aH; *itaque ilico* c; *itaque* DES. [21] cEH; *Hocta* aR; *Otta* D; *Octo* S. [22] aDEHS; *Hebissa* c; *Eosa* R. [23] DEHRS (with *Cheldric* in margin in D); *Cherdihc* a; *Kardich* c. [24] R; *.ccc.* aDEHS; *300* c. [25] aHR; *autem* c; om. DES. [26...26] aDEHS; *Hengisti atque alii uenerunt per inuitacionem* R. [27] cE (& R); *inuitationem* aHS. [28] aH (& R); *Heng'* DES. [29] cDERS; *Brittones* aH. [30] ER; *proditionem* acDHS. [31] aDHRS; *et* cE. [32...32] aR; *iam fere totam* cDES; *fere totam iam* H. [33] acDERS; om. H. [34] cDERS; om. aH. [35] cDERS; *his* aH. [36] acH; *Uortig'* DES; *Uortigrinus* R. [37] aHR; *uxorem* cDES. [38] acDHRS; *ipsorum* E. [39] acER; *adquiescere* DHS. [40] aHRS; *itaque* c; *ergo* DE. [41] cDERS; *Brittones* aH. [42...42] cDES; *apud se regem* aHR. [43] aDERS; *London'* c; *Lundonie* H. [44] EHR; *Wortimer,* altered to *Wortimerum* a; *Uortinerium* c; *Uortimerum* D; *Uortimen* S. [45] cDERS; *.iiii.* aH. [46...46] aHR; *primum prelium fuit* c; *prelium primum* DES. [47] aDERS; *fluuium* cH. [48] cDE (with *Derwerin* in margin in D); *Derwent* aS; *Deruuent* H; *Detewend* R. [49] acHR; *secundum autem* DES. [50] aDERS (with *Epilford* in margin in D); *Episford* c; *Epiford* H. [51] aDES (altered to *Kartigernus* in a); *Catigernus* c; *Kartigernus* H; *Tamgernus* R. [52] acH; *Uortig'* DES; *Uortigrini* R. [53] acDEHS; *wlnerauerunt* R. [54] cDERS; *tertium* aH. [55] cERS; *Cantie* aDH. [56] acDEHR; om. (with *de* suprascript) S. [57] cDERS; *Brittannie* aH. [58] acDERS; *huc atque* H.

contriti preliis et[59] afflicti impetum Britonum[60] sustinere non ualentes naues ingressi sunt et insulam Thaneth[61] pro refugio adierunt. At Britones[62] nichilominus insequentes nauali[63] [64]prelio cottidie illos[64] infestabant et undique telis ac sagittis circumueniebant. Cumque diucius[65] talem[66] assultum[67] sustinere nequirent, coartati[68] undique et [69]fame iam[69] afflicti miserunt Uortigernum[70] regem suum, qui cum illis in omnibus affuerat socius, ad filium suum Uortimerium,[71] petentes licenciam[72] abeundi absque detrimento sui. Et dum [73]colloquium inde[73] Britones[74] cum Uortigerno[75] haberent, Saxones elapsi maria sulcare remis et uento ceperunt relictisque mulierculis[76] suis [77]et liberis[77] Germaniam[78] redierunt.[79]

[102] Uictoria itaque potiti Britones[1] cum rege suo Uortimerio[2] possessiones conciuibus[3] suis ereptas[4] reddere primo non distulerunt. Deinde iubente et annitente[5] sancto Germano Autisiodorensi[6] episcopo ecclesias[7] dirutas renouare et fidem Christi in quibusdam locis corruptam[8] restaurare non destiterunt[9] donec ad perfectum reconciliati fuerunt.[10] Ad confirmandam[11] enim fidem, que per heresim primum Peligianam,[12] deinde per istos gentiles Saxones, in Britannia[13] corrupta erat, uenerat sanctus Germanus cum Lupo Trecacensi[14] episcopo missi a papa Romano ut uerbo predicacionis[15] et luce ewangelii[16] [17]gens que[17]

[59] acDERS; *atque* H. [60] cDERS; *Brittonum* aH. [61] R; *Teneth* a; *Thanet* cDES (with *Thaneth* in margin of D); *Tharneth* H. [62] cDERS; *Brittones* aH. [63] acDEHS; *naualli* R. [64...64] R; *cotidie prelio illos* aH; *cotidie illos prelio* c; *illos cotidie prelio* DES. [65] cERS; *diutius* aDH. [66] acDERS; *tale* H. [67] aDHRS; *insultum* cE. [68] acHRS; *coarctati* D; *coarti* E. [69...69] acDHRS; *iam fame* E. [70] acH; *Uortig'* DES; *Uortigrinum* R. [71] HR; *Wortimerium* a; *Uortinerium* c; *Uortim'* DE; *Uortime'* S. [72] ER; *licentiam* acDHS. [73...73] acDEHS; *inde colloquium* R. [74] cDERS; *Brittones* aH. [75] acH; *Uortig'* DES; *Uortigrino* R. [76] aDHRS (corrected from *mulieculis* in a); *mulieribus* cE. [77...77] acDERS; om. H. [78] acDEHRS (corrected from *Germani* in R). [79] aDEHRS (corrected from *reddiderunt* in R); om. c.

§102 [1] cDERS; *Brittones* aH. [2] HR; *Wortimerio* a; *Uortinerio* c; *Uortim'* D; *Uort'* ES. [3] aDERS; *cum ciuibus* cH. [4] aDEHR; *eleptas* c; *erreptas* S. [5] DEH; *annuente* acS; *amittente* R. [6] HR; *Autissiodorensi* ac (tampered in c); *Altisiodorensi* D; *Autusiodorensi* ES. [7] aHR; *ecclesias Christi* cDES. [8] acDEHS; om. R. [9] acDHR; *destituerunt* ES (altered to *destiterunt* in S). [10] acDEHR; *sunt* S. [11] acDHRS; *confirmandum* E. [12] R; *Arrianam* aH; *Arrianam uel Pelagianam* cDES. [13] cDERS; *Brittannia* aH. [14] aDEHS; *Treuerensi* c; *Trecasensi* R. [15] ER; *predicationis* acDHS. [16] cDRS; *euangelii* aH; *euuangelii* E. [17] cH; *gens* (or *genus* in D?) aDR (with *que* added in margin in D); *genus* ES.

errorum[18] tenebris et[19] ignorantie[20] a statu fidei suscepte deciderat[21] [22]iterum eorum[22] admonitionibus[23] Deo per omnia cooperante corroboraretur[24] et ecclesie catholice redderetur. Multa per eos [25]miracula fecit Deus[25] in regno Britannie[26] que Gildas[27] in tractatu suo luculenter exposuit. Postquam ergo[28] restituta est fides Christi per totum regnum[29] Britannie[30] ad integrum hostesque deleti qui[31] et fidem et populum inpugnabant,[32] inuidia dyaboli[33] qui Ronwen[34] nouercam Uortimerii[35] ad hoc nephas[36] instigauit[37] ueneno periit Uortimerius.[38] [39]Qui conuocans[39] milites et bellatores per quos uicerat indicata morte distribuit eis aurum et argentum et quicquid[40] ab attauis[41] [42]in thesauris suis[42] antea congestum[43] fuerat, exhortans ut pro patria pugnantes eam ab hostili irruptione[44] tuerentur. Precepit quoque piramidem[45] in litore[46] maris a parte Germanie strui in qua collocato eius corpore terrori esset Saxonibus et uniuersis barbaris. At ubi defunctus est, postposita pyramide[47] in Urbe Trinouantum illum sepelierunt.

[103] Uortigernus[1] postea in regem restitutus precibus coniugis sue misit in Germaniam pro Hengisto[2] ut iterum in Britanniam[3] rediret, sed priuatim et[4] cum paucis ne iterum discordia inter se et Britones[5] oriretur. Hengistus[6] ergo[7] audito obitu Uortimerii[8] letus efficitur et nauigio parato cum trecentis[9] milibus[10] armatorum sulcauit[11] equora

[18] acHR; *errorum quod* DES (with *quod* deleted from D). [19] acHR; om. DES (but *et* suprascript in D). [20] aDEHS; *ignorancia* a; *ignorancie* c. [21] acDEHRS (corrected from *desiderat* in R). [22...22] acEHRS (*erat* deleted before *eorum* in c); *eorum iterum* D. [23] cDHS; *ammonitionibus* a; *admonicionibus* E; *admonicibus* R. [24] acDERS; *corroborentur* H. [25...25] aH; *Deus fecit miracula* cDES; *miracula Deus* R. [26] cDERS; *Brittannie* aH. [27] acDERS; *Gildad* H. [28] acEHRS; *igitur* D. [29] acDEHS; *regni* R. [30] cDERS; *Brittannie* aH. [31] cDEHS; *que* R. [32] HRS; *impugnabant* cDE. [33] DRS; *diaboli* cEH. [34] cDES; *Ronuuen* H; *Ronwem* (or *Ronwein* ?) R. [35] HRS; *Uortinerii* c; *Uortim'* DE. [36] cDERS; *nefas* H. [37] cDEHS; *instiganum* R. [38] EHRS; *Uortim'* D. [39...39] R; *Conuocans ergo* c; *Conuocans itaque Uortim'* DES; *Conuocans* H. [40] cDEHS; *quidquid* R. [41] DEHS; *athauis* c; *attanis* R. [42...42] cHR; *suis in thesauris* DES. [43] cDEHS; *gestum* (with *con−* suprascript) R. [44] acDHRS; *irrupcione* E. [45] EHRS; *p. pyramidem* a; *pirammidem* c; *pyramidem* D. [46] aDERS; *littore* cH. [47] aDR; *piramide* EHS; *apiramide* c.

§103 [1] acHS; *Uortig'* DE; *Uortigrinus* R. [2] acHR; *Heng'* DES (with −*isto* in margin in S). [3] cDERS; *Brittanniam* aH. [4] acDEHS; om. R. [5] cDERS; *Brittones* aH. [6] acHRS; *Heng'* DE. [7] acDHR; *autem* E; *itaque* S. [8] HR; *Wortimerii* a; *Uortinerii* c; *Uortimeri* D; *Uortim'* ES. [9] R; *.ccc.* aDEHS; *300* c. [10] acDEH; *militibus* R; *nauibus* S. [11] acDEHRS (corrected from *sulcacauit* in S).

usque in Britanniam.[12] Sed[13] cum tante multitudinis exercitus Uortiger-no[14] et principibus regni nunciatus[15] esset, expauit rex et ceteri indignati sunt;[16] initoque consilio[17] memores[18] amonitionis[19] Uortimerii[20] consti-tuerunt preliari tamquam[21] cum hostibus atque[22] a litoribus[23] expellere antequam terram occuparent. Quod cum Hengisto[24] per internuncios[25] indicatum[26] foret,[27] excogitauit malignum apud se consilium illudque per complices[28] suos, sceleris sui conscios,[29] tractare cepit, [30]uidelicet ut regem[30] et gentem suam sub specie pacis adoriretur[31] et[32] dispositioni regis et optimatum[33] regni committeret quatinus de tanto numero Saxonum suorum [34]quot[35] uellent[36] secum remanere,[34] quot[37] in Germa-niam redire sub optentu[38] pacis decernerent: pacem enim querebant et cum pace et tranquillitate in regno Britannie,[39] in quo [40]plurimum iam[40] laborauerant cum ipsis, degere toto euo[41] suo affectabant. Quod cum per internuncios[42] regi suisque manifestasset,[43] placuit eis opcio[44] huiuscemodi, nichil[45] uerentes de prodicione[46] Saxonum. Die igitur[47] statuta[48] [49]mandauit cum legatis rex Hengisto[49] ut cum paucis adueniret.

[104] Interea Hengistus[1] noua prodicione[2] usus precepit [3]suis commili-tonibus[3] quos ad id facinus [4]ex omni multitudine[4] elegerat ut unusquisque cultrum ex utraque parte incidentem infra caligas in

---

[12] cDERS; *Brittanniam* aH. [13] acDHRS; *Set* E. [14] acH; *Uortig'* DES; *Uortigrino* R. [15] cDERS; *nuntiatus* aH. [16] acH; om. DERS. [17] acDEHR; *concilio* S. [18] aHR; *prudenciores* c; *seniores* DES. [19] H; *ammonitione* a; *amonitione* c; *admonitione* D; *ammonicione* ERS. [20] HR; *Wortimerii* a; *Uortinerii* c; *Uortig'* DES. [21] cDR; om. aH; *tanquam* ES. [22] aHR; *et* DES. [23] ERS; *littore* aH; *litore* D. [24] acHR; *Heng'* DES. [25] cDERS; *internuntios* aH. [26] aHR; *nunciatum* cE; *intimatum* DS. [27] aEHRS; *esset* c; *fuisset* D. [28] acDERS; *conplices* H. [29] aDHRS; *socios* c; *concios* E. [30...30] cDERS; *ut regem uidelicet* aH. [31] acHR; *adiret* DES. [32] aEHRS; *et se* D. [33] acDHRS (corrected from *opimatum* in a); *optumatum* E. [34...34] acDERS; om. H. [35] acDES; om. H; *quod* R. [36] acDRS; *uellet* E; om. H. [37] acDEHS; *quod* R. [38] aDER; *obtentu* cHS. [39] cDERS; *Brittannie* aH. [40...40] aR; *plurimum ante* c; *iam plurimum* DES; *plurimum* H. [41] aHR; *corde* c; *desiderio* DES. [42] DERS; *internuntios* aH; *nuncios* c. [43] cDERS; *manifestassent* aH. [44] ERS; *optio* aDH; *optatio* c. [45] acHR; *nil* DES. [46] ERS; *proditione* acDH. [47] acDEHS; om. R. [48] acHR; *statuto* DES. [49...49] R; *cum legatis mandauit rex Hengisto* aH; *mandauit rex Hengisto per legatos* c; *mandauit rex cum legatis Heng'* DES.

§104 [1] acHR; *Heng'* DES. [2] ERS; *proditione* acDH. [3...3] aHR; *commilitonibus suis* cDES. [4...4] acHR; *cum multitudine omni* DES (with *cum* and *omni* underpointed and *ex omni* added suprascript in D).

uaginis reconderet et, cum uentum foret ad colloquium, dato a se [5]hoc signo[5] prodicionis,[6] 'Nimet[7] eowre[8] seaxas!',[9] statim extractis cultris uniuersos occuparent inermes et interficerent.[10] Nec mora[11] die prestituta,[12] que fuit kalendis Maii,[13] iuxta cenobium Ambrii conuenerunt [14]Britones et Saxones,[14] sicut condictum[15] fuerat, sine armis pacem constituere.[16] Ut autem horam prodicioni[17] sue ydoneam[18] nactus fuisset Hengistus,[19] uociferatus est lingua sua: 'Nimet[20] eoyre[21] seaxas!'[22] Ipse autem regem per clamidem arripiens tenuit donec in alios scelus[23] perficeretur.[24] Extractis ilico cultris sicut premoniti fuerant, uniuersos fere principes nil tale metuentes[25] iugulauerunt circiter .cccclx., omnes barones aut[26] consules.[27]

[105] Dum autem fieret quasi de ouibus hec cedes, Britones[1] qui euadere periculum potuerunt aut fugiendo aut lapides in hostes mittendo et palis et fustibus defendendo plures interemerunt.[2] Eldol[3] uero consul Claudiocestrie sustulit palum quem [4]forte offenderat[4] et defensioni uacauit et multos per palum confractis ceruicibus ad tartara legauit; nec prius destitit donec .lxx. ex illis palo suo[5] interfectis diuertit se[6] ab eis equumque uelocem ascendens[7] ciuitatem suam quam cicius[8] potuit adiit.[9] Peracto itaque[10] scelere uoluerunt regem ipsum interficere mortemque comminantes uinxerunt eum fortiter loris postulaueruntque [11]sibi ciuitates[11] et castra municionesque[12] regni

5...5 aR; *signo hoc* cDES; *signo* H. 6 ERS; *proditionis* acDH. 7 R; *Nemet* a; *Nimeth* c; *Nimat* DEH (with *Nymeth* in margin in D); *Nimed* S. 8 R; *oure* a; *or* c; *hore* (with *oure* in margin) D; *ore* (altered to *yore*) E; *eoure* H; *ore* S. 9 R (preceded by deleted *sex*); *saxes* aS; *sexes* c; *saxas* DE; *sexas* H. 10 acDEHS; *occiderent* R. 11 acDHRS; *om.* E. 12 acEHRS (*die* after *prestituta* in c); *prestatuta* D. 13 acDERS; *Mai* H. 14...14 aHR (*Brittones* in aH); *Saxones et Britones* cDES. 15 acDEHS; *conditum* R. 16 acDEHS; *constitute* R. 17 ERS; *proditionis* a; *proditioni* cDH. 18 R; *idoneam* aH; *aptam* cDES. 19 acHR; *Heng'* DES. 20 R; *Nemet* a; *Nimeth* c; *Nimat* DEH; *Nimed* S. 21 R; *oure* a; *or* c; *ore* DES; *eoure* H. 22 R; *saxes* aS; *sexes* c; *saxas* DE; *sexas* H. 23 acDHRS; *om.* E. 24 aHR; *perficeretur inceptum* cDES (with *regem* deleted before *inceptum* in c). 25 acDEHS; *uerentes* R. 26 aDEHS; *et* c; *atque* R. 27 acDEHRS; after *consules*, *Quorum corpora beatus Eldadus postmodum christiano more sepeliuit haut longe a Kaercaraduc, quod Salesbyria dicitur, in cimiterio quodam iuxta cenobium Ambrii abbatis qui olim ipsius fundator exstiterat* added (from vulgate text) in margin of S.

§105 1 cDERS; *Brittones* aH. 2 acDHRS; *interimerunt* E. 3 acDEHS; *Edol* R. 4...4 aHR; *forte tenebat* DES (with *casu inuenerat* added [from vulgate text?] in margin in D). 5 acHR; *om.* DES. 6 aR; *sese* cDEHS. 7 aEHRS; *conscendens* c; *inscendens* D. 8 cER; *citius* aDHS. 9 acDHRS; *adiuit* E. 10 acDEHS; *igitur* R. 11...11 cDERS; *sibi ciuitates suas* a; *ciuitates sibi* H. 12 cEHRS; *munitionesque* aD.

omnes[13] contradi[14] si mortis periculum euadere uellet. Cumque id iureiurando confirmasset,[15] soluentes eum[16] a uinculis Urbem Trinouantum primitus adeuntes susceperunt, deinde Eboracum et Lyndocolinum[17] [18]necnon et[18] [19]Wentanam ciuitatem.[19] Ut ergo[20] ab eis euadere potuit Uortigernus,[21] secessit in partibus[22] Kambrie, ignorans quid sibi agendum foret contra nefandam[23] gentem.

[106] Uocatis denique magis suis consuluit quid faceret. Dixeruntque omnes pariter ut edificaret sibi turrim fortissimam que[1] foret sibi munimentum contra [2]hostes nefarios[2] qui dolo sibi regnum subripuerant.[3] Peragratis igitur quibuscumque locis ut in congruo loco turrim statueret, uenit tandem ad montem Erir,[4] ubi[5] coadunatis cementariis et artificibus diuersis cepit fundamenta turris iacere. Et cum ponerentur in fundamento lapides cum cemento, quicquid[6] in die ponebatur in nocte absorbebatur ita ut nescirent[7] quorsum opus euanesceret. Cumque[8] id Uortigernus[9] comperisset,[10] consuluit iterum magos ut rei causam indicarent. Qui dixerunt ut iuuenem sine patre quereret quesitumque[11] interficeret et [12]sanguine ipsius[12] [13]cementum et lapides[13] aspergerentur. Id[14] profecto [15]asserebant certissimum experimentum[15] ut fundamentum staret. Nec mora mittuntur legati per prouincias Demecie[16] querere talem hominem. Qui cum in urbem que[17] Kaermerdin[18] dicitur uenissent, inuenerunt [19]pueros et iuuenes[19] utriusque sexus[20] ante portam ciuitatis ludentes. Accesseruntque[21] ad ludum [22]ut aspicerent cum ceteris,[22] explorantes[23] quod querebant. Interea lis

---

[13] acHR; *omnes sibi* DES. [14] aDEHR; *tradi* cS. [15] acDEHRS (corrected from *firmasset* in D). [16] acH; om. DERS. [17] R; *Lindocolinum* a; *Lincoliam* c; *Lindicolinum ciuitatem* D; *Lindicolium ciuitatem* E; *Lincolinum* H; *Lindicolium* S. [18...18] aHRS; *sed et* c; *et* DE. [19] HR; *Guintoniam ciuitatem* a; *Wintoniam ciuitatem* c; *Wintoniam* DES. [20] acHR; *autem* DES. [21] acH; *Uortig'* DES; *Uortigrinus* R. [22] aHR; *partes* cDES. [23] aDHRS; *nephandam* cE.

§106 [1] acDEHR; *quo* S. [2...2] aHR; *hostes nephandos* c; *nefarios hostes* D; *nepharios hostes* E; *nefarias gentes* S. [3] HRS; *surripuerant* aD; *surripuerunt* cE. [4] aDEHR (with *Ereri* in margin in D); *Eryri* c; *Heir* S. [5] acDEHRS (corrected from *ut* in H). [6] acDEHS; *quidquid* R. [7] acDHRS; *nesciret* E. [8] acDERS; *Cunque* H. [9] acH; *Uortig'* DES; *Uortigrinus* R. [10] acDERS; *conperisset* H. [11] cDERS; *quesitum* a; *inuentumque* H. [12...12] acDERS; *ipsius sanguine* H. [13...13] acHR; *lapides et cementum* DES. [14] aHR; *Quo* c; *Quod* DES. [15...15] acR; *asserebant experimentum certissimum* DES; *certissimum experimentum asserebant* H. [16] cERS (glossed *id est Suthwallie* in S); *Demetie* aDH. [17] acDEHS; *qui* R. [18] DEHS; *Kermerdin* a; *Kaermirdin nunc* c; *Kerimdin* (?) R. [19...19] acDEHS; *iuuenes et pueros* R. [20] acHR; *etatis* DES. [21] acDEHR; *Accesserunt* S. [22...22] acDES; *cum ceteris* H; *cum ceteris ut aspicerent* R. [23] acDERS; *explorabant* H.

exoritur[24] inter duos[25] iuuenes, quorum unus Merlinus [26]dicebatur, alter Dinabucius.[26] Certantibus ergo illis [27]dixit Dinabucius ad Merlinum:[27] 'Quid mecum, fatue, contendis? Non est [28]equa nobis[28] natiuitatis prosapia: ego enim ex regibus [29]duxi originem,[29] tu autem ignoras quis tibi pater sit.' Audientes itaque legati exploratores Uortigerni[30] iuuenes in hunc modum decertantes, intuentes in[31] Merlinum[32] quesierunt a circumstantibus quis esset uel unde oriundus. Responderunt dicentes quia nesciretur[33] quis [34]ei pater esset,[34] sed mater que[35] eum genuerat filia regis Demecie[36] in ecclesia sancti Petri monialis[37] adhuc in eadem urbe uiueret.

[107] Festinantes igitur uenerunt ad [1]urbis prefectum[1] preceperuntque[2] ex parte regis ut Merlinus cum matre sua ad regem mitteretur. Prefectus illico[3] compleuit iussum[4] regis mittens Merlinum matremque eius ad eum.[5] Cumque in presentia[6] eius[7] adducti fuissent, excepit [8]rex diligenter illos[8] et cepit a matre perquirere de quo uiro iuuenem concepisset. Cui illa ait: 'Uiuit anima tua, rex,[9] et uiuit anima mea quia neminem agnoui qui illum in me generauerit.[10] Unum autem scio quia, cum essem in thalamo parentum puella, apparuit michi quidam in specie formosa [11]iuuenis, ut[11] uidebatur, et amplectens me strictis brachiis sepissime deosculabatur et statim euanescebat ita ut indicium[12] hominis non appareret;[13] loquebatur[14] aliquando non comparens.[15] Cumque in hunc modum[16] me diu[17] frequentasset, tandem in specie humana miscuit se michi et grauidam dereliquit. Sciat ergo prudentia tua me aliter uirum non cognouisse.' Admirans[18] autem Uortigernus[19]

---

[24] aDERS; *oritur* cH. [25] acDERS; *.ii.* H. [26...26] acHR (*Dinabutius* in aH); *alter Dinabutius dicebatur* DES. [27...27] cHR (*Dinabutius* in H); *Dinabutius dixit ad Merlinum* a; *dixit ad Merlinum Dinabutius* DES. [28...28] cDRS; *nobis equa* aH; *nobis* E. [29...29] aH; *originem duxi* cDES; *duxi origenem* R. [30] acH; *Uortig'* DES; *Uortigrini* R. [31] acDEHS; om. R. [32] acDEHR; *Merelinum* S. [33] acHR; *nescierunt* DES. [34...34] cR; *ei pater fuisset* aH; *pater ei esset* DES. [35] acDEHS; *qui* R. [36] cEHRS; *Demetie* aD. [37] acHR; *sanctimonialis* DES.

§107 [1...1] acDERS (*preceptum* deleted before *prefectum* in R); *urbem prefatam* H. [2] acDEHR; *et* [added suprascript] *preceperunt* S. [3] cRS; *ilico* aDEH. [4] acDERS; *iussa* H. [5] acDERS; *regem* H. [6] aDHRS; *presencia* cE. [7] acDERS; *regis* H. [8...8] aR; *illos rex et diligenter* c; *rex diligenter eos* DES; *illos rex diligenter* H. [9] acDEHR; om. S. [10] acHR; *generauit* DES. [11...11] ac; *qui iuuenis* DEHS; *iuuenis* R. [12] acDERS; *inditium* H. [13] acEHRS; *apparebat* D. [14] DERS; *et loquebatur* a; *loquebaturque* cH. [15] acDERS; *conparens* H. [16] acDEHS; om. R. [17] acDEHS; om. R. [18] acDEHR; *Ammirans* S. [19] acH; *Uortig'* DES; *Uortigrinus* R.

99

hos mulieris sermones ad se uocari[20] fecit[21] Maugancium[22] magum ut
sibi ediceret si[23] id quod [24]dixerat mulier[24] fieri potuisset. Adductus
ergo magus coram rege auditisque[25] hiis[26] que mater Merlini edixerat
inquit:[27] 'In libris philosophorum et plurimis ystoriis[28] reperimus[29]
multos huiuscemodi habuisse generaciones.[30] Nam, ut Apuleius[31] de
deo Socratis[32] perhibet, inter lunam et terram[33] habitant spiritus
inmundi[34] quos incubos demones uocant. Hii[35] partim habent naturam
hominum, partim uero angelorum et, cum uolunt, assumunt sibi
[36]humanas figuras[36] et cum mulieribus coeunt. Forsitan aliquis eorum
huic mulieri stuprum intulit et in ea iuuenem hunc generauit.'

[108] Cumque omnia hec auscultasset,[1] Merlinus accessit ad regem et
ait: 'Utquid in presentia[2] tua huc adducti sumus?' Cui rex, 'Magi,'
[3]inquit, 'mei[3] dederunt consilium ut hominem sine patre perquirerem
quatinus opus inceptum sanguine ipsius irroratum[4] firmius staret.
Uolens enim turrim edificare, non possunt fundamenta eius in loco
isto consistere [5]quin quod[5] in die construitur in nocte a[6] terra
deuoretur.'[7] Tunc ait regi[8] Merlinus: 'Iube magos tuos[9] adesse et
conuincam illos per omnia mentitos.' Asciti[10] ergo magi sederunt
coram rege. Quibus ait Merlinus: 'Nescientes quid fundamenta [11]in-
cepte turris inpediat[11] laudauistis regi ut sanguis meus funderetur[12] in
cementum quasi opus ideo constare deberet. Sed dicite michi, si magi
estis, quid sub[13] fundamento lateat. Nam aliquid sub illo esse oportet
quod structuram stare non permittit.' Attoniti ergo magi conticuerunt
omnes. Tunc intendens Merlinus in[14] regem dixit: 'Domine mi rex,
uoca operarios et iube fodere terram loci huius usquequo[15] perueniatur

[20] acHR; *uocare* DES. [21] acDEHR; om. S. [22] cR; *Maugantium* aH; *Magantium* DS
(with *Mauganum* in margin in D); *Magancium* E. [23] acDHRS; *quod si* E. [24...24] ac-
DEH; *mulier edixerat* R; *diceret mulier* S. [25] acDEHS; *auditis* R. [26] cDERS; *his* aH.
[27] cDEHR; *dixit regi* a; *inquid* S. [28] R; *hystoriis* aS; *historiis* cDEH. [29] cDERS;
repperimus aH. [30] R; *generationem* aDH; *generationes* c; *generacionem* ES. [31] cDER;
Appuleius phylosophus a; *Appuleius* HS. [32] cDES; *sacratis* aHR. [33] acDERS; *solem* H.
[34] acDHRS; *immundi* E. [35] cDERS; *Hi* aH. [36...36] acEHS (*naturas deleted before
figuras* in E); *humanas* D; *figuras humanas* R.

§108 [1] aH; *ascultasset* cDERS. [2] aDHRS; *presencia* cE. [3...3] aDEHS; *inquid mei* c; *mei
inquid* R. [4] acDEHS; *uxoratum* (with *irroratum* in margin) R. [5...5] acDERS; *nam
quicquid* H. [6] acDHRS; *in* E. [7] acDES; *deuoratur* HR (altered from *deuoretur* in R).
[8] aHR; om. cDES. [9] aDERS; om. c; *istos* H. [10] acDERS; *Astantes* H. [11...11] acH; *turris
incepte impediat* DE; *turris impediat incepte* R; *turris incepte inpediat* S. [12] acDHRS;
fundaretur E. [13] acHR; *in* DES. [14] acHR; *ad* DES. [15] acDES; *quousque* H; *usque* R.

ad stagnum quod subter¹⁶ latet,¹⁷ pro quo ¹⁸stare opus¹⁸ non ualet.'
Quod cum factum esset, repertum est stagnum sicut dixerat Merlinus
et credidit ¹⁹rex illi¹⁹ in hiis²⁰ et²¹ aliis que locutus est ²²postea
Merlinus.²² Uertens se deinde Merlinus ad magos, 'Dicite,' inquid,²³
'mendaces et fatui, si nostis quid²⁴ sit²⁵ sub stagno.' Nec²⁶ unum
uerbum proferentes obmutuerunt. 'Precipe,' ait ad regem Merlinus,
'hauriri stagnum per riuulos²⁷ et uidebis in fundo duos concauos
lapides et in illis duos dracones dormientes.' Credidit ergo²⁸ rex quia
uerum²⁹ prius dixerat de stagno et fecit hauriri³⁰ stagnum; sed super
omnia Merlinum ammirabatur.³¹ Ammirabantur³² etiam cuncti qui
aderant tantam in eo sapientiam,³³ existimantes numen esse in illo.³⁴

[111] Sedente¹ itaque Uortigerno² super ripam exhausti³ stagni egressi
sunt duo dracones de predictis rupibus concauis, quorum unus erat
albus, alter rubeus. Cumque inuicem appropinquassent, commiserunt
diram pugnam cernentibus cunctis ita ut ignis de ore ⁴et naribus eorum⁴
exalaret. Preualuit autem⁵ albus draco rubeumque⁶ usque ad extremita-
tem lacus⁷ fugauit. At ille cum se expulsum doluisset, fecit impetum in
album et retro ire coegit. Illis ergo in hunc modum certantibus precepit
rex Ambrosio Merlino – sic enim cognomen erat ei – dicere quid
prelium draconum portenderet.⁸ Mox ille in fletum erumpens⁹ spiritum
hausit prophetie¹⁰ et ait:

¹⁶ aHR; *subtus* cDES. ¹⁷ acDEHR; *lateat* S. ¹⁸⁻¹⁸ aHR; *opus stare* cDES. ¹⁹⁻¹⁹ aHR;
illi rex c; *ei rex* DES. ²⁰ cDERS; *his* aH. ²¹ acDEHR; om. S. ²²⁻²² aHR; *Merlinus* c;
postea DES. ²³ aR; *quid* c; *inquit* DEHS. ²⁴ acDEHR; *uerbum* deleted after *quid* in S.
²⁵ aHR; *lateat* cDES. ²⁶ aHR; *Qui nec* c; *Illi uero non* DES. ²⁷ acDEHS; *uerulos*
(with *riuulos* in margin) R. ²⁸ cDERS; *ergo ei* a; om. H. ²⁹ acDEHR; *uerbum* S.
³⁰ acDEHR; *haurire* S. ³¹ aHR (corrected from *ammirabantur* in H); *admirabatur*
cDES. ³² aHR; *Admirabantur* cDES. ³³ acDHRS; *sapienciam* E. ³⁴ acDEHRS; after
illo, Explicit liber sextus. Incipit septimus de prophetiis Merlini in aR, and *Explicit liber
.vi. Incipit .vii.* in H. From this point to the middle of §178 (p. 174 below) the text of c
is entirely vulgate.

§§109–10 of the vulgate text are omitted from the First Variant version, although they
and a partial commentary on the *Prophetie Merlini* are found in the margin of E, pp.
158–60 (see Introduction, pp. lxxxiv–vi).

§111 ¹ aDHRS; <S>*edente* E. ² aH; *Uortig'* DES; *Uortigrinus* R. ³ aDEHS; *hausti*
R. ⁴⁻⁴ aHR; *eorum et naribus* DES. ⁵ aHR; *ergo* DES. ⁶ aDEHR; *et rubeum* S.
⁷ aDERS; *laci* H. ⁸ aDEHS; *pretenderet* R. ⁹ aDEHS; *prorumpit* R. ¹⁰ aDHRS;
prophecie E.

[112] (1) 'Ue rubeo draconi: nam exterminacio[1] eius festinat. Cauernas ipsius[2] occupabit albus draco qui Saxones quos inuitasti significat. Rubeus uero[3] gentem designat Britannie[4] que[5] ab albo opprimetur. Montes itaque eius[6] ut ualles equabuntur et [7]flumina uallium[7] sanguine manabunt. Cultus religionis delebitur et ruina ecclesiarum patebit.

(2) Preualebit tandem oppressa et seuicie exterorum[8] resistet. Aper etenim[9] Cornubie succursum prestabit et colla eorum sub pedibus suis conculcabit. Insule occeani potestati ipsius[10] subdentur et Gallicanos saltus possidebit. Tremebit Romulea domus seuitiam[11] ipsius et exitus eius dubius erit. In ore populorum celebrabitur et actus eius cibus erit narrantibus.

(3) Sex[12] posteri eius sequentur sceptrum sed post ipsos exurget Germanicus uermis. Sublimabit[13] illum equoreus lupus quem[14] Affricana[15] nemora commitabuntur.[16] Delebitur iterum religio et transmutacio[17] primarum sedium erit. Dignitas Londonie[18] adornabit Doroberniam et [19]pastor Eboracensis[19] septimus[20] in Armorico[21] regno frequentabitur. Meneuia pallio Urbis Legionum induetur et predicator[22] Hybernie[23] propter infantem[24] in utero crescentem obmutescet. Pluet sanguineus ymber[25] et dira fames mortales[26] afficiet.

(4) Hiis[27] superuenientibus dolebit rubeus sed emenso labore uigebit.[28] Tunc infortunium albi festinabit et edificia ortulorum eius diruentur. Sceptrigeri[29] .vii. perimentur et unus eorum sanctificabitur. Uentres matrum secabuntur et infantes abortiui erunt. Erit ingens supplicium hominum ut indigene restituantur. Qui faciet[30] hec eneum uirum induet et per multa tempora super[31] eneum equum portas Londonie[32] seruabit.

---

§112 [1] ER; *exterminatio* aDHS. [2] DERS; *illius* aH. [3] aHR; *ergo* DES. [4] DERS; *Brittannie* aH. [5] aDES; *qui* HR. [6] aDEHR; om. S. [7]...[7] aHR; *ualles eius* DES. [8] aDERS; *exteriorum* H. [9] aDEHS (corrected from *enim* in D); *enim* R. [10] aHR; *illius* DES. [11] HR; *seuiciam* aDES. [12] aDES; *Sed* HR. [13] DER; *Sullimabit* aHS. [14] aDERS; *qm* (with suprascript *e*) H. [15] aDERS; *Affricani* H. [16] RS; *comitabuntur* aDEH. [17] DERS; *transmutatio* aH. [18] aDERS; *Lundonie* H. [19]...[19] DERS (glossed *id est sanctus Sampson* in S); *Eboracensis pastor* aH. [20] RS; *.vii.* aDE; *unus* H. [21] aDEHR; *Armarico* S. [22] aDEHRS (glossed *id est Patricius* in S). [23] ERS; *Hibernie* aDH. [24] aDEHRS (glossed *id est sanctum Dauid* in S). [25] aDRS; *imber* EH. [26] aDEHRS (corrected from *motales* in H). [27] DERS; *His* aH. [28] DES; *rugebit* aHR. [29] aDEHS; *Septueri* R. [30] DERS; *facit* aH. [31] aDEHRS (suprascript in R). [32] aDERS; *Lundonie* H.

(5) Exinde[33] in proprios mores reuertetur rubeus draco et in seipsum seuire laborabit. Superueniet itaque ulcio[34] tonantis[35] quia omnis ager colonos decipiet. Arripiet[36] mortalitas populum cunctasque nationes[37] euacuabit. Residui natale solum deserent et exteras culturas seminabunt. Rex benedictus[38] [39]parabit nauigium[39] et in aula .xii.[40] inter beatos annumerabitur.[41] Erit miseranda regni[42] desolacio[43] et aree[44] messium infructuosos[45] saltus redibunt.

(6) Replebuntur iterum ortuli nostri alieno semine et in extremitate stagni languebit rubeus.

(7) Exin[46] coronabitur Germanicus uermis et eneus princeps humiliabitur.[47] Terminus illi positus est quem transuolare nequibit. [113] Centum namque .l.[1] annis in[2] inquietudine et subiectione manebit, ter centum uero insidebit.

(8) Tunc exurget in illum acquilo[3] et flores quos zephirus[4] procreauit eripiet. Erit deauracio[5] in templis nec acumen[6] gladiorum cessabit. Uix obtinebit[7] cauernas suas Germanicus draco quia ulcio[8] prodicionis[9] eius superueniet.

(9) Uigebit tandem paulisper set decimacio[10] Neustrie[11] nocebit. Populus namque in ligno et [12]ferreis tunicis[12] superueniet qui uindictam de nequicia[13] eius sumet. Restaurabit pristinis incolis mansiones et ruina alienigenarum patebit. Germen albi draconis ex oɩ tulis nostris abradetur et reliquie generationis[14] eius decimabuntur;[15] iugum [16]perpetue[17] seruitutis[16] ferent matremque suam ligonibus et aratris uulnerabunt.[18]

---

33 aHRS; *Exin* DE (altered to *Exinde* in E). 34 ER; *ultio* aDHS. 35 aDEHS; *donantis* R. 36 aH; *Accipiet* DES; *Diripiet* R. 37 aDHRS; *naciones* E. 38 aDEHRS (glossed *id est Cadualladrus* in S). 39...39 aH; *nauigium parabit* DES; *parauit nauigium* R. 40 aDERS; *duodecimi* H. 41 aHR; *collocabitur* DES. 42 aDERS; om. H. 43 ERS; *desolatio* aDH. 44 aDEHS; *aeree* R. 45 aRS; *infruticosos* DE; *in* [suprascript] *infructuosos* H. 46 aDERS (altered to *Exinde* in E); *Exinde* H. 47 aHR; *humabitur* DES.

§113 1 aDHRS; *quinquaginta* E. 2 DEHS; om. aR. 3 R; *aquilo* aDEHS. 4 aDERS; *zephyrus* H. 5 ER; *deauratio* aDHS. 6 aDEHS; *accumen* R. 7 DERS; *optinebit* aH. 8 ERS; *ultio* aDH. 9 aERS; *proditionis* DH. 10 ERS; *decimatio* aDH. 11 aDEHS; *uentrie* R. 12...12 aDES; *tunicis ferreis* H; *fereis* R. 13 DERS; *nequitia* aH. 14 aDHRS; *generacionis* E. 15 aHR; om. DES (with *decimabuntur* in margin in D). 16...16 aDERS; *seruitutis perpetue* H. 17 aDERS (& H). The body of the *Prophetie* (from this point to the middle of no.73) are excised from S with the marginal note (fo.67v): '*Hic absciduntur obscene predictiones Merlini. Utpote per concilium Tridentinum ultimum condemnate*'. 18 aDEH; *wlnerabunt* R.

(10) Succedent duo dracones quorum alter inuidie spiculo suffocabitur, alter uero sub umbra nominis[19] redibit.

(11) Succedet leo iusticie[20] ad cuius rugitum Gallicane turres et insulani dracones tremebunt. In diebus eius aurum ex lilio[21] et urtica extorquebitur et argentum ex ungulis mugiencium[22] manabit. Calamistrati [23]uaria uellera[23] uestibunt et exterior habitus interiora signabit. Pedes latrancium[24] truncabuntur. Pacem habebunt fere, humanitas supplicium dolebit. Findetur forma commercii, dimidium[25] rotundum erit. Peribit miluorum rapacitas et dentes luporum ebetabuntur.[26]

(12) Catuli[27] leonis in equoreos pisces transformabuntur et aquila eius super montem Arauium nidificabit.[28] Uenedotia[29] rubebit[30] materno sanguine et domus Corinei .vi.[31] fratres interficiet. Nocturnis lacrimis madebit insula unde omnes ad omnia prouocabuntur.[32]

[114] (13) [1]Nitentur posteri transuolare superna sed fauor nouorum sublimabitur.[2] [1]Nocebit possidenti ex impiis pietas donec sese genitore induerit. Apri igitur[3] dentibus accinctus[4] cacumina moncium[5] et umbram[6] galeati transcendet.

(14) Indignabitur Albania et conuocatis collateralibus sanguinem effundere uacabit.[7] Dabitur maxillis eius frenum quod in Armorico sinu fabricabitur. Deaurabit illud aquila rupti federis et tertia nidificacione[8] gaudebit.

(15) Euigilabunt rugientes[9] catuli et postpositis nemoribus infra [10]ciuitatum menia[10] uenabuntur. Stragem non minimam ex obstantibus[11]

[19] aDER; *noui* H. [20] aEHR; om. D (with *iusticie* in margin). Glossed *id est rex Henricus* (in text) in R, the same gloss being present in the margin of a. [21] DEH; *ilio* a; *lolio* R. [22] R; *mugientium* aDEH. [23...23] aDER; *uellera uaria* H. [24] aER; *latrantium* DH. [25] aDER (preceded by suprascript *et* in a); *et dimidium* H. [26] R; *hebetabuntur* aDEH. [27] aDEHR (with *Catuli* repeated in margin in D). [28] DEHR (corrected from *nidicabit* in R); *nidificabat* a. [29] aDHR; *Uenedocia* E. [30] aDEH (altered from *rudebit* in D); *rudebit* R. [31] DER; *septem* a; *.vii.* H. [32] aDEHR; after *prouocabuntur*, the interpolated prophecy (see Wright, *Historia Regum Britannie*, I.xi, n.10), *Ue tibi, Neustria, quia in te cerebrum leonis effundetur*, is added in the margin of D.

§114 [1...1] aDER; om. H. [2] DR; *sullimabitur* aE; om. H. [3] aDHR; *enim* E. [4] aDEH; *accuietur* (?) R. [5] ER; *montium* aDH. [6] DEH; *umbra* a; *humbram* R. [7] aDER; *non uacabit* H. [8] ER; *nidificatione* aDH. [9] DER (with *regentis* in margin of D); *rugientis* aH. [10...10] aER; *ciuitatem menia* D; *menia ciuitatum* H. [11] aDEH; *optantibus* R.

facient et linguas taurorum[12] abscident. Colla rugiencium[13] onerabunt[14] cathenis[15] et auita tempora renouabunt.

(16) Exin de primo in quartum, de quarto in tercium,[16] de tercio[17] in secundum rotabitur pollex in oleo.

(17) Sextus Ybernie[18] menia[19] subuertet et nemora in planiciem[20] mutabit. Diuersas portiones[21] in unum reducet et capite leonis coronabitur. Principium eius uago affectui[22] subiacebit[23] set finis ipsius ad superos conuolabit. Renouabit namque beatorum sedes per patrias et pastores in congruis locis[24] locabit. Duas urbes duobus palliis induet et uirginea munera uirginibus donabit. Promerebitur inde fauorem tonantis[25] et inter beatos collocabitur.

[115] (18) Egredietur ex eo linx penetrans omnia que ruine proprie gentis imminebit.[1] Per illam enim utramque insulam amittet Neustria et pristina dignitate spoliabitur.

(19) Deinde reuertentur ciues in insulam; nam discidium alienigenarum orietur. Niueus quoque senex in niueo equo fluuium Perironis[2] diuertet et cum candida uirga[3] molendinum super ipsum metabitur.

(20) Cadwaladrus[4] [5]uocabit Conanum[5] et Albaniam in societatem accipiet. Tunc erit strages alienigenarum, tunc flumina sanguine manabunt. Tunc erumpent Armorici montes et dyademate[6] Bruti coronabuntur. Replebitur Kambria leticia[7] et robora Cornubie uirescent.[8] Nomine Bruti uocabitur insula et nuncupacio[9] extraneorum peribit.

(21) Ex Conano procedet[10] aper bellicosus qui infra Gallicana nemora acumen[11] dencium[12] suorum exercebit. Truncabit namque queque[13]

---

[12] aDEH; *thaurorum* R. [13] ER; *rugientium* aDH. [14] aDER; *honerabunt* H. [15] DR; *catenis* aEH. [16] ER; *tertium* aDH. [17] ER; *tertio* aDH. [18] R; *Hibernie* aDH; *Hybernie* E. [19] aDHR; *menie* E. [20] DER; *planitiem* aH. [21] aDHR; *porciones* E. [22] aDEH; *effectui* R. [23] aDER; *succumbet* H. [24] aDER; *sedibus* H. [25] aDEH; *donantis* R.

§115 [1] aDHR; *iminebit* E. [2] DE; *per Ironis* (before *fluuium*) a; *Peryronis* H; *Peritonis* R. [3] aDEH; *lingua* R. [4] aDE; *Kaduualadrus* H; *Catwaladrus* R. [5]...[5] aDER; *Conanum uocabit* H. [6] ER; *diademate* aH; *dyademati* D. [7] aDEHR (with a final *e* suprascript in R). [8] aDEHR (but altered to *reuirescent* in D). [9] ER; *nuncupatio* aDH. [10] aDEH; *precedet* R. [11] aDHR; *acumen* tampered in text, repeated in margin in E. [12] R; *dentium* aDEH. [13] aDER; om. H.

maiora robora, minoribus uero tutelam prestabit. Tremebunt illum Arabes et Affricani: nam impetum cursus sui in ulteriorem Hispaniam[14] protendet.[15]

(22) Succedet hyrcus[16] uenerii[17] castri aurea habens cornua et argenteam barbam qui [18]ex naribus suis tantam[18] efflabit nebulam quanta tota superficies insule[19] obumbrabitur.[20]

(23) Pax erit in tempore suo et ubertate glebe multiplicabuntur segetes. [21]Mulieres incessu[22] serpentes fient et omnis[23] gressus earum[24] superbia replebitur.[25] [21] Renouabuntur castra ueneris nec[26] cessabunt sagitte cupidinis uulnerare.[27] Fons Anne[28] uertetur in sanguinem et duo reges duellum propter leenam de Uado[29] Baculi committent. Omnis humus luxuriabit et humanitas fornicari non desinet.

(24) Omnia hec tria secula uidebunt donec sepulti reges in urbe Londoniarum[30] propalabuntur.[31]

(25) Redibit iterum fames, redibit mortalitas; et desolacionem[32] urbium dolebunt ciues.

(26) Superueniet aper commercii qui dispersos [33]greges ad amissa pascua[33] reuocabit. Pectus eius cibus erit egentibus et lingua[34] eius sedabit sicientes.[35] Ex ore ipsius procedent flumina que arentes hominum fauces rigabunt.

(27) Exin super turrim Londoniarum[36] procreabitur arbor que[37] tribus solummodo ramis contenta superficiem tocius[38] insule latitudine foliorum[39] obumbrabit. Huic aduersarius boreas[40] superueniet atque iniquo flatu suo tercium[41] illi ramum eripiet.

---

[14] aDE; *Yspaniam* H; *Hypaniam* (with suprascript *s*) R. [15] aDEH; *procedet* R. [16] DHR; *hircus* aE. [17] aEH; *uenerei* D; *ueneri* R. [18...18] aR; *tantam ex naribus suis* DE; *ex naribus tantam* H. [19] aHR; *terre* DE (with *insule* in margin of D). [20] aDEH; *obhumbrabitur* R. [21...21] aHR; om. DE (with *Mulieres in incessu serpentes fient et omnis gressus earum superbia replebitur* in margin of D). [22] aH; om. DE; *incestu* R. [23] aR; om. DE; *omnes* H. [24] a; om. DE; *eorum* HR. [25] aR; om. DE; *replebuntur* H. [26] aDEH; *non* R. [27] aDEH; *wlnerare* R. [28] aHR; *Amne* DE (with *Ampne* in margin of D). [29] aHR; *Uallo* DE. [30] aDER; *Lundoniarum* H. [31] aDEH; *propallabuntur* R. [32] R; *desolationem* aH; *desolatione* D; *desolacione* E. [33...33] aDEH; *reges admissa paschua* R. [34] aDEH; *ligua* R. [35] aHR; *sitientes* DE. [36] aDER; *Lundoniarum* H. [37] aDER; *qui* H. [38] ER; *totius* aDH. [39] aDEH (corrected from *filiorum* in H); *filiorum* R. [40] aDHR; *borias* E. [41] ER; *tertium* aDH.

(28) Duo uero residui locum extirpati occupabunt donec alter alterum foliorum[42] multitudine adnichilabit.[43] Deinde uero locum duorum optinebit[44] ipse[45] et uolucres exterarum[46] regionum sustentabit. Patriis uolatilibus[47] nociuus[48] habebitur:[49] nam timore umbre eius [50]liberos uolatus amittent.

(29) Succedet asinus nequicie[51] in fabricatores auri[50] uelox, sed in luporum rapacitatem piger.

[116] (30) In diebus illis ardebunt quercus per nemora et in ramis tiliarum nascentur glandes. Sabrinum mare per .vii. ostia[1] discurret et fluuius Osche per .vii. menses feruebit. Pisces illius calore morientur et ex eis procreabuntur serpentes. Frigebunt Badonis balnea[2] et salubres aque eorum[3] mortem generabunt. Londonia[4] necem .xx. milium[5] lugebit et [6]Thamensis fluuius[6] in sanguinem mutabitur. Cucullati ad nuptias[7] prouocabuntur et clamor eorum in montibus Alpium audietur.

(31) Tres[8] fontes in urbe Wintonia[9] erumpent [10]quorum riuuli[10] insulam in tres porciones[11] secabunt. Qui bibet de uno diuturniori[12] uita fruetur nec superueniente[13] languore[14] grauabitur. Qui bibet de altero indeficienti fame peribit et in facie ipsius pallor[15] et horror sedebit.[16] Qui bibet de tertio[17] [18]subita morte[18] periclitabitur nec corpus ipsius subire poterit sepulcrum.[19] Tantam ingluuiem[20] uitare[21] uolentes diuersis tegumentis eam[22] occultare nitentur. Quecumque[23] ergo moles superposita fuerit formam alterius corporis recipiet. Terra namque[24] in lapides, lapides in lignum,[25] lignum[26] in cineres, cinis in aquam, si superiecta fuerint, uertentur.

---

42 aDEH; *filiarum* R. 43 DHR; *annichilabit* aE. 44 aEHR; *obtinebit* D. 45 aDER; *om.* H. 46 aDH; erasure from text (with *exterarum* in margin) E; *exterrarum* R. 47 aDEH; *uolatibus* R. 48 aDEH; *nociuis* R. 49 aDHR; *erit* underpointed before *habebitur* in E. 50...50 aDEH; *liberi non auri* R. 51 aDE; *nequitie* H; om. R.

§116 1 aDER; *hostia* H. 2 aDHR; *balnia* E. 3 aHR; *om.* DE. 4 DER; *Lundonia* aH. 5 a; *miliorum* DEHR. 6...6 HR; *Tamensis fluuius* a; *Thamensis* DE. 7 aDHR; *nupcias* E. 8 aDHR; <*T*>*res* E. 9 aDER; *Guintonia* H. 10...10 aHR; *riuuli quorum* DE. 11 aHR; *portiones* D; *partes seu porciones* E. 12 aDHR; *diuturnior* E. 13 HR; *superuenienti* aDE. 14 aDER; *langore* H. 15 aDER; *semper pallor* H. 16 aDER; *insidebit* H. 17 aDH; *tercio* E; *tercia* R. 18...18 aHR; *morte subita* DE. 19 aER; *sepulchrum* DH. 20 aDEH; *ingluuiam* R. 21 aDER; *om.* H. 22 aDHR; *eum* E. 23 aDR; *Quecunque* E; *Cuicumque* H. 24 aDER; *nanque* H. 25 D; *ligna* a; *lingnum* E; *limpham* HR (with the marginal note *limpha id est lignum* in R). 26 DEH; *ligna* a; *lingnum* R.

(32) Ad hec ex urbe [27]canuti nemoris[27] eliminabitur puella ut medele curam adhibeat. Que ut omnes artes[28] inierit, solo hanelitu[29] suo fontes nociuos[30] siccabit.

(33) Exin ut sese[31] salubri liquore refecerit, gestabit in dextera sua nemus Colidonis,[32] in sinistra uero murorum Londonie[33] propugnacula. Quacumque[34] incedet, passus sulphureos faciet qui duplici[35] flamma fumabunt.[36] Fumus ille excecabit[37] Rutenos et cibum submarinis conficiet. Lacrimis miserandis manabit ipsa et clamore horrido replebit insulam.

(34) Interficiet eam ceruus .x. ramorum quorum quatuor[38] aurea dyademata[39] gestabunt. Sex uero residui in cornua bubalorum uertentur que nephando[40] sonitu tres[41] insulas Britannie[42] commouebunt.

(35) Excitabitur Danerium[43] nemus et in humanam uocem erumpens clamabit: "Ascende,[44] Kambria, et iunge lateri tuo Cornubiam et dic Wintonie:[45] 'Absorbebit te tellus. Transfer sedem pastoris[46] ubi naues applicant[47] et cetera membra[48] capud[49] sequantur.[50] Festinat[51] namque dies qua[52] ciues ob [53]scelera periurii[53] peribunt. Candor lanarum nocuit[54] atque [55]tincture ipsarum[55] diuersitas. Ue periure genti quia urbs inclita propter eam ruet!'."

(36) Gaudebunt naues aucmentacione[56] tanta et unum ex duobus fiet. Reedificabit eam hericius[57] honeratus[58] pomis ad quorum odorem diuersorum nemorum [59]conuolabunt uolucres.[59] Adiciet palacium[60] ingens et sexcentis[61] turribus uallabit illud.

[27...27] aR; *canuti* DE (with *nemoris* suprascript in D); *Kanuti nemoris* H. [28] aDEH; *arces* R. [29] DR; *anhelitu* aEH. [30] aH; *uicinos* DE (with *nociuos* in margin in D); om. R. [31] DER; *se* aH. [32] aER; *Calidonis* D; *Kolidonis* H. [33] aDER (after *propugnacula* in a); *Lundonie* H. [34] aDR; *Quocumque* EH. [35] DER; *dupplici* aH. [36] aDER; *flammabunt* H. [37] aDER; *excitabit* H. [38] DR; *.iiii.* aEH. [39] R; *diademata* aH; *cornua* DE (with *dyademata* in margin in D). [40] ER; *nefando* aDH. [41] aDER; *.iii.* H. [42] DER; *Brittannie* aH. [43] DE (with *Daneum* in margin of D); *Danerum* a; *Dauerium* H; *Danorum* R. [44] DEH (altered to *Accede* in D); *Accede* a; *Accende* R. [45] aDER; *Guintonie* H. [46] aDEHR (with *pastoralem* suprascript in D). [47] aDEH; *applicantur* R. [48] aDER; *menbra* H. [49] EHR; *caput* aD. [50] aDER; *sequentur* H. [51] aEHR; *Festinant* D. [52] aH; om. DE; *quia* R. [53...53] aHR; *periurii scelera* DE. [54] aDER; *pdocebit* H. [55...55] a; *ipsarum* DE; *rerum ipsarum* H; *tincture earum* R. [56] R; *augmentatione* aH; *augmentacione* DE. [57] aDEH; *henricus* R. [58] DR; *oneratus* aEH. [59...59] DE; *uolucres conuolabunt* aH; *conuolabant uolucres* (with second *a* of *conuolabant* underpointed) R. [60] aDER; *palatium* H. [61] R; *scescentis* a; *.c.* DE (with *.vi. centis* in margin of D); *.dc.* H.

(37) Inuidebit ergo Londonia[62] et muros suos tripliciter augebit. Circuibit eam undique Thamensis[63] fluuius et rumor operis transcendet Alpes. Occultabit infra hericius poma[64] et subterraneas[65] uias[66] machinabitur.

(38) In tempore illo loquentur lapides et mare quo ad Galliam nauigatur infra breue spacium[67] contrahetur. In utraque ripa audietur homo ab homine et solidum insule dilatabitur. Reuelabuntur occulta submarinorum et Gallia pre timore tremebit.

(39) Post hec ex Calaterio nemore procedet ardea que insulam per biennium circumuolabit.[68] Nocturno clamore conuocabit uolatilia et omne genus uolucrum associabit sibi. In culturis mortalium irruent et omnia genera[69] messium deuorabunt.

(40) Sequetur fames populum atque dira mortalitas famem. At cum [70]calamitas tanta[70] cessauerit, adibit detestabilis ales uallem Galahes[71] atque eam in excelsum montem leuabit. In cacumine quoque ipsius plantabit[72] quercum atque infra ramos nidificabit.

(41) Tria oua procreabuntur in nido ex quibus uulpes[73] et lupus et ursus egredientur. Deuorabit uulpes matrem et asininum[74] capud[75] gestabit. Monstro igitur assumpto terrebit fratres suos ipsosque in Neustriam fugabit.

(42) At illi[76] excitabunt aprum dentosum in illam[77] et nauigio reuecti[78] cum uulpe[79] congredientur. Que cum [80]certamen inierit,[80] finget se defunctam et aprum in pietatem mouebit. Mox adibit ipse cadauer; dum[81] superstabit, hanelabit[82] in oculos eius et faciem. At ipsa non oblita preteriti doli mordebit sinistrum pedem ipsius[83] totumque ex corpore euellet. Saltu quoque facto eripiet ei dextram[84] aurem et caudam et [85]infra cauernas moncium[86] delitebit.[87]

---

[62] aDER; *Lundonia* H. [63] aER; *Tamensis* DH. [64] DER (with *sua* suprascript in D); *poma sua* aH. [65] aDHR; *subterranias* E. [66] aDEH; om. R. [67] DER; *spatium* aH. [68] aHR; *conuolabit* DE (with *circumuolabit* in margin in D). [69] aDEHR (with *grana* in margin of D). [70...70] aDER; *tanta calamitas* H. [71] HR; *Galabes* aDE (with *Galaes* in margin of D). [72] aDEH; *plantauit* R. [73] DEH; *uulpis* a; *wlpes* R. [74] aHR; *asinum* D; *asinium* E. [75] aDER; *caput* H. [76] aDHR; *illa* E. [77] aH; *illa* DER. [78] aDEHR (corrected from *aduecti* in D). [79] aDEH; *wlpe* R. [80...80] aHR; *certamine uicta fuerit* DE (with *certamen inierit* in margin in D). [81] aDER; *dumque* H. [82] R; *anelabit* a; *anhelabit* DEH. [83] aHR; *illius* DE. [84] EHR; *dexteram* aD. [85...85] aDHR; bis in E. [86] ER; *montium* aDH. [87] aDEH; *delicebit* R.

(43) Aper ergo illusus requiret lupum et ursum ut ei amissa membra[88] restituant. Qui ut causam inierint, promittent ei duos[89] pedes et aures et caudam[85] et [90]ex eis[90] porcina membra[91] component. Acquiescet[92] ipse promissamque restauracionem[93] expectabit.

(44) Interim descendet uulpes[94] de montibus et sese in lupum mutabit. Et quasi colloquium habitura cum apro adibit illum callideque[95] totum[96] deuorabit. Exin transuertet sese[97] in aprum et quasi sine membris expectabit germanos. Sed et[98] ipsos postquam aduenerint[99] subito[100] dente interficiet atque capite leonis coronabitur.

(45) In diebus eius nascetur serpens qui neci mortalium iminebit.[101] Longitudine sua circuibit Londoniam[102] et quosque pretereuntes deuorabit.

(46) Bos montanus capud[103] lupi assumet dentesque suos in fabrica Sabrine dealbabit. Associabit sibi greges Albanorum et Kambrie qui Thamensem potando siccabunt.[104]

(47) Uocabit asinus hyrcum[105] prolixe barbe et formam ipsius mutuabitur.[106] Indignabitur igitur[107] montanus uocatoque lupo cornutus taurus[108] in ipsos fiet. Ut autem seuicie[109] indulserit, deuorabit carnes eorum et ossa sed in cacumine Uriani cremabitur.

(48) Fauille rogi mutabuntur in cignos[110] qui in sicco quasi in flumine natabunt. Deuorabunt pisces in piscibus et homines in hominibus deglucient.[111] Superueniente uero senectute efficientur submarini luces atque submarinas insidias machinabuntur. Submergent naualia et argentum non minimum congregabunt.

(49) Fluctuabit iterum Thamensis[112] conuocatisque fluminibus ultra [113]metas aluei[113] procedet. Urbes uicinas occultabit oppositosque montes subuertet.

---

[88] aDER; *menbra* H. [89] aDER; *.ii.* H. [90...90] aHR; *ei* DE (altered to *ex eis* in D). [91] aDER; *menbra* H. [92] aER; *Adquiescet* DH. [93] ER; *restaurationem* aDH. [94] DEH; *uulpis* a; *wlpes* R. [95] DEH; *callide* aR. [96] DER; *ipsum totum* aH. [97] DER; *se* aH. [98] aDEH; om. R. [99] aDEHR (corrected from *superuenerint* in E). [100] aDHR; om. E. [101] DER; *imminebit* aH. [102] DER; *Londonia* a; *Lundoniam* H. [103] DR; *caput* aEH. [104] aEHR; *exsiccabunt* D. [105] aER (corrected from *hycum* in a); *hyrcum* omitted from text, but added in margin of D; *yrcum* H. [106] DER; *mutuabit* a; *mutabit* H. [107] aHR; *ergo* DE. [108] aDEH; *thaurus* R. [109] ER; *seuitie* aD; *fini seuitie* H. [110] aDEH; *signos* R. [111] ER; *deglutient* aDH. [112] DER; *Tamensis fluuius* a; *Thamensis fluuius* H. [113...113] aHR; *aluei metas* DE.

(50) Adhibebit[114] sibi fontem[115] Galahes,[116] dolo et nequicia[117] repleti.[118] Orientur ex eo sediciones[119] prouocantes Uenedotos[120] ad prelia. Conuenient nemorum robora et cum saxis Geuisseorum[121] congredientur. Aduolabit coruus cum miluis et corpora peremptorum deuorabit.

(51) Super muros Claudiocestrie nidificabit bubo et in nido suo procreabitur asinus. Educabit eum serpens Maluernie[122] et in plures dolos commouebit. Sumpto dyademate[123] transcendet excelsa et horrido rugitu[124] populum patrie terrebit.

(52) In diebus eius titubabunt[125] montes Pacaii[126] et prouintie nemoribus suis spoliabuntur. Superueniet namque[127] uermis ignei anhelitus[128] qui emisso uapore comburet[129] arbores.

(53) Egredientur ex eo .vii. leones capitibus hyrcorum[130] turpati.[131] Fetore narium mulieres corrumpent[132] et proprias communes facient. Nesciet pater filium proprium [133]quia more[133] pecudum lasciuient.[134]

(54) Superueniet uero gygas[135] nequicie[136] qui [137]oculorum acumine[137] terrebit uniuersos. Exurget in illum draco Wigornie[138] et eum exterminare conabitur. Facto autem congressu superabitur draco et nequicia[139] uictoris opprimetur. Ascendet namque draconem et exuta ueste insidebit nudus. Feret illum ad sublimia[140] draco [141]erectaque cauda uerberabit nudatum. Resumpto iterum[142] uigore gigas[143] fauces illius cum gladio[141] confringet. Implicabitur tandem sub cauda sua draco et uenenatus interibit.

(55) Succedet post illum Totonesius[144] aper et dyra[145] tyrannide[146] opprimet populum. Eliminabit Claudiocestria leonem[147] qui diuersis preliis inquietabit seuientem. Conculcabit eum sub[148] pedibus suis apertisque faucibus terrebit.

114 aDER; *Adibebit* H. 115 DER; *fontes* aH. 116 HR; *Galabes* aDE. 117 ER; *nequitia* aDH. 118 aEHR; *repletum* (with *repleti* in margin) D. 119 DER; *seditiones* aH. 120 aEHR; *Uenedocos* D. 121 aDE; *Geuuisseorum* H; *Gewiseorum* R. 122 aDEH; *Maluerne* R. 123 DR; *diademate* aEH. 124 DER; *rachanatu* a; *rechanatu* H. 125 aDHR (with *titulabunt* in margin of D); *titulabunt* E. 126 aR; om. DEH (with *Pachay* in margin of D). 127 aDER; *nanque* H. 128 aEHR; *hanelitus* D. 129 aDER; *conburet* H. 130 aDER; *yrcorum* H. 131 aEHR; *turbati* (with *turpati* in margin) D. 132 aHR; *erumpent* DE. 133...133 aDEH; *qui amore* R. 134 aDHR; *laciuient* E. 135 EHR; *gigas* aD. 136 DER; *nequitie* aH. 137...137 aHR; *acumine oculorum* DE. 138 aDHR; *Wygornie* E. 139 DER; *nequitie* a; *nequitia* H. 140 DR; *sullimia* aEH. 141...141 aDER; om. H. 142 aR; *itaque* DE; om. H. 143 aR; *gygas* DE; om. H. 144 aDER; *Tottonesius* H. 145 R; *dira* aDEH. 146 aDER; *tirannide* H. 147 aDEH; *leonenem* R. 148 aHR; *cum* DE.

(56) Cum regno tamen litigabit leo et terga nobilium transcendet. Superueniet taurus litigio et leonem dextro[149] pede percutiet.[150] Expellet eum[151] per regni diuersoria[152] sed cornua sua in muros Exonie[153] confringet.

(57) Uindicabit leonem uulpes[154] Kaerdubali[155] et totum [156]suis dentibus[156] consumet.

(58) Circumcinget eam Lindocolinus[157] coluber presenciamque[158] suam [159]draconibus multis[159] horribili[160] sibilo testabitur. Congredientur deinde dracones et alter alterum dilaniabit.[161] Opprimet alatus carentem alis et ungues in genas uenenatas configet. Ad certamen conuenient alii et alius alium interficiet.

(59) Succedet quintus[162] interfectis; residuos[163] diuersis machinationibus confringet.[164] Transcendet uiuus[165] cum gladio et capud[166] a corpore separabit. Exuta ueste ascendet alium et dextram[167] caude leuamque iniciet. Superabit eum nudus cum nichil indutus proficeret.[168] Ceteros tormentabit a dorso et in rotunditatem regni compellet.

(60) Superueniet leo rugiens immani feritate timendus. Ter quinque porciones[169] in unum reducet et solus possidebit populum.

(61) Splendebit colore niueo ac candidum populum generabit.

(62) Delicie[170] principes eneruabunt[171] et [172]subditi[173] in beluas mutabuntur.[172] Orietur in illis leo humano cruore turgidus. Supponetur ei in segete falcifer qui, dum laborabit mente, opprimetur ab illo.

(63) Sedabit illos Eboracensis auriga expulsoque domino in currum quem ducit ascendet. Abstracto gladio minabitur orienti et rotarum suarum uestigia replebit[174] sanguine. Fiet deinde piscis in equore qui[175] sibilo serpentis reuocatus[176] coibit cum illo.

---

[149] aDEH; *dextra* R. [150] aDHR; *percuciet* E. [151] aDER; *illum* H. [152] aEH; *diuersatoria* DR (with *diuersoria* in margin in D). [153] aDEH; *Oxonie* R. [154] DEH; *uulpis* a; *wlpes* R. [155] DEH (corrected from *Kaerdubiali* in D); *Caerdubali* a; *Caerdubialis* R. [156...156] aHR; *dentibus suis* DE. [157] aHR; *Lindicolinus* DE. [158] ER; *presentiamque* aDH. [159...159] aHR; *multis draconibus* DE. [160] aEHR; *horrido* D. [161] D; *dilaniet* aEHR. [162] DER; *.v.* aH. [163] aDER; *et residuos* H. [164] aEHR; *interficiet* deleted before *confringet* in D. [165] HR; *dorsum uiuus* a; *unus* DE. [166] HR; *caput* aDE. [167] ER; *dexteram* aDH. [168] aDER; *profecerit* H. [169] ER; *portiones* aDH. [170] DER; *Delitie* aH. [171] aEHR; *enumerabunt* (with *eneruabunt* in margin) D. [172...172] aDEHR; underlined in H. [173] aHR; *subiti* DE (altered to *subditi* by suprascript *d* in D). [174] aER; *implebit* D; *repleuit* H. [175] aDEH; *qui de* R. [176] aDEH; *ter uocatus* R.

(64) Nascentur [177]inde tres tauri[178] fulgurantes qui consumptis pascuis conuertentur in[177] arbores. Gestabit primus flagellum uipereum et [179]a postgenito[179] dorsum suum diuertet. Nitetur ipse flagellum ei eripere sed ab ultimo corripietur. Auertent mutuo [180]a sese[180] facies[181] donec uenenatum cifum[182] proiecerint.

(65) Succedet ei colonus Albanie cui a dorso imminebit[183] serpens. [184]Uacabit ipse[185] tellurem subuertere[184] ut patrie segetibus candeant. Laborabit serpens uenenum diffundere ne herbe in messes proueniant. Letali clade deficiet populus et menia urbium desolabuntur.

(66) Dabitur in remedium Urbs[186] Claudii que alumpnam[187] flagellantis interponet. Stateram namque medicine gestabit et in breui renouabitur insula.

(67) Deinde duo subsequentur sceptrum quibus cornutus[188] draco ministrabit. Adueniet alter in ferro et uolantem[189] equitabit[190] serpentem. Nudato corpore insidebit dorso et dexteram caude iniciet. Clamore ipsius excitabuntur maria et timorem secundo[191] inicient.

(68) Secundus itaque sociabitur leoni et [192]exorta lite congressum facient. Mutuis cladibus succumbent[193] mutuo sed feritas[192] belue preualebit.

(69) Superueniet quidam in timpano[194] et cythara[195] et demulcebit leonis seuiciam.[196] Pacificabuntur ergo naciones[197] regni et leonem ad stateram prouocabunt. Locata[198] sede ad pensas studebit sed palmas in Albaniam extendet. Tristabuntur igitur aquilonales[199] prouincie[200] et ostia[201] templorum reserabunt.[202]

(70) Signifer lupus conducet turmas et Cornubiam cauda sua circumcinget. Resistet ei miles [203]in curru[203] qui populum [204]illum in aprum[204]

177...177 aDER; om. H. 178 aDE; om. H; *thauri* R. 179...179 HR; *postgenito* a; *a primogenito* DE. 180...180 aDER; suprascript in H. 181 aDER; *facies suas* H. 182 HR; *ciphum* aDE. 183 aDH; *iminebit* E; *innuebit* (?) R. 184...184 aDEHR; underlined in H. 185 DER; *ille* aH. 186 aDHR (tampered in D); *Urbis* E. 187 aDEH; *alumpciam* R. 188 aDEH; *coadiutus* R. 189 aR; *uolabit* DEH (with *uolantem* in margin of D). 190 aDER; *equitantem* H. 191 aDEH; *sidero* R. 192...192 aDER; om. H. 193 aDE; om. H; *subcumbent* R. 194 EHR; *tympano* aD. 195 aDER; *cithara* H. 196 DER; *seuitiam* aH. 197 R; *naciones* aDEH. 198 aDHR; *Locuta* E. 199 aDHR; *aquilones* E. 200 DER; *prouintie* aH. 201 aDER; *hostia* H. 202 aHR; *reserabuntur* DE. 203...203 aDEH; *incursum* R. 204...204 aDEH; *aprum in illum* R.

mutabit.²⁰⁵ Uastabit igitur aper prouincias sed in profundo Sabrine occultabit capud.²⁰⁶

(71) Amplexabitur homo leonem in uino et fulgor²⁰⁷ auri oculos intuencium²⁰⁸ excecabit. Candebit argentum in circuitu et diuersa torcularia uexabit. [117] Inposito¹ uino inebriabuntur mortales postpositoque celo in terram respicient.

(72) Ab eis uultus auertent sidera² et solitum cursum confundent. Arebunt segetes ³hiis indignantibus³ et humor conuexi negabitur. Radices et rami uices mutabunt nouitasque rei erit in miraculum.

(73) Splendor solis ⁴electro Mercurii⁴ languebit et erit horror inspicientibus. Mutabit clypeum⁵ Stilbon⁶ Archadie, uocabit Uenerem galea Martis. Galea⁷ Martis umbram conficiet, transibit terminos furor Mercurii. Nudabit ensem Orion ferreus,⁸ uexabit nubes Phebus equoreus. Exibit Iupiter licitas semitas et Uenus deseret statutas lineas. Saturni syderis⁹ liuido corruet et falce recurua mortales¹⁰ perimet. Bissenus numerus domorum syderum¹¹ deflebit hospites ita transcurrere. Omittent Gemini¹² complexus solitos et Urnam¹³ in fontes prouocabunt. Pensa Libre oblique¹⁴ pendebunt¹⁵ donec Aries recurua cornua sua¹⁶ supponat.¹⁷ Cauda Scorpionis procreabit fulgura et Cancer cum sole litigabit. Ascendet Uirgo dorsum Sagittarii et flores uirgineos obfuscabit.¹⁸ Currus lune turbabit zodiacum et in fletum prorumpent Pleyades.¹⁹ Officio²⁰ iam²¹ nulla redibunt²² sed²³ ²⁴clausa ianua²⁴ in crepidinibus Adriane²⁵ delitebit.

---

²⁰⁵ aE; *minabit* DHR. ²⁰⁶ DR; *caput* aEH. ²⁰⁷ aDHR; *fulgur* E. ²⁰⁸ ER; *intuentium* aDH.

§117 ¹ HR; *Imposito* aDE. ² aEHR; *sydera* D. ³...³ DER; *his indignantibus* a; *indignantibus his* H. ⁴...⁴ aH; om. DE (but *electro Mercurii* suprascript in D); *electos Mercurii* R. ⁵ R; *clipeum* aDE; om. H. ⁶ aDER; *Stylbon* H. ⁷ aDEH; *Galeam* R. ⁸ aDEH; *fereus* R. ⁹ DER (with *sydus* in margin of D); *sideris* a; *sidus* H. ¹⁰ aHR; *homines* DE. ¹¹ R; *siderum* aDEH. ¹² DR (tampered in D); *genu* a; *genua* EH. ¹³ aDER; *urinas* H. ¹⁴ aDEH; *obliqui* R. ¹⁵ aDER; *pendebit* H. ¹⁶ aDEHRS. The lacuna in S ends at this point. ¹⁷ DRS; *subponat* aEH. ¹⁸ DERS; *obfuscauit* a; *offuscabit* H. ¹⁹ R; *Pliades* a; *Pleiades* DES; *Plyades* H. ²⁰ ERS; *Officia* aDH. ²¹ aERS; *Iani* DH. ²² aEHRS; *ridebunt* D. ²³ aDHRS; *set* E. ²⁴...²⁴ aH; *ianua clausa* DES; *clauda ianua* R. ²⁵ R; *Adriagne* (altered from *Adrigne*) a; *Adrianne* DEHS.

(74) In ictu radii exurgent[26] equora et[27] puluis ueterum renouabitur. Confligent uenti diro[28] sufflamine[29] et sonitum inter sydera[30] conficient.'[31]

[118] Cum[1] igitur hec et alia[2] prophetasset Merlinus, ambiguitate uerborum suorum astantes in admiracionem[3] commouit. Uortigernus[4] uero pre ceteris admirans[5] et sensum iuuenis et uaticinia collaudat. Neminem enim presens etas produxerat qui ora[6] sua in hunc modum coram ipso soluisset. Scire igitur uolens modum exitus sui ex hac uita rogauit iuuenem ut sibi[7] indicaret quid[8] intelligeret. Cui Merlinus: 'Ignem filiorum Constantini caue, si ualueris.[9] Iam naues parant, iam Armoricanum[10] litus deserunt,[11] iam uela per equora pandunt. Petent Britanniam,[12] inuadent Saxonicam[13] [14]gentem, nephandum[15] populum subiugabunt. Sed prius te intra turrim inclusum[16] comburent.[14] Malo tuo patrem eorum prodidisti et Saxones contra eos inuitasti. Inuitasti eos tibi in[17] presidium et ecce superuenerunt in tuum supplicium.[18] Imminent[19] tibi duo[20] funera nec est promptum quod prius uites.[21] Hinc enim[22] regnum tuum deuastant Saxones et leto tuo incumbent. Hinc autem applicant duo[23] fratres, Aurelius et Uther, qui mortem fratris[24] sui[25] in te uindicare nitentur.[26] Quere tibi diffugium, si potes; cras Totonesium[27] portum tenebunt. Rubebunt[28] sanguine[29] Saxonum facies et interfecto Hengisto[30] Aurelius coronabitur. Pacificabit naciones,[31] restaurabit ecclesias; sed ueneno deficiet. Succedet ei germanus suus Utherpendragon cuius dies anticipabuntur ueneno. Aderunt tante prodicioni[32] posteri tui quos aper Cornubie deuorabit.'

26 aEHRS; *surgent* D. 27 aDEHS; *quia* R. 28 aDEHS; *dira* R. 29 DERS; *flamine* aH. 30 ERS; *sidera* aDH. 31 aDEHRS. After *conficient*, *Explicit liber septimus. Incipit liber* [om. R] *octauus* in aR; and *Explicit prophetia Merlini liber .vii.. Incipit .viii.* in H.

§118 1 aDHRS; <C>*um* E. 2 aDHR; *alia plurima* ES. 3 RS; *ammirationem* aD; *ammiracionem* E; *amirationem* H. 4 aH; *Uortig'* DES; *Uortigrinus* R. 5 R; *ammirans* aDES; *amirans* H. 6 aDEH; *hora* RS. 7 aHR; om. DES. 8 DS; *quod* aEHR. 9 aDES; *uolueris* HR. 10 aHRS; *Armoricum* DE. 11 aHR; *deserent* DES. 12 DERS; *Brittanniam* aH. 13 aDERS; *Saxonicanam* H. 14...14 aDERS; om. H. 15 ER; *nefandum* aDS; om. H. 16 aDES; om. H; *conclusum* (with *in*− suprascript) R. 17 DERS; *ad* aH. 18 aDERS; *supplitium* H. 19 R; *Imminent* aDEHS. 20 aDEHR; *.ii.* S. 21 aDERS; *euites* H. 22 DERS; om. aH. 23 aDERS; *.ii.* H. 24 DES; *patris* aHR (altered to *fratris* in a). 25 aDEHS; *tui* R. 26 DERS; *niterentur* a; *nituntur* H. 27 DER; *Totonensium* aS; *Tottonesium* H. 28 aEHR; *Rudebunt* DS (with *Rubebunt* in margin in D). 29 aDEHR; *sanguinem* S 30 aHR; *Heng'* DES. 31 ERS; *nationes* aDH. 32 DERS; *proditioni* aH.

[119] Nec mora cum[1] crastina dies illuxit,[2] applicuerunt fratres in loco quo[3] predixerat Merlinus. Rumore[4] itaque eorum diuulgato conuenerunt Britones[5] qui in tanta clade [6]dispersi fuerant[6] et societate suorum roborati hylariores[7] efficiuntur. Moxque[8] Aurelius in regem erectus est atque hostes persequi secum[9] omnes cohortatur:[10] sed[11] prius Uortigernum[12] qui patrem[13] et fratrem eius[14] dolo extinxerat. Conuertit ergo exercitum in Kambriam ad opidum[15] Genoreu,[16] quod[17] situm erat[18] in nacione[19] Herging,[20] super fluuium Guaie[21] in monte qui Cloarcius[22] nuncupatur. In quo forti munimento Uortigernus[23] se receperat[24] ut ab hostibus [25]suis se ibidem[25] tueretur. Quo cum peruenisset Ambrosius[26] cum exercitu, affatur[27] Eldol[28] ducem Claudiocestrie, dicens: 'Memento, dux nobilis, qualiter te et pater et frater meus [29]dilexerint et honorauerint[29] et de periuro isto et doloso qui eos prodidit faciamus[30] ulcionem.'[31] Nec mora diuersis machinacionibus[32] incumbunt, murum diruere festinant. Postremo igne adhibito[33] turris simul cum Uortigerno[34] et omnibus qui cum eo aderant in cineres concremata est.[35]

[120] Hiis[1] pro uoto patratis conuertit rex exercitum persequi Saxones qui audita [2]fama eorum[2] trans Humbrum[3] diffugerant[4] ut Scocia[5] eis ad munimentum et defensionem pateret. Ducens itaque [6]Aurelius Ambrosius rex per longum Britannie exercitum[6] post hostes in tanto itinere augmentum suscepit[7] exercitus de Britonibus[8] hinc inde confluentibus[9]

§119 ¹ aHR; om. DES. ² aHRS; *illuxit et* DE. ³ aDER; *quem* HS. ⁴ aDHRS; <R>*umore* E. ⁵ DERS; *Brittones* aH. ⁶...⁶ aHR; *fuerant dispersi* DES. ⁷ ERS; *hillariores* a; *hilariores* D; *ilariores* H. ⁸ DEHR; *Meret* (deleted) S. ⁹ DERS; om. H. ¹⁰ DHS; *hortatur* E; *corortantur* R. ¹¹ DHRS; *set* E. ¹² H; *Uortig'* DES; *Uortigrinum* R. ¹³ EHRS; *et patrem* D. ¹⁴ HR; *eorum* DES. ¹⁵ DERS; *oppidum* aH. ¹⁶ aDES; *Genoreum* H; *Genoreci* R. ¹⁷ aDEHS; *qui* R. ¹⁸ aDHRS; om. E. ¹⁹ ERS; *natione* aDH. ²⁰ aDEHRS (corrected from *Erging* in E). ²¹ aDEHS; *Guare* R. ²² ERS; *Cloartius* aD (with *Dewarthus* in margin of D); *Claortius* H. ²³ aH; *Uortig'* DES; *Uortigrinus* R. ²⁴ aDERS; *recepit* H. ²⁵...²⁵ aR; *suis ibidem se* DE; *se* HS. ²⁶ aHR; *Aurelius* DES. ²⁷ DERS; *effatur* H. ²⁸ DHRS (with *Eydol* in margin of D); *Eydol* E. ²⁹...²⁹ DHRS; *dilexerunt et honorauerunt* E. ³⁰ DERS; *facimus* (corrected to *faciamus* by suprascript *a*) H. ³¹ ER; *ultionem* aDH. ³² ERS; *machinationibus* aDH. ³³ aDERS; *adibito* H. ³⁴ aH; *Uortig'* DES; *Uortigrino* R. ³⁵ aDEHRS (corrected from *sunt* in D).

§120 ¹ DERS; *His* aH. ²...² aDEHS; *eorum fama* R. ³ aDEHS; *Humbram* R. ⁴ aDEHS; *diffugerunt* R. ⁵ ERS; *Scotia* aDH. ⁶...⁶ R; *rex Ambrosius Aurelius per longum Brittannie exercitum* aH; *rex Ambrosius Aurelius exercitum per longum Britannie* DES. ⁷ aHR; *accepit* DES. ⁸ DERS; *Brittonibus* a; *Brittannibus* H. ⁹ DES; *circumfluentibus* a; *circumuenientibus* H; *superfluentibus* R.

ut arene[10] maris comparari posset.[11] Sed cum preteriret, urbes et castra et maxime ecclesias a gentilibus[12] hostibus[13] destructas indoluit, restauracionem[14] promittens post triumphum.

[121] At Hengistus[1] conuocans in unum Saxones suos sic hortabatur[2] eos,[3] dicens: 'Nolite terreri, fratres et commilitones mei, a superuenientibus pueris quorum audacia[4] nullis adhuc populis nota temerario [5]se ausu[5] in nos bellatores notissimos et exercitatissimos ingerere festinat.[6] Nolite, inquam,[7] timere eorum de diuersis nacionibus[8] congregatam multitudinem quorum [9]in preliis multociens experti estis[9] inbellem[10] [11]inualitudinem.[12] Mementote uictores semper extitisse et de eis[13] stragem non modicam[11] cum paucis peregisse. Dux quoque eorum qui indoctum ducit exercitum necdum ad uirilem peruenit etatem, magis puerilibus exercitatus lusibus quam bellis. Fauentibus ergo diis nostris inuictissimis et fugari et[14] prosterni necesse est illos[15] qui necdum arma ferre nouerunt et quorum inbecillis[16] est bellandi astucia.'[17] Et cum omnes hoc modo animasset Hengistus,[18] dato signo in hostes iter tendit ut subitum et furtiuum impetum[19] in illos faceret Britonesque[20] incautos et inparatos[21] occuparet. Sed quomodo posset imparatos[22] reperire[23] qui semper in armis etiam[24] noctis excubias in castris munierunt?[25] Aurelius ergo sciens hostes prope adesse dispositis turmis prior campum adiit in quo bellum [26]futurum sibi[26] aptum existimauit.[27] Tria milia ex Armoricanis[28] equitibus[29] [30]iussit equis insidere.[30] Ipse cum ceteris pedestri milite acies ordinauit et duxit.

[10] aEHRS; *harene* D. [11] aDEHRS (corrected from *possit* in R). [12] aDRS (corrected from *gentibus* in a?); *gentibus* EH. [13] aDEHS; om. R. [14] aERS; *restaurationem* DH.

§121 [1] aHR; *Heng'* DES. [2] aDHRS; *hortatur* E. [3] aDERS; om. H. [4] DERS; *audatia* aH. [5]...5 aDEHS; *ausu se* R. [6] a; *festinant* DEHRS. [7] aDHRS; *inquit* E. [8] ERS; *nationibus* aDH. [9]...9 aHR (*multotiens* in aH); *experti estis in bellis multociens* DES (*multotiens* in S). [10] aEHS; *imbellem* D; *inbecillem* R. [11]...11 aDERS; om. H. [12] DES; *ualitudinem* aR; om. H. [13] aDER; om. H; *hiis* S. [14] aDEHR; om. S. [15] aDEHS; *eos* R. [16] DERS; *inbecilla* aH. [17] aR; *astutia* DHS; *hastucia* E. [18] aHR; *Heng'* DES. [19] aDERS; *inpetum* H. [20] DERS; *Brittonesque* aH. [21] aEHRS; *imparatos* D. [22] aDERS; *inparatos* H. [23] DERS; *repperire* aH. [24] aDERS; *in* H. [25] aDERS; *se munierunt* H. [26]...26 aDERS; *sibi futurum* H. [27] aHR; *existimabat* DES. [28] DERS; *Moricanis* aH (with *Ar–* suprascript in H). [29] DERS (with *militibus* underpointed before *equitibus* in E); *militibus* aH. [30]...30 aHR; *equis insidere iussit* DES.

Demetas in collibus, Uenedotos in prope sitis nemoribus locauit ea prouidencia[31] ut, si hostes ad[32] ea diffugerent, adessent qui[33] exciperent.

[122] Interea accessit [1]Eldol[2] dux Claudiocestrie[1] ad regem et ait: 'Sola dies pro omnibus [3]uite mee diebus[3] michi[4] sufficeret si congredi[5] cum Hengisto[6] copiam [7]michi fortuna[7] daret.[8] Reminiscerer[9] namque diei qua sine armis conuenimus quasi pacem commissuri in campo iuxta cenobium Ambrii,[10] ubi proditor ille cum cultris repositis omnes interemit[11] preter me solum qui reperto palo ad defensionem uix euasi.[12] Iugulati sunt ea die .cccclxxx.[13] inter duces et consules ac proceres qui omnes conuenerant ad pacem componendam.'[14]

[123] Dum talia referret[1] Eldol,[2] ecce Hengistus[3] cum suis partem [4]campi non minimam[4] occupauit. Dispositis[5] ex utraque parte cuneis[6] congrediuntur atque mutuos ictus ingeminant; hinc Britones,[7] hinc Saxones uulnerati cadunt. Hortatur Aurelius suos ut pro patria et[8] libertate uiriliter pugnent. Monet[9] Hengistus[10] Saxones[11] quatinus[12] omni spe fuge postposita fortiter feriant. Fit prelium anceps; nunc isti,[13] nunc illi[14] superiores fiunt. Clamor ad sydera[15] tollitur. Christiani Deum omnipotentem inuocant, illi deos suos et deas supplices exorant. Dumque diu taliter decertarent, preualuit christianus exercitus atque Saxones fugere coegit. Hengistus[16] igitur ut uidit suos christianis cedere, confestim fugiens petiuit[17] oppidum[18] Kaerconan,[19] quod nunc Cunungeburg[20] appellatur. Insequitur Aurelius et in itinere quoscum-

---

31 ERS; *prouidentia* aDH. 32 aDERS; *ex* H. 33 aDEHS; *quid* R.

§122 [1]...[1] aDERS; *dux Claudiocestrie Eldol* H. [2] DRS & H (with *Eydol* in margin of D); *Eldon* a; *Eydol* E. [3]...[3] aEHRS; *diebus uite mee* D. [4] HR; om. aDES (with *michi* suprascript before *sufficeret* in D). [5] aHR; *congrediendi* DES. [6] aHR; *Heng'* DES. [7]...[7] DERS; *fortuna michi* aH. [8] aDES; *faceret* HR. [9] DES; *Reminiscor* a; *Reminisceret* HR. [10] DERS; *Ambrie* aH. [11] aHR; *peremit* DES. [12] aHR; *uacaui* DES. [13] DHR; *.cccclxx.* aES. [14] aHR; *constituendam* DS; *constituendum* E.

§123 [1] aDEH; *referet* RS. [2] DHS; *Eldon* a; *Eydol* E; *Edol* R. [3] aHR; *Heng'* DES. [4]...[4] aHR; *non modicam campi* D; *campi non modicam* ES. [5] aDERS; *dispositisque* H. [6] aDHRS; om. E. [7] DERS; *Brittones* aH. [8] DEHS; *et pro* R. [9] aDEHS; *Mouet* R. [10] aHR; *Heng'* DES. [11] aR; *Saxones suos* DES; *suos Saxones* H. [12] aDEHS; *quatenus* R. [13] aHR; *illi* DES. [14] aHR; *isti* DE; *ite* S. [15] ERS; *sidera* aDH. [16] aHR; *Heng'* DES. [17] aDHRS; *pitiuit* E. [18] aHR; *opidum* DES. [19] aDE; *Kaerkonan* H; *Kaeconan* R; *Kaerconau* S. [20] a; *Conumgeburc* DE; *Kunungeburg* H; *Cunuligeburg* R; *Conumgesbure* S.

que[21] reperit uel in[22] interitum uel in seruitutem[23] redigit.[24] Cumque
uidisset Hengistus[25] quia insequeretur eum Aurelius, noluit introire
oppidum[26] sed conuocato in turmas populo iterum preliari disponit[27]
malens uitam in gladio et hasta committere[28] quam murorum[29] tui-
tione.[30] Adueniens itaque Aurelius conglomeratis simul[31] aciebus suis
cepit iterum pugnam reparare, Saxones econtra acriter resistere, quippe
pro uita tantum dimicantes nullum sibi existimabant diffugium prouenire.[32] Et forte [33]preualuissent in illo prelio Saxones, nisi[34] equestris
turma Armoricanorum[35] superuenisset[33] que constituta in priori prelio
fuerat ad presidium. Cesserunt igitur[36] Saxones confutati atque[37] de
stacione[38] sua pulsi dilapsique[39] fugam arripiunt quidam,[40] quidam
fortiter resistentes cum Hengisto[41] se defendebant.

[124] Tunc Eldol[1] locum congrediendi cum Hengisto[2] nactus quod
desiderabat opere compleuit.[3] Congressi namque ipse et Hengistus[4]
singulare certamen inierunt. Qui dum mutuos[5] enses alter in alterum
inmitterent,[6] excuciebantur[7] ex ictibus ignes[8] acsi fulgura coruscarent.[9]
Dumque in hunc modum decertarent,[10] superuenit Gorlois dux Cornubie cum suis quibus preerat[11] turmas Saxonum infestans. Quem[12] cum
aspexisset Eldol,[13] securior factus cepit Hengistum[14] per nasale[15] cassidis
atque totis uiribus utens[16] ipsum intra[17] suorum acies extraxit[18] magno-
que fluctuans gaudio [19]uoce clara[19] dixit: 'Desiderium meum impleuit
Deus! Prosternite, uiri, ambrones,[20] prosternite rabidum[21] canem atque
domini sui proditorem. Uobis est in manu uictoria Hengisto[22] peremp-

21 aDERS; *quosquos* E. 22 aDEHS; om. R. 23 aDEHR; *inseruitutem* S. 24 aEHRS;
redegit D. 25 aHR; *Heng'* DES. 26 aHR; *in opidum* DES. 27 EHRS; *disposuit* aD.
28 EHRS; *finire* deleted before *committere* in D. 29 EHRS; *in murorum* D. 30 DH;
intuicione ES; *circuicione* R. 31 aHR; *iterum* DES. 32 aDHR; *preuenire* ES.
33...33 aDERS; om. H. 34 aDES; om. H; *nec* R. 35 aDR; om. H; *Armoricorum* ES.
36 aEHRS; *ergo* D. 37 aDERS; *ac* H. 38 DERS; *statione* aH. 39 DERS; *delapsique* aH.
40 aDER; om. HS. 41 aHR; *Heng'* DES.

§124 1 DHS; *Eldon* a; *Eydol* E; *Edol* R. 2 aHR; *Heng'* DES. 3 aDERS; *conpleuit* H.
4 aHR; *Heng'* DES. 5 aHR; om. DES. 6 aERS; *immitterent* D; *mitterent* H. 7 R;
excuciebantur aH; *excutiebant* D; *excuciebant* ES. 8 aDEHRS (corrected from *igneis* in
S). 9 aDHR; *choruscarent* ES. 10 aDEHR; *certarent* S. 11 aDEHRS (corrected from
preerant in S). 12 aDEHS; *Quod* R. 13 DHRS; *Eldon* a; *Eydol* E. 14 aHR; *Heng'* DES.
15 aDEHS; *uasale* R. 16 aDERS; *nitens* H. 17 aEHRS; *inter* D. 18 aDEHS; *traxit* R.
19...19 aHR; *clara uoce* DES. 20 aHR; om. DES (with *ambrones* in margin of D).
21 aDEHR; *rapidum* S. 22 aHR; *Heng'* DES.

to.' Retento itaque eo ac uinculis mancipato diffugerunt [23]omnes complices sui[23] [24]quo quemque[24] impetus duxit. Alii montana, alii nemora petebant tantum ut manus Britonum[25] feriencium[26] duriter euadere possent. Octa[27] uero [28]filius Hengisti[28] cum parte Saxonum Eboracum adiit [29]et Eosa cognatus suus[29] urbemque munierunt.

[125] Aurelius autem[1] uictor factus ad urbem supramemoratam[2] Cunungesburg[3] diuertens[4] [5]ibidem tribus[5] diebus moratus est[6] se et uulneratos[7] suos quiete reficiens. Interea mortuos iussit sepeliri[8] et fatigatos quiescere cibisque et potibus[9] indulgere. Inter hec conuocatis ducibus decernere iussit quid de Hengisto[10] ageretur. Aderat Eldadus[11] [12]Claudiocestrensis episcopus,[12] frater[13] Eldol, uir summe prudencie[14] et religionis. Hic cum Hengistum[15] coram rege uinctum[16] aspexisset, silentio[17] facto ait: 'Etsi omnes istum liberare decernerent, ego sum qui Samuelem prophetam insequens hunc in frusta[18] conciderem.[19] Nam cum Agag regem Amalech[20] uiuum in Saulis potestate uidisset, iratus secuit eum per[21] frusta[22] dicens: "Sicut[23] fecisti tu[24] matres sine liberis, [25]sic faciam hodie matrem tuam sine liberis[25] inter mulieres." Sic igitur facite de isto qui alter Agag existit.'[26] Accepit itaque Eldol gladium et extra urbem educto Hengisto[27] capite priuauit. At Aurelius, ut erat in cunctis modestus, iussit sepeliri corpus eius ac more pagano tumulari.

[126] Post hec rex [1]Eboracum ducens exercitum[1] Octam[2] filium Hengisti[3] et eos qui cum eo erant in ciuitate obsedit. Uerum ille nil[4]

[23...23] aHR; *complices sui omnes* DE; *complites sui omnes* S. [24...24] DRS; *quocumque* aEH. [25] DERS; *Brittonum* aH. [26] ERS; *furientium* aH; *ferientium* D. [27] aDEHS; *Hocca* R. [28...28] aHR; *Heng' filius* DES. [29...29] aDERS; om. H.

§125 [1] aHR; *uero* DES. [2] DEHR; *memoratam* aS (altered to *supramemoratam* in a). [3] a; *Conungesburc* DE; *Kunungesburg* H; *Cuningesburg* R; *Coningesburc* S. [4] aHR; *tendens* DES. [5...5] aDHRS; *tribus ibidem* E. [6] aDEHR; om. S. [7] aDEHR; *wlneratos* S. [8] HR; *sepiliri* a; *sepelire* DES. [9] aDEHR; *potidus* S. [10] aHR; *Heng'* DES. [11] aHR; *Eldaldus* DES. [12...12] DERS; *episcopus Claudiocestrensis* a; *episcopus Cestrensis Claudio* H. [13] aDEHS; *super* R. [14] ERS; *prudentie* aDH. [15] aHR; *Heng'* DES. [16] aHR; om. DES (with *uinctum* in margin of D). [17] aHRS; *silencio* DE. [18] aDHS; *frustra* ER. [19] aEHS; *consciderem* D; *considerem* R. [20] aDERS; *Amalec* H. [21] aHR; *in* DES. [22] aDHS; *frustra* ER. [23] aDEHR; *Sicud* S. [24] aHR; om. DES. [25...25] aDEHR; om. S. [26] aHR; *extitit* DES. [27] aHR; *Heng'* DES.

§126 [1...1] aHR; *exercitum ducens Eboracum* DES. [2] aDEHS; *Hoctam* R. [3] aHR; *Heng'* DES. [4] aDEHR; *non* (supraascript) S.

ualens resistere processit de [5]ciuitate obuiam regi[5] cathenam[6] gestans ferream[7] in manu puluere asperso capite et sese regi in hec uerba presentauit[8]: 'Uicti sunt dii mei Deumque[9] uestrum regnare non hesito qui[10] per uos tot [11]bellatores nos in armis[11] deuictos dedicioni[12] amissa libertate coegit. Suscipiat ergo celsitudo nobilitatis tue cathenam[13] istam et, nisi misericordiam adhibueris,[14] habe nos uinctos ad quodlibet supplicium[15] uel, si[16] magis placet,[17] [18]nos in seruos accipe[18] federatos omni tempore.' Motus pietate Aurelius iussit adiudicari quid in illos agendum foret. Cum autem diuersi diuersa [19]proferrent, surrexit Eldaldus[20] prefatus episcopus et sententiam[21] in eos hoc sermone disseruit: 'Gabaonite[19] ultro[22] uenerunt ad filios[23] Israel [24]misericordiam petentes[24] et impetrauerunt. Erimus ergo christiani deteriores Iudeis misericordiam abnegantes? Misericordiam petunt; habeant illam. Ampla est Britannia[25] et in multis locis deserta. Federatos itaque [26]illos sinamus[26] saltem deserta inhabitare et nobis in sempiternum[27] seruiant.' Acquieuit[28] ergo rex et omnis multitudo exercitus que aderat deditque eis rex mansionem iuxta Scociam[29] fedusque cum eis firmauit[30] obsidibus acceptis.

[127] Triumphatis itaque hostibus conuocat rex in[1] concionem[2] omnes proceres et seniores ac[3] sapienciores[4] terre infra Eboracum consulens de restauracione[5] ecclesiarum que per gentem Saxonum destructe erant, de urbium quoque reparacione[6] atque tocius[7] regni status renouacione;[8] ac[9] [10]primum ipsam[10] metropolitanam [11]Eboracensem sedem[11] atque ceteros episcopatus prouincie[12] illius ipse reedificare cepit. Emensis

5...5 aDEHS; *obuiam regi ciuitate* R. 6 DRS; *catenam* aEH. 7 aDEHRS (corrected from *ferreram* in R). 8 aDEHR; *presentans* S. 9 aDERS; *dominumque regem* H. 10 DEHR; *que* S. 11...11 DERS; *in armis bellatores nos* H. 12 ERS; *deditioni* DH. 13 DRS; *catenam* aEH. 14 aDERS; *adibueris* H. 15 aDERS; *supplitium* H. 16 DERS; om. aH. 17 DERS; *placeat* aH. 18...18 aHR; *habe nos seruos* DES. 19...19 aDERS; om. H. 20 DES; *Eldatus* aR; om. H. 21 aDRS; *sentenciam* E; om. H. 22 aDHRS; *ultra* E. 23 aDEHS; *filio* R. 24...24 DER; *petentes misericordiam* aH; *misericordiam petetes* S. 25 DERS; *Brittannia* aH. 26...26 aDEHS; *sinamus illos* R. 27 aHR; *perpetuum* DES. 28 aR; *Adquieuit* DEHS. 29 aERS; *Scotiam* DH. 30 aDEHR; *confirmauit* S.

§127 1 aDERS; *in* underpointed in H. 2 R; *contione* aD; *concione* ES; om. H. 3 aH; *atque* DES; *et* R. 4 EHRS; *sapientiores* aD. 5 ERS; *restauratione* aDH. 6 ER; *reparatione* aDH; *restauracione* S. 7 ER; *totius* aDHS. 8 ERS; *renouatione* aDH. 9 aEHRS; *At* D. 10...10 aHR; *ipsam primum* DES. 11...11 aEHRS; *sedem Eboracensem* D. 12 DERS; *prouintie* aH.

deinde .xv. diebus cum operarios in diuersis locis statuisset, adiuit urbem Londonie cui hostes nequaquam pepercerant. Cuius condolens excidio reuocat ciues undique dispersos et ciuitatem [13]a conciuibus[13] restituit. Ibidem disponit de regno legesque sopitas reuocat;[14] maiorum[15] possessiones[16] nepotibus distribuit quas[17] in tanta calamitate [18]heredes amiserant.[18] Tota itaque eius intencio[19] uersabatur circa regni restitucionem,[20] ecclesie[21] reformacionem,[22] [23]pacis ac legis renouacionem[23] et iusticie compositionem. Exin[24] petiuit[25] Wintoniam[26] ut eam sicut ceteras[27] restitueret. Cumque hec omnia peragrasset et in restauracione[28] urbium et ecclesiarum que necessaria[29] erant posuisset, monitu Eldadi[30] episcopi monasterium Ambrii[31] adiit quod[32] prope Kaercaradoc,[33] que nunc Salesberia[34] dicitur, situm[35] consules et duces regni quos Hengistus[36] interfecerat in sepultura[37] continet. Huius [38]cenobii, ut fertur,[38] fundator[39] extiterat Ambrius quidam olim, de cuius nomine locus appellatus est; in quo .ccc. fratres Deo famulabantur. [40]Ubi cum[40] sepulturas interemptorum circumspiceret,[41] motus pietate [42]in lacrimas[42] resolutus est. Postea in diuersas cogitaciones[43] animum educens deliberabat[44] apud se qualiter locum faceret memorabilem.

[128] Conuocatis itaque artificibus lapidum et lignorum[1] precepit totis ingeniis uti nouamque ac mirabilem structuram adinuenire que in memoriam tantorum uirorum[2] [3]in euum constaret.[3] Cumque omnes hesitarent ad preceptum regis et ignorarent quid agerent, surrexit Tremorinus[4] Urbis Legionum archiepiscopus[5] et coram rege ait: 'Si

13...13 DERS; *conciuibus* a; *aconciuibus* H. 14 DERS; *renouat* aH. 15 aDERS; *morum* altered to *mortuorum* in H. 16 DEHRS (corrected from *possessionibus* in R); *amissas possessiones* a. 17 aD; *qui* EH; *que* RS. 18...18 aDERS; *amiserant heredes* H. 19 ERS; *intentio* aDH. 20 DERS; *restaurationem* aH. 21 aDEHR; *ecclesiarum* S. 22 ERS; *reformationem* aDH. 23...23 aDRS (*renouationem* in aDS); *pacis ac legum renouacionem* E; om. H. 24 aDEHR; *Exinde* S. 25 aDERS; *petunt* H. 26 aDRS; *Wyntoniam* E; *Guintoniam* H. 27 aDERS; *alias* H. 28 ERS; *restauratione* aDH (corrected from *restaratione* in a). 29 aDERS; *necesse* H. 30 aHR; *Eldaldi* DES. 31 aDERS; *Ambri* H. 32 aDERS; *quod* followed by suprascript *est* in H. 33 aDERS; *Kaerkaradoc* H. 34 aDEHS; *Salisberia* (altered from *Sallisberia*) R. 35 aDERS; *quod* H. 36 aHR; *Heng'* DES. 37 aDEHS; *sepulturam* R. 38...38 aDEHS; *ut fertur cenobii* R. 39 aDEHS; *fudator* R. 40...40 aH; *Ut autem* DES; *Uir cum* R. 41 aDEHRS (with *circumspexisset* in margin of D). 42...42 DERS; om. aH. 43 DER; *cogitationes* aHS. 44 aDHRS; *diliberabat* E.

§128 1 aDEHS; *lingnorum* R. 2 aDEHS; om. R. 3...3 aDERS; *constaret in euum* H. 4 aDERS; *Tremorius* H. 5 aDERS; *episcopus* H.

Merlinum uatem ad hoc opus ⁶quod disponis mirabile⁶ peragendum inuitares, puto quia⁷ ipse pre ceteris omnibus⁸ qui aduocati sunt solus ingeniosus erit ad tale opus insinuandum. Quippe in toto regno tuo⁹ non est¹⁰ similis eius siue in futuris predicendis siue in ¹¹operacionibus machinandis.¹¹ Iube ergo illum uenire ut ingenio suo innitaris.' Missis itaque¹² nunciis in regionem¹³ Gewisseorum¹⁴ ad fontem Galahes,¹⁵ quem solitus fuerat¹⁶ frequentare, adductus est ad regem. Excepit illum rex cum honore rogauitque ut de futuris aliqua¹⁷ ¹⁸prediceret sibi¹⁸ quatinus que uentura erant in diebus suis presagiret. Cui Merlinus, 'Non sunt,' inquit,¹⁹ 'reuelanda huiusmodi misteria²⁰ nisi cum summa necessitas incubuerit. Nam si ea in derisionem aut²¹ uanam iactanciam²² proferrem, taceret spiritus qui me docet nec ²³per me²³ ualerem aliter loqui quam ceteri homines. ²⁴De hiis ergo pro quibus huc adductus sum, si uultis, edicam consilium meum.' Cui rex, 'Nouo,'²⁴ ait, 'et inaudito opere uellem decorare sepulturam uirorum qui pro pace constituenda²⁵ hic tamquam²⁶ oues iugulati sunt.' At Merlinus, 'Si desideras,' inquit,²⁷ 'quod dicis perfecte facere, pro Chorea²⁸ Gigantum²⁹ mittendum ³⁰tibi est³⁰ que est in Killarao³¹ monte Hybernie.³² Est etenim³³ structura lapidum quam nemo huius etatis construeret nisi ingenium ³⁴artem subuectaret.³⁴ Grandes sunt lapides et inportabiles;³⁵ nec est aliquis cuius uirtuti cedant nisi sit mechanica³⁶ arte eruditus. Qui si³⁷ eo³⁸ modo quo ibidem positi sunt circa plateam hanc locabuntur, in eternum stabunt.'

---

⁶...⁶ aHR; *mirabile quod disponis* DES. ⁷ aEHR; *quod* DS. ⁸ aEHRS; *omnibus mortalibus* D. ⁹ aDERS; om. H. ¹⁰ DERS; *est* suprascript in H. ¹¹...¹¹ aDHRS (*operationibus* in aDH); *machinandis operacionibus* E. ¹² aDHRS; *ergo* E. ¹³ DRS; *regione* aEH. ¹⁴ aR; *Geuisseorum* DES; *Geuuisseorum* H. ¹⁵ R; *Galabes* aDEHS (with *fons Galabes in regione Geuuisseorum* in margin in D). ¹⁶ aHR; *erat* DES. ¹⁷ aDEHR; *omnia* S. ¹⁸...¹⁸ aHR; *sibi prediceret* DES. ¹⁹ DHR; *inquid* a; om. ES. ²⁰ EHRS; *mysteria* aD. ²¹ aDERS; *ad* H. ²² ERS; *iactantiam* aDH. ²³...²³ aDERS; om. H. ²⁴...²⁴ aDERS; om. H. ²⁵ aHR; *statuenda* DES. ²⁶ DR; *tanquam* aEHS. ²⁷ ER; *inquid* aDHS. ²⁸ aDEHS; *Corea* R. ²⁹ HS; *Gygantum* aDE; *Gigancium* R. ³⁰...³⁰ aHR; *est tibi* DES. ³¹ aH; *Killario* DES (with *Kyllarao* in margin of D); *Killamo* R. ³² ERS; *Hibernie* aD; *Ybernie* H. ³³ aDEHS (corrected from *enim* in a); *enim* R. ³⁴...³⁴ aHRS; *et artem subnectaret* DE (but with *et* deleted from D). ³⁵ HRS; *importabiles* aDE. ³⁶ DERS (with *mathematica* in margin of D); *mechania* aH. ³⁷ aDHRS; *si* suprascript in E. ³⁸ aHR; *eodem* DES.

[129] Ad [1]uerba hec[1] solutus Aurelius in risum cum aliis qui aderant ait [2]nequaquam intelligere se[2] posse qualiter id fieret ut tam grandes et inconpositi[3] lapides ex tam longinquo ueherentur, acsi Britannia[4] lapidibus careret qui ad operacionem[5] sufficerent. Tunc Merlinus: 'Ne mouearis,[6] rex, super hiis[7] que dixi neque falsum[8] existimes quia[9] mistici[10] sunt lapides illi[11] de quibus [12]nobis sermo est[12] et ad diuersa medicamenta salubres. Gygantes[13] [14]asportauerunt olim eos[14] ex ultimis finibus Affrice et posuerunt illic dum Hyberniam[15] inhabitarent. Erat autem causa ut balnea infra[16] eos conficerent [17]ad usus[17] hominum salubres.[18] Lauati enim[19] lapides et[20] infra balnea ea aqua diffusa[21] multorum generum[22] infirmitates curabat,[23] dum balnearentur egroti. Mixta cum herbarum succis uulnera[24] quelibet sanabat.[25] Non est ibi[26] lapis qui[27] medicamento careat.'[28] Cum igitur hec audissent[29] [30]qui aderant Britones,[30] hortati sunt pro lapidibus mittere. Eligitur ergo Utherpendragon[31] frater regis ad id negocium,[32] licet ipse ultro se ingereret, ut regnum uidelicet[33] Hybernie[34] uideret et populum. Eligitur et ipse Merlinus cuius ingenio et auxilio agenda[35] tractentur. Parato itaque nauigio cum .xv.[36] milibus armatorum Hyberniam[37] adeunt ac prosperis uelis litora[38] intrant.

[130] Ea tempestate regnabat in Hybernia[1] Gyllomanius[2] rex. Qui cum audisset Britones[3] applicuisse in terra sua, collecto exercitu perrexit[4] obuiam eis. Et cum didicisset causam aduentus eorum, astantibus risit et ait: 'Non est mirandum si ignauam[5] gentem Britonum[6] Saxones

§129 [1...1] aDEHR; *hec uerba* S. [2...2] R; *se nequaquam intelligere* aH; *nequaquam se intelligere* DES. [3] R; *incompositi* aEHS; *tam incompositi* D. [4] DERS; *Brittannia* aH. [5] ERS; *operationem* aDH. [6] aDERS; *moueris* H. [7] DERS; *his* a; *is* H. [8] aHR; *fictum* DES. [9] aDHR; *quibus* E; om. S. [10] aEHRS; *mystici* D. [11] aH; *isti* DES; om. R. [12...12] aR; *nobis est sermo* DES; *sermo nobis est* H. [13] DR; *Gigantes* aEHS. [14...14] R; *olim asportauerunt eos* aH; *eos asportauerunt olim* DS; *eos asportauerunt* E. [15] DES; *Hiberniam* a; *Yberniam* HR. [16] aEHRS; *inter* D. [17...17] aDEHS; *aduersus* R. [18] aHR; *salubria* DES. [19] aDEHR; *uero* S. [20] aHR; om. DES. [21] DERS; *effusa* aH. [22] aHR; om. DES. [23] aHR; *curabant* DES. [24] aDEHS; *wlnera* R. [25] aHR; *curabant* DES. [26] aDERS; om. H. [27] aDEHS; *que* R. [28] aDEHR; *caret* S. [29] aDEHR; *audiisent* S. [30...30] DERS; *Brittones* aH. [31] aDHRS; *Utherpendr'* E. [32] DERS; *negotium* aH. [33] aDES; om. HR. [34] DERS; *Hibernie* a; *Ybernie* H. [35] aDEHS; om. R. [36] aDERS; *.xii.* H. [37] DES; *Hiberniam* aR; *Yberniam* H. [38] DERS; *littora* aH.

§130 [1] DERS; *Hibernia* a; *Ybernia* H. [2] R; *Gillomanius* a; *Gillomanus* DES (with *Gillomonius* in margin in D); *Gillomannus* H. [3] DERS; *Brittones* aH. [4] aDEHR; *perexit* S. [5] aDEHS (with *ignaram* in margin of D); *ignauem* R. [6] DERS; *Brittonum* aH.

deuastare potuerunt, cum Britones[7] bruti sint[8] et fatui. Quis enim[9] [10]fatuitatem eorum satis ammirari posset?[10] Numquid[11] meliora sunt saxa Hybernie[12] quam Britannie[13] ad quodlibet opus? Armate uos, uiri, et defendite patriam uestram ab ignauis et brutis animalibus, quia[14] dum [15]uita michi[15] inerit[16] non [17]auferent etiam minimum lapillum[17] Choree.' Uther igitur[18] ut uidit[19] illos[20] ad preliandum uenire[21] paratos, agmen suorum[22] dirigit in illos. Nec mora preualuerunt Britones.[23] Hyberniensibusque[24] laceratis atque[25] deuictis regem suum Gylloma-nium[26] in fugam coegerunt. Potiti uictoria Killaraum[27] montem adeunt duce Merlino lapidumque structuram secundum quod coniector eorum Merlinus edixerat reperiunt.[28] Circumstantibus itaque cunctis ait Mer-linus: 'Utimini[29] uiribus uestris quantum potestis[30] et uideamus si lapides istos integros deponere ualueritis.' Quod cum fecissent, nullo modo potuerunt saxa mouere uel minimum lapillum excidere. Defi-cientibus igitur cunctis [31]solutus in risum [32]Merlinus ait:[32] 'Ut sciatis animi ingenium [33]preualere fortitudini corporis,[33] [31] ecce lapidum hec structura, que [34]uestris uiribus[34] non cessit, leuius quam credi potest nostris iam[35] machinacionibus[36] deponetur.' Et paulisper insusurrans motu labiorum[37] tamquam[38] ad oracionem[39] precepit ut adhiberent[40] manus et asportarent quo uellent. Depositis itaque mox lapidibus ad naues leuiter delatos intus locauerunt et sic cum gaudio et ammira-cione[41] in Britanniam[42] reuertuntur. Rex autem Aurelius eorum congra-tulans reditui ex diuersis regni sui[43] partibus iussit clerum et populum conuenire[44] ut [45]tantorum uirorum celebracionem honore summo[45]

---

7 DERS; *Brittones* aH. 8 DEH; *sunt* aS; *sunt* altered to *sint* in R. 9 aDEHR; *uero* S. 10...10 R; *eorum fatuitatem satis admirari posset* a; *eorum satis admirari possit fatuitatem* DES; *eorum fatuitatem satis admirari possit* H. 11 HRS; *Nunquid* a; *Numquid enim* DE. 12 DERS; *Hibernie* a; *Ybernie* H. 13 DERS; *Brittannie* aH. 14 aDERS; *quod* H. 15...15 aHR; *michi uita* DES. 16 aDEHR; *fuerit* S. 17...17 aDER; *auferetur etiam minimus lapidum* H; *auferent uel minimum lapillum* S. 18 aDEHS; *ergo* R. 19 aDEHR; *uidet* S. 20 aDEHR; *eos* S. 21 aHR; om. DES. 22 aHR; *suum* DES. 23 DERS; *Brittones* aH. 24 DE; *Hibernensibusque* a; *Yberniensibusque* H; *Hybernien-sisque* R; *Hyberniencibus* S. 25 aEHRS; *et destructis atque* D. 26 R; *Gillomanium* a; *Gillomanum* DES; *Gillomannum* H. 27 aDEHR; *Kyllaraum* S. 28 DEHR; *repperiunt* a; *repereunt* S. 29 aEHRS; *Utamini* D. 30 DERS; *poterant* H. 31...31 aDERS; om. H. 32...32 aR; *ait Merlinus* DES; om. H. 33...33 aR; *fortitudini corporis preualere* DES; om. H. 34...34 aHR; *uiribus uestris* DES. 35 aDEHS; *autem* R. 36 ERS; *machinationibus* aDH. 37 aDERS; *labiorum suorum* H. 38 R; *tanquam* aDEHS. 39 ER; *orationem* aDHS. 40 aDERS; *adiberent* H. 41 R; *ammiratione* aH; *admiratione* D; *admiracione* ES. 42 DERS; *Brittanniam* aH. 43 DERS; om. aH. 44 aDEHS; *conuenirent* R. 45...45 aHR (*celebrationem* in aH); *honore summo tantorum uirorum celebracionem* DES.

perficeret.[46] Ad edictum ergo eius conueniunt pontifices et clerus populusque innumerabilis in monte[47] Ambrii. Et die[48] penthecostes[49] rex imposito capiti[50] dyademate[51] festum regaliter [52]tribus diebus ibidem[52] celebrauit functique epulis cum gaudio et exultacione[53] ymno-rum[54] omnes affuerunt. Quarta autem die honores ecclesiasticos qui personis carebant secundum auctoritatem canonicam distribuit. Ebora-censi ecclesie, que pastore carebat, Sampsonem,[55] [56]illustrem et[56] religiosum uirum, metropolitanum prefecit. Urbem uero Legionum et eius ecclesiam Dubricio[57] nichilominus prudenti[58] uiro decorauit. Statutisque regni legibus atque omnibus que in tanta celebracione[59] constituenda erant patratis compositis[60] lapidibus a Merlino in sepultu-ram et circa Choream sicut [61]in Hibernia prius fuerant[61] dimissa concione[62] omnes cum leticia redierunt ad propria.

[131] Eodem tempore Pascencius[1] Uortigerni[2] filius qui in Germaniam[3] diffugerat congregato undecumque exercitu nauigioque[4] comparato[5] applicuit in aquilonaribus[6] Britannie[7] partibus atque eas uastare cepit. Sed [8]rex Aurelius[8] ut audiuit, collecto exercitu ei obuiam uenit et commissa pugna deuictus Pascencius[9] fugit.

[132] Nec ultra ausus est redire in Germaniam sed cum paucis ad Gyllomanium[1] [2]Hybernie regem[2] se contulit.[3] Et cum infortunium suum ei notificasset, miseratus Gyllomanius[4] promisit se[5] laturum auxilium conquerens de iniuria Britonum[6] qui nuper Choream Gygan-

---

[46] aDR; *proficeret* ES; *perficerent* H. [47] aDERS; *montem* H. [48] aDEHS; *dies* R. [49] R; *pentecostes* aDEHS. [50] aEHRS; *capiti suo* D. [51] DERS; *diademate* aH. [52...52] aR; *ibidem tribus diebus* DEHS. [53] DERS; *exultatione* aH. [54] aDHR; *hymnorum* ES. [55] DRS; *Samsonem* aE; *Sansonem* H. [56...56] DERS (*illustrem* corrected from *illustri* in R); om. aH. [57] aEHRS; *Dubritio* D. [58] aDHRS; *prudenci* E. [59] ES; *celebratione* aDH; *religione celebracione* R. [60] aHR; *compositisque* DES. [61...61] aHR (*Ybernia* in H); *prius fuerant in Hybernia* DES (*Hibernia* in D). [62] R; *contione* aDEHS (corrected from *contentione* in S).

§131 [1] R; *Pascentius* aDEHS. [2] aH; *Uortig'* DES; *Uortigrini* R. [3] aDERS; *Germania* H. [4] DERS; *nauigio* H. [5] EHRS; *parato* D. [6] aRS; *aquilonalibus* DEH. [7] DERS; *Brittannie* aH. [8...8] DERS; *Aurelius rex* aH. [9] R; *Pascentius* DEHS.

§132 [1] R; *Gillomanium* a; *Gillomnaum* DES; *Gillomannum* H. [2...2] R; *regem* aH; *regem Hibernie* D; *regem Hybernie* ES. [3] aEHRS; *transtulit* D. [4] R; *Gillomanius* a; *Gillomanus* DES; *Gillomannus* H. [5] aDEHR; *ei* S. [6] DERS; *Brittonum* aH.

tum[7] de Hybernia[8] asportauerant. Federe itaque inter se facto naues ingrediuntur cum suo exercitu et ad Meneuiam urbem applicuerunt. Interea [9]rex Aurelius[9] Wintonie[10] infirmatus lecto decubuit. Qui audiens Pascencium[11] et Hybernienses[12] applicuisse[13] misit [14]Uther fratrem suum[14] cum exercitu ualido in Kambriam contra illos ut de regno suo disturbaret.[15] Et dum iter faceret, exercitum congregando moram fecit in itinere quod longum erat et ualde laboriosum. Accedens[16] interim unus ex Saxonibus nomine Eappa[17] qui linguam Britonum[18] edidicerat[19] ad Pascencium[20] ait se regem Aurelium cito perempturum si sibi darentur argenti [21]mille libre.[21] Pactus est ei[22] Pascencius[23] quod petebat et amplius si regni dyadema per eum acquireret.[24] Ille [25]promissis ditatus[25] iter uersus Wintoniam[26] arripuit, ubi regem Aurelium infirmatum audierat esse.[27] [28]Obiter minister[28] fraudis se dolo armauit; nam ueste monachi se induit atque corona capud[29] falso coronauit sicque Wintoniam[30] ueniens ad thalamum regis accessit et se[31] [32]medicum finxit. Quo intromisso promisit statim infra breue tempus regi salutem si sibi se[33] [32] committere uellet. Omnes qui aderant congratulati[34] sunt et magnam ei pecunie[35] mercedem[36] promiserunt si dictis facta compensaret. Nec mora pocionem[37] temperans uenenatam regi bibendam porrexit. Qua hausta iussus[38] est a nequissimo ambrone[39] sabanis cooperiri[40] et[41] obdormire.[42] Paruit ille atque obdormiuit sperans salutem[43] optatam consequi posse. At priusquam[44] nox incumberet, ueneno intra uiscera grassante periit. Medicus autem dolosus ab oculis omnium lapsus[45] euasit[46] atque per fugam uite reseruatur.

[7] aDR; *Gigantum* EHS. [8] aERS; *Hibernia* D; *Ybernia* H. [9...9] aDERS; *Aurelius rex* H. [10] aDHR; *Wyntonie* ES. [11] ER; *Pascentium* aDHS. [12] ERS; *Hibernienses* aD; *Ybernienses* H. [13] aHR; *aduenisse* DES. [14...14] aH; *Utherp' fratrem suum* DE; *fratrem suum Utherpendragon* R; *post Uther fratrem suum* S. [15] aDHRS; *disturbarent* E. [16] aDEHS; *Excedens* R. [17] aDEHRS (with *Cappa* in margin of D). [18] DERS; *Brittonum* aH. [19] EHRS (corrected from *edicerat* in H); *didicerat* D. [20] ER; *Pascentium* aDHS. [21...21] DERS; *libre mille* H. [22] HR; om. DES. [23] R; *Pascentius* DEHS. [24] R; *adquireret* DEHS. [25...25] DEHS; *ditatus promissis* R. [26] DHRS; *Wyntoniam* E. [27] DERS; om. H. [28...28] R; *Ob iter iniustum* DES (with *iniustum* underpointed and *minister* in margin in D); *Ille minister mortis* H. [29] HRS; *caput* DE. [30] DRS; *Wyntoniam* E; *Uuintoniam* H. [31] DERS; *sese* H. [32...32] DERS; om. H. [33] DER; om. S (& H). [34] RS; *gratulati* DE; *gtulati* H. [35] DEHR; *pecuniam* S. [36] DERS; *partem* H. [37] ES; *potionem* DH; *poticionem* R. [38] DEHS; *iussum* R. [39] DERS; *abrone* H. [40] DEHS; *cooperti* R. [41] HR; *atque* DES. [42] DEHS; *obdormiuit* R. [43] aDHRS; om. E. [44] HR; *postquam* DES (with *priusquam* in margin of D). [45] EHRS; *elapsus* D. [46] DEHRS (corrected from *euadit* in R).

[133] Hec dum Wintonie[1] agerentur, apparuit stella mire magnitudinis et claritatis, quam[2] [3]cometam dicunt,[3] uno[4] contenta radio. A radio uero procedebat globus igneus in similitudinem draconis [5]extensus, de cuius ore procedebant duo[6] radii: quorum unus radiorum longitudinem[5] ultra Gallicana [7]regna uidebatur[7] extendere; alter uero[8] uersus[9] Hybernicum[10] mare uergens in .vii. minores radios terminabatur. Apparente itaque[11] tali sydere perculsi[12] sunt omnes metu et admiracione[13] qui uiderunt.[14] Uther igitur conuocans Merlinum ad radium stelle interrogat[15] uatem[16] quid [17]portendat tale[17] signum. Mox ille in fletum erumpens spiritu [18]cepit deficere[18] pre dolore cordis. Reuersus postea in se exclamauit[19] et dicit:[20] 'O dampnum irrecuperabile! O populum orbatum Britannie[21] defuncto Aurelio nobilissimo rege!' Uther[22] audiens fratris mortem tristis factus est ualde[23] et fleuit amare. Merlinus autem dolorem eius delinire cupiens[24] prosecutus ait: 'Festina, dux nobilissime, festina hostes presentes deuincere; nam tibi debetur [25]dominium tocius[25] Britannie.[26] Uictoria [27]de hiis tibi[27] parata[28] est et multas [29]tibi post hos[29] subdes naciones.[30] Te etenim sydus[31] istud signat[32] et igneus draco sub sydere.[33] Radius autem[34] qui uersus Gallicanam plagam porrigitur filium tibi futurum portendit potentissimum, cuius potestas usque ad montes Alpium protendetur. Alter uero[35] radius filiam designat[36] nascituram cuius filii et nepotes regnum Britannie[37] succedenter habebunt.'

§133 [1] aDHRS; *Wyntonie* E. [2] aDEHS; *quod* R. [3...3] DERS; *dicunt* a; *dicunt plyadem* H. [4] aDEHS; *una* R. [5...5] aDEHR; om. S. [6] aDER; *.ii.* H; om. S. [7...7] DERS; *uidebatur regna* aH. [8] DRS; om. EH. [9] EHRS; om. (with *uersus* in margin) D. [10] ERS; *Hibernicum* aD; *Ybernicum* H. [11] aDEHS; *autem* R. [12] aHR; *percussi* DES. [13] ERS; *ammiratione* a; *admiratione* D; *amiratione* H. [14] aDEHS; *uiderit* R. [15] DHRS; *interrogabat* E. [16] DERS; om. H. [17...17] HR; *tale portenderet* DES. [18...18] DEHS; *deficere cepit* R. [19] DEHRS (corrected from *exclamat* in H). [20] DHRS; *dixit* E. [21] DERS; *Brittannie* H. [22] aDEHRS (with *autem* in margin in D). [23] aDEHS; om. R. [24] aHR; *uolens* DES. [25...25] ES; *dominium totius* DH; *tocius dominium* R. [26] DERS; *Brittannie* H. [27...27] DERS; *tibi de his* H. [28] HRS; *patrata* DE (with *parata* in margin of D). [29...29] HR; *post hos* (with *tibi* in margin) D; *post hos tibi* ES. [30] ERS; *nationes* DH. [31] aDER; *sidus* HS. [32] DHR; *significat* aES. [33] aDER; *sidere* HS. [34] DERS; *uero* aH. [35] DERS; *autem* aH. [36] DERS; *significat* aH. [37] DERS; *Brittannie* aH.

[134] Uther igitur nocte illa in castris quiescens aurora illucescente[1] [2]exercitum legionibus ordinatis[2] in hostes producit. Illi econtra copias suas [3]obuiam educunt[3] atque inuicem congrediuntur. Gladiis extractis cominus[4] res agitur consertoque[5] prelio Uther interfectis Gyllomanio[6] et Pascencio[7] triumpho potitur ut ueritas coniectoris probaretur. Fugientibus igitur barbaris ad naues magna [8]de eis strages[8] antequam ad naues peruenirent a Britonibus[9] facta est et innumeri trucidati sunt. Dux itaque uictor retro iter agens obuios habuit nuncios[10] qui fratris casum indicauerunt[11] ipsumque iam ab episcopis sepultum iuxta cenobium Ambrii in Chorea Gygantum[12] cum ceteris terre ducibus qui ibidem, sicut dictum[13] est, sepulti fuerant. Ita[14] enim rex [15]uiuens adhuc[15] se sepeliri iusserat.

[135] Ueniens ergo[1] Uther Wintoniam[2] conuocato clero et populo omnibus expetentibus[3] et acclamantibus illum[4] regem fieri suscepit dyadema[5] regni Britannie[6] et in regem sublimatus[7] est. Reminiscens autem [8]interpretacionis Merlini quam de sydere[9] fecerat iussit fabricari duos dracones ex auro purissimo[8] et unum in [10]ecclesia episcopali[10] Wintonie[11] obtulit;[12] alterum[13] sibi ad ferendum[14] in[15] prelia[16] retinuit. Ab illo ergo tempore[17] appellatus est Utherpendragon, hoc est Britannice[18] 'capud[19] draconis', sicut Merlinus eum [20]per draconem in regem[20] prophetauerat.[21]

[136] Interea Octa[1] filius Hengisti[2] et Eosa cognatus suus, cum soluti essent a federe quod [3]Aurelio pepigerant,[3] moliti sunt inquietudinem[4]

§134 [1] DES; *illuscente* HR. [2...2] HR; *legionibus ordinatis exercitum* DES. [3...3] HR; *producunt* DES. [4] DHS; *comminus* E; *quo* deleted before *cominus* in R. [5] DEHS; *confectoque* R. [6] R; *Gillomanio* a; *Gillomano* DES; *Gillomanno* H. [7] R; *Pascentio* DEHS. [8...8] DEHS; *strages de eis* R. [9] DERS; *Brittonibus* H. [10] DERS; *nuntios* H. [11] HR; *nunciauerunt* DES. [12] DR; *Gigantum* EHS. [13] aHR; *predictum* DES. [14] aHR; *Ibi* DES. [15...15] aR; *adhuc uiuens* DEHS.

§135 [1] aDEHS; *igitur* R. [2] aDHRS; *Wyntoniam* E. [3] aH; *petentibus* DES; *expectantibus* R. [4] aHR; *ipsum* DES. [5] DERS; *diadema* aH. [6] DERS; *Brittannie* aH. [7] DR; *sullimatus* aEHS. [8...8] aDERS; om. H. [9] aDER; om. H; *sidere* S. [10...10] aDEHS; *episcopali ecclesia* R. [11] aDHRS; *Wyntonie* E. [12] DR; *optulit* aEHS. [13] aHR; *et alterum* DES. [14] aDERS; *deferendum* H. [15] aDEHR; *ad* S. [16] aDERS; *prelio* H. [17] aHRS; *ipse* DE. [18] DERS (with *latine* in margin in D); *Brittannice* aH. [19] DRS; *caput* aEH. [20...20] aHR; *in regem per draconem* DES. [21] aDHRS; *interpretauerat* E.

§136 [1] aDEHS; *Hocca* R. [2] aHR; *Heng'* DES. [3...3] aHR; *pepigerant Aurelio* DES. [4] aDHRS; *iniquitatem* E.

toti regno Britannie[5] inferre,[6] associantes sibi Saxones quos Pascencius[7] secum adduxerat, nunciosque[8] suos in Germaniam mittunt ut sibi auxilia inuitarent. Maxima itaque multitudine stipati omnes prouincias ab Albania usque Eboracum occupant ipsamque[9] urbem Eboracum[10] obsidione uallant. Superueniens autem [11]rex Uther[11] cum exercitu grandi obsidioni, congrediuntur [12]Britones Saxonibus;[12] [13]quibus uiriliter primo impetu restiterunt Saxones[13] atque eorum irrupciones[14] tolerantes[15] tandem illos in fugam propulerunt.[16] Saxones autem insecuti[17] sunt eos cedentes usque ad montem Damen[18] dum sol diem stare permitteret. Erat autem mons ille arduus in cacumine, coriletum habens circa radicem, in cacumine [19]saxa prerupta[19] latebris ferarum habilia. Ascendentes uero montem Britones[20] pro castris se munierunt in[21] coriletis et rupibus et nocte ibidem quieuerunt. A media autem nocte excitati conuenerunt[22] simul ut consilium caperent qualiter hostes inuaderent. Commiserunt igitur[23] omnes Gorloi[24] duci Cornubie sententiam tractandam, qui et ipse consilii magni erat atque etatis mature. 'Non [25]est opus,'[25] inquid,[26] 'ambagibus uanis[27] aut magnis circumlocucionibus.[28] Dum adhuc noctis umbra inuoluimur, utendum [29]est nobis[29] audacia et fortitudine: necessitas hec belli non habet legem ut turmis dispositis et aciebus pugnemus. Quoquo modo liberemus animas nostras et precemur Deum[30] omnipotentem, quem forte peccando offendimus, ut liberet nos ab imminentibus[31] aduersariis qui et ipsi [32]inimici sunt[32] Dei uiui, ydolorum[33] cultores. Confitentes itaque peccata nostra et emendacionem[34] promittentes descendamus [35]ad eos quiete et sine strepitu armorum[35] et circumueniamus illos[36] inopinate

---

[5] DERS; *Brittannie* H. [6] aDEHR; om. S. [7] R; *Pascentius* aDEHS. [8] DERS; *nunciosque* aH. [9] aR; *ipsam* DEHS. [10] H; *Eboracam* a; *Eboraicam* D; *Eboricam* E; *Eboraycum* R; om. S. [11...11] R; *rex Utherpendragon* a; *Uther rex* DES; *Uther* H. [12...12] aHR (*Brittones* in aH); *Saxonibus Britones* DES. [13...13] aDERS; *sed Saxones primo impetu uiriliter restiterunt* H. [14] ER; *irruptiones* aDHS. [15] aDHRS; *tollerantes* E. [16] DEHS; *compulerunt* a; *protulerunt* R. [17] aDERS; *insequti* H. [18] DERS; *Danien* a; *Clamen* (?) H. [19...19] aDEHS; *prerupta saxa* R. [20] DERS; *Brittones* aH. [21] aDEHS; *et* R. [22] aDEHS; *uenerunt* R. [23] aEHRS; *ergo* D. [24] aDES; *Gorloy* HR. [25...25] DERS; *opus est* aH. [26] RS; *inquit* aDE; om. H (with *Qui ait* suprascript before *Non opus est*). [27] aDHRS; *nanis* (with *uanis* in margin) E. [28] ES; *circumlocutionibus* aDH; *circumlocutacionibus* R. [29...29] R; *nobis est* aH; *est* DES. [30] aDERS; *Deum patrem* H. [31] aDHRS; *iminentibus* E. [32...32] aDEHS; *sunt inimici* R. [33] ER; *idolorum* aHS; *et ydolorum* D. [34] ERS; *emendationem* aDH. [35...35] R; *quiete et sine armorum strepitu ad eos* aH; *quiete et sine strepitu armorum ad eos* DES. [36] aHR; *eos* DES.

nichil[37] tale de nobis timentes; fugatis enim nobis[38] et uelud[39] obsessis securiores dormiunt expectantes ut in luce nos comprehendant. Paretur ergo unusquisque nostrum cicius[40] [41]et siqua sarcina est hic dimittatur[41] ut [42]postpositis omnibus tantum pro uita et libertate[42] solliciti simus. Iam si fortiter[43] egerimus, uictoria in [44]manibus nostris[44] [45]sita est;[45] nam si Deus pro nobis, quis contra nos?' Placuit[46] regi simulque christianis omnibus qui [47]aderant Britonibus[47] consilium Gorlois[48] et unanimiter se inuicem cohortantes inuadunt[49] hostes [50]sompno oppressos;[50] feriunt precordialiter, [51]obtruncant, uulnerant et[51] illidunt[52] et tamquam[53] leones [54]in armenta[54] seuiunt et fugam hesternam uindicant. Hostes uero attoniti nec arma capescere[55] neque de loco [56]cedere aliquo pacto[56] poterant. Sic Britones[57] [58]cedentes omni nisu[58] instabant.[59] Quotquot euasere[60] [61]periculum fugiendo[61] noctis beneficio computauerunt. Captiui retenti sunt Octa[62] et Eosa duces eorum et Saxones [63]per uirtutem Iesu Christi[63] penitus dissipati.

[137] Post hanc uictoriam animatus[1] rex ulterius [2]progressus est[2] uersus Scociam[3] uenitque ad urbem Alclud illique prouincie disposuit[4] et pacem ubique renouauit. Circuiuit etiam omnem Scotorum[5] regionem rebellemque populum a sua feritate deposuit, tantam ubique[6] iusticiam cum terrore et moderacione[7] [8]agens quantam alter ante se nemo fecerat. Denique pacificatis omnibus Londoniam reuersus est Octa et[8] Eosa [9]pre se[9] in uinculis mancipatis; quos in carcerem[10] trudi precepit donec

---

[37] aEHRS; *nil* D. [38] DERS; om. aH. [39] aDRS; *uelut* EH. [40] R; *ocius* a; *honus* (with *ocius* in margin) D; *onus* ES; *otius* H. [41...41] aDEHS; om. R. [42...42] aHR; *tantum pro uita et libertate omnibus postpositis* DES. [43] aDERS; *forte* H. [44...44] R; *manus nostra* a; *manus nostras* DEHS. [45...45] aEHRS; *est sita* D. [46] aDEHR; *Placuitque* S. [47...47] R; *aderant baronibus* aH; *aderant* DES. [48] aDES; *Gorloys* H; *ad* deleted before *Gorlois* in R. [49] DEHS; *inuadent* R. [50...50] DERS; *oppressos sompno* H. [51...51] DHR (*wlnerant* in R); *uulnerant obtruncant et* E; *obtruncant obiugulant lacerant et* S. [52] DEHS; *illudunt* R. [53] DRS; *tanquam* E; om. H. [54...54] DER (corrected from *in armata* in D); *inarmati* (altered to *inanimati*) H; *in armata* (with *hostes* suprascript) S. [55] RS; *capesere* aDEH. [56...56] HR; *aliquo pacto recedere* D; *aliquo pacto cedere* ES. [57] DERS; *Brittones* H. [58...58] H; *omni nisu cedentes* DES; *cedentes omni uisu* R. [59] DEHS; *uastabant* R. [60] DEHS; *euadere* R. [61...61] DERS; *fugiendo periculum* H. [62] aDEHS; *Hocca* R. [63...63] R; *per uirtutem Christi Iesu* aH; erasure in D; *per uirtutem Christi* ES.

§137 [1] aHR; *animatus est* DES. [2...2] aHR; *progredi* DES. [3] ERS; *Scotiam* aDH. [4] aDERS; *disponit* H. [5] DER; *Scothorum* aS; *Scottorum* H. [6] aDERS; *hic* H. [7] ERS; *moderatione* aDH. [8...8] aDERS; om. H. [9...9] aDEHS; *posse* R. [10] S; *carcere* aDER; *carce* H.

adiudicaret quod[11] supplicium de eis sumeret. Festo igitur paschali superueniente [12]ibidem rex[12] suscepto dyademate[13] cum magno sumptuum[14] apparatu sicut[15] decebat diem pasche ascitis omnibus [16]regni proceribus[16] cum suis uxoribus et familiis celebrauit. Suscepit eos rex cum summo[17] honore et epulati sunt cum [18]magna leticia[18] et exultacione[19] regi congratulantes quod cum tanto honore eos inuitasset. Sed[20] quia in conuiuiis [21]tetra solet[21] esse libido insidiatrix et inimica[22] leticie,[23] nequaquam preterire uoluit hostis humani generis quin huic interesset conuiuio.[24] Aderat namque inter ceteras Gorlois[25] ducis Cornubie uxor nomine Igerna[26] cuius pulcritudo omnes Britannie[27] mulieres superabat. Quam cum ex aduerso [28]respexisset rex tamquam Dauid[28] in Bersabee,[29] subito Sathana mediante incaluit et postpositis omnibus curam amoris sui totam in eam uertit atque fercula multimoda sibi gratulando dirigebat,[30] aurea quoque pocula [31]familiaribus internunciis cum salutacionibus iocundis,[31] sicut assolet inter amantes[32] fieri, quandoque clam, quandoque palam mittebat. Quod cum marito compertum esset, – quis enim ignem[33] celare potest, presertim flamma estuante? – statim de curia absque regis licencia[34] iratus abscedens Cornubiam petit atque uxorem a conspectibus[35] regis subtraxit: quam super omnia diligebat Gorlois.[36] Iratus itaque rex [37]misit post eum[37] precipiens redire ut de illata [38]iniuria sibi[38] satisfaceret. Ille uero renuens iter suum peregit quo tendebat. Indignatus itaque rex iureiurando asseruit se [39]in illum omni nisu[39] animaduersurum et in omnem terram suam nisi ad prestitutam[40] diem rediret et satisfaceret de iniuria et [41]constituit diem.[41] Transacto igitur die [42]collecto exercitu[42] [43]insecutus est[43] iniurias ducis sui atque Cornubiam ferro ac flammis uastare

[11] aDEHS; *quid* R. [12...12] aEHRS; om. (from text), added in margin in D. [13] DERS; *diademate* aH. [14] aDEHR; *sumptu et* S. [15] aR; *sicud* DEHS. [16...16] aHR; *proceribus regni* DES. [17] aEHRS; *magno* D. [18...18] R; *summa leticia* a; *gaudio magno* DES; *leticia magna* H. [19] ERS; *exultatione* aDH. [20] aDHRS; *Set* E. [21...21] DERS; *solet* a; *solet persepe* H. [22] aDEHS; *inunica* (?) R. [23] aDEHRS (corrected from *leticia* in R). [24] aDEHS; *conuiuia* R. [25] aDERS; *Gorloys* H. [26] aERS; *Ygerna* DH. [27] DERS; *Brittannie* aH. [28...28] aDERS (*tanquam* in aDES); *aspexisset tamquam Dauid rex* H. [29] aDEHS (with *Bersaben* in margin of D); *Bertabee* R. [30] aDEHR; *derigebat* S. [31...31] aHR (*internuntiis* in aH; *salutationibus* in H); *cum salutacionibus iocundis familiaribus internunciis* DES. [32] aHR; *amatores* DES. [33] aDEHR; om. S. [34] ERS; *licentia* aDH. [35] aHR; *conspectu* DES. [36] aDERS; *Gorloys* H. [37...37] aDRS; *post eum misit* EH. [38...38] aDEHS; *sibi iniuria* R. [39...39] aHR; *omni nisu in ipsum* DES. [40] aR; *presentem* DES (with *prestitutam* in margin of D); *prestitutum* H. [41...41] aHR; *diem constituit* DES. [42...42] aHR; *exercitu collecto* DES. [43...43] aR; *insequitur* DES; *insequtus est* H.

contendit. At Gorlois[44] nullam habens copiam resistendi castrum quoddam muniuit ubi se cum ualida manu suorum inclusit[45] et uxorem suam,[46] pro qua magis timebat,[47] in oppido[48] Tintagol[49] super litus maris sito et undique uallibus preruptis ac mari circumsepto [50]cum custodibus reclusit.[50] Adueniens igitur rex castro quo erat Gorlois[51] undique obsedit eum ita ut a nulla parte posset ei prouenire auxilium. Considerat[52] namque Gorlois[53] ut ab[54] Hybernia,[55] si necesse foret, subsidium haberet sicut[56] per legatos suos quos illuc direxerat [57]rex ille[57] pepigerat. Cumque per ebdomadam unam [58]iam obsidio[58] durasset, rex Uther de amore Igerne[59] pro qua totum certamen erat reminiscens uocauit ad se quendam[60] fidelem et sibi familiarem, Ulfin[61] nomine de Ridcaradoch,[62] et reuelauit ei affectum et amorem suum,[63] dicens: 'Uror[64] nimis amore Igerne[65] [66]uxoris huius ducis[66] quem obsedimus[67] nec corporis mei aut uite periculum euadere existimo nisi ea potitus fuero. Tu igitur adhibe[68] diligenciam,[69] sicut[70] me amas,[71] ut ea fruar aut scias me [72]diu sustinere[72] non posse quin mortis periculum incurram.' Ad hec[73] Ulfin:[74] 'Nemo, mi domine, [75]tibi melius consilium dare[75] ualet ex omnibus qui terram tuam incolunt quam Merlinus uates; qui si operam dederit, poteris compos esse desiderii tui.' Credulus ille iussit[76] Merlinum ad se uenire:[77] nam et ipse cum ceteris ad obsidionem uenerat. Et expositis [78]angustiarum causis[78] mox regem alacriorem reddidit, inquiens: 'Ut pociaris,[79] rex, desiderio tuo necesse est nouis artibus[80] uti: nam castrum quo Igerna[81] quam diligis retinetur[82] adeo fortis munimenti est loci situ[83] ut nullus introitus pateat alter quam

---

[44] aDERS; *Gorloys* H. [45] aHR; om. DES (with *inclusit* in margin of D). [46] aHR; om. DES. [47] aHR; *timebat inclusit scilicet* DES. [48] aHR; *opido* DES. [49] aR; *Tyndageol* D; *Tindageol* E; *Tyntagol* H; *Tintageol* S. [50...50] aHR; om. DES. [51] aDERS; *Gorloys* H. [52] aR; *Considerauerat* DES; *Considerabat* H. [53] aDERS; *Gorloys* H. [54] aDERS; *ad* H. [55] DER; *Hibernia* aS; *Yberniam* H. [56] aR; *sicud* DEHS. [57...57] aDER; *rex illi* H; *ille rex* S. [58...58] aH; *obsidium iam* D; *obsidio iam* ES; *iam obsidium* R. [59] aES; *Ygerne* DH; *Igrine* R. [60] DEHS; *quamdam* a; *quidam* R. [61] aHR; *Ulphyn* D; *Ulphin* ES. [62] aDRS; *Ridcaradech* E; *Ridkaradoc* H. [63] aDEHS; om. R. [64] aDEHS; *Uxor* R. [65] aES; *Ygerna* DH; *Igrine* R. [66...66] R; *huius ducis uxoris* aH; *uxoris istius ducis* DES. [67] aEHRS; *obsidemus* D. [68] aDERS; *adibe* H. [69] ERS; *diligentiam* aDH. [70] aR; *sicud* DEHS. [71] aHR; *diligis* DES. [72...72] DERS; *sustinere diu* aH. [73] aDEHR; *hoc* S. [74] aHR; *Ulphyn* D; *Ulphin* ES. [75...75] aH; *melius tibi dare consilium* DES; *tibi melius dare* R. [76] aHR; om. DES. [77] aDHR (with *iubet* in margin of D); *uenire iussit* E; *uenire fecit* S. [78...78] DES; *cordis angustiis* H; *causarum angustiis* R. [79] ERS; *potiaris* aDH. [80] aDEHRS (corrected from *legibus* in H). [81] aES; *Ygerna* DH; *Ingrina* R. [82] aHR; *continetur* DES. [83] aDERS; *situs* H.

[84]angusta rupes que a tribus armatis prohiberi potest toti exercitui tuo. Uerum quia in hac necessitate[84] meum queris consilium et auxilium, studebo quantum potero ut arte mea uoluntatem tuam expleas. Noui medicaminibus meis mutare hominum figuras ita ut per omnia is[85] uideatur [86]similis esse[86] cuius formam arte magica inpressero.[87] Si ergo parere uis, actibus[88] meis faciam te [89]per omnia similem[89] Gorlois[90] ut nichil differas ab eo uel[91] [92]facie uel incessu[92] eroque tecum quasi unus ex famulis Gorlois[93] transmutatus; Ulfin[94] quoque in Iordanum familiarem illius[95] transformabo[96] sicque tuto [97]poteris adire[97] oppidum[98] Tintagol[99] atque aditum habere.'[100] Paruit[101] itaque rex dictis et actibus Merlini commissaque familiaribus suis obsidione crepusculo ingressus est castrum Tintagol[102] tamquam[103] esset Gorlois[104] receptusque[105] gratanter ab Igerna[106] post oscula desiderata collocatus est una in cubili[107] atque desiderio suo satisfecit. Concepit eadem nocte Igerna[108] celeberimum[109] illum Arthurum[110] qui postquam adultus est [111]probitate sua[111] [112]toto orbe[112] enituit.

[138] Interea dum compertum esset in obsidione[1] regem abesse, exercitus inconsulte agens oppidum[2] adit;[3] muros inuadit et[4] machinas muro[5] apponere aggreditur.[6] Dux obsessus uidens se suosque nimis interius artari[7] atque grandinem telorum desuper iactari prouocatus ad bellum agmine ordinato exiuit et se hostibus parua manu[8] inseruit. Qui mox hostili multitudine circumuentus confossus[9] cecidit et pars

---

84...84 aDERS; om. H. 85 DEHR; his a; hiis S. 86...86 R; similis eius aDES; esse et similis H. 87 aHRS; impressero DE. 88 aEHRS; artibus D. 89...89 DERS; similem per omnia aH. 90 aDERS; Gorloys H. 91 aDEHR; in S. 92...92 DERS; incessu uel facie aH. 93 aDERS; Gorloys H. 94 aHR; Ulphyn D; Ulphin ES. 95 aHR; eius DES. 96 aEHRS; transmutabo D. 97...97 aEHRS; adire poteris D. 98 HR; om. a; opidum DES. 99 aHR; Tyndageol D; Tindageol E; Tintageol S. 100 aHR; adire DES (with habere in margin of D). 101 aDEHS; Parauit R. 102 R; Tyndageol D; Tindageol E; Tyntagol H; Tintageol S. 103 R; tanquam DEHS. 104 R; Gorl' DES (with -ois in margin in S); Gorloys H. 105 DEHR; Receptus est S. 106 ES; Ygerna DH; Igrina R. 107 DERS; cubiculo H. 108 aES; Ygerna DH; Igrina R. 109 R; celeberrimum aDEH; celleberimum S. 110 R; Arturum aDEHS. 111...111 aH; om. DES; proceritate sua R. 112...112 aHRS; toti orbi D; toto orbi E.

§138 1 aDEHS; obsidionem R. 2 aHR; opidum DES. 3 DER; adit aHS. 4 aHR; atque DES. 5 aHR; muris DES. 6 aHR (altered from ingreditur in R); congreditur DES. 7 EHRS; arctari aD. 8 HR; manu suorum DES. 9 aDEHS; confessus R.

quedam suorum secum; pars autem dissipata in fugam se dedit. Capto itaque oppido[10] festinauerunt nuncii ad Igernam[11] qui et necem ducis[12] et obsidionis euentum[13] indicarent. Sed cum regem [14]in specie Gorlois iuxta illam[14] sedere uidissent, erubescentes ammirabantur[15] ipsum quem in obsidione interfectum[16] didicerant ita incolumem preuenisse. Uther autem rex[17] tales deridens rumigerulos tamquam[18] mendaces dicebat: 'Non equidem me[19] ut mortuum dolere debetis, sed uiuum,[20] sicut[21] nunc[22] cernitis, congaudete; neque enim omni rumori credendum est. Doleo tamen oppidi[23] mei capcionem[24] et meorum interfectionem: unde timendum est ne superueniat rex et nos inopinatos[25] hic intercipiat. Ibo igitur obuiam ei et pacificabo me si potero cum ipso ne deterius quid contingat.' [26]Amplexans itaque[26] Igernam[27] atque deosculans deliniensque egressus uenit ad exercitum, exuta specie et forma Gorlois[28] quam susceperat. Cumque rei euentum [29]didicisset, de morte ducis sui[29] subtristem se simulans, de Igerna[30] a maritali copula soluta non modicum gaudens, reuersus ad oppidum[31] Tintagol[32] cepit illud et Igernam[33] simul uotoque suo potitus est. Nuptiis[34] igitur legittime[35] atque magnifice celebratis commanserunt pariter[36] rex et [37]regina Igerna.[37] [38]Partusque tempore[38] genuit [39]illum Arthurum[39] famosum. Deinde concipiens peperit filiam nomine Annam.

[139] Cumque dies multi et tempora preterissent, occupauit infirmitas regem eumque pluribus diebus uexauit. Interim custodes carceris qui Octam[1] et Eosam[2] reclusos[3] seruabant[4] tedio[5] affecti atque[6] promissio-

---

10 HR; *opido* DES. 11 aES; *Ygernam* DH; *Igrinam* R. 12 aDEHS; *ducum* R. 13 aEHR; *aduentum* (in text) with *euentum* in margin D; *o* deleted before *euentum* in S. 14...14 HR (*Gorloys* in H); *in specie Gorlois illam* (altered to *illuc*) a; *iuxta illam in specie Gorlois* DES. 15 aEHRS; *admirabantur* D. 16 DEHR; *interfici* S. 17 DERS; om. H. 18 R; *tanquam* aDEHS. 19 aDERS; *est* H. 20 aHR; *uiuo* DES. 21 aEHRS; *ut* D. 22 aDERS; om. H. 23 aHR; *opidi* DES. 24 ER; *captionem* aDHS. 25 aDEHS; *inoppinatos* R. 26...26 aR; *Amplexansque* DES; *Amplexatus itaque* H. 27 aES; *Ygernam* DH; *Igrinam* R. 28 aDERS; *Gorloys* H. 29...29 aHR; *de morte ducis sui didicisset* DES. 30 aES; *Ygerna* DH; *Igrina* R. 31 aHR; *opidum* DES. 32 aR; *Tyndageol* D; *Tintageol* E; *Tyntagol* H; *Tintageol* S. 33 aES; *Ygerna* DH; *Igrina* R. 34 aDHRS; *Nupciis* E. 35 aDERS; *legitime* H. 36 aEHRS; *simul* D. 37...37 a; *Ygerna regina* DH; *Igerna regina* ES; *regina Igrina* R. 38...38 aDEHR; *Partus est* S. 39...39 R; *Arturum illum* aH; *illum Arturum* DES.

§139 1 DEHS; *Octa* a; *Occa* R. 2 DEHS; *Eosa* aR. 3 aHR; *inclusos* DES. 4 aDEHS; *reseruabant* R. 5 aDERS; *atque tedio* H. 6 aDERS; *et* H.

nibus illorum[7] illecti[8] in Germaniam cum eis diffugium fecerunt. Deinde minis et terroribus totam Britanniam[9] perculerunt. Uenientes itaque in terram suam classem parauerunt non modicam atque cum magna armatorum manu [10]redierunt quantocius[11] in Albaniam ingressique[12] regionem ferro ac flammis uastabant[13] terram.[14] Eligitur[10] itaque [15]dux Leil nomine[15] de Lodonesia,[16] cui rex Annam[17] filiam suam[18] locauerat nupciali[19] thalamo, eique committitur exercitus Britonum[20] contra hostes deducendus regnique curam suscepit dum rex infirmitate teneretur. Hic in hostes progressus sepe ab eis repulsus,[21] sepe superior factus ad naues usque diffugere coegit.[22]

[140] Fuitque inter eos diu[1] anceps bellum donec[2] rex Uther audita suorum segnicia[3] ipse feretro impositus se ad exercitum deportari[4] fecit.

[141] Perductus itaque Uerolamium ad urbem, in qua Saxones se receperant propter eius aduentum quem timebant, obsedit urbem et[1] menia [2]cum machinis[2] diruere cepit. Quod cum uidissent Saxones et se uiliter[3] inclusos sensissent, egredientes diluculo de ciuitate ad campestre prelium Britones[4] prouocauerunt. Nec mora deuictis Saxonibus cessit uictoria Britonibus[5] et Octa[6] et Eosa[7] ibidem obtruncantur. Unde in tantam leticiam rex Uther emersit[8] ut feretro prosiliens nil sibi doloris [9]de infirmitate contestans[9] in risum solutus tamquam[10] sanus ac[11] ualidus factus suos exhylarabat[12] atque [13]insequi Saxones[13] fugientes accelerabat,[14] nisi hoc sui dissuasissent ne eum infirmitas grauior[15] occuparet.

[7] aHR; *eorum* DES. [8] aHR; *allecti* DES. [9] DERS; *Brittanniam* aH. 10...10 aDERS; om. H. [11] aR; *quam citius* D; *quam cicius* ES; om. H. [12] aDER; om. H; *Ingressi* S. [13] aDES; om. H; *uastabunt* R. [14] aR; *eam* DES; om. H. 15...15 HR; *dux Lot nomine* a; *Leil nomine dux* DES. [16] aDERS; *Lundonesia* H. [17] DERS; om. aH. [18] aDEHR; om. S. [19] ER; *nuptiali* aDHS. [20] DERS; *Brittonum* aH. [21] HR; *expulsus* DES. [22] DEHS; *cogebat* R.

§140 (entire First-Variant chapter absent from a) [1] DERS; om. H. [2] DHRS; *dum* E. [3] ERS; *segnicie* D; *segnitia* H. [4] RS; *deportare* DEH.

§141 [1] HR; *atque* DES. 2...2 DERS; om. H. [3] aEHRS; *uiriliter* D. [4] DERS; *Brittones* aH. [5] DERS; *Brittonibus* aH. [6] aDEHS; *Occa* R. [7] aDEHRS (tampered in R?). [8] aDEHS; *emersitur* R. 9...9 aDEHS; *contestans de infirmitate* R. [10] DR; *tanquam* EHS. [11] DHRS; *et* H. [12] R; *exhilarauit* DE; *exilarauit* H; *exhylarauit* S. 13...13 DERS; *Saxones insequi* H. [14] ER; *adcelerabat* DH; *accelerasset* S. [15] HR; om. DES (with *grauior* in margin of D).

[142] Dimisso ergo[1] exercitu ipse remansit [2]cum paucis Uerolamium[2] indulgens quieti et corporis refectioni. Sed nec sic[3] deuicti et[4] fugati Saxones ab iniquitate [5]et malicia sua[5] cessauerunt. Quod enim armis et iure belli exercere[6] non poterant, hoc ueneficiis et prodicione[7] pessima agere machinati sunt. Mittunt ergo in [8]paupere cultu[8] quosdam maleficos[9] Uerolamium qui, cum didicissent [10]regem adhuc[10] egrotare nec perfecte conualuisse, explorantes aditum quo ad ipsum pertingerent interficiendum, non inuenientes deliberauerunt apud se ut [11]quoquo modo[11] illum ueneno extinguerent. Et cum morati essent ibidem aliquamdiu, didicerunt quia[12] de fonte nitidissimo qui prope aulam fluebat solitus esset rex cottidie[13] potare. Quo comperto[14] inficiunt fontem ueneno[15] et abeuntes rei euentum expectabant.[16] Ut autem gustauit rex aquam, [17]festine mortuus est[17] ut ueritas Merlini coniectoris et eius uaticinium compleretur. Multi etiam[18] [19]de fonte illo potantes[19] perierunt donec comperta[20] malicia[21] tumulum[22] terre superapposuerunt.[23] Delatum est autem[24] corpus regis[25] ad cenobium Ambrii et ibi traditum sepulture iuxta Aurelium fratrem suum et[26] infra Choream Gygantum.[27]

[143] Conuenientes[1] igitur [2]post mortem regis optimates tocius terre[2] in ciuitatem[3] Silcestrie Dubricio[4] Urbis[5] Legionum archiepiscopo suggerente Arthurum[6] filium eius in regem consecrauerunt.[7] Et[8] erat tunc Arthurus[9] .xv. annorum iuuenis, magne uirtutis[10] et audacie atque

§142 [1] aDER; *igitur* HS. [2...2] aDEHS; *Uerolamium cum paucis* R. [3] aDERS; *sic* suprascript in H. [4] aHR; *atque* DES. [5...5] aDERS; *sua et malitia* H. [6] aDEHS; *excitare* R. [7] ERS; *proditione* aDH. [8...8] aDEHS; *cultu paupere* R. [9] EHR; *malificos* aDS. [10...10] aDEHS; *adhuc regem* R. [11...11] aDES; *quomodo* H; *quando* R. [12] aEHRS; *quod* D. [13] R; *cotidie* aDEHS. [14] aDERS; *conperto* H. [15] aDEHRS (corrected from *uenoeno* in R). [16] aDEHR; *exspectabant* S. [17...17] aR; *mortuus est festine* DES; *festine motus est* H. [18] DERS; *autem* aH. [19...19] aDEHS; *potantes de fonte illo* R. [20] aDERS; *conperta* H. [21] aDERS (corrected from *malia* in a); *malitia* H. [22] aEHR; *cumulum* DS. [23] aDERS (corrected from *superappasuerunt* in a; and from *super posuerunt* in E); *super opposuerunt* H. [24] DERS; om. H. [25] HR; *eius* DES. [26] DEHS; om. R. [27] DHR; *Gigantum* ES. After *Gygantum*, *Explicit liber octauus* [.viii. H]. *Incipit nonus* HR (rubric also present in a), followed by *De Arturo* in H.

§143 [1] aDHRS;<C>onuenientes E. [2...2] aHR (*totius* in a); *optimates totius terre post mortem regis* DES (*tocius* in E). [3] DERS; *ciuitate* aH. [4] EHRS; *Dubritio* aD. [5] aDEHS; *Urbs* R. [6] R; *Arturum* aDEHS. [7] aHR; *sublimauerunt* D; *sullimauerunt* ES. [8] aHR; om. DES. [9] R; *Arturus* aDEHS. [10] aDEHS; om. R.

largitatis: unde populo [11]ac principibus tocius regni[11] gratus et acceptus erat. Insignibus itaque[12] regiis iniciatus mox Saxones inuadere decreuit[13] per quos et pater et patruus eius dolo perierant, per quos etiam tota terra turbata[14] erat. Congregato igitur exercitu Eboracum uenit. Colgrinus autem, qui post Octam[15] et Eosam Saxones regebat, ut audiuit quia[16] nouus rex Britonum[17] surrexerat, cum graui multitudine Saxonum suorum et Scotorum[18] et Pictorum obuiam Arthuro[19] uenit et iuxta flumen Duglas[20] congressi, utrorumque exercitus in magna parte cecidit, uictoria tandem Britonibus[21] fauente et Colgrino dedecorose fugiente; quem insequens Arthurus[22] festino pede infra Eboracum ingressum[23] obsedit. Baldulfus[24] frater [25]Colgrini audita fratris fuga cum .vi. milibus uirorum Eboracum[26] petit[27] atque in spacio .x. miliariorum[28] [25] ab urbe in nemore delituit, uolens nocturnam et inopinatam irruptionem[29] obsidioni inferre. Erat autem tunc [30]ipse Baldulfus[30] quando frater pugnauerat expectans[31] aduentum Cheldrici[32] ducis[33] Germanorum iuxta maritima; qui in auxilium eorum uenturus erat. At Arthurus[34] a metatoribus[35] premunitus quod in nemore delitescerent Saxones misso Cadore[36] duce Cornubie cum [37].vi. centis[37] militibus[38] et tribus milibus peditum, eadem nocte superuenientes[39] hostibus maiorem partem[40] interfecerunt et Baldulfum[41] in fugam coegerunt. Qui cum suos amisisset et de auxilio quod fratri ferre sperauerat [42]se frustratum[42] uidisset, anxius quid faceret uel quomodo aut quo aditu ad [43]fratris colloquium[43] peruenire posset,[44] meditatus est apud se quod habitum[45] ioculatoris assumeret et capillis cum barba semirasis in castra

[11...11] aDERS (*totius* in aD); *totius regni ac principibus* H. [12] aDEHS; om. R. [13] EHRS (tampered in R); om. a; *decernit* D. [14] aDEHS; *turba* R. [15] aDEHS; *Occam* R. [16] aEHR; *quod* DS. [17] DERS; *Brittonum* aH. [18] DERS; *Scottorum* aH. [19] ER; *Arturo* aDHS. [20] DERS; *Dulgis* aH. [21] DERS; *Brittonibus* aH. [22] R; *Arturus* aDEHS. [23] aDEHRS (*ingressum* in margin in E). [24] aHR; *Baldulfus uero* DE; *Baldulphus uero* S. [25...25] aDERS; om. H. [26] aDER; om. S (& H). [27] aDES; om. H; *peciit* R. [28] aS (altered from *miliorum* in S); *miliorum* DE (with *miliarum* in margin of D); om. H; *miliarum* R. [29] aDHRS; *irrupcionem* E. [30...30] DER; *Baldulfus ipse* aH; *ipse Baldulphus* S. [31] aDEHR; *exspectans* S. [32] aDERS; *Childerici* H. [33] aHR; *regis* DES. [34] R; *Arturus* aDEHS. [35] aH; *metoribus* DES (with *metatoribus* in margin of D); *mecatoribus* (sic) R. [36] aDERS; *Kadore* H. [37] R; *secentis* a; *.dc.* DE (with *sexcentis* suprascript in D); *.vi.* H; om. (from text) with *sexcentis* in margin S. [38] DERS; *milibus* aH (with *militum* suprascript in H). [39] aDEHS; *superuenientis* R. [40] aHR; *partem eorum* DES. [41] aDEHR; *Baldulphum* S. [42...42] aHR; *frustratum se* DES (*frustatum* in E). [43...43] aDEHS; *colloquium fratris* R. [44] aDEHS; *potuisset* R. [45] aDEHS; *abitum* R.

cantitando cum[46] cythara[47] cepit deambulare et cytharistam[48] se finxit. Cumque nulli iam suspectus esset, accessit paulatim ad murum ciuitatis et agnitum se cum funibus infra[49] trahi fecit et cum germano [50]quod cupiebat[50] prolocutus est. Interea dum de[51] egressione et fuga despera-rent – circumuallati enim[52] undique obsidione fuerant – rumor innotuit[53] Cheldricum[54] cum .dc. nauibus in Albania applicuisse. Quod cum iam notum ac[55] diuulgatum [56]per omnes foret,[56] suaserunt[57] maiores natu in exercitu regi suo obsidionem dimittere ne tante multitudini impares[58] forte resistere non preualerent.[59]

[144] Paruit igitur rex Arthurus[1] seniorum[2] consilio et dimissa obsi-dione Londoniam[3] adiit. Ibi conuocato clero et populo querit consi-lium qualiter expugnare possit adueniencium[4] multitudinem barbaro-rum. Communi tandem assensu cognatos suos Britones[5] de Armorico tractu ad tante necessitatis auxilium ascire decreuerunt. Erat autem tunc temporis Britonum[6] illorum rex[7] Hoelus, filius sororis[8] Arthuri[9] ex Budicio[10] rege Armoricanorum[11] generatus. Unde audita necessitate fratrum nauigium parant collectisque .xv. milibus armatorum proximo uentorum flatu ac prospero Hamonis Portum intrant.

[145] Excepti[1] a rege Arthuro[2] sicut[3] decebat honorifice urbem Kaerliudcoit,[4] que Lindicolinia[5] [6]nostra lingua[6] dicitur, festinanter adeunt, que ab hostibus supramemoratis obsidebatur. Quo cum peruenissent, prelium ante urbem[7] mox commissum est;[8] in quo tanta cedes [9]Saxonum facta est[9] quanta nec antea nec postea [10]audita fuit.[10]

[46] aDEH; *in* R; om. S. [47] aDEH; *cythera* R; *cithara* S. [48] aDEHR (tampered in R); *cytharistam* S. [49] aHR; *intra* DES. [50]...[50] aDEHS; bis in R. [51] DS; om. aEHR. [52] aDEHRS (corrected from *eum* in R). [53] aDEH; *intonuit* RS. [54] aDES; *Chyldericum* H; *Celdricum* R. [55] aDHRS; *et* E. [56]...[56] aHR; *esset in omnibus* DES. [57] aDE; *dissuaserunt* HR; *ac suaserunt* S. [58] DER; *ui impares* a; *inpares* HS. [59] aHR; *ualerent* DES.

§144 [1] R; *Arturus* aDEHS. [2] aDEHS; *seniorum suorum* R. [3] aDERS; *Lundoniam* H. [4] ERS; *aduentantium* aDH. [5] DERS; *Brittones* aH. [6] DERS; *Brittonum* aH. [7] aDERS; *dux* H. [8] aDEHRS (with *Anne* in margin of D). [9] R; *Arturi* aDEHS. [10] aDEHS; *Bucio* R. [11] aDHRS; *Armoricorum* E.

§145 [1] aDEHS; *exceptique* R. [2] R; *Arturo* aDERS. [3] aR; *sicud* DEHS. [4] aDES (with *Kayrllwitchoyt* in margin of D); *Kaerluidcoit* H; *Kaerlindoit* R. [5] ER; *Lindicolina* a; *Lindicolnia* D; *Lindocolina* H; *Lindicollinia* S. [6]...[6] aDERS; *lingua nostra* H. [7] aDEHS; *urbes* R. [8] DES; om. aHR. [9]...[9] aDEHS; *facta est Saxonum* R. [10]...[10] aDEHS; *fuit audita* R.

Ceciderunt namque partim armis interfecti, partim fluminibus submersi fugientes relictaque[11] obsidione omnes pariter fugam arripiunt. Quos persequi non cessauerunt[12] Britones[13] usque dum uenirent[14] in siluam Colidonis.[15] Illuc ex fuga undique confluentes et suas cohortes reparantes silua tegente [16]resistere Britonibus temptant.[16] At Britones[17] circumfusi[18] partem silue cedentes egressum eis ea[19] parte prohibuerunt atque[20] tribus [21]diebus ibidem[21] obsidentes fame coactos dedicioni[22] coegerunt,[23] conuencione[24] taliter facta ut relictis armis et sarcinis et omnibus que habebant tantum cum[25] uita et nauibus in terram suam redire sinerentur. Pacti sunt[26] quoque [27]se tributum omni anno[27] de Germania daturos,[28] obsides plures transmittere fide eorum mediante.[29] Tunc rex Arthurus[30] sumpto festinanter consilio peticioni eorum acquieuit.[31]

[146] Cumque illi iam in altum[1] [2]sulcarent equora,[2] redeuntes in se piguit pactionis patrate [3]retortisque uelis redierunt in Britanniam atque[4] Totonesium intrant portum. Euntes[5] igitur in[3] terram, totam patriam illam[6] igne uastauerunt ex transuerso usque Sabrinum mare, depopulantes colonos et armis suis priuantes de quibus ipsos letiferis uulneribus[7] sauciabant. Inde arrepto[8] itinere uersus pagum Badonis urbem obsident et regionem dissipare[9] non cessant. Quod cum regi nunciatum[10] esset, qui adhuc Scotos[11] et Pictos expugnare[12] parabat, ammirans[13] perfidiam Saxonum de eorum obsidibus mox supplicium sumit et relictis Scotis[14] Saxones persequi festinat. Sed magno dolore cruciatur quod[15] Hoelum nepotem suum [16]post se[16] in ciuitate Aldclud[17]

[11] DEHR; *relicta* S. [12] aDHRS; *cessarunt* E. [13] DERS; *Brittones* aH. [14] DERS; *peruenirent* aH. [15] aE; *Calidonis* DRS; *Kolidonis* H. [16...16] aR (*Brittonibus* in a); *Britonibus temptat resistere* DES; *Brittonibus resistere temptant* H. [17] DERS; *Brittones* H. [18] DHRS; om. E. [19] DEHR; *a* S. [20] DEHS; *et* R. [21...21] HR; *ibidem diebus* DES. [22] ER; *deditioni* DH; *dicioni* S. [23] DERS; *uegerunt* H. [24] DERS; *conuentione* H. [25] aDEHS; *cura* R. [26] aDERS; om. H. [27...27] aDHR; *omni anno tributum* E; *se tributum omni amao* (sic) S. [28] aHR; *reddituros* DES. [29] aDEHRS (with *Et istum bellum dicitur Cad Coydkelydon* [cf. *Historia Brittonum*, §56] at foot of folio in D). [30] ER; *Arturus* aDHS. [31] aDR; *adquieuit* EHS.

§146 [1] aDERS; *altum* suprascript in H. [2...2] aDERS; *equora sulcarent* H. [3...3] aDERS; om. H. [4] aERS; *atque* underpointed in D; om. H. [5] a; *Exeuntes* DES; om. H; *Errantes* R. [6] aHR; om. DES (with *illam* suprascript in D). [7] aDEH; *wlneribus* RS. [8] aDEHS; *arepto* R. [9] aHR; *uastare* DES. [10] aDERS; *nuntiatum* H. [11] DERS; *Scottos* aH. [12] aDHRS; *expupnare* E. [13] EHRS; *admirans* aD. [14] DRS; *Scottis* aEH. [15] aDERS; *quia* H. [16...16] aDEHS; *posse* R. [17] DERS; *Alclud* a; *Aldud* H.

¹⁸dimittere morbo opressum¹⁸ coactus est accelerans obsidionem Saxonum dirimere. Quo cum peruenisset, ¹⁹armare militem iussit.¹⁹

[147] Ac seipsum armis suis muniuit loricam uestiens tanto rege[1] dignam, auream galeam simulacro draconis[2] insculptam capiti imponens, humeris clipeum[3] uocabulo Pridwen,[4] in quo sancte Marie ymago[5] impressa[6] sui memoriam dabat. Accinctusque[7] gladio nomine Caliburno,[8] in insula Auallonis, ut aiunt, mira arte fabricato, dexteram[9] muniuit lancea nomine Ron: hec erat rigida latoque ferro, hostium cladibus apta. Deinde dispositis[10] cateruis Saxones aggreditur expugnare. At[11] illi [12]sustinere non ualentes[12] eius impetum[13] proximum occupant montem[14] in quo tamquam[15] ex oppido[16] se defendunt. Arthuro[17] itaque [18]post eos montem uiriliter[18] ascendente atque suos magnanima uoce inclamante[19] montis cacumen post paululum[20] adeptus est atque dextra leuaque hostium phalanges strauit. Plusquam .cccc. tam ab Arthuro[21] quam a suis illo primo impetu[22] ceciderunt; inter quos Colgrinus et Baldulfus[23] interfecti sunt et cede peracta [24]multa milia[24] [25]ibi Saxonum[25] perierunt. Cheldricus[26] uix [27]per fugam elapsus[27] euasit atque[28] uersus naues suas redire conatur.

[148] Sed rex mittens Cadorem[1] ducem Cornubie [2]post eos cum .x. milibus equitum[2] persequi iussit, dum ipse rediens Albaniam[3] de

---

^{18...18} aDERS (*oppressum* in aD); *morbo oppressum dimittere* H. ^{19...19} R; *iussit armare militem* DES; *armare milites iussit* H.

§147 ¹ HRS; *regi* DE. ² DERS; om. H. ³ DEHS; *clipei* R. ⁴ DES; *Priduuen* H; *Priawen* R. ⁵ DHRS; *imago* E. ⁶ aDERS; *inpressa* H. ⁷ HR; *Accinctus est* aS; *Accinctusque est* DE. ⁸ aDS (with *Caledwlch* in margin of D) *Caleburno* E; *Kaliburno* H; *Caliburna* R. ⁹ R; *dexteram suam* a; *dextram* DEHS. ¹⁰ aHR; *expositis* DES. ¹¹ DEHS; *et* R. ^{12...12} R; *non ualentes sustinere* DES; *non sustinere ualentes* H. ¹³ DERS; *inpetum* H. ¹⁴ DEHRS (corrected from *mortem* in R). ¹⁵ R; *tanquam* DEHS. ¹⁶ HR; *opido* DES. ¹⁷ R; *Arturo* DEHS. ^{18...18} DERS; *uiriliter montem* H. ¹⁹ HR; *acclamante* DES. ²⁰ HS; *paulum* DE; *paulus* R. ²¹ R; *Arturo* DEHS. ²² DERS; *inpetu* H. ²³ DH; *Baldulphus* ERS. ^{24...24} DEHRS (with *.xv. milia* in margin of D). ^{25...25} HR; *Saxonum ibi* DES. ²⁶ aDE; *Cheldericus rex* H; *Celdricus* R; *et Cheldricus* S. ^{27...27} aR; *elapsus per fugam* DES; *per fugam* followed by suprascript *elapsus* H. ²⁸ aDHRS; *atque per fugam* E.

§148 ¹ aDES; *Kadorem* H; *Candorem* R. ^{2...2} aHR; *cum .x. milibus equitum post eos* DES (with *milibus* altered from *militum* and *equitum* in margin in E). ³ DERS; *in Albaniam* aH.

Scottis⁴ et Pictis triumpharet. ⁵Nunciatum enim⁵ ei fuerat illos⁶ in urbe Aldclud⁷ Hoelum nepotem suum obsedisse qui ibi, ut dictum est, remanserat infirmitate⁸ grauatus. Dux autem Cornubie cum .x.⁹ milibus Cheldricum¹⁰ insequens preterire illum uolens alia uia prior ad portum nauium descendit et naues manu armatorum pagensium Britonum¹¹ muniuit ne accessum, ¹²si uenirent, ad naues ulterius¹² haberent. Ipse uero hostibus ex aduerso obuians per montes et colles et nemora dispersos persequitur nec quieuit ¹³donec perempto¹³ Cheldrico¹⁴ cum multis aliis ceteros in dedicionem¹⁵ coegit.

[149] Peractis igitur pro uoto omnibus dux Cornubie post Arthurum¹ iter² arripiens uenit Aldclud³ quam rex ab⁴ obsidione barbarica iam liberauerat,⁵ nepote suo Hoelo sano recepto. ⁶Deinde duxerat⁶ exercitum⁷ ⁸Mireif ciuitatem⁸ Albanie, ubi audierat hostes se recepisse. Quo cum perueniret, deserentes⁹ municionem¹⁰ Scoti¹¹ et Picti ingressi sunt stagnum Lumonoy¹² atque insulas que infra stagnum¹³ erant¹⁴ occupauerunt refugium querentes. Hoc stagnum .lx. continebat¹⁵ insulas, .lx. flumina a montibus Albanie ¹⁶fluencia recipiens¹⁶ nec ex tot fluminibus de stagno labitur ¹⁷in mare¹⁷ preter¹⁸ unum. In insulis autem huius loci¹⁹ .lx. rupes feruntur²⁰ esse totidem ²¹aquilarum nidos²¹ continentes; que singulis annis conuenientes prodigium quod in regno futurum esset celso clamore communiter edito notificabant. Ubi dum predicti hostes presidio fruerentur, Arthurus²² collecto undique²³

---

⁴ EHR; *Scotis* aDS. ⁵...⁵ aR; *Nunciatum* DES (with *enim* in margin in D); *Nuntiatum* (with *enim* suprascript) H. ⁶ aR; *eos* DEHS. ⁷ aDER; *Alclud* HS. ⁸ aDERS; *in* deleted before *infirmitate* in H. ⁹ aDEHR; *decem* S. ¹⁰ aDES; *Chyldericum* H; *Celdricum* R. ¹¹ DERS; *Brittonum* aH. ¹²...¹² aHR; *ad naues si uenirent ultra* DES. ¹³...¹³ aDEHRS (partially in margin in D). ¹⁴ aDES; *Chylderico* H; *Celdrico* R. ¹⁵ ERS; *deditionem* aDH.

§149 ¹ R; *Arturum* aDEHS. ² aDEHS; *d* deleted before *iter* R. ³ DERS; *Alclud* aH. ⁴ aDES; *ab* suprascript in H; *ad* R. ⁵ aDERS; *deliberauerat* H. ⁶...⁶ aH; *Inde duxit* D; *Duxit inde* ES; *Duxerat deinde* R. ⁷ aDERS; *exercitum in* (suprascript) H. ⁸...⁸ aDERS; *ciuitatem Murielf* H. ⁹ DERS; om. aH. ¹⁰ ERS; *munitionem* aDH. ¹¹ DERS; *Scotti* aH. ¹² HR; *Lumonoi* aDES (with *Llumonii* in margin of D). ¹³ aHR; om. DES. ¹⁴ aDEHR; *erat* S. ¹⁵ aEHRS; *continet* D (with *continebat* in margin). ¹⁶...¹⁶ R; *fluentia recipiens* aH; *recipiens fluentia* D; *recipiens fluencia* ES. ¹⁷...¹⁷ ES; *in mari* aHR; om. D. ¹⁸ aEHRS; *nisi* D (with *preter* in margin). ¹⁹ DES; *laci* aHR. ²⁰ aDERS; *ma*-[fo 42r]*nifestum est* (from vulgate text), with *ma* over an erasure H (see Introduction, p. lxxxvii). From this point H's text is entirely vulgate. ²¹...²¹ aDES; *nidos aquilarum* R. ²² R; *Arturus* DES. ²³ R; *undecumque* DES.

nauigio per flumina nauigabilia stagnum intrat atque per .xv. dies eos
obsidendo tanta afflixit fame ut milia morerentur. Dumque [24]illos in
hunc modum[24] opprimeret, Gyllamurius[25] rex Hybernie[26] [27]cum magna
classe superuenit[27] ut eis auxilium ferret. Quo audito Arthurus[28]
dimissis[29] Scotis[30] ad Hybernienses[31] uertit[32] arma. Quos statim deuictos
ad naues fugere compulit et Hyberniam[33] redire. Postea rediens ad
stagnum quod dimiserat perseuerauit[34] Scotos[35] et Pictos infestare
donec episcopi omnes miserande patrie cum omni clero suo reliquias
sanctorum et cruces [36]in manibus ferentes[36] conuenerunt atque regem
nudis pedibus flexisque[37] genibus adeuntes pro se populoque suo nimis
afflicto misericordiam eius exorabant suppliciter ut saltem ecclesiis et
populo inbelli[38] misericordiam prestaret atque arma ab interfectione
[39]gentis misere[39] contineret, adicientes se satis penas luisse pro Saxonum
superbia quibus illi non consenserant nisi coacti: nunc permitteret[40]
eius generosa nobilitas portiunculam[41] gentis sue que remanserat in Dei
cultu[42] perseuerare, seruitutis iugum perpetue sub eius dominio ferre,
et uectigalia qualicumque federatos reddere. Commotus ergo rex
[43]pietate super afflictos[43] ueniam donauit atque expugnacionem[44] eorum
dimisit.

[150] Interim explorat[1] Hoelus situm prefati stagni ammiraturque[2] tot
flumina, tot insulas, tot rupes, tot aquilarum nidos numero adesse.
Cumque id mirum duceret, respondit ei rex magis esse mirandum aliud
stagnum quod in eadem prouincia haut[3] longe situm erat, longitudinem
et latitudinem eque[4] habens .xx. pedum, altitudinem .v.[5] pedum: in
quadrum sic siue hominum arte siue natura constitutum .iiii. genera
piscium infra quatuor[6] angulos continens[7] nec in aliqua partium[8] pisces
alterius partis reperiri.[9] Adiecit etiam aliud [10]stagnum esse[10] in partibus

24...24 aR; *in hunc modum eos* DES. 25 R; *Gillamurius* aDES. 26 RS; *Hibernie* aDE.
27...27 aDES; *superuenit cum magna classe* R. 28 R; *Arturus* aDES. 29 aDERS (corrected
from *dmissis* in E). 30 DRS; *Scottis* a; *Scoctis* E. 31 ERS; *Hibernienses* aD. 32 aR; *infert*
DES (with *uertit* in margin in D). 33 ERS; *Hiberniam* aD. 34 aDER; *perseuerat* S.
35 DRS; *Scottos* a; *Scoctos* E. 36...36 aR; *ferentes in manibus* DES. 37 aR; *flexis* DES
(with *-que* suprascript in D). 38 R; *imbelli* aDES. 39...39 aR; *misere gentis* DES.
40 aDES; *permittet* R. 41 aR; *porciunculam* DES. 42 aR; *cultum* DES. 43...43 aDS; *super
afflictos pietate* E; *pietate super afflictas* R. 44 ERS; *expugnationem* aD.

§150 1 aR; *exquirit* DES (with *explorat* in margin of D). 2 aRS; *admiraturque* DE.
3 aDES; *hau* R. 4 aR; *equo* DES. 5 aDER; *quinque* S. 6 RS; *.iiii.* aDE. 7 DES;
continentem aR. 8 aDRS; *parcium* E. 9 aR; *reperire* DES (with <*is*>*tud stagnum
dicitur* <*Fin*>*naun* Wrhelic [cf. *Historia Brittonum*, §70] in margin in D). 10...10 aR;
esse stagnum DES.

Gualliarum[11] prope Sabrinam quod pagenses terre Liliguan[12] apellant[13] quod, cum in ipsum mare refluctuat, recipitur in modum uoraginis sorbendoque fluctus nullatenus repletur ut riparum margines operiat. At dum mare decrescit, eructat adinstar montis aquas absortas quibus demum[14] ripas rigat et aspergit. Interim si gens patrie eius[15] facie uersa prope accederet, recepta in uestibus undarum aspergine uel uix uel numquam[16] elabi ualeret quin a stagno uoraretur. Tergo autem uerso non est irroracio[17] timenda etiamsi in ripis astaret.

[151] Hiis itaque gestis rex sonitu buccine sue[1] atque lituorum[2] toti exercitui signum donauit regressionis ad propria ueniensque Eboracum festum natalis Domini instantis ibidem celebrauit. Ubi[3] uisa sacrarum ecclesiarum desolacione[4] atque templorum semiustorum tociusque[5] urbis destructione a pagana gente facta[6] corde indoluit et de reparacione[7] ciuitatis et ecclesiarum cogitauit. Conuocato deinde clero et populo Pyramum[8] capellanum suum[9] sedi illi metropolitanum prefecit. Cui et ecclesiarum curam renouandarum[10] iniunxit. Uiros ac mulieres ciuitatis indigenas per Saxones in regiones longinquas expulsos[11] data[12] pace reuocauit, quos patriis honoribus restituit.

[152] Inter quos inuenti sunt tres fratres regali prosapia orti, Loth uidelicet atque Urianus et Anguselus,[1] qui antequam Saxones [2]in terra[2] preualuissent tocius[3] terre illius ab Albania usque Humbrum [4]principatum tenebant.[4] Hos igitur ut ceteros paterno affectu suscipiens reddidit[5] Anguselo[6] regiam potestatem Scotorum[7] fratemque suum Urianum sceptro Murefensium[8] insigniuit; Loth autem, qui tempore

---

[11] aR; *Walliarum* DE; *Gualiarum* S. [12] S; *Linliguram* a; *Lilingua* DE; *Linliguaei* R. [13] ERS; *appellant* aD. [14] aR; *deinde* DES. [15] aDES; *illius* R. [16] aDES; *numcquam* R. [17] R; *irroratio* a; *retractacio* (with *irroratio* in margin) D; *retractio* ES.

§151 [1] aR; om. DES. [2] aDER; *limorum* S. [3] aDES; *Ut* R. [4] ERS; *desolatione* aD. [5] ER; *totiusque* aD; *totius* S. [6] aDER; om. S. [7] ERS; *reparatione* aD. [8] DR; *Piramum* aES. [9] aDES; *sui* R. [10] aDES; *renouandorum* R. [11] DES; *expulsas* aR. [12] aDES; *dare* deleted before *data* in R.

§152 [1] RS; *Auguselus* aDE. [2]...[2] ERS; om. aD. [3] ERS; *totius* aD. [4]...[4] aDES; *principabant tenerent* R. [5] aDER; *reddit* S. [6] RS; *Auguselo* aDE. [7] DRS; *Scottorum* a; *Scoctorum* E. [8] aR; *Mireifensium* D; *Mirefensium* ES.

Aurelii sororem ipsius duxerat,[9] ex qua[10] Walwanum et Modredum genuerat, ad consulatum Lodonesie[11] ceterarumque prouinciarum que ei pertinebant remisit. Denique[12] cum in pristinam dignitatem reduxisset tocius[13] regni statum, Arthurus[14] ipse duxit uxorem nomine Guenhauerham[15] ex nobili genere Romanorum ortam, pulcram satis ac[16] decoram, in thalamis Cadoris[17] ducis Cornubie honeste educatam.

[153] Sequenti subinde estate classem parauit atque Hyberniam[1] adiuit ut eam dominio suo subiugaret. Applicanti ergo sibi Gyllamurius[2] rex predictus cum gente sua obuiam uenit quasi bello dimicaturus. Sed[3] cum preliari cepissent, gens eius nuda et inermis non ferens telorum grandinem a Britonibus missam lacerata fugit et per nemora dispersa latuit quo ei refugii patuit locus. Nec mora captus est Gyllamurius[4] et regi Arthuro[5] adductus. Qui mox dedicioni[6] se tradens datis obsidibus[7] tributo ascripto suscepit Hybernie[8] regnum sub[9] Arthuro[10] possidendum. Subiugatis itaque [11]Hybernie partibus[11] in Hyslandiam[12] direxit nauigium atque eam [13]similiter populo debellato[13] subiugauit. Interea diuulgato rumore per ceteras insulas quod ei nemo in armis coequari uel resistere posset, Doldauius[14] rex Gothlandie[15] et Gunuasius rex Orchadum[16] ultro uenere[17] ad eum precauentes eius expugnacionem[18] superatis hostibus dampnosam promissoque uectigali et facta subiectione obsidibusque[19] datis quisque ad terram suam abiit ab Arthuro[20] rege ulterius possidendam. Reuersus deinde[21] in Britanniam statum[22] regni .xii. [23]continuis annis[23] semper meliorando confirmauit.

[154] Tunc ex generosi [1]sui animi[1] consilio et prouidencia[2] inuitatis[3] quibusque ex longe positis regnis familiam suam cepit augmentare

[9] aERS; *duxerat* (with *Goear nomine* in margin in D; see Introduction, p. lxxxii). [10] aDES; *quo* R. [11] aDER; *Ladonesie* S. [12] aDR; *Deinde* ES. [13] ERS; *totius* aD. [14] R; *Arturus* aDES. [15] R; *Guenwaram* a; *Gwennuuaram* (with *Ganhumaram* in margin) D; *Gwennewaram* ES. [16] aR; *et* DES. [17] DES; *de* deleted before *Cadoris* in R.

§153 [1] ERS; *Hiberniam* aD. [2] S; *Gillamurius* aDE; *Gyllanurius* R. [3] aDRS; *Set* E. [4] R; *Gillamurius* aDES. [5] R; *Arturo* aDES. [6] ERS; *deditioni* aD. [7] aDES; *obsidionibus* R. [8] ERS; *Hibernie* aD. [9] aDRS; *ab* E. [10] R; *Arturo* aDES. [11]...[11] R; [b]*partibus* [a]*Hibernie* a; *partibus Hibernie* D; *partibus Hybernie* ES. [12] aR; *Hislandiam* DES. [13]...[13] R; *populo debellato similiter* a; *populo similiter debellato* DES. [14] aR; *Doldanius* DES. [15] DES; *Gollandie* a; *Gallandie* R. [16] R; *Orcadum* aDES. [17] aDER; *uenire* S. [18] ERS; *expugnationem* aD. [19] aDER; *obsidibus* S. [20] R; *Arturo* aDES. [21] aERS; *inde* D. [22] aDES; *statim* R. [23]...[23] aR; *annis continuis* DES.

§154 [1]...[1] aERS; *animi sui* D. [2] ERS; *prouidentia* aD. [3] aDES; *inuitans* R.

tantamque faceciam[4] in[5] curia sua habere ut emulacionem[6] eius longe lateque manentibus populis fama celebris incuteret. Unde inclitus quisque incitatus ad famam illius nichili pendebat seipsum nisi[7] armis et indumentis ad modum familie Arthuri[8] se ornaret. Fama quoque largitatis eius omnes terre principes superabat unde quibusdam amori, quibusdam timori erat, metuentes ne regna terrarum Europe probitate sua et donorum largitate sibi subiugaret. Arthurus[9] igitur de die in diem in melius proficiens hanc eandem sentenciam[10] et uoluntatem[11] quam timebant in animo iam conceperat ut scilicet extra Britanniam se et gentem suam dilataret et nomen suum cunctis gentibus manifestaret et exaltaret. Et primum quidem parato nauigio Norwegiam[12] adit[13] ut ibi Loth sororium suum regni dyademate inuestiret. Erat namque Sichelinus[14] rex Norwegie[15] nuper defunctus; cuius nepos iste Loth fuerat regnumque suum[16] eidem destinauerat.[17] At Noruuegenses[18] indignati quod alienigenam [19]regem sibi[19] ingereret,[20] quendam [21]nomine Riculfum[21] indigenam in regem iam erexerant munitisque[22] urbibus Arthuro[23] resistere parabant. Erat tunc Walwanus[24] filius Loth [25].xv. annorum fere[25] obsequio[26] Sulpicii pape ab auunculo traditus, a quo arma recipiens uir factus est strenuus et miles audacissimus. Arthurus[27] itaque[28] Norguegensi[29] [30]litore appulsus[30] eductis ad terram nauibus cepit patriam mox ferro et igne uastare atque colonos ferreis uinculis mancipare. Quo adueniens Riculfus rex cum suis, prelium commissum est grande atque ex utraque parte multi ceciderunt. Preualuerunt tandem Britones factoque congressu Riculfum cum multis pereme-runt.[31] Uictoria itaque potitus Arthurus[32] regnum Norguegie[33] sibi subiugauit et Loth regendum tradidit; Daciamque mox adiens dominio suo subegit.

---

[4] ES; *facetiamque* (omitting *tantamque*) a; *fascetiam* D; *facesciam* R. [5] aDRS; *in* suprascript in E. [6] ERS; *emulationem* aD. [7] aDES; *ut* R. [8] R; *Arturi* aDES. [9] R; *Arturus* aDES. [10] ERS; *sententiam* aD. [11] aDER; *nobilitatem* S. [12] aR; *Norguegiam* DES (corrected from *Norgueguegiam* in S). [13] aR; *adiit* DES. [14] aR; *Sicholinus* altered to *Sichelinus* (with *Sichelinus* in margin) D; *Sicholinus* ES. [15] aR; *Norguegie* DES. [16] aDER; *suumque* S. [17] aDRS; *festinauerat* E. [18] R; *Norwengenses* a; *Norguegenses* DES. [19]...[19] R; *sibi regem* a; *sibi in regem* DES. [20] aR; *erigerat* D; *erigeret* E; *exigeret* S. [21]...[21] aDE; *Riculfum nomine* R; *nomine Riculphum* S. [22] aDES; *muratis* R. [23] R; *Arturo* aDES. [24] aDER; *Waluuanus* S. [25]...[25] aR; *fere .xv. annorum* DES. [26] DES; *in obsequio* a; *obsequi* R. [27] R; *Arturus* aDES. [28] aDRS; *igitur* E. [29] DRS; *Norwengensi* a; *Norguigensi* E. [30]...[30] R; *littore appulsus* a; *appulsus litore* DES. [31] aDS; *perimerunt* ER. [32] R; *Arturus* aDES. [33] DES; *Norwegie* a; *Norguesie* R.

[155] Quibus subactis nauigauit ad Gallias et patriam infestare cepit. Erat tunc Gallia prouincia[1] Rome subdita sicut et cetera regna[2] tribunoque Frolloni commissa qui eam[3] sub Leone imperatore regebat. Qui cum aduentum Arthuri[4] [5]in Galliam comperisset,[5] collegit omnem [6]armatum militem[6] qui [7]potestati sue[7] parebat et cum Arthuro[8] preliatus mox primo[9] congressu confusus atque deuictus fuge se dedit. Quippe Arthurum[10] committabatur[11] omnis[12] electa iuuentus[13] terrarum et insularum quas subegerat preter priuatam familiam que de preelectis[14] [15]erat bellatoribus;[15] fauebatque ei pars maxima Gallicane[16] milicie[17] quam [18]sua munifica largicione[18] sibi obnoxiam fecerat.[19] At[20] Frollo fugiens Parisius cum paucis deuenit urbemque muniuit milite armato ac cibariis quantum potuit.[21] Sed Arthurus[22] festinato gradu insequens illum in ciuitate obsedit seditque cum toto exercitu ibidem fere[23] toto mense et sic ciuitatem undique uallauit milite ut nulla spes cibariorum [24]inclusis restaret.[24] Cumque Frollo populum fame dedicioni[25] coactum cerneret, malens se periculo opponi quam populum dedicioni misit nuncios regi Arthuro[26] ut ipse secum singulare certamen iniret et cui uictoria proueniret alterius [27]regnum et populum[27] optineret. Placuit Arthuro[28] illa[29] legacio[30] datoque ex utraque parte federe conuenerunt in insulam Secane fluminis preterfluentis, populo spectante a ciuitate et ab exercitu euentum rei. Ambo erant in armis decenter ornati super equos mire uelocitatis residentes nec erat promptum agnoscere cui triumphus proueniret. Ut ergo erectis hastis in [31]aduersis partibus[31] steterunt, subdentes equis calcaria inuicem se magnis[32] ictibus[33] percusserunt. Arturus uitato [34]Frollonis ictu[34] lanceam suam in summitate pectoris illius fixit et quantum haste longitudo fuit ipsum Frollonem in terram prostrauit. Extractoque mox ense festinabat eum ferire, cum[35]

§155 [1] R; *prouintia* a; om. DES. [2] aDES; *signa* R. [3] aDES; *ea* R. [4] R; *Arturi* aDES. [5]...[5] aR; *comperisset in Galliam* DES. [6]...[6] aR; *militem armatum* DES. [7]...[7] aR; *sue potestati* DES. [8] R; *Arturo* aDES. [9] aR; *ipso* DES. [10] R; *Arturum* aDES. [11] R; *comitabatur* aDES. [12] aDES; om. (but space left) R. [13] aDRS; om. E. [14] aDRS; *electis* E. [15]...[15] aR; *bellatoribus erat* DES. [16] aDES; *Gallicana* R. [17] ERS; *militie* aD. [18]...[18] R; *sua munifica largione* a; *sua largicione munifica* D; *sua minifica largicione* E; *munifica largicione* S. [19] aERS; *faceret* deleted before *fecerat* in D. [20] aDES; *atque* R. [21] aR; *poterat* DES. [22] R; *Arturus* aDES. [23] aDER; *fero* S. [24]...[24] aR; *restaret inclusis* DES. [25] ERS; *deditioni* aD. [26] R; *Arturo* aDES. [27]...[27] aERS; *populum et regnum* D. [28] R; *Arturo* DES. [29] R; *ista* DES. [30] ERS; *legatio* D. [31]...[31] aR; *aduersa parte* DES. [32] aDES; *magis* R. [33] aERS; *ictibus* suprascript in D. [34]...[34] aDES; *ictu Frollonis* R. [35] aDRS; *Tunc* E.

Frollo uelociter erectus pretensa lancea occurrit illatoque in pectore equi Arthuri[36] letali uulnere[37] utrumque ad terram ruere fecit. Britones ergo ut regem suum in terram prostratum uiderunt, attoniti timuerunt et uix retineri potuerunt quin federe rupto in Gallos unanimes irruerent;[38] et dum federis metas egredi meditarentur,[39] erectus est [40]ocius Arthurus[40] pretensoque clipeo imminentem[41] sibi Frollonem ense excepit. Instant igitur cominus;[42] [43]mutuos ictus ingeminant,[43] alter alterius neci insistens.[44] Denique Frollo reperto aditu percussit Arthurum[45] [46]super frontem in casside[46] atque collisione cassidis uulnus[47] ei inflixit. Manante ergo sanguine cum Arthurus[48] loricam et clipeum rubere uidisset, ira succensus est uehementi erectoque ense Caliburno[49] totis uiribus per galeam in capud[50] Frollonis impressit et in duas partes dissecuit.[51] Cecidit Frollo terram[52] calcaneis pulsans nec mora spiritum in auras emisit.[53] Occurrunt continuo ciues[54] apertisque portis ciuitatem Arthuro[55] tradiderunt. Qui deinde exercitum suum in duo diuisit committens[56] partem unam Hoelo duci ad expugnadum Guitardum[57] Pictauensium[58] ducem et partes Aquitannie.[59] Ipse uero cum reliqua parte exercitus ceteras Gallie prouincias[60] subiugandas suscepit. Hoelus ergo Acquitanniam[61] ingressus urbes et castra subegit Gwitardumque[62] pluribus preliis deuictum dedicioni[63] coegit;[64] [65]Guasconiam quoque[65] ferro et igne depopulans principes terre sibi[66] subiugauit. Emensis interim .ix. annis, cum tocius[67] Gallie partes potestati sue submisisset,[68] Arthurus[69] iterum Parisius uenit festum pasce[70] celebraturus conuocatoque[71] clero et populo statum regni pace et legibus confirmauit. Tunc familiarium[72] suorum fidele seruicium et laborem diuturnum recompensans[73] Beduero[74] pincerne suo[75] Neustriam, que nunc Normannia

[36] R; *Arturi* aDES. [37] aDES; *wlnere* R. [38] aDES; *ruerent* R. [39] aR; *meditauerunt* DE; *meditabantur* (tampered) S. [40]...[40] R; *Arturus otius* a; *otius Arturus* D; *ocius Arturus* ES. [41] aDR; *iminentem* ES. [42] DRS; *comminus* aE. [43]...[43] aR; *ictus ingeminant mutuos* DES. [44] aDRS; *instans* E. [45] R; *Arturum* aDES. [46]...[46] R; *in casside super frontem* DES. [47] DE; *wlnus* RS. [48] R; *Arturus* aDES. [49] aDRS; *Caleburno* E. [50] RS; *caput* aDE. [51] aDES; *desecuit* R. [52] aDES; *super* R. [53] aDES; altered from *misit* by suprascript *e* in R. [54] aDES; *et* deleted before *ciues* in R. [55] R; *Arturo* a; *ei* DES. [56] aDER; bis in S. [57] aRS; *Gwitardum* DE. [58] aDES; *Pictauiensium* R. [59] aDR; *Aquitanie* ES. [60] aDES; *partes* R. [61] R; *Aquitaniam* aE; *Aquitanniam* D; *Acquitaniam* S. [62] aDE (corrected from *Gwitatardumque* in a); *Guitardum* RS. [63] ERS; *deditioni* aD. [64] aDRS; *subegit* (with *uel coegit* in margin) E. [65]...[65] R *Gwasconiam quoque* a; *Guasconiamque* DE; *Guasconiam* S. [66] aR; om. DES. [67] ER; *totius* aDS. [68] aDER; *summisisset* S. [69] R; *Arturus* aDES. [70] aDER; *pascale* S. [71] DER; *conuocato* (partially in margin) a; *uocatoque* S. [72] aD; *familiarum* ERS. [73] aDES; *recompescens* underpointed before *recompensans* in R. [74] aER; *Bedwero* DS. [75] aDES; *suo uenusto* R.

dicitur, donauit Keyoque[76] dapifero[77] Andegauensem prouinciam; pluribus quoque secundum meritum et generis dignitatem[78] ceteros[79] largitus[80] est honores. Pacificatis itaque quibusque ciuitatibus et populis dispositisque omnibus incipiente uere in Britanniam reuersus est.

[156] Ubi, cum sollempnitas[1] penthecostes[2] adueniret, post tot triumphos Dei[3] permissione[4] sibi concessos[5] magna exestuans[6] leticia statuit festum magno conuentu cleri et populi regioque dyademate[7] sollempniter[8] decorare. Missis ergo nunciis per omnes regiones terrarum proximas inuitauit quotquot erant in potestate sua regulos et duces ac ceteros regnorum[9] proceres ad tantam sollempnitatem[10] celebrandam[11] consilioque suorum locum delegit in Urbe Legionum cetum tantum congregare, tum quia ciuitas illa agris fertilibus[12] et pratis siluisque undique uallata, tum quia palaciis regalibus pre ceteris Britannie ciuitatibus precellebat ita ut aureis tectorum fastigiis Romam orbis dominam imitaretur. Est enim [13]ciuitas hec[13] sita in Glamorcancio[14] territorio[15] super Oscam[16] fluuium non longe a Sabrino mari omnibus copiis habundans. Preterea duabus prefulgebat[17] ecclesiis: quarum una in honore beati Aaron sanctissimi confessoris fuerat dedicata atque canonicorum conuentu regulariter famulata tertiam sedem [18]metropolitanam Britannie[18] continebat; altera in honore Iulii martiris fundata uirgineo sanctimonialium choro fulgebat. Fuerat quoque tunc temporis ciuitas hec astrologorum atque omnium arcium[19] eruditorum celebris[20] qui diligenter cursus stellarum obseruantes futura ueris argumentis predicebant. Tot igitur stematibus atque diuiciarum[21] copiis urbs preclara festiuitati predicte disponitur. Nam et mare uicinum mercium diuersarum habundanciam[22] nauigio aduectans [23]dat deliciarum[23] incrementum. Uenerunt itaque ad [24]festum regis[24] celebrandum hii reges et

---

[76] R; *Kaio* a; *Keioque* DES. [77] aDER; *suo* suprascript after *dapifero* in S. [78] aDES; *d. dignitatem* R. [79] aDES; *ceteris* R. [80] aDERS (corrected from *largitatus* in R).

§156 [1] aDRS; *solempnitas* E. [2] R; *pentecostes* aDES. [3] aDES; *dicitur* R. [4] aR; *concessione* DS; *confessione* E. [5] aR; *permissos* DES. [6] aDERS (corrected from *exestunans* in S). [7] aDER; *diademate* S. [8] DRS; *solempniter* aE. [9] aR; *magnorum honorum* DES. [10] DRS; *solempnitatem* E. [11] aDES; *per* deleted before *celebrandam* in R. [12] aR; *fertilis* DES. [13...13] aDER; *hec ciuitas* S. [14] ES; *Glamorgantio* aD; *Glamorguncio* R. [15] aDER; *territoris* S. [16] R; *Hoscam* a; *Oscham* DES. [17] aDER; *fulgebat* (with *pre-* suprascript) S. [18...18] R; *Brittannie metropolitanam* a; *Britannie metropolitanam* DES. [19] ERS; *artium* aD. [20] aR; om. DES (with *celebris* in margin of D). [21] aERS; *diuitiarum* D. [22] ERS; *habundantiam* aD. [23...23] R; *dat delitiarum* a; *deliciarum dat* DES. [24...24] aERS; *regis festum* D.

149

duces subscripti: Anguselus[25] rex Albanie; Urianus rex Murefensium;[26] Caduallo[27] Lauith rex Uenedotorum; [28]Stather rex Demetorum, id est Suthgualensium;[28] Cador dux Cornubie. Uenerunt et nobilium ciuitatum consules: Morwid[29] consul Claudiocestrie; Mauron Wigorniensis; Anaraud[30] Salesberiensis; Archgal[31] Kaergueirensis,[32] que nunc Warewic[33] appellatur; Iugein[34] ex Legecestria;[35] Cursalem ex Kaicestria;[36] Kimmare[37] dux Dorobernie; Galluc[38] Silcestrie; Urbgenius[39] ex Badone; Ionathal Dorocestrensis; Boso[40] Ridochensis,[41] id est Oxinefordie.[42] Preterea conuenerunt magne dignitatis heroes multi quos longum est enumerare uel nominare. Ex collateralibus insulis Gyllamurius[43] rex Hybernie;[44] [45]Maluasius rex Hislandie;[45] Doldauius[46] rex Gothlandie; Gunuasius[47] rex Orchadum;[48] Loth rex[49] Norguegie; Aschillus rex Dacorum; Holdinus dux Rutenorum;[50] Leodegarius consul Bolonie;[51] Beduerus[52] dux Neustrie; Borellus Cenomannensis;[53] Keyus[54] dux[55] Andegauensis; Guitardus[56] Pictauensis; .xii.[57] quoque pares Galliarum quos Gerinus Carnotensis secum adduxit; Hoelus dux Armoricanorum[58] Britonum cum heroibus sibi subditis qui tanto apparatu [59]et fastu[59] ornamentorum, mularum et equorum[60] incedebant quantum difficile est enarrare. Preter hos non remansit princeps terre citra Hyspaniam[61] qui ad istud edictum non ueniret, etiam non inuitatus; fama enim largitatis Arthuri[62] longe lateque diffusa totum fere mundum perculerat.

[25] RS; *Auguselus* aDE. [26] aE; *Mireifensium* D; *Murefenensium* R; *Murifensium* S. [27] R; *Cadwallo* aDES. [28...28] a; *Stather rex Demetorum* DE (with *Sather* in margin in D); *id est Suthgualensium* R; *Stater rex Demetorum* S. [29] aDE; *Mordwit* R; *Moruid* S. [30] aDER; *Anarud* S. [31] R; *Artgal* a; *Arthgal* DES (with *Artwail* in margin in D). [32] aDRS; *Kaercargueirensis* E. [33] aS; *Warwic* DE; *Warewich* R. [34] RS; *Iugem* aE; *Lugein* (with *Iuges* in margin) D. [35] aR; *Leicestria* DES. [36] aDE; *Karcestria* R; *Kaycestria* S. [37] aER; *Kimare* D; *Kymare* S. [38] aDES; *Galliie* R. [39] R; *Urbgennius* aDES. [40] aR; *Bado* DES (with *Bozo* in margin in D). [41] aDS; *Ridogensis* E; *Richodensis* R. [42] aDE; *Oxnefordie* R; *Exinefordie* S. [43] R; *Gillamurius* aDES. [44] ERS; *Hibernie* aD. [45...45] aDE; om. R; *Maluasius rex Islandie* S. [46] aRS; *Doldamus* D; *Doldanius* E. [47] aER; *Gunuasus* D; *Gunuarius* S. [48] RS; *Orcadum* aDE. [49] aDES; *rex* underpointed (with *dux* suprascript) R. [50] aDRS; *Ruthinorum* E. [51] aDRS; *Balonie* E. [52] aR; *Bedwerus* DES. [53] aERS; *Cenomanensis* D. [54] R; *Kaeius* a; *Keius* DS; *Keuis* E. [55] aR; om. DES. [56] DRS; *Gwittardus* a; *Gwitardus* E. [57] R; *duodecim* aDES. [58] DRS; *Armaricanorum* a; *Armoricorum* E. [59...59] aDRS; om. E. [60] aDRS; *equuorum* E. [61] DRS; *Hispaniam* aE. [62] R; *Arturi* aDES.

[157] Omnibus ergo[1] in Urbe Legionum congregatis die[2] sollempnitatis[3] regali dyademate insignitus rex ducitur a metropolitanis ad ecclesiam clero psallente ac[4] populo applaudente et .iiii. regibus .iiii. enses aureos ante ipsum ferentibus. Ex alio latere regina non minus pompose ab episcopis laureata deducebatur ad templum sanctimonialium, uoce clara [5]episcopis ac[5] clero ante illam precinentibus. Quatuor quoque regine[6] regum predictorum .iiii.[7] [8]albas columbas[8] ex more preferebant.[9] Uxoresque[10] consulum ac heroum que aderant reginam sequentes magno tripudio exultabant. Peracta processione tot organa, tot cantus in utrisque fiunt templis ut[11] pre mira consonancium uocum[12] dulcedine multi obdormirent et seipsos capere non poterant attoniti tanto gaudiorum[13] strepitu. Diuinis[14] tandem obsequiis sollempniter[15] celebratis rex[16] et regina cum omni heroum cetu domum regressi[17] regalibus ferculis[18] epulati sunt; antiquam [19]consuetudinem Troianorum[19] seruantes mares cum maribus, mulieres cum mulieribus separatim discubuerunt. Refecti denique sollempnibus[20] dapibus diuersi diuersos ludos componunt et extra ciuitatem per campos et prata se diffundunt; alii cestibus, alii palestra,[21] alii aleis ac diuersis lusibus diem illam iocunde[22] consumpserunt[23] sicque in hunc modum tres reliquos dies sollempnes[24] peregerunt.[25] Quarta uero die diuiduntur honores singulis quibusque[26] pro merito famulatus sui et ciuitatum ecclesiis, quibus deerant persone, episcopi eliguntur et abbatie distribuuntur. Beatus autem Dubricius[27] [28]heremiticam uitam[28] eligens[29] de sede archipresulatus se deposuit. In [30]cuius loco[30] sacratur Dauid auunculus[31] regis, uir religiosus ac timens Deum. In loco Sampsonis[32] Dolensis[33] presulis substituitur[34] Theliaus[35] illustris presbiter Landauie annitente[36] Hoelo duce Armoricanorum[37] cui uita et boni mores testimonium

---

§157 [1] aDER; *igitur* S. [2] DER; *in die* S. [3] DRS; *solempnitatis* E. [4] aDES; *et* R. [5...5] aR; *episcopis cum* DE; *cum episcopis et* S. [6] aDES; *regnnine* R. [7] aDER; *quatuor* S. [8...8] a; *columbas albas* DES; *columbas* R. [9] aDRS; om. E. [10] a; *Uxores quoque* DES; *Uxores* R. [11] aDES; om. R. [12] DES; om. a; *uoti* (?) R. [13] aR; *gladiorum* DES (with *gaudiorum* in margin of D). [14] aDES; *d* underpointed before *Diuinis* in R. [15] DRS; *sollemniter* a; *solempniter* E. [16] aDES; *r* underpointed before *rex* in R. [17] aDER; *egressi* S. [18] R; *epulis* DES. [19...19] R; *enim consuetudinem Troianorum* a; *Troianorum consuetudinem* DES. [20] DRS; *solennibus* a; *solempnibus* E. [21] aDES; *palestria* R. [22] DER; *iocundum* S. [23] R; *consumpsere* DES. [24] DRS; *solempnes* E. [25] R; *peregere* DES. [26] DER; *quibus* S. [27] ERS; *Dubritius* aD. [28...28] aR; *uitam heremiticam* DES. [29] aDES; *elegens* R. [30...30] aR; *loco cuius* DES. [31] aDER; *awunculus* S. [32] DES; *sancti Samsonis* a; *Sansonis* R. [33] aD; *Dalensis* ERS. [34] a (corrected from *substitutur*); *restituitur* DES; *substituuntur* R. [35] RS; *Theliauus* a; *Teliaus* DE. [36] aDES; *anitente* R. [37] DRS; *Armoricanorum Brittonum* a; *Armoricorum* E.

dederant. Episcopatus quoque Silcestrie Magaunio,[38] Wintonie[39] uero Duuiano[40] decernitur.[41] [42]Eledemio necnon[42] religioso uiro pontificalis infula[43] donatur Aldclud.[44]

[158] Dumque[1] hec aguntur,[2] ecce Romanorum legati,[3] .xii. uidelicet[4] uiri etatis mature, reuerendi uultus, ramos oliue in signum legacionis[5] in dextris ferentes moderatis passibus curiam ingrediuntur salutatoque rege cartam[6] protulerunt et regi porrexerunt a parte Lucii Romanorum principis missam in hec uerba: 'Lucius rei publice procurator Arthuro[7] regi Britannie quod meruit. Ammirans[8] uehementer ammiror[9] super tue tyrannidis proteruia; ammiror,[10] inquam,[11] et[12] iniuriam quam Rome intulisti recolligens indignor quod extra te egressus eam[13] non agnoscas nec animaduertere festinas quid sit iniustis actibus senatum Romanum offendisse, cui totum orbem famulari non ignoras. Etenim tributum quod Gayus[14] Iulius ceterique post eum principes Romani a gente Britonum susceperunt necglecto[15] senatus imperio iam per plurimos annos retinere presumpsisti. Eripuisti quoque Galliam, eripuisti nobis[16] Allobrogum[17] prouinciam omnesque occeani insulas[18] quarum reges [19]potestati Romane[19] subditi uectigalia antecessoribus[20] nostris ad supplementum erarii[21] persoluebant. Quia igitur de tantis iniuriarum excessibus Romanam dignitatem lacescere[22] non timuisti, calumpniatur te senatus atque ut reum [23]maiestatis Romane[23] uocat et inuitat quatinus mediante Augusto proximi anni Rome satisfacias senatui de hiis omnibus quibus accusaris. Sin autem ego cum exercitu Romano a senatu [24]missus trans Alpes[24] partes quas nobis[25] eripuisse gloriaris adibo atque eas te inuito Romane potestati restituam. Deinde te ipsum quocumque loco latitantem reperiam uinculis mancipatum mecum Rome adducam.' Hiis itaque[26] perlectis et auditis murmur in tanta

---

[38] DE; *Maugannio* a; *Mangaunio* R; *Magannio* S. [39] RS; *Gwintonie* a; *Wyntonie* DE. [40] aDS; *Duiuano* E; *Duuinianio* R. [41] aDRS; *discernitur* E. [42...42] ES; *Eldenio necne* a; *necnon Eledemio* D; *Eledenio necne* R. [43] aDES; *insula* R. [44] aDER; *Alsdclud* S.

§158 [1] aDES; *Cumque* R. [2] aR; *agerentur* DES. [3] aDES; om. R. [4] aDES; om. R. [5] ERS; *legationis* aD. [6] aDES; *carcham* R. [7] R; *Arturo* aDES. [8] ERS; *Admirans* aD. [9] ES; *admiror* aDR. [10] ERS; *admiror* aD. [11] aDRS; *eciam* E. [12] aDES; om. R. [13] aDES; *eam rem* R. [14] R; *Gaius* aDES. [15] R; *neglecto* aDES. [16] aERS; *quoque* (with *nobis* in margin) D. [17] aDES; *Alogobrum* deleted before *Alobrogum* in R. [18] aDERS (with *scilicet Hyberniam, Yslandiam, Orcades, Norwegiam, et Daciam* in margin in D). [19...19] aR; *Romane potestati* DES. [20] aDES; *an antecessoribus* R. [21] aDES; *errarii* R. [22] aDR; *lacessere* ES. [23...23] aR; *Romane maiestatis* DES. [24...24] aERS; *trans Alpes missus* D. [25] aDES; *uos* R. [26] aRS; *ita* DE.

heroum turba non minimum surrexit et de tributi mencione[27] legatos iniuriarum ac minarum conuiciis afficiebant. Uerum rex sedato strepitu suorum in gyganteam[28] turrim secessit, de hiis tractaturus[29] cum senioribus gentis sue. Et cum circa regem tamquam[30] in corona omnes consedissent,[31] Cador dux Cornubie prior in uerba prorumpens silencium[32] rupit et ait: 'Hucusque in timore fueram ne Britones [33]armis semper assuetos,[33] paci nunc redditos, segniores et ignauos[34] quies longa redderet laudemque[35] et famam[36] probitatis qua ceteris gentibus clariores censentur amitterent. Quippe ubi[37] armorum usus uidetur abesse, merito[38] alee et mulierum contubernia ceteraque oblectamenta adesse, [39]dubium non est[39] ut id quod erat uirtutis, quod audacie, quod honoris, quod fame, ignauia et socordia occupet. Deus igitur et eius prouidentia ut nos liberet segnicia[40] Romanos in hanc sententiam induxit[41] quatinus ad pristinum statum nostra reducatur probitas que quasi semisepulta conuiuendo[42] obdormiuit.'

[159] Hec et hiis similia illo prosequente rex silencium petens ait: 'Consocii prosperitatis et aduersitatis, quorum uirtute hactenus[1] contumaciam regum ac ducum proximorum superaui et quorum in dandis consiliis et miliciis[2] agendis expertus sum diligenciam,[3] aduertite, [4]si quid[4] [5]de uobis[5] merui, aduertite nunc quanta nobis omnibus inferuntur obprobria. Audistis Romanorum superbam legacionem,[6] audistis quoque in eorum peticionibus[7] nostram depressionem. [8]Quidquid ergo[8] a sapiente diligenter preuidetur, cum ad rem agendam[9] uentum fuerit, facilius superatur atque decernitur.[10] Facilius itaque Lucii huius inquietacionem tolerare poterimus si[11] communi studio premeditati quibus modis illam debilitare possimus preuideamus. Tributum exigit a nobis [12]sibi dari[12] debere [13]quod ui[13] a Iulio Cesare ceterisque regibus Romanis extortum a gente nostra atque uiolencia[14] surreptum dudum

---

[27] ER; *mentione* aDS. [28] DER; *giganteam* aS. [29] aDERS (corrected from *tractuturis* in S). [30] R; *tanquam* aDES. [31] aDES; *concedissent* R. [32] ERS; *silentium* D. [33]...[33] aDES; *semper assuetos armis* R. [34] aDES; *ignaues* R. [35] aDERS; (corrected from *laudamque* in S). [36] aDES; *famam omnium* R. [37] aDERS; (corrected from *uir* in S). [38] aDES; *merite* R. [39]...[39] R; *non dubium est* a; *non est dubium* DES. [40] ERS; *a segnitia* a; *a segnicie* D. [41] aERS; *adduxit* D. [42] aERS; *conniuendo* D.

§159 [1] aDES; *h hactenus* R. [2] ERS; *militiis* aD. [3] ER; *diligentiam* aDS. [4]...[4] aDES; *siqui* R. [5]...[5] aR; om. DES (with *de uobis* in margin of D). [6] ERS; *legationem* aD. [7] aERS; *petitionibus* D. [8]...[8] R; *Quod ergo* a; *Quicquid igitur* DES. [9] aDRS; *agendum* E. [10] aDER; *discernitur* S. [11] aDES; *sed* R. [12]...[12] aDR; *dari sibi* ES. [13]...[13] DE; *quia* a; *qui* R; *quod* S. [14] ER; *uiolentia* aDS.

fuisse testatur. Quod autem uiolencia[15] a populo libero subreptum[16] est[17] licet aliquando redintegrari[18] et ad pristinum statum duci. Enimuero si id quod iniustum est et ui sublatum a nobis presumunt exigere Romani, consimili ratione[19] et nos expetamus[20] ab illis uectigal quia antecessores nostri Romam quondam subegerunt et in seruitutem redegerunt.[21] Quid enim Belini tempore et Brennio duce Romanis factum fuisse a nostris Britonibus recenseam? Etsi illis excidit, [22]omnibus tamen[22] nota fuerunt qui usque Romam terras incoluerunt. Annon Constantinus nostre Helene filius ac nobis propinquus Britannie sceptro insignitus, Maximianus[23] quoque, alter post alterum imperii Romani fastigium[24] adepti sunt? Eya,[25] si subacti sunt Romani, sicut uerum est, a nostris, non habent iustiorem causam a nobis exigere tributum quam nos ab ipsis. Facessant[26] ergo exhinc [27]calumpnias liberis Britonibus[27] inferre donec iterum ferro subactos – quod Deus auertat![28] – in seruitutem redigant.[29] De Gallia autem siue insulis[30] collateralibus[31] non est illis respondendum, cum eas defendere a nobis uel nollent uel nequirent.'

[162a] Hec et hiis similia rege prosequente placuit omnibus qui aderant et collaudauerunt eius sententiam.[1] Reuersique ad Romanorum legatos responderunt eis que[2] in concione[3] rege dictante collata fuerant atque scripto mandauerunt;[4] cartisque signatis Romam[5] quantocius[6] regrediuntur narrantes Britonum constantem audaciam atque regis Arthuri[7] modestam per omnia responsionem, uirorum quoque bellatorum incomparabilem dignitatem atque diuiciarum[8] ammirabilem[9] copiam.

---

[15] ER; *uiolentia* aDS. [16] R; *surreptum* aDES. [17] aDER; *est uerbum* S. [18] aDES; *reintegrari* R. [19] aDRS; *racione* E. [20] aDES; *expectamus* R. [21] aDES; *redigerunt* R. [22...22] DE; *tamen omnibus* R; *omnibus cum* S. [23] aDES; *et Maximianus* R. [24] aDES; *uestigium* R. [25] R; *Eia* aDES. [26] ERS; *Fascesant* a; *Tacescant* D. [27...27] aR (*Brittonibus* in a); *liberis Britonibus calumpnias* DES. [28] aDES; *auertit* R. [29] aDERS (corrected from *redegant* in S). [30] aER; *de insulis* D; *de* underpointed before *insulis* in S. [31] aDES; *collaterialibus* R.

§160 is not present in the First Variant version; on the restructuring of §§161–4, see Introduction, pp. xxxvi–vii.

§162a [1] DRS; *sentenciam* E. [2] DES; *quod* R. [3] ES; *contione* D; *conticione* R. [4] DER; *mandauerant* S. [5] DES; *qui Romam* R. [6] ERS; *quantotius* D. [7] R; *Arturi* aDES. [8] ER; *diuitiarum* aDS. [9] aERS; *admirabilem* D.

[163] Lucius igitur consul Romanus[1] agnita per legatos[2] Arthuri[3] responsione indignatus mox [4]senatus consultu[4] misit per totum orientem legacionem regibus et principibus Romane potestati parentibus[5] ut quisque cum exercitu undecumque comparato Romam properarent et idibus[6] Iulii seruata[7] maiestate Romane dignitatis omnes in urbe Roma[8] conuenirent. Ad edictum itaque tante potestatis conuenerunt ocius Epystrophus[9] rex Grecorum; Mustensar rex Affricorum; Aliphatima[10] rex Hyspanie;[11] Hirtacius[12] rex Parthorum;[13] Boccus rex Medorum; Sertorius[14] Libie; Xerses Mircorum;[15] Pandrasus Egypti;[16] Micipsa rex Babilonie;[17] Politetes dux Bythinie;[18] Teucer Frigie;[19] Euander Syrie;[20] Echion Boecie;[21] Ypolitus[22] Crete, cum principibus sibi subditis. Ex senatorio ordine Lucius Catellus; Marius Lepidus; Gaius Metellus Cocta;[23] Quintus Miluius Catulus; Quintus Caritius.[24] Tot etiam confluxerunt quod .clxxx.[25] milia armatorum[26] computati essent.

[164a] Dispositis ergo[1] quibusque[2] ad iter necessariis incipientibus kalendis Iulii[3] Britanniam adire ceperunt ut contumaciam Britonum Romane potestati resistencium[4] confutarent et uectigali reddendo iterum assuescerent.

[161] Interea[1] [2]Arthurus rex[2] suos affatus[3] poscit ab omnibus[4] auxilia [5]congregandi exercitus[5] atque Romanorum[6] superbie obuiare. Promiserunt ei mox gratanter omnes sui suorumque[7] famulatum fidelem in obsequium suum quocumque eos ducere uellet quatinus nomen suum in omnes terras celebraretur.[8] Et primum Anguselus[9] rex Albanie eius

§163 [1] aDERS (with *natione Yspanus* [cf. §173] in margin in D). [2] aDES; *legacionem* R. [3] R; *Arturi* aDES. [4...4] aR; *consultu senatus* DES. [5] aDES; *patentibus* R. [6] aERS; *ydibus* D. [7] aDES; *seruare a* R. [8] DERS (corrected from *Romane dignitatis* in S); *Romana* a. [9] aDR; *Epistrophus* ES. [10] DES; *Alifantima* a; *Alifotyma* R. [11] aR; *Yspanie* D; *Hispanie* ES. [12] E; *Hyrtatius* a; *Hyrtacus* DS; *Hycacius* R. [13] aDE; *Parchorum* R; *Partorum* S. [14] aDES; *Sextorius* R. [15] ERS; *Myrcorum* aD. [16] aDRS; *Egipti* E. [17] DES; *Babylone* a; *Babilone* R. [18] aD; *Bithinie* E; *Bitunie* R; *Bitinie* S. [19] aER; *Phrigie* DS. [20] aDRS; *Sirie* E. [21] ES; *Boetie* aD; *Bocie* R. [22] aDR; *Ipolitus* ES. [23] E; om. a; *Cotta* DS; *Coctu* R. [24] aDES; *Caricius* R. [25] R; *centum .lxxx.* a; *.cclxxx.* DES. [26] aR; *armatorum preter Romanos* DES.

§164a [1] aR; *igitur* DES. [2] aDER; *quibus* S. [3] DES; *Iunii* aR. [4] ERS; *resistentium* aD.

§161 [1] aDRS; <*I*>*nterea* E. [2...2] R; *Arturus rex* a; *rex Arturus* DES. [3] aDES; *affatos* R. [4] aR; *eis* DES. [5...5] aR; *exercitum congregandi* DES. [6] aR; *Romane* DES. [7] aDES; *suorum* R. [8] DR; *celebriretur* a; *celebretur* ES. [9] R; *Auguselus* aDES.

necessitati operam[10] dare quantam posset spopondit,[11] dicens: 'Nunc[12] opus est ut [13]omnes quotquot subicimur tue dicioni[13] totis uiribus[14] et animis paremur[15] ad maiestatis tue dignitatem exaltandam et amplificandam. Nichil enim michi ante hoc facilius persuaderi[16] potuit quam cum Romanis congressum, quod nisi ultro oblatum foret omnibus nobis optandum esset. Quis enim contumaciam eorum atque iugum seruitutis liberis hominibus impositum ferre unquam[17] sine inuidia potuit, cum tam despecta gens et ignaua[18] multitudo tot uiros fortes robore atque [19]bellicis rebus[19] assuetos suis exposcant[20] sisti[21] tribunalibus atque rationem[22] de uectigalibus antiquis[23] reddi, que si umquam[24] predecessoribus data sunt, uiolencia[25] quadam et iniusta exactione a nostris tunc forte resistere non ualentibus magis extorta[26] quam[27] suscepta sunt? Aggrediamur[28] ergo semiuiros istos ut et nobis et ceteris gentibus libertatem comparemus et eorum opibus, quibus superflue habundant et unde[29] tam petulantes[30] existunt, uictoria potiti perfruamur. Ut autem noueris, domine mi rex, me uerbis operam accommodare,[31] duobus milibus armatorum equitum exceptis peditibus, qui [32]sub numero[32] facile non ueniunt, expedicionem tuam stipabo atque Romanis[33] acquilis[34] prior, [35]si placuerit,[35] occurram. Cumque deuictis Romanis eorum [36]copiis fuerimus[36] ditati, [37]Germanos adhuc rebelles necesse est[37] inuadamus quatinus tota terra Cisalpina conspectui tuo pareat.'

[162b] Hiis dictis omnes quotquot[1] aderant reges, duces ac principes ad expedicionem[2] parandam contra Romanos animati sunt et promiserunt singuli auxilium ferre quantum famulatui suo iusta descripcione[3] debebant aut eo amplius exhibere. Hoelus Armoricanorum[4] dux .x.

[10] aERS; *opem* D. [11] aES; *spospondit* DR. [12] aR; *Nunc nunc* DES. [13]...[13] R; *omnes quotquot tue subicimur ditioni* a; *quotquot ditioni tue subitimur* D; *quotquot dicione tue subicimur* E; *quotquot dicioni tue subitimur* S. [14] aDERS (with *et armis* in margin of D). [15] aDES; *patremur* R. [16] aDES; *suaderi* R. [17] aDES; *numquam* R. [18] aDERS (corrected from *ignauia* in S). [19]...[19] aDES; *armis bellicis* R. [20] aR; *poscant* DES. [21] aERS; *assisti* D. [22] aDRS; *racionem* E. [23] aDER; *antiqui* S. [24] DE; *unquam* a; *numquam* RS. [25] ERS; *uiolentia* aD. [26] aDES; *exorta*.R. [27] aDES; *qua* R. [28] aDES; *Egrediamur* R. [29] aDE; *unum* R; *inde* S. [30] DS; *peculatores* a; *peculantes* ER. [31] DER; *acommodare* S. [32]...[32] ER; *sub numerum* D; *super numerum* S. [33] DER; om. S. [34] R; *aquilis* DES. [35]...[35] DER; om. S. [36]...[36] R; *fuerimus copiis* DES. [37]...[37] DES; *necesse adhuc Germanos rebelles* R.

§162b (entire chapter absent from a) [1] R; *qui* DES. [2] ERS; *expeditionem* D. [3] ERS; *descriptione* D. [4] DRS; *Armoricorum* E.

milia armatorum forcium[5] promittit. Et ne [6]longum esset[6] omnium partes singulas describere, reges insularum adiacencium,[7] uidelicet Hybernie,[8] Hyslandie,[9] Gothlandie,[10] Orchadum,[11] Norguegie atque Dacie, .cxx. milia ad augmentum [12]regis exercitus spondent.[12] Ex[13] Galliarum uero ducatibus, Rutenorum, Portinensium,[14] Neustriensium, Cenomannorum, Andegauensium, Pictauensium,[15] .lxxx. milia equitum annumerati[16] sunt. [17]Ex ipsa Britannia .lx. milia equitum preter pedites connumerati sunt.[17]

[164b] Dispositis[1] itaque omnibus que ad tantam expedicionem[2] competebant, rex Arthurus[3] Modredo nepoti suo atque Guenhauere[4] regine regnum Britannie conseruandum dimittens[5] cum exercitu suo Portum Hamonis petit[6] et parato nauigio uento flante prospero mare ingreditur nauigandum. Dum [7]igitur altum iam pelagus[7] sulcarent, quasi media[8] noctis[9] hora rex sompno pressus obdormiuit uiditque[10] per sompnum quasi quendam ursum[11] in aere uolantem cuius[12] murmure litora tota infremebant: terribilem quoque ex aduerso draconem ab occidente aduolare cuius oculorum tamquam[13] stellarum splendore[14] tota Neustrie prouincia refulgebat; alterum uero alteri occurrentem miram [15]inire pugnam,[15] sed[16] draconem sibi sepius irruentem ursum fedo et urente hanhelitu[17] suo ad terram prosternere. Expergefactus igitur rex circumsedentibus sompnium[18] narrat et hinc atque illinc, aliis sic, aliis[19] uero sic, sompnii significacionem[20] conicere[21] temptabant.[22] Uerum Arthurus[23] se et sompnium[24] Deo committens spe bona fretus in meliorem partem eius significatum[25] conuertebat.

---

[5] ERS; *fortium* D. [6...6] R; *longum foret* DE; *longe foret* S. [7] ERS; *adiacentium* D. [8] ERS; *Hibernie* D. [9] R; *Hislandie* DES. [10] DR; *Godlandie* ES. [11] RS; *Orcadum* DE. [12...12] R; *exercitus regis promittunt* DES. [13] DES; *Et* R. [14] DS; *Portenensium* E; *Portuensium* R. [15] DES; *Pictauiensium* R. [16] DER; *annunciati* S. [17...17] DES; om. R.

§164b [1] aDERS (corrected from *Depositis* in S). [2] ERS; *expeditionem* aD. [3] R; *Arturus* aDES. [4] R; *Gunware* a; *Gwenneuuare* D; *Gwenneware* E; *Guenneware* S. [5] aDES; *dimittentes* R. [6] aDERS (corrected from *petat* in S). [7...7] R; *altum igitur iam pelagus* a; *igitur altum pelagus iam* DES. [8] aDES; *medius* R. [9] aDERS (corrected from *noctos* in R). [10] aDES; *uidique* R. [11] aDER; *uirum* S. [12] aDRS; *cum* E. [13] R; *tanquam* aDES. [14] a; *fulgore* DES; *splendorem* R. [15...15] DERS (with *ei uisum est* in margin in D); *pugnam committere* a. [16] aDRS; *set* E. [17] R; *anelitu* aS; *hanelitu* D; *anhelitu* E. [18] DS; *somnium* a; *sopnium* E; *sompnum* R. [19] aERS; *alii* D. [20] ERS; *significationem* aD. [21] aDES; *conuicere* R. [22] DER; *temptant* aS. [23] R; *Arturus* aDES. [24] DES; *somnium* a; *sompnum* R. [25] aDES; *significari* R.

157

Rubente itaque[26] aurora litora Neustrie conspiciunt[27] atque in Portum[28] Barbe fluuii applicuerunt tentoriaque figentes exercitus augmentum e[29] diuersis partibus [30]confluentis prestolabantur.[30]

[165] Interea nunciatur Arthuro[1] quendam mire magnitudinis gygantem[2] ex partibus Hyspaniarum[3] aduenisse et Helenam neptem[4] Hoeli ducis Armoricanorum[5] custodibus ui[6] eripuisse et in cacumine montis qui nunc [7]dicitur archangeli Michaelis[7] illam[8] detulisse: milites autem regionis illius[9] insecutos nichil aduersus gigantem[10] profecisse. Audito hoc rex nocte sequenti[11] assumpto Keio dapifero et familiari suo et Beduero[12] pincerna cum armigeris tantum suis clam tentoria egressus ad [13]montem prefatum[13] tendit et, cum monti appropinquaret, in modum rogi [14]ardere ignem super montem[14] cernit, aliumque super minorem montem qui non longe ab altero distat. Dubitans autem super quem illorum moncium[15] habitaret gigas[16] Beduerum[17] premisit ut rem cercius[18] exploraret. At ille inuenta nauicula nauigauit[19] ad minorem montem qui infra mare situs[20] fuerat [21]et propior[21] illis aduenientibus erat. Cuius dum cacumen ascendisset, audito ululatu femineo primum inhorruit. Deinde propius accedens mulierem reperit[22] lacrimantem iuxta tumbam cadaueris nuper humati. Erat autem mulier hec anus, puelle altrix quam asportauerat gigas[23] ex finibus Armoricanorum,[24] ut suprafatum est. Que ut conspexit[25] Beduerum[26] ad se uenientem, timuit ne a gigante[27] perciperetur. Exclamans[28] ait: 'O infelix homo, quod infortunium [29]te huc[29] adduxit[30] miseret me tui. Nam nocte hac[31] si nefandum[32] monstrum te hic offenderit, membris omnibus discerptis[33] morte turpissima morieris. Iste est sceleratissimus

---

[26] aDES; *igitur* (with *itaque* suprascript) R. [27] aR; *aspiciunt* DES. [28] R; *Portu* aDES. [29] aDES; *de* R. [30...30] DES; *confluentem prestolantur* aR.

§165 [1] R; *Arturo* aDES. [2] DR; *gigantem* aES. [3] a; *Hispaniarum* DES; *Hyspanarum* R. [4] aDES; *neptam* R. [5] DRS; *Armonicanorum* a; *Armoricorum* E. [6] aDES; *in* R. [7...7] R; *Michaelis archangeli dicitur* a; *archangeli dicitur Michaelis* DES. [8] aDER; *iam* (tampered) S. [9] aDES; *huius* R. [10] ERS; *gygantem* aD. [11] aR; *sequente* DES. [12] aR; *Bedwero* DES. [13...13] aERS; *prefatum montem* D. [14...14] aR; *ignem super montem ardere* DES. [15] RS; *montium* aDE. [16] ERS; *gyas* a; *gygas* D. [17] aR; *Bedwerum* DES. [18] ERS; *certius* aD. [19] aDES; *nauigans* R. [20] DES; *situm* aR. [21...21] aR; *propiorque* DES. [22] aDRS; *repperit* E. [23] ERS; *gygas* aD. [24] DRS; *Armonicanorum* a; *Armoricorum* E. [25] aR (with the *x* suprascript in a); *aspexit* DES. [26] aR; *Bedwerum* DES. [27] ERS; *gygante* aD. [28] aDES; *et exclamans* R. [29...29] DERS (corrected from *dehuc* in S). [30] R; *duxit* DES. [31] aDRS; om. E. [32] aR; *infandum* DES (with *nefandum* in margin of D). [33] aDES (altered from *disceptis* in a); *discriptis* R.

ille qui nuper neptim[34] ducis Hoeli [35]puellam pulcerrimam – proh
nefas![35] – meque cum illa simul aduexit et cum illa concumbere
temptans pondere magnitudinis sue [36]illam oppressit[36] atque morti[37]
addixit et hic tumulatam[38] reliquid.[39] Fuge ergo quisquis es et quantum
potes fugiendo salua te ipsum.' At ille festinum promittens ei[40]
auxilium ad Arthurum[41] reuersus est narrans ea que audierat et uiderat.
Rex ergo casum [42]ingemiscens puelle[42] tendit ad alium montem et
dimissis[43] equis[44] cum armigeris pedes ascendit montem armatus.
Ipseque precedens socios inuentum aggreditur monstrum qui ad
rogum igne succensum[45] illitus ora tabo sedebat; semesorum[46] porco-
rum partes[47] uerubus infixas[48] suppositis[49] prunis torrebat. Qui ut
respexit[50] in regem, mox festinauit ut clauam assumeret [51]suam magni
ponderis[51] et in regem dirigeret.[52] At ille pretenso clipeo euaginato
gladio ut illum prius feriat quantum potest celeri cursu properat.
Uerum gigas[53] festinato ictu clauam librat regemque interposito clipeo
tanto conamine ferit quod sonitu[54] ictus et[55] litora maris repleuit et
aures eius fere hebetauit. Arthurus[56] ergo[57] ira accensus[58] erecto ense in
frontem illius[59] uulnus[60] intulit non modicum: unde sanguinis riui per
totam faciem copiose fluentes aciem oculorum[61] illius[62] turbauerunt.
Percussus tamen acrior insurgit et uelud[63] aper in uenatorem per
uenabulum ita per gladium cecus factus ruit in regem et complectens
illum brachiis ui et pondere suo humi fere geniculando eum[64] strauit.
At rex senciens[65] monstri illius molem suis brachiis non esse tractandam elabitur in parte altera et sublato in sublime[66] ense totis uiribus in
ceruicem gigantis[67] pressit ita ut uix ensis cum cerebro extraheretur.
Mox ille mugitum magnum cum dolore emittens corruit et spiritum

---

[34] DER; *neptem* aS (corrected from *nuptem* in S). [35...35] R; *puellam pulcherrimam
quam modo hic intumulaui proh nefas* a; *proh nefas puellam pulcherrimam* D; *proth
nefas puellam pulcherrimam* E; *proh nefas puellam pulcherimam* S. [36...36] aDES;
oppressit illam R. [37] aDES; *mortem* R. [38] aDES; *tumulatum* R. [39] R; *reliquit* aDES.
[40] R; om. DES. [41] R; *Arturum* aDES. [42...42] aR; *puelle ingemiscens* DES. [43] aDER;
dimisis S. [44] aERS; om. (with *equis* in margin) D. [45] aR; *accensum* DES. [46] aDRS
(with *semiustorum* in margin of D); *semessorum* E. [47] aDER; *parter* S. [48] aDE; *infixis*
R; *infixax* S. [49] aR; *superpositis* DES. [50] aR; *aspexit* DES. [51...51] R; om. DES (with
suam magni ponderis in margin in D). [52] aDERS (corrected from *redigeret* in S).
[53] RS; *gygas* aDE. [54] aDR; *sonitum* ES. [55] aDRS; om. E. [56] R; *Arturus* aDES. [57] aR;
igitur DES. [58] aDES; *succensus* R. [59] aERS; *eius* D. [60] aDE; *wlnus* RS. [61] aDER;
occulorum S. [62] aERS; *eius* D. [63] aRS; *uelut* DE. [64] aR; om. DES. [65] ERS; *sentiens* aD.
[66] DRS; *sullime* aE. [67] ERS; *gygantis* aD.

exalauit. Beduerus[68] tunc precepto regis accedens[69] amputato eius capite [70]detulit secum[70] ad[71] castra ut spectaculum foret intuentibus. Testatus est rex se[72] non reperisse tante uirtutis alium preter Rithonem[73] gigantem[74] in Arauio[75] monte, quem similiter[76] interfecerat. [77]Iste gigas[78] ex barbis regum quos congrediendo interfecerat[77] pelles in testimonium uirtutis sue et triumphi ad induendum[79] composuerat et mandauerat Arthuro[80] ut suam[81] diligenter excoriatam[82] transmitteret: nam quemadmodum ipse ceteris preerat regibus ita in honore ceteris barbis suam superponeret;[83] sin autem ad singulare certamen inuitabat eum et cui sors uictoriam daret pelles et barbam deuicti tolleret.[84] [85]Inito itaque[85] certamine forcior[86] apparuit Arthurus[87] et eo[88] interfecto barbam et spolium tulit sicut[89] gigas[90] ille ante[91] prolocutus[92] fuerat. Hoelus uero audito neptis sue[93] infortunio ob memoriam ipsius[94] fecit basilicam edificari super corpus illius in eodem monte quo tumulata fuerat; qui mons postea nomen traxit ex sepultura puelle Tumba Helene[95] usque in hodiernum diem.

[166] Francorum igitur exercitu atque regum quos prestolatus est Arthurus[1] insimul collecto dirigit iter uersus Alpes contra Romanos. Qui cum ad[2] Albam fluuium in Burgundia[3] usque progressus esset, nunciatur [4]Romanus exercitus[4] circa Augustudunum[5] castra posuisse et tanto incedere commitatu[6] ut uix [7]eos terre illius[7] solum caperet.[8] Ut autem trans flumen castra sua metatus est [9]rex Arthurus, ex communi consilio suorum[9] legauit tres uiros ad imperatorem Romanum, Bosonem[10] uidelicet consulem de Uado Boum et Gerinum Carnotensem et nepotem suum Walwanum, mandauitque[11] ei ut a finibus Gallie

[68] aR; *Bedwerus* DES. [69] aR; *obediens* DES. [70]...[70] aDES; *secum detulit* R. [71] aDERS (corrected from *in* in S). [72] aDES; om. R. [73] aDE (altered to *Rithionem* in D); *Richonem* R; *Uithonem* S. [74] ERS; *gygantem* aD. [75] aDER; *Aruio* S. [76] aDER; *sim similiter* S. [77]...[77] aDER; om. S. [78] ER; *gygas* aD; om. S. [79] aDES; *intuendum* R. [80] R; *Arturo* aDES. [81] R; *suam ei* DES. [82] aDES; *barbam excoriatam* R. [83] aDER; *supponeret* S. [84] aDES; *tollet* R. [85]...[85] aR; *Initoque* DE; *Inito* S. [86] ERS; *fortior* aD. [87] R; *Arturus* aDES. [88] aDER; *in eo* S. [89] aDER (corrected from *secum* in a); *sicud* S. [90] ERS; *gygas* aD. [91] aERS; *antea* D. [92] aERS; *prelocutus* D. [93] aR; om. DES. [94] aR; *illius* DES. [95] aR; *puelle* DES (with *Helene* in margin of D).

§166 [1] R; *Arturus* aDES. [2] aDES; om. R. [3] aDES; *Burgundiam* R. [4]...[4] aDES; *Romanum exercitum* R. [5] aR; *Augustidunum* DES. [6] R; *comitatu* aDES. [7]...[7] aR; *terre illius eos* DES. [8] aR; *capere posset* DES. [9]...[9] R; *Arturus ex communi suorum consilio* a; *Arturus rex communi suorum consilio* DES. [10] aDES; *Bosonum* R. [11] aDER; *mandauit* S.

quantocius[12] recederet,[13] que dominio suo iure belli subdita erat quemadmodum antea Romanis[14] fuerat: sin autem sciret [15]se armis eam uelle[15] tueri quoad uiueret atque hos[16] quos secum adduxerat. Pergentes[17] itaque legati nunciauerunt Romanis que eis a rege iniuncta fuerant. Qui dum responderet quod non deberet recedere, ymmo[18] ad regendam[19] illam accedere,[20] interfuit Gayus[21] Quintilianus eiusdem nepos inquiens Britones magis iactancia [22]et minis[22] habundare quam audacia et probitate. Indignatus illico[23] Walwanus[24] extracto ense[25] quo accinctus erat irruit in eum et amputato eius capite ad equos qui secus stabant se cum sociis recepit atque simul redire ceperunt. Turbato igitur[26] per Walwanum[27] Romanorum exercitu [28]partim pede, partim equis insidentes[28] ad uindicandum mortuum suum accelerant. Insequentibus itaque[29] illis iamiamque[30] approximantibus Gerinus Carnotensis in quendam illorum[31] qui pre ceteris equo admisso armatus[32] festinabat lanceam direxit et de equo quantum hasta longa erat prostrauit. Boso quoque de Uado Boum retorquens equum suum similiter[33] alium [34]ex apropinquatoribus[34] equo deiecit. Marcellius autem Mutius[35] nobilis decurio Romanus Walwano[36] iam [37]imminens a tergo[37] manus iam[38] in eum [39]inicere gestiens[39] ut Quintilianum uindicaret repente gladium Walwani in uertice capitis sui sensit et letaliter percussus equo cadens expirauit.[40] Walwanus in uerba[41] facecie[42] prorumpens precepit ut Quintiliano socio suo in infernum renunciaret Britones[43] armis et audacia magis ualere quam minis et iactancia.[44] Romanis deinde usque insequentibus, quandoque lanceis, quandoque gladiis a[45] tergo infestabant; sed nec retinere quemquam illorum preualebant nec equo[46] deicere. Dum autem apropinquarent[47] nemori quod erat inter se et exercitum suum, prosiliunt subito de nemore .vi.

---

12 ERS; *quam citius* a; *quantotius* D. 13 aDES; *excederet* R. 14 aDES; *Romanos* R. 15...15 a; *se uelle eam* DES (bis in E, with first occurrence deleted); *se armis ea uelle* R. 16 DES (with *hii* in margin of D); *hi* a; *ii* R. 17 aERS; *Pergentesque* D. 18 R; *immo* aDES. 19 DS; *regendum* aER. 20 aDES; *propius accedere* R. 21 R; *Gaius* aDES. 22...22 aDES; *minisque* R. 23 aR; *ilico* DE; *ilieo* S. 24 aDER; *Waluanus* S. 25 aR; *gladio* DES. 26 aDES; *itaque* R. 27 aDER; *Waluanum* S. 28...28 aR; *partim equis insidentes partim pede* DE; *partim equis incidentes partim pede* S. 29 aDES; om. R. 30 aDER; *iamque* S. 31 aDES; *illo* (with *-rum* suprascript) R. 32 aR; *celerius* DES. 33 DES; *super* R. 34...34 DER (*appropinquatoribus* in E); *a propinquandoribus* S. 35 aDR; *nuncius* E; *Mucius* S. 36 aDER; *Waluano* S. 37...37 aR; *a tergo imminens* DES (*iminens* in E). 38 aR; om. DES. 39...39 aDR; *gestiens inicere* ES. 40 DER; *exspirauit* aS. 41 aERS; *hec uerba* D. 42 aERS; *facetie* D. 43 DES; *Brittones* a; *Britonis* R. 44 ERS; *iactantia* aD. 45 aDERS (corrected from *in* in S). 46 aR; *gladio* DES. 47 aDRS; *appropinquarent* E.

milia Britonum in armis fulgentibus qui ad explorandum uenerant et in eodem loco nemoroso delituerant[48] ut, si opus esset, suis auxilium ferrent. Qui ut [49]conspexerunt Romanos pluribus cateruis suos insequentes,[49] subductis calcaribus equis ac[50] clipeis pretensis, clamore signi sui aera complentes Romanis obuiant et in fugam compellunt.[51] Persequentes a tergo feriunt et quosdam uulneratos[52] prosternunt,[53] quosdam interficiunt. Quod cum Petreio[54] senatori nunciatum esset, .x.[55] milibus commitatus[56] [57]suis subuenire[57] festinat. Et progressus coegit Britones ad siluam ex qua fuerant[58] egressi[59] iterum redire. Quibus [60]hoc modo cedentibus[60] Hiderius[61] filius Nu[62] cum .v. milibus aduenit ut auxilium Britonibus ferret. Redeunt ergo [63]audacter in[63] campum et Romanis resistentibus fit pugna [64]ualida et[64] prosternuntur utrinque.[65] Cumque in hunc modum contenderent, Boso callens suorum audacem temeritatem quosdam seiunxit a ceteris et eos hoc modo affatur:[66] 'Quoniam nesciente rege nostro congredimur Romanis, cauendum [67]nobis est[67] ualde[68] ne in deteriorem partem incepti nostri[69] fortuna decidat. Nam si contigerit nos inferiores[70] esse, et nostrorum dampnum incurremus et regem offendemus.[71] Quia ergo incaute et absque ducis nostri prouisione ad certamen hoc deuenimus, elaboremus quantum[72] possumus[73] ut cum honore ad castra regrediamur et insidiemur [74]Petreio huic[74] Romanorum duci ut[75] uel uiuum uel mortuum regi nostro presentemus.' Sumentes itaque omnes qui aderant ex uerbis eius audaciam pari impetu in hostes ruunt turmasque[76] penetrant usque ad locum quo Petreius similiter [77]suos hortabatur.[77] In quem Boso irruens amplectitur illum sicut premeditatus fuerat[78] et secum in terram corruit[79]. Concurrunt[80] igitur[81] Romani ut eum eripiant, concurrunt[82] et Britones ut eum[83] abducant; et fit utrinque[84] clamor et cedes de Romanis, preualentibus Britonibus.

---

[48] aERS; *dilituerant* D. [49...49] aR; *Romanos pluribus cateruis suos insequentes conspexerunt* DES. [50] aDERS (suprascript in E). [51] aR; *propellunt* DES. [52] aDE; *wlneratos* RS. [53] R; om. a; *sternunt* DES. [54] aDES; *Petreyo* R. [55] aERS; *decem* D. [56] R; *comitatus* aDE; *commitatis* S. [57...57] DES; *subuenire* a; *subuenire* (with *suis* suprascript) R. [58] aDER; *fuant* S. [59] aDES; *progressi* R. [60...60] aDER; *cadentibus hoc modo* S. [61] DER; *Biderius* a; *Hidorius* S. [62] aR; *Nuth* DES. [63...63] aDES; *in audacter* R. [64...64] R; *ualida* a; *magna et* DES. [65] ERS; *utrimque* aD. [66] R; *affatus est* DES. [67...67] aR; *est nobis* DES. [68] aDERS (corrected from *walde* in R). [69] aDER; om. S. [70] aDER; *miseros* S. [71] aDER; *offendeus* S. [72] aR; *in quantum* DES. [73] aDER; *possimus* S. [74...74] aDES; *huic Petreio* R. [75] aDES; om. R. [76] aDER; *turmas* S. [77...77] aDES; *hortatur suos* R. [78] aDRS; *fuat* E. [79] aR; *corruere fecit* DES. [80] aDERS (corrected from *Concurruunt* in R). [81] aDES; *ergo* R. [82] aDES; om. R. [83] ER; *illum* aDS. [84] ERS; *utrimque* aD.

Extrahentes autem Petreium[85] de medio suorum duxerunt usque in fortitudinem prelii sui ac reuertentes ad Romanos multos strauerunt, quamplures retinuerunt, et cum Petreio ad castra deduxerunt. [86]Uenientes itaque ante regem racionem[87] [88]de legacione sua reddiderunt[88] et Petreium cum sociis suis[89] captiuos presentauerunt.[86] Quibus rex congratulans honorum et possessionum augmentaciones, si [90]triumphum de Romanis[90] obtineret,[91] promisit. Captiuos autem custodibus tradens consilium accepit ut eos Parisius in crastinum mitteret ne, si in castris seruarentur, casu aliquo [92]accideret quo[92] eos amitteret. Tradidit ergo eos[93] ducendos Cadori duci Bedueroque[94] necnon Borello[95] et Richero ut cum [96]suis familiis[96] eos conducerent donec uenirent[97] eo quo minime timerent Romanorum irrupcionem.[98]

[167] At Romani per exploratores[1] suos quos in exercitu Arthuri[2] habebant agnoscentes hec fieri miserunt Uulteium[3] Catellum cum .x. milibus armatis[4] et Quintum Caritium[5] senatorem, Euandrum quoque regem Syrie[6] et Sertorium Libie qui [7]iter eorum nocte illa[7] precederent atque suos liberarent. Nacti ergo locum latibulis aptum delituerunt donec Britones cum captiuis iter agentes super Romanorum insidias deuenerunt. Prosilientes mox ex insidiis [8]circumuenire Britones imparatos[8] estimauerunt atque captiuos de manibus eorum eripere. Uerum per cateruas distributi precedebant agmen Cador[9] dux Cornubie cum suis atque[10] Borellus. Post illos uero ducebantur captiui uinctis[11] manibus[12] post terga cum quingentis armatis quibus preerant Richerus et Beduerus.[13] Qui ut Romanorum insidias persenserunt, tanquam in acie pugnaturi,[14] audacter eos susceperunt, dimissis[15] in tuto loco captiuis cum paucis. Romani ergo sine ordine erumpentes[16] non

---

85 aDE; *eum Petreium* R; *Petreum* S. 86...86 aDRS; om. E. 87 aRS; *rationem* D; om. E. 88...88 aR (*legatione* in a); *reddiderunt de legacione sua* DS (*legatione* in D); om. E. 89 aDS; om. R (& E). 90...90 aR; *de Romanis triumphum* DES. 91 R; *optineret* aDES. 92...92 aR; om. DES. 93 aR; om. DES. 94 aR; *et Bedwero* D; *Bedweroque* ES. 95 aDRS; *Burello* E. 96...96 R; *famulis suis* aS; *familiis suis* DE. 97 aDES; *peruenirent* R. 98 ERS; *irruptionem* aD.

§167 1 aDER; *explorantes* S. 2 R; *Arturi* aDES. 3 R; *Uulteum* D; *Wlteum* E; *Wlteium* S. 4 R; *armatorum* DES. 5 DES; *Carucium* R. 6 DR; *Sirie* ES. 7...7 R; *nocte illa iter eorum* DES. 8...8 aR (*Brittones* in a); *Britones imparatos circumuenire* DES. 9 DES; om. aR (with *Cador* in margin of a). 10 aDES; *et* R. 11 R; *uincti* aDS; om. E. 12 aRS; *manus* DE. 13 aR; *Bedwerus* DES. 14 aDER; *pugnaturi sunt* S. 15 aDER; *dimisis* S. 16 aR; *irruentes* DES.

curabant suos per turmas disponere neque cum Britonibus congredi; ymmo[17] diffusi huc illucque[18] [19]captiuos querebant quoquo modo[19] eripere et sic ad castra redire. At Britones nulli parcentes stragem [20]magnam de Romanis primo[20] fecere.[21] Deinde rex Syrie[22] Euander et Sertorius in unum conuocantes fusas suorum cohortes[23] Britones inuadere acriter ceperunt[24] et, quia maior eorum numerus ac forcior[25] erat, mox omnes[26] eorum turmas penetrauerunt et quassauerunt; ac[27] omnino illis prostratis captiuos abduxissent, nisi Guitardus[28] Pictauensis dux [29]comperto dolo Romanorum[29] cum tribus milibus [30]uirorum bellatorum[30] superuenisset atque ab instanti[31] periculo liberasset. Reuocatis itaque [32]suis Britones[32] in hostes acrius seuiunt et omni nisu[33] eos debellare intendunt.[34] Illi congressum eorum non ferentes reliquerunt campum castra sua petentes. Britones insequentes sternunt, obtruncant, retinent captos, et suos uindicant. Ceciderunt illic[35] Uulteius[36] Catellus et Euander rex Syrie[37] cum ceteris innumerabilibus; ceteri[38] fuga dissipati sunt. Cumque redissent Britones ad campum quo [39]strages suorum facta est,[39] inuenerunt[40] inter peremptos illum inclitum Borellum Cenomanensem[41] ultimum spiritum exalantem, lancea fixum per gulam, sanguine cruentatum, et de nominatis uiris [42]ac strennuis[42] quatuor,[43] Hirelgas[44] [45]de Perirum,[45] Mauricum[46] Cardorcanensem,[47] Aliduc[48] de Tintagol,[49] et filium Hider. Traditis igitur illis[50] sepulture cum immenso fletu et planctu miserunt captiuos cum hiis quos nouiter ceperunt Parisius,[51] ad regem Arthurum[52] repedantes et spem future uictorie promittentes, cum admodum pauci de tot hostium milibus triumphassent.

[17] R; *immo* aDES. [18] aR; *atque illuc* DES. [19...19] aDR; *querebant quoquo modo captiuos* E; *captiuos querebant quomodo* S. [20...20] a; *de Romanis magnam primo* DES; *de Romanis primum magnam* R. [21] aDES; *fecere uel fecerunt* R. [22] aDR; *Sirie* ES. [23] DER; *cateruas* a; *choortes* S. [24] aDER; *perceperunt* S. [25] ER; *fortior* aDS. [26] aERS; om. D. [27] aR; *et* DES. [28] aDRS; *Gwitardus* E. [29...29] aR; *dolo Romanorum comperto* DES. [30...30] aR om DES. [31] aDES; *stanti* R. [32...32] aR (*Brittones* a); *Britones suis* DES. [33] aDE; *uisu* RS. [34] aR; *contendunt* DES. [35] aDES; *illuc* R. [36] R; *Wlteius* aDES. [37] aDR; *Sirie* ES. [38] aR; *alii* DES. [39...39] aR; *sui dissipati sunt* DES. [40] aDER; *et uenerunt* S. [41] aDR; *Cenomannensem* ES. [42...42] aR; om. DES. [43] aR; *.iiii.* DES. [44] aR; *Hirelglas* DES. [45...45] DER (corrected from *deperiturum* in E); *de Peirun* a; *de Peritum* S. [46] aR; *Mauricium* DES. [47] a; *Cadorcanensem* DES (altered to *Cardorcananensem* in D); *Cardornensem* R. [48] aDES; *Aliduch* R. [49] a (but altered to *Tintagel*); *Tindageol* D; *Tintageol* E; *Tangol* R; *Tyndageol* S. [50] DES; om. aR. [51] aDES; *apud Parisius* R. [52] R; *Arturum* aDES.

[168] At Lucius Hiberus[1] [2]Romanorum dux[2] tales casus moleste ferens animum diuersis cruciatum cogitacionibus nunc [3]h<u>c, nunc illu<c>[3] reuoluens hesitabat[4] an cepta[5] prelia cum Arthuro[6] perficiat an[7] auxilium Leonis imperatoris exspectet[8] intra Augustudunum[9] receptus. Formidans itaque bellum nocte insequente[10] ciuitatem prefatam aditurus Lengrias cum exercitibus suis[11] ingreditur. Quod ut Arthuro[12] compertum est, iter illius [13]eadem nocte[13] precedere decreuit; relictaque[14] a leua ciuitate quandam occupat uallem que Siesia[15] uocabatur, quam Lucius cum exercitu transgressurus[16] erat. Commilitones igitur suos per acies iure belli disponens legionem unam, cui prefecerat Hoelum ducem, ordinauit [17]post se[17] in equis adesse ut, si opus accidisset, quasi ad castra sese ibi recipere posset uel, si hostes fuge operam darent, illi post eos admissis equis insequerentur fugientes. Cateruas itaque septenas distribuens in unaquaque quinquies mille et .d.[18] et .lv. uiros omnibus armis instructos collocauit. Erant autem acies Britannico[19] more cum dextro et sinistro cornu in quadrum statute: quibus[20] Anguselus[21] rex Albanie et Cador dux Cornubie, unus in dextro et[22] alius in sinistro cornu, preficiuntur; secunde autem turme, que post eos incedebat,[23] duo insignes[24] consules, Gerinus uidelicet Carnotensis et Boso de Ridechen,[25] id est Oxinefordie,[26] prestituuntur;[27] tertie uero Aschil[28] rex Dacorum atque Loth Norguegensium; quarte Walwanus[29] cum duobus comitibus prefertur. Post has[30] autem fuerunt alie quatuor a dorso constitute: quarum uni preponitur Keyus[31] dapifer et Beduerus[32] pincerna; alii preficiuntur Holdinus dux Rutenorum[33] et Guitardus[34] Pictauensis; tertie Iugenis[35] de Legecestria[36] et Ionathal[37] Dorocestrensis;[38] quarte Cursalem[39] de

§168 [1] aDER; *Hyberus* S. [2...2] aR; *dux Romanorum* DES. [3...3] my emendation (see Introduction, p. xcvii); *hoc nunc illud* aDERS. [4] aDRS; *hesetabat* E. [5] a; *incepta* DES; *capta* R. [6] R; *Arturo* aDES. [7] DES; *aut* aR. [8] aDER; *inspectet* S. [9] aR; *Augustidunum* DES. [10] aR; *sequente* DES (altered to *insequente* in D). [11] aR; om. DES. [12] R; *Arturo* DES. [13...13] aDES; *nocte eadem* R. [14] aDER; *relicta* S. [15] aDES; *Sicilia* R. [16] aERS; *ingressurus* D. [17...17] aDER; *posse* S. [18] DERS (altered by erasure from *.dc.* in D); *quingentos* a. [19] DES; *Brittannico* a; *Britonico* R. [20] aDER; *in quibus* S. [21] RS; *Auguselus* aDE. [22] aDES; om. R. [23] aDERS (corrected from *incedebant* in D). [24] aDRS (corrected from *insignis* in a); *insegnes* E. [25] D; *Richeden* aES; *Richiden* R. [26] DES; *Oxineford* a; *Oxneforde* R. [27] DES; *statuuntur* aR. [28] aR; *Aschild* DES. [29] aDES; *Walwanius* R. [30] aDERS (corrected from *hos* in R). [31] R; *Keius* aDES. [32] aR; *Bedwerus* DES. [33] aDER; *Ruthenorum* S. [34] aDER; *Gintardus* S. [35] aES; *Lugenis* (with *Iugenius* in margin) D; *Ingenis* R. [36] RS; *Legecestra* aDE (altered to *Leircestra* in D). [37] aDER; *Ionatal* S. [38] aDES; *Dorostrenscensis* R. [39] aDRS; *Cursale* E.

Kaycestria[40] atque[41] Urbgenius de Badone. Ipse rex post hos [42]locum quendam eminenciorem[42] nactus cum uexillo aureo draconis legionem habebat forcium[43] uirorum in qua [44].vi. milia .dclxvi.[44] numero erant.

[169] Dispositis itaque omnibus bellicis rebus hos qui circa se aderant sic affatus est: 'Commilitones mei domestici, quorum uirtute semper et ubique triumphaui, qui Britanniam nobilem insulam terdenorum[1] regnorum [2]fecistis dominam,[2] uestre congratulor probitati quam nullatenus deficere, ymmo[3] magis ac magis uigere considero. Duos michi iam de Romanis attulistis triumphos; terčius[4] adhuc restat quem haut[5] segniter per iuuentutis uestre robur et innatam[6] audaciam tamquam[7] futurorum presagus Deo in omnibus opitulante hodie accumulari[8] confido ceteris. Sane orientalium gencium[9] segniciam[10] in nobis[11] esse existimabant Romani dum patriam uestram[12] facere tributariam et nosmetipsos sibi subiugare uolebant. Numcquid[13] nouerunt[14] que bella Dacis, que Norwegensibus,[15] que Gallorum ducibus et ceteris gentibus [16]uestra uirtute[16] peregimus atque triumphauimus? Qui igitur aduersus tam fortes et bellatores populos preualuimus, hiis semiuiris et effeminatis forciores[17] esse non desperemus? Ecce iam tota uictoria in manus nostras[18] se contulit, si hodierna [19]die tantum[19] pacienter[20] ac uiriliter stemus.' Hec[21] eo uociferante omnes uno clamore assenciunt[22] parati mortem subire potius quam ipso uiuente campum belli deserere.

[170] At Lucius Hiberus[1] compertis[2] hiis que ab Arthuro[3] rege sibi parabantur noluit ut prius cogitarat: nec potuit absque dedecore belli instantis congressum[4] uitare neque sine rei publice detrimento diffu-

---

[40] R; *Kaicestria* aS; *Kaicestra* D; *Kaycestra* E. [41] aR; *et* DES. [42...42] aDES (*eminentiorem* in aDS); *eminenciorem locum quendam* R. [43] ERS; *fortium* aD. [44...44] DES; *sex milia cescenti sexaginta sex* a; *.vi. milia .dclvi.* R.

§169 [1] a; *ceterorum* DES; *edenorum* R. [2...2] aR; *fecistis* DES (with *dominam* suprascript before *fecistis* in D). [3] R; *immo* aDES. [4] ERS; *tertius* aD. [5] aDER; *hanc* (?) S. [6] aR; *maternam* DES (with *innatam* in margin of D). [7] DR; *tanquam* aES. [8] aDES; *accul* deleted before *accumulari* in R. [9] ERS; *gentium* aD. [10] R; *segnitiam* a; *segniciem* DES. [11] aDRS; *uobis* E. [12] aR; *nostram* DES. [13] R; *Numquid* aDES. [14] aDES; *nouerit* R. [15] aR; *Norguegensibus* DES. [16...16] aDES; *uirtute uestra* R. [17] ERS; *fortiores* aD. [18] aDR; *uestras* ES. [19...19] aDR; *tantum die* ES. [20] aERS; *patienter* D. [21] aERS; *Hoc* D. [22] ERS (with *uno* underpointed after *assentiunt* in S); *assentiunt* aD.

§170 [1] aDE; *Hyberus* RS. [2] aDES; *cognitis* R. [3] R; *Arturo* aDES. [4] aDRS; om. E.

166

gium facere. Conuocatis itaque ad se [5]in unum separatim locum regibus ac ducibus imperii Romani[5] sic affatur eos, dicens: 'Patres inuictissimi, tocius[6] orbis triumphatores ac [7]Romani nominis[7] propagatores et defensores,[8] uidetis [9]mecum belli huius instantem[9] necessitatem, uidetis hostes inter [10]locum illum,[10] quo proponebamus ire, et nos acies suas ordinasse: nec[11] aliunde nobis patet iter ad presidia[12] ciuitatis nostre quam per uallem istam[13] que ab aduersariis preclusa est. Sumite animos,[14] sumite arma et ueterum uestrorum[15] memores et hostium[16] iniuriam Romane maiestati illatam[17] recolentes armorum discrimine cum multa sanguinis effusione, si oportet, uiam hanc patefacite; et eam libertatem et audaciam qua usi semper estis bellorum miliciis[18] hodie necesse est ad memoriam reuocetis et[19] ut inprobos[20] istos, qui tamquam[21] latrunculi et [22]iter uestrum obcludere[22] presumunt, dissipare et eorum robur confutare omnes unanimiter intendamus[23] ut, si perstiterint incepto,[24] triumphati atque deuicti Romane [25]subdantur potestati:[25] si fuge se dederint, uiles et abiecti terras et urbes quas se nobis subripuisse[26] gloriantur amittant et in perpetuum nobis seruientes uectigalia erario cum ceteris gentibus dependant.'[27] Ut igitur finem[28] dicendi fecit, uno omnes assensu[29] fauentes socias manus iureiurando promittunt[30] et ad[31] armandum sese festinant. Armati tandem dispositis turmis ad uallem predictam accedunt; hostes intuentur totam uallem dextra leuaque[32] obsidentes.[33]

[171][1] Postquam autem in aduersa parte hinc Britones, illinc Romani erectis steterunt signis, lituis insonantibus conueniunt et grandine sagittarum et [2]genere omnium[2] telorum primas[3] belli partes[4] lacessunt.

[5...5] aR; *separatim regibus ac ducibus imperii Romani in locum unum* (*suum* in S) DES. [6] aERS; *totius* D. [7...7] aR; *nominis Romani* DES. [8] aDRS; *defensatores* E. [9...9] R; *mecum belli huius instantem* a; *mecum huius instantis belli* DES. [10...10] aR; *illum locum* DES. [11] R; *non* aDES. [12] aR; *presidium* DES. [13] aDER; om. S. [14] aR; *animos et* DES. [15] aDR; *nostrorum* ES. [16] aR; *hostium uestrorum* D; *hostium nostrorum* ES. [17] aDER; *illata* S. [18] aERS; *militiis* D. [19] aDES; om. R. [20] RS; *improbos* aDE. [21] DR; *tanquam* aES. [22...22] R; *inter uestrum obcludere* a; *iter nostrum includere* DES. [23] aDER; *attendamus* S. [24] aERS; *in incepto* D. [25...25] aR; *potestati subdantur* DES. [26] R; *surripuisse* aES; *eripuisse* (with *surripuisse* in margin) D. [27] aDES; *dependeant* R. [28] aDES; *furem* R. [29] aDES; *affectu* R. [30] aERS; *affirmant* underpointed before *promittunt* in D. [31] aRS; om. DE (but with *ad* suprascript in D). [32] aDER; *leua* S. [33] aDES; *obsistentes* R.

§171 [1] *Bellum inter Romanos et Arthurum* (*Arturum* in a) aR; no rubric in DES. [2...2] aR; *omnium genere* DES. [3] aDES; *primis* R. [4] aERS; *acies* D.

Deinde cominus[5] gladiis et sicis[6] sese inuicem obuiant atque uulnerant.[7] Et sic diu se[8] ex utraque parte uerentes contendunt ut dubium esset quis eorum preualeret, donec Beduerus[9] et Keyus[10] agmine suo Romanos penetrantes seipsos cum magna[11] audacia periculo dederunt atque sanguine multo Romanorum fuso a turmis hostilibus circumuenti undique confossi[12] sunt. Beduerus[13] peremptus cecidit, Keyus[14] letaliter uulneratus[15] uix euasit[16] corpore Bedueri[17] secum sublato.[18] In agmine enim Medorum pariter inciderant et a rege Bocco[19] lancea pectori[20] medio fixus[21] Beduerus[22] interiit.

[172] Hirelglas[1] autem nepos Bedueri[2] ob mortem auunculi sui dolore simul et ira commotus ad uindicandum illum uehementer exarsit et cum .ccc. suorum per hostiles cateruas ueluti aper inter[3] canes dextra leuaque[4] sternens ac dissipans quantum robur equorum sibi [5]et suis uires augebant[5] ad uexillum regis Medorum peruenit, nichil uerens quid[6] sibi contingere posset dum auunculum suum uindicaret. Extracto itaque gladio regem ipsum[7] peremit peremptumque ad socios suos detraxit suis undique defendentibus ac uiam patefacientibus et iuxta corpus Bedueri[8] auunculi sui totum dilaniatum[9] et in frusta[10] concisum[11] dimisit. Deinde magno clamore in hostes ruens stragem [12]non modicam de eis[12] fecit. Signum Britonum sepius inclamando suos exhortabatur[13] quasi furore plenus ut fortiter ferirent et[14] sine pietate obtruncarent: gentiles enim [15]inimici Dei cum christianis erant[15] mixti et idcirco[16] nec ipsis[17] christianis parcendum. Illo tunc impetu corruerunt in parte Romanorum Alifatima[18] rex Hyspanie[19] et Micipsa Babiloniensis;[20]

[5] aDRS; *comminus* E. [6] R; *cesi* a; *lanceis* DES (with *et sicis* in margin in D). [7] aDE; *wlnerant* RS. [8] aR; om. DES. [9] aR; *Bedwerus* DES. [10] R; *Keius* aDES. [11] aR; *multa* DES. [12] aDERS (with *confusi* in margin of D). [13] aR; *Bedwerus* DES. [14] R; *Keius* aDES. [15] aDE; *wlneratus* RS. [16] aDES; *a* deleted before *euadit* in R. [17] aR; *Bedweri* DES. [18] aDR; *sullato* ES. [19] R; *Bocco Medorum* a; *Bocca* DES. [20] DES; *pectoris* aR. [21] aERS; *infixus* D. [22] aR; *Bedwerus* DES.

§172 [1] DE (altered to *Hirglas* in D); *Hirelgas* aR; *Hyrelglas* S. [2] aR; *Bedweri* DES. [3] aERS; *intra* D. [4] aDE; *leuam* RS. [5...5] a; *et suis uires dabant* DES; *suis augebant* R. [6] aDER; *quod* S. [7] aDES; *illum* R. [8] aR; *Bedweri* DES. [9] aR; *dilaniauit* DE; *delaniauit* S. [10] aDRS; *frustra* E. [11] aDES; *conscisum* R. [12...12] R; *de eis non modicam* aDES. [13] aDES; *hortabatur* R. [14] aR; *atque* DES. [15...15] R; *erant inimici Dei cum christianis* a; *erant inimici Dei christianis* DES. [16] DR; *iccirco* aES. [17] aDES; om. R. [18] R; *Alifantina* a; *Aliphatima* DES. [19] aRS; *Hispanie* DE. [20] a; *Babilonicensis* DES; *Babilonensis* R.

Quintus quoque[21] Miluius et Marius Lepidus senatores. Ceciderunt et[22] in parte Britonum Holdinus dux Ruthenorum[23] et Leodegarius Boloniensis; tres etiam consules Britannie, Cursalem Caicestrensis,[24] Anaraud[25] Salesberiensis, et Urbgenius[26] de Badone.

[173] Turme autem quas isti[1] regebant quassate amissis ducibus retro cesserunt donec uenirent ad aciem Armoricanorum Britonum quam Hoelus et Walwanus[2] tuebantur. Ut ergo uiderunt hii duo duces socios pre se peremptos, magis ac magis [3]in iram[3] accensi hostibus instant[4] et dextra leuaque cedunt[5] donec ad turmam imperatoris, ubi signum aquile tenebatur, peruenirent. Hic renouatur prelium et Romani, sicut[6] recentes[7] leones [8]in defessos[8] canes, [9]ruunt sine lege et[9] sine lege utrobique pereunt. At Walwanus[10] [11]semper recenti[11] uigens uigore aditum congrediendi cum Lucio querebat sternens [12]quosque sibi[12] obuios habebat Romanorum. Hoelus quoque non inferior ex alia parte fulminabat socios exhortans ut acriter ferirent; hostium ictus haut timidus suscipiens et econtra repercuciens[13] multos solus ense suo uita priuauit, quia non erat [14]tempus uacuum quin aut[14] percuteretur aut percuteret. Non erat facile agnosci quis[15] eorum alterum audacia excederet: quibus ante secula meliores non genuerunt. Tandem Walwanus acies Romanas[16] cedendo penetrans peruenit ad ipsum Lucium imperatorem quem ualde siciebat[17] inuenire. Lucius quoque non segnis, ab Hyspania[18] oriundus, prima uirtute florens multum audacie, [19]multum uigoris, multum[19] probitatis habebat. Congressus itaque cum Walwano[20] mire letatur et gloriatur quod cum uiro[21] de quo tanta fama fuerat singulare certamen iniret commissoque [22]diucius inter se[22] agone dant ictus ualidos et scuta galeasque ensibus detruncant. Et dum acriter

21 aDES; *uero* R. 22 aDES; *om.* R. 23 aR; *Rutenorum* DES. 24 a; *Kaicestrensis* DES; *Carcestrentis* R. 25 DERS (with *Gualauo* in margin of D); *Gualano* a. 26 DES; *Urbgennius* a; *Urgennus* R.

§173 1 aDER; *ipsi* S. 2 aDER; *Waluuanus* S. 3...3 aR; *ira* DES. 4 aR; *instabant* DES. 5 aR; *cedebant* DES (corrected from *credebant* in S). 6 aDER; *sicud* S. 7 aR; *om.* DES (with *recentes* in margin in D). 8...8 DRS; *indefessos* aE. 9...9 a; *sine lege ruunt* DES; *ruunt* R. 10 DES; *Walwanius* R. 11...11 R; *recenti semper* DES. 12...12 R; *quoscumque* DES. 13 ER; *repercutiens* DS. 14...14 R; *tempus quin* DES. 15 DES; *qui* R. 16 aDES; *Romanos* R. 17 aERS; *sitiebat* D. 18 RS; *Hispania* aE; *Yspania* D. 19...19 R; *multum uigoris multumque* aES; *multumque uigoris et multum* D. 20 aDER; *Waluano* S. 21 aDES; *tanto uiro* R. 22...22 aERS; *inter se diutius* D.

in hunc modum decertant, ecce Romani subito recuperantes impetum in Armoricanos²³ faciunt et imperatori suo²⁴ subueniunt; Hoelum et Walwanum²⁵ cum suis cedentes retro ad cohortes suas paulisper coegerunt.

[174] Quibus mox rex ipse Arthurus¹ cum agmine suo adhuc recenti in auxilium festinus occurrens extracto Caliburno² ense celsa uoce ³se testatur³ adesse atque retro cedentes hiis uerbis hortatur, dicens: 'Utquid fugitis?⁴ Quid pertimescitis? Ne abscedat ullus uestrum! Ecce ⁵dux uester,⁵ qui ad certamen uos adduxi,⁶ paratus, si forte⁷ contingat, pro uobis occumbere; nec, dum uita comes fuerit, uos uel campum hunc relinquam donec triumpho potitus⁸ hostes fuge aut dedicioni⁹ hodie¹⁰ compellam. Mementote dextrarum uestrarum que tot preliis exercitate omnibus aduersariis usque modo preualuerunt. Mementote libertatis uestre quam sibi subdere affectant¹¹ semiuiri isti.' Hec cum uociferatus esset, irruit in hostes, cedit, prosternit et tamquam¹² leo famelicus in animalia seuit. Nemo ei obuius esse¹³ ausus est. Diffugiunt omnes et latere magis quam pugnare querunt. Quippe nullus ¹⁴euadere poterat eorum¹⁴ quem cruento¹⁵ ense summotenus tangebat: ita erat mortiferum¹⁶ uulnus illius gladii. Hic ¹⁷duos orientales reges obuios sibi¹⁷ infortunium dedit quos abscisis¹⁸ capitibus ad tartara misit. Uiso igitur ¹⁹rege suo Britones¹⁹ in hunc modum decertare animosiores effecti aduersarios unanimiter inuadunt et cateruatim sternunt; resistunt Romani quantum possunt.

[175] Dumque sic omnibus uiribus ¹inuicem decertant,¹ ecce Morwid² consul Claudiocestrie cum legione equitum³ de nemorosis collibus,⁴ ubi ad presidium dimissus fuerat, prosiliens a dorso superuenit hostibus; et

---

²³ aDR; *Armoricos* E; *Armaricanos* S. ²⁴ aDES; om. R. ²⁵ aDER; *Waluanum* S.

§174 ¹ R; *Arturus* aDES. ² aDRS; *Caleburno* E. ³⁻³ aER; *testatur se* DS. ⁴ aDES; *fugitis ensis Arthuri* R (a displaced gloss on *Caliburno*; see Introduction, p. xc). ⁵⁻⁵ aDER; *duxerunt* S. ⁶ aDES; *adduxit* R. ⁷ aDER; *fonte* S. ⁸ aERS; *potitus hodie* D. ⁹ ERS; *deditioni* aD. ¹⁰ aERS; om. D. ¹¹ aDER; *affecant* S. ¹² DR; *tanquam* aES. ¹³ aDER; om. S. ¹⁴⁻¹⁴ aR; *eorum poterat euadere* DES. ¹⁵ aR; *cruentato* DES. ¹⁶ aDER; *mortifer* S. ¹⁷⁻¹⁷ aR; *sibi orientales duos reges obuios* DES. ¹⁸ aDRS; *abcisis* E. ¹⁹⁻¹⁹ aR (*Brittones* in a); *Britones rege suo* DES.

§175 ¹⁻¹ a; *decertant inuicem* DES; *inuicem decertarent* R. ² R; *Moruid* a; *Muruid* DES. ³ aR; *militum* DES. ⁴ aR; *uallibus* DES (with *collibus* in margin in D).

eos nil tale uerentes cedunt et[5] obtruncant et disturbatos a fronte et a tergo in fugam compellunt. Tunc multa milia orientalium pariter ac Romanorum aliis alios urgentibus[6] stipatis cateruis ceciderunt; quidam uestigiis fugiencium pressi et calcati[7] occumbunt, quidam [8]armis propriis iugulantur,[8] maior pars hostium gladiis intereunt.[9] In turbine illo Lucius ille preoccupatus[10] cuiusdam lancea confossus occubuit. Britones igitur[11] usque insistentes[12] uictoriam de Romanis omnibus seculis celebrem adepti sunt. Ut autem insequendo et cedendo exsaturati[13] sunt, reuertentes[14] spolia diripiunt et armis et spoliis Romanorum ea die ditati sunt.

[176] Rex itaque Arthurus[1] tanto triumpho glorificatus corpora suorum ab hostium cadaueribus separans quedam [2]ibidem sepulta[2] reliquid,[3] quedam[4] ad comprouinciales[5] abbacias[6] deferri[7] fecit et honorifice sepeliri. Corpus autem Bedueri[8] dilecti sui ad Neustriam ciuitatem[9] Baiocas[10] [11]a Neustriensibus[11] suis delatum [12]sepulture egregie[12] tradi precepit. Ibi[13] in cimiterio[14] ecclesie, que tunc erat in australi parte ciuitatis iuxta murum, honorifice cum magnis lamentis suorum positus est. Keius uero ad Camum[15] oppidum[16] quod ipse construxerat grauiter uulneratus[17] asportatur ac paulo post eodem ex[18] uulnere defunctus ad cenobium heremitarum in quodam nemore non longe ab oppido[19] delatus ut decuit Andegauensium[20] ducem sepultus est. Holdinus dux[21] Ruthenorum[22] Flandrias uectus in Teruana[23] ciuititate sua inhumatus[24] iacet. Ceteri autem consules et[25] proceres prout quisque ciuitate aut predio in uita sua floruit ad propria delati[26] sunt. Hostes quoque rex miseratus precepit indigenis sepelire corpusque[27]

---

5 aR; om. DES. 6 aDES; *urgentes* R. 7 aR; *galeati* DES. 8...8 aDES; *propriis armis iuguliantur* R. 9 aDES; *interiunt* R. 10 DRS; *preocupatus* aE. 11 aERS; *ergo* D. 12 aDES; *insequentes* R. 13 aDER; *exsaturitati* S. 14 aDERS (corrected from *reuertestes* in R).

§176 1 R; *Arturus* aDES. 2...2 aDES; *sepulta ibidem* R. 3 aRS; *reliquit* DE. 4 aDES; *quidam* R. 5 DER; *comprouintiales* a; *prouintiales* S. 6 aRS; *abbatias* DE. 7 aDES; *defferri* R. 8 aR; *Bedweri* DES. 9 aDES; *ciuitate* R. 10 aDES; *Boiacas* R. 11...11 DER; *ab Estrusiensibus* a; *a Neustrensibus* S. 12...12 aR; *egregie sepulture* DES. 13 aDES; *Ibique* R. 14 aER; *cymiterio* DS. 15 aES; *Kamum* D; *Cadonium* R. 16 aR; *opidum* DES. 17 aDE; *wlneratus* RS. 18 aDER; om. S. 19 aR; *opido* DES. 20 aDER; *Audegauensium* S. 21 aERS; *rex* (with *dux* in margin) D. 22 R; *Rutenorum* aDES. 23 DES; *Treuuana* aR. 24 DER; *humatus* a; *et humatus* S. 25 aR; *ac* DES. 26 aDERS (corrected from *delata* in R). 27 R; *corpus* a; *corpus quoque* DES.

Lucii[28] Rome ad senatum deferre, mandans non debere aliud tributum ex Britannia reddi. Postea uero subsequente hyeme in partibus illis moratus est et ciuitates Allobrogum subiugare uacauit. Adueniente estate dum Romam petere et Alpes transcendere cogitaret, nunciatur ei Modredum nepotem suum, cuius tutele permiserat Britanniam, eiusdem dyademate[29] per tyrannidem et prodicionem[30] usurpatum esse reginamque Guenhaueram[31] uiolato iure priorum[32] nuptiarum eidem nefando thalamo copulatam.[33]

[177] Rex[1] Arthurus[2] audita fama, ymmo[3] infamia, Modredi nepotis sui continuo dimissa inquietacione quam Romanis[4] [5]adhuc cogitarat inferre[5] Hoelo duci Armoricanorum[6] [7]exercitum Gallorum relinquens[7] ad pacificandas partes Allobrogum, ipse cum insulanis regibus eorumque exercitibus atque obiter[8] associatis sibi pluribus Britanniam rediit. Predictus autem[9] [10]proditor ille[10] Modredus[11] Cheldricum[12] Saxonum suorum ducem Germaniam[13] direxerat ut inde [14]exercitum copiosum[14] compararet spondens se illi hoc pacto daturum illam partem[15] Britannie que a flumine Humbri[16] usque in Scociam[17] porrigitur et simul quicquid[18] in Cancia[19] tempore Uortigerni[20] Horsus et Hengistus[21] possederant. At ille peracta[22] legacione cum octingentis nauibus bellatorum Saxonum plenis rediens applicuit et federe dato huic tanquam regi suo parebat.[23] Associauerat quoque Scotos, Pictos,[24] Hybernienses[25] et quoscumque sciebat [26]ante habuisse[26] auunculum suum odio. Erant autem omnes numero quasi .lxxx. milia tam paganorum quam christianorum, quorum multitudine uallatus Arthuro[27] in Rutupi

---

[28] aERS; *Lutii* D. [29] DRS; *diademate* aE. [30] ER; *proditionem* aDS. [31] R; *Gunuuaram* a; *Gwenneuuaram* D; *Gwennewaram* E; *Guennewaram* S. [32] aDES; *primo* R. [33] aDERS; after *copulatam*, *Explicit liber decimus. Incipit liber* [om. R] *undecimus* in aR.

§177 [1] aDRS; <R>ex E. [2] R; *Arturus* aDES. [3] R; *immo* aDES. [4] DERS (altered to *Romanorum*, with *Leoni regi* [from the vulgate text] in margin, in D); *Leoni Romanorum regi* a. [5]...5 R; *inferre disposuerat* a; *adhuc inferre cogitarat* DS; *inferre adhuc cogitarat* E. [6] DRS; *Armaricanorum* a; *Armoricorum* E. [7]...7 aR; *relinquens Gallorum exercitum* DES. [8] ERS; *ob iter* aD. [9] aDER; *iam* S. [10]...10 aDES; *ille proditor* R. [11] aDER; *Medredus* S. [12] aDES; *Celdricum* R. [13] aR; *in Germaniam* DE; *in Germania* S. [14]...14 aR; *copiosum exercitum* DES. [15] aDES; *parte* R. [16] aDES; *Humbrie* R. [17] ER; *Scotiam* aDS. [18] aDES; *quidquid* R. [19] ERS; *Cantia* aD. [20] aDS; *Wortigerni* E; *Uortigrini* R. [21] aR; *Heng'* DES. [22] aR; *pacta* DES. [23] aDRS; *parebant* E. [24] aERS; *et Pictos* D. [25] ERS; *Hibernienses* aD. [26]...26 R; *odio habuisse* (with *odio* omitted after *suum*) a; *habuisse antea* D; *habuisse ante* ES. [27] R; *Arturo* aDES.

Portu applicanti obuiam uenit et commisso prelio magnam stragem applicantibus intulit. In quo loco Auguselus rex Albanie et Walwanus nepos Arthuri[28] cum innumerabilibus corruerunt.[29] Tandem exercitus Arthuri[30] bello[31] magis assuetus post mutuam cladem Modredum et exercitum eius[32] in fugam coegerunt. Periurus igitur ille atque proditor infandus[33] sequenti nocte fugiens Wintoniam[34] [35]ingressus est[35] cum paucis. Quo [36]Arthurus adueniens[36] ciuitatem obsedit et, cum exercitum suum per[37] turmas in obsidionem disponeret, ille [38]agminibus suorum ac ciuium Wintoniensium in unam coniuracionem prouocatis[38] tamquam[39] preliaturus egreditur atque inito certamine fuge [40]precipitem se[40] dedit fugiensque [41]Hamonis Portum[41] petit ac cito remige euectus Cornubiam deuenit.[42] Interea Iwenus,[43] filius Uriani fratris Auguseli,[44] in regnum Albanie succedens [45]rex Albanorum[45] creatus[46] est; qui postea in [47]decertacionibus huiuscemodi[47] multis probitatibus preclaruit.[48] Guenhauera[49] autem regina auditis de tanto [50]euentu bellorum[50] nunciis confestim desperans ab Eboraco ad[51] Urbem Legionum diffugit atque in templo Iulii martiris[52] inter monachas uitam professa[53] monachalem delituit.

[178] Arthurus[1] itaque interno[2] dolore cruciatus quoniam tociens[3] manus suas euasisset proditor suus congregans quantum potuit exercitum illum usque in Cornubiam prosequitur.[4] Modredus autem [5]copiis interim[5] terra[6] marique comparatis ad fluuium Cambula[7] Arthuro[8] preliaturus occurrit.[9] Tradens fortune rei euentum atque diem extremum uite sue, si contingat, cum triumpho compensans maluit cum auunculo suo Arthuro[10] constanter dimicare atque finem rebus dubiis

---

[28] R; *Arturi* aDES. [29] DER; *eo die corruerunt* a; *corruunt* S. [30] R; *Arturi* aDES. [31] aDES; *bellum* R. [32] aERS; *suum* D. [33] ERS; *nefandus* aD. [34] aDER; *Wyntoniam* S. [35]...[35] aDES; *est ingressus* R. [36]...[36] R; *Arturus adueniens* a; *adueniens Arturus* DES. [37] aR; *in* DES. [38]...[38] aR (*coniurationem* in a; *aciuium* for *ac ciuium* in R); *agmina sua ac ciues Wyntonienses in unam coniuracionem prouocans* DES (*Wintonienses* and *coniurationem* in D). [39] DR; *tanquam* aES. [40]...[40] aR; *se precipitem* DES. [41]...[41] aR; *Portum Hamonis* DES. [42] aERS; *petit et ibi deuenit* D. [43] aDE; *Wennus* R; *Wenus* S. [44] aDES; *Auguselei* R. [45]...[45] aR; *Albanorum rex* DES. [46] aDES; *certatus* R. [47]...[47] R; *decertationibus huiusmodi* a; *huiusmodi decertacionibus* DES. [48] aERS; *claruit* D. [49] R; *Gunuuara* a; *Gwenneuuara* D; *Gwennewara* ES. [50]...[50] aR; *bellorum euentu* DES. [51] aR; *usque ad* DES. [52] aERS; *martyris* D. [53] DES; *professam* R.

§178 [1] R; *Arturus* aDES. [2] aDER; *in tanto* S. [3] ER; *totiens* aDS. [4] aER; *persequitur* DS. [5]...[5] aR; *interim copiis* DES. [6] aDES; *terram* R. [7] aDRS; *Cabula* E. [8] R; *Arturo* aDES. [9] aDER; *occurit* S. [10] R; *Arturo* aDES.

inponere[11] quam tociens[12] turpiter cedere. Inito igitur[13] certamine committitur durissima[14] pugna in qua fere omnes duces qui ex utraque parte affuerant cum [15]suis cateruis[15] mutuis uulneribus[16] occubuerunt.[17] Cecidit[18] ea die Modredus cum [19]suis ducibus,[19] Cheldrico,[20] Elasio,[21] Egbricto,[22] Brunnigo[23] cum omnibus eorum Saxonibus, necnon et Gillapatric,[24] Gillamor, Gillasel,[25] Gillaruum Hyberniensibus,[26] Scoti[27] etiam et Picti cum omnibus quibus dominabantur. In parte autem Arthuri[28] Obericus[29] rex Noruegie,[30] Aschillus[31] rex Dacie, Cador Limenic,[32] Cassibellaunus[33] cum multis milibus suorum tam Britonum quam ceterarum gencium[34] quas secum adduxerat. Omnes hii eadem die perierunt iuxta flumen[35] Cambula. Sed[36] et inclitus ille Arthurus[37] letaliter uulneratus[38] est; qui illinc[39] ad sananda uulnera[40] sua in insulam[41] Auallonis[42] euectus Constantino cognato suo et filio Cadoris Cornubie Britanniam regendam dimisit anno ab incarnacione[43] Domini .dxlii..[44]

[179/180] Postea duo filii Modredi cum Saxonibus qui remanserant,[1] alter [2]Londoniam, alter uero Wintoniam[2] ingressi contra Constantinum munire ceperunt. At Constantinus cum armata manu Britonum ciuitatibus adueniens Saxones potestati sue subiugauit et alterum iuuenem Wintonie[3] in ecclesia sancti Amphibali delitescentem[4] trucidauit, alterum uero Londoniis in quodam cenobio absconditum crudeli

[11] RS; *imponere* aDE. [12] ERS; *totiens* aD. [13] aDES; *ergo* R. [14] aR; *dirissima* DES. [15...15] aR; *cateruis suis* DES. [16] aDE; *wlneribus* RS. [17] aDES; *obcubuerunt* R. [18] aDERS. From this point the text of c is partially First-Variant (although predominantly vulgate). [19...19] aR; *ducibus suis* DES. [20] DES; *Chelrico* a; *Celrico* R. [21] aDRS; *Elafio* E. [22] DES; *Egbrico* a; *Esbricto* R. [23] S; *Brunigo* a; *Brumugo* DR; *Bruningo* E. [24] aR; *Gillepatric* cES; *Gillepatrich* D. [25] aDES; *Gissasel* R. [26] ES; *Hibernienses* ac; *Hiberniensibus* D; *Hybernienses* R. [27] cRS; *Scotti* aD; *Scocti* E. [28] R; *Arturi* acDES. [29] R; *Odbericus* a; *Odberictus* c; *Odberictus* DE; *Obictus* S. [30] R; *Norwegie* ac; *Norguegie* DES. [31] aDER; *Asschillus* c; *Achillus* S. [32] S; *Limenie* aER; *Llumenic* c; *Lymenic* D. [33] aDR; *Cassibelaunus* cE; *Cassibellanus* S. [34] acERS; *gentium* D. [35] acR; *fluuium* DES. [36] acDES; *Set* E. [37] R; *Arturus* acDES. [38] acDE; *wlneratus* RS. [39] acDER; *illicum* S. [40] acDES; *wlnera* R. [41] acDES; *insula* R. [42] acDES; *Aualonis* R. [43] ERS; *incarnatione* acD. [44] aDERS; *542* c. The *Vera Historia de Morte Arturi* is interpolated between §178 and §§179/80 in R (see Introduction, p. xc).

§§179/80 [1] aDER; *remanserunt* S. [2...2] aDES (*Wyntoniam* in ES); *Londonias alter Gwintoniam* c; *Gintoniam alter Lundoniam* R. [3] aDR; *Wyntonie* ES. [4] aDES; *diletescentem* R.

morte multauit.[5] Tunc temporis[6] sanctus Daniel Bangornensis[7] ecclesie religiosus antistes migrauit ad Dominum. Tunc quoque [8]sanctus Dauid obiit[8] [9]Urbis Legionum[9] archiepiscopus sepultusque[10] est in Meneuia ciuitate infra monasterium suum, quod pre ceteris [11]sue dioceseos[11] dilexerat pro eo quod beatus Patricius, qui natiuitatem eius prophetauerat, ipsum[12] fundauit. Subrogatur sedi illius Kinnocus[13] Lampaternensis[14] ecclesie antistes et ad altiorem dignitatem [15]in metropolitanum[15] promouetur. Cum autem duobus annis regnasset Constantinus, tertio anno interfectus est[16] a Conano[17] et infra structuram lapidum, que Saxonica lingua Stanheng[18] nuncupatur, iuxta cenobium Ambrii[19] sepelitur.

[181] Conanus uero[1] regni dyademate[2] insignitus,[3] dignus laude si non foret ciuilis belli amator,[4] post multa facinora ab illo perpetrata[5] secundo regni sui anno obiit.

[182] Cui successit Uortiporius,[1] in quem [2]insurrexerunt Saxones[2] de Germania educentes magno nauigio exercitum. Sed[3] superatis hiis monarchiam totius[4] regni adeptus est [5]populum gubernans[5] [6]annis quatuor[6] cum diligencia[7] et pace.

[183] Huic successit Malgo[1] omnium fere ducum Britannie pulcherrimus et probitate preclarus, nisi [2]sodomitic<a> peste[2] fedatus[3] Deo

[5] aERS; *mulctauit* D. [6] aR; *tempore* DES. [7] aER; *Bangoriensis* c; *Bangorensis* D; *Bargornensis* S. [8...8] aR; *obiit sanctus Dauid* DES. [9...9] aERS; *Urbis Legionum* over an erasure (with *Meneuensis* suprascript) D. [10] aDER; *sepultus* S. [11...11] acR; *dyocesis sue* DES. [12] DES; *ipsam* ac; *illud* R. [13] aR; *Kynnorus* (with *Kynnocus* in margin) D; *Kinnorus* ES. [14] aES; *Lanpaternensis* D; *Lampatriensis* R. [15...15] aR; om. DES (with *in metropolit<anum>* [partially clipped] in margin in D). [16] aDS; om. ER. [17] aR; *Conano suo consanguineo* DES. [18] aDES; *Stanhens* R. [19] DES; *Ambrie* a; *Ambri* cR.

§181 [1] aDES; *autem* R. [2] DRS; *diademate* aE. [3] aDER; om. S. [4] aDES; *armator* R. [5] DES; *perpetrato* R.

§182 [1] acDRS; *Wortiporius* E. [2...2] acR; *Saxones insurrexerunt* DE; *Saxones insurexerunt* S. [3] aDRS; *Set* E. [4] DRS; *tocius* aE. [5...5] aERS; *gubernans populum* D. [6...6] R; *quatuor annis* a; *4 annis* c; *annis .iiii.* DES. [7] ER; *diligentia* aDS.

§183 [1] aDERS (altered to *Mailgo* by suprascript *i* in D). [2...2] my emendation; *sodomitica* a; *sodomitica esset peste* DES; *sodomitico peste* R. [3] aR; *fedatus et sic* DES.

sese inuisum exhibuisset: multorum tamen tyrannorum[4] depulsor, robustus armis, largior[5] ceteris. Hic totam Britanniam sibi subiugauit; adiacentes quoque insulas,[6] Hyberniam uidelicet atque Hyslandiam,[7] [8]Gothlandiam, Orcades,[8] [9]necnon Norwegiam[9] et Daciam, durissimis[10] preliis sue potestati adiecit.

[184/6] Successit Malgoni[1] Carecius[2] amator idem[3] ciuilium bellorum[4] inuisus Deo[5] et Britonibus Saxonibusque; cuius[6] inconstanciam[7] atque seuiciam Saxones ferre non ualentes miserunt nuncios ad Godmundum[8] regem Affricanorum[9] in Hyberniam[10] quam magno nauigio aduectus[11] sibi subiugauerat et adduxerunt eum in Britanniam cum .clx. milibus Affricanorum[12] bellatorum. Inito igitur federe Godmundus cum Saxonibus oppugnauit Carecium[13] regem Britonum et post plurima prelia fugere coegit et persequens eum de ciuitate in ciuitatem tandem in Cicestria[14] [15]obsedit eum.[15] Dum autem ibi moram faceret, uenit ad eum [16]de Francia Ysembertus nepos Ludouici regis Francorum[16] nauigio aduectus et cum eo iniit fedus amicicie rogans ut se uindicaret de auunculo suo rege Francorum, qui, ut aiebat, ui et iniuste illum de Francia expulerat;[17] et [18]ut ei facilius[18] acquiesceret[19] de christiano factus est paganus[20] et sacrificiis ydolorum se commaculauit.[21] Capta deinde[22] ciuitate illa[23] quam obsederat fuge iterum se dedit Carecius[24] et pertransiens totam Britanniam usque ultra Sabrinam non cessauit fugere donec peruenit[25] in Guallias.[26] At Godmundus dimisso illo[27] agros[28] depopulatus est et succendit igni urbes et municipia, uicos

---

[4] aDRS; *tirannorum* E. [5] aERS; *et largior* D. [6] aDRS; *isulas* E. [7] R; *Hislandiam* aDES. [8...8] DR; *Godlandiam Orcades* aE; *Orcades Godlandiam* S. [9...9] R; *necnon et Norguegiam* a; *Norguegiam necnon* DES. [10] acR; *dirissimis* DES.

§§184/6 On the restructuring of §§184–7 (and the omission of §185) in the First Variant version, see Introduction, pp. xxxvi–vii. [1] aDERS (altered to *Mailgoni* by suprascript *i* in D). [2] R; *Caretius* aDES. [3] aR; om. DES. [4] aDRS; *bellatorum* E. [5] aDRS; om. E. [6] aDER; om. S. [7] aERS; *inconstantiam* D. [8] aDES; *Gotmundum* R. [9] aDRS; *Affricorum* E. [10] ERS; *Hiberniam* aD. [11] aERS; *adductus* D. [12] aDRS; *Affricorum* E. [13] RS; *Caretium* aDE. [14] ES; *Cicestriam* deleted (with *Cirecestriam* suprascript) a; *Cycestria* D; *Sirestria* R. [15...15] aR; *eum obsedit* DES. [16...16] R; *de Frantia Hisembertus nepos Ludowici regis Francorum* a; *Isembartus nepos Lodouici regis Francorum de Francia* DES (with *Ysembartus* in D; and *Lodeuici* in S). [17] aDER; *expulauit* (tampered) S. [18...18] aDES; *non facilius ei* R. [19] R; *adquiesceret* aDES. [20] aDES; *xan* deleted before *paganus* in R. [21] aDES; *maculauit* (with *com-* suprascript) R. [22] aDES; *demum* R. [23] aDES; om. R. [24] RS; *Caretius* aDE. [25] aR; *ueniret* DES. [26] R; *Gualias* a; *Gwallias* DES. [27] aR; *eo* DES. [28] aDER; om. S.

et castra necnon et monasteria et omnes regionis ecclesias depredatus est et ferro et igne ad terram diruit[29] colonosque cum mulierculis partim necauit, partim abduxit; nec quieuit donec omnem[30] terre superficiem fere a mari usque ad mare exussit.[31] Fugiunt episcopi de sedibus suis et presbiteri[32] simul[33] reliquias[34] sanctorum secum asportantes, monachi et moniales et uniuersi [35]quotquot Affricanorum[35] gladium euadere potuerunt; et desolata est terra ab omni specie[36] sua, [37]maxime Loegria[37] que pars Britannie melior extiterat.

[186/7] Postquam infaustus ille tyrannus[1] totam regionem illam[2] deuastauit, Saxonibus tenendam dimisit atque ad Gallias cum Ysembarto[3] transiuit. Hinc [4]Angli Saxones[4] uocati sunt qui Loegriam[5] possederunt[6] et ab eis Anglia terra postmodum dicta est. Britonibus[7] enim[8] fugatis ac[9] dispersis amisit terra nomen Britannie sicque Angli in ea super reliquias Britonum regnare ceperunt et Britones regni dyadema[10] [11]in perpetuum[11] amiserunt nec postea pristinam dignitatem recuperare[12] potuerunt. Secesserant itaque eorum reliquie partim in Cornubiam, partim in Guallias,[13] ubi nemoribus obtecti in montibus et speluncis cum feris[14] degentes longo tempore delituerunt donec reuocata audacia irrupciones[15] in Anglos Saxones crebras[16] facere conati sunt et sic diu perseuerauere[17] ut [18]nec Saxones in illos, nec illi in Saxones[18] preualerent.[19] Creati sunt interea plurimi reges Anglorum Saxonum qui in diuersis partibus Loegrie[20] regnauerunt; inter quos fuit Edelbertus[21] rex Cancie,[22] uir illustris et magne pietatis.

---

[29] aDES; *irruit* R. [30] aDERS (corrected from *omnes* in R). [31] cR; *excussit* aDES (with the c underpointed in D). [32] aDES; *presbiteris* R. [33] aDES; *suis* underpointed before *simul* in R. [34] DES; *cum reliquiis* aR. [35]...[35] acDS; *quotquot Affricorum* E; *quoque Affricanorum quotquot* R. [36] aDER; *defensione* c; *spe* S. [37]...[37] aE; *Loegria maxime* D; *maxime Loegrina* R; *maxime Leogria* S.

§§186/7 [1] aDRS; *tirannus* E. [2] aDERS (corrected from *illama* in S). [3] DR; *Ysembardo* a; *Isembarto* ES. [4]...[4] R; *bAngli aSaxones* a; *Saxones Angli* DES. [5] aDER; *Leogriam* S. [6] aDS; *possiderunt* ER. [7] DES; *Brittonibus* a; *Britonis* R. [8] aDER; om. S. [9] aR; *atque* DES. [10] DRS; *diadema* aE. [11]...[11] R; *imperpetuum* a; om. DES. [12] aR; *nisi post longum tempus recuperare* DES. [13] R; *Gualias* a; *Gwallias* DE; *Gwalias* E. [14] aDERS; the remainder of this chapter and §§188–203(part) are missing from a, because of a lacuna between fos 62v–63r (see Introduction, p. lxxviii). [15] ERS; *irruptiones* D. [16] DRS; *crebrius* E. [17] DE; *preseuerare* RS. [18]...[18] R; *nec illi in Saxones nec Saxones in illos* DES. [19] DRS; *preualuerunt* (with *seu preualerent* in margin) E. [20] DER; *Leogrie* S. [21] R; *Aethelbrictus* DES. [22] ERS; *Cantie* D.

[188] Cuius temporibus missus est beatus Augustinus a beato Gregorio papa Romano in Angliam ut Anglis uerbum uite predicaret. Qui fugatis Britonibus christianis adhuc in errore gentilitatis perseuerabant. Ueniens itaque Augustinus[1] in Canciam[2] susceptus est a rege Edelberto[3] gratanter et eo permittente et concedente uerbum Dei genti [4]Anglorum predicauit[4] et[5] signo fidei eos insigniuit. Deinde non multo post [6]rex Edelbertus[6] ipse cum ceteris baptismatis sacramentum consecutus est. Suscepta igitur [7]ab Anglis in Cancia[7] christianitate diffusa est per totam Loegriam[8] fides Iesu Christi usque ad fines Britonum.[9] Quo perueniens beatus Augustinus[10] inuenit in prouincia Britonum – quam tunc possidebant – .vii. episcopatus et unum archiepiscopatum et abbacias[11] quam plures in quibus grex Domini ordinem ecclesiasticum tenebat; inter quos erat abbas[12] Dinoot[13] nomine liberalibus artibus inbutus[14] in Bangor ciuitate presidens bis mille fere monachis. Qui per diuersas mansiones diuisi labore manuum uictum sibi acquirebant[15] et in .vii. porciones[16] diuidebant prout singulis quibusque[17] opus erat; sed et nulla porcionum[18] minus continebat quam .ccc.[19] monachos. Augustino itaque petenti subiectionem ab eis sibi debere fieri, utpote metropolitano et tocius regni primati, et communem ewangelizandi[20] [21]laborem secum[21] susciperent in gentem Anglorum, renuerunt omnes pariter et[22] episcopi et abbates dicentes nullam ei subiectionem debere facere nec inimicis suis communicare pro eo quod et[23] regno et lingua et sacerdocio[24] [25]et consuetudinibus omnino diuisi essent:[25] presertim cum gens illa maledicta illis foret exosa, utpote que de propriis sedibus illos[26] uiolenter eiecerat,[27] et adhuc [28]eis uim[28] inferre perseuerarent. Neque enim aiebant Anglis magis quam canibus communicare uelle;[29] preterea ipsi proprium metropolitanum tamquam[30] primatem[31] et regem[32] cum regni sui dyademate[33] sibi prefecerant quibus potius[34]

---

§188 [1] DR; *Aug'* ES. [2] ERS; *Cantiam* D. [3] R; *Athelbricto* DES. [4...4] R; *predicauit Anglorum* DES. [5] DER; *in* S. [6...6] R; *Athelbrictus rex* DES. [7...7] R; *in Cancia ab Anglis* DES (*Cantia* in D). [8] DER; *Leogriam* S. [9] DES; *Britannie* underpointed before *Britonum* in R. [10] DR; *Aug'* ES. [11] RS; *abbatias* DE. [12] R; om. DES. [13] RS; *Dynoot* DE. [14] R; *eruditus* DES. [15] R; *adquirebant* DES. [16] ER; *portiones* DS. [17] DRS; *quibus* E. [18] ER; *portionum* DS. [19] ERS; *.cccc.* D. [20] RS; *euuangelizandi* DE. [21...21] R; *secum laborem* DES. [22] R; om. DES. [23] R; om. DES. [24] ERS; *sacerdotio* D. [25...25] R; *essent diuisi et etiam consuetudinibus* DES. [26] R; *eos* DES. [27] R; *eiecerant* DES. [28...28] R; *uim eis* DES. [29] DES; *uolebant* R. [30] R; *quasi* DES. [31] DER; *primatum* S. [32] ER; *regnum* DS. [33] DRS; *diademate* E. [34] DRS; *pocius* E.

³⁵obedire secundum legem Dei³⁵ satagebant et,³⁶ quia ipsi priores baptismi gratiam consecuti fuerant, indignum uidebatur et contra morem ecclesiasticum fieri ut posteris et barbaris ³⁷inimicis ullatenus³⁷ subderentur.

[189] Edebertus[1] ergo rex Canciorum[2] ut audiuit Britones[3] dedignantes[4] subiectionem facere Augustino[5] et predicacionem[6] eius spernere, grauissime[7] ferens misit ad regem Edelfridum[8] Nordamhumbrorum et ceteros subregulos Saxonum rogans ut collecto exercitu in ciuitatem Bangor abbatem Dinoot[9] cum ceteris [10]Augustini predicacionem[10] spernentibus perditum irent. Qui mox regis preceptis acquiescentes[11] [12]exercitum grandem producunt[12] et prouinciam Britonum petentes uenerunt Legecestriam,[13] ubi Brochinail[14] consul urbis[15] eiusdem cum exercitu suo [16]eorum aduentum[16] prestolabatur ut dimicaret cum eis. Qui pauciori [17]numero militum[17] resistens Anglis insistentibus attrociter[18] in fugam uersus est amisso exercitu. Edelfrido[19] itaque ciuitate capta occurrerunt ciues[20] et populi qui terrore suo se intra incluserant obuiam[21] ut pro salute sua supplicarent. Uenerant quoque[22] ad eandem ciuitatem monachi et heremite, uiri religiosi, quamplures ex diuersis Britonum prouinciis et maxime de Bangor ut pro salute populi sui[23] intercederent apud regem Edelfridum[24] et ceteros regulos; quos diri et funesti barbari, cum intellexissent causam quare aduenissent, tamquam[25] ouium[26] greges[27] in caulas usque ad duo milia .cc.[28] trucidauerunt absque misericordia et de confessoribus martires fecerunt. Cumque[29] ulterius progrederentur ut urbem[30] Bangornensium[31] adirent atque cedem inceptam peragerent, Britonum duces audita eorum

35...35 R; *secundum legem Dei obedire* DES. 36 DES; om. R. 37...37 DES; *in tunicis nullatenus* R.

§189 1 R; *Athelbrictus* DES. 2 ERS; *Cantiorum* D. 3 DRS; om. E. 4 R; *indignantes* DES. 5 DER; *Aug'* S. 6 ERS; *predicationem* D. 7 cR; *grauiter* DES. 8 R; *Ethelfridum* DES. 9 ERS; *Dynoot* D. 10...10 R; *predicationem Augustini* D; *predicacionem Aug'* ES. 11 DR; *acquiescens* (with *-tes* in margin) E; *acquiescentes* S. 12...12 R; *exercitum magnum producunt* DS; *producunt exercitum magnum* E. 13 RS; *Legrecestram* DE (with *Leyrcestram* in margin of D). 14 DER; *Brochmail* S. 15 DER; *urbs* S. 16...16 R; *aduentum eorum* DES. 17...17 R; *militum numero* DES. 18 R; *atrociter* DES. 19 R; *Ethelfrido* DES. 20 R; *ciues obuiam* DES. 21 R; om. DES. 22 R; *itaque* DES. 23 R; om. DES. 24 R; *Ethelfridum* DES. 25 DR; *tanquam* ES. 26 DES; *obuium* R. 27 DES; *re* underpointed before *greges* in R. 28 R; *et .cc.* DES. 29 DES; *Cumque ut* R. 30 R; *ciuitatem* DES. 31 E; *Bangorensium* D; *Bargorniensium* R; *Bargornensium* S.

insania in unum conuenerunt, Bledricus uidelicet dux Cornubie et Margadud[32] rex Demetorum, Cadwanus[33] quoque rex Uenedotorum,[34] et conserto prelio ipsum regem[35] Edelfridum[36] uulneratum[37] Dei auxilio in fugam propulerunt et totum fere eius exercitum extinxerunt. In parte quoque Britonum cecidit Bledricus[38] dux.

[190] Post hec conuenerunt principes Britonum in ciuitatem[1] Legecestrie[2] communemque assensum simul habuerunt ut Cadwanum[3] sibi regem facerent eoque duce Edelfridum[4] ultra Humbrum insequerentur. Cumque id [5]nunciatum esset Edelfrido,[5] associauit[6] sibi omnes reges Saxonum obuiusque Cadwano[7] perrexit. Qui cum cateruas suas ex utraque parte statuissent[8] ad bellum, interuenerunt amici eorum pacemque inter eos tali pacto fecerunt ut Edelfridus[9] trans Humbrum, Cadwanus[10] uero citra Humbrum Britanniam possideret. Cum autem Deo preside conuentionem[11] huiusmodi[12] iureiurando atque obsidibus datis comfirmassent, orta est tanta amicicia[13] inter eos ut omnia sua communia haberent. [14]Lapso itaque[14] tempore natus est Caduano ex propria coniuge filius nomine Cadwallo; sub eodem quoque tempore peperit et[15] uxor Edelfridi[16] filium nomine Edwinum.[17]

[191/92] Hii[1] post mortem parentum dyademate[2] insigniti susceperunt [3]curam regnorum[3] agendam secundum antecessorum institucionem et amiciciam quam[4] prius patres eorum tenuerant[5] inter se ipsi statuere tenendam.[6] Emenso deinde biennio rogauit Edwinus[7] Cadwallonem ut sibi dyadema[8] liceret habere celebraretque statutas sollempnitates[9] in partibus Nordamhumbrorum quemadmodum ipse citra Humbrum

---

[32] DERS (with *Maredud* in margin in D). [33] R; *Caduanus* DES. [34] DRS; *Uenodotorum* E. [35] R; om. DES. [36] R; *Ethelfridum* DE; *Etheldridum* S. [37] DES; *wlneratum* R. [38] DES; *Bledriacus* R.

§190 [1] R; *urbem* DES. [2] RS; *Legrecestrie* DE (with *Leyrcestrie* in margin of D). [3] R; *Caduanum* DES. [4] R; *Ethelfridum* DES. [5...5] R; *Ethelfrido nunciatum esset* DES. [6] DES; *associauis* R. [7] R; *Caduano* DES. [8] DERS (corrected from *statuerunt* in R). [9] R; *Ethelfridus* DES. [10] R; *Caduanus* DES. [11] DRS; *conuencionem* E. [12] ERS; *huius* D. [13] DER; *amicitia* S. [14...14] R; *Elapso deinde* DES. [15] R; om. DES. [16] R; *Ethelfridi* DE; *Etheldridi* S. [17] DERS (corrected from *Edwinclii* [?] in S).

§§191/2 [1] DER; om. (with *Qui* suprascript) S. [2] DRS; *diademate* E. [3...3] R; *regnorum curam* DES. [4] DES; *qua* R. [5] ERS; *tenuerunt* D. [6] DRS; *tenendum* E. [7] DES; *Eadwinus* R. [8] DR; *diadema* ES. [9] DRS; *solempnitates* E.

antiquo more consueuerat. Cumque inde iuxta fluuium Duglas colloquium haberent, disponentibus sapiencioribus[10] et antiquioribus qua
ratione id melius fieri posset, Cadwallone in altera parte fluminis
existente consilio Briani nepotis sui, qui forte secum aderat, penituit
eum incepte pactionis mandauitque Edwino quod nullatenus a consi-
liariis suis impetrare poterat quatinus permisissent eum peticioni eius
acquiescere.[11] Aiebant enim contra ius ueterumque tradicionem esse
regnum unius corone duobus coronatis summitti[12] debere. Iratus itaque
Edwinus dimisso colloquio reuersus est in Nordamhumbriam asserens
se sine licencia[13] Cadwallonis regali dyademate[14] iniciaturum.[15] Quod
cum Cadwalloni[16] esset nunciatum, intimauit[17] ei per legatos se
amputaturum [18]ei capud[18] sub dyademate si infra regnum Britannie
coronari presumeret.

[193] Orta igitur inter eos discordia, cum utrorumque homines [1]magis
bellum[1] quam pacem[2] affectantes[3] sese plurimis decertacionibus inquie-
tassent, conuenerunt ambo iuxta Humbrum factoque congressu amisit
[4]Cadwallo multa milia sociorum[4] et in fugam uersus est. Arreptoque
per Albaniam itinere transfretauit in Hyberniam.[5] At Edwinus ut
triumpho potitus fuit, duxit exercitum suum per prouincias[6] Britonum
combustisque ciuitatibus ciues et colonos pluribus affecit tormentis.
Dum ergo sic seuiret in Britones, conabatur Cadwallo clam reuerti et
[7]in aliquo portu applicare;[7] nec poterat quia per magum quendam qui
uenerat ad Edwinum de Hyspania aduentum illius presciebat et,
quocumque portu applicare destinabat, armato milite [8]illi obuius[8] erat.
Nomen magi[9] Pellitus dicebatur et[10] uolatu auium cursuque[11] stellarum
predicebat regi[12] omnia que ei accidere poterant: unde[13] ualde [14]ei erat
carus.[14] Interea consilium querit Cadwallo quid[15] inter hec [16]agendum
sit[16] et tandem [17]deliberauit apud se[17] ut [18]regem Armoricanorum

---

[10] R; *sapientioribus* DES. [11] R; *adquiescere* DES. [12] RS; *submitti* DE. [13] ER; *licentia*
DS. [14] DR; *diademate* ES. [15] R; *insigniturum* DES. [16] DRS; *Cadwallano* E. [17] R;
interminauit DES. [18...18] R; *capud eius* DES.

§193 [1...1] R; *bellum magis* DES. [2] ERS; om. (but *pacem* in margin) D. [3] DERS
(corrected from *affectassent* in D). [4...4] R; *multa milia suorum Cadwallo* DES. [5] RS;
Hiberniam DE. [6] DRS; *prouinciam* E. [7...7] R; *applicare in aliquo portu* DES.
[8...8] DER; *obuius illi* S. [9] R; *illius magi* DES. [10] R; *qui* DES. [11] DE; *cursu* R; *cursum*
S. [12] R; *ei* DES. [13] R; *inde* DES. [14...14] R; *carus ei erat* DES. [15] R; *quid ei* DES.
[16...16] R; *sit agendum* DES. [17...17] R; *apud se deliberauit* DES.

Salomonem cognatum suum peteret[18] quatinus [19]consilio eius[19] et auxilio in regnum suum restitueretur.

[194/5] Pandens itaque uela iter flexit uersus Armoricum regnum[1] et transfretauit et applicuit in portum Kidalete urbis ueniensque[2] ad regem Salomonem gratanter ab illo et honorifice susceptus est. Cumque causam aduentus eius didicisset, mox sibi [3]ferre auxilium[3] quantum preualeret[4] spopondit.[5] Sed[6] quia hyemis[7] tempus[8] instabat et [9]opus erat maiori consilio[9] ad tantam rem peragendam, hyemandum [10]illi secum[10] erat ut post hyemem collecto[11] exercitu nauibusque paratis hostes Saxonicos uiriliter inuaderent.

[196] Interim[1] consilium ineunt[2] ut magus ille Pellitus aliquo modo perimeretur[3] ne machinaciones[4] eorum et [5]aduentus eorum[5] in Britanniam detegantur.[6] Premiserunt Brianum Cadwallonis nepotem ut curam [7]eius rei[7] ageret quatinus clam ex insidiis prorumpens magum interimeret[8] et a prestigiis suis et maleficiis arte dyabolica comparatis[9] Britanniam liberaret. Nauigans ergo ille applicuit [10]ad Portum[10] Hamonis et exiens in[11] terram de naui finxit sese pauperculum uilibus pannis obsitum fecitque[12] sibi [13]fieri baculum[13] in summitate ferreum et acutum ualde, tanquam peregrinus de longa peregrinacione[14] aduectus esset.[15] Deinde perrexit Eboracum quo audierat degere regem Edwinum et, cum ingrederetur ciuitatem, associauit se pauperibus qui regis elemosinam petebant. Eunte autem illo[16] et redeunte ac deambulante cum ceteris egressa est soror eius de triclinio regine baiulans[17] peluim in

---

18...18 DES (*suumque* in ES, corrected to *suum* in S); *Salomonem apud* [underpointed] *Armoricanorum peteret cognatum suum* R. 19...19 R; *eius consilio* DE; *ei consilio* S.

§§194/5 1 DER; *regum* R. 2 DER; *ueniens* S. 3...3 DES; *auxilium fere* R. 4 R; *ualeret* DES. 5 ES; *spospondit* DR. 6 DRS; *Set* E. 7 DRS (corrected from *hymemis* in R); *hiemis* E. 8 DES; *tempore* R. 9...9 R; *maiori consilio opus erat* DES. 10...10 ERS; *secum illi* D. 11 DES; *collectoque* R.

§196 1 R; *Interea* DES. 2 DES; *iniunt* R. 3 DRS; *perimetur* E. 4 ERS; *machinationes* D. 5...5 R; *aduentum* DES. 6 R; *detegeret* DES. 7...7 R; *rei huius* DES. 8 R (corrected from *interiemeret*); *perimeret* DES. 9 R; om. DES. 10...10 R; *in Portu* DES. 11 R; *ad* DES. 12 DES; *fecit* R. 13...13 R; *baculum fieri* DES. 14 ERS; *peregrinatione* D. 15 DES; om. R. 16 R; *eo* DES. 17 DER; corrected from *baiolans* in S.

manu ut de fonte proximo aquam hauriret. Illam enim rapuerat Edwinus ex urbe Wigorniensium[18] dum [19]post fugam Cadwallonis in prouincias Britonum[19] deseuiret. Cum ergo ante Brianum preteriret, agnouit eam Brianus et in fletum solutus eam [20]uoce dimissa[20] uocauit. Que cum illius faciem propius intueretur, agnito fratre in lacrimas collapsa[21] est atque osculis[22] prelibatis familiaribus collocuti sunt inuicem[23] sermonibus. At illa indicauit [24]breuiter fratri[24] quasi aliud loquens statum curie[25] et magum quem querebat, qui forte tunc inter pauperes deambulabat, digito demonstrauit et agnoscere fecit. Qui mox dimissa sorore intromisit se infra turbam pauperum. Et cum[26] aditum feriendi reperisset, erexit burdonem[27] et infixit in pectore magi cadensque[28] in terram magus mortuus est. Mox proiecto [29]Brianus in terram[29] baculo inter pauperes[30] pannosos pannosus ipse delituit nulli astancium[31] suspectus. Dehinc[32] egressus[33] cum ceteris propero gradu [34]relinquens ciuitatem[34] et totam regionem illam Exoniam[35] usque peruenit, ubi conuocatis Britonibus de Cornubia et de finitimis[36] locis notificauit Cadwallonis aduentum fore[37] in proximum cum grandi exercitu ad eorum omnium liberacionem[38] et palmam: ciuitatesque et oppida[39] munirent et sibi conseruarent; misitque citam legacionem[40] ad Cadwallonem. Diuulgato itaque hoc rumore Peanda [41]Merciorum rex[41] cum magna multitudine Saxonum ab Edwino missus uenit[42] Exoniam[43] et obsedit eam.

[197] Interea applicuit Cadwallo ad portum Totonesium cum .x. milibus militum bellatorum quos ei rex Salomon cognatus suus tradiderat petiuitque[1] celeriter Exoniam.[2] Ut ergo cominus[3] uidit exercitum Peande circa ciuitatem, dimisit milites suos in quatuor[4] partes et sic[5] per turmas hostes undique inuasit. Consertoque[6] prelio captus est Peanda et exercitus eius peremptus. Cumque ille aditum

[18] DRS; *Wygorniensium* E. [19]...[19] R; *in prouincias Britonum post fugam Cadwallonis* DES. [20]...[20] R; *demissa uoce* D; *dimissa uoce* ES. [21] DER; *colapsa* S. [22] DERS (corrected from *oculis* in E). [23] R; om. DES. [24]...[24] R; *fratri breuiter* DES. [25] R; *regni* DES. [26] DES; *tum* R. [27] DRS; *burtonem* E. [28] DES; *cadens* R. [29]...[29] R; *in terram Brianus* DES. [30] DRS; om. E. [31] ERS; *astantium* D. [32] DES; *Dehinc ciuitatem* R. [33] DERS (altered from *ingressus* in R). [34]...[34] R; *ciuitatem relinquens* DES. [35] DS; *Oxoniam* ER. [36] DRS; *finictimis* E. [37] DRS; om. E. [38] ES; *liberationem* D; *deliberacionem* R. [39] R; *opida* DES. [40] ES; *legationem* D; *legionem* R. [41]...[41] R; *rex Merciorum* DS; *rex Merceorum* E. [42] DRS; om. E. [43] DES; *Oxoniam* R.

§197 [1] DER; *petuntque* S. [2] DES; *Oxoniam* R. [3] DRS; *comminus* E. [4] ERS; *.iiii.* D. [5] R; om. DES. [6] R; *Conserto itaque* DES.

alium non haberet, subdidit se Cadwalloni[7] fide sua et adiuracione[8] promittens datis[9] obsidibus sese cum illo Saxones inquietaturum. Conuocauit itaque Cadwallo[10] proceres suos multo tempore a se delapsos et desolatos atque uerbis consolatoriis eos[11] exhortans[12] congregauit quantum potuit exercitum atque in Nordamhumbriam contra Edwinum regem duxit; patriamque totam in transitu suo [13]non cessauit uastare[13] ferroque[14] et igne trucidare atque cremare quoscumque hostes inuenit. Audiens autem hoc Edwinus rex conuocauit omnes sibi subditos [15]Anglorum regulos[15] cum exercitibus eorum et in campo qui Hedfeld[16] appellatur obuiam ueniens Britonibus[17] bellum commisit sibi suisque cruentum. In quo bello interficitur ipse et totus fere populus cum regulis qui cum eo uenerant necnon et filius eius Osfridus cum Golboldo[18] rege Orchadum[19] qui in auxilium[20] eorum uenerat.

[198] Confecto[1] itaque prelio et uictoria patrata uniuersas Cadwallo [2]prouincias Saxonum[2] perlustrans ita [3]in totum[3] [4]Saxonum Anglorum[4] genus debachatus est et omnis exercitus eius ut [5]ne quidem sexui muliebri[5] uel paruulorum etati parceret, multos inauditis tormentis afficiens, ceteros diuersis mortibus puniens. Post hec commisit prelium cum Osrico[6] qui Edwino successerat et interfecit eum et duos nepotes eius quos post illum regnare sperabat[7] sed et Eadanum[8] regem Scotorum[9] qui eis in auxilium uenerat.

[199] Hiis itaque omnibus interemptis successit Oswaldus in regnum Nordamhumbrorum; quem [1]rex Cadwallo, mox ut[1] audiuit, cum grandi exercitu inuasit atque fugauit usque ad murum quem Seuerus

---

[7] DRS; *Cadualloni* E. [8] ERS; *adiuratione* D. [9] R; *datisque* DES. [10] DRS; *Caduallo* E. [11] DERS (corrected from *eorum* in S). [12] DER; *exortans* S. [13...13] R; *uastare non cessauit* DES. [14] DES; *ferro* R. [15...15] R; *regulos Anglorum* DES (with *populos* deleted before *regulos* in D). [16] DES; *Helfelt* R. [17] R; om. DES. [18] R; *Godbaldo* DES. [19] R; *Orcadum* DES. [20] DES; *auxilio* R.

§198 [1] R; *Facto* DES. [2...2] R (with *s* before *Saxonum*); *Saxonum prouincias* DES. [3...3] DERS (corrected from *motum* in S). [4...4] R; *Anglorum Saxonum* DES. [5...5] R; *nec sexui quidem muliebri* DS (*sexui* corrected from *serui* in S); *nec sexui muliebri quidem* E. [6] DES; *Osneo* R. [7] DERS (corrected from *superabat* in S). [8] DR; *Cadaum* ES (tampered in E). [9] RS; *Scottorum* D; *Scoctorum* E.

§199 [1...1] R; *mox ut Cadwallo* DES.

imperator olim inter Britanniam Scociamque[2] construxerat. Ut ergo uidit illum in remotas partes[3] fugientem, noluit uexare seipsum et[4] totum exercitum suum insequendo eum, sed misit Peandam Merciorum regem cum quadam [5]sui exercitus parte[5] ut eum debellaret. Quo comperto Oswaldus noluit diucius[6] fugere sed mansit in loco qui dicitur Heuenfeld,[7] id est 'celestis campus', expectans Peandam insequentem ibique erexit [8]dominicam crucem[8] et indixit commilitonibus suis[9] ut orationem[10] ad Deum facerent in hec uerba: 'Flectamus genua omnes et Deum omnipotentem, unum ac[11] uerum, in commune deprecemur ut nos ab exercitu superbo[12] Britannici regis et eius nefandi[13] ducis defendat. Scit enim ipse quia iusta[14] pro salute gentis nostre bella suscepimus.'[15] Fecerunt ergo omnes ut iusserat et sic diluculo in hostes progressi secundum fidei sue meritum uictoria potiti sunt. Fugiens ergo[16] Peanda uenit ad Cadwallonem dolens quod sic ab Oswaldo deuictus esset et fugatus. At Cadwallo acri insurgens ira collecto exercitu Oswaldum persecutus est et conserto cum illo prelio in loco qui Burne uocatur[17] irruit in eum Peanda et interfecit.

[200] Oswaldo itaque perempto et martyre[1] effecto successit ei in regnum Oswi[2] frater eius, qui cum Cadwallone pacem constituens multa donaria auri et argenti dedit et amiciciam cum eo confirmauit et se sibi[3] subdidit; et sic ex tunc toti Britannie imperauit rex Cadwallo. Nec mora insurrexerunt in Oswi[4] Alfridus filius eius et Oiwald[5] filius fratris eius. Sed cum preualere ei nequissent, secesserunt ad Peandam[6] regem implorantes auxilium contra Oswi.[7] At Peanda timens pacem a rege Cadwallone constitutam[8] infringere distulit inquietacionem Oswi[9] sine licencia[10] regis inferre donec illum aliquo modo incitaret quatinus uel[11] ipse in Oswi[12] insurgeret uel[13] sibi[14] copiam [15]cum eo congrediendi[15] concederet.[16] Quadam igitur sollempnitate[17] penthecostes[18] cum rex

2 ER; *et Scotiam* DS. 3 R; *regiones* DES. 4 R; *atque* DES. 5...5 R; *parte exercitus sui* DES. 6 ERS; *ulterius* D. 7 DER; *Hedenfeld* S. 8...8 DER; *dominicam* preceded by suprascript *crucem* S. 9 R; om. DES. 10 DRS; *oracionem* E. 11 DES; om. R. 12 DRS; om. E. 13 DRS; *nepfandi* E. 14 R; *iuste* DES. 15 R; *suscipimus* DES. 16 R; *igitiur* DES. 17 R; *dicitur* DES.

§200 1 ERS; *martire* D. 2 DRS; *Oswy* E. 3 R; *ei* DES. 4 DRS; *Oswy* E. 5 DE; *Orwald* R; *Oswal* S. 6 DES; *Piandam* R. 7 DRS; *Oswy* E. 8 DES; om. R. 9 DRS; *Oswy* E. 10 ER; *licentia* DS. 11 ERS; om. D. 12 DRS; *Oswy* E. 13 DER; *et* S. 14 DES; *ipse* R. 15...15 R; *congrediendi cum eo* DS; *cum eo congrediendi cum eo* E. 16 DES; *succederet* R. 17 DRS; *solempnitate* E. 18 R; *pentecostes* DES.

Cadwallo in Londonia[19] ciuitate festum celebraret et omnes[20] Anglorum reges et Britonum duces preter Oswi[21] adessent, adiuit Peanda
regem et quesiuit ab eo cur Oswi[22] solus abesset a cetu baronum
suorum; cui [23]rex cum responderet[23] infirmitatis causa interueniente
eum detineri posse, adiecit Peanda dicens nequaquam sic esse, sed
illum propter Saxones [24]misisse in Germaniam[24] ut fratrem suum
Oswaldum in se et in ceteros uindicaret.[25] Addidit quoque illum pacem
contra ius suum infregisse, utpote[26] qui Alfridum et Oywald[27] bello
inquietatos a propria patria expulerit.[28] Petiuit ergo licenciam ut [29]illum
uel[29] interficeret uel de regno fugaret. Rex itaque Cadwallo hec audiens
emisit Peandam et familiares suos atque optimates conuocans quesiuit[30]
quid super hiis esset agendum. [31]Tacentibus ergo[31] aliis Margadud rex
Demetorum pre ceteris respondit: 'Domine mi rex, quoniam omne
genus Anglorum [32]tibi infestum semper[32] fuisse nouimus et propter eius
perfidiam te ex finibus Britannie illud[33] expulsurum proposuisti, cur
[34]pacem eos inter nos[34] habere pateris?[35] Eia[36] ergo permitte saltem ut
ipsimet[37] inter se ipsos oppugnantes[38] se consumant et mutuis cladibus
affecti uniuersi a regno exterminentur. Peanda iste de[39] illis est et
eandem perfidiam quam in genus suum machinatur ne dubites quin in
[40]te ipsum tuosque[40] exerceat, si locum et tempus innate prodicionis[41]
habuerit. Da igitur ei licenciam ut in Oswi[42] insurgat et debachari[43]
inuicem permitte ut sic ciuili discordia exorta alter alterum perimens
omnes a patria deleantur.' Hiis itaque dictis omnis procerum concio[44]
consensit et rex Peande peticionem fieri concessit. Ille uero letus
discedens collecto exercitu transiuit Humbrum super Oswi[45] et [46]ferro
et igne terram eiusdem[46] uastare cepit. Cumque immaniter[47] atque
crudeliter superbia elatus in Oswi[48] deseuiret, mandauit ei Oswi[49] ut
sibi[50] parceret et donaria [51]auri et argenti multa[51] daret. Cum autem

---

[19] R; *Badonia* DES. [20] R; *uniuersi* DES. [21] DRS; *Oswy* E. [22] DRS; *Oswy* E. [23]...[23] R;
cum responderet rex DES. [24]...[24] DER; *in Germaniam* (followed by suprascript *misisse*)
S. [25] DERS (corrected from *uindicat* in D). [26] DES; om. R. [27] D; *Oidwald* E;
Oswaldum R; *Oswald* S. [28] ERS; *expulerat* D. [29]...[29] R; *uel illum* DES. [30] R; *quesiuit
ab eis* DES. [31]...[31] DES; *Tacenti uero* R. [32]...[32] R; *semper sibi inuisum* DES. [33] DES;
om. R. [34]...[34] R; *inter nos pacem* DES. [35] DERS (corrected from *pateritis* in S). [36] R;
Eya DES. [37] DES; *ipsemet* R. [38] ER; *obpugnantes* DS. [39] R; *ex* DES. [40]...[40] DE; *ipse in
te tuosque* R; *in te ipsum et* [suprascript] *tuos* S. [41] ERS; *proditionis* D. [42] DRS; *Oswy*
E. [43] DER; *debacari* S. [44] ERS; *contio* D. [45] DRS; *Oswy* E. [46]...[46] R; *terram eiusdem
ferro et igne* DES. [47] DES; *immaaniter* (sic) R. [48] DRS; *Oswy* E. [49] DRS; *Oswy* E.
[50] R; *ei* DES. [51]...[51] DER; *multa auri et argenti* S.

⁵²nec sic⁵² a proposito Peanda cessare uellet nec precibus nec⁵³ muneribus eius acquiesceret,⁵⁴ rex Oswi⁵⁵ diuinum expetens auxilium cum Peanda ⁵⁶decreuit pugnare⁵⁶ et conuenientes iuxta fluuium Winied⁵⁷ prelium inierunt. Sed⁵⁸ licet Oswi⁵⁹ minorem numero habuisset exercitum, superior tamen Deo auxiliante factus est et Peanda cum .xxx. ducibus perempto⁶⁰ uictoriam adeptus est. Post Peandam Wilfridus⁶¹ filius eius donante Cadwallone successit ei in regnum Merciorum. Qui consociatis sibi Eba⁶² et Edberto ducibus rebellauit aduersum⁶³ Oswi.⁶⁴ Sed iubente ac prohibente ⁶⁵tandem Cadwallone rege⁶⁵ pacem habuerunt ⁶⁶inter se adinuicem.⁶⁶

[201] Completis postea .xlviii. annis Cadwallo¹ infirmitate grauatus .xv. kalendis Decembris obiit. Cuius corpus Britones balsamo et aromatibus conditum in enea² statua posuerunt atque super eneum equum ipsam statuam,³ armis decoratam, collocauerunt. Deinde super occidentalem portam⁴ Londonie erexerunt in signum uictorie ad terrorem Saxonum. Sed et ecclesiam subtus in honore beati Martini edificauerunt in qua pro ipso et fidelibus⁵ ⁶omnibus defunctis⁶ diuina celebrarentur obsequia.

[202] Successit Cadwalloni in regnum filius suus Cadwalladrus.¹ Cuius temporibus ciuile discidium inter Britones ortum est. Mater namque eius soror Peande fuerat, ex nobili quidem ²Gewisseorum genere² edita, eamque Cadwallo post factam cum fratre concordiam in societatem thori acceperat et inde³ Cadwalladrum⁴ genuerat. Dum ergo regnaret Cadwalladrus⁵ et se omnibus amabilem prestaret, decidit in lectum⁶ et languore corripitur magno.

---

⁵²...⁵² DES; *sic ne* R. ⁵³ DES; *aut* R. ⁵⁴ R; *adquiesceret* DES. ⁵⁵ DRS; *Oswy* E. ⁵⁶...⁵⁶ R; *dimicare decreuit* DS; *dimicare decernit* E. ⁵⁷ DES; *Wumed* R. ⁵⁸ DRS; *Set* E. ⁵⁹ DRS; *Oswy* E. ⁶⁰ R; *peremptis* DES. ⁶¹ R; *Wlfridus* DES. ⁶² ERS; *Ebba* D. ⁶³ R; *aduersus* DES. ⁶⁴ DRS; *Oswy* E. ⁶⁵...⁶⁵ R; *rege Cadwallone* DES. ⁶⁶...⁶⁶ DES; *ad se inuicem* R.

§201 ¹ ERS; *Cadwal* D. ² DERS (corrected from *enia* in S). ³ DERS (corrected from *statutam* in S). ⁴ DES; *portem* (altered from *partem*) R. ⁵ ERS; *pro fidelibus* D. ⁶...⁶ R; *defunctis omnibus* DES.

§202 ¹ R; *Cadwaladrus* DES. ²...² R; *genere Geuisseorum* D; *genere Gewisseorum* ES. ³ R; *ex ea* DES. ⁴ R; *Cadwaladrum* DES. ⁵ R; *Cadwaladrus* DES. ⁶ DER; *lecto* S.

[203] Quo languente discordia, ut dictum est, afficiuntur Britones et opulentam[1] patriam dissensione detestabili destruere totis uiribus conantur. Accessit interea aliud[2] infortunium: fames uidelicet dira insipientem [3]affecit populum[3] adeo ut preter uenacionem[4] et herbarum surculos[5] deficerent eis ciborum solacia. Quam famem [6]continuo pestifera[6] mortis lues subsecuta est que in breui tantam[7] populi stragem fecit ut uiui [8]mortuos uix[8] sepelire possent. Ad cuius mortalitatis excidium[9] – miserabile ac pauendum[10] spectaculum! – multi[11] siue in domo siue in agro attoniti[12] passim moriebantur sine egrotacione, aeris tantum, ut ferebatur,[13] corrupcione.[14] Nonulli quoque stantes et loquentes, edentes[15] et bibentes subito expirabant. Unde reliqui stupefacti transmarinam fugam quam plurimi inierunt. Ipse quoque rex Cadwalladrus[16] ad Armoricam[17] cum paucis [18]nauigio effugit[18] et inter nauigandum fertur has lugubres uoces ad Deum protulisse:[19] 'Ue nobis miseris et peccatoribus, qui ob immania scelera nostra quibus Deum offendimus hanc tribulationem[20] et dispersionem patimur; gentem et patriam amittimus. Timendum [21]est ualde nobis[21] ne post[22] hanc celestem patriam perdamus[23] et [24]eterna hereditate priuemur.[24] Domine, miserere nobis; [25]tempus et locum[25] penitencie misericorditer permitte.[26] Ne irascaris nimis ut, si uel terrena caremus[27] ac presenti hereditate, illa omnino non[28] frustremur ad quam boni omnes quos in hac uita elegisti laborant peruenire. Exterminat nos de terra nostra potestas ulcionis[29] tue, quos nec olim Romani uel quelibet gens robustior eradicare potuit. Uere peccauimus ultra modum coram te et angelis tuis qui digni[30] non[31] sumus ut conuersi ad penitenciam terras quas incoluimus[32] inhabitemus. Expellimur flagello iracundie[33] tue quia serui nequissimi spreuimus, dum licuit, ueniam misericordie tue.

§203 1 DES; *opilentam* R. 2 R; *et aliud* DES. 3...3 R; *populum afficiens* DES. 4 ERS; *uenationem* D. 5 DES; *oculos* R. 6...6 DRS; *pestifera continuo* E. 7 DE; *tanta* R; *copiam* deleted after *tantam* S. 8...8 ERS; *uix mortuos* D. 9 DES; *exscidium* R. 10 R; *impatiendum* D; *paciendum* ES. 11 DER; *multa* S. 12 DES; *pauore attoniti* R. 13 R; *fertur* DES. 14 ERS; *corruptione* D. 15 aDERS; the lacuna in a (from §§186/7) ends at this point. 16 R; *Cadwaiadrus* aDES. 17 aDES; *Armonicam* R. 18...18 aDES; *effugit nauigio* R. 19 aR; *emississe* DES. 20 aDRS; *tribulacionem* E. 21...21 aR; *nobis ualde est* c; *est nobis ualde* DE; *nobis est ualde* S. 22 aDERS (partially in margin in E). 23 aR; *amittamus* DES. 24...24 aR (*priuemur* corrected from *priiuemur* in R); *eterna priuemur hereditate* c; *hereditate eterna priuemur* DES. 25...25 cR; *et tempus et locum* a; *et tempus* D; *locum et tempus* ES. 26 acR; *nobis permitte* DES. 27 acERS; *careamus* D. 28 DES; om. a; *ne* cR. 29 ERS; *ultionis* aD. 30 aDRS; om. E. 31 aDES; om. R. 32 ac; *coluimus* DES; *incolimus* R. 33 aER; *iracondie* cDS.

Experimur nunc seueritatem iudicantis[34] qui, dum tempus habuimus, noluimus[35] flectere lumina ad paternitatem uocantis. Frustra patriam nostram aduersus hostes te adiuuante tociens[36] expugnauimus, tociens[37] expulsi te donante recuperauimus, si sic olim decreueras uniuersum genus nostrum extirpare de terra uiuencium.[38] Sed placabilis esto, quesumus,[39] super maliciam nostram et conuerte [40]luctum nostrum[40] in gaudium ut de periculo mortis erepti uiuentes tibi Domino Deo nostro, cuius[41] serui esse debemus, in perpetuum famulemur.[42] Redeant ergo Romani, redeant Scoti[43] et Picti, redeant Saxones[44] perfidi et ceteri, quibus patet Britannia ira Dei deserta, quam illi desertam facere nequiuerunt. Non nos fortitudo illorum expellit sed summi regis indignacio et potencia.'[45]

[204] Ut igitur[1] hos et alios gemitus rex Cadwalladrus[2] nauigando expleuit, in Armorico litore appulsus est. Ueniensque[3] ad Alanum [4]regem Salomonis[4] nepotem susceptus est[5] benigne cum omnibus suis mansitque cum eo quamdiu uoluit. Britannia igitur ciuibus suis uiduata[6] ac desolata per .xi. annos ab incolis exceptis paucis Britonibus horrenda et inculta fuit; Saxonibus quoque Anglis eadem tempestate ingrata,[7] quia in illa sine intermissione extinguebantur. Quorum residui, cum feralis illa lues cessasset, miserunt in Germaniam propter conciues suos ut desolacionem[8] suam aliis ciuibus supplerent. Illi uero[9] nichil hesitantes, ut audierunt terram ab incolis orbatam,[10] festinato[11] itinere cum innumerabili multitudine uirorum ac mulierum nauigantes [12]applicuerunt in partibus Nordamhumbrie[12] et ab Albania usque in[13] Cornubiam uniuersam[14] terram occupauerunt. Nec [15]enim supererat[15] quisquam qui prohiberet uel commaneret in locis desertis [16]preter paucas reliquias[16] Britonum qui superfuerunt et de[17] prefata mortalitate

---

[34] acDER; *mendicantis* S. [35] acDE; *uolumus* R; *nolumus* (altered from *uolumus*) S. [36] ERS; *totiens* aD. [37] ERS; *totiens* aD. [38] ERS; *uiuentium* aD. [39] aR; om. cDES. [40...40] acDES; *nostrum luctum* R. [41] aERS; *cui* cD. [42] acDES; *usque famulemur* R. [43] DRS; *Scotti* a; *Scocti* E. [44] aRS; *et Saxones* DE. [45] ERS; *potentia* acD.

§204 [1] aERS; *ergo* cD. [2] aR; *Cadwaladrus* cDES. [3] aDES; *Ueniens* R. [4...4] aR; *Salomonis regis* DES. [5] aDES; *est ab eo* R. [6] aDERS (corrected from *iduata* in S). [7] aERS; *ingrata similiter intereuntibus* D. [8] ER; *desolationem* aDS. [9] aR; *autem* DES. [10] aDERS (corrected from *orbitam* in S). [11] aERS; *festino* D. [12...12] aDES; *in partibus Nordamhumbrie applicuerunt* R. [13] aR; *ad* DS; om. E. [14] aR; *totam* DES. [15...15] aR; *erat* DES. [16...16] DES; *preter pauce reliquie* a; *nisi pauce reliquie* R. [17] aDES; *in* (with *de* suprascript) R.

euaserunt uel postea nati sunt. Illi abdita nemorum inhabitant in[18] Gualiis[19] tantum et in Cornubia commanentes. Ab illo ergo[20] tempore potestas Britonum cessauit et Angli in totum regnum[21] regnare ceperunt, Adestano[22] rege facto qui primus inter eos dyadema[23] portauit. Pacem et concordiam tamquam[24] fratres inter se habentes agros coluerunt, ciuitates et oppida[25] reedificauerunt[26] et magistratus et potestates in urbibus constituentes leges quas de terra sua aduexerant[27] subiectis populis tradiderunt seruandas; ducatus et honores prout Britones ante habuerant inter se diuidentes summa pace et securitate[28] terram desiderabilem incoluerunt.

[205] Cumque magnum temporis spacium [1]emensum esset[1] et populus Anglorum, sicut[2] dictum est, in Britannia roboratus et augmentatus fuisset, recordatus Cadwalladrus[3] regni sui amissi, iam a prefata colluuione purificati, quesiuit merens[4] ab Alano cognato suo consilium et auxilium ut[5] potestati pristine restitueretur. Quod cum ab illo[6] impetrasset, intonuit ei uox diuina, dum classem pararet, ut[7] ceptis suis desisteret. Preuiderat enim Deus Britones in Britannia, que tunc Anglis [8]tradita erat,[8] amplius non regnare donec tempus illud compleretur[9] quod Merlinus Arthuro[10] prophetauerat. Precepit etiam[11] illi ut Romam ad Sergium papam [12]properaret ubi[12] peracta penitencia inter beatos[13] reciperetur. Dicebat etiam[14] populum[15] Britonum per meritum [16]sue fidei in posterum Britanniam fore adepturum,[16] cum fatale tempus compleretur. Nec id tamen[17] antea futurum quam Britones reliquiis corporis sui potiti illas in Britanniam a Roma asportarent. Tum[18] demum reuelatis sanctorum quorundam reliquiis que propter pagano-rum terrorem dudum abscondite fuerant amissum regnum recupera-rent. Quod cum auribus beati uiri intimatum fuisset, tamquam[19] in

---

[18] aDER; *et* S. [19] aDER; *Gwalliis* S. [20] aDRS; *autem* E. [21] aDES; om. R. [22] aDERS (altered to *Adelstano* by suprascript *l* in S); *Cedelstano* c. [23] cDER; *diadema* aS. [24] R; *tanquam* acDES. [25] aR; *opida* cDES. [26] acDER; *redificauerunt* S. [27] aR; *adduxerant* cDES. [28] acR; *tranquillitate* DES.

§205 [1...1] aR; *esset emensum* DES. [2] aDER; *sicud* S. [3] aR; *Cadwaladrus* DES. [4] aR; om. DES. [5] aDES; *non* (?) R. [6] aR; *eo* DES. [7] DES; *ut a* a; *nec* R. [8...8] aDE; *tradiderat* R; *irradiata* [altered from *iradiata*] *erat* S. [9] aR; *ueniret* DES. [10] R; *antea* a; om. DES. [11] aDRS; *enim* E. [12...12] aDES; *properabat ut* R. [13] aDRS; *sanctos* E. [14] aDER; *in* S. [15] aR; *populo* DES. [16...16] aR (*Brittanniam* in a; *in* omitted from R); *fidei sue Britanniam in posterum fore tradendam* DE; *fidei sue Britanniam in posterum fore* S. [17] aDES; *cum* R. [18] aR; *Tunc* DES. [19] DR; *tanquam* acES.

extasi[20] ex uisione turbatus uenit ad Alanum regem et indicauit ei quod [21]sibi celitus releuatum[21] fuerat.

[206] Tunc Alanus sumptis[1] de armariis libris et conuocatis sapiencioribus[2] [3]terre sue[3] philosophis cepit[4] per eos scrutari que de propheciis[5] aquile[6] que[7] Sestonie[8] prophetauerat,[9] que de carminibus Sibille[10] ac Merlini in scriptis suis reperissent [11]sibi exponendo[11] notificarent ut uideret[12] an reuelacio[13] Cadwalladri[14] oraculis eorum concordaret. Et cum omnia hec[15] perscrutasset[16] et nullam discrepanciam[17] eorum reperisset,[18] suggessit Cadwalladro[19] ut diuine[20] prouidencie[21] pareret et quod ei celitus[22] reuelatum[23] fuerat perficeret, filium autem[24] suum [25]Iuor aµcλ Yni[25] nepotem suum[26] ad regendas[27] Britonum reliquias in Britanniam dirigeret[28] ne gens[29] eorum omnino interiret aut[30] libertatem barbarica irrupcione[31] amitteret. Mox ergo Cadwalladrus[32] abrenuncians[33] secularibus pompis recto itinere uenit Romam, ubi a Sergio papa honorifice susceptus et criminum suorum omnium coram ipso confessione puro[34] corde facta[35] languore inopino correptus .xii. die kalendarum[36] Maiarum[37] anno [38]ab incarnacione[38] Domini[39] .dclxxxix.[40] a [41]carnis contagione[41] solutus [42]celestis curie ianuam coronandus[42] ingressus est.

---

20 acDER; *extassi* S. 21...21 R; *celitus sibi reuelatum* a; *ei celitus indicatum* DES.

§206 P's final extract begins here with the note, 'The last chapter in this Manuscript is as followeth'. 1 aDEPRS (corrected from *sumptus* in R). 2 ERS; *sapientioribus* acDP (altered from *sapientibus* in c). 3...3 acDERS; *terrae suae* P. 4 acDERS; *caepit* P. 5 cERS; *prophetiis* aDP. 6 acDERS; *aquilae* P. 7 acDERS; *quam* P. 8 DEPS; *Exonie* a; *Testonie* c; *Scestonie* R. 9 DERS; *locuta est* a; *prophetauit* cP. 10 cDERS; *Sybille* a; *Sibyllae* P. 11...11 aDERS; *ex expondo* P. 12 cDERS; *uiderent* aP. 13 DER; *reuelatio* acPS. 14 R; *Cadwaladri* acDEPS. 15 aDERS; *haec* P. 16 aDERS; *perscrutatus est* P. 17 cERS; *discrepantiam* aDP. 18 cDEPS; *repperisset* a; *reperasset* R. 19 aR; *Cadwadro* c; *Cadwaladro* DEPS. 20 aDERS; *diuinae* P. 21 ERS; *prouidentie* aD; *prouidencie et dispositioni* c; *prouidentiae* P. 22 aDERS; *caelitus* P. 23 aPR; *indicatum* DES. 24 aDERS; *uero* P. 25...25 my emendation; *Iuor Ayni* a; *Iuorum uel* DS; *Yuorum uel* E; *Ifor Ann* P; *Inor Ayni* R. 26 aPR; om. DES. 27 aDERS; *regendum* P. 28 aDEPS; *erigeret* R. 29 RS; *genus* aDEP (with *gens .q.* suprascript in P). 30 aDEPS; *ante* R. 31 ERS; *irruptione* aDP. 32 aR; *Cadwaladrus* DEPS. 33 aDERS; *renuncians* P. 34 acDERS; *pio* P. 35 aDERS; *factam* P. 36 acDERS; *Calend.* P. 37 acDES; *Maii* P; *Maiorum* R. 38...38 acPR (*incarnatione* in acP); *incarnationis* D; *incarnacionis* ES. 39 acDEPS; om. R. 40 RS; *secentesimo octogesimo nono* a; *689* c; *dclxxx. nono* DE; *dclxxxxix* P. 41...41 aPR; *contagione carnis* cDES. 42...42 aDRS; *coronandus celestis curie ianuam* E; *celestis c'ie [.q. an ciuitatis] januam coronandus* P.

[207] Iuor autem[1] cum .xii. nauibus in Kambriam uenit et conuocatis Britonum[2] reliquiis[3] [4]ex cauernis et[4] nemoribus cum multitudine quam secum adduxerat[5] Saxones[6] inuadere mox decreuit et eos uiriliter per .xlviii. annos oppugnauit. Sed[7] Iuor de hac uita discedente[8] Britones propter ciuile discidium[9] nullo modo Saxonibus resistere potuerunt. Nam ulcio[10] diuina in tantum executa est Britones ut de omnibus bellis uicti discederent. Tunc autem[11] Britones sunt appellati[12] Gwalenses, siue[13] a Gwalone[14] duce eorum siue a Galaes regina siue a barbarie uocabulum trahentes. [15]Degenerati autem a Brittanica nobilitate Gualenses qui in parte boreali Anglie remanserunt numquam postea Loegriam[15] uel ceteras[16] australes partes recuperauerunt.

[208] Regum autem[1] eorum[2] acta qui ab illo tempore in Guualliis[3] successerunt et fortunas successoribus meis scribendas dimitto ego, Galfridus Arthurus[4] Monemutensis,[5] qui hanc hystoriam[6] Britonum de eorum lingua in nostram transferre curaui.[7]

§207 This chapter is found in R in the following shorter form: *Degenerati autem a Britannica nobilitate Guallenses qui in parte boriali Anglie remanserunt numquam postea Loegriam uel ceteras australes partes recuperauerunt. Gualense autem uocabulum* [sic] *siue a Gualone duce eorum siue a Galaes regina siue a barbarie trahentes duxerunt.* 1 DES; *uero* P. 2 cDES; om. P. 3 cDES; *reliqiis* P. 4...4 DES; *de* P. 5 DES; *adduxerant* c; *abduxerat* P. 6 DEP; *et Saxones* S. 7 DPS; *Set* E. 8 DPS; *decedente* c; *descedente* E. 9 DES; *dissidium* P. 10 E; *ultio* DP; *ratio* S. 11 DES; *uero* P. 12 DEP; *appelati* S. 13 DES; om. P. 14 DES; *Gwallone* P; *Gualone* R (above). 15...15 a (compare R, above); *Degenerati autem Britanni qui in parte boreali insule remanserunt numquam Loegriam* c; *Sed illi Britones qui in parte boreali* [*boriali* ES] *Anglie* [*Angliae* P] *remanserunt a lingua Britannica* [*Britannica lingua* PS] *degenerati numquam* [*nunquam* P] *Loegriam* [*Leogriam* S] DEPS. 16 aDES; *caeteras* P.

§208 1 aDERS; *uero* P. 2 aR; om. DEPS. 3 a; *Gwalliis* DS; *Gwaliis* E; *Gwalia* P; *Gualis* R. 4 PR; *Arturus* aDES. 5 aPRS; *Monemuthensis* DE. 6 aERS; *historiam* DP. 7 aDEPRS. After *curaui*: *Explicit historia Brittonum correcta et abbreuiata* (with *et cum uulgari Galfrido non concordat* added in a later [Parker's?] hand) a; *Explicit tractatus* c; *Explicit* (with *historia Britonum* added) D; *Explicit* E; *Explicit historia Britonum a magistro Galfrido Monemutensi in Latinum translata* P; *Explicit hystoria Britonum a Galfrido Arthuro de Britannico in Latinum translata est* [*est* underpointed]. *Deo gracias* R; *Qui scripsit carmen sit benedictus amen* S.

Index Nominum

Variant forms are recorded in brackets; all references are to Faral's chapters, except those in brackets which give *Prophetia Merlini* numbers.

Androgeus 53, 56, 61, 62, 63, 64
Angarad 27
Angli (Angli Saxones, Saxones Angli) 34, 186/7, 188, 189, 197, 198, 200, 204, 205
Anglicus 39
Angues 27
Anguselus (Auguselus) 152, 156, 161, 168, 177
Anna 138, 139
Anor 27
Antenor 17, 22
Antigonus 9, 10, 11, 12
Appollo 30
Apuleius 107
Aquitani 18, 87
Arabes 115 (21)
Archgal 156
Archgallo 50, 52
Archmail 52
Aries 117 (73)
Armoricani (Armoricani Britones) 87, 88, 121, 123, 144, 156, 157, 162b, 165, 173, 177, 193
Arthurus 137, 138, 143, 144, 145, 147, 149, 152, 153, 154, 155, 156, 158, 162a, 163, 161, 164b, 165, 166, 167, 168, 170, 174, 176, 177, 178, 205
Aruiragus 65, 66, 67, 68, 69, 70
Asaph 27
Ascanius 6
Aschillus (Aschil) 156, 168, 178
Asclepiodotus 76, 77, 78
Assarach (Assaracus) 27
Assaracus 7, 8
Auguselus see Anguselus
Augustinus 188, 189
Augustus Cesar 64, 86
Aurelius Ambrosius 93, 118, 119, 120, 121, 123, 125, 126, 129, 130, 131, 132, 133, 136, 142, 152
Azarias 29

Baldulfus 143, 147
Bangornenses 189
Basianus 75
Beduerus 155, 156, 165, 166, 167, 168, 171, 172, 176
Belinus I 35, 36, 37, 38, 39, 40, 41, 42, 43, 44, 159
Belinus II 56

194

Gwitardus   see Guitardus
Gyldas (Gildas)   39, 72, 102
Gyllamurius   149, 153, 156
Gyllomanius   130, 132, 134

Habren   24, 25
Hector I   22
Hector II   27
Helena I   78, 80, 159
Helena II   165
Helenus   7
Heli   53
Heli sacerdos   22
Hengistus   98, 99, 100, 101, 103, 104, 118, 121, 122, 123, 124, 125, 126, 127, 136, 177
Henninus   31
Hider   167
Hiderius filius Nu   166
Hireglas   61
Hirelgas de Perirum   167
Hirelglas   172
Hirtacius   163
Hoelus   144, 146, 148, 149, 150, 155, 156, 157, 162b, 165, 168, 173, 177
Holdinus   156, 168, 172, 176
Homerus   19, 25
Horsus   98, 100, 101, 177
Humbaltus   84
Humber   24
Huni   24, 88
Hybernienses   130, 132, 149, 177, 178

Iago I   33
Iago II   195
Iagon   27
Ianus   31
Idwallo   52
Iesus   see Christus
Ieu   29
Igerna   137, 138
Indon   33
Ingenius   51, 52
Innogen   14, 15, 23
Innogin   27

Loelinus   79, 80
Loth   152, 154, 156, 168
Lucius   72, 73
Lucius Catellus   163
Lucius Hiberus   158, 159, 163, 166, 170, 173, 175, 176
Lud   53
Ludouicus   184/6
Lupus Trecacensis episcopus   102

Maddan   24, 25, 26
Magaunius   157
Maglaunus   31
Mailure   27
Malgo   183, 184/6
Malim   26
Maluasius   156
Marcellius Mutius   166
Marcia   47
Marciana lex   47
Margadud I   27
Margadud II   189, 200
Marganus I (Morganus)   32
Marganus II   52
Maria   147
Marius I   70
Marius II   79
Marius Lepidus   163, 172
Mars   117 (73)
Martinus   201
Maugancius   107
Mauricius   81, 82
Mauricus Cardorcanensis   167
Mauron   156
Maxencius   79
Maximianus   81, 82, 83, 84, 86, 87, 88, 89, 159
Maximianus Herculius   77
Medi   163, 171, 172
Medlan   27
Melga   88, 91
Menbricius I   14
Menbritius II (Membricius)   26, 27
Merchenelaga   47
Mercii   196, 199, 200

Mercurius 98, 117 (73)
Merianus 52
Merlinus (Merlinus Ambrosius) 106, 107, 108, 111, 118, 119, 128, 129, 130, 133, 135, 137, 142, 205, 206
Methael 27
Micipsa 163, 172
Minerua 30
Mirci 163
Modredus 152, 164b, 176, 177, 178, 179/180, 191
Molmuntine leges 34, 39
Moriani 35, 48
Morpidus 48
Moruid 27
Morwid consul Claudiocestrie 156, 175
Murefenses 152, 156
Mustensar 163

Nathan 27
Nennius 53, 56, 57
Nest 27
Neustrienses 162b, 176
Nordamhumbri 189, 191/2, 199
Norguegensis 154
Norguegenses (Norgueguenses, Norguengenses, Noruegienses, Noruuegenses, Norwegenses) 35, 36, 37, 89, 91, 95, 154, 168, 169
Nu 166

Obericus 178
Octa 101, 124, 126, 136, 137, 139, 141, 143
Octauius 80, 81, 83
Oiwald (Oywald) 200
Orion 117 (73)
Osee 32
Osfridus 197
Osricus 198
Oswaldus 199, 200
Oswi 200
Otidas 27
Ourar 27

Pandrasus I 7, 8, 9, 10, 14, 15
Pandrasus II 163
Parthi 163

Index Locorum

Affricana nemora 112 (3)
Affrica 17, 129
Akalon 9
Alba Longa 6
Alba fluuius 166
Albania 23, 24, 27, 31, 34, 37, 39, 51, 56, 70, 72, 74, 75, 80, 83, 88, 89, 91, 98, 101,
   114 (14), 115 (20), 116 (65), (69), 136, 139, 143, 148, 149, 152, 156, 161, 168, 177,
   193, 204
Albion 5, 21
Aldclud (Alclud) 27, 50, 137, 146, 148, 149, 157
Alpes 43, 77, 116 (30), (37), 133, 158, 166, 176
Ambrii cenobium (monasterium, mons) 104, 122, 127, 130, 134, 142, 179/180
Amphibali ecclesia 93, 179/180
Andegauensis prouincia 155
Anglia 186/7, 188, 207
Anne fons 115 (23)
Apulia 43
Aquileia 86
Aquitania (Acquitannia, Aquitannia) 17, 18, 19, 155
Arauius mons 113 (12), 165
Archadia 117 (73)
Are Philistinorum 17
Armenicanus tractus   see Armoricus tractus
Armorica (Armorica Britannia) 87, 92, 203
Armoricum (Armoricanum) litus 118, 204
Armorici montes 115 (20)
Armoricum regnum 84, 112 (3), 194/5
Armoricus sinus 114 (14)
Armoricus (Armenicanus) tractus 5, 99, 144
Auallonis insula 147, 178
Augustudunum 166, 168
Autisiodorensis 102
Azare see Montes Azare

Babilonia 163
Babiloniensis 172
Badon (Bada) 30, 116 (30), 146, 156, 168, 172
Baioce 176
Bangor 188, 189
Bangornensis 179/180
Belnesgata 44
Bethleem 64
Boecia 163
Bolonia 156
Boloniensis 172
Britannia (Britannie) 5, 21, 23, 27, 28, 31, 32, 34, 36, 37, 39, 41, 44, 46, 54, 58, 59,
    61, 62, 63, 65, 67, 68, 69, 70, 72, 75, 76, 77, 79, 80, 81, 82, 83, 84, 86, 87, 88, 89, 91,
    93, 95, 100, 101, 102, 103, 112 (1), 116 (34), 118, 120, 126, 129, 130, 131, 133, 135,
    136, 137, 139, 144, 146, 153, 154, 155, 156, 158, 159, 164a, 162b, 164b, 169, 172,
    176, 177, 178, 183, 184/6, 186/7, 190, 191/2, 196, 199, 200, 203, 204, 205, 206
Britannia [i.e. Brittany] 84
Britannia altera 84
Britannia minor 92, 96
Burgundia 166
Burne 199
Bythinia 163

Caicestrensis 172
Calaterium nemus 37, 50, 166 (39)
Cambula fluuius 178
Camum 176
Cancia 53, 98, 100, 101, 177, 186/7, 188
Cantuaria 29, 98
Cardorcanensis 167
Carnotensis 156, 166, 168
Castellum Puellarum 27
Castrum Corrigie 99
Cathenesia 35, 70
Catinensium litus 39
Cennomannensis 156, 167
Chorea Gigantum 128, 130, 132, 134, 142
Cicestria 184/6
Cisalpina terra 161
Claudiocestrensis 125
Claudiocestria 68, 69, 73, 105, 116 (51), (55), 119, 122, 156, 175
Cloarcius mons 119
Colecestria 78

Colidonis nemus (silua)   116 (33), 145
Columpne Herculis   17
Corineia   21
Cornubia   21, 25, 31, 34, 35, 53, 56, 64, 72, 76, 81, 87, 112 (2), 115 (20), 116 (35),
    (70), 118, 124, 136, 137, 143, 148, 149, 152, 156, 158, 167, 168, 177, 178, 186/7,
    189, 196, 204
Cornubiense mare   39
Creta   163
Cunungeburg   123, 125

Dacia   38, 45, 154, 162b, 178, 183
Damen mons   136
Danerium nemus   116 (35)
Deira   72, 74, 89, 101
Demecia   44, 56, 68, 106, 157, 200
Demeticum mare   39
Demeticus ducatus   68
Derte flumen   20
Derwend   101
Dolensis   157
Dorobernia (Dorobernum)   56, 62, 98, 112 (3), 156
Dorocestrensis   156, 168
Duglas flumen   143, 191/2

Eboracensis   72, 112 (3), 116 (63), 127, 130
Eboracum   38, 50, 63, 72, 74, 78, 105, 124, 126, 127, 136, 143, 151, 177, 196
Egyptus   163
Episfrod   101
Erir mons   106
Europa   154
Exonia   69, 116 (56), 196, 197

Flandrie   176
Francia   184/6
Frigia   163

Galabroc   76
Galahes fons (uallis)   116 (40), (50), 128
Gallia (Gallie)   5, 19, 27, 31, 33, 40, 41, 42, 56, 63, 69, 84, 86, 116 (38), 120, 155, 156,
    158, 159, 162b, 166, 195
Gallica nemora   115 (21)
Gallicana litora   37
Gallicana plaga   133

Maisuram   80
Malua flumen   17
Maluernia   116 (51)
Mauritania 17
Meneuia   39, 112 (3), 132, 179/180
Mons Dolorosus   27
Mons archangeli Michaelis   165
Montes Azare   17
Montis Agned, oppidum   27
Montis Paladur, oppidum   29
Mureif   149

Nantgallin   76
Neustria   41, 113 (9), 115 (18), 116 (41), 155, 156, 164b, 176
Norguegia (Noruegia, Norwegia)   35, 80, 154, 156, 162b, 178, 183
Normannia   155
Nordamhumbria (Nordanhymbria, Nordhamhumbria)   35, 36, 48, 191/2, 197, 204
Noua Troia   22

Odnea   60
Orchades (Orcades)   46, 68, 153, 156, 162b, 183, 197
Osca (Oscha, Uscha)   44, 72, 116 (30), 156
Oxinefordia   156, 168

Pacaii montes   116 (52)
Parisius   155, 166, 167
Perirum (Perironis fluuius)   115 (19), 167
Petri, ecclesia sancti   106
Porcestria   65, 67
Portlud   53
Portus Barbe fluuii   164b
Portus Hamonis   39, 66, 144, 164b, 177, 196

Redonum   85
Ridcaradoch   137
Ridichen   168
Ridochensis   156
Roma   32, 43, 44, 63, 64, 66, 68, 69, 71, 72, 74, 75, 76, 78, 79, 81, 86, 88, 89, 90, 91, 155, 156, 158, 159, 162a, 163, 176, 205, 206
Romulea domus   112 (2)
Ruscicada   17
Rutupi Portus   62, 69, 177

Sabrina (Sabrinum flumen, Sabrinus fluuius)   23, 25, 68, 72, 116 (46), (70), 150, 184/6
Sabrinum mare   116 (30), 146, 156
Salesberia   127, 180
Salesberiensis   156, 172
Saxonica tellus   98
Scithia   70, 74
Scocia   23, 74, 95, 101, 120, 126, 137, 177, 199
Secana   155
Sephtonia (Sestonia)   29, 206
Siesia   168
Silcestria   93, 143, 156, 157
Sparatinum   9
Sora   31
Stanheng   179/180
Stura   25
Syria   163, 167

Teruana ciuitas   176
Thamensis (Thamensis fluuius)   22, 44, 56, 59, 88, 116 (30), (37), (46), (49)
Thancastre   99
Thaneth   101
Tintagol   137, 138, 167
Totonesium portus (litus)   20, 69, 93, 118, 146, 197
Totonesius   116 (55)
Trecacensis   102
Treueri ciuitas   86
Troia   6, 7, 8, 16, 22, 54
Tumba Helene   165
Turonum ciuitas (ciuitas Turonis)   19, 20

Uadum Baculi   115 (23)
Uadum Boum   166
Uenedocia (Uenedotia)   56, 113 (12)
Uerolamium   141, 142
Uerolamius   77
Urbs Claudii   116 (66)
Urbs Legionum   44, 46, 72, 77, 112 (3), 128, 130, 143, 156, 157, 177, 179/180
Urbs Trinouantum   22, 24, 30, 34, 41, 44, 49, 51, 53, 56, 57, 59, 61, 62, 102, 105
Uriani cacumen   116 (47)
Uscha   see Osca

Warewic 156
Wentana ciuitas 105
Westmaria (Westmarialanda) 70, 80
Wigornia 116 (54)
Wigorniensis 156
Winied fluuius 200
Wintonia (Guentonia) 29, 67, 80, 94, 116 (30), (35), 127, 132, 133, 135, 157, 177, 179/180
Wintoniensis 94, 177

Ybernia see Hybernia
Ytalia 6, 22, 27, 29, 43, 44